Politics in a Pandemic

Jacinda Ardern and New Zealand's 2020 Election

PREVIOUS BOOKS IN THIS SERIES

The 1987 General Election: What Happened?
The 1990 General Election: Perspectives on Political Change in New Zealand
Double Decision: The 1993 Election and Referendum in New Zealand

Published by Dunmore Press:

From Campaign to Coalition: New Zealand's First General Election Under Proportional Representation

Published by Victoria University Press:

Left Turn: The New Zealand General Election of 1999
New Zealand Votes: The General Election of 2002
The Baubles of Office: The New Zealand General Election of 2005
Key to Victory: The New Zealand General Election of 2008
Kicking the Tyres: The New Zealand General Election and Electoral Referendum of 2011
Moments of Truth: The New Zealand General Election of 2014
Stardust and Substance: The New Zealand General Election of 2017

Politics in a Pandemic
Jacinda Ardern and New Zealand's 2020 Election

Edited by Stephen Levine

VICTORIA UNIVERSITY OF WELLINGTON PRESS

VICTORIA UNIVERSITY OF WELLINGTON PRESS
Victoria University of Wellington
PO Box 600 Wellington
vup.wgtn.ac.nz

First published 2021

A catalogue record for this book is available from the National Library of New Zealand.

ISBN 9781776564330

Printed by YourBooks, Wellington

CONTENTS

IMAGES, FIGURES AND TABLES

Images

Colour section 1 (between pages 190 and 191)

Colour section 2 (between pages 262 and 263)

Colour section 3 (between pages 300 and 301)

Figures

Tables

‘No harm shall befall you, nor shall any plague come near your tent’

(Psalms, 91:10)

To all those responsible for keeping us safe and healthy
in troubled times

FOREWORD

I want to start my reflections on this campaign by acknowledging that I am privileged to be the Speaker of two rather strange Parliaments. In the 52nd Parliament the largest party was not in government, and at the time there was some disbelief that this was possible under MMP. And now, in the 53rd Parliament, we have the first one-party majority government under MMP in New Zealand. Again, many thought this would not be possible.

As Speaker, because of the majority the government has, additional responsibility falls on me to ensure that parliamentary processes are properly maintained. This is because there is not the traditional coalition partner 'handbrake'. As a result, there will always be a temptation for governments to push through legislation, as occurred frequently in the pre-MMP days.

On the role of Speaker, I foresee that there will be a place for a political science student in the future to write about the changing role of the Speaker under MMP and their relationship with elections. We have not yet had a Speaker run for a constituency under MMP.

When I became Speaker I undertook some consultation with previous Speakers on what their role was during election campaigns. The feedback indicated that they had increasingly pulled back from being involved in campaigns. Back in the early days of MMP there was also much more frequent attendance by Speakers at a party's caucus and conferences. We have moved away from that, and our system in terms of the role of the Speaker is now much more like the United Kingdom's than Australia's.

However, for me it was slightly strange to not be involved. This campaign was the first time I have not done door knocking or phoning in a campaign since 1972. When you are a candidate for the first time it's slightly nerve-racking when you go out door-knocking for the first time each day; then you realise people are much nicer at the door than you expect them to be. I did miss not participating in it this campaign.

During the campaign a day doesn't often go by without there being some sort of reference on the part of candidates or members of

Parliament, and the Speaker being involved in the judgement of those being appropriate or not. It seems wrong to be constantly sitting in judgement of my colleagues and at the same time campaigning with or against them: hence why Speakers have distanced themselves.

My one comment about how the 2020 campaign felt to me . . . I live in Wainuiomata, and traditionally I have done a lot of work taking older or less able-bodied voters to the polls. It has always been part of my role, but with early voting it has become easier to access voting places.

Early in the voting period, on a Tuesday, which was superannuation day and also Gold Card discount day at the local supermarket, I ran into a group of three women, two of whom I knew to be strong Labour supporters. The third woman, one of their dear friends, was a long-time activist in the National Party for the vast majority of the time that I had lived in Wainuiomata, including being a past office branch holder.

One of the first two women reminded me of my long-term role taking them to vote and suggested that to save them the taxi fare I take them to the polls and then home. I thought that two for one is not a brilliant ratio in Wainuiomata but it's not bad, so I agreed.

While dropping the third woman off first after the vote, she told us, 'You know I'm in my 80s and I've voted every time I could and I've always been a National Party supporter. But this time I voted Labour for the first time and I've done it because she cares about us old people.' She was of course referring to the prime minister.

And at that point it didn't matter what polling had been done. I knew that if people like this woman were voting for the Labour Party then the result was going to be pretty extraordinary. So at that stage I did get the sense of the tidal wave that was going to crash down.

I am happy to have opened this post-election conference at Parliament, and I look forward to reading the book and learning what happened around me during the campaign. I thank Professor Levine, who I have known for 45 years and for whom I have a longstanding respect, for his continued work to produce the book every election, and more importantly for encouraging people to share at least in a limited way their thoughts about what happened and why.

Rt Hon Trevor Mallard
Speaker
New Zealand House of Representatives

PREFACE

Stephen Levine

> 'Thou shalt not be afraid of the terror by night, nor of the arrow that flieth by day; nor of the pestilence that walketh in darkness . . .'
>
> (Psalms 91:5–6)

Politics in a Plague Year

The year 2020 will no doubt be remembered everywhere for the worldwide pandemic that struck, suddenly and unexpectedly, with a virus – Covid-19 – emanating from China and spreading steadily and stealthily across the globe. Inevitably New Zealand, though geographically remote even in an interconnected globalised world, became caught up in the expanding pandemic, its consequences affecting all New Zealanders in one way or another. International travel became, for the most part, a thing of the past. Airline terminals were silenced; airport runways abandoned. Cruise ships stopped calling at New Zealand ports. International students, mostly from China, remained overseas. A nationwide lockdown brought social life to a standstill; schools and universities closed their doors, students remaining at home. New norms were established, including exhortations about handwashing and the use of hand sanitisers. Handshakes and hugs were discouraged, elbow bumps becoming a more or less acceptable substitute. Elements of a new vocabulary emerged, 'social distancing' a key feature. Places of business – shops and banks, buses and trains – that would previously have had misgivings about masked customers coming through their doors now required them to do so.

Charles Dickens' *A Tale of Two Cities* describes an epoch: 'It was the best of times, it was the worst of times'. For many of those living through the 2020 pandemic it can only have been 'the worst of times'. At least in New Zealand people had the good sense to comply with the needs of the moment, so that together all would be able, as best we could, to survive and ultimately prevail over the deadly challenge that had suddenly arisen to confront us.

In this, an election year, the country's politics could not but be affected. Parliament, along with everything else, came to a virtual halt, the building closed as part of the nationwide lockdown, a unifying constraint on otherwise partisan combatants. When Parliament resumed, limits were placed on the number of members able to sit in the debating chamber. Those allowed to be there practised social distancing, keeping their distance from adversaries and allies alike. When a new Covid-19 outbreak emerged, the election date itself was changed and campaigns were temporarily disrupted. In 2020, voters accustomed in election years to having candidates and party canvassers come to their doors were likely to be spared such experiences. An altogether original sight, intermittently viewed, was of masked candidates, appealing for votes. In the end, as ever, an election was held, voters and candidates adapting to circumstances, allowing the democratic process to continue unabated.

Every three years New Zealand holds regularly scheduled parliamentary elections. Since 1987 these elections have been followed by post-election conferences, organised by the country's oldest political science programme, which is based at Victoria University of Wellington, in the nation's capital, not far from Parliament.

These triennial conferences were instituted to allow political figures, journalists, commentators and academics an opportunity to provide their own reflections and insights about the election that had just passed, while memory of the campaign and all that transpired was still fresh. Subsequently, these conference presentations, supplemented by other contributions, have been published, providing a record of 12 New Zealand elections over five decades.

In this 'plague year', the conference and this publication were also influenced by the pandemic and the steps taken to combat it. Initially, all of the conference planning went very smoothly. The Legislative Council Chamber (premises of New Zealand's former upper house, disbanded on New Year's Day, 1951) was booked for the event; the adjacent Grand Hall was made available for refreshments during the breaks. A date – 9 December – was set. Invitations were sent out. The first to accept, with a brief text message from his BlackBerry, was the leader of the National Party, Simon Bridges. All was proceeding according to plan.

Then matters began to unravel. The country went into lockdown. The National Party changed its leader. Todd Muller's office was contacted; a second invitation was dispatched and duly accepted. On 14 July, however, the National Party found itself again without a leader: Todd Muller announced his resignation. A university colleague, hearing the news on morning radio, remarked to his wife, 'Stephen's not going to be happy about this.' Rightly puzzled, she responded, 'Stephen? What does Stephen have to do with this?' He replied: 'He's going to have to invite another National Party leader to the conference.' And so it was, with Judith Collins agreeing very readily to participate.

In August a renewed Covid-19 outbreak occurred and the election date was changed. It was unclear whether the conference could be held and, if so, how many people would be allowed to attend, with potential restrictions on the numbers of people permitted to be present and how they would be accommodated: seated; standing; how many metres apart. Even the catering arrangements became provisional, linked to limits on numbers, subject to change.

With a country precariously situated between Covid-19 outbreaks, and with no guarantee that there would not be a renewed nationwide lockdown, thinking about anything other than the ongoing threat to our collective health and well-being, and the safety and security of our own families and friends, seemed something of an indulgence. The international news slid steadily from bad to worse, casualty figures rising from the tens, to the hundreds, to the thousands, and eventually on into the millions. Nevertheless, the country's election preparations continued, as did arrangements for a post-election gathering, although conference advertising remained vague, the details sketchy.

Priorities

In recognition of the impact that the pandemic was having on us all, it seemed only right that the keynote address should focus on the pandemic and that it should be given by an individual with unquestioned expertise and authority. A conversation with a former parliamentary intern, Brodie Fraser, led to Professor Michael Baker being invited to participate. It would be the first time he had ever attended, let alone spoken at, a political science conference. It would also be the first post-election conference in which an epidemiologist had been invited to speak; indeed, more than one participant had to take special care to articulate the word correctly.

Professor Baker's address to the conference established, from the outset, what proved to be an overarching theme. The Covid-19 pandemic established parameters around which the election campaign came to be fought. The election outcome, though as always influenced by a variety of factors, was likewise shaped significantly by the pandemic and by perceptions of the prime minister's handling of it. As such, the pandemic has been an ever-present element in both the conference presentations and this book.

Each of the party leaders make reference to the pandemic in their chapters. The prime minister's conference contribution was given in a pre-recorded video, the first post-election conference 'remote' message. Her chapter emphasises the decision-making dilemmas in dealing with the pandemic as well as the effect of Covid-19 on Labour's campaign. Jacinda Ardern's chapter is followed by a contribution from Chris Hipkins, the minister responsible for the government's Covid-19 response – and as Leader of the House, a minister with a good grasp of the newly elected government's plans for the 2020–2023 period – providing a further view of Labour's pandemic preparations and overall governing agenda. James Shaw and Marama Davidson, the Greens' co-leaders, offer a perspective on the success of their 2020 campaign (nationwide and in Auckland Central), which led to them retaining their position as Labour's governing partner (formalised via a post-election 'cooperation agreement' reprinted in Appendix 2). Leaders of two opposition parties – Judith Collins (National) and David Seymour (ACT) – conclude the second segment of the book with their own personal perspectives on their parties' 2020 campaigns and electoral fortunes.

Arrivals and departures

The outlook of the parliamentary contributors is complemented by the book's many other contributors. Veteran journalist/author Colin James – contributor to each of the 12 books in this election series – provides historical context on New Zealand's elections and political leadership, from Norman Kirk through to Jacinda Ardern, offering an overview on New Zealand elections and events over nearly 50 years.

Periods of political exile and return feature in two chapters. Margaret Joiner considers New Zealand First – gone from Parliament (for the second time in its history) as a result of its 2020 electoral performance – against a background of populism, an at times ill-defined aspect of politics that has gained heightened international attention in recent years. The Māori Party – absent from Parliament following former co-leader Te Ururoa Flavell's 2017 loss of his Waiariki seat – is a focus of Lara Greaves and Ella Morgan's chapter, which also looks more broadly at election outcomes in the Māori electorates and the overall importance of the 2020 election for Māori. Ayca Arkilic draws attention to New Zealand's Muslim community, generally overlooked in political commentary, whose perspective on the 2020 election was greatly affected by the 2019 Christchurch mosque attacks, a deeply disturbing event for the community and the entire country.

Perspectives on politics

Two chapters provide case studies of campaign contests in particular electorates. While most election coverage rightly focuses on the overall struggle among the country's political parties and party leaders, and the rivalry between prospective prime ministers, under MMP voters cast ballots not only for parties but for electoral candidates as well. Bonnie Hayvice's position as an intern in Victoria University's parliamentary internship programme gave her a first-hand view of Chlöe Swarbrick's successful Auckland Central campaign, one of the major stories of election night. Campbell Garrett's internship with Kieran McAnulty likewise offered him an opportunity not only to become involved in the effort to win the Wairarapa electorate, but to observe an election campaign that unfolded in the shadow of a pandemic. The Wairarapa chapter also offered a rare opportunity to revisit and update a previously published electorate case study on former MP Georgina Beyer's capture of the seat in 2002.

A nationwide perspective – a survey-based overview of factors contributing to Labour's successful re-election, by UMR's Stephen Mills, Thomas Butt and Marcus Downs – draws upon the firm's opinion poll findings, documenting New Zealanders' views about the prime minister, rival party leaders, the various political parties, and the issues of greatest concern, the Covid-19 pandemic among them. A data-based snapshot of leaders' 'word clouds' and voters' likes and dislikes represents one way of understanding what happened in the election and why.

Two other chapters offer alternative visual perspectives on the 2020 election. Mike Grimshaw views the election campaign – and the pandemic-influenced events of the year – through the work of New

Zealand's leading political cartoonists. Few observers of New Zealand politics will have seen all, even most, of these shrewd and vivid images. Nigel S. Roberts, academic and inveterate photographer, assesses one of the campaign's most impermanent elements – election billboards, which are required to be taken down the day before the election – giving insights into the messages and strategies adopted by political parties as they seek to sum themselves up at a glance for motorists and passers-by.

Messages and the media

Any election involves politicians and the public engaging with the media in one way or another. Broadcast, print and online media are represented in the book both by those in the profession and by academic observers.

Two of New Zealand's most respected political journalists, Tova O'Brien and Henry Cooke, offer personal reflections on the 2020 election: its personalities, ups-and-downs, and the outcome. Their observations complement those of the prime minister and other party leaders, offering insights based on direct experience of the news (and newsmakers) on which they have been reporting.

A former journalist, Mark Boyd, now an academic, draws on his experience and his research in documenting mainstream media coverage of the election. In 2020, traditional news sources continued to serve as an important source of information about parties, policies and potential prime ministers, influencing voters' perceptions without the extreme bias increasingly seen elsewhere.

Sarah Bickerton reflects on the evolution of New Zealand's digital campaigning – from websites through to the various social media platforms available in 2020, drawing attention, as well, to trends in academic research into the topic. Her chapter also highlights social media use by politicians and political parties, noting hopes for more genuine interactive engagement.

Among the most high-profile events in a modern election campaign are televised leaders' debates, a feature of democratic politics since John F. Kennedy and Richard M. Nixon faced one another on US television in the 1960 election. As he did in the 2017 election book, Geoffrey Craig analyses each of the New Zealand leaders' debates, drawing attention to not only the political leaders' performances but also that of the moderators selected to preside over the televised confrontations.

Fund-raising, by one means or another, has long been a significant part of overseas politics, particularly in the United States, where campaigning is an enormously expensive undertaking for parties and candidates. New Zealand's electoral politics, by contrast, has seldom involved much of a focus on electoral financing, as it is regulated in ways that would be transformative in a US setting. Notwithstanding the relatively small amounts of money involved, the absence of much attention being given to the topic does not mean that all is entirely as it should be. This series of election studies has not previously dwelt on how New Zealand's political parties are financed, but the 2020 election saw some commentary devoted to it; Michael Macaulay offers a more extended analysis of the role of money in New Zealand electoral politics, highlighting unresolved issues.

Issues and policies

The 2020 parliamentary elections were accompanied by two nationwide referendums dealing with topics often described as conscience issues, left to the collective judgment of the public rather than MPs. Lara Greaves and Luke Oldfield discuss the two referendums – the proposed legalisation of cannabis, and the legalisation of end-of-life decisions by terminally ill patients – analysing what was at stake, the outcome in each instance, and the campaigns undertaken to influence New Zealanders' thinking (and voting) on these sensitive subjects.

When Jacinda Ardern swept to power in 2017 – her emergence as Labour Party leader upending what had until that point seemed a fairly low-key fourth successive election victory for National – she had a presence, and policies, but no governance record of her own to defend. Standing for re-election in 2020, she was in a different position.

As in *Stardust and Substance*, in which a host of National government policies were reviewed and critiqued after the party's nine years in office, so too in this book several major policy areas are examined. Two of them are (or ought to be) perennials, pivotal in considering a government's record. Simon Chapple looks at the government's economic policies, considering whether the attempt to introduce an approach focused on people's 'well-being' – anticipated in Girol Karacaoglu and Joey Au's chapter in *Stardust and Substance* – has produced much of a difference, rhetoric aside. Inevitably, the impact of Covid-19 on New Zealand's economy, and on the government's economic policies, is also considered. Robert Ayson examines the Labour-led government's foreign and defence policies, topics not often critical to a New Zealand government's re-election hopes but vital all the same in assessing the character and quality of an administration's record.

More electorally significant, and more closely aligned with the government's first-term performance, are the remaining three chapters in the 'public policy issues' section. The first, not surprisingly, is epidemiologist Michael Baker's discussion of the Covid-19 emergency and the government's performance in responding to it. The chapter looks more broadly at the pandemic – the available policy options and the consequences of the policies adopted – while charting, in some detail, how matters evolved as the 2020 pandemic unfolded. Brodie Fraser looks at one of the issues highlighted by Labour in opposition and given considerable emphasis while in government – housing – noting false starts, the difficulties encountered, and the magnitude of the challenge facing even the most determined of governments. Ayca Arkilic's chapter on the Christchurch mosque attacks, noted earlier, draws attention to one of the signature features of Prime Minister Ardern's first term, brought about in the immediate aftermath of the attacks. The changes made to New Zealand's firearms laws, implemented in a disciplined and steadfast manner, had international effects, the prime minister emerging as a role model and virtual miracle worker for perpetually frustrated US gun control advocates.

International perspectives

In the past, New Zealanders' interest in international events has not always been reciprocated by outsiders' curiosity about developments taking place in this country, although the previous election book, *Stardust and Substance*, provided several studies of how the 2017 election looked to overseas observers. Subsequently, owing initially to the Christchurch mosque attacks and Ardern's response, interest in New Zealand's politics and political leadership grew. Much of the attention paid was supportive, the prime minister's leadership gaining high praise. This accelerated in 2020, attracted by New Zealand's response to Covid-19 and the prime minister's role in leading that response. During the lead-up to the 2020 election and throughout the campaign, academics specialising in New Zealand politics were approached by journalists from every continent except Antarctica, all eager for insights, comments and soundbites. Accordingly, in this book, the way that the New Zealand election campaign was viewed from overseas is the subject of five chapters, offering perspectives from Chile, Canada, Western Europe, Australia and the United Kingdom, with Ayca Arkilic's chapter providing insight into media coverage in Muslim-majority countries (particularly Turkey).

The 2020 outcome

The election result itself is discussed from several perspectives. The overview given in the opening chapter is preceded by reflections in the book's Foreword from the Speaker of the New Zealand House of Representatives, Trevor Mallard. Veteran political scientists Nigel S. Roberts and Therese Arseneau provide detailed and definitive discussion of special votes, an oft-discussed feature of television commentary on the election but (as they point out) one not always well understood. Their chapter clarifies what 'special votes' actually are, accompanied by a systematic analysis of trends and the impact of special votes at the 2020 election.

A book of record on a country's election needs to move beyond the campaigns and votes to provide clarity about the overall outcome. Through several successive volumes political scientist and consultant Stephen Church has identified, discussed and analysed the options available to post-election party representatives (and, where appropriate, negotiators), given the numbers of parliamentary seats won by the various parties. In New Zealand's parliamentary system this is not always simple or straightforward. Even in 2020, with Labour gaining a majority of Parliament's 120 seats, determining the post-election arrangements (including the allocation of ministerial portfolios) required some consideration.

Finally, the epilogue offers a preliminary perspective on Jacinda Ardern's prime ministerial leadership, set against an established academic framework for the study of a leader's political performance, and speculates on how she will fare over the next three years and beyond.

As with previous publications, this 2020 New Zealand election volume includes primary documents – Labour's post-election cooperation agreement with the Greens and the Governor-General's 'Speech from the Throne' outlining the government's plans for the 2020–2023 period – as well as listings of the members elected in 2020 to the 53rd Parliament and the MPs awarded ministerial portfolios (both within and outside Cabinet).

*****

Acknowledgements

This book continues an effort to record and document New Zealand's elections, for the interested public; for students and scholars; for journalists, commentators and public officials, both in New Zealand and elsewhere. New Zealand's politics, particularly in recent years, have revealed a capacity to surprise and intermittently inspire, both within this country and overseas, and it is appropriate to respond to that interest with thoughtful, well-presented commentary, spotlighting significant elements of the country's politics, from one election to the next. Ultimately, these books share a commitment to the view that forgetfulness – about politics and political history – is to be avoided where possible, and that a healthier and more rational politics can best be achieved by knowledge of the past, as part of a country's heritage and political culture.

As editor I am happy to express my gratitude to all those who participated at the post-election conference and/or as contributing authors to this volume. Support from the prime minister, party leaders and the Speaker is particularly appreciated. It is gratifying that the value of these post-election conferences and books is recognised through their participation.

Apart from the participants' contributions, assistance with conference arrangements and manuscript preparation came from several sources. At Parliament, Jessie Manning (the Speaker's Senior Private Secretary) and Roland Todd (Speaker's Assistant) were, as always, very helpful at all times, whenever approached, facilitating arrangements for the conference venue and the Speaker's involvement. Other parliamentary staff likewise assisted in arranging their party leaders' participation.

Any all-day conference requires catering arrangements; as previously, Sophie Tavoi once again was able to assist, ensuring that all went entirely according to plan. Flawless technical support, allowing for powerpoint presentations and the prime minister's pre-recorded video to proceed without any difficulties, was provided by Nyssa Edgecombe (Operations Manager, Soundtech Ltd.) and her team, and is gratefully acknowledged.

At Victoria University of Wellington, the most important individual in assisting with organising the post-election conference was Jonette Crysell, School Manager at Victoria University's School of History, Philosophy, Political Science and International Relations. Over a period of months, going well beyond a strict reading of her job description, Jonette assisted with various arrangements and communications, displaying, at all times, good judgment, efficiency, and a calm, good-natured demeanour. Assistance was also provided by administrative assistants Yan Ma (conference arrangements) and Henry Beckford (manuscript preparation). A special thanks also to parliamentary intern Logan Byrne for some much appreciated last-minute editorial assistance. As previously, Victoria University's Colin McDiarmid brought his photographic skills – and, crucially, his camera – to the conference, taking some superb photos.

This is the seventh book in this New Zealand elections series to be published by Victoria University of Wellington Press. It has also been my pleasure to have had four other books published by them over the years. I am happy to take the opportunity to thank the publisher, Fergus Barrowman, for his warm support for these endeavours. As always, the book's copy editor, Kyleigh Hodgson, brought her meticulous eye, technical skills and scrupulous professionalism to the task, going through the manuscript with great care – for which much thanks. Thanks also to Kate Guthrie for preparing the book's comprehensive index.

To those who attended the post-election conference, your presence – your interest and enthusiasm – contributed significantly to the atmosphere at the event. And it was, as ever, good to see so many familiar faces.

In December 2020, New Zealand was one of the few places in the world where a conference such as we had – approximately 120 people sitting together indoors, maskless, at a normal distance from one another – could have safely been held. We were, in this respect as in others, most fortunate, and it is appropriate, in looking back at that event and ahead to the future, to be grateful for all that we have been able to enjoy.

Overview of the Election

1

POLITICS IN A PANDEMIC: NEW ZEALAND'S 2020 ELECTION

Stephen Levine

17 October 2020

Election day brought largely fine weather – mostly sunny, scattered clouds and rain – and a high voter turnout, although many people had already voted days and weeks before the actual polling day. At 7.00 pm the polls closed. Now the country waited. On television, experienced commentators sat together, offering speculative comments about likely outcomes as they awaited the first electorate-by-electorate returns. The party leaders were in New Zealand's largest city, Auckland – Prime Minister Jacinda Ardern (Labour), Judith Collins (National), David Seymour (ACT), James Shaw and Marama Davidson (Greens) – or (in the case of New Zealand First's Winston Peters) just north of it. With the rest of the country all they could do was await the outcome. The first results were expected to be announced shortly after 8.00 pm.

Nine months earlier: 28 January 2020

With the summer holiday break nearing an end, Jacinda Ardern called a press conference in Wellington. Following her predecessor John Key's example, she was giving early notice of the election date. New Zealanders were to go to the polls on Saturday, 19 September, almost to the day the same date as in 2017 – Saturday, 23 September – when she was able to lead a revived Labour Party to a result good enough to bring the party back to power in a coalition with New Zealand First and the Greens.

Meanwhile, in China's Wuhan province, an outbreak of a virus labelled Covid-19 (coronavirus) is claiming victims. Life in New Zealand continues as normal for the moment. This is shortly to change.

February 2020

New Zealand begins, prudently, to take precautions. A ban on travellers arriving from China is instituted on 3 February, initially for two weeks. As the international outbreak becomes more severe and the news more disturbing the government's border closure is extended for a further eight days from 15 February. On 18 February China's ambassador to New Zealand calls for trade and travel restrictions to be lifted, describing them as contrary to World Health Organisation advice. On 24 February the prime minister announces a further eight-day extension, on public health advice, predicting, even so, that it is 'highly likely' that the virus will eventually reach New Zealand.

On 28 February New Zealand has its first reported case of Covid-19.

March 2020

On 14 March the government announces that anyone entering the country from anywhere apart from the Pacific will need to self-isolate for 14 days. Five days later New Zealand's borders are closed to all but New Zealand citizens and permanent residents; all indoor gatherings of more than 100 people are ordered cancelled. On 21 March a four-tiered alert system is introduced; New Zealand is on alert level 2. Two days later the prime minister places New Zealand at alert level 3. A further two days and, on 25 March, the prime minister announces a national state of emergency. New Zealand is at alert level 4, the entire country in self-isolation. The nationwide lockdown closes schools and businesses; internal travel is restricted, people are required to remain in their homes. Hand sanitisers are in; hugs and handshakes are out. New Zealand, its streets quiet, its footpaths empty, enters a reality more suited to the *Twilight Zone*, an imagined dystopia (although teddy bears make an appearance in home and car windows, offering a form of uplift and comfort).

New Zealand remains at alert level 4 for close to two months. Only 'essential people' are allowed out; others remain indoors.

Regular televised briefings from the prime minister and the Director-General of Health, Dr Ashley Bloomfield, provide information and evidence-based commentary, calling upon New Zealanders to 'unite against Covid-19'. Jacinda Ardern and her government have put the country on something approaching a war footing, fighting against an unseen yet altogether too lethal adversary. On 29 March New Zealand reports its first Covid-19-related fatality. There will be 24 further deaths before the end of the year.

Apart from healthcare consequences – pressures on hospitals and other medical facilities; the need for supplies of personal protective equipment (for medical personnel) and masks – the pandemic emergency has other effects. Commemorations of the 15 March 2019 Christchurch attacks are cancelled. On 17 March the government announces a $12.1 billion package to support workers, businesses and the healthcare system. The country's tertiary education sector, deprived of international student revenue, experiences financial crisis (while introducing 'remote learning' systems). The tourism sector begins a year-long struggle to survive in the absence of international travellers.

A special parliamentary committee – the Epidemic Response Committee – is set up to scrutinise the government's management of the pandemic. Established on 25 March, chaired by National Party leader Simon Bridges and with more Opposition members (five National MPs and ACT's sole MP David Seymour) than members from government parties (three Labour, one New Zealand First, one Green), the committee meets for nine weeks over video conference, its hearings of experts, ministers, members of the public and officials livestreamed until its disestablishment on 26 May.

As transmission of the virus comes under control, the government's policies and the prime minister's performance win high praise, both internationally and domestically. Awareness of the extent of the pandemic elsewhere, with steadily rising numbers of cases and fatalities in the United States, the United Kingdom and Europe, adds further to New Zealanders' appreciation of its government's approach. The Covid-19 Public Health Response Act, enacted (63–57) on 13 May over National and ACT objections, gives police the power to enforce Covid-19 restrictions. Its enactment takes place hours ahead of New Zealand's move to alert level 2. On 14 May the government announces a budget which includes a $50 billion Covid rescue package, with an extension to an emergency wage subsidy and free trades training; the National opposition denounces what it describes as a 'campaign bribe'.

On 14 May, its state of emergency ended, New Zealand goes from alert level 3 to 2; travel between regions is able to resume, schools reopen; gatherings are limited to ten people. A week earlier, on 5 May, Prime Minister Ardern takes part (remotely) in an Australian cabinet meeting.

At the same time an international survey ranks New Zealand tops for its government's Covid-19 response, including the prime minister's 'personal style and empathy' and the alert-level system, with Germany coming second and Singapore third. The prime minister is praised by the *New York Times* for having provided a 'masterclass on how to respond' (Manhire 2020).

The year had begun with poll-driven stories predicting a close election, with the National Party preserving a lead over Labour that stretched back to the 2017 election itself (when National won more votes than Labour but was unable to form a majority coalition). The first *1 News* Colmar Brunton poll of 2020 (released on 13 February) has National, at 46 per cent, coming to power in coalition with ACT (at 2 per cent). Labour remains in second place, at 41 per cent, with the Greens at 5 per cent and New Zealand First at 3 per cent (and unable to return to Parliament) (Cheng 2020). Jacinda Ardern is 'preferred prime minister' for 42 per cent of those polled, with National Party leader Simon Bridges at 11 per cent support. Judith Collins and Winston Peters are both at 3 per cent.

Polls in May, as the lockdown comes to an end, see a dramatic reversal in poll numbers: Labour holds a commanding lead which, if retained, will allow the party to govern without a coalition partner, something no party has been able to do since the introduction of the mixed-member proportional (MMP) system in 1996. On 18 May a *Newshub*–Reid Research poll gives Labour 56.5 per cent of the vote – up 14 per cent – while National falls 12.7 per cent down to 30.6 per cent. The result, if confirmed at the election, will give Labour 72 seats in Parliament. Simon Bridges observes:

> Governments the world over have seen a boost following Covid-19. We've seen wall-to-wall coverage of the government during the crisis. But that wasn't an election campaign, which will be about our economic future. National has the team and the track record for jobs and growth and that will put us in a much stronger position as we head towards the election (Moir 2020b).

22 May 2020

A week later, on 21 May – with New Zealand at alert level 2 and the state of emergency allowed to expire – a *1 News* Colmar Brunton poll puts the National Party, led by Simon Bridges, at 29 per cent support, a decline of

17 per cent from its previous poll. Support for Labour rises to 59 per cent, its best result in the poll's history. Jacinda Ardern's 63 per cent support as 'preferred prime minister' is the poll's highest ever figure for any prime minister; Bridges is at 5 per cent (Trevett 2020).

A leadership challenge comes from Todd Muller (MP for Bay of Plenty since 2014), with Nikki Kaye (MP for Auckland Central since 2008 and, perhaps not coincidentally, successful in defeating Jacinda Ardern for the seat in 2011 and 2014) as his deputy. Bridges calls an emergency National Party caucus meeting for the following day, declaring that he is 'very confident' that he has the numbers: 'The overwhelming majority of the caucus are behind me.' Observing that the polls reflect coverage of the government during the Covid-19 pandemic, he describes the prime minister as likeable but adds, 'My view of politics is it's not just a popularity contest, it's a contest of ideas and policies and plans and the ability to deliver' (Theunissen 2020).

Former National Prime Minister Jim Bolger announces his support for Muller on Radio New Zealand: 'Todd has the ability to work well with all . . . he will work with others to achieve the right goal' (RNZ 2020c). The caucus elects Muller as National's new leader, the Covid-19 virus claiming two further victims in Simon Bridges and his deputy, Paula Bennett. Bridges becomes only the second National Party leader removed by his colleagues without having the opportunity to lead the party at a general election, following in the footsteps of Jim McLay, who was chosen in November 1984 to succeed Robert Muldoon, and subsequently systematically undermined by the former prime minister and deposed in March 1986. Prior to Muller's elevation a commentator observed: 'Todd's not an inspiring guy. I don't think he's going to inspire Mullermania . . .' (David Cormack, quoted in RNZ 2020d). Another predicted,

> Victory for National can't be absolutely ruled out, but to get there Muller will have to be the most capable opposition leader in history . . . Muller wasn't chosen to win an election, he was chosen to avoid a rout. . . . There isn't going to be any 'Mullermania' to spark a great revival (Wilson 2020a).

On 25 May Muller reshuffles his caucus; MP Amy Adams, who had announced her retirement, alters her plans and is ranked third, with a new portfolio, Covid-19 recovery. Judith Collins remains in fourth spot, taking on economic and regional development as well as the position of shadow attorney-general and responsibility for rehabilitation of the Pike River coal mine. Following the leadership change, a *1 News* Colmar Brunton poll sees National rise nine percentage points (to 38 per cent), but with Labour still far ahead, at 50 per cent (Coughlan 2020a).

On 19 June Housing Minister Megan Woods takes responsibility for the managed isolation and quarantine of returning New Zealanders after two individuals leave isolation without being tested (*Dominion Post* 2020a). The New Zealand defence force is brought in to review border control processes, oversee quarantine facilities and provide additional organisational discipline. On 2 July the Covid-19 Recovery (Fast-track Consenting) Act, introduced on 16 June, is enacted to advance 11 'shovel ready' infrastructure projects in housing, environment and transport.

14 July 2020

On 14 July – Bastille Day in France, celebrating revolutionary change – Todd Muller resigns, 53 days after succeeding Simon Bridges. It is exactly 36 years since a previous National leader, Robert Muldoon, called what proved to be a momentous 'snap election', bringing David Lange, Roger Douglas and the fourth Labour government to power.

Muller explains his early morning resignation: 'The role has taken a heavy toll on me personally, and on my family, and this has become untenable from a health perspective,' adding, 'It has become clear to me that I am not the best person to be Leader of the Opposition and Leader of the New Zealand National Party at this critical time for New Zealand' (National Party 2020). Reactions from other party leaders are not entirely unsympathetic. The prime minister observes that 'no matter what side of Parliament you're sitting, politics is a difficult place'. David Seymour comments that 'being a leader of a political party on the national stage is an extremely competitive and bruising role'. Winston Peters' summing-up is more acerbic: 'Leading a divided and incompetent caucus would have tested even the best leader' (RNZ 2020f).

Later that morning National's parliamentary caucus elects Judith Collins – a veteran MP (first elected to Parliament in 2002) and a former Cabinet minister – as the party's new leader. Gerry Brownlee becomes deputy leader. National's leadership travails send some MPs to the exits, Amy Adams, Nikki Kaye and Paula Bennett announcing that they will not be seeking re-election to Parliament. Simon Bridges says of the leadership change: 'I'll make no secret that I voted for Mark Mitchell. . . . But now we've got Judith and I think she's going to do a really good job' (Moir 2020c). As in 1999, when Jenny Shipley and Helen Clark led National and Labour at the general election, the country can be assured that whatever the election outcome New Zealand will continue to be led by a woman prime minister.

Collins' election as leader comes after previous unsuccessful efforts, losing to Bill English in 2016 and to Simon Bridges in 2018. She brings her two predecessors to National's front bench: Simon Bridges at the number four spot (with responsibility for justice and foreign affairs), Todd Muller at number eight (responsible for trade). Her first media conference as leader sees her entire caucus surrounding her in a show of unity. The change of leadership comes with National's election hoardings – its message declaring 'Strong Team. More Jobs. Better Economy.' – ready to go up, a photo of Todd Muller and Nikki Kaye side by side (see chapter 22).

In February Simon Bridges had ruled out working with New Zealand First after the election: 'If they hold the balance of power after the next election, we're not working with them,' adding, 'I can't trust them and I don't think New Zealanders can' (RNZ 2020a). Shortly after becoming leader Collins announces that while the leadership may have changed, the decision not to work with New Zealand First had not (Jones 2020). Neither, however, had National's prospects. A *Newshub*–Reid Research poll has National falling to 25.1 per cent support, with Labour rising (to 60.9 per cent). Jacinda Ardern's support as 'preferred prime minister' is at 62 per cent, Collins at 14.6 per cent (McCulloch 2020a), the results highlighting the absence of any 'bump' in support for National following the party's latest leadership change.

August 2020

On 11 August, a renewed Covid-19 outbreak in Auckland ends 102 days in which New Zealand has been free of newly reported cases. Mystery surrounds how the outbreak occurred, but the impact is swift. On 12 August Auckland moves to alert level 3 – a lockdown that sees checkpoints at roads into the city, with entry only by special permission from the Ministry of Health – and the rest of the country slips back to alert level 2. The chilling threat of a new nationwide lockdown is real, the impact on the 2020 election immediate. Political parties suspend their campaigns. The formal dissolution of Parliament – scheduled to occur at 11 am on 12 August – is postponed; the moment comes and goes, none of the ceremonial trappings on the front steps of Parliament taking place. Instead, the prime minister is speaking to the media, announcing that Parliament – having adjourned on 6 August – is to be recalled. On 18 August Parliament resumes. It is an emptier-than-usual debating chamber, with social distancing separating those present, and with many MPs advised to remain outside Wellington, in their home communities.

National MPs challenge ministers, assigning blame for the renewed Auckland outbreak. Deficiencies at the border are uncovered, with the prime minister admitting that the behaviour of frontline staff did not conform to expectations. The prime minister had stated in July that all frontline border staff were being regularly tested. It turns out that that wasn't happening.

Following complaints from Judith Collins, Winston Peters and David Seymour that the Auckland outbreak and subsequent restrictions have made it impossible for campaigning to occur, on 17 August the prime minister announces that the 19 September election date is to be moved. The ease with which New Zealand's political system is able to adapt to evolving circumstances – perhaps too readily taken for granted – is well on display. Disregarding suggestions that the election be put off until 2021, the prime minister announces that it will now be held on 17 October and that there will be no further postponements. The decision is accepted by her adversaries amid the prospect of renewed campaigning.

With an election campaign in abeyance – only roadside hoardings to show for it – and the renewed Auckland outbreak leading to a revival of anti-Covid-19 measures (social distancing; the wearing of masks on all public transport), the spectre of the 2019 Christchurch mosque attacks is also revived. The mass murderer, having pleaded guilty to 51 counts of murder, 40 counts of attempted murder and one count of terrorism, is in court as survivors recount their memories of what occurred. After four days, on 27 August the presiding judge issues his sentencing verdict: for the first time a defendant is given a life sentence without parole, the harshest sentence on New Zealand's statute books in the absence of capital punishment, which was abolished in 1961 (Brown 2020). New Zealand First leader Winston Peters dissents from other leaders' satisfaction with the verdict, calling for the murderer, an Australian citizen, to be returned to that country to serve out his sentence: 'I don't think the New Zealand taxpayers, after all this misery, should go ahead and be mugged and brutalised a second time year upon year at enormous cost.' It is revealed that special security measures will cost $3.6 million over two years. ACT's leader David Seymour describes it as 'legally impracticable to send him back to Australia', adding, 'I'm really saddened that Mr Peters has tried to make a political point on a day such as today' (McCullough 2020a).

With Auckland still at alert level 3 – a virtual lockdown – National calls for tougher anti-Covid-19 measures, proposing a new border agency reporting to a single minister with the mandate of keeping the country free of Covid-19 and other pandemic threats. The rest of the country moves to alert level 1 on 22 September. Auckland moves to alert level 2 on 30 August; it remains at that level until 7 October – ten days before the election – when it at last joins the rest of the country at alert level 1.

As the election campaign resumes, Parliament is scheduled to dissolve on 6 September. Wellington's weather prevents the ceremony from taking place on the front steps of Parliament (RNZ 2020m). It is, instead, moved indoors, where, at alert level 2, the few interested members of the public, on Parliament's grounds to witness the event, are unable to attend. Political party television and radio ads, postponed to 13 September due to the election date change, are released for the enlightenment of the New Zealand public following the Governor-General's issuance of the writ for the election to be held.

The parties campaign . . .

Small parties make earnest efforts to put their programmes, policies and personnel before the public. The Opportunities Party (TOP) launches its campaign on 24 July, a universal basic income one of its key offerings. With its slogan – 'Don't Leave Change to Chance' – the party (which made its first appearance at the 2017 election) seeks to offer itself as a fresh alternative, its social policies not dissimilar to those of Labour and the Greens. A campaign letter declares that 'Covid-19 has shown that our current way of doing things is no longer fit for purpose', describing New Zealand as a country with 'record high rents, an entire generation who cannot afford to buy their first home, and an environment and climate crisis', and claiming that 'successive governments have ignored expert research and policy advice about how to solve these huge problems'.

The One Party – 'the only explicitly Christian party running for office at this election' (Braae 2020) – brings opposition to the 2020 abortion law changes and concerns about the euthanasia referendum as campaign themes, stressing the need for a more religious approach to be taken in New Zealand's increasingly secular society. Its slogans – 'It's Time'; 'Your choice determines the morality and freedoms of our nation'; 'Advance the Kingdom' – support a vision intended 'to stir the hearts of the nation to arise and pursue righteous change in Aotearoa New Zealand' (One Party 2019). A mooted accord with another small party, Advance New Zealand, fails to eventuate, although an agreement not to compete in Waiariki against a Destiny Church–backed Vision NZ candidate (Hannah Tamaki) is honoured in return for that party promising not to stand a candidate against the One Party's Te Tai Tokerau candidate (Janice Arahanga-Epiha).

A broader conservative approach, taken by the New Conservative Party, calls to 'Save New Zealand' from a myriad of policies considered to be misguided, including: government debt – 'Every New Zealander owes $32,000 in Government debt'; ease of abortion 'up to full term'; spending '$1.4 billion of taxpayer dollars overseas annually on the UN's Paris 2015 Agreement'; the legalisation of 'Medicinal Marijuana'; and spending 'over ½ million dollars on a playground at Parliament'. The party promises 'to make voters important again by making citizens initiated referenda binding'; 'to make taxpayers important again by good stewardship of the taxes paid'; 'to make families important again'; 'to make New Zealand important again by protecting our sovereignty and putting the interests of New Zealand ahead of international agreements made by non-elected officials' (New Conservative Party 2020). A brochure declaring 'Keep NZ Ours' sounds a populist note. In October a High Court judge dismisses the party's bid to be included in a televised multi-party debate; it had been excluded on the basis that it was polling below TVNZ's three per cent threshold and that the party had not been in Parliament for the past two election cycles. The party's leader, Leighton Baker, describes its absence from the debate as unfair and incompatible with a healthy democracy (Smith 2020), arguing that it is 'a credible minor party with strong opposition' on the two referendum questions, the legalisation of cannabis and the euthanasia legislation.

On 26 July former National MP Jami-Lee Ross announces that his Advance New Zealand Party has merged with the New Zealand Public Party, hopeful that the seat of Te Tai Tokerau might be won by co-leader Billy Te Kahika. Subsequent polling suggests that this is largely wishful thinking, a poll released on 8 October showing Billy Te Kahika with 'almost no support' in the electorate (RNZ 2020u).

Launching Advance New Zealand, Ross states that the party would repeal the Covid-19 Public Health Response Act and remove foreign interference in New Zealand's politics, calling for the suspension of New Zealand's free trade agreement within China: 'The number one problem with the establishment parties is that no one wants to stand up to the biggest threat – China', indicating that he supports independence for Hong Kong and Taiwan (RNZ 2020i). In September, excluded from a minor party leaders' debate (the 3 October Newshub Nation PowerBrokers), the party takes legal action against MediaWorks, seeking 'judicial intervention' in order to allow New Zealanders to hear 'a range of opinions from political parties' (RNZ 2020o). The High Court rejects the effort, stating that the criteria used – that a party needed to 'have won a list or electorate seat within the last two parliamentary terms' – is neither unreasonable nor arbitrary (RNZ 2020s). The two co-leaders describe the ruling as 'another example of the media stacking the deck against democracy' (Advance New Zealand 2020).

In September, while claiming that Advance New Zealand is tapping into 'growing voter dissatisfaction with the main parties' and that the party will be 'competitive on October 17', Jami-Lee Ross announces that he will not be standing in Botany – the electorate that he had won as a National candidate in 2011, 2014 and 2017 – but will be hoping to return to Parliament on the party's list, describing the Te Tai Tokerau contest as 'a three-way race': 'We had to decide which one of us should focus on running the nationwide campaign, which one should focus on the seat. I'm running the nationwide campaign and Billy's gonna win [the electorate]' (Forrester 2020). A rally organised by the co-leaders in Auckland on 12 September protests the government's use of lockdowns and other Covid-19 restrictions. With 'several thousand people packed into Aotea Square with no social distancing and few wearing masks', the police choose not to intervene, alert-level-2 rules going unenforced (Scotcher 2020c).

The Māori Party's effort to return to Parliament opens by making clear that it will not be seeking to work with National (as it had done in the past), the party's president stating that it prefers to work with Labour (Moir and Patterson 2020). Matters become less clear when former Labour MP and party co-leader John Tamihere (the party's candidate in Tāmaki Makaurau) states that the party hopes to gain sufficient votes to be able to negotiate with either a National/ACT bloc or Labour/Greens (Moir 2020a). Subsequently Tamihere announces the party's 2020 policies, including establishment of a Māori Parliament, registering all Māori on the Māori electoral roll (while ensuring that they can switch to the general roll at any time), entrenching the Māori parliamentary seats (making their abolition more difficult) and reducing MMP's 5 per cent party vote threshold to 2.5 per cent (RNZ 2020p). The party also pledges to officially change the country's name to 'Aotearoa' and to replace Pākehā place names with Māori names (RNZ 2020n).

Public discourse involving smaller parties with parliamentary representation – ACT, New Zealand First and the Greens – becomes increasingly adversarial as the brief campaign goes on. ACT's leader David Seymour, taking a dismissive view of New Zealand First, states that the party has 'let down a lot of people', adding, 'I don't think they deserve to be in any Parliament let alone New Zealand's' (Hollingworth 2020). Seymour is also critical of the government's Covid-19 response, stating that the government lacked a strategy for dealing with the pandemic's consequences and that 'the goal should be smart borders that people and money can come through, but not Covid-19'; he calls for an open debate about how long New Zealand should keep its borders closed (Devlin and Clent 2020). ACT party president Tim Jago tells those attending the party's campaign launch in Auckland that ACT is 'aiming to get as high as 6 or 7 per cent of the party vote, which would give ACT eight MPs' (Robson 2020a). Calling for New Zealanders to 'Party Vote ACT, To Change Your Future', ACT declares that it has 'a real plan' to 'jump-start the economy', offering to cut GST to 10 per cent and give more support to small businesses, 'essential for New Zealand's economic recovery' (ACT 2020).

With National's support weakening and ACT's rising, National leader Judith Collins continues National's practice of endorsing David Seymour's candidacy in the Epsom electorate he has represented since 2014. Collins asks Epsom voters to give their party vote to National but their 'first tick' to Seymour, saying, 'I think he's a very good local MP and I would welcome him being part of a National–ACT government.' Seymour's cheerful response – 'It would be churlish for me to turn off any endorsement' (Robson 2020b) – reflects his party's consistent polling above the 5 per cent threshold as well as his own level of support as the electorate's incumbent MP.

On 25 July the Green Party releases its 'policy vision document', focusing on three main areas: healthy nature, fairer communities and a clean economy (Dreaver 2020). Its policy programme includes spending more on solar panels for state houses, the funds coming from the $50 billion Covid-19 Response and Recovery Fund (RNZ 2020e). A Green Party flyer highlights 'warm homes and fair wages so everyone has what they need to live a good life'; 'strong protections for the wild places we love so they thrive for generations to come'; and 'bold climate action so our communities are resilient and no one is left behind on the route to a cleaner future'. Voters are urged to join those 'acting now for a cleaner, fairer Aotearoa' (Green Party 2020).

Having launched their wealth tax policy in June, co-leader James Shaw indicates that the Greens want to introduce a 1 per cent wealth tax for those with a net worth over a million dollars but states that the proposal is not one of the party's bottom lines. Cognisant of Jacinda Ardern's popularity, Shaw argues that the best way to ensure she continues as prime minister is to 'party vote Green': 'Frankly they are going to need us if they're going to be able to form a government because they're polling just shy of 50 per cent. They're going to need a partner to get them over the line and we are the partner they want to have.' He declares that the Greens want Ardern to continue as prime minister, stating, 'A vote for the Greens is the most powerful vote you can wield in order to ensure Jacinda Ardern continues as prime minister and we have a strong Labour–Green government' (McCullough 2020b).

While looking forward to a renewed Labour-led government, Shaw is less keen on continuing collaboration with New Zealand First, describing the party as 'a millstone' (Walls 2020a). As an example, New Zealand First's unwillingness to agree on a light rail system to be built from downtown Auckland to the airport means that the project is unable to gain approval prior to the election. New Zealand First leader Winston Peters states 'frankly this is a matter people and parties can campaign on' (Scotcher 2020b). James Shaw's response is that he's 'always disappointed in New Zealand First', expressing frustration with the decision and with the party more generally (Scotcher 2020a).

Unlike National's arrangement with David Seymour in Epsom, Labour states that it will not enter into a deal with the Greens to allow

Chlöe Swarbrick to win the Auckland Central seat, its refusal to do so coming at a time when the Greens are still hovering at around 5 per cent in pre-election polls (Robson 2020c). In May the release of the Greens' party list finds Swarbrick (ranked seventh in 2017) moved to third place in the party's rankings.

James Shaw's 2020 campaign does not proceed without mishap. Criticised by Judith Collins for allegedly holding up the process of approving government grants for a variety of infrastructure projects in order for a grant to be provided to Taranaki Green School, despite the Greens having a policy against public funding for private schools – Collins calls for his resignation on 2 September – Shaw apologises for an error in judgment (RNZ 2020l). When Shaw indicates that he had been given 'verbal sign-off' from the Minister of Education, Chris Hipkins, Hipkins notes that he was 'not one of the ministers involved in decisions around the "shovel ready" projects, so it was not a matter for me to sign off, or otherwise' (Patterson 2020d). The saga becomes a distraction in the Greens' campaign at a time when polling suggests the party is still vulnerable; there is also internal dissatisfaction within the Greens over the incident. Shaw issues numerous apologies, demonstrating a gift for understatement with his observation that 'it didn't work out well' (Wilson 2020b).

New Zealand First

On 19 July New Zealand First launches its campaign in Auckland with 'Back Your Future' as its slogan and party leader (and founder) Winston Peters giving the keynote speech. Election policy includes reintroducing a universal family benefit, allowing families to use the programme to put down a deposit on a first home (Moir 2020e).

Other policy includes a focus on immigration: allowing no more than 15,000 people to come into New Zealand annually, all highly skilled workers, is described by Peters as a coalition agreement bottom line. The immigration policy includes bringing immigrants to towns and smaller cities under a new rural visa scheme, and a nationwide review to create a 30-year population plan, part of an attempt to identify the desired level of New Zealand's future population numbers (Bonnett 2020). The rural visa would introduce a legal obligation on foreign workers to stay in their specified place of settlement until becoming residents. Peters indicates that a renewed coalition agreement with Labour will need to see New

Zealand First placed in charge of immigration. Jacinda Ardern responds that when the coalition was formed in 2017, 'immigration was an issue' but 'we maintained our position', adding, 'ultimately I think it is going to be a different debate at this election given the circumstances with Covid we find ourselves in' (RNZ 2020h).

The party also focuses on law-and-order issues; an additional 1000 frontline police are to be recruited as Peters warns of higher crime rates due to Covid-19 bringing increased unemployment and an economic downturn. New Zealand First's 'Safer Kiwi Communities' policy includes legislating to ensure that 'when courts are sentencing or otherwise dealing with offenders, they must prioritise the needs of the victim first, then the community second, then last, the offender' (*Scoop* 2020b). Overall, the party's policies, including the revived family benefit, emphasise traditional New Zealand First themes and ideas, with presumed appeal to older voters (Moir 2020f).

Peters' evinces little regret over his post-2017 election decision to enter a coalition with Labour, giving Jacinda Ardern the opportunity to become prime minister. He argues that Labour 'lacked experience in government' after New Zealand had endured 'nine long years of neglect by the National Party', and that New Zealand First has 'used common sense to hold Labour and the Greens to account. We've opposed woke pixie dust. We've defended socially conservative values.' In his view, a 2020 vote for New Zealand First represents a chance for voters to 'take out some necessary insurance' –

> against the ideological urge to tax, tax, tax; insurance against big government and the view that nanny state knows best; insurance against the folly that taxpayers' money can solve any problem; insurance against extremism – from either side of politics; and insurance against any who would seek to govern alone.

Among his contributions as a coalition partner Peters cites New Zealand First's ability to disrupt plans for a capital gains tax and Auckland light rail: 'we have stopped bad, uncosted ideas' (*Scoop* 2020a).

Other party leaders, not surprisingly, take a different view of New Zealand First governing as a partner. Of National's stance – to not work with New Zealand First – Peters remains sceptical: 'Well, I've heard it all before and the first call on election night is from them' (Moir 2020d).

A David Seymour tweet on 19 July ignites an exchange: 'Winston Peters' swansong promise to slash immigration is tragic. Peters himself will soon be retired and will require a care worker to help him get dressed and go for a walk. He'll discover that such facilities can't function without migrant workers.' Peters' response:

> I've spent much of my career respecting and working for retirees. You seem to want to euthanise them. As for your nasty comments about my physical – I reckon you'd last 10 seconds in the ring with me. There'd be three hits – you hitting me, me hitting you, and the ambulance hitting 100. Thank your lucky stars I'm not into physical violence' (*Otago Daily Times* 2020).

Relations between New Zealand First and the Greens are little better than those between Peters and Seymour. Peters' advice to voters – to give New Zealand First their party vote 'to take out some insurance in this campaign to ensure you don't get the nightmare government I know you're going to get' – leads Shaw to observe: 'Well, I think that the nightmare that he's got is that he's not going to be back in Parliament,' adding, 'My experience of working with New Zealand First as a party in government is that rather than a force of moderation, they're a force of chaos.'

Peters raises the spectre of a Labour–Green government without a New Zealand First presence: 'If you think a red-green government is safe for you then you're in cloud cuckoo land. They know everything about how to spend your money, and not one idea about how to make some.' Speaking in Wellington, Peters describes his 2017–2020 coalition experience less than positively: 'I've never had three years so difficult, trying to manage circumstances when you're surrounded by plain inexperience.' Jacinda Ardern takes a high-minded approach to Peters' rhetoric: 'Look, I put it down to an election period. You can also find many comments from the deputy prime minister talking about what we've managed to achieve as a government, which I've got the sense he's been proud of' (Moir 2020g). At his campaign launch Peters notes with satisfaction that the coalition had lasted for the full three years despite some predictions to the contrary. As for the prime minister, Peters stresses that he is

> not campaigning against her, quite the contrary. Let me tell you that we made a decision in 2017 to go with a change style of

> leadership. We don't resile from that. But we did promise all of our experience and understanding and common sense to the government. And we've done both those things. I'm not going to go and campaign against the last three years (Patterson 2020c).

During the campaign Labour and New Zealand First are unable to agree on what should be done in the wake of plans for production to end at the South Island's Tiwai Point aluminium smelter. There are further clashes between the Greens and New Zealand First when on 29 July Green MPs vote in favour of a members' bill from National MP David Carter to abolish the 'waka jumping' law (introduced at New Zealand First's behest to ensure MPs who quit their party are made to leave Parliament). The measure – the Electoral (Integrity) Amendment Act 2018 – had been agreed to in the Labour–New Zealand First coalition agreement; the Greens voted for the Act (despite opposing it) but declare, in July, that the party had made no commitment not to vote subsequently in support of its repeal.

New Zealand First's prospects are complicated by investigations and legal issues. There are ongoing matters relating to overpayments of Peters' superannuation (subsequently repaid) and alleged breaches of privacy. Peters' legal action against several individuals is unsuccessful when the High Court rules in April that Peters has been unable to establish that any of the defendants were the ones responsible for the leak of his personal superannuation information; he appeals against the ruling. Subsequently, in July, he is ordered to pay nearly $320,000 in costs after failing to prove that the privacy breach had been made by the four individuals taken to court: two former National ministers, the former head of the Ministry of Social Development and the State Services Commissioner (RNZ 2020g); he states that the ruling will be appealed.

A further issue involves an investigation by the Serious Fraud Office (SFO) into the New Zealand First Foundation, further complicating matters in September with the election only three weeks away. Peters is critical of the timing of the SFO's announcement: 'While we respect its independence, the SFO cannot justify its timing. The foundation is an entirely separate entity from the New Zealand First party but that will be lost on some and deliberately confused, sadly, by others' (RNZ 2020q). New Zealand First's attempt in the High Court to delay the SFO's announcement – charging two people of 'obtaining by deception', neither of them a minister, a sitting MP, a candidate, or a current New

Zealand First member – fails when a judge rules that there is 'significant public interest in the New Zealand voting public being informed during an election campaign about criminal charges of serious fraud against people or organisations related to political parties'. The SFO matter had begun when police, in February 2020, decided to refer inquiries about New Zealand First Foundation donations to the SFO, following a complaint to the Electoral Commission in 2019 about whether the party and the Foundation were complying with requirements for donations and loans. The Electoral Commission concluded that the Foundation had received donations that should have been treated as party donations, referring the matter to the police (RNZ 2020b).

Peters makes known his views on the difficulties of campaigning with Covid-19 restrictions: 'It's the worst campaign environment that I've been involved in because, not only is it in the cold months of the year, but it's in circumstances in which people cannot be meeting, can't assemble in halls and you can't have a traditional political dialogue,' given alert level restrictions (Doyle 2020). Aboard his campaign bus, the slogan 'Back Your Future' written on the side, the party's tours around the country – both North and South Island – have little apparent effect.

In August, with opinion polls suggesting that New Zealand First might not be back in Parliament, Peters observes, 'Look, one of these days I'll have a lovely retirement – but not yet,' stating, 'I'm not going out there to lose.' Peters campaigns on his experience: 'Our idea is to go out there and say to people "you've done so well" but things are never more precarious than they are now. Now, it's about the economy and you do need serious experienced politicians who have been here before and know what they're doing' (Patterson 2020c).

Characteristically, Peters is dismissive of the polls, describing them as 'of no value to anyone': 'I have been to Warsaw. It is the capital of Poland. That's where Poles live. That's all I do when I talk about polls. All the rest is just ridiculous' (Ensor 2020).

National

'Strong Team' is removed from National's campaign slogan – 'Strong Team. More Jobs. Better Economy.' – in the wake of leadership changes, retirements and internal party divisions. Other elements of National's messaging, however, remain largely unaltered. The party promises to replace the Resource Management Act 1991 with more 'development-friendly' legislation and get rid of KiwiBuild (described by Collins as 'the biggest public policy failure in a generation'). On 17 July she announces a proposed infrastructure upgrade to the country's transport network, including a rail link to Auckland's airport.

National's official launch of its election campaign takes place on 20 September. Its finance spokesperson, Paul Goldsmith, soon acknowledges 'an irritating mistake', a $4 billion 'hole' in the party's economic policy, saying that National would borrow the missing funds, while promising $4.7 billion in tax cuts. Minister of Finance Grant Robertson describes National's economic plan as 'irresponsible and unaffordable', its error undermining the party's 'credibility' (Moir 2020h). National, in turn, claims that there is a $10 billion hole in Labour's economic plan (Patterson 2020e), with projects (such as 100 per cent renewable electricity by 2030 and light rail for Auckland) included without the funding to achieve them.

Due to Covid-19 restrictions Collins' virtual launch takes place at Avalon Studios in Lower Hutt. Only 100 socially distanced people are allowed to attend; others view the event via livestream. Collins promises listeners and viewers that 'You will not find a National government wasting taxpayers' money on expensive failures like KiwiBuild, light rail and a pet Green School,' declaring, 'Our policies will grow the economy, not the bureaucracy' (Walls 2020b). On the campaign trail in Nelson, with National polling under 30 per cent, Collins is encouraged to be tougher, to embrace her 'crusher' image: she replies, 'I'm often accused of being too nice' (McCulloch 2020b).

In October, an email from National MP Denise Lee to members of the National caucus, leaked to *Newshub*, accuses Collins of making improvised policy and failing to consult with her party's own spokesperson, indicative of 'incredibly poor form' and 'a shockingly bad example of poor leadership'. Another National MP characterises Collins as 'making up policy on the hoof'. Collins responds that during an election campaign 'leaders do make decisions, that's part of leadership, sometimes the leader just has to go out and make that announcement and that's the way it works'. While Denise Lee responds that the email 'was intended for internal purposes only' and that she completely disagreed 'with the actions of the person who leaked the email' (*1 News* 2020a), the incident, nine days before the election, leaves National's leader having to talk about internal criticism of her leadership from an ill-disciplined and divided caucus, rather than about National's policies and its critique of the government's record. It is a Laurel-and-Hardy moment: Judith Collins, exasperated, might well have gazed at her caucus colleague and observed, 'Here's another nice mess you've gotten me into.'

On 16 October, the day before the election, Collins responds to questions anticipating National having a poor result. Noting that she became leader when polling showed National far behind she rules out resigning afterwards, irrespective of the outcome. As for ACT's growth of support, she remarks that 'the people who decide to vote for ACT are doing so because they want a National-led government' (RNZ 2020v). Collins' attacks are directed towards both left and right: she objects to the Greens' wealth tax and ACT's flat tax (*1 News* 2020b), and disagrees with ACT's proposal to cut benefits: 'They're polling significantly lower than us. We're not going down a cutting of benefits for people who can't put food on the table' (RNZ 2020r).

Collins stands by National's assertion that the party has a 'strong team', saying that it reflects the front bench's 'breadth of experience'. On the campaign trail she seeks to project confidence, advising an interviewer, 'I'm always a very confident person, particularly when I know I'm right' (Patterson 2020a). She sums up her party's outlook, distinguishing National from Labour: 'We believe in people, more than we believe in big government' (Cook 2020).

Labour

On 4 July Labour's campaign is launched with the slogan 'Let's Keep Moving' – the successor to 2017's 'Let's do this' – campaign chair MP Megan Woods stating that the words are a rallying cry for New Zealanders to 'keep the country moving in the right direction under Jacinda Ardern's leadership'. Woods describes Labour as having a plan to 'respond, recover and rebuild' following the Covid-19 pandemic.

Speaking at the Labour Party's Congress in Wellington on 5 July, Jacinda Ardern highlights persistent challenges – climate change; reducing inequality and poverty – while stating that the government is making the biggest investment in infrastructure in her lifetime, helping with economic recovery.

Labour's 'five-point recovery plan' to 'keep us moving' is framed by the government's Covid-19 response: 'By protecting our health, we can recover faster. Going hard and early to stamp out the virus with a strong health response has saved lives, and puts us on a path to faster recovery.' The five points include: 'Investing in our people by supporting 1.7 million Kiwis through the Wage Subsidy Scheme and making all apprenticeships free'; 'Creating jobs by investing in shovel-ready infrastructure projects. We're creating 20,000 jobs, with 11,000 more to protect our environment'; 'Preparing for the future by investing in waste management and renewable electricity, and decarbonising our economy'; 'Supporting small businesses to help them get through, with interest free loans, tax refunds, and targeted support to sectors like tourism'; 'Backing our exporters with practical support and a continued focus on negotiating trade agreements' (New Zealand Labour Party 2020).

A Labour Party flyer includes a statement from the prime minister: 'Together, we've made a good start', 'together' being consistent with the prime minister's rhetoric about 'unity' and the 'team of 5 million'. The statement sums up the approach taken to the pandemic: 'By going hard and early against Covid – and because of the unity we showed and sacrifices everyone made – we've set ourselves up for a strong recovery. Now, as we keep fighting the virus, it's also vital we take advantage of the opportunities ahead. That's why we're rolling out a clear plan that protects health, creates jobs, and keeps the economy moving. Giving your Party Vote to Labour will keep up that momentum with a strong, stable government. Let's stick together and build on what we've started. Let's keep moving' – the statement underscored by Ardern's scarcely legible signature.

While National is dealing with problems within its caucus – two MPs announce that they will not be seeking re-election (see chapter 13, endnote 1) – the government is also caught up in matters which in other circumstances might have proved politically damaging. On 2 July the Minister of Health, David Clark, resigns following disclosures about his behaviour during the lockdown and his comments about Covid-19 testing lapses at the border, suggesting that the Director-General of Health Dr Ashley Bloomfield was in some way responsible. The prime minister declares that 'we need as a country, as a government, as a Cabinet, to be totally focused on our Covid response. Anything regardless of origins – anything that acts as an unnecessary distraction to that – we just simply couldn't afford.'

Less than three weeks later, on 22 July, another minister, Iain Lees-Galloway, is dismissed following admission of an affair with a former staffer. Accepting the decision, he apologises to the prime minister and 'to anyone who has been hurt by my actions'; the prime minister states that the minister had 'opened himself up to accusations of improperly using his office', his lack of judgment causing her 'to lose my confidence in him as a minister'. The difficulties with the two ministers, quickly and decisively resolved, have little effect on campaign dynamics.

Labour's Auckland launch of its campaign, on 8 August, includes a promise to invest $311 million to help unemployed New Zealanders into jobs, the prime minister's speech summarising Labour's key achievements and acknowledging some shortfalls: 'We haven't always achieved everything we set out to, and there have been lessons for us in that. We wanted more homes for first home buyers. We wanted light rail in Auckland. But we've had to accept that sometimes when you try things that have never been done before, you won't always succeed, but that doesn't mean you should give up' (RNZ 2020j).

On 16 October, following polling showing Labour with a strong lead over National, the prime minister observes that she has proved that she can work with three parties and that she could also work with two. Governing alone, however, would be preferable. 'My final pitch to voters continues to be that I'm looking for a strong mandate for Labour. Every vote that comes to Labour does enable us to form a strong stable government; it means that we can get on with things faster.' She notes, 'There's no doubt the more complex the arrangement that you have in government, the slower that recovery would be so that's why I'm looking for that simplicity and that mandate.' Regarding New Zealand First, she again refrains from criticising the party or its leader: 'I feel like it would be disingenuous to go and make statements about a party that I worked constructively with for the past three years.' Deflecting criticism about continued child poverty and the ongoing threat from global warming, she comments, 'We made and legislated the work that we are doing on child poverty – and I am not finished yet. I take some flattery in the idea that I would resolve a decades-long problem in three years but I can't. I'm proud of the work that we have done on climate change; it's more than any government has done ever in New Zealand on that issue' (RNZ 2020w).

The prime minister comments to an interviewer in August: 'I will not feel satisfied until I feel – and probably the job will never feel done for me – until I feel we're living up to our reputation that we are a country that cares for its most vulnerable' (Patterson 2020b). Her closing statement in a press conference on 24 August is similarly reflective: 'In a world where

2020 has frankly been terrible, we are strong, we have been kind, and we are doing really well.'

Looking to the future, speaking at a rally at Wellington's Michael Fowler Centre six days before the election, the prime minister offers a vision for the future: 'Imagine, if you will, that it's 2030. We are now a country where children living in poverty has halved, where we've ended our housing wait list, where health inequalities based on race, wealth and geographical location no longer exist, where every New Zealand child knows their history and our nation's history, where we've overcome the digital divide' (Coughlan 2020b).

On 6 September Jacinda Ardern introduces a 'September surprise', a campaign promise to provide New Zealanders with a new public holiday: 'Matariki will be a distinctly New Zealand holiday and a time for reflection, celebration and to look to the future as we take increasing pride in our unique national identity' (Cooke 2020). This is an immediate winner on multiple levels, combining the promotion of Māori culture with the appeal of a day off work, as consistent with the prime minister's 'relentlessly positive' outlook as any policy initiative yet taken. It is possible to feel sympathy for National: all the party is able to do, in reply, is to observe that the holiday is a fine idea but one which raises concerns about its impact on businesses – a hopeless, Scrooge-like position for a hapless party.

Voting in a pandemic

The Electoral Commission responded to the pandemic in a variety of ways, intending to allow for enrolment and voting to safely proceed. A flyer distributed to voters includes information on how to avoid infection while voting:

> Get ready to vote before you go to help keep everyone's visit to a voting place shorter . . . Hand sanitiser will be available at all voting places, please use it when you enter and when you leave. Physical distancing will be practised and our team will be on hand to help make sure everyone is safe. Face masks will be available at voting places if you need one (Electoral Commission 2020).

In the background to the general election campaign, divisions over two referendums (see chapter 23) continue. Family First issues a brochure describing the 2020 election in stark terms: 'This year it's a matter of life and death. Your votes will literally change lives.' The brochure urges a 'no' vote on both the euthanasia and cannabis referendums and states that while New Zealand's 'response to the health and economic threats of Covid-19 have been especially important this year', 'focusing on economics and other issues while ignoring social values will actually make society's present problems worse in the long term' (Family First 2020). A commentator notes: 'No one would have predicted when David Seymour's End of Life Choice Bill was passed by Parliament last November [2019] that the referendum required to bring the legislation into force would be held against the backdrop of a deadly global pandemic' (Adams 2020).

Voters wanting to know more about referendum details are able to access information from a government website. The government distributes at least two flyers to voters identifying the subject of the two referendums and the specific voting choices available, supported by a website from which further information can be obtained (New Zealand Government 2020). Although the referendums are for voters to decide, MPs and the parties they represent are not forbidden from stating their views. In August Judith Collins states that the entire National Party caucus has decided to vote against legalisation of cannabis, reflecting concerns 'about the mental health of New Zealanders' and opposition to 'a decision that tells younger people in particular that this is something that won't do you any harm'. The prime minister's reticence as to her own voting preference allows Collins to describe the referendum as 'a very crucial vote for people. New Zealanders need to know where the prime minister stands on this.' Ardern's position remains: 'people should vote in favour or oppose' based on their own views (RNZ 2020k).

A youth-led campaign to enlarge the franchise through court action to give 16- and 17-year-olds the vote – 'Make it 16' – proves fruitless. The High Court, unconvinced that restricting voting to those aged 18 and over was inconsistent with New Zealand's Bill of Rights Act, rules that current arrangements are a justified limit on the right to be free of discrimination on the basis of age, citing other laws that also distinguish between those over and those under the age of 18 (RNZ 2020t).

17 October 2020 – the election results

As the results come into the television studios the trend – a Labour landslide – is evident right from the start.

The National Party's parliamentary caucus was already going to be very different from the one elected in 2017. Thirteen MPs had announced their retirement, including a former Speaker and minister, David Carter; a once high-profile media personality, Maggie Barry; two former deputy leaders, Paula Bennett and Nikki Kaye; former ministers Amy Adams, Nathan Guy, Anne Tolley and Nicky Wagner; and MPs Sarah Dowie, Alastair Scott, Jian Yang, Hamish Walker and Andrew Falloon. Many of these MPs' electorate seats are captured by Labour Party candidates: Anne Tolley's East Coast seat by Labour's Kiri Allan; Nathan Guy's Ōtaki seat by Terisa Ngobi; Paula Bennett's Upper Harbour seat by Vanushi Walters; Alastair Scott's Wairarapa seat by Kieran McAnulty (see chapter 30). Nikki Kaye's Auckland Central seat is won by the Greens' Chlöe Swarbrick (see chapter 31).

To the list of retiring MPs is added a steadily lengthening roll of National electorate MPs defeated in their constituencies: Dan Bidois – Northcote; Harete Hipango – Whanganui; Matt King – Northland; Denise Lee – Maungakiekie; Tim Macindoe – Hamilton West; Jonathan Young – New Plymouth; and Lawrence Yule – Tukituki. Five other National MPs also lose their electorate seats – David Bennett, defeated in Hamilton East; Chris Bishop, in Hutt South; deputy leader Gerry Brownlee, in Ilam; Shane Reti, in Whangārei; and Nick Smith, a former Minister and an electorate MP since 1990, in Nelson – but are able to return to Parliament by virtue of their ranking on the party's list. Other National Party list MPs are less fortunate, unable to return to Parliament owing to National's weak party vote, which brings in only ten MPs alongside National's 23 surviving electorate MPs. Gone as a result are Kanwaljit Singh Bakshi, Paulo Garcia, Joanne Hayes, Brett Hudson, Agnes Loheni, Alfred Ngaro and Parmjeet Parmar.

The Labour Party emerges as the voters' preferred party in 71 of the country's 72 constituencies, winning the party vote in every electorate apart from Epsom (where National receives 37 per cent support, Labour 36 per cent). National even loses the party vote in Judith Collins' own electorate, Papakura, capturing just 36.9 per cent of the party vote against Labour's 42.5 per cent, although Collins wins the seat with a 5,583-vote margin of victory over her Labour opponent.

Labour's victory is a 'landslide', of course, although its magnitude can be exaggerated. While becoming the first party to win an absolute majority since 1951, it did so by a decimal point – 50.01 per cent. Looked at from a different perspective this also means that half the country voted for parties other than Labour.

Labour's 65 parliamentary seats (compared with National's 33) is impressive, but is only 54 per cent of the total 120 seats. In the first-past-the-post era, Labour under Norman Kirk won 55 of 87 seats (to National's 32) – a much more substantial 63 per cent of the House; three years later, these figures were reversed when National won.

In 2014 – two general elections ago – the New Zealand Labour Party received 604,535 party votes, suffering its third successive defeat to a John Key–led National Party. Three years later Labour's party vote total rose to 956,184 votes, Jacinda Ardern leading the party to a second-place finish, electorally, forming a coalition government afterwards to become prime minister. In 2020 Labour's party vote total rose again, to 1,443,545, a gain of nearly 500,000 votes. In just two elections the Labour Party has more than doubled its vote: an extraordinary achievement.

Wellington's *Dominion Post* (2020b) describes National's defeat as 'dramatic and humiliating'. All the campaigning – on the road and in broadcast studios, including a series of one-on-one debates with the prime minister (see chapter 25) – has had little effect on Labour's substantial months-long advantage. The election outcome reflects not only satisfaction with the government's performance in curbing the spread of Covid-19, but the absence of persuasive evidence that any other party, any other leader, could have done any better.

Among New Zealand's smaller parties there are mixed results. The Greens' performance sees the party in no danger of vanishing from Parliament, its ten seats including Chlöe Swarbrick's Auckland Central triumph. ACT's result – ten seats – exceeds its party president's expectations. As for New Zealand First, its campaign, forever in the doldrums, never managed to ignite that spark of late enthusiasm characteristic of some of the party's previous efforts. The party's leader, ranked number 1 on the party's list, did not contest an electorate; none of the party's candidates who did so came even close to winning a seat.

In 2020 the only Labour MP to lose their electorate seat is Tamati Coffey, defeated in Waiariki (which he won in 2017, defeating the then Māori Party leader, Te Ururoa Flavell). Returned to Parliament as a list MP, his electorate defeat by Rawiri Waititi gives the Māori Party renewed parliamentary life (see chapter 28 for discussion of the Māori Party and the results in the Māori electorates). In winning Waiariki – and thus becoming exempt from MMP's 5 per cent threshold – the party found that

Table 1.1: The results of the 2020 New Zealand general election

Party	Number of party votes	Percentage of party votes	Percentage difference from 2017 to 2020	Total number of seats won	Percentage of seats won	Number of electorate votes	Percentage of electorate votes	Percentage difference from 2017 to 2020	Electorate seats	List seats
Labour	1,443,545	50.0	+13.1	65	54	1,357,501	48.1	+10.2	46	19
National	738,275	25.6	-18.8	33	28	963,845	34.1	-10.0	23	10
Green	226,757	7.9	+1.6	10	8	162,245	5.7	-1.2	1	9
ACT	219,031	7.6	+7.1	10	8	97,697	3.5	+2.5	1	9
Māori	33,630	1.2	0.0	2	2	60,837	2.2	+0.1	1	1
TOP	43,449	1.5	-0.9	0	-	25,181	0.9	-0.1	0	0
NZ First	75,020	2.6	-4.6	0	-	30,209	1.1	-4.3	0	0
New Cons.	42,613	1.5	+1.3	0	-	49,598	1.8	+1.6	0	0
Others	64,100	2.1	+1.3	0	-	77,085	2.6	+1.3	0	0
Total	2,886,420	100.0		120	100.0	2,824,198	100.0		72	48

Turnout: 82.2%

Notes: NZ First = New Zealand First; New Cons. = New Conservative Party; TOP = The Opportunites Party. The total given at the bottom of the Table – for the numbers of party votes and of electorate votes – excludes 'informal' votes (i.e., votes cast but not counted for any party or candidate).

Source: Electoral Commission, '2020 General Election and Referendums – Official Result'; '2017 General Election – Official Result'.

by the time 'special votes' had been counted its 1.2 per cent of the party vote was just enough to gain a second seat, bringing its co-leader Debbie Ngarewa-Packer, placed first on the Māori Party list, into Parliament.

New Zealand First had no such luck: despite winning 2.6 per cent of the party vote its failure to win an electorate seat kept the party out of Parliament altogether. New Zealand First's departure from Parliament is neither unexpected (given its poor pre-election polling) nor unprecedented. Many other parties have come and gone from Parliament and from most voters' memories. They include Social Credit; Jim Anderton's NewLabour and Peter Dunne's United Future (both, like New Zealand First, essentially parties centring in large measure around a particular individual); the Alliance (of which NewLabour had been a part); and Hone Harawira's Mana Party.

Of course, political parties can leave and return, as New Zealand First did in the past and as the Māori Party did in 2020; at the same time a party's name can remain the same even as its message, outlook and conduct 'evolve'. The Māori Party that returned to Parliament in 2020 is not the same as its earlier incarnation (in Parliament from 2005 to 2017, supporting a National-led government from 2008 to 2017). The 2020 version appears to regard both National and Labour with more or less equivalent and undisguised disdain, its previous collaboration with National, in particular, highly unlikely to be repeated any time soon. The party appears equally uncomfortable collaborating with some of Parliament's protocols: neckties became optional for male MPs after co-leader Rawiri Waititi objected to the requirement and was required to leave the debating chamber until the rule was relaxed – probably not what motivated those who voted for him.[1]

24 November 2020

Members of the new Parliament are sworn in (in alphabetical order) on 24 November. Most (78 MPs) have been through this before; 42 MPs take the oath of allegiance for the first time. Five are National MPs; nine from ACT; three from the Greens; two from the Māori Party; and 23 from Labour, more than one-third of its parliamentary membership. Among the 120 MPs are a record number of women: 58 (near-parity). The electoral outcome gives two parties – Labour and the Greens – a majority of women MPs: 36 of Labour's 65 MPs (exceeding the party's goal of 50 per cent), seven of the Greens' ten MPs. National has ten women MPs, nearly one-third of its caucus. ACT's ten MPs include four women, among them Brooke van Velden, the party's deputy leader. The Māori Party's two MPs include its female co-leader.

The 2020 election continued to achieve the result expected of MMP when the electoral system was recommended to New Zealanders in 1986 by the Royal Commission on the Electoral System: namely, making Parliament a more diverse (and representative) institution, with more women, Māori and ethnic minorities among its MPs. The 2020 election sees a number of firsts: New Zealand's first African MP (Labour's Ibrahim Omer, born in Eritrea); the first Sri Lanka–born MP (Labour's Vanushi Walters); and the country's first Latin American MP (the Greens' Ricardo Menéndez March, born in Mexico). Dr Gaurav Sharma (in Hamilton West) and Priyanca Radhakrishnan (in Maungakiekie, previously a list MP) become the first Indian MPs to win electorate seats. The new Parliament includes eight Asian and ten Pasifika MPs, with 25 MPs of Māori descent, distributed amongst every political party: Labour (15), ACT (3), Greens (3), National (2) and the Māori Party (2). Of the 72 electorate MPs, 16 represent South Island seats (ten won by Labour), 49 North Island seats (30 won by Labour); seven represent Māori electorates (six won by Labour).

The transformation of Parliament (over a period of several decades) from an institution composed almost exclusively of white males is also reflected in the composition of Jacinda Ardern's ministry. Five of the ten top-ranked ministers (and eight of the 20 Cabinet members) are women, as are two of the four ministers outside Cabinet, one of the two Cooperation Agreement ministers and one of the two Parliamentary Under-Secretaries. The ministry (including those outside Cabinet) includes at least eight MPs with Māori ancestry, as well as four Pasifika MPs (with family links to the Cook Islands, Tokelau, Sāmoa and Tonga) and two Asian MPs.

Over a period of weeks and months, each of the 42 MPs elected for the first time receive the traditional opportunity to give a 'maiden speech', stating why they have stood for Parliament and what they hope to accomplish.

25 November 2020

The Speaker, Trevor Mallard, is elected to a second term, describing it as 'an honour and a privilege' (*1 News* 2020c). All begins well, the prime minister congratulating him in these terms: 'Mr Speaker-Elect, or, as one of my front-bench colleagues muttered, "You again",' before moving on to more serious matters, declaring, with reference to Parliament's prayer: 'You have brought about significant change,' adding: 'I will forever remember when we reopened a session of Parliament after the 15th of March [2019] and you chose to begin it with a prayer delivered by a member of the Muslim community.' Her assessment of the Speaker's outlook approximates a role description if the position were to be properly advertised: 'You have a true commitment to this place, to the people within it, and ultimately a love of the people that it serves. What more could we ask for in a Speaker.'

With no hint of clashes to come – by March 2021 she is calling adamantly for his removal – Judith Collins notes that between the Speaker and herself there has, over time, been the 'odd clash', but adds, 'I like to think that we have a mutual respect for each other's work ethic and responsibility and sense of what a privilege it is to be here as a member of Parliament.' The Speaker's position is confirmed by the Governor-General at a ceremony at Government House the following day.

The aftermath

In the aftermath of the election National Party President Peter Goodfellow partly blames the party's poor showing on 'the celebrity Labour government', describing the government's response to Covid-19 as 'tyrannical' (RNZ 2020y). Former Speaker David Carter, elected to National's board, takes a different view: 'I think the problems the National Party had at the last election were entirely of National's making,' adding, 'They needed to be a unified team with a credible message. National failed to do that, and the voters of New Zealand recognised it and responded accordingly. The faults lay with ourselves' (Moir 2020i).

Judith Collins follows the election by taking stock of her depleted caucus, producing a new shadow Cabinet following one-on-one meetings with each National MP. Gerry Brownlee is replaced by Dr Shane Reti, who describes his elevation to the deputy leader position as 'a privilege and a dream' (RNZ 2020x). Andrew Bayly is installed at number three, in the newly created role of Shadow Treasurer, with Michael Woodhouse (ranked fourth) given the Finance portfolio. The top 20 positions include six of National's ten women MPs. Simon Bridges remains on the front bench (ranked seventh); Todd Muller is ranked nineteenth. Meeting with the National Party caucus on 20 October Collins says, 'It's onwards and upwards for us and we are determined to be the best opposition ever' (Whyte 2020).

Jacinda Ardern also engages in a post-election reshuffle, necessitated by the departure of New Zealand First (with its four Cabinet ministers and one Parliamentary Under-Secretary position). With Winston Peters' departure Nanaia Mahuta gains his Foreign Affairs portfolio – the first woman, and the first Māori woman, to hold the role. Dr Ayesha Verrall, a new MP, goes straight into Cabinet – an unusual though not unprecedented elevation – and is given several ministerial responsibilities (see this book's Appendix 4 for the complete Cabinet line-up). David Clark – who surrendered his Health portfolio following one too many adverse news stories focusing on a lack of judgment – is returned to Cabinet with several portfolios. Also brought back as a Minister outside Cabinet (after having lost the prime minister's confidence in 2018 as a result of problematic behaviour involving a staff member) is Meka Whaitiri. Minister of Finance Grant Robertson is elevated to the position of Deputy Prime Minister, succeeding – if not altogether replacing – Winston Peters. In total, Jacinda Ardern's second-term Cabinet includes seven new faces around the Cabinet table, with three additional Labour MPs elevated to positions outside Cabinet (either as a minister or parliamentary under-secretary). Chris Hipkins takes up the new role of Minister for Covid-19 Response among his other responsibilities.

Apart from the Cabinet reshuffle the newly returned Labour-led government gets right down to business, showing what a parliamentary majority can quickly achieve. Without having to negotiate with other parties, legislation is enacted on drug testing; creating a new top tax rate; declaring a climate emergency, and committing the government and the public service to achieving carbon neutrality by 2025 (Wilson 2020c). The first Colmar Brunton poll since the election, taken in December, has Labour's support at 53 per cent, National's at 25 per cent. Jacinda Ardern receives 58 per cent support as 'preferred prime minister', with Judith Collins at 12 per cent.

In an end-of-session interview, following the parliamentary adjournment on 9 December, the prime minister observes that 'we've demonstrated just how resilient we are as a nation . . . I have faith we'll get through'. Looking at her own circumstances and outlook she states that 'the weight that people place on me will be never be any greater than the weight I place on myself,' commenting, at the same time, that 'I'm naturally an optimist' (Patterson 2020f).

17 October 2020 – later that election night . . .

As at any New Zealand general election, the election night proceedings are not complete without speeches, some regretful, others celebratory.

Winston Peters, speaking in Russell in front of a sign, 'Force for the North', expresses appreciation for those who 'got on the bus and travelled 12,000 kilometres from one end of the country to the other'. The election itself is depicted, accurately, as unique: 'This was an election that, because of Covid-19 and extended lockdowns, was like no other this country has ever seen even in wartime.' Characteristically, Peters' final words of the night are mischievously enigmatic: 'For in any challenge it is the preparedness to stand up and take on the challenge, win or lose, that really matters,' concluding, 'And as for the next challenge we'll all have to wait and see.'

James Shaw, speaking at the Grid X building by Auckland's waterfront, describes the prime minister as 'a remarkable leader', expressing delight with the night's results for the Greens and speaking graciously of Winston Peters: 'He's given 40 years of service to this country and I don't think anybody can take that away [from] him.' He observes that despite their differences 'everything we've done over the course of the last three years we did together', and 'ultimately I would just have to say he's deserved his retirement.'

David Seymour, triumphant, arriving to his election-night function by sea, congratulates Labour 'on an historic outcome for the MMP era' while welcoming 'more ACT MPs to go out and hear the aspirations and concerns of New Zealanders', and to work holding the government accountable, assisting ACT to take a more active role in Parliament, at select committees and at Question Time.

At Westhaven, in Auckland, Judith Collins begins by saying 'We always knew it was going to be tough, didn't we?' and finds herself remarking – in the face of chants of 'Judith, Judith' – that with 'that sort of welcome you'd think we won!' Noting that she had been party leader for only three months – 14 July to 17 October – she thanks National voters for their 'trust and confidence', describing the party as committed to seeking 'a better way forward'. Promising that National will be 'a robust opposition' she says that 'we – the National Party – will take time to reflect, and we will review and we will change. National will re-emerge from this loss a stronger, disciplined, more connected party.' Her election night speech concludes with Collins unexpectedly channelling Arnold Schwarzenegger in *The Terminator*: 'I say to everybody' (pause) 'we will be back'.

The election night belongs, of course, to the prime minister. Speaking to a rapturous audience at the Auckland Town Hall, having had a concession telephone call from Judith Collins and with each of the other party leaders having already spoken, Jacinda Ardern chooses to give a speech that is more than a late-night celebration of victory, seeing in the occasion 'a teachable moment', offering ideas and images that transform her remarks into something more distinctive.

Standing behind a lectern with 'Let's keep moving' and 'Labour' emblazoned on it, the prime minister expresses thanks for the support received, in electorates both urban and rural, in seats that Labour expected to win and in ones that were unexpected. There is room for humour – 'to those amongst you who may not have supported Labour before; and the results tell me there were a few of you' – as she moves on to express her thanks and her commitment not to take their support for granted. Her approach is in any event generous: 'And I can promise you – I will govern for every New Zealander.'

The election outcome leaves little doubt as to the mandate received: 'Tonight's result has been strong and it is clear that Labour will lead the government for the next three years.' The election has taken place in extraordinary circumstances, in the midst of a pandemic with all that that has involved.[2] 'This has not been an ordinary election and it's not an ordinary time. It's been full of uncertainty and anxiety and we set out to be an antidote to that.' Now, with an election rewarding Labour with a substantial increase in support, the prime minister gives a glimpse of what she hopes to achieve with her second term.

'This is our opportunity to build an economy that works for everyone, to keep creating decent jobs, to upskill and train our people, to protect our environment and address our climate challenges, to take on poverty and inequality', 'to turn all of the uncertainty and hard times into cause for hope and optimism', to 'govern as we campaigned – positively, with optimism about our future, with a relentless focus on recovery that brings New Zealanders with us to deliver long-lasting change.' With 'the mandate to accelerate our response, and our recovery' the prime minister declares: 'Now more than ever is the time to keep going, to keep working, to grab hold of the opportunities that lay in front of us, so let's step forward together. Let's keep moving!'

The speech is given in the midst of a turbulent United States presidential election campaign, one accompanied by crude and unruly televised debates, altogether without precedent. Against that background (but without mentioning the US by name) the prime minister speaks of New Zealand's election with an outward-looking perspective, setting the country's experience up as an example, a point of contrast, noting that:

> governing for every New Zealander has never been so important more than it has been now. We are living in an increasingly polarised world, a place where more and more people have lost the ability to see one another's point of view. I hope that this election New Zealand has shown that this is not who we are, that as a nation we can listen and we can debate. After all, we are too small to lose sight of other people's perspective. Elections aren't always great at bringing people together but they also don't need to tear one another apart.

Reflecting on the prime minister's victory, with her election night promise to govern 'for all New Zealanders', *The Economist* (2020) describes Jacinda Ardern as 'New Zealand's most popular leader in generations', publishing results of a survey placing her at the top of a table of world leaders in terms of net approval rating.

Alongside policies and the prime minister's performance – in the Beehive, in Parliament, in television studios and in person, campaigning around the country – there is room, even in New Zealand, for prose lifted beyond the prosaic to have an effect. Former US First Lady Eleanor Roosevelt is sometimes associated with a phrase, both attributed to her and descriptive of her outlook: 'It is better to light a candle than to curse the darkness.' In similar spirit, on 17 October Jacinda Ardern said:

> We know the next few years will not be easy. The last few have not been easy either, but there have been chinks of light that have shone through even the darkest of times. That light has been our nation's determination, our support for one another, our sense of resolve, and that light has always been more powerful than the most overwhelming darkness.

She went on to say:

> Yes, policies, ideas and having a plan matters, but it will only be as good as the people that it works to support. And I cannot imagine a people I would feel more privileged to work on behalf of, and to work alongside, and to be Prime Minister for.

Warm sentiments; and in New Zealand in 2020 the feeling, it seems, was mutual.

Party Leaders' Perspectives

2

THE PRIME MINISTER'S REFLECTIONS – CAMPAIGNING IN THE MIDST OF A PANDEMIC

Jacinda Ardern

Kia ora to everyone at the Victoria University of Wellington 2020 post-election conference, and a special mention to today's host, Professor Stephen Levine. I hope you're all having a fantastic day, and enjoying the insights, analysis and anecdotes that have been shared so far. I'm really sorry I can't be there to relive with you what at least from the inside felt like a fairly unusual election campaign in what has been an incredibly unusual year. However, as you're watching this today I will be in Whakatāne joining the commemorations to mark the first anniversary of the Whakaari / White Island tragedy. And in a roundabout kind of way that is actually where I want to start my reflections on this election campaign.

The past three years have been marked by terrible moments, events and challenges I certainly didn't anticipate New Zealand would have to face when I spoke at this conference three years ago. I won't spend too much time recounting the last term, but I do want to acknowledge that together our country has been through a lot. After the March 15 attacks and the Whakaari tragedy – two events that would have been tough enough by themselves – it seemed almost unbelievable that the nation was once again required to pull together due to a global pandemic. The 'team of five million' did pull through and did so in a way that speaks volumes about New Zealanders and our values. But Covid-19 presented a lot of challenges, some immediate and urgent, some more insidious and long-term, and some that we're only learning the full impact of.

I think it's fair to say that 2020 threw a lot of spanners our way, even before we factored in trying to run a successful election campaign in the middle of a pandemic. Surprisingly, despite Covid, there was a lot about this year's campaign that operated pretty much as expected. There were the early starts, and long nights, the hoardings on every street corner, and the teams of enthusiastic and dedicated volunteers ready to do their bit for the cause, just like every election before. However, outside of these constants, Covid's impact on the 2020 campaign was huge. There were the instantly noticeable changes, like the elbow bumps instead of hugs and handshakes, alongside the invisible but still very much present changes: in particular, for me, the lingering anxiety that every phone call would be the one that brought news of a new outbreak. Then there were perhaps the biggest impacts of all, including the change of the election date.

Even before New Zealand went into lockdown I faced questions from the media about postponing the election and if the virus would derail our democratic process. We worked closely with the Electoral Commission to prepare for all eventualities. For a long time it seemed that the election would go ahead as planned despite the pandemic. This all changed on our first official day of campaigning. We had just passed 100 days with no new community-transmitted cases of Covid, and the focus for most people, it seemed, had decidedly shifted to getting our economy moving and safely reopening the borders. That first day in Whanganui was a busy one, but for the most part it was a perfectly normal day on the campaign trail. After a tour of the Sarjeant Gallery Redevelopment I stopped in to meet a number of small business owners to talk about how their recovery was going. We visited a local face mask manufacturing company, and then took part in the media obligations that come with any campaign. We had just finished the last scheduled event of the day – an afternoon tea with local Labour Party members – when I had a call from Wellington. That was when the fairly usual day changed into something else. That call confirmed the situation we'd been planning for but had hoped wouldn't happen. Our 100 days free of no new cases was officially over. It was a long night in the Beehive as we set in motion our resurgence plan and did everything necessary to keep Auckland and New Zealand safe. Again, one of the first questions put to me was if it would now lead to the postponement of the election, and this time the question was a bit more urgent than it had been in March. Now there were only 39 days until polls were supposed to close.

I had the choice in front of me. I sought advice from the Electoral Commission and spoke with leaders of every party in Parliament along with checking in with both Business New Zealand and the Council of Trade Unions. It was a difficult decision. I absolutely understood the magnitude of pushing back the election, but I also understood the magnitude of continuing on with an election at a time when there might have been questions raised about whether or not it was fair and safe. New Zealanders deserve to have both certainty and a balanced decision. And so, after much consideration, right here at this desk [the prime minister's Beehive office], I made the call to postpone the election for four weeks. The election was now to be 17 October. And it would take place on that date no matter what happened, because I'd also decided that we could not change the election date again. After all, the most certain time in a pandemic is oddly in the midst of an outbreak. It was not a decision I made lightly. I had utmost faith in our systems and processes. I was sure that the 'team of five million' would once again beat the virus. And the early signs indicated that the new outbreak was under control. But even with that reassurance no one knew what the next few months would bring. It was something I thought about and planned for every single day until 17 October.

Despite the extra month we now had there wasn't a lot of time for Labour to reconsider or reprioritise our election strategy. Our attention and focus was almost solely on containing the Auckland resurgence and keeping all of New Zealand safe. That meant that in September, when Labour officially started campaigning again, our plan pretty much followed the same blueprint we had prepared earlier in the year. There's a lot to that plan, too much to go through today in any great detail, so I just want to touch upon two elements.

The first was our strategy to go everywhere. Long before the campaign got underway we made a conscious decision to hit the road – really hit the road: we wouldn't just travel to traditionally Labour-friendly electorates. This didn't change when we restarted our campaign. I wanted to get right across New Zealand, to meet with people from all backgrounds and political persuasions, to hear how Covid had impacted their families and their businesses. I wanted to see first-hand how communities were coping and if the policies and support we put in place were working as we intended. It wasn't just an election campaign. It was a large focus group. I hadn't spent nearly as much time mixing amongst people in 2020 and I wanted to make up for that.

This choice led to some logistical challenges. We were nearly stranded by snow in Invercargill. There were a lot of meals eaten on the go as we criss-crossed the country in our campaign van. However, overall, I think that this decision was incredibly valuable. And apart from the ongoing battle of trying to overcome car sickness as I kept up with paperwork from the back seat it was the part of the campaign I enjoyed the most. It's always heart-warming to hear from the Labour faithful and meet with the volunteers and members living there, giving their all to the party, day in and day out. It's something that politicians of all stripes enjoy. But if you only talk to those on your side you run the risk of misjudging the true impact of what you're doing and missing important insights. I didn't want 'candidate-itis' – also known as 'drinking your own Kool-Aid' – to be an issue for us in this election. I wanted to make sure we heard everything from everyone, and that meant going everywhere.

Our amazing candidates were on the ground from the far north to the deep south, listening to people's concerns, taking their feedback on board. This included both in Labour strongholds and in the electorates where, as the old joke goes, 'even a post could win by a landslide if it was wearing a blue ribbon'. It's hard to truly quantify the impact of that decision we made to really campaign hard everywhere. I'll leave that to others. But it goes without saying how humbled we have been to welcome 23 new MPs to Parliament.

The second element of our plan I wanted to touch on was our decision to campaign on the big issues – in spite of Covid. I was adamant that the big issues facing our country – the issues we campaigned on in 2017 and had spent three years making progress on – were still an important part of our platform. I wasn't going to stop talking about them just because we found ourselves in the middle of a global pandemic. Yes, we were completely focused on Covid, and New Zealand's recovery, but that didn't mean that these long-term challenges had disappeared. Instead, I wanted to use the campaign as an opportunity to set out our plan for 'double-duty' solutions, initiatives that would not only create jobs and support our economic recovery in the short term, but would also help us tackle the long-term challenges, like housing, climate change and child poverty.

I didn't believe – and I still don't believe – that we should have to choose between growing our economy and building a better future. We can and should do both. In fact, it's more important now than ever. This was a key part of our election message, and I spent a lot of the campaign sounding like a broken record, repeating the planks of our five-point 'rebuild and recovery' plan, and talking about this idea of 'double-duty' solutions as I travelled about the country. But again, I think this early decision paid off. We are now in the privileged position of being able to get started on these solutions, and in doing so we're laying the foundations, I hope, for a better future for us and our children and grandchildren.

After what felt like an almost endless campaign we made it to 17 October largely in one piece. And then came the familiar nervous hours as we waited to find out how, or if, that hard work would manifest. Election nights are always a nerve-racking time no matter what the polls say. I don't think even in our most optimistic moments that anyone within the Labour camp would have predicted the result that came in on election night. It's not a result any of us take for granted. As I said on election night, we will be a party that governs for every New Zealander. That doesn't mean our government can or will represent the views of every New Zealander, all of the time. But it does mean that we will focus on the things that matter most. That means that we will listen; do the things we said we would do; and focus on 'building back better'. And I hope that you've seen that reflected in the programme we've already started rolling out.

After the last election, at this same conference, I referred to 2017 as 'the most extraordinary year of my life'. I think the past three years – and in fact the past nine months – have shown that perhaps I spoke a little prematurely. This time around, I'm going to refrain from making any bold statements that might come back to haunt me in future years. Instead, I want to finish with a big 'thank you' to everyone who played a role in 2020. This is the year of the 'team of five million', where we learned to value the simple things – human contact; gatherings; one another – but where we also proved the lengths we can and will go to in order to look after one another. I will forever be humbled to have represented New Zealand in 2020, and to still be here in 2021. May it be a less memorable year.

Nō reira.

Tēnā koutou, tēnā koutou, tēnā koutou katoa.

3

COVID-19 AND THE 'TEAM OF FIVE MILLION'

Chris Hipkins

It's fantastic to be here this morning to reflect on the year that has been and the road ahead. As we gather here today, in what we've now all come to know as a mass gathering, it's worth reflecting that in many other parts of the world right now restrictions imposed in the battle against Covid-19 make gatherings like this impossible. It's a real testament to our 'team of five million' that we are here today to reflect on our recent general election – an election that was free, fair and conducted relatively normally, albeit with a slight delay, despite the havoc that Covid-19 has caused around the globe.

2020 is a year that none of us will forget anytime soon, and most of us are eager to see the back of. I'm reminded of a line from *Peanuts* cartoon creator Charles M. Schulz, who once said: 'Life is like a ten-speed bicycle; most of us have gears we never use.' Well, I can say that in 2020, we used them all.

Our challenges were many, varied and complex. I recall the Cabinet teleconference held shortly before Waitangi Day where we discussed the closure of the border between New Zealand and China. It seemed like such a monumental and unprecedented decision. Yet only weeks later we were closing the border almost completely.

The Cabinet decision to move New Zealand as a whole to the newly defined Covid-19 alert level 3 and then two days later to alert level 4 was already being done in the context of our new reality. We had already adopted continuity of government protocols so that when that decision was made, half of the Cabinet were in the room and the other half were dialling in via teleconference. Things were moving fast and the pace wouldn't let up for most of the year. In those early days and weeks, the election was far from all of our minds. If I did allow myself a moment to reflect on it, I have to confess I did so with a sense of foreboding. How the public would respond to a government that effectively shut the country down for four weeks was anybody's guess, but I never imagined we as a country would respond so positively and comprehensively as we all did.

Looking back, there was a whole raft of things that contributed to our collective success, but if I had to pick one to raise above all others, I would say it was honesty. As a government, we were as open and upfront as we could be about the challenge ahead. We sought to share information as it came to hand, explain what we were doing and why we were doing it, and when mistakes were made, as was inevitable in such an unprecedented set of circumstances, we owned them and set about correcting them. As a result, New Zealanders' trust and confidence in the government's overall response to Covid-19 has remained strong. In fact, it is one of the strongest in the world.

I've been invited today to speak about the road ahead for our government, both as Minister for Covid-19 Response but also as the Leader of the House. I mention all of the above because the challenges we have faced in 2020 will very much define our work over the next term of Parliament. We will continue to deal with the greatest public health emergency since the global flu pandemic a century ago. The ensuing economic shock represents the largest global downturn since the Great Depression. While we can take some comfort from the success we have achieved through our collective efforts and the fact that our defences continue to strengthen, as evidenced by our success in stamping out recent incursions without the need to escalate alert levels, we can't ignore the reality that Covid-19 rages on around the globe. When New Zealand went into lockdown, there were 413,000 cases of Covid-19 worldwide. Two weeks ago we reached a new peak in the number of cases reported in a single day – over 779,000 people were diagnosed with the virus on the 28th of November alone. Over 1.5 million people have lost their lives to Covid-19. So when the government's priorities for the next three years were set out in the Speech from the Throne, it should come as no surprise that the very first of these is keeping New Zealanders safe from Covid-19. This is followed closely by our priorities to accelerate our economic recovery and lay the foundations for a better future.

Our work to keep New Zealanders safe from Covid-19 will be based around three main pillars. First, keeping it out. Through border restrictions, 14 days of managed isolation for all those entering the country, tight health and safety requirements for those working at and across the border, and regular surveillance testing of those at risk of coming into contact with the virus at the border, we aim to avoid Covid-19 making its way into our community in the first place.

But there is no room for complacency. We have to stay vigilant and be prepared for it, which is what the second pillar of our elimination strategy is based on. Regular testing in the community and strong public health measures will help us to pick up any cases of Covid-19 before they can spread.

We can all prepare by keeping good records of our movements and contacts. That will help us with the third pillar of our strategy, which is to stamp it out quickly if cases are detected. Today I announced that we will be adding Bluetooth functionality to the New Zealand Covid Tracer app. I can't speak strongly enough about just how important it is for us all to be prepared to identify all of our recent contacts in the event we need to do so as part of our contact tracing efforts. Being able to rapidly identify all potential sources of infection for any new case, and all the people that the virus could possibly have been passed onto, and isolate those people quickly is the way we avoid future alert level escalation and continue to enjoy the freedoms we could too easily take for granted.

Looking ahead, there is light on the horizon. Recent breakthroughs in vaccine development give us reason to hope. By this time next year, New Zealand should be in possession of enough vaccines to immunise our entire population several times over. But the road between now and then won't be a smooth one. Our Covid-19 immunisation campaign will be the biggest public health campaign New Zealand has ever seen. We are likely to find ourselves distributing and administering multiple vaccines at the same time, each with different logistical issues and potentially different target populations.We have to be prepared to combat public reluctance around immunisation, some based on lack of information, some based on complete misinformation that is too easily spread.

We also need to start thinking about opening up again when it is safe to do so. While the prospects for vaccination are looking incredibly encouraging, we need to accept that the world isn't just going to revert back to the way it was pre-Covid-19 with the flick of a switch. The global economy is likely to take some time to recover. It could be a while before we again see the level of global mobility that we did before Covid-19. That's why accelerating our own economic recovery is so important.

The government's five-point economic plan aims to foster jobs and growth:

- $42 billion of infrastructure investment to future proof the economy
- Training and job creation opportunities to support workers and businesses
- Support for small businesses to grow and thrive
- Programmes to bolster our exports
- Policies that prepare New Zealand for the future by making the most of our competitive advantage in renewable energy and waste reduction.

The second of those is near and dear to my own heart. After the global financial crisis, we saw a reduction in vocational education and training. Apprentices were often the first to be laid off when the going got tough. We're still suffering from skill shortages today that we exacerbated by those decisions. We can't afford to repeat those mistakes. In the early stages of our Covid response the government focused heavily on growing training and apprenticeships. We launched a comprehensive support package for apprentices and their employers, assuring job security for existing apprentices and creating openings for new ones. Thousands of New Zealanders have embraced the opportunity to take up a trade and train for free. It's a win for them and a win for us. They get valuable new skills, and we secure the workforce we need for the huge programme of activity that lies ahead.

Which brings me back to the final theme in the Speech from the Throne: laying the foundations for a better future, or – to use the global catchphrase – 'building back better'. Covid-19 didn't create problems like inequality and the digital divide, but it sure did amplify them. As a government we will be focused on tackling the root causes of inequality, including some of the tough and complex intergenerational issues that are too easily confined to the too-hard basket.

Finally, as we look to the term ahead, we will all continue to evolve and adapt to the new normal. Our Covid-19 experience showed us that there are different and better ways to do things. Remote working has never been more possible. Parliament has adopted new ways of working too, and we've shown that while our historical conventions remain important, we can evolve and adapt when the need arises. 2020 will go down in history as one of the most challenging any of us have ever faced. We've seen New Zealand at its best. We came together by staying apart. We all made the sacrifices that were asked of us and we're all enjoying the benefits that have flowed from that. So let's stay focused, and – to use a phrase that you'll hear a lot more of very soon – let's stay vigilant so we can make summer unstoppable.

4

GROWING GREEN SUPPORT FROM A POSITION OF GOVERNMENT

Marama Davidson and James Shaw

The late afternoon sun streamed through the windows above Karangahape Road in the Auckland Central electorate, bathing the crowd in a promise of the coming summer. It was three days before election day and the Green Party was holding our final big campaign rally.

Early voting had been open for more than a week and we knew millions of New Zealanders had already made up their mind. We were both carrying the exhaustion of a hard-fought election campaign but the energy in the room was electric. When our speeches were over, the crowd stuck around and danced to live music by rappers Church & AP. 'School Strike for Climate' kids who were voting for the first time in 2020 moved to the front of the crowd, ducking between long-time Green Party supporters. We both got a good feeling. No matter the result on election day, it was clear to us then that the Greens had run a strong campaign.

Students of politics in Aotearoa will know that one of the golden rules of MMP is that when small parties go into government, they lose voters at the next election. Three days after that campaign rally on K' Road, the Green Party broke that rule, increasing our vote and restoring our parliamentary caucus to double digits. We did it by putting forward bold policy solutions to move the public debate; strategically focusing our messages about our priorities and our relationship with the Labour Party; and empowering an extensive campaign on the ground. The Green Party's Chlöe Swarbrick is now the MP for Auckland Central, the party's first electorate seat win since 1999.

Political positioning

Two things defined politics in Aotearoa as we went into the 2020 election campaign: the popularity of Labour Prime Minister Jacinda Ardern, and the government's response to Covid-19. Opinion polling suggested that most people who were considering voting Green liked the prime minister, and most New Zealanders supported the government's world-leading Covid-19 response. We made a decision, the right one, to publicly endorse the government's handling of Covid-19. This placed the Green Party alongside the prime minister and the 'team of five million', rather than in opposition.

Ardern's popularity also influenced the Green Party's overall political positioning. We heard loud and clear from our supporters that their preferred option was a two-party government with the Greens and Labour. Our core message became that the Greens wanted to work in partnership with Labour to go 'further and faster' than Labour would alone. This reflected the positive working relationship between the two parties and also the Green Party's points of difference. We were publicly proud of our achievements as part of the government from 2017 to 2020. And we had plans to build on those achievements, while also acknowledging that the dynamics of the multi-party government had sometimes limited the ability to deliver our preferred policy solutions.

Our approach to Covid-19 demonstrated what this looked like in practice. We were unequivocally supportive of the government's overall health-first approach, but we also embraced specific points of difference. For example, we called for greater income support for essential workers and rent relief for small businesses; we endorsed the actions taken by some rural Māori communities to protect themselves against the pandemic; and we negotiated exemptions to managed isolation and quarantine fees for New Zealanders returning from overseas to live. We stressed the importance of using Covid-19 economic stimulus investments to promote a low-carbon future to keep our planet stable and ensure nature thrives.

We think that this approach built trust in the Green Party: trust that we would not undermine the popular and effective health-first, science-based leadership of Ardern during the pandemic, and at the same time, trust that we would not fall silent on particular issues of importance.

In contrast, the government's other support partner from 2017 to 2020, New Zealand First, openly criticised the government's Covid-19 response, despite its leader Winston Peters being at the Cabinet table where the government's response was decided, in his role as Deputy Prime Minister. This may have negatively affected trust in New Zealand First, because they were effectively criticising decisions they had been part of making. Their broader message of being a 'handbrake' on the Labour Party's agenda was the direct opposite of the Green Party's 'further and faster' message. Voters on the centre-left clearly didn't want a handbrake, and those on the centre-right seemed to abandon New Zealand First for other reasons, probably to do with trust. New Zealand First was not re-elected in 2020.

Bold policy solutions

For decades, the Green Party has played an important role pushing the boundaries of public policy conversations in Aotearoa. Working with NGOs (non-governmental organisations) and other campaign groups, we have helped bring into the mainstream political discourse issues like climate change, the pollution of rivers and the financial sanctions faced by single beneficiary mothers who refuse to name the father of their children.

In our first ever experience as part of a government, from 2017 to 2020, we could finally begin implementing the policy solutions that we'd been relentlessly pursuing for 30 years. But being in government comes with challenges and while our achievements were substantial, we did have to make compromises that sometimes disappointed our supporters. This might have had the effect of moderating some of our bold policies for the 2020 campaign, as some other smaller political parties have done. But in 2020, we believed many New Zealanders wanted to hear bold policy ideas and it was our job to put those forward.

Announcing policies during an election campaign is an important way of expressing the Green Party's values and showing voters we have solutions to the issues they care about. Anchored in our party's core values, we developed six major policy packages across the themes of climate change action, reducing economic inequality and protecting nature. The six major policies gave us a small number of key themes and messages we could focus on throughout the campaign, rather than trying to talk about everything all the time.

We aimed for our priority policies to truly meet the scale of the challenges facing the country, so that they were transformational rather than incremental. For example, our housing policy aimed to completely clear the waiting list for state homes. And our transport policy went beyond the usual urban projects to include a ten-year plan to build high-speed passenger rail between major cities as an alternative to driving and domestic air travel.

Our Māori campaign extended this approach. The Green Party has worked hard to establish a record of aligning with Māori political aspirations, grounded in the place of Te Tiriti o Waitangi in our party's charter. Our consistent advocacy of bold policy solutions for issues impacting Māori gave us a proud platform to stand on, including in the live TV debates.

The Green Party also published a full policy manifesto at the same time as we officially launched our election campaign. *Think Ahead: Our Green Vision for Aotearoa* laid out a suite of solutions across a range of areas. The broader manifesto meant people and sector groups with particular interests (for example, animal welfare or workers' rights) could clearly see our priorities for those specific areas. It also meant our candidates, our volunteer doorknockers and people browsing the party's website had easily accessible key points in most major policy areas.

The wealth tax

Our wealth tax policy became a flashpoint. Originally, we'd announced it early in the campaign as part of our Poverty Action Plan. The wealth tax would pay for a Guaranteed Minimum Income that would have lifted hundreds of thousands of people out of poverty. It would also rebalance the tax system away from relying on the wages and salaries of working people, and towards taxing accumulated wealth such as investment properties. The timing was intended to set the scene for what truly transformational policy looked like; Labour, National and New Zealand First had not yet announced any substantive policies.

We specifically designed the wealth tax with a threshold that meant only 6 per cent of New Zealanders would pay a tax on their assets worth over $1 million. With the revenue from that, we calculated that we could ensure everyone had enough income to live with dignity. This resonated with a lot of people, whose sense of community, fairness and helping out was growing in the immediate context of Covid-19. It also occurred against the background of the broader structural wealth inequality that has got worse in recent decades, most obviously in the housing market and with persistent child poverty.

The backlash from the National Party was swift, but in their haste they made mathematical errors which discredited their critiques of the wealth tax and undermined their brand as a party that is strong on economic issues. In the final weeks of the campaign, National reignited their attacks on the wealth tax on social media and through statements to the news media. The Advertising Standards Authority found at least one of National's online attack ads to be misleading.[1] A conservative lobby group ran a major direct mail campaign, sending letters to people who they thought might be impacted by the tax.

National's campaign refocused attention on the Green Party's wealth tax and, by extension, the Green Party. By the time election day arrived, our research showed that a huge majority of people who were considering voting Green had heard of the wealth tax policy, and it had a strong net positive rating among those people, meaning it is likely to have attracted many more people to vote Green than it deterred.

Prior to this, the prime minister had ruled out a capital gains tax in 2019 despite the Labour Party campaigning for one for about a decade. The public debate about structural economic inequality and the housing market had been left somewhat directionless. Our wealth tax put a bold new idea on the table, one which mainstream commentators have now added to the menu of potential policy interventions that governments should consider.

Our field campaign

As the co-leaders of the party, we spend a lot of time focusing on getting our messages out to voters through the media. But we also know that face-to-face contact is essential to build our party's support. Growing our support and our movement happens bit by bit, community by community, by meeting people where they are and taking them with us – not by winning over the so-called median swing voter.

In 2020, we hired more professional organisers to support our volunteers. At least 7,137 people volunteered their time to help with the Green Party campaign, around 1,000 more than in 2017. We focused our efforts in urban centres with historically strong Green support, looking to bring back some voters who had turned away from the Greens in the 2017 general election. And then Covid-19 hit.

We joined other political parties and put our campaign on hold. All our public communications simply echoed the public health messages. Then, as we got back into it, our extensive face-to-face campaign plan had to change quickly. Unable to knock on doors while Covid-19 alert levels were raised, our volunteers hit the phones instead, chalking up 206,000 contacts with voters nationwide. We also expanded our text messaging programmes to reach younger voters less likely to own a landline phone. As a party, we had 68 per cent more conversations with voters than in the previous 2017 election campaign.

We moved events online to Zoom 'town halls', which were oversubscribed. Ironically, this meant we were actually able to attend more events than we could have in person. Online events made it easy to speak with volunteers and supporters in different parts of the country, all in one day. This was a silver lining for both of us, because as party co-leaders we both experience the tension of needing to campaign nationwide but also in our home communities.

The second Auckland lockdown in August threw everyone out again and led to the election itself being postponed. We encouraged our campaign teams to take a break and reset mentally. Election campaigns are marathons, but everyone has to sprint at the end. A delayed election creates the risk that people start sprinting too soon and collapse before the finish line.

The last few weeks were a whirlwind of public rallies, TV debates, doorknocking and our final policy announcements. The final campaign rally on K' Road in Auckland Central brought it all to a head, in a place that just a few days later would turn from a National-held seat to the Green Party's first electorate seat in two decades. (See this book's chapter 31 by Bonnie Hayvice for more discussion of Chlöe Swarbrick's successful Auckland Central campaign.)

2020: Growing the Greens

The 2020 election can be seen as an evolution in MMP politics for Aotearoa, and for the Green Party itself. We proved that small parties can grow their support when in government with larger parties. We proved that Green Party electorate candidates running 'two tick' campaigns can boost the party vote in those electorates too and, in the case of Auckland Central, win. And we did not simply trade voters with the other parties of the centre-left bloc: support for the Greens, Labour and te Pāti Māori all grew.

In Parliament's adjournment debate before the election, one of this chapter's authors, James Shaw, had reflected on the Green Party's achievements during our first ever term as part of a multi-party government. They were significant: from the Zero Carbon Act, ending new offshore oil and gas exploration, and greater protections for Māui and Hector's dolphins, to record investment in conservation, cycleways, and the prevention of sexual and domestic violence. If that was it, and we were not returned to Parliament, there was a lot to be proud of. But we also knew that there was plenty more work to do. The 226,754 New Zealanders who voted for us have entrusted us to continue that work. With an enlarged caucus and strong party organisation, our success in the 2020 election means that we will.

5

NATIONAL: THE LEADER'S PERSPECTIVE

Judith Collins

Thank you, Professor Stephen Levine, for organising the 2020 post-election conference. I acknowledge the guest speaker, Professor Michael Baker. I think it is very unfair that I am following a media superstar. Who thought we would all know how to say 'epidemiologist' as part of our lessons this year. I would also like to acknowledge all the other speakers.

I understand these post-election conferences started in 1987 and have resulted in 11 books. In preparation for today, I had a look at some of the books from recent years and I was struck by how many election campaigns were described as extraordinary, unpredictable or bizarre. So I will wait with bated breath for the book on the 2020 election! I expect it will be described as extraordinary, unpredictable and bizarre. In the meantime, I appreciate this opportunity to give my perspective on it.

Sometimes it seems like a lifetime ago, but it is not quite five months since I became the leader of the National Party. I try to remember it by recalling that it was Bastille Day. It has been a tumultuous five months for me, at the end of a difficult three years for the National Party culminating in a significant loss at the 2020 election. National gained just 26 per cent of the party vote compared with 44 per cent in 2017. We lost over 400,000 votes and with just 33 MPs our caucus and our Opposition resources have been seriously depleted. It has been very tough to see so many of our talented and hard-working MPs and their staff leave Parliament and their electorates.

When some of my colleagues asked me to take over the leadership the night before Todd Muller announced his resignation as leader, I had serious reservations. My first reaction was 'no'. I think my second was 'why'. It was eight weeks out from the original election date and we had just been plunged into chaos. I wouldn't quite describe it as a poisoned chalice but it was hardly a golden ticket either. The political timing and conditions were far from ideal. We were up against a first-term government with an incredibly popular leader. The government was widely perceived to have done a good job in managing the response to Covid-19. Whilst it had failed to deliver on most of its promises from 2017, including child poverty reduction, KiwiBuild and light rail, all that had been swept away by Covid-19. In contrast, we appeared to be in disarray.

I spoke to my husband, whose reaction was the same as mine. I decided to sleep on it. By the morning, I had decided if there was ever a time I needed to step up, it was now. And I am an optimist: I genuinely believed the election was still winnable by us if things went our way and if we could give New Zealanders a reason to change the government. Unfortunately we didn't do that.

Despite the result, our team had some great moments on the campaign. Lots of things went well, especially when you allow for the speed we had to do everything under. But it is undeniable that a lot went wrong too. The impact of events beyond our control, Covid-19, and then the second lockdown in the middle of the election campaign all had a significant impact. But we were also let down by avoidable mistakes, and self-inflicted distractions and wounds.

When he became leader in May 2020 Todd Muller had established a new team of senior staff; most of them hadn't worked together before. I kept that team in place, bringing in a couple of additional people. The circumstances of the leadership change meant there was no time to do anything else. The campaign machine or infrastructure of past elections had massively thinned out. The new campaign team had been forced together at short notice. Covid-19 lockdowns and two leadership changes meant we were not as well organised or prepared for an election as we had been in the past. There were also problems with our policy platform, issues with campaign management, themes, messaging and discipline – and, of course, distractions and scandals of our own making.

Within days of becoming the leader I was managing the fallout from the Hamish Walker / Michelle Boag scandal, the resignations of Nikki Kaye and Amy Adams and then the Andrew Falloon scandal. And unfortunately, we were plagued by other problems throughout the campaign. I inherited the campaign themes that had been announced by Todd Muller on 8 July 2020. Those themes were responsible economic management; delivering infrastructure; reskilling and retraining our workforce; a greener, smarter future; and building stronger communities. The themes had been set and some collateral had been produced but we never managed to get any real traction with our campaign themes. And our themes were frequently undermined by events, mistakes and distractions.

Firstly, *events*: there is no doubt the second lockdown had a major impact and put paid to big events around the country. Prior to the second lockdown we'd been able to hold big public meetings and had some great, well-attended meetings in places like Taupō, Palmerston North and Ōtaki. That all came to a standstill with the second lockdown. Our large campaign launch in Auckland had to be abandoned. We couldn't campaign around the country. Logistically it was a nightmare and it was very difficult to generate media interest in our policies.

Secondly, *mistakes*, such as the 'fiscal hole', were a major blow to our campaign. Our polling had indicated that National was considered the strongest party on the economy and that this was the area we should focus on, rather than health and the response to Covid-19, where Labour was considered stronger. However, we had issues with our economic narrative from very early on in the campaign. The 30 per cent debt target that had been announced in July led to speculation by our opponents that such a target could only be achieved by $80 billion in austerity measures. Then we had the $4 billion 'fiscal hole' story which broke on the morning of our belated 'virtual' campaign launch, two days after the release of our economic plan and short-term tax relief package. In a complete role reversal from 2017, we were coming under considerable media pressure over our numbers. It was a significant dent to our economic credibility and made it that much harder for us to convince New Zealanders that they should entrust us to oversee the economic recovery. Even though our fiscal plan had been independently costed, reviewed and endorsed we were unable to convincingly counter the 'fiscal hole' allegations that continued throughout the campaign.

Thirdly, *distractions*: while the country was focused on Covid-19, the National Party looked like it was far too focused on tittle-tattle and internal politics. We did not spend enough time talking about the things that matter to New Zealanders – issues like jobs, debt, housing, transport, health, education, law and order. When we did talk about them, our message was often drowned out by destabilising distractions and scandals. Our law and order policy announcement was overshadowed by the untidiness of the Auckland Central candidate re-selection in the wake of Nikki Kaye's resignation. Our housing policy announcement was obliterated by the leak of Denise Lee's email. The email was leaked just before my media stand-up and the media were far more interested in the leaked email than our housing policy. The first I knew of Denise Lee's concerns and the email was after the housing announcement. The destabilisation from this leak was a body blow to the National Party that we never recovered from. The combination of events, mistakes and distractions meant we did not look like a credible alternative government. We did not look like a government in waiting. And it was reflected in our election result and our reduced caucus.

Despite our shock and disappointment at the result, New Zealanders have spoken and we must listen. We must analyse what worked and what didn't and heed the lessons from our defeat. To that end, the National Party has announced a comprehensive external review, overseen by a review panel. The review will consider election preparedness, candidate selection, caucus performance and the election campaign, including strategy, narrative and selection. The panel is composed of experienced people who were not involved in the day-to-day running of the campaign. It has a wide mandate to seek feedback from anyone and explore any areas it chooses. We are taking this review extremely seriously. We will take the recommendations on board, institute change where it is needed, and rebuild.

The next three years will be incredibly important for this country as we recover from the economic damage caused by Covid-19. The National Party may not be in government, but as the Opposition we have one of the most important jobs in the country. We will be a strong and effective Opposition who will hold the government to account each and every day. The Labour Party may have 'unbridled power' in terms of numbers but the Opposition will keep the government on its toes. And we will build an alternative vision over the next three years that reflects the National Party values of individual freedom and choice, personal responsibility, limited government, competitive enterprise, equal citizenship and opportunity. I know what an honour it is to be the Leader of the Opposition and I am proud to lead a team of such talented and effective MPs. I have huge confidence in our caucus and our staff. We have taken a battering but we have got up and we are working together very well. Thank you for the opportunity to speak today at this conference. It is a privilege to do so.

6

ACT II

David Seymour

After sinking to the worst result in its history in 2017 – 0.5 per cent of the party vote – ACT achieved its best ever result in 2020. ACT's share of the party vote – 7.6 per cent – delivered ten times as many MPs as in 2017, and was also fractionally better than its previous high-water mark of 7.1 per cent in 2002.

Perhaps most significantly, the support was widespread. ACT broke the 5 per cent threshold in every territorial local authority except Wellington and Hutt City. Exit polling showed support nearly constant across age, location type, employment and income, with strong support from European, Chinese and Māori voters but less support from Pacific and Indian voters. ACT's support does not look like the profile of a 'niche party' with a particular support base so much as the foundation of a big tent. ACT's 2020 result promises a second ACT after the halcyon period of 1996–2005 and the long winter of 2005–2020.[1]

How did it happen? The lazy narrative is that an extraordinary series of disasters within the rival National Party has temporarily helped ACT. National's woes were certainly a factor. However, ACT's result occurred against the tide of a massive swing to incumbency as voters credited the government for New Zealand's performance through Covid-19. Furthermore, exit polls show only a bare majority of ACT's new support coming from former National voters. The real story is far more interesting. It involves an array of talented people coming together, mostly voluntarily, to execute a sound strategy like clockwork. That was only possible because of a sustained build up over three years. The rest of this chapter tells that story.

Epsom

Core to ACT's overall strategy was holding the Auckland seat of Epsom. Holding a seat meant that we could claim, accurately, that every party vote for ACT would count regardless of whether ACT's total party votes reached 5 per cent. The strategy in Epsom was, as in previous elections, to appeal to voters that a candidate vote for ACT would add more MPs to the right and that the candidate would be a good local MP.

The most important work was done over the preceding three years on the second premise. Helping even five constituents a day means that 10 per cent of voters have had direct contact with the candidate or his office since the last election. Our research showed that even amongst voters who did not favour the first message, the candidate was widely respected as a good local MP. Furthermore, a combination of three factors – the tide going out on National, the remoteness of a single seat making a major difference to the election result, and ACT exceeding the 5 per cent threshold in polls for months before the election – all reduced the effectiveness of the first message. This sentiment showed up in 23 per cent of Labour Party votes and 10 per cent of Green Party votes being split with ACT candidate votes.

Polling as early as June showed the ACT candidate 31 points ahead of the nearest rival. Even so, the Epsom campaign was still vigorous. We used direct mail, geotargeted online videos, and held 47 hugely popular street corner meetings, with some attended by more than 100 people. This fitted our theme of hearing the voter, with each meeting starting with brief comments and an invitation for comments and questions. Beyond actual attendees, we received a lot of positive feedback on the concept, for going out to meet and hear from residents.

Rebounding

In the previous edition of this series, a chapter in *Stardust and Substance* (Seymour 2018) candidly told the story of why ACT failed in 2017. A quick review of it is a useful background for the path from 0.5 per cent to 7.6 per cent. In 2017, the campaign pursued too many voters, who were often mutually antagonistic, with policy prescriptions that were too complex, and without a clearly recognised brand of its own to fall back on. That year's campaign also failed to gain sufficient coverage for voters to be aware of, let alone understand it, and it relied far too much on old technology in the form of direct mail. In early 2018 I knew we needed to do things differently. I travelled to Berlin where I was hosted by the Friedrich Naumann Foundation, a charity affiliated to the centrist Free Democratic Party (FDP), with a mission of promoting democracy in

Germany and around the world. The FDP had faced similar difficulties, having exited the Bundestag in 2013, the first time since their post-war formation. They rebounded to win 10.7 per cent of the vote in an election held on 24 September, the day after New Zealand's 2017 ballot. More than anything else, I learned from them that recovery was possible. I also learned that it required innovation and that it required having a positive programme. Over the past three years ACT has adopted both of these lessons, in some cases borrowing directly from the FDP.

We gave the party a clear programme: ACT, for Freedom. We copied the FDP's approach to party conferences, as a performance in an auditorium. A rapid-fire series of speeches, over in two hours, replaced a two-day ordeal tolerable only for the hardiest political enthusiasts. Like us, the FDP's yellow-and-blue colour scheme had become fatigued. We followed their introduction of magenta, giving a scheme of three colours that make a combination, spaced equidistantly around a colour spectrum wheel. I recognised that, despite being sporadically in the political news for three years, few people outside of the Epsom electorate knew me. Appearing on *Dancing with the Stars* changed that beyond anything I could have imagined. Although fewer than 10 per cent of New Zealanders watched the show on any given Sunday or Monday night, nearly everyone was conscious of it at some level.

Events

With the marketing, purpose and name recognition all set, the rest of the parliamentary term was left to what former British Prime Minister Harold Macmillan described as 'events'. The government's responses to the March 2019 Christchurch terror attacks and the Covid-19 epidemic would give ACT an opportunity to reach more voters than had heard the party's message in a decade.

The terrible tragedy in Christchurch required, and still requires, a sound policy response to its underlying causes. The failings were a broken firearms licensing system and a failure of focus on the part of security and intelligence services. The government's responses were not only ineffective but divisive, opening them up to criticisms that many New Zealanders felt were needed. Inexplicably, the government responded to an attack on democracy by throwing away its normal lawmaking process and rushing through ultimately ineffective laws that marginalised – almost blamed – licensed firearms owners. For ACT, it was natural to draw on long-held principles of property rights, due process and a primary focus on public policy and oppose rushed firearms laws in the wake of March 15. This opposition had obvious appeal to licensed firearms owners, but we also started to detect in focus groups a perception that ACT would do hard things and stand on principle. A second policy where the government promised, but in this case did not deliver, involved restricting speech. The irony of responding to an attack on our free society this way was not lost on a wider range of voters than those affected by the firearms laws. Once again, it was natural for ACT to stand for basic personal liberties, even if it meant standing alone in New Zealand politics.

These stances increased ACT's attention, but polling by November 2019 was still not much more than 1 per cent. However, there were more events to come. November also featured saturation coverage of ACT's long march to pass End of Life Choice legislation, an effort ending with success. This achievement, which would be ratified after a referendum campaign concurrent with the 2020 general election, complemented ACT's position as a party that could take on hard issues. Whatever New Zealand First's motivations were for insisting the bill be ratified by referendum, it helped that the election was accompanied by an issue that I and our deputy leader were closely associated with. The law also positioned me as one of the few politicians in the 2017–2020 term who had made a positive change. Even government ministers were wracked by failures in KiwiBuild, light rail, and measles vaccination, among other examples.

However, none of these events moved the dial as much as the government's response to the Covid-19 epidemic. The closure of Parliament and the establishment of an Epidemic Response Select Committee meant that I went from being one of 57 opposition MPs to one of six. Furthermore, the committee's meetings were livestreamed across the country, who were at home, in lockdown, effectively under house arrest.

These circumstances allowed me to execute ACT's mantra of 'offering constructive criticism where necessary, helpful suggestions where possible, and asking questions that needed answers'. The positive feedback from these sessions was overwhelming, and ACT's polling began to rise steadily towards the election.

We were fortunate that ACT has always been a party of great faith in its mission. We stood 57 candidates, many of whom signed up for the party's School of Practical Politics programme in June 2019, long before our polling began to rise. The party's membership managed to rival National and Labour in the laborious job of erecting hoardings, even in sparsely populated parts of the country.

Strategy

Amongst the broken play of Covid-19 began a campaign that would start mid-year, only to stop for a three-week lockdown in August, have the election date delayed, and finally end in mid-October. ACT's strategy was to represent voters from a range of sectors which had been affected by the government's regulatory largesse. These not only included licensed firearms owners and people concerned about free speech, but farmers, landlords, employers and small business owners. It especially included those affected by Covid-19, such as tourist operators and small business owners not favoured by the government's seemingly arbitrary restrictions.

It also pointed to the enormous amounts of debt that the government promised to take on in battling Covid. During the Covid period, Treasury forecast that interest on public debt would exceed expenditure on education in years to come, and there was considerable concern that the government was simply using the cushion of cheap debt to cover inadequacies in its performance at managing the pandemic.

ACT's message was that while the impact of Covid seemed impossibly hard, it was possible to rebuild from it a country we could be truly proud of, by electing a genuinely independent team to hold them *all* accountable. It built on ACT's track record of standing up for people and finding a better way forward in difficult times. Discipline on message was a key feature of the campaign: rebuilding after Covid, managing debt and improving mental health services, as well as ACT's pledge that the party's MPs would sit on the cross benches and hold them all accountable.

Tactics

Tactically, ACT had far greater options than previously. The final campaign budget was roughly twice what had been spent in 2017, but there was also a major boost in volunteers in general and skilled volunteers in particular. ACT had been building momentum over several years, and more and more people wanted to come to the party. Among many other volunteers and paid staff, we had a supporter who was a professional videographer to capture the campaign as it happened; a market researcher giving invaluable research advice; a volunteer who worked on databases professionally, volunteering his skills full time; another, prior to beginning university, who constructed alternative budgets better than National's, working with only a spreadsheet.

Direct mail, apart from Epsom, was out. Digital campaigning was in. Public and street corner meetings, as part of a nationwide bus tour, were in. So was building a wider team. When we put the faces of eight candidates on the side of our bus, we thought it was daring. The election night result far exceeded our early expectations.

Our research involved extensive focus groups – many done by Zoom in a Covid world – and two major polls tested voter sentiment and issues. Being able to do research throughout the campaign meant that we were able to refine our message to connect our policy offerings with voters' issue agendas. We knew we were making progress when a female focus-group participant said: 'National only cares about money, ACT cares about people.' This was a major reversal of prior expectations.

Public meetings followed the same format as street corner meetings but were larger in attendance and longer in duration. The bus travelled literally from Cape Reinga in the far north to Tiwai Point on the South Island's southern coast, stopping for over 140 public meetings. The largest of these meetings was attended by over 300 people; altogether we engaged literally thousands of people. When over 100 people turned up to a public meeting in Te Anau, in Fiordland, by the South Island's largest lake, we knew the momentum was with us.

Our digital campaign involved extensive online and social media advertising, on platforms from Snapchat to Google Ads. Expenditure on these rivalled our 2017 campaign's entire spending. They allowed us to reach voters regardless of the mainstream media's issue agenda and appeared to drive much of ACT's polling increase. Our digital team was excellent; volunteers often created shareable relevant content better and faster than more polished agency-produced content.

Earned media was much more forthcoming. As ACT's polling increased so did our coverage, although we certainly faced long weeks with little or no television coverage early in the campaign. For a long time New Zealand First appeared far more frequently on television, not because they were doing anything reportable but because journalists were following them in anticipation of a decision by the Serious Fraud Office about alleged donation irregularities. However, we also changed our tactics in recognition of how to get coverage. I jumped out of a plane over the Mackenzie Country, by the Southern Alps, and both networks had cameras waiting when I landed. One commentator breathlessly told a morning talk show that he 'just couldn't stop watching because he wondered what I was going to do next' (I drove the campaign bus around a racetrack). In my previous chapter in this book series, I lamented the lack of coverage; this time, we figured, if you can't beat 'em, join 'em.

Conclusion

ACT's campaign (and its rise from one to ten seats) would have been the political story of 2020 had it not been for two other exceptional achievements: Labour gained the first outright majority in the MMP era and the Greens survived a term as a Confidence and Supply partner to increase their share of the vote. The context does not change ACT's achievement though. More than anything, it shows that a long commitment to executing a strategy, and a little luck along the way, can achieve results in politics.

The 2020 New Zealand election

– views from overseas

7

JACINDAMANIA IN CANADA: COVERAGE IN THE GREAT WHITE NORTH

Tina Marie Barton

For Canadians, Jacinda Ardern and the Labour Party's decisive 2020 election victory seemed a foregone conclusion. The featured headlines rang enthusiastic on election day. 'New Zealand's Ardern wins 2nd mandate in election landslide', proclaimed an article in the Canadian Broadcasting Corporation (CBC), connecting Ardern's soaring popularity with her successful leadership to defeat Covid-19 in New Zealand (CBC 2020a). Similarly, the *Globe and Mail* headline trumpeted 'Ardern leads Labour to landslide N.Z. election victory after successful COVID-19 strategy' (*Globe and Mail* 2020). Such emotive language was also reflected in the *Toronto Sun*, the daily tabloid for Canada's largest city, with the headline 'New Zealand's Jacinda Ardern wins "historic" re-election for crushing COVID-19' (*Toronto Sun* 2020).

Since gaining power in 2017, Jacinda Ardern's reputation for leadership has grown from strength to strength in New Zealand, Canada and indeed around the world. At the same time Canada was living its own new era of liberal governance in almost parallel timing. In 2015, Canada voted in the youthful, yoga-loving, feminist Justin Trudeau, who soon showed his progressive side in legalising cannabis and appointing a gender-balanced Cabinet. When asked why, about the latter, Trudeau responded 'because it's 2015' (Ditchburn 2015). Indeed, following Ardern's 2017 victory, the Canadian media was quick to draw parallels to the leadership shift in Canada, grouping Ardern and Trudeau together as part of 'a generational change' (Withers 2017). A *Newsweek* story republished by *Yahoo Finance* (Canada) proclaimed Jacinda Ardern 'the New "Trudeau-Like" Leader of New Zealand' (Sanders 2017). The comparison was easy against a backdrop where the people of Canada, like New Zealand, had voted out a reign of conservative-led governments.

However, Ardern went on to further distinguish herself to Canada and the world with what became her signature response – a blend of compassion and decisiveness in the face of a series of unheralded events in New Zealand. Ardern's surprise announcement of pregnancy shortly after becoming prime minister was swiftly followed by her commitment to return to governing after just six weeks of maternity leave. This tone reflected a theme rising to prominence in Canada at that time, along the lines of 'It's time to move over, (white) men, women are leaders too'. (While Canada was celebrating its 150th anniversary as a nation, Indigenous leaders and non-profit groups were challenging the public and private sector to check their colonialism and revisit the power dynamics around Indigenous peoples, women and minority groups.) The following year, newspapers in Canada and globally were swift to hail Ardern as the first world leader to bring her baby to the United Nations' annual summit (*CTV News* staff 2018), with some articles emphasising the positive reception from the United Nations, based on the need to increase female leaders from their current 5 per cent representation (Joseph 2018).

Ardern continued to impress the Canadian public with her unique response to the series of unprecedented tragedies that unfolded in her first term, from the devastating March 2019 Christchurch mosque shooting, to the unexpected Whakaari / White Island volcanic eruption in December 2019, to the onset of the global Covid-19 pandemic in March 2020. Following Ardern's handling of the mosque shooting, the *Globe and Mail*'s deputy head of editing, Carol Toller, wrote an impassioned column extolling Ardern as 'the leader the world needs right now' (Toller 2019). Toller praised Ardern's 'fresh, deeply principled approach' and refusal 'to be defined by old-school conventions'. Canada's *Global News* reflected on 'why New Zealand's Jacinda Ardern has the world's attention' (Gerster 2019a) – the biggest reasons being that Ardern was 'using rhetoric of love and respect and compassion and understanding' alongside 'solace and steel'.

Ardern's swift action to ban high-powered weapons, including most semi-automatics, large-capacity magazines and some pump-action shotguns, similarly gripped Canada's attention. There has been much attention to gun control in recent years as Canada has grappled with an increase in shooting rampages, starting with the 2014 assault on Parliament Hill, then the 2017 Quebec mosque attack, and more recently with the Nova Scotia shooter who killed 22 people in April 2020. New

Zealand's actions to address gun violence have been closely followed. Some commentators, including at the *Globe and Mail*, proclaimed 'New Zealand's gun ban shows the way . . . will Canada be as bold?' (Renzetti 2019). An opinion piece in *Global News* criticised various levels of government in Canada for 'failing to meet the challenge of growing far-right movements and the climate that nurtures them' and for keeping government responses clandestine, in stark contrast to Ardern, who, the article highlighted, had called for a public inquiry within a week of the attack (Elghawaby 2019). In contrast, a columnist for Canada's national magazine, *Maclean's*, countered that while New Zealand had been widely praised for its gun crackdown, it was 'mostly just catching up to Canada's existing laws' already in place for decades (Gurney 2019). Despite the varying opinions, it is indisputable that New Zealand's parliament moved much faster to ban military-style weapons – within a month of the mosque shooting – whereas while the Liberal Party made firearms regulations a component of its 2015 election platform, it took almost four years for Bill C71: An Act to amend certain Acts and Regulations in relation to firearms to come into effect in Canada in June 2019.[1]

Throughout all these high-stakes tragedies, Ardern signalled to the world that a compassionate touch can both reassure the public and mobilise policy quickly. In addition, Ardern's selflessness particularly resonated with the Canadian public. When the Covid-19 pandemic affected New Zealand businesses (for a much shorter period than the rest of the world), Canadians were taken by the Ardern-led decision that all Members of Parliament would take a 20 per cent pay cut for six months in solidarity. Canada's *Global News* was moved to conduct a public opinion poll, finding that 66 per cent of those polled believed their Members should also take a salary cut (Breen 2020). Canada's parliamentarians did not act upon this recommendation.

For all the popularity of Ardern in Canada, in looking back on the news coverage, one thing is strikingly apparent. Coverage in Canada is predominantly shaped by reprints of syndicated press stories from New Zealand. While Canada's larger publications, notably the *Globe and Mail*, *Global News*, *Vancouver Sun* and *National Post* (to name a few examples), do offer some independent coverage and analysis on occasion, by and large these papers and most others use Reuters and Associated Press stories from New Zealand to inform the Canadian public. With the mass proliferation of freely accessible internet and social media content, media outlets across the world can no longer afford to entrench their correspondents in foreign locations to produce original news stories as they once could. In any case, on account of its distance from Canada and its smaller-scale economy, a New Zealand bureau would not likely be on the shortlist for Canadian media. While there are no surprises about the lack of diversity of media coverage, it is worth highlighting the consequences. Canadians' knowledge of New Zealand affairs is informed by reporting that, while fair and balanced, lacks the caustic humour and more fringe perspectives offered by *The Spinoff* or *Newsroom*, to name a few alternative New Zealand publications.

When Canada does produce its own analysis of New Zealand affairs, such articles are insightful in reflecting the issues that have attracted Canadians' attention. For example, roaring property prices have become a major issue in Vancouver and Toronto in recent years, partly attributed to foreign buyers flooding the market and driving up prices. When Canadian politicians and the media looked around the world for solutions, New Zealand's foreign housing ownership ban, initiated by Ardern, caught their eye. Some were inspired by New Zealand's solution and suggested similarly affected provinces in Canada should follow suit, as featured by the CBC (Hennig 2018; Britten 2018), *Toronto Star* (Hutchings 2019) and *Financial Post* (Francis 2018); others questioned the policy's efficacy (Tencer 2018; Gerster 2019b). In the *Huffington Post* (Canada), Tencer's headline was that Canadians should be careful what they wished for. While calling New Zealand a 'trailblazer' (a term frequently associated with New Zealand in Canadian media) the article cited chief economists in Canada who said that implementing a ban similar to New Zealand's would accomplish less than Vancouver's 15 per cent tax on residential property transfers to foreign buyers already had. Gerster's article in *Global News* asked whether New Zealand's strategy was the right one for Canada. (The consensus among her sources was 'no'. Some said that improving housing affordability was the ultimate goal, whereas others recommended policy levers to discourage housing from being bought primarily for investment purposes, regardless of the owner's nationality.)

Another trademark of Ardern's leadership that captured attention in Canada was the competence of her more traditionally female style of compassion and care (Titleman Colla 2020; Delvoie 2020; Marshall 2020). In British Columbia, Green candidate James Marshall readily compared the provincial Green Party leader Sonia Furstenau with Ardern, noting their similar leadership styles (calm, non-combative) and advocacy efforts. Furstenau has long championed a shorter work week and was quick to praise Ardern's idea to encourage more weekend travel and support the domestic tourism industry (Fletcher 2020). Furstenau and the Green Party have also promoted a 'wellness budget' type of approach for a significant number of years, although Marshall (2020) noted that the concept had not received the same media attention in Canada as it did in New Zealand following Ardern's budget announcement in May 2020. In the *Globe and Mail*, Titleman Colla (2020) highlighted how female leaders in Germany, Denmark and New Zealand managed the coronavirus crisis very well; and that it appeared few female leaders handled it poorly. She referenced Ardern as 'one of the most touted stars' for shining a spotlight on the leadership traits needed across countries, companies and communities in these times: transparency, decisiveness, empathy and authenticity. Meanwhile, Delvoie's article in the *Gananoque Reporter* brought Ardern's leadership to the attention of a small waterside Ontario town with just over 5,000 residents, signalling that Ardern was of interest in Canadian communities both large and small.

On the downside, it seems the distance from New Zealand can occasionally result in blatantly inaccurate perspectives. In one 2020 election coverage example, the Canadian reporter referenced Ardern as having been elected to power in 2017, seemingly oblivious to Ardern's complex negotiations with New Zealand First and the Green Party that had made it so. The reporter wrote: 'Ardern was first elected in a 2017 election she was supposed to lose by a landslide in large part because of her charisma and communication skills' (Drolet 2020).

In the lead-up to the 2020 election, Ardern's opponents suffered a fate worse than lack of breadth – a lack of coverage. In Canada, the search term 'Jacinda Ardern' was significantly more popular throughout the year than searches for any of her opponents or for the New Zealand election itself. *Google Trends* assigns a value out of 100 relative to search interest, with 100 representing peak popularity and 0 indicating not enough data for the term. Among Canadian searches, *Google Trends* showed an average value of 25 for Ardern in 2020, compared to values between zero and nine for 'New Zealand election' (Google 2020). In fact, the only time 'New Zealand election' exceeded 'Jacinda Ardern' in search interest was the week of the election (October 11–17) when the election soared to a score of 100 compared to 87 for Ardern. That same week, 'Judith Collins' peaked at a value of eight. Throughout the year, searches for 'Judith Collins', 'Todd Muller' and 'Simon Bridges' typically received a value of zero, except for a few tiny peaks at three upon change-of-leadership announcements from the National Party.

Focusing on the latest leader, the treatment of Judith Collins in Canadian media was no different than in New Zealand media, given that the stories were typically reprints from Reuters – as seen in *The National Post* (2020) and *The Chronicle Herald* (2020) – or the Associated Press – as seen in CBC (2020b) and *CTV News* (2020). In these examples, Judith Collins was referred to as 'Crusher Collins', a 'long-serving lawmaker' and an 'admirer of former British Prime Minister Margaret Thatcher'.

As mentioned at the outset, there were no surprises for Canada that Ardern emerged from the 2020 election with a resounding victory. Although election articles mentioned the demise of New Zealand First and the rise of the ACT Party, these outcomes received only brief coverage – the focus in Canadian media remained squarely on Ardern. Meanwhile, in the days following the election, the results of New Zealand's referendums on legalising euthanasia and cannabis seemingly captured almost as much attention in Canadian media as the election result itself. Again, stories were mostly reprints of Nick Perry's Associated Press dispatches from New Zealand, as seen with *Globe and Mail* (Perry 2020a), *Global News* (Perry 2020b) and *CTV News* (Perry 2020c), and republication of Colin Packham's Reuters article, in the *National Post* (Packham 2020a) and *The Guardian P.E.I.* (Packham 2020b).

In the weeks following, there was interest in the new role for New Zealand's Green Party, particularly in Canada's most western province – likely spurred by the British Columbia provincial election underway at the time. Ardern's offering of ministerial portfolios outside of Cabinet to two Green Party MPs under a 'cooperation agreement' yielded interest, especially as Ardern had won a majority and did not need to form any alliances. In British Columbia, the snap election called by the incumbent New Democratic Party resulted in their majority governance, which meant they no longer required support from the provincial Green Party. Green leader Furstenau praised Ardern's 'collaborative leadership' style and criticised the provincial New Democratic Party

(NDP) and Liberal Party leaders for not following Ardern's example, for instead being stuck in an 'old way of thinking' that prioritised power and partisanship (Harnett and Duffy 2020). As a side note, following Canada's 2019 federal election that kept the Liberal Party in power, no official coalitions were formed; however, the Liberals had to make policy concessions for Covid-related unemployment benefits, sick leave and childcare programmes in order to secure the necessary support of the NDP and survive a vital confidence vote on the Speech from the Throne in September 2020 (Baker 2020; Levitz and Bryden 2020). The Liberals again depended on NDP support a month later to survive a second confidence vote. With Canada's first-past-the-post electoral system, coalitions are less common than in New Zealand, although debate over electoral reform resurfaces from time to time, sometimes with reference to New Zealand's electoral system.

With respect to Ardern's 2020 Cabinet picks, the appointment of Nanaia Mahuta as Minister for Foreign Affairs captured the most attention among Cabinet appointees in Canada (and around the world). That said, media coverage was not extensive, mostly reprints of Associated Press stories, as seen in outlets including *CP24* (Perry 2020d), *Yahoo News Canada* (Perry 2020e) and *Toronto City News* (Perry 2020d), or stories via Reuters as seen in the *National Post* (Moloney and Bhalla 2020). However, Canada's French radio station, *Ici Radio-Canada*, did write its own article about the appointment, with a headline (in French) that emphasised how New Zealand's Minister of Foreign Affairs was Māori – 'Une ministre des Affaires étrangères maorie pour la Nouvelle-Zélande' (Villeneuve 2020). Filed under 'Indigenous' (in French) the story, which drew upon articles from New Zealand and the United Kingdom, highlighted that Mahuta was the first Indigenous person and woman to be appointed to this post. It also briefly and respectfully described her moko kauae.

New Zealand's relationship with Māori and its inclusion of designated Māori seats under a separate Māori roll are also developments monitored in Canada. Canadians have acknowledged that 'Maori are far ahead in asserting their rights' compared to Indigenous peoples in Canada (Ball 2018). In this connection *The Conversation* (Canada edition) discussed 'what Canada can learn from New Zealand on electoral reform' (O'Sullivan 2019); a political scientist contributing to the *Globe and Mail* had previously asserted 'there can be no electoral reform without indigenous input' (Williams 2016); and the Munk School of Global Affairs and Public Policy proposed 'Virtual Indigenous Districts', modelled after New Zealand's Māori seats (Martin 2020).

Looking to the future, Canada can be expected to continue to pay great attention to New Zealand's treatment of and governance by Indigenous peoples, its handling of the pandemic, management of assault weapons, and affordable housing policies. Yet if the current infatuation continues, it may be that 'Jacindamania' outshines all.

8

THE 2020 NEW ZEALAND ELECTION – THE VIEW FROM AUSTRALIA

Nicholas Economou and Zareh Ghazarian

In May 2019, an opinion poll reported in the *New Zealand Herald* showed that Prime Minister Jacinda Ardern had been ranked as 'Australia's most trusted politician' (*New Zealand Herald* 2019). This finding was partly a reflection of the dismay Australians had at the time about their own leaders. It was also an indication that Australians were closely watching Ms Ardern's conduct as prime minister at arguably one of New Zealand's darkest hours (arising from the appalling March 2019 Christchurch mosque attacks) and were impressed with what they saw.

Sadly, the Christchurch massacre was not the only major national emergency to arise during Ardern's first three years as prime minister. As was the case with its Christchurch response, the policies pursued by her Labour–New Zealand First coalition government to the onset of the dreaded Covid-19 in the first months of 2020 (an election year in New Zealand) were closely observed in Australia, even though the next Australian federal election was not due until at least August 2021. Initially derided by some in Australia, her government's 'go early, go hard' approach based on an extensive lockdown of the country would become a model, especially for the governments of the Australian states and territories (with the possible exception of New South Wales). Further, New Zealand's claim to have eradicated the disease and to be able to return to some semblance of normalcy was to become the benchmark by which the success, or otherwise, of Australian policies would be assessed. Indeed, in May 2020, Prime Minister Ardern was asked to join Australia's 'National Cabinet' – the joint meeting of heads of Australian government convened to co-ordinate Australia's response to Covid-19 (see Koslowski 2020). There was thus wide admiration in Australia for the New Zealand government's approach to Covid-19, particularly when it appeared that the 'go early, go hard' policy had been rewarded with what appeared to be the eradication of the virus (see Baker, Wilson and Anglemyer 2020).

Prior to the coronavirus outbreak, the New Zealand prime minister was to make a number of visits to Australia. In the case of a stopover in Victoria, Ardern was warmly greeted by Premier Daniel Andrews and the state's governor. There were close synergies between the political views of Ardern and the Victorian premier. Andrews heads a Labor state government and is himself a member of the party's Socialist Left faction. The Victorian premier would also institute a hard lockdown that would last nearly four months as part of his government's response to the Covid-19 crisis.

Meetings between Ardern and the Australian prime minister, Scott Morrison (Liberal Party, leading a Liberal–National coalition government), tended to be somewhat cooler. In a visit to Sydney in February 2020, this relationship was marked by failure to advance debate on some persistent trans-Tasman issues, including the Australian policy of repatriating New Zealanders convicted of committing crimes (Remeikis 2020). Throughout 2020, there was endless wrangling between the countries over travel arrangements and pandemic-related border closures.

The commonality of concerns – such as how to deal with a pandemic, how to respond to terrorism and how to manage a national disaster – provides an important basis for Australia and New Zealand to be interested in aspects of each other's politics. Mutual observations of each other's elections are also driven in part by interest in what general political trends might be at work and if they are likely to be replicated in the other jurisdiction. We have noted previously a tradition of Australian commentators looking to New Zealand for indications of what might be likely trends (see Tingle 2020). The election of Australian Labor governments in 1972 and 1983, for instance, coincided with Labour victories in New Zealand at about the same time – led by Norman Kirk (1972) and David Lange (1984). The ascendancy of Helen Clark in 1999 to the New Zealand prime ministership inspired Australian feminists, who could see an Australian woman replicating this achievement: and indeed this in due course occurred when Julia Gillard became Australia's first female prime minister in 2010. Even the emergence of Winston Peters and his New Zealand First Party was seen in Australia as being commensurate with rise of the One Nation Party in Australia, led by Pauline Hanson, notwithstanding how remote the possibility of Ms Hanson ever going into coalition with Australian Labor might be.

Consequently, Jacinda Ardern's election in 2017 seemed to suggest that a swing to the left was occurring and that Australia would soon copy New Zealand and elect a progressive federal Labor government at the 2019 poll. A new Australian Labor government would potentially have had closer policy synergies with the Ardern government. However, as things were to transpire, a swing to the left-of-centre did not materialise at the 2019 Australian election. Despite opinion polls predicting a Labor victory, the Liberal–National coalition was returned to government, with the socially conservative Scott Morrison as prime minister. Within this context, it looked as if Australian and New Zealand politics had in fact diverged, thus suggesting that perhaps the trends occurring in New Zealand politics were now an imperfect guide for Australian politics. Of course, the onset of Covid-19 might have had an influence.

Crisis and the advantage of incumbency: Comparative politics in the time of Covid

The first case of Covid-19 in Australia was detected in late January 2020, but it would take some weeks before the various Australian governments (state, territory and federal) started to undertake dramatic policy responses to address it. Initially, the Australian prime minister and his officials urged Australians not to panic about Covid-19, with Morrison famously declaring that he intended to attend a football match in Sydney at the same time that state-based health officials were urging the shutdown of civil society. Morrison cancelled plans to attend shortly thereafter. At about this time New Zealand was introducing an extensive national lockdown, the severity of which was of interest to the Australian media not least because of the contrast it presented to the sanguine approach of the Australian prime minister, already under fire for allegations of under-performance in the Australian bushfire crisis that stretched over December 2019 and into 2020 (Walter 2020).

An undercurrent of scepticism underpinned initial Australian reporting of the New Zealand lockdown, particularly with regard to the way the general public would react to having their lives so profoundly affected by government decree (Edwards 2020). There was speculation that aggrieved citizens might take their frustrations out on their government at the ballot box in 2020. At this stage, Australia was flirting with milder versions of the New Zealand restrictions, mainly via the six state and two territory governments, with the federal government's main contributions being the prohibition of entry to Australia of foreign nationals and a programme of regulated repatriation of Australian citizens from overseas. This was, of course, the beginning of Australia's hotel quarantine programme.

By the middle of 2020, the trans-Tasman divergence continued. Having instituted its hard lockdown, the New Zealand government was able to declare that, in its opinion, Covid-19 infections had been eradicated and the lockdown could end (Sternlicht 2020). In Australia, however, infection rates were increasing, especially in the state of Victoria, where the hotel quarantine programme had run into serious trouble. The state government declared its intention to impose a hard lockdown not dissimilar to that instituted in New Zealand. The other Australian states joined in with border closures and travel restrictions, all of which were very disruptive to the movement of people and goods.

In the upheaval caused by these policies, commentators speculated about how voters would respond to such drastic government policies. The prevailing view was that the voters supported their governments despite the inconvenience and the cost of lockdowns. The resumption of some sort of normalcy in New Zealand in its post-lockdown period reinforced the idea that lockdowns could work, provided the government was resolute in their execution. The order and stability of New Zealand's governance in the midst of the pandemic was contrasted with the chaotic mismanagement occurring in the United States. Thus the New Zealand approach became a model to aspire to, and the inclusion of the New Zealand prime minister in Australia's National Cabinet formalised Australian recognition of the 'Ardern approach'.

The other noteworthy feature of the Ardern government's approach was that, for New Zealand, 2020 was an election year. Choosing the harder option (admittedly on the assumption that a short, sharp response at the onset of the pandemic would require only a short period of time to take effect) was politically risky. The New Zealand election, subsequently delayed by a month due to Covid-19, would give an indication of how damaging such repressive regulations (albeit for a relatively short period of time) would be to Labour's popularity. While the Australian federal election was still some way off, a number of state and territory elections were due to be held between 2020 and 2021 and these, along with the

New Zealand contest, would be a gauge of how the public would respond to lockdowns, border closures, travel bans and all the other disruptive outcomes of public health policy at a time of pandemic.

An incumbency triumph: Australian perspectives on the New Zealand contest

At the conclusion of the New Zealand election count, Ardern emerged triumphant. Far from punishing her government for its lockdown, New Zealand voters gave the prime minister a ringing endorsement, rewarding her Labour Party with an absolute majority of seats in the House of Representatives – the very outcome that reforms to New Zealand's electoral system had tried to prevent when the mixed member proportional (MMP) system was introduced. As a consequence, Labour can now govern without the need for support from minority parties. Indeed, the decline in the fortunes of New Zealand First was another feature of the contest, although its weak performance was obscured somewhat by the large swing away from the main opposition party, the National Party.

To many Australians, the New Zealand election result reinforced the high regard in which Jacinda Ardern is held this side of the Tasman Sea. Her election victory was interpreted as a strong endorsement of her resolute leadership at a time of crisis, notwithstanding the potential unpopularity of some of the specific policies put in place as a response to the Covid-19 threat (Brockett and Thomson 2020). No less significantly, the result has also been interpreted as an indicator of voters' perceptions and behaviour – during times of crisis, in not greatly dissimilar communities – with respect to their government, the opposition and political parties. It has long been held that a crisis situation is usually an advantage to an incumbent government, provided voters believe that the government has done a reasonable job in managing it (Tavan 2019). Voters' evaluative criteria seem to include the strength and empathy of the leader, the discipline exercised by the governing party or parties, and the ability of a government to bring order and stability amidst a sense that the alternative could be chaos and disorder. Accordingly, the contentious and possibly unpopular nature of a policy (the economic and social costs of a lockdown, for example) may be less important to voters than the extent to which electors think the government is dominating, rather than being dominated by, the crisis at hand. There is no doubt that the way the

Ardern government has handled the major crises that occurred during her first prime ministerial term has been endorsed by the voters of New Zealand, including those who were once partisan supporters of the other major political party.

Indeed, the New Zealand election result also demonstrates the electoral dangers crises present for opposition parties. The collapse of the National Party's vote, accompanied by the loss of a large number of seats, was a stand-out feature of the New Zealand contest and sounds an alarm for all of Australia's opposition parties in state and federal politics. This reflects the difficult situation opposition leaders and parties find themselves in as a crisis unfolds. If a government should seek to use emergency powers and suspend the parliament, opposition parties are denied a forum in which to present their alternative views or try to keep the government accountable for its actions. To criticise government during a time of crisis runs the risk of being cast as an unreasonable critic undermining the greater national effort and siding with the enemy (the virus) rather than with those seeking to defeat it. Meanwhile, a government and the community may become so focused on the crisis that any other policy debate might find it difficult to make its way onto the agenda and this, in turn, can deny scope for issue-specific minor parties to have an impact on political debate.

Was this tendency at work in the New Zealand contest? After the collapse in National's vote, the next biggest swing was the fall in support for New Zealand First, from 7.2 per cent to 2.6 per cent, with a commensurate loss of seats from nine MPs to none. On the other hand, support for the Greens increased, as did its parliamentary representation (up from eight seats to ten). Amongst the other non-major parties, only ACT, rising to ten seats (from one), and the Māori party, with two seats, won representation. Given the strength of the Labour vote and the decline in support for the centre-right, the 2020 New Zealand election has defied one of the intentions of the electoral system – to deny major parties absolute parliamentary majorities and encourage coalition politics by reducing the hurdles to non-major party representation.

Once again, the question arises as to whether the pattern of the New Zealand election might be replicated in Australia. There has been much talk amongst Australian political commentators about voter dealignment from the major parties and the rise of a values-oriented party such as the Australian Greens. There has also been a surge in right-of-centre minor parties that have actually had some success in getting elected to the Australian Senate via its system of proportional representation. The New Zealand result hints at a consolidation of support for the incumbent government in the midst of a crisis. While this pattern may be the case at a future Australian election, equally, there is some evidence to remind us again about how divergent Australian and New Zealand politics have become.

In October 2020, Queensland went to the polls. There were some interesting similarities between the Queensland and New Zealand elections. Both involved roughly the same number of voters (slightly over 2.9 million in Queensland, slightly more than 2.8 million in New Zealand), both have a unicameral parliament, both had a Labor/Labour government, both had female leaders (Annastacia Palaszczuk, in the case of Queensland), and both had governments that had taken a hard line in the management of Covid-19. Indeed, the Queensland government pursued a controversial border closure policy that was bitterly attacked by some in the media and was opposed by both the premier of the adjacent state of New South Wales and by the prime minister (Grattan 2020).

The result of the Queensland election is contained in Table 8.1, with the key features of the New Zealand election included for comparative purposes. While the election was won reasonably comfortably by Ms Palaszczuk, there was no corresponding wipe-out of the main opposition party. Indeed, the Liberal National Party (LNP) opposition primary vote actually increased by 1.79 per cent. Support for the non-major parties remained steady, with Pauline Hanson's One Nation securing 7.1 per cent of the vote and the Greens increasing representation from one seat to two despite a 0.5 per cent decline in its statewide vote.

While the Queensland election was an endorsement of an incumbent government at a time of crisis, that endorsement was by no means as comprehensive as that won by Jacinda Ardern and her government, and both the main opposition party and the minor parties of the right-of-centre managed to either defend or actually increase their vote. With some Australian state governments taking their lead from New Zealand when it comes to managing Covid-19, the Australian electorate may be a little less willing than their New Zealand counterparts to give those hardline lockdown governments their warm approval.

Table 8.1: 2020 elections – New Zealand and Queensland compared

New Zealand			Queensland		
Total votes: 2,886,420			Total votes: 2,967,636		
Party	Vote % (swing)	Seats (change)	Party	Vote % (swing)	Seats (change)
Labour	50.0 (+13.1)	65 (+19)	ALP	39.6 (+4.1)	52 (+4)
National	25.6 (-18.8)	33 (-23)	LNP	35.9 (+1.8)	34 (-5)
Green	7.9	10 (+2)	Greens	9.4 (-0.5)	2 (+1)
ACT NZ	7.6	10 (+9)	One Nation	7.1	1
Māori	1.2	2 (+1)	Katter Australia	2.5	3
NZ First	2.6	0 (-9)	Animal Justice	0.3	
Opportunities	1.5		Civil Liberties	0.1	
New Conservative	1.5		Palmer United	0.6	
Advance NZ	1		Informed Med	0.6	
Aotearoa Legalise Cannabis	0.5		Cannabis	0.9	
ONE Party	0.3		Nth Qld First	0.2	
NZ Outdoors	0.1		Shooters, Fishers, Farmers	0.1	
TEA Party	0.1		independents	2.5	1
Sustainable NZ	0.1				
Social Credit	0.1				
Heartland	0				

Source: https://www.electionresults.govt.nz/electionresults_2020/; https://results.elections.qld.gov.au/state2020

Conclusion

Somewhat ironically, given their ideological differences and the hint of coolness that exists in their relationship, incumbent Australian prime minister Morrison would take much more solace from Jacinda Ardern's victory than would the Australian Labor opposition leader, Anthony Albanese. Ardern's success has clearly been underpinned by the advantage of incumbency during a time of crisis, as well as the perception held by the electorate that she and her government had done a pretty good job at managing Covid-19 as well as the other crises that erupted during her first term. Morrison would like to think that the Australian people will view him in the same light, although it is also the case that the Australian prime minister's standing in relation to Covid-19 will be affected by the performance of the state and territory governments to whom the Morrison government handed over much of the responsibility for the policy response to the pandemic. As usual, Australian politics is complicated by the federal factor.

This is not to say that there is not significant interest in Australia in the performance of Jacinda Ardern as a leader. The New Zealand prime minister has clearly provided a model for managing Covid-19 that has been replicated by five of the six Australian states. As that poll in the *New Zealand Herald* reminds us, Ardern is held in very high regard amongst Australians. Her role as a strong yet empathetic leader in the aftermath of the Christchurch massacre was also widely admired in Australia, not least because of the contribution made by an Australian to this appalling event. Her landslide win at the 2020 general election is also widely recognised as another of her great political achievements, but the election itself is of limited utility as an indicator as to what might happen in future Australian politics (inevitably an interest of politicians and commentators). Despite some of the important things that are held in common between the two nations, Australian and New Zealand politics remain very different indeed.

9

'AND THE WINNER IS . . . NEW ZEALAND': THE VIEW FROM THE UK

Tim Bale

'It would be a gross exaggeration,' I observed when writing about UK coverage of New Zealand's 2017 general election, 'to suggest that the media in Britain experienced "Jacindamania"' (Bale 2018, p. 99).[1] This time around things were a little different. Far from being a virtual unknown, Jacinda Ardern was already familiar to many Brits, celebrated not only for her empathetic handling of the Christchurch shootings but also for doing a far better job of coping with Covid-19 than her counterpart in Number 10 Downing Street. This, along with brief references to polling, a focus on TV debates, and discussion of the referendums being held on the legalisation of cannabis and assisted dying, provided the background to the British media's coverage of the election right throughout the campaign.[2]

Gone (for the most part anyway), then, were routine mentions of Ardern's Mormon upbringing and her time 'working for Tony Blair' in London, although references to her having become New Zealand's youngest prime minister in 150 years were commonplace, as were reminders that she was only the second world leader to have given birth whilst in office. Once again, however, there was rather more interest in Ardern, her government and the election as a whole in outlets traditionally sympathetic to the centre-left, most obviously *The Guardian* (which ran a weekly review during the campaign) and the *Independent/i* paper, both of which have a strong online presence.[3] Both are also prone to seeing New Zealand as a beacon of progressive hope in an otherwise pretty dark world, as well as taking an occasional interest in stories involving its Māori population and heritage.[4]

Indeed, one of the first stories on the election – in the *Independent* and *The Guardian* – referred to the fact that, on dissolving parliament at the start of the campaign, Ardern had promised to introduce an additional public holiday to mark the Māori New Year (Perry 2020; McLachlan 2020a). Perhaps predictably, the right-wing *Mail* chose instead to kick things off with a warning that she would be raising taxes to pay for New Zealand's coronavirus response, while the equally right-wing *Telegraph* couldn't help but notice that the country had not only 'plunged into recession' but was experiencing its 'worst slump since the Thirties' (AP 2020; Burden 2020).

While there was relatively little coverage of the first televised leaders' debate, probably because it was widely seen as a bit of a damp squib, the second, feistier affair received rather more attention (Roy 2020a, 2020b), with *The Guardian* providing the most detailed hands-on coverage of all the leaders' debates. That was due in part to a slight narrowing in the polls but mainly as a result of Ardern's admission that she had previously smoked pot, allowing the media to tie together the election and the cannabis referendum (Graham-McLay 2020a). The third, equally boisterous, debate also commanded some coverage, possibly because Ardern (the clear favourite of those newspapers that carried stories on it) was widely seen as having come out on top after what was reported as a difficult few days for her supposedly Thatcherite opponent, Judith Collins (Graham-McLay 2020b; Hunt 2020). And it was those difficulties which prompted one Kiwi comedian and writer to note in *The Guardian*:

> If a moment so far could sum up Collins' campaign, it's how she attempted to present herself as the conservative Christian candidate with photographs of her praying before she voted in what must be New Zealand's emptiest church. A generous analysis would say it was referencing Heinrich Hofmann's *Christ in the Garden of Gethsemane*. But it looked like she was praying to the sanitiser bottle in front of her. And the bottle didn't know how to overcome a 14% deficit in the polls (Nokise 2020).

Ardern, on the other hand, while she wasn't presented as immune from criticism – a supposed tendency to waffle, a failure to live up to promises made last time around on housing, the environment and poverty – continued to come over as a politician with preternatural 'star power', especially with younger voters and even those still too young to vote (Roy 2020c). Hardly surprising, then, that in most of the British media coverage (with *The Guardian* an honourable, if partial exception), policies took second place, although that didn't mean that they were completely ignored (Graham-McLay 2020c). Three days out from the election, for instance, the *Independent* noted that

> Labour has campaigned on free dental for beneficiaries, lunches for underprivileged children, gender-neutral bathrooms in schools, more social housing, investment in New Zealand's provinces, free university fees and trade deals with the UK and EU.
>
> Meanwhile, National has pointed to 70,000 people losing their jobs since March and projections that 100,000 more will do so over the next two years. It has promised substantial road improvements and 'responsible economic management' to support businesses to recover from Covid-19. Tax cuts for middle-income earners will provide much-needed stimulus, Ms Collins said (Marshall 2020).

London's widely read freesheet, the *Evening Standard*, had a go the same day as well and, like a number of outlets as polling day grew closer, also provided readers not just with a sense of where the parties stood and the government's record but also with a brief explainer on MMP (Roach 2020).

In that respect, at least, so far, so 2017. But there was one obvious difference, namely the relative absence of attention paid to Winston Peters, although his 'brutal' put-down of a Covid-19 denier just before polling day earned him an admiring mention (Stickings 2020). He was, though, along with the leaders of the other parties (save Ardern, who declined the invitation), interviewed in election year by *The Guardian*, which helpfully pointed readers to all those interviews on the eve of the contest (Farrer 2020b). What happened to New Zealand First on election day – deftly covered in the same paper, incidentally – suggested that the decision to pay it little heed in the run-up was a good call (Graham-McLay 2020d).

Also a good call – at least for those of us more than casually interested in New Zealand politics – was *The Guardian*'s decision to live-blog the election: an heroic exercise, conducted (with the help of colleagues) by Helen Sullivan and Mattha Busby, which eventually ran to well over 10,000 words and ran from 6.30 on Saturday morning to just past 2.00 on Saturday afternoon. In fact, by mid-morning even those papers that had thus far paid little or no attention to the election were jumping on the bandwagon to record Labour's (or more often than not the prime minister's) win. The nation's top-selling red-top tabloid, the *Sun*, opted, characteristically, for a pun: 'ARD WORK New Zealand PM Jacinda Ardern claims landslide general election victory after Covid response' – a headline which was typical of nearly all the results coverage inasmuch as it put the result down almost entirely to the government's much-admired handling of the pandemic (Maynard 2020). The *Sun* was alone, however, in publishing a pen portrait of Ardern's partner, Clarke Gayford (Carter 2020).

A subsidiary theme in most of the immediate post-election coverage was, not surprisingly, the sheer scale of the win and the fact that New Zealand's proportional representation system looked likely to produce a single-party majority. That said, one title in that part of the UK that had itself experienced such an outcome – Scotland – found time to make the first of a few mentions, in the light of Boris Johnson tweeting his congratulations, of an eight-year-old tweet of Ardern's that revealed she hadn't (at least back then) been much of a fan of his.[5]

It didn't take long, though, for British titles to run pieces looking to the future: indeed, Saturday afternoon had barely begun when one commentator in the *Independent* was noting that 'In 2017, Ardern had a lot of work to do to prove she was more than "Jacindamania". Now, she has to prove that as well as being really nice, she can get stuff done' (Stewart 2020; Van Veen 2020). That didn't, however, prevent another of the paper's commentators drawing some lessons from her victory for the British Labour leader, Keir Starmer:

> What Ardern calls her 'team of 5 million' evidently doesn't suffer from the same vicious culture wars tearing societies apart in the Americas and in Europe. New Zealand might well turn out to be sui generis, a Nordic-style paradise in the sunny Pacific. Yet not so very long ago New Zealand was a far more chauvinistic, socially conservative society than the New Jacindaland of the 2020s. Leftish, vaguely progressive ideas and policies can change countries and win elections, even in today's world and in the most superficially unlikely of places (O'Grady 2020b).

Elsewhere, attention swiftly turned to the composition of the new parliament, with the media, after touching lightly on some of the ups and downs of some of the smaller parties and enjoying Tova O'Brien's viral 'roasting' of Advance New Zealand's Jami-Lee Ross, highlighting the fact that New Zealand's legislature was now apparently 'the world's most openly gay parliament'.[6] There was also some belated interest in the result from the BBC, which, although it hadn't given the election campaign much coverage save for a piece it called '[t]he plight of Maori and Pacifica citizens' (BBC 2020a), did carry pieces on its website about newly elected Labour MP Ibrahim Omer, originally from Eritrea, and about New Zealand's newly appointed Foreign Minister, Nanaia Mahuta (BBC 2020b, 2020c). Perhaps, with the end of the pandemic in sight, we can look forward to Mahuta and maybe even Ardern visiting London, thereby providing a refreshing contrast with most of those currently involved in governing (or what passes for governing) the UK.

10

JACINDA ARDERN'S ELECTION – A EUROPEAN PERSPECTIVE

Aljoscha Kertesz

Introduction

New Zealand's prime minister Jacinda Ardern is the Ryan Gosling of politicians: 'Almost too nice to be true. Above all, too good' is how she is described in the German newspaper *Süddeutsche Zeitung* (Wichert 2020). This chapter attempts to paint a comprehensive picture of how the general election in New Zealand was reported and evaluated in European media, focusing on the prime minister, her record in office, and parallels with the United States presidential election that took place at the same time. The chapter also notes issues overlooked by the European media. Given the many languages and wide-ranging media diversity of Europe, this is a challenge; I primarily focus on German-language media, due to the availability of articles and my familiarity with the language.

New Zealand's prime minister – a role model for Europe's social democrats

Prime Minister Jacinda Ardern is sometimes depicted in European media as a pleasant crisis manager who played a significant role in the Labour Party's 2020 election victory: 'the triumph was first and foremost Ardern's personal success' (Senzel 2020). Ardern's talents as a crisis manager seem to be widely recognised in New Zealand; even her harshest critics have praised the communication skills of the former fish-and-chip-shop worker and political science graduate, as well as her accessibility to people on the street and her normality (Wälterlin 2020d). Barbara Barkhausen (2020a), while noting that Ardern has faced criticism from both the left wing of her coalition government and the opposition parties, says she is the Pacific island nation's best-known prime minister thus far, and calls her an 'international political star'. *Tagesschau.de*, the online portal of the most watched news programme on German television, pointed out that Ardern was sometimes greeted like a rock star during the election campaign. Shopping malls where she appeared could scarcely hold the crowds (Senzel 2020). A similar picture was painted by an Italian online newspaper, which reported that thousands of students greeted the prime minister like a rock star (*affaritaliani.it* 2020) – images unimaginable for any politician in Europe, even in the early days of French president Emmanuel Macron's political career.

At the end of 2020 social democrats were heads of government in only six European countries (Friedrich Ebert Stiftung 2021). In his guest article 'Centre to Purpose' for *Die Zeit*, political scientist Michael Bröning explains that Ardern is a beacon of hope for social democrats worldwide although her politics at home are not at all classically left-wing (Bröning 2020). Barbara Barkhausen claims that Ardern's charisma, emotional style and forthright approach resurrected the country's social democrat Labour Party – who only made it to government in 2017 through a coalition with right-wing populists (New Zealand First) and the Greens – from practical irrelevance (Barkhausen 2020a). With so much to praise, it's little wonder that beleaguered social democrats in Europe are turning their eyes to New Zealand, trying to learn from her success. In the summer of 2018 the former leader of the German Social Democrats and vice president of the Socialist International, Kurt Beck, proclaimed during a visit by Ardern to Friedrich Ebert Stiftung, the German social democratic think tank: 'We hope for inspiration, you are a role model' (Hasel 2018).

However, the learning effect for political apparatchiks could be rather small. The media, insofar as they address the topic, agree that Labour's success is more to do with Ardern as a person and her very personal way of doing politics, and less with a convincing social democratic programme: 'Her victory is based less on social democratic content than on her personal style of politics, in which she repeatedly convinced through successful crisis management' (Hansen 2020). Ardern is described in many articles as a progressive politician. In a *Deutsche Welle* (2020) report, she is portrayed as a kind of icon in this field, considered a champion of progressive politics in an era of right-wing populist rulers, warm words where one might wish for a little more analytical underpinning. She was only the second woman ever to give birth to a child while serving as head of government, then took the child with her to Parliament and to the UN General Assembly, with her partner lending a hand, upending the traditional male and female roles. However, using this alone as evidence of progressive politics falls short of the mark.

Mathieu von Rohr sums it up well in his article when he describes Ardern as an exceptional political talent: approachable, modern, popular. She has become a global celebrity and icon of the left, with the election result primarily due to her personal popularity. She fits in perfectly with the spirit of the times, conveying clear messages about the climate and equality – and at the same time appealing to the middle of society (von Rohr 2020). The learning effect lies less in the shaping of a social democratic programme for the 21st century, and more in the selling of policies, in a Europe in which the traditional social democrats are only a shadow of their former selves.

Unblemished Covid-19 record of the prime minister

In early September 2020, the Institut für Weltwirtschaft (Institute for World Economy) presented a study showing that governments that successfully contained the pandemic and enacted strict countermeasures were the big winners in the Covid-19 crisis. Dithering governments that relied on easing to support the economy fared much worse, especially as Covid case rates rose. From February to July 2020, trends in infection rates were the key driver of political poll numbers (Warlimont 2020). This study, conducted in more than 35 states, gave a clear indication of who would win the New Zealand election. New Zealand's small number of Covid-19 cases could only mean victory for the incumbent, Jacinda Ardern. The fact that Ardern was already far ahead in the polls at the time was, of course, another indication.

In fact, all the European newspapers that examined the issue in more detail attest to the New Zealand prime minister's first-rate crisis management. The Dutch newspaper *de Volkskrant* wrote that the 'monster victory' was mainly due to Ardern's successful Covid strategy (Visser 2020). The Italian newspaper *Il Post* also described the government's response as the main reason for Labour's success, pointing out that Ardern's popularity had been declining before the Covid crisis because of unkept election promises (*Il Post* 2020). France's *Le Figaro* called the expected re-election logical given Ardern's brilliant crisis management, listing as evidence the low figures of only 25 dead and 1,876 infected

(Plesse 2020). The Italian newspaper *Il Fatto Quotidiano* (2020) also noted New Zealand's low Covid-19 numbers, observing that Ardern was only truly 'consecrated' as a result of the fight against the coronavirus. Employing the same imagery, the German newspaper *Badische Zeitung* called Jacinda Ardern New Zealand's 'Mother Teresa' (Abel 2020), and the Belgian newspaper *De Standaard* referred to her as 'Saint Jacinda' (Delbeke 2020). *Tagesschau.de* called her 'Jacinderella', a term of limited appeal in much of the non-English-speaking world since Cinderella has a different name in their respective languages (Senzel 2020).

Somewhat less euphoric, Miguel Sanches wrote in the *Berliner Morgenpost* that Ardern was only riding a wave of popularity after twice bringing the Covid-19 pandemic under control: first, at the outbreak, and again when a second wave occurred. His article highlighted the fact that women in particular had shown leadership during the Covid crisis around the world, especially compared to male leaders who took the virus more lightly, including US president Donald Trump, Brazilian president Jair Bolsonaro and British prime minister Boris Johnson. Sanches counted the 'caretaker from New Zealand' alongside German chancellor Angela Merkel in this special group of women (Sanches 2020).

Süddeutsche Zeitung reported polls showing that almost 90 per cent of New Zealanders believed that their government had taken the right measures, a remarkable figure to be achieved in a democracy (Wichert 2020). Three and a half months later, the same newspaper noted that the race between Labour and the National Party had been competitive over the previous two and a half years and that it was only with the Covid crisis in March 2020 that Ardern was able to pull clear (Haselsteiner 2020).

While many newspapers left it at the mere statement that New Zealand under Ardern had defeated the virus, Till Fähnders explained to his readers *how* the New Zealand prime minister had succeeded. When the coronavirus came, Ardern did the opposite of leaders such as Trump, Bolsonaro and Johnson. She took the threat seriously from the start, listened to the advice of experts, closed New Zealand's borders early and imposed one of the world's toughest lockdowns. The economic consequences were glaring, but it managed to push the number of new local infections to zero, twice in a row. For this decisiveness, New Zealanders had now overwhelmingly rewarded her with a second term (Fähnders 2020b). In her article 'New Zealand's high-flyer', Anke Richter also describes in more detail the leadership strategy Ardern used to master the crisis and become 'currently the world's most successful head of government in the fight against Covid-19': through tough measures flanked by soft words, along with social media expertise (Richter 2020a).

European newspapers, from left to right, paid tribute to Ardern for her crisis management in responding to the pandemic. Barbara Barkhausen (2020b) presented a Bloomberg Media survey confirming New Zealand's response to the coronavirus pandemic as the best in the world: the country received top marks in political stability, economic recovery, virus control and social resilience. In the face of so much approval, not only did the opposition have a hard time scoring at the ballot box, but there was hardly any room for critical voices in the field.

Balance sheet in general – still room for improvement

While the European media's evaluation of New Zealand's fight against the Covid crisis was positive across the board, numerous articles focused on unfulfilled election promises that the prime minister carried with her as an unwelcome legacy of her first term in office. Ardern promised a lot when taking office in 2017 – reducing child poverty, building social housing, stricter environmental protection – and most of these promises had not been implemented to the extent hoped for, giving the head of government a poor report card (Wälterlin 2020c).

Under the title 'Acclaimed in the world, criticized in New Zealand – Jacinda Ardern's record', Esther Blank informed readers of *Neue Zürcher Zeitung* that Ardern faced tougher scrutiny at home than her global cult status would suggest (Blank 2020a). She mentioned the unfulfilled promises on housing as an example, and the criticism from environmentalists and the Greens that the government was not moving fast enough on environmental protection. The fiscally conservative *Frankfurter Allgemeine Zeitung* noted that election promises had not been implemented and that hardly any progress had been made in building 100,000 affordable homes or significantly reducing child poverty (Fähnders 2020a). On the latter point, *Merkur* readers learned that, according to UNICEF, there was hardly any other industrialised country where there were as many suicides among young people as in New Zealand, and Māori continued to be particularly affected (*Merkur* 2020). Readers of the Dutch *rtlnieuws* (2020) were also advised that Ardern was having a tough time before Covid because of her government's undelivered election promises. European media occasionally supplied two reasons why the balance was significantly weaker than Ardern's global standing in the media would suggest.

In an article with the telling title 'Smiling against the crises', Barkhausen (2020b) admitted that the government's lack of progress on domestic policy was due to them being in more or less permanent crisis mode for much of the previous three years. The March 2019 massacre in Christchurch, the December 2019 volcanic eruption on Whakaari / White Island and the Covid-19 pandemic made the implementation of election promises difficult, although the Austrian *Der Standard* claimed that not even an earthquake could shake the New Zealand prime minister considered possibly the most effective leader on the planet (Wälterlin 2020b).

Some media outlets pointed out that New Zealand First – the party which, by choosing to go into coalition with Labour following the 2017 election, made the Ardern government possible, but which exited Parliament as a result of its poor 2020 electoral performance – was also part of the problem. The populist New Zealand First had blocked or slowed down many of Labour's domestic social reforms on housing and reducing child poverty (*Le Monde* 2020). *Le Parisien* (2020) wrote that Ardern's absolute majority as a result of her 2020 victory will now give her a freer hand in domestic politics. *Die Tageszeitung* (*taz*) noted that this could also be seen as a problem. Until now, Ardern has always been able to point to blockades erected by her right-wing populist coalition partner as a 'brake' on progress. That excuse is now gone. If economic problems persist, she will have to decide from whom to demand greater sacrifices and whose solidarity to insist upon (Hansen 2020, Wälterlin 2020d). The bottom line, according to these journalists, is that the young prime minister will have no excuses in her second term, given her clear parliamentary majority, if she does not implement the election promises she announced: unless, of course, the Covid crisis brings the economy to its knees.

The Dutch *rtlnieuws* wrote that it remains to be seen how long Ardern's surge in popularity will last, given that New Zealand's closed borders have ensured that tourism has been flat (*rtlnieuws* 2020). And it was once again Urs Wälterlin who stated that Ardern will need all her talent in the coming months to bring people together, to keep society together. For the Covid crisis has also had devastating consequences for New Zealand's economy. Unemployment, combined with persistent abject poverty in parts of the population and an extreme lack of affordable housing, threaten to undermine the middle class. The quality of life of the very people who today cheer Ardern is at risk (Wälterlin 2020d).

Similarly, Germany's public service broadcaster ARD called Ardern 'the caretaker', and told viewers that she must now deliver, as her supporters expect tangible results (Ratzow 2020). *Frankfurter Allgemeine Zeitung*'s economic correspondent for South Asia/Pacific had some immediate advice for the prime minister: she will have to become an economic leader in order to succeed. The 40-year-old Ardern, who once described capitalism as 'a plain mistake' in the eyes of poor New Zealanders, promised higher minimum wages, the planting of one billion trees by 2028, 100 per cent renewable energy supply by 2030 and longer sick leave. In making such promises, she raised expectations. But even Ardern will not be able to perform miracles (Hein 2020).

In the shadow of the United States election

Reading the multitude of newspaper articles drawing a comparison between the general election in New Zealand and the presidential election in the United States, which took place almost simultaneously, one got the impression that two systems were fighting for global supremacy, at least as far as the fight against the Covid-19 pandemic was concerned. However, these were not so much ideological blocs as two completely different characters, each cultivating a distinctly different political style. In a variety of articles, Ardern was readily described as the absolute opposite of Trump – the 'anti-Trump' (Richter 2020b; Radio Erft 2020; Hein 2020; Blank 2020b).

Anke Richter, writing as a correspondent for *Die Zeit* from Christchurch, informed us that Ardern had already been dubbed 'the anti-Trump' since the Christchurch mosque attacks, due to her empathetic nature and swift post-attack ban on the sale of automatic weapons. This combination – a tough crackdown and empathetic words – again had an effect in combating the Covid crisis (Richter 2020a). In his article entitled 'The Communicator', Urs Wälterlin described the prime minister adeptly switching from changing diapers in a 'grubby sweater' to negotiating economic relations with Donald Trump, noting that she 'can even reel in this chauvinist' (Wälterlin 2020a). In Austria's *Der Standard* he described Ardern's communication style as the opposite of Trump's: hope instead of fear, uniting instead of dividing, compassion instead of rejection (Wälterlin 2020b).

Under the title 'Ardern responds after Trump attacks over Corona cases', Germany's *Spiegel online* described how Ardern countered in no uncertain terms the US president's untenable statements that a huge wave of new Covid-19 cases was spreading in New Zealand, exposing the Trump campaign's use of indefensible fake news. For in fact, as the article noted, it was the US which had the most Covid-infected people in the world, while New Zealand was considered the model to emulate in the global fight against the virus (Hassenkamp 2020). A similar story was run by France's *Le Figaro* newspaper, which also reminded its readers that it was not the first time that these two leaders had confronted each other verbally: shortly after his 2016 presidential victory, when Trump met Ardern at a summit in Vietnam, he had joked that she had 'caused a lot of upset in her country', and Ardern had responded, referring to the protests that followed Trump's election, 'You know, no one marched when I was elected' (*Le Figaro* 2020).

Several media outlets compared the televised leaders' debates in each country. After the moderators in the US had let the first such encounter between the presidential candidates Donald Trump and Joe Biden completely slip out of their hands, articles could be found drawing a contrast with New Zealand, in which the showdown between rival leaders was conducted far more sedately. *Spiegel online* (2020) reported that Jacinda Ardern and her opponent Judith Collins presented themselves honestly and appropriately. *Der Standard* described the debate as a 'rather mild fight' (Wälterlin 2020b), and the Swiss newspaper *Neue Zürcher Zeitung* noted the lack of personal attacks and outbursts that made the almost simultaneous debate of the US presidential candidates descend into ugly chaos (Blank 2020a).

Far away from any coverage of an election campaign, Thomas Borchert informed his readers that, according to the bookmakers, a woman had a good chance of winning the Nobel Peace Prize in 2020, with frontrunners including Greta Thunberg and Jacinda Ardern, both of whom were well ahead of Donald Trump (Borchert 2020).

What wasn't actually in the media?

The majority of Europeans, especially in Germany, receive their news through regional daily newspapers. These are strong in terms of local and regional content, with most of their international content coming from news agencies such as Deutsche Presse Agentur, Agence France Press or even Associated Press. Thus, while basic information about the New Zealand election was given in regional newspapers, little was provided in terms of real depth. Regional dailies may have printed, at most, a single article around the time of the election, reporting more generally on the issues and the outcome.

National dailies maintain a dense network of overseas correspondents to cover the region, including Tim Fähnders (*Frankfurter Allgemeine Zeitung*, based in Singapore), Barbara Barkhausen (a freelance journalist, writing from Sydney for *Die Welt*, *Neues Deutschland*, *Frankfurter Rundschau*, *Der Tagesspiegel* and the Austrian daily *Die Presse*), Urs Wälterlin (writing from Canberra for Germany's *taz*, Austria's *Der Standard* and Switzerland's *SRF*) and Anke Richter (a freelance journalist based in Christchurch, published in the German newspapers *Der Freitag*, *Die Zeit* and *Frankfurter Allgemeine Zeitung*). The reports of the overseas correspondents are characterised by depth and expertise. But despite such analysis, some facts went unreported. Competition from other international news was simply too great. When regional dailies usually reserve only one of their pages each day for coverage from abroad, it is little wonder that some topics would have received little, if any, mention.

This included, for example, the strengthening of ACT. While the moderate performance of National, the success of Labour, the growth of the Greens and the exodus from Parliament of the New Zealand First Party were extensively reported, the rise of ACT, from one to ten seats, was hardly mentioned, and a thematic classification of that party can be found only in two articles, one a guest article by political scientist and SPD member Michael Bröning (2020), the other by Felix Haselsteiner (2020).

National's weakness was often mentioned but seldom analysed in any detail. For example, readers in Europe rarely learned about the comparatively late replacement of the party's leaders; under normal circumstances this alone could have been blamed as a reason for National's defeat. Few media outlets enlightened their readers about National's leadership problems. In the Belgian newspaper *De Standaard*, Charlotte van Campenhout (2020) dedicated a whole portrait to Judith Collins before the election, in which she also explained her 'Crusher' nickname. Writing on the televised debate between Ardern and Collins, Urs

Wälterlin (2020b) handed out positive points for Collins' performance and strong leadership, while noting that against Ardern's charisma she had little chance of electoral success.

By far the most in-depth analysis of the National Party's dilemma appeared not in a newspaper, but in an extensive report by the conservative think tank Konrad Adenauer Stiftung (Gorawantschy and Wagner 2020). The Australia and Pacific regional office of the think tank, which is close to Germany's Christian Democratic Union, considered the fate of the National Party in a multi-page analysis, reporting on an almost inflationary attrition of party leaders, resignations and retirements by members of the shadow cabinet, and the party's difficult search for unity and cohesion. Ultimately, the authors explained, National had yet to come to terms with its defeat in the 2017 general election. The analysis, freely available on its website, was realistic and well-informed, though probably read by only a handful of members of the German ministerial bureaucracy.

There were also very few comparisons between Jacinda Ardern and German Chancellor Angela Merkel, despite certain parallels between the two. No one would think of describing Angela Merkel as a rock star, as some newspapers have done with Jacinda Ardern, but various comparisons were made between the two politicians after the 2017 election due to their similarly balance-oriented political styles and policies aimed at the broad mass of the middle. This time around, Felix Haselsteiner (2020) observed that Ardern is sometimes called 'Aunty' by her supporters, while Merkel is sometimes referred to as 'Mutti' (mommy). In both cases there is the reassuring, deeper statement that 'Aunty' or 'Mutti' will take care of the people, especially in a time of crisis. At least up to now, the assumption seems justified, albeit with a high economic price.

Conclusion

Although in-depth discussion of New Zealand political events took place only in a few national media, the expansion of digital platforms means that readers of European newspapers had the chance to at least obtain a certain level of knowledge about New Zealand political events. Such in-depth analyses of other countries' domestic politics are more readily available than ever for those with an interest in learning about them.[1]

European media gave more attention to New Zealand's government than usual in 2020. The increasing coverage in the media's digital offerings may have helped, but the global pandemic and the prime minister's first-class crisis management certainly played their part in the stronger focus placed on New Zealand and its leader. This level of interest seems to be ongoing as New Zealand's relative success in combatting Covid-19 continues: in February 2021, several media outlets in Europe showed photos of a concert with thousands of spectators in Wellington, a rare sight in Europe where such gatherings are currently banned due to the pandemic. Outside of a pandemic, such photos – depicting a life back to 'normal' – would not have been worth editors' or readers' attention. In this sense, a heightened interest in New Zealand's politics reflects an abnormal state of affairs, and it is likely to subside if and when the Covid-19 experience begins to fade into history.

11

A FARAWAY BUT CLOSE RELATIONSHIP – THE VIEW FROM CHILE

Valentina Jofré Méndez

In 2017 the Chilean media covering the New Zealand elections focused on the novelty of Jacinda Ardern being the youngest prime minister since 1856, and the third woman in the country's history to assume the position of head of government; in 2020 the angle was very different. During 2020 'Jacindamania' became a kind of global idolatry for Ardern's work leading the fight against the coronavirus pandemic. In April, when most countries were going through the first wave of the pandemic, Ardern declared that New Zealand had 'won the battle' against the virus.

'She has plenty of what any world leader would like to have,' said one Chilean television commentator (Apud 2020). *La Tercera* devoted two whole pages to a profile on Jacinda Ardern, highlighting the performance of the prime minister in the face of the terrorist attack in March 2019 and the Covid-19 crisis (Jofré 2020).

As the election date came closer, eyes turned to Ardern's campaign and her competition with another woman, the conservative candidate Judith Collins. 'Ardern finds a rival in what seemed like an easy re-election', headlined the Chilean newspaper *El Mercurio* in July 2020. The same newspaper wrote an article on both candidates the day before the elections in October. 'Analysts agree that charisma, kindness and calm are Ardern's strengths' said the article, which also mentioned that the 'broken promises' of her previous term could take away some important votes (Caldera 2020).

The global phenomenon of Ardern and her model of modernity attracted attention in Chile, which has already had a woman president twice: Michelle Bachelet (2006–2010 and 2014–2018). Ardern's story appeared on almost every network and in the print media. Her hobby as a DJ and having given birth while governing the country were undoubtedly the most interesting aspects for this South American nation.

It is clear that her outstanding leadership in the fight against Covid-19 helped her win a new mandate and dissipate mistrust regarding any management shortcomings, according to what New Zealand analysts told me when I was writing about the electoral process. It may even have convinced many Chileans (28 per cent) that Chile should follow a political and economic model like that of New Zealand, according to a 2020 survey (Plaza Pública 2020), although the second most popular option was Sweden's model, which 17 per cent of Chileans preferred.

The elections and the following months

Despite New Zealand being 9,131 km distant from Chile, the New Zealand elections were closely followed by both the media and the Chilean government. The government 'followed the process with special attention', according to the Chilean Foreign Ministry, and the triumph of the prime minister's party, which achieved a parliamentary majority, was highlighted by the Chilean administration. On a more personal note, President Sebastián Piñera sent a letter congratulating Prime Minister Jacinda Ardern, highlighting the impeccable process and civic spirit of the New Zealand people. From the Ministry of Foreign Affairs came assurances that they had observed Ardern's successful policy in relation to Covid-19 very closely and with great interest.

After Ardern's triumph and the start of her second term, the Chilean news media became interested in the nomination of Māori MP Nanaia Mahuta as Minister of Foreign Affairs. Chile was discussing at the same moment the issue of seats reserved for indigenous peoples in the Constitutional Convention (the body that will draft Chile's new Constitution), a process that emerged after the 'social outbreak' of 2019: a series of massive protests against social and economic inequality and deficiencies in Chile's public health, education and pension systems. 'While Chile is fighting for reserved seats: New Zealand Prime Minister appoints Māori woman as Foreign Minister', headlined a Chilean web newspaper (*El Desconcierto* 2020).

Chileans' interest in the New Zealand government's agreements and negotiations with the country's indigenous people is not new. Chile has maintained decades of minimal relationship and dialogue between the State and the Mapuche community, indigenous people living in Chile and Argentina who, according to the 2017 census, make up 9.93 per cent of Chile's population. At present, there are initiatives on the part of the

Mapuche to recover their historic lands, which today are held by private companies.

In 2020 *La Tercera* interviewed Christopher Finlayson, former Minister for Treaty of Waitangi Negotiations, who signed numerous agreements with Māori during his nine years in office (2008–2017). When asked, 'Based on your experience as a negotiator, what would you recommend to a country that must reach agreements with its indigenous peoples?', Finlayson replied:

> The New Zealand experience can provide a guide, but ultimately, the one Chile chooses must be a Chilean formula. I think it is very important for the government to address the issue in all its magnitude, to be prepared to apologise. In my experience as someone who worked on this with Māori, there is nothing more powerful than forgiveness and the promise of a better relationship. Money is secondary. It is important, but the ability of the Crown to stand up and say 'I'm sorry', we were wrong, we did not treat them well and we promise to do better in the future, is much more powerful (Iglesias 2020).

New Zealand and Chile have maintained diplomatic relations for 75 years. This relationship was strengthened after Chile's return to democracy following the military dictatorship of Augusto Pinochet (1973–1990). It has now transcended bilateral agreements, economic interests and even electoral processes, to become, instead, a phenomenon of admiration. It may seem a cliché to say so, but when it is the Chilean authorities themselves who speak of New Zealand as an example to follow, we can speak of 'admiration'.[1]

Both are southern hemisphere countries, with enormous maritime zones extending out into the Pacific, with a fluid relationship and a broad agenda that includes issues such as the digital economy, climate change and the treatment of indigenous peoples, among many others. But they differ greatly in their models of society, their economic outcomes (including GDP per capita) and their levels of human development and inequality. Chile's current Minister of Finance, Ignacio Briones, reflected this 'admiration' very clearly in October 2020:

> I have always set a country like New Zealand as a reference. I think it is a model to follow, it is a reference for many reasons,

> but partly because it combines the elements that we are talking about here. It is a tremendously dynamic economy, tremendously competitive, an extraordinary climate for doing business, but also with a tremendously modern State (Briones 2020).

It is not surprising that Chile is looking out for models that make sense to it, since it is on the verge of drafting a new Constitution. At this time New Zealand has emerged as a kind of social democratic paradise, worth keeping an eye on. This admiration has also permeated the Chilean business sector, which aspires to rapid economic growth and is today trying to overcome the two consecutive crises that have hit the country: the 'social outbreak' of 2019 and the coronavirus pandemic of 2020.

Successful Chilean businessman Nicolás Ibáñez is the owner of Drake Group, whose business portfolio includes the Papa John's pizza chain in Chile, Spain, Costa Rica and Panama; real estate companies; the private bank Hampden & Co.; and The Borders distillery in the United Kingdom, among others. In an interview with the economic newspaper *Pulso*, Ibáñez observed that in Chile it is necessary to:

> take advantage of channeling the re-founding illusion to direct the impulses towards the achievement of a national aspiration and identity that is realistic, practical and effective, so that Chile follows its own course, definitely abandoning the Latin American traps and moving towards being a fully developed country, with a high level of inclusion and social cohesion, such as New Zealand, for example (Villagrán 2020).

Chilean historian Joaquín Fermandois, an expert in the history of Chilean foreign policy, describes the comparison with New Zealand (and the admiration shown for it) as follows: '100 years ago, Argentina was at the same level of development as Canada, Australia and New Zealand. Not so now. So this issue of comparing Latin America with New Zealand is important because it says why can't we be like them? It's quite a question.' Fermandois explained to me that New Zealand is presented as an example to follow as it has a 'model that is interesting because it is a country that has developed based on natural resources, some renewable and others not. Chile has made progress in renewable natural resources. And we are "neighbours"; we are in the Pacific'.

The Chilean government has observed with interest New Zealand's development model, considering both countries to be 'likeminded'.

Every Chilean president since the return to democracy in 1990 has visited New Zealand. In 2018 President Sebastián Piñera was in New Zealand to strengthen commercial ties, and Prime Minister Jacinda Ardern praised Chile as 'one of our closest and oldest partners in Latin America'. In 2019, visits were made to Chile by the former Deputy Prime Minister and Minister of Foreign Affairs, Winston Peters, and the then Minister of Māori Affairs, Nanaia Mahuta. In 2020, the planned visits by Chile's Minister of Finance, Ignacio Briones, and Minister of Science, Technology, Knowledge and Innovation, Andrés Couve Correa, were suspended as a result of the pandemic.

While diplomatic relations between the two countries continue to advance, opportunities for cooperation continue through shared membership in the Asia-Pacific Economic Cooperation (APEC) and the Comprehensive and Progressive Agreement for Trans-Pacific Partnership (TPP-11). Chile has yet to ratify the TPP-11, because the agreement has brought forth a wave of criticism that the government prefers not to revive, for now, in the midst of a pandemic and with a polarised social climate linked to the ongoing constitutional process. Despite Chile's internal conflicts, it continues to see New Zealand as an example worthy of close observation – by Chile, and South America more generally.

Media Perspectives

12

COVERING THE 2020 ELECTION: PLATFORMS AND THE PLAGUE

Henry Cooke

It was a very hot day in Havelock North and Simon Bridges was having a very good time. The National leader had just ruled out working with Winston Peters after the election (New Zealand National Party 2020a). The half dozen reporters following him around had something to ask about that wasn't either a government announcement or some kind of scandal. Public polls from around this point in early 2020 had National ahead of Labour; some polls even had the right bloc of National and ACT ahead of the left bloc of Labour and the Greens (O'Brien 2020; Colmar Brunton 2020a).

I was with him walking around the streets of Havelock North in my role as a political reporter for *Stuff* and its stable of newspapers. It's a very blue town – or it was at the start of 2020 at least – and Bridges seemed to be getting a good reception, with the public telling him repeatedly that they backed his call on Peters, right in front of the cameras. Labour itself was knee-deep in problems borne of working with New Zealand First, from Auckland light rail being halted to serious charges being raised about its foundation (Malpass 2020).

National didn't necessarily look on track to win, but it certainly looked to be a nail-biter of an election. Twenty-five days later, New Zealand would see its first Covid-19 case. Just over 100 days later Simon Bridges would be ousted as leader. And by the end of the year, National would not just lose the election, but be decimated, losing 23 seats and more than 400,000 party votes (Electoral Commission 2020). Indeed, after winning Havelock North by over 3,500 party votes in 2017, National ended up losing the town to Labour in 2020 (Electoral Commission 2020). Some of that loss had to do with a walkabout.

No election result can be explained with a single cause, but two massive and intermingling influences emerge as key to the result. One was a massive news event and the other a structural force. The news event was Covid-19, and the structural force was the increasing diversity of platforms politicians use in an attempt to reach voters – and how these interact with traditional political reporting.

Going through us and going around us

Election campaigns are traditionally thought to happen *on the ground*: in shopping malls, at candidate forums, and finally in the polling booth itself.

But as small as New Zealand is, you can't shake everyone's hands. There are obviously huge benefits to in-person mobilisation efforts, but for the candidates themselves this is essentially theatre: the real battle is being fought in the wider public sphere.

This used to be where my colleagues and I – the mainstream media – dominated. We wrote the news stories about the policies, analysed the performances on the stump, and hosted the debates. We still perform much of this role, but the internet has allowed politicians to go *around* us in a massive way. Politicians can talk to thousands of voters with Facebook livestreams, with tweets and Instagram posts, with targeted social media advertising, and in many other ways. This was happening before the internet of course – direct mail campaigns upturned American politics decades ago – but it has been amplified even further (Perlstein 2020).

The advantages for a politician are obvious. Your message can go out to both your fans and detractors, unmediated by the professional decision-making of reporters and editors. You get to push the issues you care about, not just the ones the media does. And you can talk about the issues that the media are talking about without their framing or the direct quotes from your opposition you are likely to see in a political story. It's also obvious that we find this upsetting.

This does not mean the media are abandoned or irrelevant. We are still one of the most effective ways to reach large swathes of voters and being seen to ignore us or avoid us can be extremely problematic. We may not control the entire public sphere any longer, but we do control a large part of it – and our presence can lend a feeling of objectivity and truth.

However, there is advantage in going straight through us to your own audience, even if we are the ones asking the questions. That is what happened at the most consequential political events of the year: the

1 pm Covid-19 briefings. Instead of seeing our finished stories or video packages in the 6 pm news, the public got to hear the news as we heard it, and then watch us question politicians and officials on its import. The press conference, usually a part of the story creation process mostly hidden from the public, became the story itself.

How Covid-19 maimed the National Party

This shift gave Jacinda Ardern an excellent stage to show off what was a world-leading response. New Zealand has come out of Covid-19 with fewer deaths, fewer days in lockdown, and fewer job losses than the countries we compare ourselves to (Lowy Institute 2021; Radio New Zealand 2021). Ardern and Health Director Dr Ashley Bloomfield's communication strategy has been cited as a major factor in this success (McGuire et al. 2020; Friedman 2020). As the government took action, both in economic and health policy, it had the attention of the nation – and the nation clearly liked what it was seeing. Polls on the government's performance shot into the stratosphere and Labour's polling hit record highs, staying very strong ever since (Colmar Brunton 2020b).

The 1 pm Beehive press conferences were the stage for this response, and typify the tension between going around us and going through us. They were broadcast live and in full by many outlets, and because of a somewhat recent technical change to the Beehive Theatrette (where they are held) our questions as reporters were also picked up (TVNZ 2020; Walls 2020). The audience was massive – over 3.3 million people tuned into the 1 pm briefing on either TV1 or TV3 throughout the year, with average daily viewers at almost 1.5 million in April, a figure roughly double what a typical 6 pm news bulletin reaches (Donnell 2020; Nielsen 2020).

Bloomfield and Ardern knew this and used it to their advantage – giving long preambles before opening up to questions, and often noting that they were directly addressing the audience. It also gave audiences a better chance to see how we work every day, and this proved problematic. It is a journalist's job to be skeptical of power, and the nature of broadcasting sometimes requires a question to be asked repeatedly in order to get a response that will make sense within a package (a politician saying 'yes' is rarely useful). We also compete with each other for the scarce time in each press conference by interrupting each other. For viewers this appeared as rudeness and cynicism.

Reporters got used to their questions being criticised by many in the public for being insufficiently respectful or on-topic, with *Newshub*'s political editor Tova O'Brien emerging as a particular villain (Walls 2020; Oliver 2021). Instead of a conduit of information, we were seen by some as an obstruction, our questions themselves needless interventions (Brettkelly 2020). I would argue that it was also a significant contributor to the popularity of the prime minister and Labour rising so swiftly – viewers were getting an unfiltered look at the prime minister deftly answering questions from a faceless bunch of whingers. I would go so far as to say the election was won not on the campaign trail but on that stage in the theatrette.

But going straight to the viewers also has its risks, as Bridges soon found. Labour's popularity completely destabilised National and Bridges' hold on the leadership. Bridges had survived as leader despite very poor personal ratings in part because of the strength of the party vote polling – as this began to fall, the party's image of stability cracked (Cooke and Coughlan 2020; Colmar Brunton 2020b). The natural thing for an Opposition to do is criticise government actions, and for New Zealand parties to compare our performance to Australia's, as Bridges did (Whyte 2020). This seemed to jar with a public who were in a patriotic mood.

Things got particularly acute after Bridges – or at least, his Facebook account – did what Ardern had been doing for weeks, going around the media and directly to the public. His Facebook page featured a post in his name harshly criticising the extension of the level 4 lockdown, saying 'The decision for New Zealand to stay locked down in Level 4 shows the Government hasn't done the groundwork required to have us ready,' and musing that the extended lockdown could do more harm than it prevented (Bridges 2020). This drew so much negative feedback that several news stories were written about it, and his MPs started to murmur about his judgment as leader (Small 2020). Eventually these hints of a leadership challenge would harden into a caucus coup, and the months of infighting and leaks that National itself blames for its loss (Cooke 2020c).

Ironically, this post itself was a carbon copy of a press release, and my own reporting suggests it was only a mistake that led to it being posted in that form (Cooke and Coughlan 2020; New Zealand National Party 2020b). Had it remained as a press release it is likely the public outrage would have been far smaller. Press releases are designed to go to the media and be chopped up into small segments that find their way into news stories, meaning a relentlessly negative tone – as found in Bridges' post – is far less relentless and is balanced with other views. Instead it went straight to the public, and the public hated it. Going through the media obviously has some advantages.

The long days and long nights of a long campaign

As the actual campaign started, paused, then restarted, we in the news media took back some control. We are the ones who run the debates. We are the ones packaging news at 6 pm, in newspapers and online.

Politicians during campaigns structure much of their days around appearances in the news media, which in turn means reporters structure much of their days around following politicians, often a logistical challenge given we don't have the luxury of free flights and chauffeured cars. This makes us very busy, which is probably advantageous for politicians keen to make sure we cover the big issue *they* are talking about on any given day, rather than fossicking around for something more complicated.

Here's a typical day, September 29, to give a sense of how busy reporters are.

At 8 am Collins held a press conference in central Auckland announcing National's new policy of doubling the funding for the Serious Fraud Office. At 10 am Ardern held a press conference in South Auckland to announce a raft of health policies. At 10.30 am ACT leader David Seymour began a whole day of campaign activities across Auckland. At 1 pm Green Party co-leader James Shaw announced a multi-billion-dollar transport policy in central Auckland, held a press conference, then headed out for a 'walkabout' around Britomart. At 1 pm two new Covid-19 cases were announced. At 5 pm New Zealand First leader Winston Peters and the Serious Fraud Office simultaneously announced the decision made in the New Zealand First Foundation case.

Reporters were at each of these events. Typically, each announcement or speech is followed by a 20-minute press conference or 'stand up' with reporters. Many of us would be filing live updates from our phones for rolling coverage, as well as planning out longer stories or analysis. The tension between covering what everyone else is covering – the announcements themselves – and what you personally want to cover is ever present. The press conferences give you a chance to probe the politicians and hopefully find out something new.

There are also 'walkabouts' – key elements of the campaign calendar not often seen outside of elections. A politician walks somewhere between 100 metres and one kilometre around a suburb or mall, depending on how much they get mobbed. Journalists are told about the walkabout in advance and turn up to see how the public react to politicians in real life, even if they know it is a bit of a trick, because walkabouts are typically planned for areas where a party has strong support anyway. These events are ostensibly for the public, but there's a reason politicians invite the media along too: images of politicians out in the 'real world' with a smiling public makes them look popular, even if the polls disagree and the politician is in an atypical area.

While they are somewhat contrived, walkabouts are still useful for reporters and far from risk-free for politicians. Journalists get an opportunity to see how voters view politicians, to talk to them about what they care about, and to see if the public cares about what politicians are talking about. A good example is that walkabout Bridges had in Havelock North at the beginning of the chapter – everyone he met seemed genuinely happy with the decision to sideline Peters. By contrast, Collins' floundering campaign ran into stronger headwinds on an awkward walkabout in Ponsonby, when news media revealed one of the 'fans' Collins ran into was in fact the head of the National Party's campaign in that area (Manch 2020).

We aren't the only ones at these media events anymore. Again, politicians attempt to go around us as well as through us. Each party would have its own videographers taking footage or photos of the press conferences and speeches, which were released directly on social media (New Zealand Labour 2020; New Zealand National Party 2020c). Journalists and our microphones are often present in these posts, the news media acting as a kind of prop, a signifier of legitimacy. After all, normal folk don't have legions of reporters following them around.

There was also a huge number of posts sent out by parties and candidates that were totally disconnected from the day-to-day events of the news media's campaign trail. Hundreds of thousands were spent on Facebook and Google ads, appearing alongside hundreds of non-sponsored posts 'fact-checking' other parties and promoting one's own policies (Hancock 2020). Politicians often appeared to use these platforms to say the kind of things that cynical reporters wouldn't let them get away with (Cooke 2020a).

Despite our busy schedules, I don't think it is responsible of the news media to leave this area of the campaign solely to the parties. If things are being said online that are misleading, lack context, or are plain wrong, reporters should endeavour to correct them, using their sizeable platforms to do so. My own publication *Stuff* launched a fact-checking platform called 'The Whole Truth', which often ended up correcting or at least adding context to posts made online (*Stuff* 2020). Often this would require detailed policy research, but sometimes it was as simple as correcting an incorrect quote being spread by MPs online (Pullar-Strecker 2020; Cooke 2020a).

Knowing when to intervene

There is an opportunity cost to fact-checking, and a value judgment. Each one of these fact-checks requires time and a certain willingness to *intervene* in the political discourse, rather than just transcribe it. Sometimes the appropriateness of this is obvious – you should tell the public if a party leader is directly lying – but often things are a little more grey, with politicians making statements that are true but lack context, or seem designed to distract. Fact-checks are just one of several proper interventions the media can make in political discourse – from polls to big investigative scoops.

Intervention came more to the fore in the last weeks of the 2020 campaign as the usual source of campaign news dried up: new policies. Because so many people were expected to (and did) vote early, campaigns got almost all of their large announcements out well before the final weeks, when attention to the campaign was at its peak (Ensor 2020). By my tallying, the week of 12 September – a month before the election – saw eight new National Party policies and five new Labour ones. The week of 12 October, just before the election, saw just two National Party policies.

This led to press conferences where no one had anything new to talk about, allowing the odd storyline of Collins' beliefs on the relationship between obesity and personal responsibility to bloom in the final days of the campaign (Burrows 2020). As the clear underdog, Collins needed traction, and attempted to get some with a campaign against the wealth tax – a Green Party policy (McKay 2020). MMP offers many opportunities to attack an opponent for the policy of a likely ally, but most reporters found this attack hard to take seriously, as Labour had repeatedly said that it would not introduce a wealth tax, while the Green Party had made clear that it was not a 'bottom line' for them (Radio New Zealand 2020). This led to several combative press conferences, where reporters basically just asked Collins why the public should trust her version of the future over the very clear statements made by Ardern (Harman 2020; Cooke 2020b). Collins eventually went on to complain that she felt the press gallery were acting as press secretaries for Ardern (Newstalk ZB 2020).

This kind of tension between reporters and politicians is nothing new. It is generally when we make some kind of intervention that it happens – essentially, when we push back against something that a politician is saying, rather than just repeating it. Sometimes readers really do just deserve a crisp summation of what a politician has said, alongside reaction from their opponent – plenty of good political reporting looks like this. But we are not stenographers and should not be afraid to intervene on the side of truth and clarity for our readers. I believe you can do this while being completely fair to politicians – in fact, it is often required in order to be fair – but this is fertile ground for debate.

Reporters and their editors have agency here, and can change the course of elections with their actions. The *New Zealand Herald*'s decision to report on the fact that Covid-19 patient data had been leaked to them by a National MP – something other outlets with the same information did not do – led to the resignation of that MP, and a scandal that undoubtedly contributed to National's loss (Moir 2020). We kid ourselves if we pretend we are just recorders of the political discourse; we are actors too. And in a world where more and more of the political discourse is moving away from areas we control, we must be more assertive than ever.

13

THE 2020 ELECTION: A TELEVISION JOURNALIST'S PERSPECTIVE

Tova O'Brien

Introduction

Back in January 2020 when we were young, carefree and full of hope the political year started like any other with the set pieces – Labour's caucus retreat at a vineyard, Rātana celebrations, Waitangi. It is the perfect way to come back to politics after a break – i.e., you're not in Parliament. Because although Parliament is lifeblood for Press Gallery journalists – we're part of the fabric, stitched into the fleur-de-lis carpet, just as trampled on sometimes – we really, really love getting out, talking to so-called 'real people' and observing the politicians in the real world. It's illuminating and great fun, which is why we also live for election year and the campaign – six to eight weeks of unbridled, adrenaline-soaked, relentless, exhausting, exhilarating politics in the wild.

So 2020 started in the field and was set to conclude thus. Then the wheels came off entirely in a way none of us could have ever predicted. Covid, coups, conspiracies, scandal, ministerial screw ups, a sexting MP, leaks, lies, leadership. It was immense. Even if we set Covid aside for a second – which we all wish we could – we have just lived through one of the most tumultuous years in New Zealand politics. With all that in mind my eyes were bulging, bloodshot and bagged by the time campaign o'clock came around. We were still ready, the *Newshub* politics team was pumped, but we were terrified of what lay ahead given the year had been so full of noise.

And so it began – a filthy electorate campaign in central Auckland with a senior National Party figure calling up talkback in the middle of the night pretending to be Merv from Manurewa to undermine one of his party's own candidates. The crazy looked set to continue.

Then . . . like so much of the year . . . handbrake . . . Covid.

Back to Wellington, back to Covid, back to the 1 pm presser and all its social media baggage.

Reset. Campaign round two and, miraculously, clear air. The clouds parted; the political gods shone through. The pressure had been released; the hyperdrive of 2020 went down a gear. We finally had policy to discuss – Matariki, drug harm reduction, business loans, tax, energy, electric vehicles, border policy: that was just the first week from the major parties.

Labour / Covid campaign

But despite the unexpected volume and breadth of policy this was, as the prime minister said, a Covid campaign. It was Covid that helped determine the outcome, Covid that cemented Jacinda Ardern's reputation for strong leadership in a crisis – something we already knew following the Christchurch terror attack and the Whakaari / White Island disaster the year before.

Ask Ardern pre-election campaign about her leadership and the hellish trifecta of crises that beset us and she would kick to the broader team, showing humility. Whether you believe it was entirely genuine or not, she never wanted to make it about her. Come the campaign, it was a different story. Labour knew it was their not-so-secret weapon, a bazooka of political power. So often politics is about nuance, reading between the lines; the slightest change of language can mean so much. During a campaign subtlety goes out the window. Labour brazenly played the Covid card. During a rally in Wellington in the final throes of the campaign, Ardern trumpeted her leadership in a crisis: 'You truly get to know your government and your leaders when disasters strike . . . the alternative is an opposition party that is focused on itself.'

It was also writ large in the political advertising Labour released, carefully workshopped and focus-grouped down to the letter: Jacinda Ardern prime ministerial in her ninth-floor office, calm, competent and in charge, with accents of Labour red and the portrait of Michael Joseph Savage placed just so.

All that said, I struggle to see how National could have won the election even if Covid hadn't happened.

Tale of two leaders

Elections in New Zealand are presidential and although I think Jacinda Ardern and Judith Collins share a lot of leadership traits – both are smart, ambitious, decisive – the public's reception of them on the campaign could not have been more starkly different.

Ardern's barnstorming of every Westfield in the country, like a cashed-up mall rat, and her street walkabouts said it all. She was absolutely thronged by adoring fans, some nearly in tears as they thanked her for 'keeping us safe'. Journalists were crushed in the stampede. Parents were flinging their children into the blind gauntlet of backwards-walking camera operators wedged together in a single rolling mass. 'Get your picture with Aunty Jacinda!' they demanded of their young. A priceless selfie was worth a minor maiming or a touch of trampling. The rallies of students, the filled town halls – it was quintessential 'rah-rah Ja-cin-dah'.

Then there was Collins. Turned away from a Ponsonby Road shop where she wasn't wanted, National Party apparatchiks planted along a walkabout route to heap pre-arranged praise on their leader and boss as she passed by. It was dire.

National

What a litany of failure. Own goals, friendly fire and faux pas. The National Party's *annus horribilis* was a remarkable exercise in political mismanagement. It was like an episode of *The Thick of It* had a baby out of wedlock in a church with an episode of *House of Cards* and somehow an episode of *The Office* was the surrogate. They were like Labour during its nine years in opposition, but off the back of the John Key era, when they looked like such a grown-up party, it was surprising to see National derail itself so spectacularly. National could not catch a break and – barring Covid – the party only had itself to blame. Now it's engaging in a wide-ranging, forensic, post-election post-mortem review. It'll take ages, cost money, trigger PTSD within the caucus, foment blame. I could save them the trouble; any New Zealander with half an eye on politics in 2020 could.

The party came into the campaign with one leg severed (the first coup), an arm chopped off (the second leadership change), two fingers amputated (Andrew Falloon, the sexting MP, and Hamish Walker, the MP who leaked Covid patients' details)[1] and several stubbed toes (including declaring Pākehā MP Paul Goldsmith Māori to make up for a lack of diversity). It was always going to struggle to make it across the finish line. Then, remarkably, it shot itself in its remaining foot. Paul Goldsmith's 'fiscal hole' undermined National's sacred domain of responsible economic management while simultaneously blowing to pieces its one chance at a cracker, vote-winning election bribe – its tax cuts.

Gaffes became a theme of National's campaign: Gerry Brownlee's Covid conspiracy theorising ('interesting series of facts'); Judith Collins praying in front of media she'd invited, then pretending she didn't want us there; her fat shaming and blaming ('We all have to own up to our little weaknesses'); Brownlee's blowout – swearing at a young reporter ('Your people give me the shits. They're bloody lazy as buggery').

You couldn't make this stuff up.

But it was an MP most New Zealanders would have struggled to place, Denise Lee, who lopped the head off this weird anatomical analogy I've adopted. She emailed the entire caucus with a supermarket list of strongly worded complaints about the leadership – an attack on the leadership, *during* an election campaign – which was leaked to *Newshub*'s Jenna Lynch. Firstly, you only send emails like this to the whole caucus if you want it to go further. This was meant for public consumption. Secondly, if you're passionate enough about a party to become an MP, in theory you love your party. You may not like the leader, you may not like something they've done. In normal times, sure – you might leak about it, agitate, blow the whistle. During a campaign you're supposed to put the party first. Do whatever you can to try to win. This email and subsequent leak so close to an election were the king hit that destroyed any chance of National securing a win.

New Zealand First

Gone but not forgotten, Winston Peters is still the most recognisable man in New Zealand politics: the kingmaker, game changer, muckraker, piss taker and ballbreaker.

Peters had a lot going for him this term. He started out as a statesman, had a successful stint (subbing for Ardern) as Acting Prime Minister, was well-regarded in foreign affairs. His ministers did well splashing cash around the regions and with the Defence Force. He flexed his coalition muscle. He could have run a more positive campaign by playing more to those strengths and trying to get some of Ardern's stardust to rub off on him rather than attacking the government of which he was a part.

But, like everyone, Peters struggled to get a word in edgeways during Covid. Throw in the Serious Fraud Office investigation into New Zealand

First Foundation donations, top it all off with some bad advice from an ill-informed cabinet and advisors, and there was a confluence and display of all the bad bits of Winston Peters.

ACT

With all due respect to David Seymour and his band of merry newbies, the 900 per cent increase in his party is less about him and more about the National Party's aforementioned howlers. That's not to take away from the fact he had a very good term. Once he got past the desperate attention grabs in fluoro lycra he did the hard mahi on euthanasia, working tirelessly and across the aisle to get a piece of legislation he truly cared about passed.

His opposition to gun reform, on the other hand, was more about political opportunism. That's politics though – they all do what they can to hold onto or increase their power.

And it all worked. It really became a reality for me when I spent a day with Seymour in Arrowtown – that's when I truly clocked the groundswell. Almost everyone that Seymour wombled up to in the small town pledged him their support. Even David Seymour was surprised. Seeing Seymour's teenie tiny dinky little ACT Party bus climbing through the majestic ranges of Central Otago was the perfect visual representation of what Decision 2020 was going to mean for Seymour. David was about to become Goliath.

Māori Party

Bloody brilliant. First up, ten points to Rawiri Waititi, the only person in New Zealand who could flip a Labour seat in the epoch of Juggernaut Jacinda. Then doubling their presence in Parliament on the specials, coat-tailing in Debbie Ngarewa-Packer. And from the second they walked through the doors at Parliament they've been an almighty presence.

'A pebble in the shoe of government', Waititi said in his maiden speech. A Māori voice in every piece of legislation to come to the House. It's particularly great to have an effective Māori opposition when there are so many Māori ministers in government. Those ministers have their work cut out for them: Labour has no excuses, no blaming New Zealand First and Winston Peters this term. Inequality and the disproportionate representation of Māori in all the wrong statistics has to be addressed.

And a lot of those ministers should be worried about the Māori Party for political survival reasons too. Many of them are elected in Māori seats. At the rate the Māori Party is going, if they keep up the momentum and do what they've promised to do, it's easy to see them increasing their party share in Parliament in 2023 and taking the fight to Labour big-time in the Māori electorates.

Greens

There was a very real risk the Green Party wouldn't make it back this election. The party hovers around the 5 per cent threshold and when the Green School schmozzle was revealed, alienating many in the Green base, that could have spelled game over. The Greens played some pretty deft politics in the wake of the mess, James Shaw apologising 18 million times and then talking up the risk to their political future.

They exploited it and it paid off. Fear of the Greens being ousted got their supporters back onside; fear of a Labour-only government too: that bit didn't work out so well for them. The Greens have been attempting to strike the right balance of sitting at the table in government while simultaneously wanting to knock the table over. So far they've got it about right: speaking out on housing, voting against the government's top tax rate.

Advance New Zealand

Advance New Zealand was the only other party – and I use the term loosely – to exit Parliament following the election. For their leader Jami-Lee Ross I have just two words: good riddance.[2]

Election night

Even those who foresaw the drubbing for National and the landslide for Labour probably didn't foresee the great electorate flip of 2020, the red tsunami ripping through the country, toppling not just the marginal National seats Labour was targeting, but also National Party fortresses like Ilam, Maungakiekie and other safe majority seats. They just kept flipping from blue to red. It was bloody murder for National, the final physical manifestation of everything we'd been seeing play out on the campaign trail.

It's still incredible (as someone who's only really known MMP) looking down at the Parliament from the press gallery and seeing the government benches extend beyond the right of the House to the seats normally reserved for the Opposition. As journalists in Parliament, we're excited about this term. With a single-party majority government for the first time under MMP, accountability has never been so important. We can't wait to help keep them honest, but in the meantime: farewell 2020. We leave you wiser than when we arrived, having all aged about a decade in eight months.

14

A TALE OF TWO CAMPAIGNS – COVID VS CHAOS: MAINSTREAM MEDIA COVERAGE OF THE LEAD-UP TO ELECTION 2020

Mark Boyd

The 2020 New Zealand general election campaign was the 'Covid campaign' – it was about which of the two major parties, Labour or National, and which of their leaders, could keep the country safe from the scourge and manage its economy back to good health. That was the perception of the public, the politicians and the media covering the campaign. But it was very much in the interests of the incumbent party, Labour, and its leader, Jacinda Ardern, to frame the campaign that way and to sell themselves to the voting public through the media. They were successful beyond expectations, helped by a dysfunctional campaign by the main opposition party, National, which descended into chaos, bordering on farce, in the final fortnight leading up to election day. Once again, the media went along for the ride.

This chapter examines the 2020 campaign coverage in the month leading up to election day, Saturday 17 October, on the two main television bulletins, TVNZ's *1 News* and TV3's *Newshub Live*, which both go to air at 6 pm, and in the pages of the two daily newspapers with the highest circulation: Auckland's *New Zealand Herald* and the Wellington-based *Dominion Post*. These are the flagship mastheads of the two main print news companies, respectively New Zealand Media and Entertainment (NZME), and Stuff, formerly the Australian-owned Fairfax Media.

Mainstream media

Most voters in modern democracies still get their political information during election campaigns from mainstream media – especially television, and to a lesser extent newspapers and radio (despite the growing popularity of online sources). This holds in two countries with great influence on

New Zealand politics and culture: Australia (Australian Election Study 2016; Carson and McNair 2018) and the United Kingdom (British Election Study 2017). Increasing numbers, particularly the young, do get their campaign news online. In only one campaign for which full data is available, the 2016 United States presidential election, have more people got their campaign news from the internet than from traditional news media. But in that election, older Americans, who vote in much greater numbers than their younger counterparts, used traditional media more than online sources (American National Election Study 2016). And even a master of direct communication through social media, Donald Trump, benefited from extensive free media coverage (Crotty 2018).

Analysis of mainstream media coverage of the campaign is an important contribution to a comprehensive review of an election. Mainstream media still dominates in New Zealand (New Zealand Election Study [NZES] 2011; 2014; 2017). Among frequent users of news media, voters were three times as likely to get their campaign news from television than from online sources, and nearly twice as likely to get it from reading newspapers. More than 40 per cent of voters did not access any campaign news at all online, much higher than those who ignored it on television or in newspapers (NZES 2017). In the months prior to the 2020 election campaign, an average of almost a million viewers watched the main 6 pm news bulletins each evening on TVNZ (741,000) and TV3 (242,000) (Dillane 2020). Over the same period, 1.8 million New Zealanders read the *New Zealand Herald* at least once a week, either in print or online, and 430,000 read the *Dominion Post*. Another 2.4 million read other daily papers, most of them with almost identical campaign stories to those in the main NZME or Stuff newspapers (Roy Morgan 2020).

Methodology

The television bulletins and newspapers were analysed in two data sets. The first, covering all campaign news in the 31 days leading up to election day, was analysed at the story level, with each discrete story on television timed to the second, and newspaper stories measured by column centimetres. Coverage of the referendums on end-of-life choice and legalisation of cannabis was not included. Each story was coded for which politician or party was the main subject and what was addressed, including policy areas and non-policy topics such as general campaign activities, opinion polls and voting, and scandals, among others. The stories were also coded for tone, with *negativity* covering attack, criticism or denigration, either by one politician to another, or by a journalist towards a politician or other target. *Positivity* was indicated by praise, endorsement and unchallenged exposition of positions, particularly policy. Neutrality covered straight reporting of events or statements.

At the story level, a definitive category was assigned to a story if at least 50 per cent of its content covered that category. Stories with less content than that in any one category were classified as 'mixed'. Total campaign coverage was around four hours on each of the television networks, with *1 News* running 129 stories and *Newshub* 135. Both daily papers publish six days a week: to provide comparability with the seven-day television bulletins, the respective Sunday offerings, NZME's *Herald on Sunday* and Stuff's *Sunday Star-Times*, were included. There were more than 8,000 column centimetres in the NZME publications, covering 320 stories, and 191 stories totalling more than 6,000 column centimetres put out by Stuff (Table 14.1).

Table 14.1: Amount of coverage of 2020 election campaign by mainstream news outlets

	31-day	7-day
1 News minutes	237.6	44.8
Newshub minutes	244.4	51.8
New Zealand Herald column cm	8,521	1,112
Dominion Post column cm	6,314	1,070

The second data set was much more fine-grained, analysing coverage sentence-by-sentence in a smaller 'seven-day sample'. This started with the first day of the 31-day story-level analysis, 16 September, then every fifth day subsequently, with the last day being election eve, 16 October. This meant that every unit of analysis, averaging six seconds on television and 1.4 column centimetres in print, was assigned a specific subject (usually a politician or party; a policy or non-policy topic) and tone – positive, negative or neutral. Total data for the more detailed set was 45 minutes on *1 News*, 52 minutes on *Newshub*, and slightly more than 1,000 column centimetres in each of the newspapers. The 'seven-day' sample has been shown to be statistically representative of the full 31-day period in a previous study (Boyd 2019).

The quantitative data was augmented by interviews with journalists and press secretaries to gain their insights into what they saw on the campaign trail, how they either covered it or managed it, and their reactions to the quantitative findings. Interviews were done with senior political reporters from each of the four outlets, news managers, and the chief press secretaries for the two major parties, Labour and National.

How the campaign was covered

All the major news outlets went into the campaign with the best of intentions as to how to cover it. TVNZ planned to 'cover the campaign as comprehensively as we possibly could to enable voters to make the most sensible decisions' (O'Sullivan 2020). TV3 was similar, with a slightly more populist stance of 'trying to make our stories informative and entertaining to engage as many people with the politics and the policies as possible' (O'Brien 2021). NZME aimed for 'fair and balanced coverage' of both policies and personalities, coverage of the latter meaning 'voteability is the overall thing you're looking at' (Rowe 2021). And Stuff's coverage, like TV3's, was audience-focused, with an objective 'to produce relevant and interesting stories for our readers' (Malpass 2020).

On the other side of the competition for control of the news agenda, the major party press secretaries had quite different strategies. Labour, with the advantage of incumbency and historically high opinion poll figures, angled its campaign around the popularity of Jacinda Ardern, looking to 'generate significant positive media coverage for the Prime Minister through our events, and to ensure the public understood the strategic reason for voting for Labour' (Campbell 2020). The strategy largely worked, with images appearing almost daily of Ardern being mobbed in shopping malls, and accepting accolades from adoring fans. As one of the on-the-road reporters described it, 'everyone's coming up to Jacinda Ardern and thanking her for saving their lives' (O'Brien 2021). But apart from the positive images, and with a relative dearth of new policy from Labour, the party's media campaign relied on a 'small target strategy. The best thing was to not either expose ourselves or unnecessarily rock the boat' (Campbell 2020).

Against the well-planned and efficiently executed strategy of Labour, National went into the campaign at a distinct disadvantage. Its polling figures were around half of Labour's, against a background of organisational dysfunction, the party having had three leaders in as many months in the middle of the year. Its objective was 'to be as strong an alternative as we possibly could be to possibly one of the most popular governments of the time' (Wilson 2020). But achieving that was no easy task for the party's chief press secretary, who had been hired by Todd Muller and stayed on under Judith Collins. She said she was 'parachuted in on a suicide mission . . . chaos reigned from the moment I arrived' (Wilson 2020). Part of the problem was selling a leader with a polarising personality. Collins, dubbed 'Crusher' early in her political career, alienated many voters, although she also had a devoted following. The same split existed within the National Party, a large section of its caucus thinking 'she was unelectable, which proved to be the case, and the fact that the election went longer just really proved why that was' (Malpass 2020).

Both major parties revealed a large amount of policy in the campaign's early stages. While much of it addressed the need to boost economic recovery from the Covid-19 lockdowns, this was particularly the case for Labour, which also touted its success in controlling the virus. As one news executive said, Labour's 'fairly slick campaign . . . was quite a deliberate attempt to make all things about Covid, which I think did limit that policy debate to a certain perspective' (Symons 2020). Such a tightly focused, personality-based strategy is a hallmark of the 'modern' campaign (Norris et al 1999). This raises the question of whether there is a role for the media to highlight the strategy, pushing back against it if it is seen to be too shallow or manipulative. Stuff's senior reporter resisted that suggestion:

> It comes back to what is your job during a campaign. Is your job to report what happens, and then analyse it a bit, or is your job to say 'actually, Labour, you're much too slick' and go on a bit of a war against the Labour machine? There is a time to do that, but it seems to me that the time to do that is if they're feeding out lies and misinformation and whatever else, which they weren't, they were operating within the normal parameters of a campaign, trying to maximise their positives and minimise their negatives (Malpass 2020).

National also addressed the Covid issue, both in terms of health and economic recovery, but it released a wider range of policies than Labour. National's press secretary thought this worked *against* the party: 'We also had a lot of policy. Now that's an affliction for all opposition parties and, in hindsight, I thought we needed less, but more thought out, policies that we rammed home better and longer.' She saw no disadvantage for Labour in taking the opposite path: 'They had little in the way of policy because they knew they didn't have to have policy, because they had the golden jewel, they had Jacinda. And all she had to do basically was smile and wave' (Wilson 2020). But National's media campaign was also undermined by regular exposés of incorrect figures in its economic policy, described as 'a complete own goal' (Wilson 2020), as well as gaffes by Judith Collins and leaks against her by caucus members. These became more frequent in the campaign's final two weeks.

One incident which received considerable media attention, and indicated the lack of organisation both within the National campaign and in its media strategy, was coverage of Judith Collins praying in a church next to the polling station where she cast her advance vote on 4 October. When criticised for this, she claimed that the media had intruded on a private moment. However, Collins' own press secretary disputes that stance, saying 'it was a stitch-up by her [Collins]. To my mind that was a blatant pitch to the Christian vote' (Wilson 2020). The journalists tended to agree, calling Collins' claim of a media ambush 'a really poorly reverse-engineered excuse' (O'Brien 2021), that it 'played into a lot of people's views of Judith Collins that she's a bit untrustworthy, and a bit disingenuous' (Malpass 2020), the episode 'a distraction' (Trevett 2020).

Jacinda Ardern was also criticised for gaffes, but they were much less frequent than those of Collins and her team. Only two had any coverage: when Ardern was seen taking selfies with a tightly packed group of students in Palmerston North in contravention of social-distancing rules, and when she made an affordable housing policy announcement in the Auckland suburb of Birkenhead in front of a multi-million dollar house being built for an overseas tech entrepreneur. In the last week of the campaign, Collins' missteps became almost farcical, with extensive coverage of a staged walkabout in Auckland's Ponsonby Road, where supposedly random members of the public who greeted her warmly turned out to be National Party members. When she tried to engage with a real member of the public, in an optometrist's shop, she was turned away. That same week, Collins was extensively criticised for stating that obesity was the result of personal choices. Meanwhile, Labour and Ardern coasted to the finish line, with their only negative coverage around a spat over whether Labour would consider a Green Party proposal for a wealth tax if it needed the Greens' support in forming a government.

National's dysfunctional campaign meant it got more coverage than Labour in all of the media outlets analysed, and its coverage was more negative. But all of the journalists interviewed denied that this indicated any sort of bias, insisting they were simply covering the campaign as it unfolded. As one put it, 'to the extent of negative and positive, you can't be dishonest about what you're seeing on the ground' (Trevett 2020). National's press secretary acknowledged the flaws, describing the Ponsonby Road embarrassment as 'an operational stuff-up of the highest order', the antithesis of 'Ardern going to shopping malls and being mobbed' and indicating that National 'was more fixated on itself than it was on the people of New Zealand' (Wilson 2020).

Fair coverage? – the major parties

The first question that many observers of media coverage of election campaigns ask is: was it fair? Did comparable parties get comparable coverage, both quantitatively (total amount) and qualitatively (was it positive or negative?). The designation 'comparable parties' is crucial in the New Zealand context with its multi-party MMP electoral system. Given that only two parties, Labour and National, have been able to form governments (with minor parties in support) since the advent of MMP in 1996, it is reasonable to expect that these two major parties will get roughly similar amounts of coverage. But precisely because all the governments they have formed over the past 24 years have needed those support parties, it is also reasonable to expect that the minor parties will also receive a fair share of coverage. The problem is how to define that. One benchmark is the parties' performance in opinion polls, and then, in retrospect, in the share of the votes received in the election. Another factor to consider is the 'advantage of incumbency', where the lead governing party usually gets more coverage simply by holding the reins of government.

In 2020, all of the mainstream media outlets in this analysis gave more coverage to the opposition party than to the incumbent. Apart from the *Dominion Post*, all the news outlets gave around 60 per cent of their major party coverage to National, with the Wellington paper also favouring it, although only by a slim margin (Table 14.2). When a party, especially one in opposition, gets more coverage than its support would indicate, that coverage is often more negative. This was definitely the case for two parties which received disproportionately heavy coverage in the 2014 campaign, National and the Internet Mana alliance (Boyd and Bahador 2014).

Table 14.2: Coverage of parties by mainstream news outlets – 31 days (%)

	Labour	National	Green	NZ First	ACT	Māori	Other
1 News	24.7	36.0	10.4	15.6	7.4	2.4	3.5
Newshub	26.4	42.5	7.7	15.7	3.3	1.5	2.9
NZ Herald	28.7	38.9	10.0	10.5	6.7	2.9	2.5
Dom Post	32.5	32.7	3.3	14.6	2.1	3.2	11.5
2020 vote	50.0	25.6	7.9	2.6	7.6	1.2	5.1

Despite being in opposition and trailing Labour in the polls by up to 30 per cent, National got almost two-thirds of major party coverage in most outlets. But as Table 14.3 shows, the share of its coverage that was negative was significantly greater than that given to the Labour Party.

Table 14.3: Negative tone in major party coverage by mainstream news outlets – 7 days (%)

	Labour	**National**
1 News	19.1	34.5
Newshub	26.8	48.0
New Zealand Herald	31.2	41.0
Dominion Post	28.4	36.0

Only TVNZ kept a detailed log of its output, timing how much coverage was given the parties and politicians. But this was a guide, rather than an attempt to give comparable parties equal coverage, with one of their news managers saying 'there were certainly no edicts that we need to do more on one than the other at all. We try and be as even handed as we possibly can' (O'Sullivan 2020). And the network's political editor admitted that the combination of Labour's low-key campaign and National's woes worked in the governing party's favour: 'We probably fell into the trap of Jacinda Ardern's agenda a little bit more because of the Covid stuff, and probably because National were self-imploding we didn't focus as much on their policy messages that they were wanting to get across' (Mutch McKay 2020).

TV3 did not track its coverage by minutes, saying, 'you kind of do it by your gut a bit' (O'Brien 2020). At Stuff, the focus was more on straight news reporting, with their political editor saying 'we've tried to do a lot less opinion than we were doing previously, we've tried to do more news, and where we've done opinion we try to make it more analytical' (Malpass 2020). And although NZME has measured column centimetres in the past, its senior writer said 'you try and be 50/50 on the big two parties, but when there's an obvious difference in how they're viewed by people, you can't get to the point where you're lying about it and pretending Judith is as popular as Jacinda' (Trevett 2020).

Fair coverage? – the minor parties

If the benchmark for 'fair' coverage of the minor parties is their final vote, then all four outlets were more than fair. As Table 14.2 shows, they all gave at least 30 per cent of their coverage to minor parties, substantially more than those parties' total vote share of less than 25 per cent. New Zealand First got several times more coverage than its vote share in all news outlets; ACT was relatively undercovered, the Green Party even more so. Te Pāti Māori got coverage at least double its vote share in most outlets, despite running a campaign firmly aiming at the electorate vote. Most outlets gave only passing coverage to the micro parties, such as TOP and the New Conservatives, except for the *Dominion Post*. This can largely be attributed to an extensive, multi-page exposé of allegations of questionable practices by the co-leader of Advance New Zealand, Billy Te Kahika.

Despite his considerable coverage, Winston Peters' campaign was rather lacklustre. Story after story on television showed him addressing small crowds or wandering around shopping centres, with tepid engagement with voters. This was also often reflected in his print coverage. His style of electioneering was also hobbled by Covid restrictions in the early part of the campaign. As one reporter said, 'everything he did well, he couldn't do it. Like he couldn't go around rest homes, he likes to talk to a crowd, he's not so comfortable with the one-on-one interactions' (Trevett 2020). Conversely, the politician Peters often characterised as his nemesis, ACT's David Seymour, 'played a blinder to be honest, and he pretty much did it single-handedly with his staff' (Trevett 2020). For the Greens, its low level of coverage did not seem to put the party at a disadvantage, given that they increased their party vote and won an electorate seat, Auckland Central. Judith Collins' strident attacks on the Greens' proposed wealth tax in the last week of the campaign kept them in the news and may even have enhanced their standing among more left-wing voters. The only negative story about the Greens, involving allegations of questionable funding of a 'green' school in Taranaki, was very early in the campaign, meaning the one-month postponement of election day may have worked in their favour (Mutch McKay 2020).

Follow the leader

Concentration on party leaders by news media – 'presidentialisation' – is now firmly entrenched in New Zealand (Miller 2015; Sharp 2004). Television particularly focuses on leaders, with cameras assigned to them on the campaign trail, and their use in sound bites. This was also reinforced by the major leaders' debates, two of which were shown on TVNZ, one on TV3, and one online by Stuff. The television debates got around a million viewers each, and all four were extensively analysed in follow-up stories in all media (Boyd 2020). As Table 14.4 shows, both television networks were almost identical in their overall proportion of leader coverage, at around 55 per cent, as were the newspapers, at close to 50 per cent.

Table 14.4: Coverage given to party leaders as a proportion of total party coverage by mainstream news outlets – 31 days (%)

	Labour	National	Green	NZ First	ACT	Māori	Other	All
1 News	66.7	64.5	21.7	71.2	0.0	100.0	0.0	55.5
Newshub	43.5	55.0	26.0	81.5	59.4	0.0	66.7	54.2
NZ Herald	45.2	54.1	34.8	65.2	64.9	16.8	8.3	49.3
Dom Post	45.8	31.0	8.0	78.2	75.0	51.5	83.0	49.7

Although this was lower than the heavily presidential 2017 campaign, characterised by 'Jacindamania', it was much higher than in 2014 (Boyd 2019). TVNZ was particularly leader-focused in 2020, with both Collins and Ardern receiving around two thirds of their parties' coverage on *1 News*. With the exception of the *Dominion Post*, the other outlets covered Collins more heavily than Ardern. Among the minor leaders, as always, Winston Peters had the highest overall coverage of any party leader.

The 'policy light' campaign?

At the beginning of August, the prime minister warned voters not to expect any 'large-scale' policies from the Labour Party in the campaign, and that her 'big focus' would be on the Covid-19 recovery (Walls 2020). This instantly drew fire from Judith Collins, who accused Ardern of 'hiding' and being 'incapable of delivering anything but slogans' (Cooke 2020). Despite this, the proportion of policy covered in all outlets was considerably more than what they ran in the 'Dirty Politics' election campaign of 2014 (Boyd and Bahador 2015, p. 158), though not as much, at least on television, as in 2017, when part of Jacinda Ardern's vow of 'relentless positivity' was to concentrate on substantial policy matters (Boyd 2019, p. 89). On television in 2020, *Newshub* ran considerably more policy than *1 News*, the *New Zealand Herald* more than the *Dominion Post* (Table 14.5). Both major parties, but particularly Labour, 'front-loaded' their policy announcements early in the campaign. This was partly because of the one-month election day postponement, but also in expectation of high numbers of advance voters. These exceeded predictions, with more than two thirds of voters casting a ballot before election day, and one third of the total votes being cast at least a week before (Electoral Commission 2020).

Table 14.5. Coverage of policy and non-policy issues by mainstream news outlets – 31 days (%)

	Policy	Non-policy
1 News	37.8	62.2
Newshub	45.0	55.0
New Zealand Herald	47.4	52.6
Dominion Post	37.6	62.4

Coverage of policy showed a distinct difference between the 17 days leading up to the start of advance voting and the subsequent two weeks. As Table 14.6 shows, the proportion of coverage dealing with policy was at least twice as high in all news outlets in the earlier period. But this was also because there was much heavier coverage of non-policy issues, including gaffes and leaks by National and opinion poll stories, in the latter period. The polls always have considerable significance in New Zealand elections, especially when minor parties are close to the 5 per cent threshold for representation in Parliament, and even more so when such parties appear unlikely to win an electorate seat (which would enable them to enter Parliament even if failing to get 5 per cent). Much of the 2020 coverage of the Green Party and New Zealand First was framed around their standing in the polls. Another point of speculation in all outlets was whether Labour could get enough votes to govern alone.

Table 14.6: Stories covering policy in mainstream news outlets, 16 September to 16 October – 31 days (%)

	16 September–2 October	3–16 October
1 News	56.7	20.7
Newshub	58.4	29.3
New Zealand Herald	62.9	27.6
Dominion Post	64.5	31.7

Positive or negative – the tone of the coverage

The four news outlets showed marked variance in the tone of their coverage. *Newshub*'s coverage was almost twice as negative as that seen on *1 News*, and the *Dominion Post* slightly more negative than the *New Zealand Herald* (Table 14.7). But both *Newshub* and the *Herald* were more positive than their competitors in each medium, suggesting that their coverage was more opinionated. This is indicated by the fact that their proportion of neutral and mixed coverage was just over 50 per cent, compared to more than 60 per cent on *1 News* and in the *Dominion Post*. The greater amount of opinionated coverage in the *Herald* can be explained by the fact that it has a large stable of guest writers, many conservative, such as Mike Hosking and Richard Prebble, although it also features some with more centrist or left-leaning views, such as Josie Pagani. NZME's senior writers also provided stories which included some opinion. Stuff ran fewer opinion pieces; most of its analysis was by Luke Malpass, who tended to write in a more neutral style.

Table 14.7: Tone of all coverage by mainstream news outlets – 31 days (%)

	Negative	Positive	Neutral/Mixed
1 News	15.0	16.1	68.9
Newshub	28.7	19.5	51.8
NZ Herald	18.7	30.9	50.4
Dom Post	19.8	18.5	61.7

Conclusion

New Zealand voters were not left wanting for information about the election campaign in their mainstream media outlets, whether it was news reporting of politicians' campaigns and straight coverage of their policies, both on television and in print, or more opinionated guest columns and analysis pieces in the newspapers. Both across the spectrum of the media, and within the content of each outlet, there was comprehensive coverage of parties, politicians and policies. There appeared to be little, if any, partisan bias, apart from pieces from guest columnists whose political affiliations were well-known, and usually flagged in the copy.

Where bias was apparent, it was structural. Judith Collins and National were given considerably more coverage than Jacinda Ardern and Labour, both because of the novelty of Collins as National leader, and because her mishaps, and the leaks by members of her caucus, were intrinsically newsworthy. This also meant that coverage of the opposition was more negative. Conversely, Labour's 'policy light' campaign, which largely consisted of Jacinda Ardern being mobbed by fans, many thankful for her government's handling of the Covid crisis, garnered at worst neutral, and often positive, coverage. As Labour's Press Secretary said:

> The [press] gallery tends to hunt as a pack, but they tend to do it when they smell blood, and I think National offered them a target in that regard. They didn't particularly come after us, but we also didn't particularly provide many opportunities for them to do so. If it bleeds, it leads, and National were definitely bleeding (Campbell 2020).

New Zealand's news media does not exhibit the extreme bias seen in the hyperpartisan coverage of politics on websites and cable television in the United States, or in many of the daily papers, particularly those controlled by the Murdoch family, in the United Kingdom and Australia. This may go some way to explaining why New Zealand voters continue to use mainstream media as their primary source of election campaign news. While the 2020 coverage was firmly based on traditional news values, to National's detriment and Labour's advantage, it reflected what was happening in the campaign. Many voters had made their minds up well before the height of the campaign, reflected in the large numbers who voted early. But those who wanted information to help them make their choice in the month leading up to election day were well-served by the traditional source – mainstream media.

15

SOCIAL MEDIA, ONLINE POLITICS AND THE 2020 ELECTION

Sarah Hendrica Bickerton

Online technology was supposed to transform politics, democratising it, making it easier, allowing everyone to contribute and directly interact with politicians and policies. The reality, however, has been far from this imagined revolution. When it comes to online politics in New Zealand, not only has the majority of focus been on elections, but it has also tended to be top-down rather than bottom-up and citizen-focused. In large part this has been because New Zealand parties and politicians have employed social media in much the same way as they have more traditional radio and television technologies – mono-directionally. New Zealand's 2020 election was no different from prior elections in this regard.

This chapter explores this approach to online election politics at the 2020 New Zealand election, first looking at prior analysis of online technology and social media use in New Zealand elections, and then at party political websites and their use in disseminating election policy.

Online politics at New Zealand elections

A consistent theme for online media and politics in New Zealand has been the use of websites as party political vehicles (Barker 2004; Roper 1998), particularly as they were one of the earliest online platforms used by New Zealand political parties. However, websites have continued to be used merely as tools of generalised broadcast with very little targeting. A study of the 1996 election noted that 'a lack of knowledge of the potential of the medium has resulted in the content and format of the sites resembling those of more traditional media, with little or no attempt at appealing to any one of a variety of publics' (Roper 1998, p. 77). The study also found that 'during the election campaign period, *none* of the New Zealand party political web sites *allowed for open, direct interaction with or between users*' (Roper 1998, p. 78, emphasis added).

What this suggests is that interactional spaces online have been seen as something to be kept separate from political parties' traditional political engagement. Research into the 2002 election showed that information online 'can be provided through other forms of media including party information leaflets and flyers, through newspapers, radio and television' (Barker 2004, p. 84). In other words, online media were being treated with the same mass media approach as traditional media.

A change in this theme was seen at the 2005 New Zealand election; not only was there a change in the degree to which online media were used by political parties, but attention paid by researchers also increased (Fitzjohn and Salmond 2007; Hopkins and Matheson 2005; Pedersen 2005, 2007). Websites remained the dominant form of online political expression during the period leading up to the election; more participatory features were included, such as being able to join the party or donate money, but interactive features for online engagement were again left off these spaces (Pedersen 2007), with engagement remaining top-down (Pedersen 2005).

The only real shifts in this theme of mono-directional political engagement have been via the inclusion of new online technologies as they developed, supplementing websites, such as in 2005, at the first election in which blogging gained prominence in New Zealand (Fitzjohn and Salmond 2007; Hopkins and Matheson 2005). Similarly, the inclusion in 2008 of what were at the time referred to as 'Web 2.0' features (Goode 2010) did result in a limited shift away from solely passive information delivery (Shaw 2009).

A study of internet use amongst New Zealand households at the 2008 election showed that while 78 per cent of New Zealanders were using the internet, only 15 per cent of those did so to specifically seek out information about political parties or members of Parliament (de Ronde 2010). This contrasted with the fact that a third of internet users used online spaces to gather information on government services and almost two thirds used the internet for news gathering. What this suggests is that online users in 2008 were at the very least not using online political party electioneering spaces for political content. A content analysis of party websites in 2008 (Lips and Gong 2009) showed that providing for direct personal interaction on websites was limited despite the use of Web 2.0 features. Political participation online remained top-down.

Edwin de Ronde (2010) noted that parties had moved away from merely using sites as analogues of printed campaign material, and were using more multimedia and linking to other online locations (though this remained broadcast focused). This included YouTube (Goode 2010; Salmond 2010) and the arrival of Facebook as a tool for political parties (Kean 2010). However, Facebook's use by political parties and MPs was not consistent, nor was it used to its full potential, particularly when it came to interacting with the public directly (Kean 2010). This contrasted markedly with the use of Facebook in United States elections at that time. Social media use in the 2008 election tended to focus on traditional websites (Chen 2009), with political parties again failing to use online media to its full potential, particularly its interactive and participatory features (Murchison 2015). This lack of interactive engagement did not change at the 2011 election despite further development in social media technologies.

One exception was an increase in the role of Facebook, anticipated by Kean (2010). However, Murchison and Deos (2012) found that 'overall, we were surprised by the extremely small extent of interaction using Facebook in the final 31 days of the election campaign . . . in general, New Zealand's parties did not use their Facebook pages predominantly for direct interaction with potential voters' (p. 246). And the content-based analysis carried out by Ross, Fountaine and Comrie (2015) on MPs' Facebook pages found little change in MPs' overall approach: 'Most politicians do not invite dialogue with readers of their posts, rarely get involved in comment threads and mostly take a monologic approach, using Facebook as a way of broadcasting information rather than as a medium enabling two-way flow' (p. 251).

Asking how MPs conceptualised their social media use, Ross and Burger (2014) found a disconnect between the rhetoric MPs expressed around citizen engagement and their use of social media to just distribute information about themselves (mono-directional) in order to increase their visibility and make themselves '"hip" to the public' (p. 46). There were also gender-based differences among MPs: women had a higher volume of posts as well as a higher number of personal anecdotes, while men were more likely to use photographs, particularly of themselves (Ross, Fountaine and Comrie 2015).

MPs did see Facebook and Twitter as having considerably different audiences: Facebook was more general and diverse, Twitter was a space for 'political "junkies"' (Ross and Burger 2014, p. 55). This was consistent with international research (Kreiss, Lawrence and McGregor 2018). Twitter was also seen as a space for timeliness, breaking news and instant media. As such, users had to be strategic in their use of the medium (consistent with Murchison's (2015) content analysis of Twitter). The primary focus in 2014 across all social media forms was getting users to share content generated by the political parties, which, while a form of online political participation, did not result in two-way communication (Beveridge 2015) in any substantial way. Developments between the 2011 and 2014 elections in social media interaction between politicians and the public were for the most part changes in degree, not in kind.

The consistent finding about New Zealand's online election practices is that interaction by political parties and politicians remains mono-directional and prescriptive. Online media, and by extension social media, operate in more or less the same frame as other forms of mass media. Actual interactive political discussion and debate are kept at a distance if not entirely absent. From the academic research it is apparent that online political participation by political parties and politicians is being funnelled through to support traditional offline forms of engagement (such as voting, attendance at campaign events and what individuals can do to support candidates and parties).

Old stalwarts

This was the historical context of parties' online election politics going into the 2020 election. The consistent theme – online technologies being employed in a mono-directional manner – was, again, largely followed, with some differences. Websites were again used in the 2020 election, in much the same way as at previous elections. Analysis of election policies announced on the websites of eight different political parties in the run-up to the election made it apparent that the websites were for the most part serving their principal function as repositories of information (Gender Justice Collective 2020).

The most prolific of the political parties in posting policy documents on their website were the National and Green parties; the least active in this respect were the Māori Party (which left updating to the very end, with little detail) and New Zealand First (whose site received scant updating). Party policies were gradually added to sections of party websites over time during the campaign, though not at a consistent rate nor in an organised manner, making it difficult to find what was new or updated. Often policy announcement documents were structured differently, lacking consistency even within the same party, which made comparison more difficult.

The websites themselves lacked interactional features beyond a few basics: information collection, sign-up forms, solicitation of donations (in a perfunctory way) and basic surveys. But given there were other priorities for political parties' online engagements, it was apparent that for a number of New Zealand parties the websites had become afterthoughts in their digital strategies. Nor had the approach changed markedly from previous elections. To a certain extent party political websites have arrived in the 'mature technology' niche, their accepted use and form largely settled, and we should not expect to find major shifts in future elections.

The 'Team of 5 Million' effect

The social media context for the 2020 New Zealand election was, of course, the Covid-19 pandemic and the government's response. Part of that response, particularly during lockdowns, involved daily press briefings in the early afternoon, detailing new pandemic numbers, responses and policy updates. The briefings were invariably headed by Prime Minister Jacinda Ardern and/or the Director-General of Health, Dr Ashley Bloomfield. They were carried live by the various media networks, which naturally involved being broadcast on TV and radio, but they were also streamed online, via either the official Covid-19 unit or platforms such as YouTube and Facebook.

What this meant is that daily, for months, as the country moved towards the election, it became a matter of routine for many New Zealanders to have the prime minister in their homes – where most of the country's residents were to be found, 24 hours a day, 7 days a week, with the country in lockdown. This was a media vehicle that the prime minister had used prior to the pandemic. One of the most renowned was her Facebook livestream, sans makeup, from inside her own home, in casual clothing while on parental leave with her newborn child. There were also 'off-the-cuff' videostreams on Facebook and Instagram from her Beehive office in vertical video (a performatively more personal format due to associations with video calls) before and after said leave.

As such, the New Zealand public were very familiar with the prime minister's personal-connection approach to media, and particularly social media. That this approach was continued as an electioneering vehicle was not surprising. It allowed for seamless transitions between official election appearances, pandemic updates and more casual livestreams, and gave the prime minister a personal, direct connection with New Zealand voters, bypassing traditional media. This effectively handed agenda-setting power and control over framing the public discourse to politicians, the government and the prime minister, rather than the political media.

That bypass became particularly visible on social media with criticism that the political media received over their behaviour during the Q&A sessions following the formal announcements at the daily Covid-19 press briefings. Following traditional practice, the sessions were free-flowing, with journalists speaking over each other, using raised voices, asking follow-up questions, repeatedly challenging the prime minister, Dr Bloomfield and others over points of clarification, pressuring for responses and quotable statements. This was how political press briefings had always been held. However, for many on social media this previously hidden part of journalism and political practice sat uncomfortably with the personal connection they felt they had with the prime minister, Dr Bloomfield and other participants. As a result, across many social media platforms, political journalists were criticised for their conduct (Vowles 2020).

Many in the media responded, correctly, that those who were challenging them were merely seeing behind the scenes: this was how political journalism had always been done, both politicians and journalists were familiar with it, and there were strategic and established reasons for this kind of holding-to-account. However, the context in which these briefings were occurring had now changed.

The public had developed a direct personal connection to the prime minister (and to Dr Bloomfield) as seen in the continuing high approval numbers for Ardern's handling of the pandemic. And many perceived the journalists as getting in the way of that connection and/or behaving in inappropriate ways towards someone they felt that connection with. The prime minister had bypassed the journalists in creating that connection via social media, and many of the journalists were not shifting with that change in context.

However, the sense of personal connection was effectively an illusion. While using social media in innovative and nuanced ways, it was still mono-directional broadcast campaigning. If anything, by bypassing traditional media, Ardern could keep even tighter control over the message. As she had done prior to attaining the leadership, Ardern avoided those forms of social media that lent themselves to interaction (such as Twitter, where her account tended to function merely for putting out press releases), gravitating to those platforms (like Facebook and Instagram) that afforded the appearance of intimate connection while allowing her to retain control.

The prime minister's approach was seamless. She had set it up pre-pandemic, perfected it over the course of the pandemic, and by the time the election came around the technique was established and accepted. As noted, it was both innovative and not innovative; it allowed Ardern to bypass political media in new ways, while still controlling the message and not being truly interactive.

Twitter: Tweeting on the sidelines

Twitter was largely sidelined in its impact, which is interesting given that it is the medium that most lends itself to interactivity. In my own experience researching online New Zealand political participation, Twitter use by New Zealand politicians outside of elections falls into three types: those tweeting from their own accounts, with varying degrees of personability and frequency; those whose postings come from social media managers or teams; and those whose accounts are largely press releases, with little, if any, interactive aspects.

The prime minister's Twitter account was largely a combination of press briefings and posts from her social media team. It had been like this since the leadup to the 2017 election. This was in marked contrast to her use of Instagram or Facebook, which both showed considerably higher levels of engagement (though, again, not interaction). In comparison, Judith Collins, prior to becoming National Party leader, had an extensive Twitter presence, using the platform for actual interactive engagement far more frequently. After becoming party leader her account became far more managed.

On Twitter, the most engaging and interactive parties were the New Conservative Party and The Opportunities Party (TOP). Both had a large number of replies and quote-tweets during the campaign period, as well as posting more traditional press releases, speeches, campaign events and news articles. The Greens, ACT and the Māori Party were a little behind these two in terms of two-way interaction, but did include replies as well as the more traditional materials mentioned above. Replies for these parties included responses to tweets that were directed at them as well as to indirect tweets that mentioned them, suggesting that they used keyword searches (such as for party name) to increase engagement. Labour, National and New Zealand First all stuck to using Twitter in a largely broadcast manner, with few or no replies, just press releases, speeches, campaign events and comments on news articles. Although all these parties used Twitter, Twitter itself had little impact on the election, nor was its capacity for bi-directional interaction fully used.

YouTube: Reaching new audiences

A number of parties used YouTube for political advertising, including Labour, National and the Greens. Most parties had a YouTube presence, providing their own content via party accounts (though with relatively low follower-counts, even for the prime minister), which was supplemented with party political advertising both on their own accounts and between YouTube videos on other topics. But who sees this advertising?

YouTube uses advanced viewership algorithms to determine who is most likely to watch what videos (including, of course, location data), selling that targeting information to advertisers. Users can opt out of such advertising by paying for YouTube Premium, which provides videos ad-free. As a result, those most likely to see the advertising are those who cannot, or choose not to, pay for the privilege of ad-free content. Labour's advertising continued to position the prime minister as a figurehead. National did the same with Judith Collins. By contrast, the Greens included Chlöe Swarbrick, the party's Auckland Central candidate. Considering YouTube's demographics, it appears that the Greens thought appealing to the youth vote would work better than a more traditional party leadership approach. Given that Collins had neither the social media presence of Ardern (particularly not when it came to video, where the prime minister had a considerable presence), nor the youth recognition of Swarbrick, the choice to front her on this medium suggests a social media strategy that did not differentiate between platforms.

Facebook: Misinformation and deplatforming

Overall, the biggest users of Facebook were the Labour Party and Jacinda Ardern (Victoria University of Wellington 2020a). Second was the Māori Party, with considerable input from party co-leader John Tamihere;

the Māori Party did much of its event organisation and coordination via Facebook. Next came National, with Advance New Zealand close behind. Most of Advance New Zealand's Facebook content came from co-leader Billy Te Kahika, as its other co-leader, Jami-Lee Ross, did not post to Facebook during the campaign. The Greens were the next most frequent posters, with the New Conservative Party and TOP behind them. The bottom two were New Zealand First and ACT, the latter preferring to engage with the public on Twitter.

The overwhelming majority of posts involved policy and/or issues, undermining the popular view that social media posts lack substance. Some parties responded to the growing appeal of advance voting, with Labour, National, the Māori Party, the Greens and Advance New Zealand all actively campaigning on Facebook from the beginning of advance voting through to election day. ACT stepped up its Facebook efforts at the start of advance voting, then fell back until the campaign's last two weeks when it put in renewed effort. New Zealand First, however, was consistent in its low overall use of Facebook. In general, New Zealand's political parties were not very interactive on Facebook (Victoria University of Wellington 2020b), which is consistent with the pattern noted in this chapter.

Most parties maintained a positive tone at the beginning of the campaign. For a period early in the campaign Judith Collins had a higher 'positivity' ranking than Jacinda Ardern, but National (and its leader) trended negative over time as election day came closer. The prime minister apparently began with a more neutral incumbent 'governing' tone. An exception to incumbent parties' positivity was New Zealand First, which started out negative and became increasingly so as the campaign went on. The Greens and, to a lesser extent, the Māori Party remained positive in their posts throughout the campaign.

Researchers analysing parties' Facebook posts for misinformation and 'half-truths' found overall levels to be very low. However, where misinformation and 'half-truths' did feature, these tended to involve posts by Advance New Zealand. Preliminary results showed that 31 per cent of the party's Facebook posts were considered 'half-truths' and 6 per cent were fake (Election 2020). As these results came to light and were being reported in traditional media, Facebook was also conducting its own investigation; two days before the election Facebook decided to take down the party's page: a first for a New Zealand political party.

Concluding thoughts

Over the past quarter century, online media has evolved from a novelty to a mature technology, part of a palette of options within contemporary election toolkits. Overall, it has not transformed elections, instead becoming embedded into the political milieu of the more traditional election tools, reflecting the same structures, arrangements and practices.

While we can certainly see innovation in approach in the likes of Jacinda Ardern's live direct-to-the-public videos, or the use of YouTube advertising, or even political meme creation by parties' youth wings, the lack of true online interactive engagement that we have witnessed in the stagnation of websites, the underuse of the likes of Twitter, and the potential for misinformation and disinformation, is nonetheless replicated by even these 'innovations'.

The absence of truly bi-directional interaction between politicians and the public is a continuation of past decades' approaches to political communication and online technologies. There is little reason to expect that this will change any time soon. For New Zealand elections, the traditional relationship between the voting public and elected politicians looks likely to remain in place online.

16

'GETTING CLOSER TO THE TRUTH': THE 2020 ELECTION CARTOONS AS COMMENTARY, PROTEST AND CRITIQUE

Mike Grimshaw

The editorial cartoon holds a long-standing and invaluable role in political commentary and analysis. I paraphrase the French thinker Jean Baudrillard's quote about terrorism (Baudrillard 2003, p. 59) in my book on the cartoon history of religion in New Zealand, writing that 'the editorial cartoon merely crystalizes all the ingredients in suspension' (Grimshaw 2019, p. iv). I feel this is a useful way to consider the editorial cartoons that arise during an election campaign, because the editorial cartoon does not create a political situation or event, but rather gathers together the ingredients that arise out of the event, comment or action of the politician and political party – or the response of the general public – and succinctly and incisively represents them.

One role of the editorial cartoon is to attract readership. Ian F. Grant, founder of the New Zealand Cartoon Archive, has described the decision of the *National Business Review* to hire Bob Brockie as cartoonist as 'the very deliberate intention of annoying the hell out of our business readership . . . as Lord Beaverbrook did with David Low, [I] knew that a cartoon irritant would stimulate interest and readership' (Grimshaw 2019, p. 3). (Sadly, the *NBR* no longer hosts a resident editorial cartoonist.)

Editorial cartoons also provide social criticism via satire and commentary; they are, in the words of the great New Zealand cartoonist Sir Gordon Minhinnick (1902–1992), 'an act of protest' that operates as 'a negative conception usually against some thing or somebody' (Grant 1980, p. 2). These cartoons demand that the cartoonist, the newspaper publishing them and the readership accept or reject the ideas they represent; they demand engagement. Editorial cartoons are therefore a very effective 'thinking tool' within society and politics:

they signal not only that which may be thought and considered but also that which readers may not have thought and considered. Editorial cartoons reflect society back to itself: either confirming views, opinions and attitudes, or confronting readers with views and opinions they may otherwise never engage with or too easily dismiss. Moreover, to engage with such cartoons requires an understanding and recognition of the personalities and issues depicted; they require a political and societal literacy. This means editorial cartoons are not passive observations nor merely amusement or distraction. The success of a cartoon is therefore not whether you agree with it or like what it says – nor that you may disagree with it and dislike it. The success is that you understand it – for understanding is neither agreement nor disagreement. Cartoonists must be able to express ideas in understandable images, words and allusions, and their audience needs to understand how editorial cartoons operate as well as what they express. As American triple-Pulitzer-prize-winning cartoonist Jeff McNelly states:

> Cartoonists violate every rule of ethical journalism . . . They misquote, trifle with truth, make science fiction out of politics and sometimes should be held for personal libel. But when the smoke clears, the cartoonist has been getting closer to the truth than the guys who wrote political opinion (Lamb 2004, p. 42).

For example, the 2020 election campaign can be summed up by Slane's cartoon 'Candidate Covid' (Image 16.1). Here the Covid-19 virus disconcerts and disrupts both major party leaders, not only with its malevolent presence but also by its statement that it is 'the only truly transformative candidate', negating the claims of both Labour and National that they would transform New Zealand. Certainly, from a post-election perspective, as the Labour government settled into its term of office, it seemed there was little truly transformative on the horizon except the ongoing impact of Covid-19.

This cartoon reminds us that Covid-19 created a global transformation far greater than any politician could achieve, despite their election promises. Here the source of Slane's cartoon is also in itself representative of the impact of Covid-19, for it was to be found in a resurrected *Listener* that had fallen victim to the economic effects of Covid-19 earlier in 2020. The collapse of the *Listener*, *North & South* and *Metro* magazines not only severely impacted local journalism; it also brought to an end three major outlets for cartoonists during the election. (While all three have since returned to publication, *Metro* and *North & South* no longer feature socio-political cartoons.) This is important, for the political cartoon thrives in the circulation of the public media, especially in accessible print media. This is also how cartoon literacy and associated socio-political literacy thrives. In other words, editorial cartoons are public documents that engage minds and stimulate conversations.

This was the first election campaign not covered by the *Listener* since 1939; the first not covered by *Metro* or *North & South* since they began in 1981 and 1986; and it was not only political commentary and assessment that was absent: it was also their political cartoons on the election. A cartoon in a physical newspaper or magazine reaches a different audience to one circulating online, often behind paywalls.

The *New Zealand Herald* kept its stable of cartoonists – Rod Emmerson, Guy Body and Peter Bromhead –but for all those who did not or could not access the physical paper copy, the cartoons were kept behind a paywall and then, when free of this, were hidden behind user analytics. To have an ongoing reminder of political cartoons meant ensuring your personal analytics made them appear on your *New Zealand Herald* webpage. You may have been a follower of Rod Emmerson's Twitter account and so had both a preview and record of his *Herald* cartoons, but this again is another form of digital gatekeeping that stops the editorial cartoon from becoming a truly accessible public document. To access the cartoons of Guy Body and Peter Bromhead on the online *Herald* again required the link-through of a cartoon search or deliberately refocusing your analytics to ensure cartoons came up on your online *Herald* feed.

On the other hand, the forced sell-off of *Stuff*, its purchase by Sinead Boucher and the subsequent reformatting suddenly meant editorial cartoons were always present and available in *Stuff* online. No longer was it a matter of clicking through or searching for cartoons; the online *Stuff* perspectives page operated in a very similar fashion to a physical newspaper. Not only that, but a back catalogue of *Stuff* cartoons was also available for each of their three cartoonists – Sharon Murdoch, Jim Hubbard and Jeff Bell. It was heartening to see, for *Stuff* at least, the restoration of editorial/political cartoons to their role as part of an easily accessible public media and political debate.

In the case of the *Otago Daily Times,* in the absence of a physical copy, it was necessary to go directly to Shaun Yeo's Facebook site. Similarly, as noted, it was easier to go to Rod Emmerson's Twitter account than to the *Herald* to see what comment he was making. As for Malcolm Evans and Garrick Tremain, the best and easiest access to their cartoons was via their respective websites.

The movement of political cartoons from newspapers to social media in 2020 made them potentially more widely available, and yet less available, depending on who you were and what you knew. The shift to more and more people getting news from online news sites meant – except for *Stuff* – that access to political cartoons depended on paywalls and analytics; or what Twitter feeds or Facebook links you followed; or if you knew the websites of cartoonists. In this context the democratic function of the political cartoon changed. The circulation and accessibility of the political cartoon increasingly depended on what social media it linked into, which increasingly mirrored political parties' social media direct access campaigning. Here all leaders could be seen – though they may deny it – using the Donald Trump/populist playbook, circumventing mainstream media. In this they had learned, finally, from the political cartoon because the cartoon works on 'affect' and 'effect': what they make us feel and what effect they wish to provide and provoke. The cartoon provides a type of counter-narrative to what is supposed to be rational, reasonable, perhaps impartial critique and analysis. This is why a political cartoon history of the election provides an important insight not only into the election but also into the electorate, as cartoonists tap into the wider 'zeitgeist' while also, to varying degrees, reflecting and directing it.

From a political cartoon viewpoint, the 2020 election campaign went through a number of distinct phases. While some of these might match what other commentators emphasised, the importance of cartoons is that they give a different election narrative, focusing on what may or may not be considered important in more official perspectives, providing a type of popular – indeed, populist – counternarrative.[1]

The election year in cartoons . . .

At the end of January 2020 Jeff Bell signalled the start of a showdown in which Simon Bridges was on the back foot against Jacinda Ardern's politics of 'niceness' (Image 16.2). His cartoon notes that Ardern's 'niceness' is always political and always strategic; it is not niceness in and of itself – no matter how it is spun. That is, 'niceness' and 'kindness' are political tools and phrases deliberately employed for political purposes, used to gain the upper hand, both politically and in a deliberately populist fashion – 'kindness' especially being astutely employed during the Covid-19 lockdown and the election campaign.

In February, Sharon Murdoch's cartoon on party donations (Image 16.3), featuring Paula Bennett, Simon Bridges and Jami-Lee Ross, signalled the real start of the election campaign. Yet what is most telling is that very soon neither Bennett nor Bridges were National Party leaders and Jami-Lee Ross had assumed – for many – an even more diabolical form: not as a scapegoat, but rather as a conspiracy party co-leader with Billy Te Kahika for Advance New Zealand. This party ran its own Facebook-focused campaign in which they took and altered cartoons by American alt-right cartoonist Ben Garrison (Molyneux 2020; see Image 16.4).

A review of editorial cartoons also enables us to remember the topics and issues of a particular time. For example, political party donations were, we may have soon forgotten, the focus story at the start of the election year (Image 16.5); the tarnish of these early disputes and scandals was one from which neither the National nor New Zealand First parties would fully recover.

Yet, as the cartoons throughout the campaign demonstrated, the real story, besides Covid-19, was the 'presidential' nature of the election. The question for National, and one which the party could never adequately answer, was who they could put up to match the 'presidential' power of Jacinda Ardern. In this it became apparent that most cartoonists were on the side of Ardern; the one real exception was veteran cartoonist Garrick Tremain, who would critique both Ardern and Collins – yet in the process demonstrating attitudes that for many were out of step with liberal views in 2020. If the party leaders were both males, would they have been portrayed as streetwalking rent boys (Image 16.6)?

Problematic as Tremain's cartoon is, it does raise a deeper question of what happens when the vast majority of political cartoonists during an election campaign seem to be, either intentionally or by default, part of a wider Labour Party – or perhaps, more accurately, a Jacinda Ardern party. Tremain articulates a counterpoint to the status quo and gives access to a political and social outlook not often expressed in New Zealand's cartoons or media. In this, Tremain could be said to represent talkback radio, while most other cartoonists were more Radio New Zealand – or perhaps Tremain is the last cartoonist of provincial New Zealand, the last non-metropolitan cartoonist? (While Malcolm Evans has a long history of rural-topic cartoons, most of his political cartoons could be said to be more sympathetic to a left-wing, non-neoliberal urban critique.)

The election year had a reboot with the arrival of Covid-19. Going back to the first Colmar Brunton poll in February 2020, National was actually leading in the polls, with the distinct possibility that a National–ACT coalition could take power (Radio New Zealand 2020). Covid-19 changed everything, giving Jacinda Ardern the platform and public focus to turn a party-political contest into a leadership- and personality-focused one. The signs were there in that February 2020 poll: Ardern was more popular than her party and was 31 per cent more popular than the leader of the party Labour trailed in the polls. The cartoonists had already noted this, their focus always being far more pro-Ardern than her party, representing the election and electorate shift away from party to leadership. If a party does not have a leader who captures the popular mood it does not matter how well it may be rating as a party: it is, it seems, leadership that now wins elections.

Bromhead's cartoon (Image 16.7) illustrates the way Ardern's Covid-19 response enabled capture of the media and the public mood, allowing her to easily increase her popularity over Bridges. In doing so Ardern took Labour with her, rather than the other way around.

Of course, Ardern's popularity was also (perhaps deliberately) linked to the performance of Director-General of Health Dr Ashley Bloomfield and his daily Covid-19 updates. Bloomfield was the only public figure whose popularity could exceed that of the prime minister. While he was resolutely non-political in his appearances, his mahi and mana were politically appropriated by Ardern at every opportunity. Cartoons depicting Bloomfield tended to posit him as a pop-culture superhero (Image 16.8) and pop-culture saint for Apostle hot sauce (Chumko 2020; *TVNZ News* 2020).[2]

More interesting is the manner in which the prime minister and Bloomfield were linked as a twin act of Covid-19 leadership, adding to Ardern's political capital. As became evident, the central definition of political popularity was the status quo soft populism of Jacinda Ardern: a leader who knew how to turn every opportunity into an election campaign moment. Ardern's politically astute use of her daily Covid-19 public briefings effectively marginalised all other political leaders and politicians to secondary status – at best. This is recognised in Jeff Bell's use of two famous images of wartime propaganda: Kitchener from World War I and Rosie the Riveter from World War II (Image 16.9). In this cartoon Ardern is reimagined as both military leader and iconic symbol of wartime female worker, mobilised in the war against Covid-19. If she (in both guises) provides the leadership (as command and inspiration) it is Bloomfield who provides the news; while it is a double act, Ardern remains firmly in control.

The ongoing effect of this capture of media attention and focus was recognised even when it was time to relaunch the election campaign with the end of the Covid-19 lockdown; here the exit from lockdown – and all other events – was presented by Jeff Bell as the result of the Ardern–Bloomfield double-act (Image 16.10).

In fact, for such a public figure, it was impossible to find a cartoon that critiqued Bloomfield. The closest would be those that raised, briefly, issues of miscommunication on border security leakages but even here the damage was seen to be affecting the prime minister more than Dr Bloomfield (Image 16.11). This cartoon by Murdoch is interesting in the way it mixes allusions to create its message. The Achilles heel is from Greek mythology and Homer's *Iliad*, yet Ardern is dressed as Joan of Arc; in the background Bloomfield and Cabinet minister Chris Hipkins appear as English archers. As in all cartoons, the image's historical accuracy is less important than the message being conveyed, and in the end this proved to be only a flesh wound.

In Yeo's cartoon (Image 16.12) the text and image combine to signal a resourcing and communication breakdown, yet Ardern is, by her absence, not the focus of either, with Bloomfield shown trying to cope as best he can – on his own.

The question of Simon Bridges' popularity – both inside and outside the National Party – signalled the central drama of the election for National: could *anyone* credibly challenge Ardern? Bridges' attempts at his own version of Ardern-style populism badly misfired, creating unfortunate comparisons (Image 16.13). It soon became clear, both inside and outside National, that Bridges had to be replaced (Image 16.14): but by whom?

Bridges' replacement by Todd Muller (Images 16.15 and 16.16) did little to rebalance the election campaign. Muller seemed to be selected to lead a National Party focused on policy not personality, which was either a misreading of the public mood or a miscalculated gamble given the presidential nature of modern politics.

Ostensibly elected leader with an unofficial mandate to 'make National great again', Muller's missteps with his Trump campaign MAGA cap were a gift to cartoonists from across the political spectrum (Images 16.17–16.20). Could Muller escape making yet another naive leadership gaffe? Or did National need to escape from his leadership (Image 16.21)? What was excused as a bumpy start became an ever-increasing list of missteps and failures, culminating in dissenting email leaks from within National's caucus, making Muller and National the focus of cartoonists for all the wrong reasons (Images 16.22–16.24).

Labour suffered its own version of political naivete and ineptitude, in its case from Minister of Health David Clark. Somewhat strangely (or perhaps not) kept out of the Bloomfield–Ardern team's daily Covid-19 briefings, banished (or returning) to Dunedin for more family time, Clark became the focus of widespread ridicule and anger for his repeated failures to follow the social distancing and lockdown advice given by his own health department officials (Images 16.25 and 16.26). Even more damaging was Clark's well-documented 'throwing Dr Bloomfield under the bus', caught on TV3 news (O'Brien) – a moment of incredible political ineptitude given Bloomfield's popularity and one that, undertaken by a trained theologian[3] against a popular saint, was analogous to both iconoclastic failure and an act of heresy (Images 16.27 and 16.28). As cartoonist Sharon Murdoch explained on her Twitter feed discussing this cartoon, by blaming Bloomfield, Clark had become a target even for those supporting Labour.[4] Clark's repeated failures were too damaging for a party and a leader who repeatedly emphasised her leadership qualities over those of her National opponents, so he was removed from the Health portfolio in July 2020 (Images 16.29 and 16.30).

Who could take his place? There was, it appeared, a paucity of talent in Labour; Megan Woods had already taken over Housing from the inept Phil Twyford and it was left to Chris Hipkins to add the Health portfolio to that of Education, in doing so embodying the positive, 'we can do it' (or rather, in reality, 'only a very select few can do it') ethos and slogan of Labour under Ardern (Image 16.31).

Yet if Clark and Twyford had proved they were not up to their portfolios, Todd Muller decided that the National Party leadership came with too great a burden. Following the ongoing drama of leaked National Party emails and the meddling of former party president Michelle Boag (Images 16.32 and 16.33), he resigned.

This left the way open for Judith Collins to at last claim the role she had been seeking for many years. What this role actually entailed – in this year, with this party – was open to conjecture (Image 16.34). Elected leader of a party struggling in the polls and with a new deputy in Gerry Brownlee, it seemed there would be little that Collins could do – or would not do – to try and halt National's ongoing decline against the combination of Ardern and Covid-19 (Image 16.35).

Collins' rise to leadership provided new drama to an election that seemed to be one Labour would win by default. National's new leadership team claimed their experience and political capital would triumph. Yet if Collins was the new captain of a sinking ship, Ardern remained challenged by the legacy of the first Labour government's truly transformative leadership. The feeling was (and is) that the use of Michael Joseph Savage as icon in background shots of Ardern and other Labour leaders had to be matched by truly progressive politics and a proper recalibration of the Welfare State in the face of ongoing and growing inequity (Image 16.36).

Yet the election of Collins and her new deputy Brownlee signalled a shift in National that made many uncomfortable; in particular, a number of experienced National women MPs decided they would not contest the election under Collins' leadership (Image 16.37). Cartoonists suggested that part of the reason was the possible return of character assassination and autocratic politics that National had last practised under Prime Minister Robert Muldoon. While Winston Peters was often portrayed looking back to Muldoon for inspiration and tactics (Image 16.38), Judith Collins was perceived as about to institute a return to Muldoon-style populism as well, now with a touch of Thatcherism (Image 16.39). If Labour was presenting itself as a 21st century forward-looking party, National was seen as following New Zealand First, looking to the past for inspiration.

Meanwhile, Winston Peters found 2020 one campaign too far. If Collins was attempting to channel the spirit of National past, Peters discovered that the New Zealand he claimed to represent no longer wanted either him or his party (Images 16.40 and 16.41). In an increasingly fractious campaign Labour and New Zealand First sought to distance themselves from each other – a move far more successfully undertaken by one coalition partner than the other. Shane Jones was seen as just as problematic as Winston Peters; together they suffered the fatal ignominy of populist politicians who had become highly unpopular with the electorate (Images 16.42–16.46). New Zealand First's scuppering of light rail for Auckland was at the time conveniently seen as part of a wider constraint upon Labour enacting a capital gains tax; and yet Labour's decision to rule out such a tax contributed to its expanded success within the centre of New Zealand politics. The more New Zealand First could be viewed as the problem in the coalition government, the more Labour stood to gain in its move to the populist centre (Images 16.47 and 16.48). In retrospect, the cartoonists stated – more often and more clearly than anyone else – that this election was to be the end of New Zealand First and Winston Peters, proving that cartoonists (Images 16.49–16.51) often have a better sense of the electorate than many commentators and pollsters.

Far more successful was the rise of ACT under its leader David Seymour, to the point where his party (which originally arose out of both Labour and National) was seen as a possible 'kingmaker', occupying the traditional role held by Peters and New Zealand First (Images 16.52 and 16.53). Seymour and ACT benefitted not only from National's self-destruction and the collapse of New Zealand First, but also from their ability to provide a genuine point of difference, backed up by Seymour's success in achieving a referendum on euthanasia – though not all saw this as positive (Image 16.54). Yet as ACT rose in the polls, there were growing concerns as to who exactly might come into Parliament along with Seymour, with ACT having courted support from the gun lobby. *New Zealand Herald* cartoonist Emmerson particularly focused on the rise of ACT (Images 16.55–16.57), signalling the outlook and concerns of the *Herald* and wider Auckland.

While support for ACT rose following dissatisfaction with National and New Zealand First, the Greens were effectively and deliberately sidelined by Labour (Image 16.58) and by the decision of Greens' co-leader James Shaw to demand funding for a private school in the wealthy seaside town of Ōakura in Taranaki (Images 16.59–16.61).

The Greens thought they would be more successful with their support of the cannabis referendum, but in the end, despite Chlöe Swarbrick winning Auckland Central (and a modest increase in their number of MPs, from eight to ten), the Greens found themselves even more marginalised than in the previous coalition government – and without a win on the cannabis vote (Images 16.62–16.64). With the

Greens deciding to enter into a supporting role with the new Labour government, questions were again raised about James Shaw's political judgment (Images 16.65–16.69).

What can't be denied is the entertainment value that Judith Collins brought to the election campaign. The leaders' debates became compulsory viewing, not so much for what was or was not said, but for the relish (and expressive eyebrows) Collins brought to them – and the wider campaign (Image 16.70). If John Campbell was strangely muted and underwhelming as a debate host, the same could not be said of Paddy Gower's participatory investigative journalism into the cannabis debate, or his gonzo-style coverage and commentary on election night (Image 16.71).

The election was ultimately less a clash of policies and parties than of leaders, generations and political style. Many cartoons depicted an Ardern versus Collins double act in a presidential style match-up more of personalities than of policies (Images 16.72–16.76). Ardern's ability to dominate the narrative against all of her rivals was made most explicit in Emmerson's cartoon of responses about how to rebuild New Zealand's economy and society post-Covid-19 (Image 16.77). In the end, only one party – or leader – was able to successfully maintain the election machine (Image 16.78), which meant Labour was able to win an unprecedented number of National electorates (Images 16.79–16.80).

It was, in the end, the Covid-19 election (Image 16.81) and the real issues lay ahead (Images 16.82 and 16.83). As veteran cartoonist Malcolm Evans observed, 'the Evans cartoon that best sums up the election is that which highlights Labour's terror at the thought that it might have to live up to the mandate it's been given, and [the] electorate's expectation[s]' (Image 16.84).[5]

16.1: Chris Slane, 'Candidate Covid' (*The Listener*)

16.2: Jeff Bell, 'Election 2020 – First Shots Fired!' (*Stuff*)

16.3: Sharon Murdoch, 'Election Special: A Behind-the-Scenes Look at the Management of Party Donations' (*Stuff*)

16.4: Advance NZ, 'What happens when good Kiwi Couch Potatoes do nothing'

16.5: Malcolm Walker, 'Electoral Donations'

16.6: Garrick Tremain, 'Just one more week on the streets'

16.7: Peter Bromhead, 'At least you're practicing good social distancing, Simon . . .'

16.8: Jeff Bell, 'Dr Ashley Bloomfield, superhero'
(*Stuff*)

16.9: Jeff Bell, 'Your Country Needs You . . .'
(*Stuff*)

16.10: Jeff Bell, 'Right! Let's Get This Thing Started, Shall We??'
(*Stuff*)

16.11: Sharon Murdoch, 'The Border Patrol "Incident" (as it later became known)' (*Stuff*)

16.12: Shaun Yeo, 'Border' (*Otago Daily Times*)

16.13: Garrick Tremain, 'Amazing!! The more he campaigns the more he reminds me of somebody . . .'

16.14: Garrick Tremain, 'Taking a dive . . .'

16.15: Peter Bromhead, 'Good luck, Todd!'

16.16: Jeff Bell, 'Easy! What's Next?'
(*Stuff*)

16.17: Garrick Tremain, 'Quite harmless . . . all part of his U.S. political memorabilia'

16.18: Garrick Tremain, 'That hat . . .'

16.19: Peter Bromhead, 'Stuff to put away . . .'

16.20: Rod Emmerson, 'National's madness'
(*New Zealand Herald*)

16.21: Shaun Yeo, 'Another escapee . . .'
(*Otago Daily Times*)

16.22: Sharon Murdoch, 'Blatting down the motorway in your new Crown Pragmatic'
(*Stuff*)

16.23: Guy Body, 'Ferris Muller's Way Off'
(*New Zealand Herald*)

16.24: Shaun Yeo, 'Leak Scandal'
(*Otago Daily Times*)

16.25: Rod Emmerson, 'The David Clark Covid-19 Executive Test' (*New Zealand Herald*)

16.26: Malcolm Evans, 'Something could be arranged!'

16.27: Garrick Tremain, 'Where can I find Ashley Bloomfield?'

16.28: Sharon Murdoch, 'Covid Response'
(*Stuff*)

16.29: Rod Emmerson, 'I'm the Health Minister and I'm social distancing' (*New Zealand Herald*)

16.30: Garrick Tremain, 'HMS Cabinet'

16.31: Jeff Bell, 'Labour Reveal New Slogan' (*Stuff*)

16.32: Guy Body, 'Aaa-Tchooo!!!' (*New Zealand Herald*)

16.33: Rod Emmerson, '. . . Obviously, my work here is done . . .'
(*New Zealand Herald*)

16.34: Rod Emmerson, 'A poisoned chalice?'
(*New Zealand Herald*)

16.35: Sharon Murdoch, 'Jude & Gerry's Bar & Grill (previously Simon & Paula's Chop House)' (*Stuff*)

16.36: Guy Body, 'Those vivid Coronavirus dreams –' (*New Zealand Herald*)

16.37: Rod Emmerson, 'Breakout . . .'
(*New Zealand Herald*)

16.38: Guy Body, 'Theory & Practice of Muldoonism'
(*New Zealand Herald*)

16.39: Jeff Bell, 'Heh Heh Heh!'
(*Stuff*)

16.40: Garrick Tremain, 'Meanwhile, on the bus to . . . nowhere'

16.41: Garrick Tremain, 'Taxidermist'

16.42: Sharon Murdoch, 'Election Vocabulary: Today's word is "woke"'
(*Stuff*)

16.43 Rod Emmerson, 'Polar Polls'
(*New Zealand Herald*)

16.44: Sharon Murdoch, 'Winston's points of difference'
(*Stuff*)

16.45: Rod Emmerson, 'Off the charts . . .'
(*New Zealand Herald*)

16.46: Peter Bromhead, 'A matter of political stature . . .'
(*New Zealand Herald*)

16.47: Rod Emmerson, 'Waiting for the light rail . . .' (*New Zealand Herald*)

16.48: Rod Emmerson, 'Phasing out NZ First . . .' (*New Zealand Herald*)

16.49: Shaun Yeo, 'Winston's Last Stand' (*Otago Daily Times*)

16.50: Rod Emmerson, 'New Zealand First's Farewell Tour' (*New Zealand Herald*)

16.51: Shaun Yeo, 'Your polls are rubbish!'
(*Otago Daily Times*)

16.52: Rod Emmerson, 'Your highest priority at the moment . . .'
(*New Zealand Herald*)

16.53: Rod Emmerson, 'And I'd just like to thank Judith and Winston . . .' (*New Zealand Herald*)

16.54: Sharon Murdoch, 'Death and Taxes' (*Stuff*)

16.55: Rod Emmerson, '. . . Don't vote the gun nut out . . .'
(*New Zealand Herald*)

16.56: Rod Emmerson, 'David Seymour – Pied Piper'
(*New Zealand Herald*)

16.57: Rod Emmerson, 'The inorganic rubbish collector' (*New Zealand Herald*)

16.58: Jim Hubbard, 'Green Party Wealth Tax Proposal' (*Stuff*)

16.59: Rod Emmerson, 'Back to school'
(*New Zealand Herald*)

16.60: Rod Emmerson, 'Shovel Ready . . .'
(*New Zealand Herald*)

16.61: Garrick Tremain, 'Greens Private School'

16.62: Rod Emmerson, 'The Reefer-endum'
(*New Zealand Herald*)

16.63: Rod Emmerson, 'OK Boomers'
(*New Zealand Herald*)

16.64: Sharon Murdoch, 'Kiwis think about cannabis law reform & give their considered opinion' (*Stuff*)

16.65: Malcolm Evans, 'Remember remember the 5th of November!'

16.66: Guy Body, 'Thanks James – now sit there and look important' (*New Zealand Herald*)

16.67: Rod Emmerson, 'Red, with a spot of Green'
(*New Zealand Herald*)

16.68: Jim Hubbard, 'Cheers!'
(*Stuff*)

16.69: Jeff Bell, 'Social distancing'
(*Stuff*)

16.70: Rod Emmerson, 'The Leaders' Debate . . .'
(*New Zealand Herald*)

16.71: Rod Emmerson, 'Paddy Gower's leaders' debates warning' (*New Zealand Herald*)

16.72: Rod Emmerson, 'The Fairy Tale Election?' (*New Zealand Herald*)

16.73: Jim Hubbard, 'Let's have a clean fight!'
(*Stuff*)

16.74: Rod Emmerson, 'Updated Campaign Slogans'
(*New Zealand Herald*)

16.75: Shaun Yeo, 'Stardust / Crusher'
(*Otago Daily Times*)

16.76: Guy Body, 'Jeepers – are those eyebrows starting to arch?'
(*New Zealand Herald*)

16.77: Rod Emmerson, 'Shovel-ready projects' (*New Zealand Herald*)

16.78: Guy Body, 'Election machine' (*New Zealand Herald*)

16.79: Malcolm Evans, 'On the farm . . .'

16.80: Rod Emmerson, 'We have a mandate!'
(*New Zealand Herald*)

16.81: Jim Hubbard, 'The Covid-19 election'
(*Stuff*)

16.82: Sharon Murdoch, 'The second book'
(*Stuff*)

16.83: Garrick Tremain, 'Our top priority . . .'

16.84: Malcolm Evans, 'No excuse . . .'

Public Policy Issues and Jacinda Ardern's Government

17

THE 2020 ELECTION, THE COVID-19 EMERGENCY, AND THE NEED TO IMPROVE OUR RESPONSE CAPACITY FOR EVEN MORE SERIOUS THREATS

Michael G. Baker

The Covid-19 pandemic was the largest public health emergency faced by New Zealand since the 1918 influenza pandemic. It dominated public life throughout 2020. The New Zealand government's response was the most decisive among OECD countries and included two distinct features: a short and intense lockdown and an explicit elimination strategy which has been largely successful at achieving sustained Zero-Covid in the community. This strategy gave New Zealand the lowest Covid-19 mortality rate in the OECD and less economic contraction than many countries pursuing suppression and mitigation strategies. The effective response to this event is likely to have strongly influenced the results of the 2020 New Zealand election.

This chapter aims to briefly describe the Aotearoa New Zealand Covid-19 response; summarise the impact of this response; and identify some of the major policy and political implications of this event. Written from a public health policy perspective, it summarises how the Covid-19 pandemic and response provided a strong context for the 2020 election, but it does not provide a detailed political analysis of how the emergency influenced the outcome of that election.

Assessing pandemics

Pandemics are epidemics that have spread to multiple countries. There is no precise definition for these events or any process for declaring them. By contrast, Public Health Emergencies of International Concern (PHEIC) are defined in international law (World Health Organization 2008). On 30 January 2020, the WHO Director-General declared that the Covid-19 pandemic constituted a PHEIC.

Pandemics can be assessed according to four main characteristics (Kvalsvig and Baker 2021):

1. Transmissibility
2. Severity and distribution of health impacts
3. Controllability
4. Certainty of information and stability of the threat.

With new emerging diseases, these key characteristics are poorly understood at first, and the likely population health impact is not known. Consequently, there is an important role for disease modelling to generate future scenarios based on plausible parameters and assess the impact of various interventions.

Disease modelling was carried out for the New Zealand Ministry of Health in February and March 2020 and provided an indication that the impact of the Covid-19 pandemic on New Zealand would be severe (Wilson et al. 2020). Under the most plausible scenario, New Zealand could expect to see 28,300 patients hospitalised (0.6 per cent of the population) and 12,700 deaths (0.3 per cent of the population). To put this number in perspective, that mortality would have been equivalent to 25 seasonal influenza seasons stacked on top of each other, and more than the number of people killed in the 1918 influenza pandemic where 9,000 died in eight weeks (though the risk of death during that pandemic was higher, at 0.8 per cent of the population).

There was also considerable concern about the impact of the Covid-19 pandemic on minorities. Previous influenza pandemics caused markedly higher mortality for Māori compared with Europeans, including the recent 2009 pandemic (Wilson et al. 2012).

Strategic choices for a pandemic response

The strategic choices for responding to serious infectious diseases and pandemics are shown in Figure 17.1 (adapted from Kvalsvig and Baker 2021). Pandemic plans have been largely developed with a focus on pandemic influenza, the most consistent recurring pandemic threat. Such plans use a mitigation approach to 'flatten the curve' and reduce the impact on healthcare systems. In some countries, notably Sweden, Netherlands and the United Kingdom, this approach was described as 'herd immunity' as there was an initial expectation that the virus would continue infecting people widely until herd immunity was established.

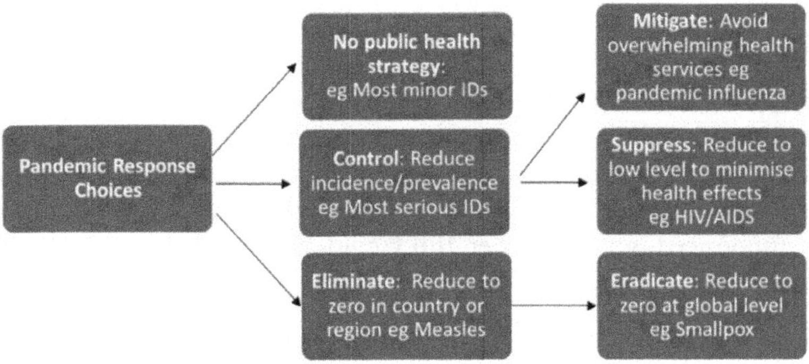

Figure 17.1: Broad response strategies for managing serious emerging and pandemic diseases (IDs = infectious diseases)

The suppression strategy has the goal of flattening the epidemic curve further than the mitigation strategy to minimise cases to within health sector capacity but without expecting to end community transmission. As the pandemic intensified, most countries in Europe and North America adopted this approach to reduce transmission and the harms of Covid-19 infection. This strategy required countries to have prolonged periods going in and out of lockdowns.

The alternative approach of elimination was not initially adopted by any Western countries. However, China's success in containing the pandemic showed that this virus could be eliminated even after widespread community transmission (WHO-China Joint Mission 2020). A number of other Asian jurisdictions also achieved success in containing the pandemic at an early stage, notably Taiwan (Wang, Ng and Brook 2020), Hong Kong (Cowling et al. 2020) and South Korea (Kang et al. 2020). Covid-19 elimination can be defined as 'The absence of newly diagnosed SARS-CoV-2 virus infections from community transmission, within a defined jurisdiction or region, for a specified period (e.g., 28 days since the last known case in the community was placed into isolation)' (Baker, Wilson and Blakely 2020).

By the end of January 2020, the pandemic's spread from China to surrounding countries indicated that this would be a serious global pandemic (Wu, Leung and Leung 2020). New Zealand rolled out its existing national influenza pandemic plan as the basis for its response (Ministry of Health 2017). By the end of February 2020, evidence from

China showed that Covid-19 could be eliminated (Aylward and Liang 2020). A further 'light-bulb moment' came in early March 2020 when community transmission was starting in New Zealand. Because the country did not have the systems in place to manage high-volume testing and contact tracing, a 'lockdown' was needed to interrupt and eliminate transmission. New Zealand effectively adopted an elimination strategy on 23 March when the decision to pursue rapid and intense lockdown was announced, with just over 100 Covid-19 cases and no deaths. That move to alert level 4 was scheduled for 11:59 pm on 25 March 2020.

Components of the COVID-19 elimination strategy

The elimination strategy has four main components (Baker et al. 2020; Baker, Kvalsvig and Verrall 2020; Baker, Wilson and Anglemyer 2020):

1. *Exclusion of cases:* Border management to exclude cases. This measure requires highly effective quarantine facilities and associated personnel, systems and technical support, notably for testing.
2. *Case and outbreak management:* Testing and contact-tracing systems to manage high volumes of cases that may occur in an outbreak, and the associated isolation/quarantine facilities.
3. *Preventing community transmission:* Physical distancing and travel restrictions to reduce levels of contact, and mass masking to reduce virus transmission. Vaccination is increasingly available to reduce transmission. These measures were organised into a four-level alert system.
4. *Social safety net:* A wage subsidy scheme and many other forms of support were introduced to protect vulnerable populations and those losing jobs and income as a result of the pandemic response.

Impact of the elimination strategy

The major desired impact of the elimination strategy is to reduce the rate of Covid-19 infection in the community to zero and sustain it at that level. Such a decline was seen in New Zealand following the first major lockdown in March–May 2020, lasting for more than 100 days without another case (Baker, Wilson and Anglemyer 2020; Jeffries et al. 2020).

Understanding of Covid-19 elimination has been enhanced by whole-genome sequencing of SARS-CoV-2 viruses isolated in New Zealand. This work found that the whole genome sequences isolated in New Zealand were representative of global virus diversity (245 separate introductions of the virus out of the 649 cases considered). This work also discovered that only about one in five (19 per cent) of virus introductions resulted in transmission lineages of more than one additional case (Geoghegan et al. 2020). A national serological study has also confirmed the low levels of Covid-19 infection in New Zealand (Carlton et al. 2021).

A key population health indicator is the Covid-19 mortality rate, which provides a basis for international comparisons. Because New Zealand minimised case numbers, deaths were also low, giving New Zealand a Covid-19 morality rate of 5 per million, the lowest in the OECD (Baker, Wilson and Blakely 2020). The public health measures used as part of the Covid-19 response also greatly reduced circulation of other respiratory pathogens, notably influenza (Huang et al. 2021). This is the likely cause for the reduced overall mortality seen in 2020. Countries like New Zealand that pursued elimination also had better economic recoveries than countries that used mitigation and suppression approaches (Baker, Wilson and Blakely 2020).

The Covid-19 response did create some adverse effects: 30 per cent of people surveyed during lockdown reported moderate to severe psychological distress, 16 per cent reported moderate to high levels of anxiety, and 39 per cent reported low well-being; well above baseline measures. Suicidal ideation was reported by 6 per cent of respondents, and 2 per cent reported suicide attempts (Every-Palmer et al. 2020). By contrast, 64 per cent reported 'silver linings', such as enjoying working from home, spending more time with family, and a quieter, less polluted environment (Jenkins et al. 2021).

Future scenarios

At the time of the post-election conference in December 2020 the world was still largely in its first pandemic wave. Up until then, resurgences and declines in Covid-19 incidence were largely driven by the actions (and inactions) of governments. However, that situation was changing rapidly with the emergency of SARS-CoV-2 variants that were more transmissible, and therefore harder to control and more likely to infect more people and overwhelm health care systems.

The other major development towards the end of 2020 was the first evidence that Covid-19 vaccines are highly effective and safe. The first announcement was by Pfizer on 9 November 2020. This development also introduced the first of the new class of mRNA vaccines. The evidence of vaccine effectiveness has continued to strengthen subsequently.

There are two main scenarios for the future development of the Covid-19 pandemic:

- *Endemic infection* where SARS-CoV-2 continues to circulate, particularly in children, and vaccination (potentially with a regular booster and some use of public health measures) is used to protect vulnerable groups, as is done with seasonal influenza.
- *Progressive elimination* where growing parts of the globe are protected from infection with a combination of public health measures and vaccination. Even global eradication might become feasible and could be pursued, depending on the balance of evidence regarding the harm caused by infection and the ease and effectiveness of widespread vaccination.

Multiple uncertainties limit our ability to decide on an optimal long-term strategy. These uncertainties include the duration of immunity, the performance of the vaccine in children, and the extent of potential vaccine escape variants. There are also uncertainties about the prevalence of long-term consequences from Covid-19 infection. Elimination remains a useful interim strategy to protect public health while an optimal strategy emerges (Baker, Wilson and Blakely 2020).

Policy and political implications

The following policy choices could support New Zealand transitioning to a society that provides a higher level of performance in health, equity and sustainability. These items have been described in a range of sources, including articles in *The Conversation* (Baker, Kvalsvig and Wilson 2020a, 2020b).

1. Improving evidence-informed decision-making, particularly in crises

There are several ways in which decision-making processes could be improved, particularly for public health emergencies:

- Improve cross-party engagement in shaping and taking responsibility for the response, e.g., reconvene and continue the Epidemic Response Committee of parliamentarians to support development of political consensus around the pandemic response.

- Ensure high-level, multidisciplinary, strategic science input into the response, e.g. Covid-19 science council/rōpū to provide well-informed strategic advice about the response.
- Support evidence and evaluation of the response, e.g. develop a well-resourced research and development strategy to support a high level of research and evaluation of the response, proportionate to the scale of the multi-billion-dollar response.
- Support access to full information on the pandemic and response, e.g. provide comprehensive data reporting via suitable websites to support active scrutiny and analysis of the response by scientists and journalists.
- Ensure comprehensive review of the pandemic and response, e.g. begin planning for an official inquiry to maximise learning from this event.

2. Adapting responses to future threats ('all hazards' approach)

A major constraint for the New Zealand pandemic responses was that previous plans were focused on a single disease: influenza (Ministry of Health 2017). Future plans need to be far more adaptable to the much wider range of serious infectious disease threats (Boyd, Baker and Wilson 2020). It would also be useful if these frameworks could be adaptable to other major threats such as climate change, or broader goals such as promoting greater equity.

3. Building effective public health infrastructure

The Covid-19 response has shown the limitations of New Zealand's national public health infrastructure. In response to this threat, the country assembled a workable national public health agency, including:

- A ministerial position (Covid Response Minister) and Covid Cabinet Committee
- A Covid-19 directorate in the Ministry of Health
- An all-of-government group in the Department of Prime Minister and Cabinet
- A range of science advisory groups, including the Ministry of Health Technical Advisory Group (TAG)
- A nationally coordinated public health laboratory service to provide high-volume testing and specialised genome testing (Geoghegan et al. 2020)

- A nationally coordinated system of local public health services run through public health units
- A set of specialised Managed Isolation and Quarantine (MIQ) facilities run through a dedicated organisation based in MBIE.

As part of upgrading our public health infrastructure we can learn from the success of jurisdictions like Taiwan that delivered an even more effective Covid-19 response than New Zealand without the need for lockdown. A key difference was that Taiwan had a dedicated national public health agency (Summers et al. 2020; Lu et al. 2020). The government has clearly recognised the need to upgrade New Zealand's public health infrastructure. Its White Paper, released on 21 April 2021, outlined the need for a dedicated public health agency as part of an extensive upgrade of the health system (New Zealand Government 2021). The pandemic also demonstrated the need for specialised quarantine facilities as a key part of national infrastructure.

4. Supporting effective global health institutions

The World Health Organization (WHO) has multiple critical global public health functions that are needed to support the prevention and control of emerging infectious diseases and pandemics. These functions include:

- Supporting early outbreak detection, notably through the International Health Regulations (2005)
- Coordinating investigations
- Coordinating vaccine development and distribution
- Supporting outbreak prevention e.g. ending wet markets.

The performance of the WHO during the pandemic has been criticised for multiple reasons, including its slowness in responding and its advice, which appeared to lag behind best practice. A review identifying improvements (the Independent Panel for Pandemic Preparedness and Response, appointed by the WHO) issued its report on 12 May 2021, 'calling on the global community to end the Covid-19 pandemic by immediately implementing a series of bold recommendations to redistribute, fund, and increase the availability of and manufacturing capacity for vaccines, and to apply proven public health measures urgently and consistently in every country'. The Panel also recommended that governments (and the international community) 'immediately adopt a package of reforms to transform the global pandemic preparedness and response system and prevent a future pandemic' (Scoop 2021).

5. Seizing public health opportunities provided by the Covid-19 reset

One of the positive aspects of the successful Covid-19 pandemic response in New Zealand is that it can provide an opportunity to review and reset approaches to economic and social policy. More specifically, there are activities that have a positive impact on public health, equity and sustainability whose uptake may have been advanced by New Zealand's Covid-19 response. Examples of such opportunities include:

- increased support for active government interventions
- increased trust in benefits of collective action
- greater use of infection control measures
- more innovative healthcare delivery
- increased focus on mental well-being and connectedness
- increased focus on food quality, security, and sovereignty
- increased focus on universal basic income
- increased awareness of quality and safety of workplaces
- reduced commuting and associated reductions in road crashes and air pollution
- elimination of homelessness.

Conclusion

The Covid-19 pandemic had the potential to kill an estimated 13,000 New Zealanders (0.3 per cent of the population) as well as magnify ethnic health inequities. The New Zealand government's decisive response, featuring a rapid and intense lockdown and an explicit elimination strategy, gave New Zealand the lowest Covid-19 mortality in the OECD and less economic contraction than many countries pursuing less aggressive strategies.

This success is likely to have contributed to the electoral success of the Labour Party in the October 2020 general election, but while this may have been the 'Covid-driven election', there is little evidence that the election drove the Covid response. Instead, the major elements of the Covid-19 response appear to have been informed by science.

The success of the Covid-19 response appears to be supporting much needed investment in public health infrastructure, including the proposed creation of a public health agency and national public health service. Optimistically, we may now look forward to a golden age of science-informed policy-making and collective action to respond to the many major public health, equity and sustainability challenges we face both nationally and globally.

18

WELL-BEING AND THE COVID CRUNCH: THE ECONOMY AND THE 2020 ELECTION

Simon Chapple

Background

This chapter addresses some of the more interesting dimensions of the relationships between the economy and the 2020 election.

In 2017, the Labour coalition government inherited a modestly performing economy from National and its coalition partners. Economic growth was being primarily generated by historically high and sustained rates of net immigration (Figure 18.1). This tacit economic growth strategy, which might be described along the lines of the Lewis model – economic development with unlimited supplies of labour (Lewis 1954) – had been the default growth model since 2014. While absolute levels of GDP growth were consequently solid (Figure 18.2), productivity growth had stalled, falling effectively to zero (Figure 18.3). Unemployment, while continuing to fall from the 2008 Global Financial Crisis (GFC), remained at or slightly above norms achieved prior to the crisis (Figure 18.4).

Within this modestly performing, net immigration-driven economy, there existed significant inherited economic imbalances, which arguably were exacerbated by the growth drivers. The most prominent economic imbalance involved the housing market, with housing prices climbing to increasingly unaffordable levels (Figure 18.5; Demographia 2020). In addition, high and migration-driven rates of population growth, along with burgeoning numbers of international visitors, were placing increasing pressure on physical infrastructure and the natural environment. The political economy of acceptance of this growth model had been generated by a rapid escalation in relative asset prices of houses, given high voting rates of home owners and their middle New Zealand role as 'swing' voters and power brokers, whom neither main political party appear interested in crossing if they are to retain (or gain) the Treasury benches.

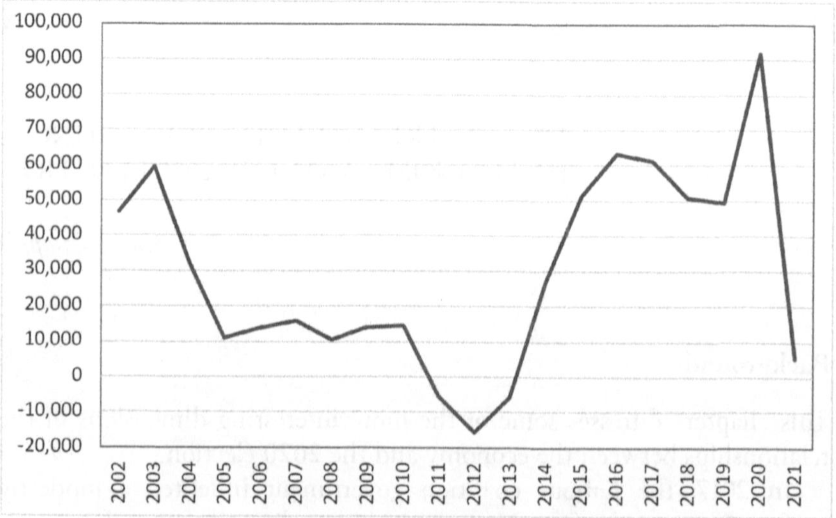

Figure 18.1: Annual net migration, March years

Source: Statistics New Zealand, https://www.stats.govt.nz/information-releases/international-migration-april-2021-infoshare-tables, (accessed 13 August 2021).

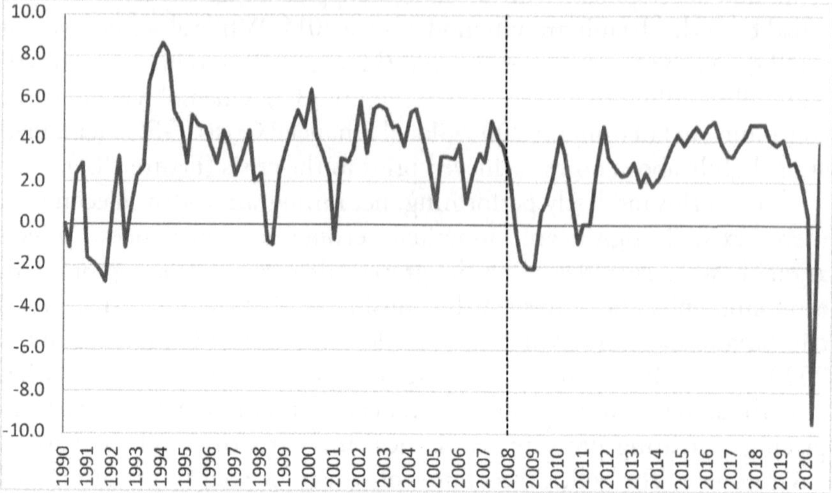

Figure 18.2: Annual GDP growth, 1990–2020

Source: Reserve Bank of New Zealand, https://www.rbnz.govt.nz/statistics/ (accessed 27 January 2021). Dashed line indicates the Global Financial Crisis.

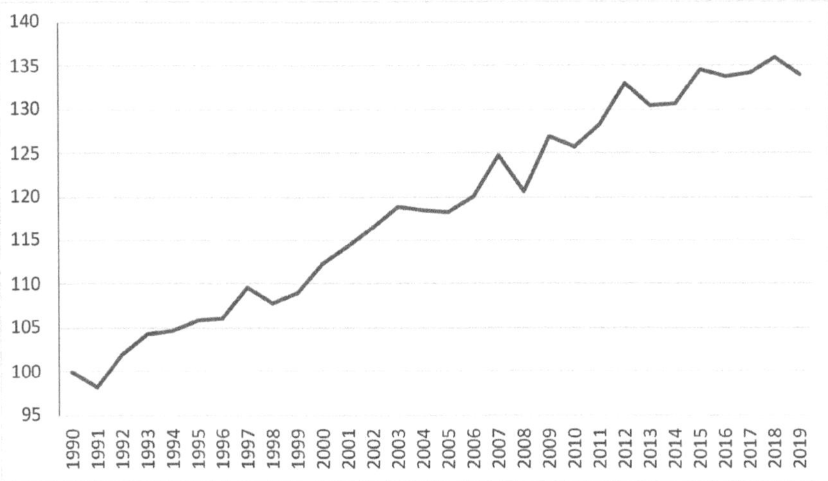

Figure 18.3: Recent productivity stalls: GDP per hour worked, 1990–2019

Source: OECD, https://stats.oecd.org/Index.aspx?DataSetCode=PDB_LV# (accessed 24 February 2021)

Figure 18.4: Unemployment rate, 1990–2020

Source: Statistics New Zealand, *Household Labour Force Survey*, Infoshare https://www.stats.govt.nz/tools/stats-infoshare (accessed 29 January 2021)

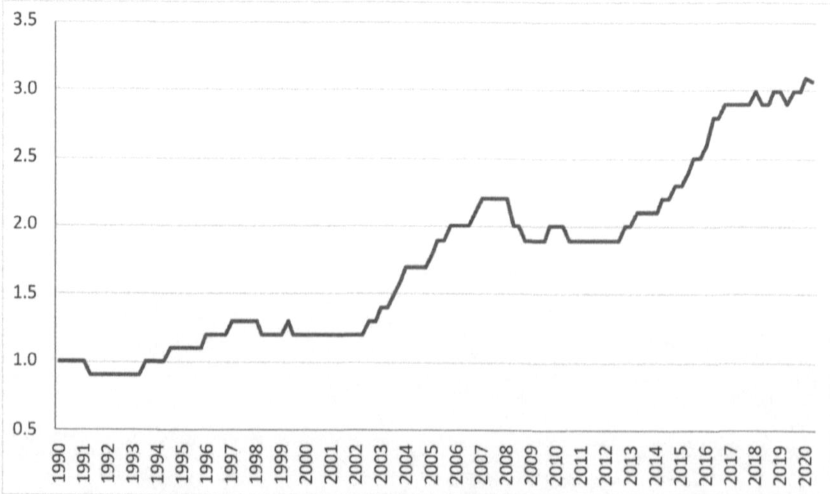

Figure 18.5: Increasingly out of reach: House prices relative to consumer prices, 1990 to 2020

Source: Reserve Bank of New Zealand, https://www.rbnz.govt.nz/statistics/key-graphs/key-graph-house-price-values (accessed 17 January 2021)

By early 2020, on the cusp of the Covid-19 shock, little about this growth model had fundamentally changed. The economy was still performing modestly, with flat productivity. Net migration had remained at historical highs through 2018 and 2019 and into the first quarter of 2020. Economic development and capital accumulation were still being driven by migration, rather than productivity. Following a rise as a consequence of the 2008 Global Financial Crisis, unemployment was still continuing a slow and steady march downwards.

A well-being approach to economic policy?

Despite minimal change in the dominant model of capital accumulation, as a strategic move following its election in 2017 the Labour coalition adopted an explicitly well-being focused approach to economic policy, picking up on extensive work undertaken at the Treasury under the previous government and in the context of significant ongoing movements in that direction by international agencies, including the OECD (in the aftermath of the 2009 Stiglitz report to the Sarkozy government in France on better measuring economic success). At the same time they dropped the previous National government's social investment approach as a broad budget coordination device, perhaps because of its logical limitations, perhaps because its ultimate goals – reducing the size of government while concomitantly improving people's lives – were not consistent with their underlying political philosophy (Chapple 2017). This new strategic well-being approach was operationalised in the government's 2019 'Wellbeing Budget' (New Zealand Government 2019). This more expansive approach to assessing the success of economic policies had been part of the international policy environment for some time and is well discussed in the previous volume in this series considering the 2017 New Zealand election (Karacaoglu and Au 2018).

The Wellbeing Budget stated that it was about tackling New Zealand's long-term challenges, by focusing on five priorities, which were fairly loosely shoe-horned in under the 'well-being' rubric:

- Taking mental health seriously
- Improving child well-being
- Supporting Māori and Pasifika aspirations
- Building a productive nation
- Transforming the economy.

In that budget, the Minister of Finance, Grant Robertson, unveiled considerable new spending for mental health services and child poverty as well as measures to tackle family violence. It has been argued that with that budget, New Zealand became the first Western country to place well-being priorities at the centre of its governance philosophy, instructing its ministries to design policies to improve well-being, rather than remaining focused on monetary indicators such as GDP, which measure the volume of market transactions. However, this world-leader claim, made in some quarters of the international press (Roy 2019), while appealing to Kiwi prejudices, has been rather oversold, as Arthur Grimes (2019) has pointed out. Well-being budgets, Grimes argues, have been delivered in New Zealand from at least the 1890s, when the Liberal Government introduced old age pensions and free primary education, and built the first state houses. In any case, of course, back in the 1890s there was little in the way of regular national income measurement around which to coordinate a budget strategy.

So, what about the 2019 budget recognised 'well-being' in new ways? Economist Richard Layard (2011) has noted that if public policy were organised around well-being, it would focus much more strongly on issues of (1) mental health and (2) unemployment. Of course, unemployment and mental health are in many respects strongly connected, with causality likely running in both directions. There is strong evidence that unemployment and poor mental health have substantial negative effects on people's satisfaction with their lives (Winkelmann and Winkelmann 1998; Fergusson et al. 2014).

As Grimes (2019) points out, the 2019 budget had a clear focus on mental health, recognising the strong links between mental health problems and low life satisfaction, a primary indicator of people's well-being as whole. In addition, major initiatives to address family and sexual violence also have a strong well-being focus as they are likely causes of (or contributors to) poor mental health. Grimes notes several weaknesses, however, in the strategic approach. He sees a major weakness in the lack of announced higher level policy targets or explicit metrics, including well-funded, high quality, independent evaluations of the success or otherwise of new spending programmes. These sorts of feedback loops are essential if new spending decisions are to achieve higher levels of well-being. New Zealand does not have a strong tradition of such feedback loops, and, as normal, there is almost no appetite for the installation of these feedback loops either amongst the political classes or in the upper echelons of the public service.

A further longstanding weakness that at least the first well-being budget did not address was the evaluation and direction of existing or baseline spending. New spending is always and inevitably small in comparison to existing spending, which is notoriously difficult to change. How would (or should) a well-being budget address re-allocation of departmental baselines? This was a question that was neither asked nor answered in the 2019 budget.

Lastly, in the 2019 budget the government missed a major trick in not making unemployment one of its central well-being priorities. Considerable research shows that when people become unemployed, their well-being, measured by their self-assessed life satisfaction, falls sharply (Layard 2011; Winkelmann and Winkelmann 1998). Should they remain without a job, the unemployed do not adapt to this new and traumatising experience. Instead, their well-being remains low until they are re-employed. Research suggests that the main impact of unemployment on well-being is not through people's lower incomes, but through loss of social status, life structure and purpose, and a positive social context.

In addition to being a direct cause of low well-being, unemployment is also strongly connected to other 2019 well-being budget priorities. Parental unemployment is a major cause of child poverty and hence relevant to child well-being, one of five budget priorities. Unemployment is also likely to affect mental health and associated alcohol and drug problems, another priority. A third budget priority relates to Māori and Pacific people, who suffer from significantly higher chances of unemployment than other ethnic groups. Given these two groups are over-represented among the unemployed, lower overall unemployment would also contribute to progress in achieving that priority.

In 2019 budget documents Treasury forecast unemployment to decline moderately to 4 per cent in 2019, rising slightly to 4.3 per cent by 2023. While some might trumpet this as success, it is poor by New Zealand's historical standards. Between 1956 and 1981, New Zealand's unemployment was never above 2 per cent and often below 1 per cent. In the mid-1980s, the then 4 per cent rate was considered unacceptably high and, indeed, offered as a rationale for the economic reforms of the time.

Treasury's budget assessment of the unemployment rate at which the economy is stable (strictly speaking, their estimate of the 'Non-Accelerating Inflation Rate of Unemployment' or NAIRU) is 4.25 per cent. Following informal discussions by the author with Treasury about the range of possible estimates around the 4.25 per cent number, officials indicated they had no direct sense of its considerable imprecision in terms of actual policy purposes. But they did suggest that estimating the rate using different statistical models delivered quite different results, although the size of these differences went unstated.

The conclusion that different statistical models can generate quite different stable unemployment rates comes from recent work at the Reserve Bank of New Zealand (Jacob and Wong 2018). The Reserve Bank takes two approaches to estimating the stable unemployment rate and the results can differ at times by more than 2 per cent. Consequently, it is difficult to take the precise 4.25 per cent unemployment estimate, used to justify the do-nothing approach, seriously as a hard policy constraint.

It should be acknowledged that the well-being budget did contain some new employment initiatives. But they were minor in scale and really amount to fiddling around the micro-edges of a macro-unemployment problem. Even in today's globalised trading economies, much lower unemployment rates than New Zealand's current 4.4 per cent are achievable. For example, the best OECD performer in 2019 was the Czech Republic, with an unemployment rate of 2.1 per cent. Japan was next at 2.4 per cent, with Iceland at 2.7 per cent.

The questioning of the very notion of a stable unemployment rate, and the suggestion that macro policies can have significant impacts on unemployment, is also attracting serious intellectual attention internationally. Top US economist Lawrence Summers remarked that 'the issue that's preoccupied monetary policy for the generation before the financial crisis – the avoidance of inflation – is no longer the top one'. Rather, for Summers, that top issue was 'getting to full employment' (Condon, Lima and Jackson 2018).

In terms of their well-being approach, the government has fairly obviously missed an opportunity to use macroeconomic tools to test whether New Zealand can once again have low rates of unemployment, as it used to between 1938 and the early 1980s when rates lay between 0 and 2 per cent (Chapple 1996).

Since the 1938 Social Security Act – a well-being focused piece of legislation if ever there was one – New Zealand has had a welfare system designed to work best when high numbers of New Zealanders are in work. Despite all the changes to the working-age welfare system since the 1970s, it still functions best when the unemployment rate is considerably lower than what we have settled for today. Full employment and low rates of unemployment were what post-war left-wing economist Wolfgang Rosenberg accurately described in the late 1970s as the fulcrum of New Zealand's social welfare system. Perhaps much lower unemployment should once again be the fulcrum of what in the 21st century might better be described as New Zealand's *social well-being* system. To place it in such a position of prominence would be to inaugurate economic policies considerably more transformational than this coalition government has thus far delivered.

To give the Labour coalition its due on the unemployment focus front, it should be acknowledged that the government has changed the Reserve Bank structure to better include labour market goals, though how effectively remains to be seen. In 2018 the government amended the Reserve Bank Act to give the Reserve Bank an additional major economic objective besides maintaining stable prices: 'supporting maximum sustainable employment'. While recognition of the (implicitly paid) job market as central to generating well-being was important in legislation, the government again missed a major trick here. All the evidence suggests that what matters for well-being is not unemployment *per se*, but being in a state of unemployment: people who want a paid job and don't have one. It is unclear, from a well-being perspective, why the government didn't write well-being into the Act.

The Covid-19 sideswipe

The arrival of the Covid-19 virus in New Zealand at the end of the first quarter of 2020 dominated the background and trajectory of the 2020 election campaign and was a critical factor behind the eventual result. Covid pulled attention away from the *explicitly* well-being focused approach of the 2019 budget to an *implicitly* well-being focused approach to responding to Covid, with public debate and the policy response driven not by economists but by epidemiologists and public health experts.

What happened to the economy during Covid? Covid resulted in an almost immediate halt to cross-border population movement – a massive de-globalisation, occurring almost overnight. Figure 18.6 shows the broad picture of Covid de-globalisation: human cross-border movements plummeted in 2020. After growing at a staggering average rate of 5 per cent per annum in the last three decades, human globalisation reverted in 2020 to levels not seen for 30 years. The 2020 figures do not reveal the true extent of this de-globalisation since the data for 2020 includes only the first three months of the year, which were much more normal than subsequently. With this striking de-globalisation, gone was the net migration growth which had driven New Zealand's dominant economic growth model since 2014. Effectively gone, too, were the international tourist and export education industries.

The consequence of this shock was a massive fall in GDP of nearly 10 per cent per annum (Figure 18.2). During New Zealand's alert level 4 lockdown, well-being amongst those who lost jobs, compared to those who remained employed, was significantly lower (Habibi et al. 2021). Essential workers also experienced more stress and worry than other workers. The longer-term upward movement in unemployment (Figure 18.4) was, however, considerably more muted than anticipated and so, presumably, were resulting declines in well-being. Overall, the traditional economic indicators suggest an economy which was much more robust to the de-

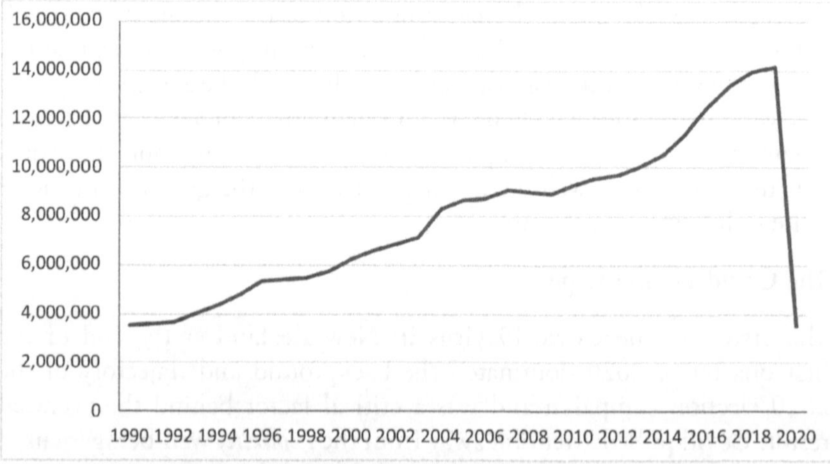

Figure 18.6: International population turnover, New Zealand (total arrivals and departures, December years) [January–March 2020]

Source: Statistics New Zealand

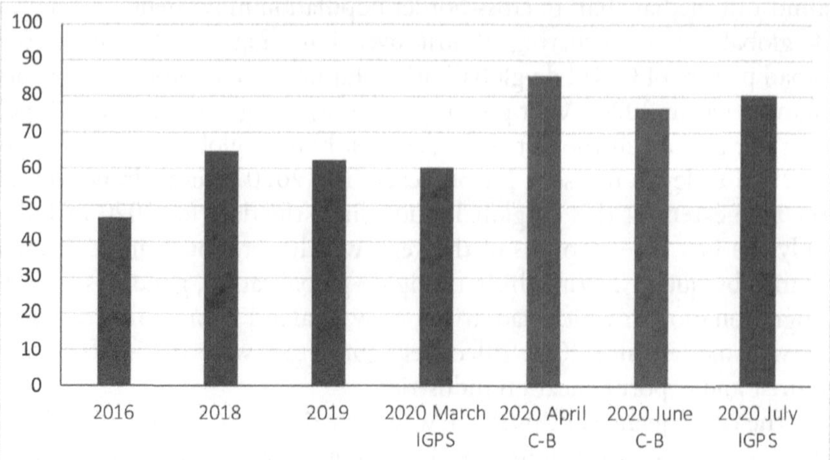

Figure 18.7: Trust in government (%) to solve national problems: a sustained rise post-April 2020 lockdown

Source: IGPS; Colmar Brunton

Note: Each bar represents the proportion of respondents who ticked 'a great deal' or 'a reasonable amount' of trust in government to solve national problems from the IGPS survey 2016–2020 (March). It charts two additional observations (April and June) collected by Colmar Brunton (C-B) for their 'Covid Times Survey' and then a July figure collected from the second wave of the IGPS/Roy McKenzie Covid-19 survey.

globalisation which occurred than many anticipated; and the economic data since lockdown has, generally, continued to surprise on the upside (Reserve Bank of New Zealand 2021). This more robust economy includes a stronger labour market and lower than expected unemployment rates (4.9 per cent, for example, in the December 2020 quarter) which, as discussed above, are critical to a fuller understanding of the impact of economic performance on well-being. The economic resilience of the country also is likely to have considerably aided the Labour Party's 2020 election victory. Covid also distracted from the 2017–2020 government's modest economic performance.

Part of the reason for the more robust performance on traditional economic indicators is likely to have been the positive government response to the Covid-19 crisis. A generous government response to stabilise the economy was aided by low fiscal debt levels and, arguably, the proximity of the election. In addition to loosening monetary policy, from late March until early June 2020, the government introduced a wage subsidy scheme for employers and the self-employed who would otherwise have had to lay off staff or reduce hours due to Covid. In addition, the government created a Covid Income Relief Payment, which offered temporary and short-term support for people who lost their jobs between March and October 2020 because of Covid. A further reason for the unexpectedly strong economic performance may simply be that the economic and well-being benefits of globalisation have been somewhat over-emphasised.

In terms of wider indicators of well-being, one important and unanticipated factor was the popularity of the Level 4 lockdown amongst many, not simply as a preventive measure, but in and of itself. The IGPS/Roy McKenzie Centre Covid-19 lockdown survey allowed people to report their experiences of the Level 4 lockdown, both positive and negative, in an open-field response. Many people mentioned the positive impact of the lockdown in freeing up time to spend with family members. Two thirds of responses were positive or mixed (43 per cent positive, 23 per cent mixed), and just over one third (35 per cent) were negative about their experiences during lockdown. Several interesting socio-demographic patterns in well-being emerged. There were few gender differences, but younger people tended to offer more positive comments and older people more negative comments, although the differences were not great. Second, New Zealand Europeans were less likely to offer positive responses than non-Māori minority ethnic groups. Māori fell in between the majority and other minorities. Third, in terms of socioeconomic status, those in the bottom two income bands were noticeably more likely to offer a negative comment, as were people without a tertiary education, suggesting that lockdown may have exacerbated pre-existing inequalities in well-being (Chapple et al. 2020).

Lifting the well-being eyes (both before and after lockdown) to issues of trust, there was strong evidence of a sustained rise in trust in the government to deal with problems, which almost certainly was reflected in economic confidence and thus resilience. Figure 18.7 reveals that, following its large rise between 2016 and 2018, the slow erosion in government trust 2018 to March 2020 was reversed during the Level 4 lockdown and largely sustained at very high levels thereafter. This rise in trust probably reflects 'a rally round the flag' phenomenon, but, regardless, is an important component of people's well-being as well as an indicator of their confidence in the future, which is critical in terms of people's employment and investment decisions.

Looking forward – the economic challenges post-election

In addition to the major challenges of coming out of Covid in an uncertain domestic and international economic environment, this majority government faces a large number of other serious challenges critical to long-term well-being and hence to their economic management. These challenges include inter-connected environmental challenges (climate change, fresh water, biodiversity), social challenges (inequality, child poverty) and economic challenges (high house prices, managing macro-policy in a low-interest environment, poor productivity performance). They will face these in a global geopolitical environment of the most profound uncertainty to be confronted since the 1930s. Many of these challenges involve thorny issues associated with the design of effective inter-generational governance mechanisms. How the government addresses these major challenges – in particular and most immediately the pressingly vexed issue of housing prices and quality – will determine the strength of its arguments for re-election in 2023 and, more long-term, its place in the political history of the country. Ultimately, the assessment of the success or failure of that effort will be for others – voters and historians – to make.

19

HOUSING AND THE SIXTH LABOUR GOVERNMENT

Brodie Fraser

Inheritance

The Sixth Labour Government (formed in coalition with New Zealand First, and confidence and supply with the Green Party of Aotearoa New Zealand) came to power in large part due to the sustained housing crisis that New Zealand continues to experience. Labour campaigned strongly on housing policies at the 2017 election, and there were high expectations and optimism for how the government would handle the housing crisis (Davison 2017; Satherley and Owen 2017). As outlined in the housing chapter of the 2017 election instalment of this series, the Fifth National Government had failed to acknowledge even the existence of the housing crisis, let alone its increasing scale (Schrader 2018).

A Roy Morgan poll released in February 2017 found that 41 per cent of participants viewed housing to be one of the most important problems facing the country (interest.co.nz 2017). Such public sentiment set the tone for the 2017 election, with housing quickly becoming one of the top election issues. Leaders' debates included a considerable amount of time spent on housing issues, and political parties released a range of housing policies in response to demand that the increasing housing crisis be addressed and resolved (Davison 2017). Following the election results and the protracted formation of government, the incoming Sixth Labour Government's Speech from the Throne, delivered by Governor-General Dame Patsy Reddy, stated housing to be one of the government's top priorities. The speech noted that 'this will be a government of aspiration. It aspires to make this a nation . . . where everyone can have decent housing' (Reddy 2017).

This chapter outlines several key developments relevant to housing policy during the 52nd Parliament, structured in a loose chronological order, outlining some of the highs and lows of the government's record. Housing is a large and often complicated policy arena comprising many parts. It is thus not possible to include every aspect of what occurred in the space over the past three years. However, this chapter gives an overview of the housing arena during the 2017–2020 period, providing an overview of the main issues (as well as a guide to additional sources).

Housing Stocktake Report

Shortly after taking office, the then Minister of Housing, Phil Twyford, commissioned a stocktake report (Johnson et al. 2018) into the state of the country's housing. The report, painting a dire picture of the housing crisis, focused on eight key areas: market renting, home ownership, new housing, state and other social housing, housing assistance, homelessness and emergency housing, security of tenure, and the social costs and benefits of housing quality. The number of households renting is increasing, and renters pay a higher proportion of their income on housing than homeowners. Furthermore, Māori and Pasifika households are more likely to rent, and rental properties are generally in worse condition than owner-occupied houses, with health implications that subsequently affect Māori and Pasifika at disproportionate rates. Security of tenure in the rental market has been declining and overall home ownership rates are decreasing. The report also noted increasing rates of homelessness, with government funding weighted towards emergency housing (see the section on homelessness later in this chapter); Housing First funding had been increased. The stocktake report outlined a number of other issues with the housing market, contributing to an understanding of New Zealand's housing crisis.

KiwiBuild

One of the first housing-related policies that the government announced was its 'KiwiBuild' programme. KiwiBuild began as an election policy which committed the government to building 100,000 affordable homes over 10 years, half of them in Auckland (Cooke 2019b). It was an aspirational policy aimed at supporting first home buyers. Popular with the public, KiwiBuild faced many setbacks, with a number of high-profile missed targets. The target for the first year of the policy was to have 1000 homes built; this was removed when it became evident that the government would struggle to reach

100 homes (Cooke 2019b). Another setback KiwiBuild faced was an employment relations case, with KiwiBuild Chief Executive Stephen Barclay initiating the dispute after he abruptly stopped working for the unit (Cooke 2019a). Employees, contractors and various stakeholders had complained about Barclay's leadership behaviour (Cooke 2019a). Eventually, KiwiBuild's problems became so numerous that Twyford was reshuffled out of the housing portfolio, with Megan Woods assuming the role (Cooke 2019c). Despite setbacks with the rolling out of the policy, the demand for KiwiBuild homes was, and remains, high: 36,000 people registered with the ballot in the first three weeks after it was opened (Cooke 2019b). Ideally, the government will be able to scale up the number of homes built in its second term, and continue to ensure that those who wish to enter the property market are able to do so.

Healthy Homes Guarantee

The Healthy Homes Guarantee Act passed in 2017, amending the Residential Tenancy Act (RTA), creating standards for heating, insulation, ventilation, moisture ingress, drainage and draught stopping, and improving the quality of housing stock (Tenancy Services 2019). The housing stock in Aotearoa has repeatedly been found to be of bad quality, which is directly linked to a number of poor health outcomes, particularly for low income, Māori, and Pacific families (Baker et al. 2013; Howden-Chapman et al. 2007, 2008; Oliver et al. 2017; Rangiwhetu et al. 2017; Shorter et al. 2018). Per the Healthy Homes Guarantee Act, private landlords must meet the standards within 90 days of any new, or renewed, tenancies by 1 July 2021; all Kāinga Ora and registered community housing houses must be compliant by 1 July 2023; and all rentals must be compliant by 1 July 2024 (Tenancy Services 2019). Despite the necessary improvements the Healthy Homes Guarantee Act has made, and will make, to the standard of houses, more is still needed to ensure that everyone lives in a warm, dry and safe home. We know that poor housing quality directly leads to poor health outcomes – which becomes a racial justice issue when, as the Housing Stocktake Report showed, Māori and Pasifika families are more likely to live in rental housing, which is of poorer quality than owner-occupied housing (Johnson et al. 2018). It is imperative, then, that the government continue to legislate to improve the building code and the overall quality of the country's houses. The Healthy Homes Guarantee Act could be a way for the government to start discussing the need to update and improve the building code, to ensure housing in Aotearoa can be as well built as possible in order to keep its inhabitants healthy and safe from the inevitable changes in weather extremes and patterns associated with increased climate change.

Kāinga Ora and HUD

Another significant element of housing policy during this government's first term was the creation of the Ministry of Housing and Urban Development (HUD) and Kāinga Ora (a Crown agency intended to transform housing and urban development). HUD was formed in late 2018, bringing together disparate functions from the Ministry of Business, Innovation and Employment (MBIE) and the Ministry of Social Development (MSD), as well as the monitoring of Kāinga Ora and Tāmaki Redevelopment Company from Treasury. HUD opened to some criticism; staff were spread across several office buildings, no permanent chief executive had been appointed, and its budget was smaller than Treasury had advised was reasonable (Cooke 2018). Kāinga Ora was formed in late 2019, bringing together Housing New Zealand, the KiwiBuild unit, and the Homes, Land, Community development subsidiary. One of the key aims of these changes was to bring together multiple government departments and agencies working in the housing and urban development area in order to have a more unified sector with clear leadership (Cooke 2018; Twyford 2019; Woods 2019).

The government received criticism for the ever-increasing social housing waiting list; Kāinga Ora's waiting list increased steadily over the government's first term, hitting new records almost every time the numbers were released (Cooke 2019d, 2019e, 2020a, 2020b, 2020c, 2021). In November 2020 the waiting list hit a new high, with 22,409 households waiting for a social housing placement. The government attributed this in part to people feeling more hopeful about getting on the waiting list since it came to power. It seems unlikely, however, that this reason alone is enough to account for the rise from 5,844 households in September 2017 to over 22,000 in November 2020 (Cooke 2020a, 2021). Kāinga Ora manages over 60,000 homes, indicating that the demand will require at least a third more housing to be either acquired or built as quickly as possible (Kāinga Ora 2020). There have also been several instances in which Kāinga Ora has made headlines due to the poor quality of some of its homes (Carroll 2020; Cook 2020; Robson 2020).

Kāinga Ora has experienced some positives: the sale of state houses has ended under this government, new construction and refurbishments of existing properties continue to be scaled up, and the agency's borrowing power has been raised. One of the earliest housing policies the new government enacted was to stop the sale of state houses that the National Government had attempted to push, a policy which had become increasingly unpopular during National's last year in government when several sales fell through as the housing crisis continued to worsen (Schrader 2018). Importantly, new construction of state housing has continued, with over 4,000 Kāinga Ora homes built since mid-2018 (HUD 2020e). A final notable change was that Kāinga Ora's borrowing power was lifted by $4 billion, allowing it more financial 'headroom' in order to increase the number of homes it is able to build and retrofit (Hickey 2020a). Overall, positive progress has indeed been made in the social housing space; however, there remains an urgent need for more housing placements so that some of Aotearoa's most precarious have warm, dry, safe homes.

Homelessness

Prior to the government's election, homelessness had become a growing public concern, with a 2016 cross-party inquiry into homelessness jointly conducted by the Labour Party, the Green Party, and the Māori Party (Labour Party et al. 2016; Little 2016). Rates of homelessness have been steadily increasing, with 41,000 New Zealanders, or nearly 0.9 per cent of the population, counted as homeless in the 2018 census (Amore 2016; Amore et al. 2020). Young people, Māori and Pasifika are all over-represented in these statistics (Amore et al. 2020). June 2020 saw over 1,000 people in Housing First, over 3,000 in transitional housing and over 9,000 seeking emergency housing special needs grants (HUD 2020c). The government has committed to addressing rising homelessness, and has increased funding for Housing First programmes to address this problem. Housing First was initially funded by the Fifth National-led Government, but the Sixth Labour-led Government increased funding for Housing First services from $16.5 million to $63.4 million in Budget 2018 (Adams 2017; Twyford 2018). The funding increase has allowed for Housing First services to be rolled out across the country (HUD 2020b). In addition, the government released a Homelessness Action Plan in early 2020, a cross-government strategy for reducing and ending homelessness in Aotearoa (Ministry of Housing and Urban Development 2020a). The plan is an important piece of work that brings together several ministries and provides a clear set of actions and accountability measures, divided into four action areas: prevention, supply, support and system enablers (HUD 2020a). This should go a long way to ensuring that the national response to homelessness is coordinated and coherent.

However, the government's record on homelessness has not been perfect. Motels are being paid millions of dollars by the government as emergency housing providers (*Stuff* 2019). These motels are often of poor quality and are not a long-term solution to housing need (Fonseka 2020a; Tso 2020). Furthermore, clients in emergency accommodation are now having to pay some of the costs themselves, which the government says is to incentivise them into transitional, private or social housing (Fonseka 2020b). However, it is questionable as to how effectively this will incentivise people to leave emergency accommodation when there is a shortage of both private and social housing available, and when we see steadily increasing rental prices in the private market.

Poverty and homelessness are intricately linked (Johnsen and Watts 2014; Nooe and Patterson 2010; Shinn 2010). In order to effectively address homelessness, we must address poverty. It will not be enough to only fund housing services; we need to be lifting people out of poverty and address rising housing costs too. The first policy change that needs to happen is the implementation of all of the Welfare Expert Advisory Group's recommendations, and as quickly as possible. This should begin with the immediate lifting of benefits by at least 40 per cent of their current rates (Welfare Expert Advisory Group 2019). It is imperative that the government acts quickly to provide a more supportive and comprehensive social safety net to those who are most precarious and at risk of experiencing homelessness. In addition to implementing the Welfare Expert Advisory Group's recommendations, the government would also do well to implement all of the recommendations from the Mental Health and Addictions Inquiry to ensure that people who struggle with poor mental health and/or addictions are able to receive the support they need (Paterson et al. 2018).

House prices and affordability

House prices and affordability have been one of the main housing issues the Labour Government has failed to adequately address. November 2020 saw house prices increase at their fastest rate in 16 years (Radio New Zealand 2020). This came during the Covid-19 pandemic, which was predicted to cause the housing market to crash. This did not eventuate due to the size of the housing market and the fact that it was the first market to be bailed out, with efforts such as the Reserve Bank removing high loan-to-value ratio lending (Hickey 2020b). In spite of predictions of crashes and rising demand for affordability, house prices (and rental prices) continue to rise. In the quarter ending 30 June 2020, the government provided $878.6 million in housing support in response to exceptionally high demand for financial support to pay for housing costs (HUD 2020d). A sixth of all property in Aotearoa is owned by investors (i.e., people who own more than 20 properties), meaning our housing market is currently serving to deepen material inequalities (Johnston 2020). Prime Minister Ardern has ruled out implementing a capital gains tax (one of many measures needed to address the housing crisis), once even blaming the public for their refusal to accept increased taxes (*1 News* 2020). This is despite the fact that prime ministers are able to implement important and useful policy even when such policy may be unpopular.

Residential Tenancy Act

In the renting domain, the government made an additional amendment to the Residential Tenancy Act (RTA) in 2020. Unlike the Healthy Homes Guarantee Act, the 2020 RTA amendment sought to make changes to the nature of renting, rather than to rental houses themselves. These changes include: limiting rent increases to once every 12 months; increasing the notice landlords need to give when evicting tenants; landlords no longer being allowed to prevent tenants from making minor changes to a property; prohibition of rental price bidding; and increased maximum Tenancy Tribunal compensation. Importantly, tenants experiencing family violence can withdraw from a tenancy without financial repercussions and only have to give two days' notice (Tenancy Services 2020). While these changes serve to give tenants slightly more power in the rental dynamic, there is much more that needs to be done in order to dampen the excessive amount of power landlords hold. Renting in Aotearoa is far from equal.

The next three years

Following a phenomenally successful 2020 election, Ardern has an historic MMP majority in Parliament and unprecedented levels of political capital, both of which have the potential to result in sweeping, positive change. The Sixth Labour Government certainly focused a lot of its energy on addressing the housing crisis throughout its first term: however, it is far from enough. Labour's second term brings with it the ability to implement policy without the potential of being slowed down by coalition partners. Nevertheless, it seems unlikely that we will see the scale of change needed to address the ongoing housing crisis in a comprehensive and long-lasting manner. One of the most notable indications of this is, as noted, the Prime Minister ruling out implementing a capital gains tax, despite research showing support for the proposal (Dann 2019; Small 2020). As over half of Labour's 2017–2020 caucus own more than one house (Wevers 2020), some may perhaps be hesitant to jeopardise their pecuniary interests.

The 2020 Speech from the Throne once again noted that addressing the housing crisis would be a priority for the government (Reddy 2020). If it is truly to address the crisis, a wide range of policy initiatives will need to be taken. Fortunately for Labour, there are a number of different policy changes to choose from. For low-income households and those most in need, the government could: refurbish all state housing and ensure all new houses meet appropriate requirements; have fully accessible universal design, for people with varying levels of accessibility needs; increase the proportion of the housing stock which is state and community housing to at least 25 per cent of the total; and implement the Welfare Expert Advisory Group's recommendations, to ensure that beneficiaries are able to better afford housing and related costs.

For renters, changes might include: implementing short- or medium-term rental caps; extending the Covid-19 related temporary halt to rental price increases; and legislating further amendments to the RTA in order to increase the privacy, rights and agency of renters, to enable renters to live long-term in warm, dry, affordable houses, dwellings that feel like home. It would be beneficial to many if 'renting for life' were a stable, affordable option for those not aspiring to home ownership.

We could look to international examples where renting for life is the norm and consider the possibility of the state and/or iwi (if they so wish) owning the majority of rental housing. Renters could then have long-term security of tenure. This would reduce residential mobility, which has been shown to adversely impact on a range of outcomes, especially for children (Nathan et al. 2019). The current model of private rentals with one-year tenancies is clearly not working; rents are ever-increasing, properties are poorly maintained and households that rent are forced to move frequently. We need to dream bigger when it comes to reforming the rental market; the recent RTA amendments, while useful, seem laughably minor – allowing tenants to put a nail into a wall without needing landlord permission does little to improve their health and well-being. We can do better for renters. It is important that the housing market take into account those not seeking home ownership; New Zealand has a long-standing obsession with everyone owning a home and 'getting on the property ladder'. However, many do not wish to own a home, merely to have long-term stability and the ability to make a house feel like a home (e.g., through painting walls or making a garden, which, even if given permission, many renters do not do as they do not wish to spend their money on their landlord's property if they know they are going to have to pack up and move in a year).

Other much needed changes include immediate strengthening of the building code to match other similar climates internationally – see Hindley (2020) for a comparison of the climates and building codes of Dunedin and Dublin – with near immediate effect (where possible) for new homes, and timely retrofits for existing dwellings. Other changes, too, could include the implementation of a full capital gains tax, or changes to the bright-line test (instituted in 2015, whereby investment properties sold within two years of purchase could be taxed), making it applicable to a greater number of people.[1] Finally, policies to incentivise first home *building* over first home *buying* could, potentially, help to increase the available housing stock. These are only some of the many housing-related policies which need to be considered (and, of course, implemented) in order to more genuinely address the housing crisis.

The Sixth Labour-led Government spent much of its first term attempting to alleviate the housing crisis, with limited success. Now in its second term, with a majority in Parliament, Labour has the ability to act in a swift and strong manner to enact a wide range of measures in addressing a crisis of considerable (and accelerating) severity. While the Labour Government has certainly not denied the existence of the housing crisis, as the National Government did before it, it still has a long way to go in rectifying the current situation. It should be possible to multi-task – to combat the housing crisis as well as the Covid-19 pandemic – and move beyond slogans, with the mantra 'to build better' bringing meaningful, positive change, so that – in the words of the government's first initial statement of policy, the 2017 Speech from the Throne – 'everyone can have decent housing'.

20

THE CHRISTCHURCH SHOOTING AND THE 2020 NEW ZEALAND ELECTION

Ayca Arkilic

This chapter involves a brief description of the 2019 Christchurch terrorist attacks; Prime Minister Jacinda Ardern's, the Labour government's, and the New Zealand society's response to the atrocity; and New Zealand's relations with Muslims at home and abroad in the aftermath of the deadly shooting. It also looks at the effects of the mass murder on the country's counter-terrorism strategy and white supremacist violence, as well as the implications of the 2020 New Zealand election for the Muslim community in New Zealand. The chapter concludes with a section on the media coverage of the 2020 New Zealand election in the Muslim world.

The day New Zealand changed forever: The 2019 Christchurch shooting

On 15 March 2019, a 28-year-old white supremacist from Australia arrived at the Al-Noor Mosque in central Christchurch during Friday prayers. An elderly Afghan man who greeted the terrorist with the words, 'Hello, Brother', at the mosque entrance was one of the first to be shot. After killing his victim, the terrorist walked in and opened fire on some 190 innocent worshippers while live-streaming the massacre on social media. He then drove to the Linwood Islamic Centre, another mosque five kilometres east of the Al-Noor Mosque, to continue his fatal rampage. The consecutive attacks killed 51 people and injured 40, including women and children. They were the deadliest ever to take place in New Zealand, one of the most peaceful countries in the world (Brown 2020). Prior to the slaughter, the terrorist had published a 74-page manifesto entitled 'The Great Replacement', citing the growing Muslim population and 'white genocide' as his main motivations (Bogost 2019).

The manifesto also included hateful references to Turkey, its President Recep Tayyip Erdoğan, and the Turkish diaspora. According to analysts, this is because 'Turkey is synonymous with Islam in the eyes of Western ultra-nationalists' and the terrorist sought to 'drive a wedge' between the European members of NATO and Turkey, also an important NATO member (Sahin 2019).

The twin attacks sent shock waves across the country and the rest of the world, given the scale of the bloodshed and the clear targeting of Muslim worshippers, some of whom were foreign nationals. Two days after the incident, a high-level diplomatic delegation led by Turkish Vice President Fuat Oktay and Foreign Minister Mevlüt Çavuşoğlu met in Christchurch with then Deputy Prime Minister and Minister of Foreign Affairs Winston Peters (Cheng 2019). Although the meeting had been amicable, relations between New Zealand and Turkey were strained shortly after when Turkish President Erdoğan showed footage of the massacre at electoral rallies to garner support for his Justice and Development Party prior to the 31 March 2019 local Turkish elections. In addressing New Zealanders, Erdoğan shouted at one of these rallies:

> Your grandparents came [and] some of them returned in coffins. If you come as well, like your grandfathers, be sure that you will be gone like your grandfathers . . . The enemies of Muslims have shown that they continue to hate us . . . They are testing us from 16,500 kilometres away, from New Zealand, with the messages they are giving from there. This is not an individual attack, it is organised.

Following these inflammatory remarks, Winston Peters left New Zealand to attend an emergency Organisation of Islamic Cooperation meeting hosted by Turkish officials in Istanbul. 'They asked me to come and I'm going to go. I certainly intend to put New Zealand's record as being an innocent party to an act of a foreigner in our country,' Peters announced before his departure (Young and Trevett 2019). Jacinda Ardern clarified that the main motivation behind Peters' trip was not to criticise Erdoğan's display of the video but to demonstrate that New Zealand is not a place that bolsters white supremacist movements. Subsequently she announced that, after a successful meeting, Erdoğan's rhetoric had changed (Walls 2019). At the meeting, Turkey's Minister of Foreign Affairs, Çavuşoğlu, thanked New Zealand's authorities for their sensitivity towards Muslims and conveyed the message that Turkey is in solidarity with New Zealand (Turkish Ministry of Foreign Affairs 2019).

The United Arab Emirates also sent a delegation to New Zealand to visit the two mosques and to console the victims' families (*The Gulf News* 2019). Other countries with a significant Muslim population, including Saudi Arabia, Kuwait, Oman, Jordan, Egypt, Morocco, Indonesia, Malaysia, Afghanistan, Pakistan and Bangladesh, similarly condemned the atrocity, extending their sympathies and condolences to the victims, their families and New Zealand society. Iran's Foreign Ministry condemned the mosque attacks as 'brutal' and 'inhuman' and urged New Zealand authorities to find the perpetrators behind the massacre, its Minister of Foreign Affairs, Javad Zarif, stating that 'the West must end its "hypocrisy" of demonizing Muslims under the pretext of defending freedom of expression' (*Tehran Times* 2019). The country's leading international daily, *Tehran Times*, labelled the attacks as 'white supremacist terrorism' and indicated that 'how the counter-terrorism and law-enforcement authorities in New Zealand missed the warning is incredibly astonishing' (Mehdi 2019). The Al-Azhar Mosque and the Coptic Church in Egypt, the Muslim World League, the Arab League and the United Nations were among the institutions issuing an official statement to express their deepest sorrow and condemnation at the abhorrent attacks (*Arab News* 2019).

Jacinda Ardern immediately called out the killings as an act of terrorism and refused to use the terrorist's name. 'Many of those who will have been directly affected by this shooting may be migrants to New Zealand; they may even be refugees here. They have chosen to make New Zealand their home, and it is their home. They are us,' she said. 'The person who has perpetuated this violence against us is not. They have no place in New Zealand. There is no place in New Zealand for such acts of extreme and unprecedented violence, which it is clear this act was' (*The Guardian* 2019). 'One of his goals . . . was that he sought notoriety and we will absolutely deny him that,' she continued. Ardern wore a hijab while comforting Muslim mourners, broadcasted the Islamic call to prayer (adhan) on national television and radio, and called for a global struggle to root out racism (*BBC* 2019). Moreover, she advised that survivors would be eligible to benefit from the government's funeral grants and financial assistance (Kuruvilla 2019).

Prime Minister Ardern's warmth resonated well with Muslims all around the world. An image of her hugging a Muslim woman was projected onto the world's tallest building, the Burj Khalifa, in Dubai. Sharing the image of the tower on his Twitter account, Sheikh Mohammed bin Rashid Al Maktoum of the United Arab Emirates thanked Ardern for her 'sincere empathy and support that has won the respect of 1.5 billion Muslims' (Satherley 2019). Other Muslim leaders and institutions also praised the prime minister for her strong leadership. The Muslim World League announced that they have full 'confidence in the New Zealand Government to bring those involved in this crime to justice and to prosecute them as terrorists' (*Arab News* 2019). Sadiq Khan, the mayor of London, tweeted a picture of Ardern hugging a Muslim woman and praised her inclusivity. Negar Mortazavi, a prominent Iranian-American columnist and the host of the Iran Podcast, wrote that donning a hijab was 'a sign of respect' (Fifield 2019).

In a similar vein, in an opinion piece written a year after the wicked act, Turkish President Erdoğan expressed his gratitude to Ardern:

> In the aftermath of the Christchurch massacre, the West has certain responsibilities. Western societies and governments must reject the normalization of racism, xenophobia and Islamophobia, which has been on the rise in recent years . . . Finally, all Western leaders must learn from the courage, leadership and sincerity of New Zealand's prime minister, Jacinda Ardern, to embrace Muslims living in their respective countries (Erdoğan 2020).

Representatives of the Muslim Public Affairs Council and the Muslim Advocates in the USA also maintained that 'Ardern has done an "exceptional job" and is demonstrating how a politician should lead a country after such a horrific attack' with her 'honest, compassionate, and strong response' (Kuruvilla 2019). Arabic media sources, such as the London-based Saudi newspaper *Asharq al-Awsat*, also suggested that, with this unfortunate event, 'the world recognised New Zealand like a gift hidden in a disaster' (Utaybi 2019 cited in Öztürk 2019, p. 37). The Qatar-based international news channel, *Al Jazeera*, compared her empathetic leadership to the anti-Muslim rhetoric of other world leaders, such as France's Marine Le Pen and US President Donald Trump, and lauded her for clarifying that 'Islam is neither the "other" nor the "invader". Islam is New Zealand and those adhering to it, departed or alive, are at home in this country' (Beydoun 2019).

New Zealanders equally responded to the violent attacks with displays of love and compassion. A day after the atrocity, a Baptist church in Auckland opened its doors to Muslims, and Catholic bishops published a statement, emphasising the positive relationships they have with the Muslim community. Synagogues in the country closed on Shabbat for the first time in their history (Rohrlich 2019). The New Zealand Māori Council also expressed solidarity by calling for a nationwide haka on 22 March 2019 (Fitzgerald 2019). In the wake of the killings, a campaign was set up to encourage women across New Zealand to wear a hijab: 'We are with you, we want you to feel at home on your own streets, we love, support, and respect you,' the initiator of the campaign asserted (Paul and Birsel 2019). While some Muslims found the campaign controversial and interpreted it as a sign of 'cheap tokenism' and distraction from the root causes of 'white supremacy, systematic racism, Orientalism and bigotry', most Muslim groups, such as the Islamic Women's Council of New Zealand and the New Zealand Muslim Association, expressed their gratitude to the people of New Zealand for masterminding and participating in the campaign (Paul and Birsel 2019). The 2019 New Zealand Attitudes and Values Study, which compared the attitudes of New Zealanders before and after the attacks, also found that in the immediate days after the incident, warmth towards Muslims increased among both left-wing/liberal and right-wing/conservative individuals. However, attitudes towards Muslims among conservatives soon reverted back to pre-attack levels whereas liberals sustained their increased level of positive attitudes for a longer period (Shanaah et al. 2021, p. 15).

Counter-terrorism measures in the aftermath of the Christchurch shooting and the 2020 New Zealand election

The Labour-led government was quick to undertake significant counter-terrorism measures. Immediately after the heinous shooting, the New Zealand police shut down all mosques in the country until further notice and placed security at their gates (*Stuff* 2019). In addition, New Zealand's terrorism threat level went from low to high, all flights departing from Christchurch were cancelled (Cooke and Kirk 2019), and security checks were heightened at Parliament (Radio New Zealand 2019a). Prime Minister Ardern announced the prohibition of the sale of all military-style semi-automatic and assault rifles under stricter gun laws only six days after the attacks: 'On 15 March our history changed forever. Now, our laws will too. We are announcing action today on behalf of all New Zealanders to strengthen our gun laws and make our country a safer place,' Ardern declared (New Zealand Government 2019a). Ten days after the incident, the government also publicised the establishment of the Royal Commission of Inquiry into the Terrorist Attack in Christchurch Masjidain [mosques] on 15 March 2019 to scrutinise and report on 'the actions of the individual, the actions of relevant Public sector agencies and any changes that could prevent such terrorist attacks in the future' (Royal Commission of Inquiry 2020).

On 10 April 2019, the Arms (Prohibited Firearms, Magazines, and Parts) Amendment Act passed with a vote of 119–1. The Act, which received royal assent the following day, banned semi-automatic firearms and magazines, as well as parts that could be used to assemble prohibited firearms (New Zealand Government 2019b). As part of the government's counter-terrorism measures, a six-month gun buy-back scheme took place in 2019, which encouraged gun owners to return their prohibited firearms to 605 collection points across the country. According to New Zealand Police (2020), a total of 34,185 hand-ins were completed, with 57,716 firearms (52,597 as buy-back and 5,119 under amnesty) and 205,209 parts (198,642 as buy-back and 6,567 under amnesty) being collected. A second measure, the Arms Legislation Act, passed its final reading in Parliament on 18 June 2020, receiving royal assent on 24 June. The Act created a national gun registry to track how many firearms were in legal circulation (and who buys and sells them); reduced the length of a firearms licence from ten to five years for first-time licence holders and those who had previously had their licence revoked or allowed it to expire; introduced harsher penalties for possessing an illegal firearm; and banned further 'high-risk firearms', such as pistol-length semi-automatic rifles (New Zealand Government 2020; Devlin 2020).

In November 2020, the Royal Commission of Inquiry submitted an 800-page report entitled *Ko tō tātou kāinga tēnei* ('This is our home') to emphasise New Zealand's inclusive and welcoming identity. The report was presented to the public in December 2020. Focusing mainly on the period between 2016 and 2019, the report pointed out that 'the primary, but not exclusive, focus of the counter-terrorism resources was on what was seen as the presenting threat of Islamist extremist terrorism' while noting that Muslims in the country had long experienced racism, discrimination, hate speech and hate crime. The report acknowledged the negative consequences of secrecy about counter-terrorism measures as well as 'failings' within the firearms licensing system and the laws under which the security agencies operate. Some of the proposed policy recommendations included the formation of a Ministry of Ethnic Communities, new anti-terror and hate speech legislation, a new security and intelligence agency, and increased funding for New Zealand–specific counter-terrorism strategies (Royal Commission of Inquiry 2020; Sullivan 2020).

The government also announced a second three-month gun buy-back scheme that took place between February and May 2021 (Small and Fleming 2021). While New Zealand does not have the death penalty as a form of punishment, in August 2020 the white supremacist who committed the Christchurch terrorist shooting became the first person in New Zealand to be convicted of terrorism and to be sentenced to life in prison without parole (Gillespie 2020). Additionally, the government has undertaken an extensive consultation and outreach process, provided better trauma support for the victims, initiated an international fight against online extremism through the 'Christchurch Call', and worked on a new strategy with police to protect people in crowded places (Gillespie 2021). However, despite such a strong response from the New Zealand government, white supremacy is still present in the country (Gilbert and Elley 2020; Spoonley 2020; Arkilic 2020a) and far-right fringe parties are entering into New Zealand politics as never before (O'Brien 2020). In comparing attitudes towards Muslims with attitudes towards other religious groups in New Zealand, including Hindus, Buddhists, Christians and Jews, as well as atheists, scholars have also identified that there is a substantially greater perceived threat and negativity towards Muslims compared with other groups and that, in particular, older people, Pākehā (New Zealanders of European descent), and those with a more right-wing stance report greater feelings of threat and negativity with respect to Muslims (Greaves et al. 2020).

Islam is one of New Zealand's fastest-growing religions (Onnudottir et al. 2013; Drury 2016; Arkilic 2020b), which is a concern for some xenophobic groups. A Muslim presence in the country is by no means a novel occurrence, however. In 1769 a short visit by a French ship to Northland brought the first Muslims, two Indian sailors, to New Zealand

(Drury 2015). The 1874 census recorded 17 'Mahometans', as Muslims were then called, most of whom were Chinese immigrants. By 1966, 551 Muslims from different parts of the world were living in New Zealand (Pratt 2010). Over the past few decades the Muslim population has increased exponentially. While there were about 6,000 Muslims in 1991, their numbers reached 46,146 in 2013 (Foroutan 2017). According to the 2018 census, the Muslim population stood at 60,621, forming the third largest religious group in New Zealand (Statistics New Zealand 2018). This is a striking rise, particularly given that at the same time the number of people identifying with Christianity fell by 10 per cent and the percentage of people who identified as having 'no religion' rose by around 6 per cent (Statistics New Zealand 2013; Statistics New Zealand 2018).

While early immigrants formed the majority of the country's Muslim community, both Pākehā and Māori converts have been identified from the 1960s onwards, beginning to take part in Muslim organisational life from the 1970s (Drury 2016). In the early 2000s there were between 300 and 500 converts across the country, many of whom chose Islam due to marriage or other close personal contact with Muslims (Kolig 2003; Shepard 2006). There is no official data on current numbers of converts. However, the 2018 census gave the numbers of Muslims: 39,996 from Asia; 15,780 from the Middle East, Latin America or Africa; 3,693 from Europe; 1,536 from the Pacific; and 1,116 Māori (Statistics New Zealand 2018). Islam has become an increasingly popular religion particularly among Māori. Māori Muslims form a small yet rapidly growing community given that there were only 99 Muslims of Māori ethnicity recorded in 1991 (Keber 2003).

Islam's appeal to New Zealanders increased after the Christchurch attacks. According to the International Muslim Association of New Zealand, after the fatal event three to five people a day were converting at a Wellington mosque (Hart 2019). The mosque shooting also encouraged some prominent Muslims to stand for election for the first time. For example, in 2019, the Imam of the Al-Noor Mosque, Gamal Fouda, and a well-known Muslim community advocate, Zahra Hussaini, both affiliated with the Labour Party, stood in Christchurch's city council and community board elections, a decision motivated by the March 15 shooting spree (Foon 2019; Radio New Zealand 2019b). Finally, before the Christchurch terror attack, news stories on Islam and Muslims in the New Zealand media tended to replicate 'the negative othering rhetoric' of Western media, but since 15 March 2019 the New Zealand press has embraced a more inclusive and positive narrative with respect to Islam and Muslims (Rahman 2020).

Yet Muslim representatives suggest that the threat of white supremacist violence has risen after the Christchurch attacks. For example, Ikhlaq Kashkari, the head of the New Zealand Muslim Association, reported shortly after the first anniversary of the mass murder that 'we're constantly getting messages of hate . . . There was a pause, obviously, after 15 March . . . Lately it's got quite bad. I assume it's because of the anniversary.' In a similar vein, Anjum Rahman, the spokesperson of the Islamic Women's Council of New Zealand and the founder of the Inclusive Aotearoa Collective Tāhono, pointed out that the attacks have empowered some extremists. Rahman's message needs to be taken seriously, given that she and her colleagues had met with officials prior to the Christchurch massacre to voice their concerns over discrimination, increasing levels of hate, and a more organised far-right in New Zealand. A study conducted by the University of Auckland has also found that anti-Muslim hate crimes and Islamophobic abuse have increased dramatically since the March 15 terrorist attacks (Wilson and Shastri 2020).

Security Intelligence Service officials have confirmed that several young men affiliated with white supremacist, neo-Nazi, and identitarian movements, such as the Dominion Movement and Action Zealandia, have been investigated or arrested and that the threat continues (Manch 2020), with 60 to 70 groups and 150 to 300 core right-wing activists in New Zealand (Spoonley 2020). Given New Zealand's small population, these are not trivial numbers. Experts suggest that New Zealand's terrorist list needs to be expanded. While the list includes international terror groups, such as Al-Shabaab, the IRA, and ISIL Sinai, the only white supremacist on the list is the Christchurch assassin (Scotcher 2021).

As Dr Rawiri Taonui explains, while Muslim immigrants appear to be the main target of xenophobic groups today, white supremacy dates back to the slave trade and European colonisation, which marginalised Māori. Suppression of Māori culture and language, coupled with war and land confiscations, culminated in an inter-generational cycle of poverty. Poor housing, education and health, as well as disproportionate levels of Māori incarceration, persist to this day. Taonui explains that during the 19th and early 20th centuries, racists attacked Chinese, Indian and Jewish immigrants. Chinese immigrants had to pay a poll tax to enter the country as a result of the Chinese Immigrants Act 1881 (not repealed until 1944). New Zealand citizenship was not introduced until 1948 (New Zealand residents having been 'British subjects'), with Chinese and Indian individuals lacking citizenship rights until 1952. New Zealand's second most-populous city, Christchurch, has been a particular hotbed for racism, generating a greater number of white racist groups since the 1960s than elsewhere in the country. Although it is hard to measure the full extent of white racist violence as New Zealand does not record hate-crime data, media stories and various reports indicate that Christchurch is still home to the highest number of racist violence and harassment incidents (Taonui 2019). Yet racism remains a problem not just in Christchurch but in all New Zealand communities and provincial towns, and even small white supremacist groups need to be monitored closely (cited in Keith 2019).

Jacinda Ardern's landslide victory in the 2020 New Zealand general election is a positive development for the protection of Muslim minority rights and New Zealand's fight against white supremacist terrorism. The 2020 election was characterised by an unprecedented 'historic shift' and 'tilt to the left', as 'National Party leaders were decimated in their strongholds by young Labour candidates who appealed to voters with progressive, democratic messages, and highlighted the party's success in beating coronavirus' (*Al Jazeera* 2020). There is no data on Muslim voting behaviour in New Zealand. For example, the New Zealand Election Study, which documents political behaviour in New Zealand elections, does not provide any information on the Muslim electorate due to the small sample of Muslims. However, one can suggest that, following the national trend, Muslim voters were likely increasingly drawn to the Labour Party due to Ardern's compassionate leadership, effective counter-terrorism measures, and 'go hard and go early' approach to the pandemic. In commenting on the election results, the Imam of the Al-Noor Mosque, Gamal Fouda, argued that:

> It is the policy from Jacinda Ardern and how she was able to handle the pandemic, she was able to keep the country safe. It was also the strong support for the community after March 15, which has led to us being on the world stage. We are leading and we want to continue under this leadership of Jacinda Ardern (*Star News* 2020).

Fouda now serves on Christchurch City Council's Riccarton Community Board (Christchurch City Council 2021).

With the 2020 election, the New Zealand Parliament has also become more diverse than ever in terms of the representation of international, Indigenous, women, and LGBTQIA+ politicians. Labour MP Ibrahim Omer became the first African and second Muslim MP elected to the Parliament in this election round. Omer followed in the footsteps of Labour MP Ashraf Choudhary, born in Pakistan, who had been elected as the country's first South Asian and Muslim MP in 2002 (New Zealand Parliament 2011) and had made parliamentary history by deciding to swear allegiance on the Qur'an instead of the Bible, a move that broke a 'centuries-old tradition', according to New Zealand First leader, Winston Peters (*The Times of India* 2002). In November 2020, the Islamicity Foundation's Islamicity Index ranked New Zealand as the 'most Islamic country in the world' for the second year in a row based on its adherence to Islamic principles (set forth in the Qur'an) such as integrity, consensus, religious freedoms, human rights and equality (Islamicity Foundation 2020).

The defeat of New Zealand First, a nationalist and populist party that had previously spread anti-migrant messages and campaigned on reducing immigration, was another milestone in the 2020 election. However, the rise of far-right movements and parties across the world continues to be a serious threat for the country because New Zealand's white supremacist community is closely linked to far-right networks in other countries, facilitated by internet chat rooms and social media platforms (Cohen 2019). While New Zealand's anti-terrorism efforts should not be underestimated, it is important to remember that white supremacist violence can only be eradicated with closer surveillance and strong global commitment and collaboration.

Media coverage of the 2020 New Zealand election in the Muslim world

The 2020 New Zealand election was covered extensively in the Muslim community. Ahead of the election Jacinda Ardern was presented as the favourite. For example, Turkey's state-run news agency, *Anadolu Ajansı*, stated that Ardern's 'handling of the COVID-19 situation has pushed up her chances to retain the top executive seat. Besides, her handling of the March 2019 Christchurch tragedy has won her acclaim in the Muslim community' (Ul Khaliq 2020). However, a columnist affiliated with another Turkish state-run news channel, *TRT World*, questioned whether Ardern is 'really the inclusive leader she's been made out to be', citing her 2017 power-sharing agreement with New Zealand First leader Winston Peters, who had previously promoted restrictive immigration policies, complained about an 'Asian invasion', and announced that 'New Zealand has never been a nation of Islamic immigrants' and that 'moderate and militant [Muslims] fit hand and glove everywhere they exist' in the wake of the 2005 London subway bombings. The columnist also criticised 'Ardern's 2017 election campaign, which included a proposal to cut net migration by 20,000 to 30,000 people during its three-year term' (Girijashanker 2019).

In the run-up to the election, *Al Jazeera* cited 'Jacindamania' and positioned Ardern as the 'antithesis of Donald Trump'. While also discussing some of Ardern's wrong moves during the pandemic and in relation to the country's escalating housing crisis, *Al Jazeera* assessed that Ardern was still 'on track' for her second term (Borissenko 2020).

Once her electoral victory was confirmed, Turkish media outlets, such as *Anadolu Ajansı* and *Hürriyet*, attributed Ardern's success to her sensible decisions in the aftermath of the outbreak of the Covid-19 pandemic and the Christchurch shooting. Turkish media also drew attention to Ardern's progressive leadership, young age, motherhood and special role as the third female prime minister of the country. Furthermore, Ardern was presented as a leader giving importance to minority perspectives, as evidenced by her use of Māori language in her 2020 election-night victory speech (Aytekin and Sakar 2020; *Hürriyet* 2020) and by her appointment of Nanaia Mahuta as the country's first female Māori Minister of Foreign Affairs (*Sabah* 2020). Another media channel, *CNN Türk*, echoed these remarks:

> Ardern started her victory speech in the country's Indigenous language . . . She is a leader appreciated by her own country and the world. She has become a symbol of peace after she condemned the terrorist attack, made the call to [Islamic] prayer on national television, and wore a headscarf in commemorative ceremonies (*CNN Türk* 2020).

Journalists from Egypt's most-widely circulated daily newspaper, *Al-Ahram*, similarly extolled Ardern and wrote that:

> a new feminine model of political leadership is promising to transform traditional models of power and authority . . . with its emphasis on the values of care, empathy and inclusion, and on issues such as equality, climate-change and universal healthcare . . . This model might be our only hope for a brighter future for our societies and our planet (Shehata 2020).

Indonesia, which hosts the world's largest Muslim population, covered the election extensively as well. Its daily English-language newspaper, *The Jakarta Post*, published numerous positive news articles about Ardern's victory and charisma (see, for example, Sands 2020).

According to *Al Jazeera*, the electoral outcome was Ardern's reward for 'a decisive response to COVID-19' and for her 'leadership through a series of extraordinary events that shaped her first three-year term: the gunman's massacre of 51 worshippers at two Christchurch mosques and the eruption of the White Island volcano, which killed 21'. However, it warned that despite being an international champion of progressive values, such as women's rights and social justice, Ardern is criticised for not being 'transformational' at home. *Al Jazeera* cautioned that she might suffer from an economic hangover from the pandemic, an economic recession due to severe lockdowns, a worsening housing crisis and growing inequality between New Zealand's haves and have-nots (*Al Jazeera* 2020).

Conclusion

This chapter discussed the Christchurch shooting and the 2020 election in terms of domestic and international effects. It showed that the country's response to the massacre has been compassionate and effective, as evidenced by Prime Minister Ardern's and New Zealand society's empathetic response, heightened security, the firearms legislation, and the creation of a Royal Commission of Inquiry into the Christchurch attacks. The government also initiated an extensive consultation and outreach process, provided trauma and financial support for the victims, initiated an international fight against online extremism through the 'Christchurch Call', and embarked on a new strategy with police to protect people in crowded places. Jacinda Ardern's charismatic leadership and strong counter-terrorism measures strengthened New Zealand's relations with Muslims both at home and abroad and boosted its international reputation. As analysis of media sources shows, Muslim-majority countries in the Middle East and Asia greeted the prime minister's success in the 2020 elections with delight. At the same time they noted, as do many New Zealanders, that significant challenges lie ahead, ranging from economic and quality-of-life issues to the ongoing threat of white supremacist terrorism, with many Muslims still the target of racism, discrimination and hate speech. How these varied challenges are dealt with will play a large part in defining the long-term legacy of the prime minister and her government.

21

NEW ZEALAND'S FOREIGN AND DEFENCE POLICY, 2017–2020

Robert Ayson

At about 11 o'clock on the night of the 2020 general election, Jacinda Ardern acknowledged the Labour Party's sweeping victory which had just occurred under her leadership. Imagine if she had immediately left her joyful supporters to step into a time machine conveniently hidden backstage. Walking out of that contraption into coalition negotiations three years earlier with Winston Peters, Ardern would have known about New Zealand First's political obliteration at the end of her first term in office. Is there any doubt that she would have given Peters and his colleagues less than they were demanding in 2017, knowing how little Labour would need them in three years' time?

A firmer hand from Labour would have reduced New Zealand First's healthy array of seats around the Cabinet table. Most likely this would have changed the role of one or both of two leading ministers, foreign affairs (Winston Peters) and defence (Ron Mark). Back in 2017 it was almost inevitable that New Zealand First would get one of these outward-looking portfolios. Peters had been foreign minister before and, as deputy prime minister, needed a senior role to accommodate his standing. A job that required him frequently to be offshore would not be a bad thing. Mark, a former soldier who in the run up to the election insisted that New Zealand's defence spending needed doubling, had been waiting for the minister of defence spot for much of his political career. So there was a real logic in both appointments. But in giving this portfolio pair to New Zealand First, Ardern and Labour subcontracted New Zealand's external affairs policy to a party which did not always share its more liberal and optimistic international philosophy. As the forthcoming analysis suggests, this choice would influence New Zealand's posture on global issues, and especially its approach to a rising China.

From an early wobble to growing confidence

The record of New Zealand defence and foreign policy in the 2017–2010 period is sometimes as much about these two New Zealand First personalities as it is about the international challenges that New Zealand would encounter. Their preferences were on display from the outset. In the case of Winston Peters, it was not an especially smooth start because his bugbear issue, relations with Russia, came up early. Lurking in the 2017 coalition agreement was a commitment insisted on by New Zealand First for the new government to begin negotiations on a Free Trade Agreement with Moscow and its Eurasian partners. This was odd because by that stage Putin's Russia had achieved full pariah status amongst New Zealand's traditional security partners for its brazen hybrid war campaign against Ukraine. The source of Peters' warmth towards the former superpower remains unclear, but it definitely influenced the Ardern government's response to the dramatic poisoning in the United Kingdom of two Russian expatriates, an act widely attributed to Putin's intelligence services. Rather than join its Five Eyes partners (an intelligence-sharing arrangement with the United States, Canada and Australia, as well as the UK itself) in blaming Russia, New Zealand stayed on the sidelines, with Peters throwing around some fairly unconvincing doubts about the need to hold Moscow to account (Ayson 2020).

It would take months for the Ardern government to clarify its position on Russia (and move closer to the positions of its leading security partners in so doing). But on China, another authoritarian power challenging Western influence, Wellington's response was less jarring. Early on in the new government's term Peters spoke to the Lowy Institute for International Policy in Sydney, cementing the importance of leading ally Australia in New Zealand's international outlook (Peters 2018a). His main subject was the Pacific Reset – a stepping up in New Zealand's commitment to its immediate region, for which Australia was the most obvious partner. This was headlined by a significant boost in New Zealand's aid spending in the Pacific, which in turn constituted the main portion of the extra money that Peters had secured from Cabinet to bolster the Ministry of Foreign Affairs and Trade. And what had this to do with China? In his Sydney address, and in others later on, the foreign minister argued that the influence of New Zealand and its traditional (i.e., Western) partners in the Pacific was declining, with new players becoming more significant. It was time to step up and reverse that trend. And the main source of the challenge, indicated Peters, was Beijing's increasing influence.

New Zealand's doubts about China's rise had been growing before Ardern and Peters joined forces to become the new coalition government. During the latter years of John Key's long premiership, and into the months when Bill English briefly was prime minister, National's foreign and defence ministers had become more willing to raise concerns about China's posture in the South China Sea and elsewhere (Capie 2016). But Peters brought added concerns to his office, including questions about China's 'Belt and Road' initiative. He had long been a supporter of US preponderance in Asia and took almost a pre-ANZUS crisis view of America's role in the balance of regional power. Among the members of the new Cabinet, this made Peters especially receptive to the concerns about China's behaviour which had been growing within New Zealand's national security community (and amongst its counterparts in Canberra and Washington).

But Peters did not set New Zealand's foreign policy course on his own; Ardern also had something to say. On China, the most crucial question in New Zealand's contemporary foreign policy, the prime minister and foreign minister almost created a 'good cop–bad cop' routine. Jacinda Ardern's version of New Zealand's China policy emphasised optimism and opportunity rather than risk and threat. In her inaugural prime ministerial foreign policy address, delivered in Wellington, she explained that New Zealand saw China as a partner in two important areas: trade and climate change (Ardern 2018a). This was also, indirectly, a contrast with what was going on in Washington as Donald Trump's presidency gathered steam. The 45th President saw global trade as a drain on America's greatness and he eschewed the sorts of deals like the Trans-Pacific Partnership that New Zealand had advocated. And Trump had pulled the United States out of the Paris climate change accord.

On more than one occasion Ardern would take a dim public view of Trump's xenophobia and his assaults on international cooperation. In September 2018, for example, she delivered a widely reported defence of multilateralism at the United Nations (Ardern 2018b). While not mentioning the 45th President by name, the direction of her words was clear. In the following year, when Trump called on four Democratic congresswomen of colour to go home (even though they were US citizens), Ardern voiced her disagreement in no uncertain terms (Molyneux and

Wilkins 2019). This time the rebuke was even more important given New Zealand's recent experience of white nationalist terrorism in the Christchurch mosque shootings.

In their aftermath, it was none other than Peters who was dispatched to Muslim capitals to reinforce the values of openness and tolerance that the prime minister wanted to be seen at the forefront of New Zealand's response to this tragedy. But off his own bat the foreign minister had been speaking in Washington with a more familiar agenda: to encourage the United States to check China's growing power in the Pacific (Peters 2018b). This was one occasion when the geopolitical temperatures being fanned by the foreign minister grew too hot for the prime minister. Ardern insisted that her government was not trying to pick sides in the US–China tussle (Smellie 2018).

This bad cop–good cop routine raised questions about quite what New Zealand's China (and China–US) stance really was. At the same time it created some necessary wriggle room for New Zealand. Similarly, the prime minister could take issue with the most divisive American president in recent memory without capsizing the NZ–US bilateral relationship, as officials in Wellington and Washington worked behind the scenes to keep the functional aspects functioning.

The Australia factor

If the foregoing assessment encourages the view that the entirety of New Zealand's foreign policy consists of creating a comfortable place between the United States and China, that would be a disservice to the complexity of the real situation. Unlike some Asia–Pacific countries, New Zealand does not have two great powers on its radar screen, but three. Australia may be a medium power in many such contexts, but for New Zealand its importance is much larger. And in Ardern's first term, developing tensions in trans-Tasman relations were perhaps the most complicated of all of the developments in New Zealand's interactions with the world.

Soon after she became prime minister, Ardern travelled to Canberra to affirm the unique importance of Australia in New Zealand's international relations. But she took with her the voting public's expectations that differences over the treatment of migrants would be raised with her Australian counterparts (Yaxley 2018). This would become a familiar and largely frustrating exercise. It was not just that Australia's Liberal–National coalition government continued to rebuff New Zealand's offers to receive some of the asylum seekers stuck in Australia's offshore facilities. Much more problematic was Wellington's inability to change Canberra's mind on the deportation of New Zealand nationals who had spent most of their lives in Australia and who suddenly found themselves back in the country of their birth without social connections and, in some cases, with worrying criminal records.

Ardern's subsequent observation that this problem was becoming a 'major irritant' in the trans-Tasman relationship (Ensor 2019) understated its divisiveness. The impasse was more than just another example of the power asymmetry that favours Australia. It underscored a clash of priorities between New Zealand's arguments about fairness and justice and the Morrison government's uncompromising position on national security. And this was not just about foreign policy: on both sides the disagreement was locked up in domestic politics. Compromise was always going to be much harder to find in these circumstances.

As this disagreement became the default assessment of the state of New Zealand's most important foreign relationship, the last two decades of more positive trans-Tasman visions were being rejected. In previous decades the picture drawn by the prime ministers of both countries had been one of common commitment to confronting shared external hazards. But these photo opportunities had been drying up, especially on the defence front where myths were often imagined of unbroken ANZAC camaraderie since Gallipoli. Long gone were the trans-Tasman military missions to peace and stabilisation operations in the nearer abroad – from Bougainville and Timor Leste in the late 1990s to Solomon Islands in 2003 and a limited deployment to Tonga in 2006. More recent responses to natural disasters in Fiji did not quite cut the same picture.

Further afield, there was little in the way of joint Australia–New Zealand collaboration in the long Afghanistan War, from which both countries were seeking to extricate themselves. This left the politically more controversial mission in Iraq, where in 2015 New Zealand had begun to deploy army personnel for a training mission under Australia's lead at Taji Base. But Labour had opposed the Key government's deployment decision, and by the time Ardern became prime minister, most of the heat from the ISIS period of Middle East conflict was evaporating. It was therefore Ron Mark's job not to extend the mission, but to bring the forces home. That decision was announced in the middle of 2019 (Ardern, Peters and Mark 2019).

Defence decisions aplenty

But if defence was now providing few new opportunities for operational deployments, Mark's three years as minister comprised an active period for the future of New Zealand's deployable capabilities. He secured Cabinet approval for not one but two major defence procurement choices. The second of these, announced in the last months of his role, was a no-brainer, bound to appeal to the full cross-section of New Zealand political opinion. This was for New Zealand to procure C-130J 'Super Hercules' aircraft (Block 2020), essential for transporting troops and equipment in all manner of situations: peacekeeping and stabilisation missions, and natural disasters in the Pacific and at home. The much harder accomplishment was the first – the announcement in 2018 that New Zealand would replace the P-3 Orion maritime surveillance aircraft with P-8 Poseidons (Mark 2018). Like the C-130Js these new aircraft were in use by several of New Zealand's main defence partners, including Australia. But unlike the Super Hercules, the Poseidons promised a significant combat capability for the New Zealand Defence Force, including for subsurface missions (i.e., for detecting submarines).

It's not at all surprising that a New Zealand First defence minister was a strong proponent of the P-8 purchase: Mark saw absolutely nothing wrong with a defence force able to participate in combat missions with traditional partners, including more tricky theatres beyond the South Pacific. But that this decision would happen under a Labour prime minister is more noteable. Almost twenty years earlier, Jacinda Ardern's Labour predecessor in that high office – Helen Clark – had turned down the Air Force's plans to update the already ageing P-3s with subsurface capabilities (Greener 2009). Even more surprisingly, the P-8 decision won support from the Greens, who held several portfolios in the Ardern-led government. Quite how Mark convinced them to sign off would make a wonderful subject for a postgraduate dissertation.

The public explanation for New Zealand pushing on towards a much more ambitious Defence Capability Plan (which Mark would leave for his successor to grapple with) included the argument that a much more challenging regional security environment was in the making. This was laid out in a document which appeared just days before the announcement on the P-8s. While not a fully-fledged Defence White Paper (something which had not appeared under a Labour prime minister since 1987), the 'Strategic Defence Policy Statement' featured an unusually frank account of the more strategically competitive wider region facing New Zealand and its traditional partners (New Zealand Government 2018a). This included some very direct words about China's behaviour, with particular reference to the South China Sea, an issue of considerable urgency and sensitivity in Beijing. By comparison, while the world had already become used to the trials and tribulations of living with Donald Trump in the White House, the United States got a fairly free pass. In combination with the decisions on capability, New Zealand defence policy was now closer to Australian views of the strategic universe than it had been for some time.

On China questions, New Zealand First did not hold a monopoly by virtue of its two externally facing portfolios. The growing importance of the information technology dimension for international strategy guaranteed a front seat in the growing geopolitical contest for New Zealand's intelligence agencies. These answered to senior Labour Ministers (Andrew Little, as minister responsible for both the Government Communications Security Bureau [GCSB] and the New Zealand Security Intelligence Service, and the prime minister). In 2018 there were two public occasions at which Wellington's disquiet about China's exploitation of cyber vulnerabilties burst into the public sphere. The later of these was more explicit – towards the end of the year the GCSB (which has the lead role in signals intelligence) named China as a country whose cyber activities were damaging the interests of organisations operating in New Zealand (New Zealand GCSB 2018b). Until then only Russia and North Korea had earned that unenviable spotlight.

But it was the earlier and more implicit expression of concern about China that made the headlines, and not just in New Zealand. This was the decision to reject a bid by Spark (a leading New Zealand telecommunications firm) to include Huawei (a Chinese multinational telecommunications company) in a bid for the upcoming rollout of 5G infrastructure (New Zealand GCSB 2018a). This decision was taken on national security grounds, which were not explained to the public in any detail but which the Ardern government was obliged to consider under legislation. The outcome was widely interpreted as New Zealand joining the United States and Australia in banning the Chinese company

(Tobin 2019). The reality was somewhat different: this was not a blanket ban but a single rejection, and in theory Spark would have been able to submit a new bid including Huawei. But the Ardern government did little to advertise this ambiguity, presumably content with the wider international view that New Zealand had become the latest member of the Five Eyes intelligence alliance to take an unequivocal stand.

From prosperity to security . . . and vulnerability

By the halfway point of Ardern's first term, there was enough evidence to suggest that a change in New Zealand's foreign policy priorities had well and truly occurred. Trends which began in the later years of John Key's prime ministership had been turbocharged under the new coalition. Concerns about regional security increasingly crowded out optimism about regional markets. In both cases, China's rise was the dominant factor. This would also affect what forms of international cooperation took the lion's share of public attention. The debate was no longer about how Wellington should approach what had become of the CPTPP (or TPP-11) and other free trade instruments. The gradual progress towards the Regional Comprehensive Economic Partnership (which New Zealand signed onto in November 2020) rarely made the front pages. Some attention was garnered by the prospect of a free trade agreement with the European Union, a long-term objective if ever there was one (Sachdeva 2020). By contrast, newspaper space could be guaranteed whenever New Zealand's security posture was put in a Five Eyes context. Commercial considerations (involving international trade) appeared to have been outbid by security worries.

The Ardern government would not only find itself changing what things in the region New Zealand was talking about, but also what that region ought to be called. Wellington had long been comfortable with the term 'Asia–Pacific'. This allowed for two main types of regionalism: small state regionalism with its Pacific Island Forum partners, and East Asian regionalism based on the institutional outgrowths of ASEAN (the Association of Southeast Asian Nations). These were not at the forefront of the move towards an 'Indo-Pacific' nomenclature that had become increasingly favoured by Canberra, Washington and Tokyo. These three saw a stronger emphasis on the Indian Ocean and tighter connections with India as a way to dilute some of China's influence and play to America's advantages.

New Zealand continued to keep some distance from 'the Quad' – an on-again, off-again Indo-Pacific grouping of the US, Japan, Australia and India, originally envisioned by Japan's former prime minister Shinzō Abe with much more obvious connotations of competing with China. This was a big players club. Yet once other smaller states were shifting their conceptions of the region (at least in rhetorical terms) it was hard for New Zealand to exclude itself from the emerging Indo-Pacific conversation. Once Indonesia had persuaded its ASEAN partners that it was time for a change, the writing was on Wellington's wall. New Zealand insisted that in doing so it would be guided by the principles of inclusiveness and multilateralism (Ministry of Foreign Affairs and Trade 2018). But this qualification was easily lost in the new geopolitics. The Ardern government would even depict its South Pacific interests in Indo-Pacific terms in one of the many defence assessments launched by Ron Mark (New Zealand Government 2019).

Another of these documents laid out the New Zealand Defence Force's response to the problem of climate change (New Zealand Government 2018b). But neither this problem nor the changing 'great power' picture would come to dominate New Zealand's view of the world in 2020. Along with every other nation-state on the planet, attention became fixed on a transnational non-state challenger which had no leader, capital city, armed force or purpose. This was the Covid-19 pandemic, still the primary issue of international concern as the present chapter is being written. The direct health effects on New Zealanders, as illustrated elsewhere in this book, were not as severe as they were for so many populations elsewhere. But the restrictions on travel, which the Ardern government instituted before the virus had an opportunity to spread out of control, reflected the disruption to the normal patterns of global interaction which had for so long connected New Zealand to the world. At the time of writing, a sustained trans-Tasman travel bubble with Australia, New Zealand's closest partner, was still yet to eventuate.

The daily business of foreign policy changed too. Diplomacy was still possible by 'Zoom', but international meetings were even more scripted than before, with few opportunities for the quiet corridor conversations where issues could be hammered out. And rather than a collaborative effort spearheaded at the United Nations, much of the Covid-era foreign policy seemed national and unilateral rather than global and multilateral. What the Ardern government said to its citizens had far more weight than what was being said by the World Health Organization (from which the United States' participation was removed by the Trump Administration). In the time of Covid, rather than witnessing a new era of cooperation among partners in a crisis affecting everyone, new fault lines in the political competition were being formed: the already tense relationship between Australia and China (two of New Zealand's three most important partners) headed to a new low as the Morrison government called for an investigation into the origins of the virus (Walsh 2021).

The priorities were reduced to just two: dealing with the public health crisis that the pandemic was generating, and the economic costs of the recurrent shutdowns. Not much else, including New Zealand's international engagement, mattered nearly as much. But Wellington did seek to find some partners in initial efforts to create safe space for value chains and other international connections. Rather than 'coalitions of the willing' (familiar to multi-country military engagements, as in the 2003 invasion of Iraq), these were 'coalitions of the trusted'. Reminiscent of the P4 group of countries who had opened their economies to each other as a forerunner to the much wider TPP (New Zealand, Singapore, Chile and Brunei), New Zealand entered into some building block collaborations that would hopefully be the start of something more extensive (Ministry of Foreign Affairs and Trade 2020). But the overall picture was of a world beset by an interruption of the international connections that had for decades been taken for granted. In particular, this meant far fewer visitors to New Zealand – tourists, international students, sportspeople and migrants.

This temporarily closed world – entertained by countries like New Zealand which otherwise sought openness – brought some irony to the arguments of nationalism and populism. 'America First' and 'Brexit' were illiberal movements which argued for new restrictions on migration to the United States and the United Kingdom. But as Covid-19 spread like wildfire, it was often leaders with liberal sentiments who were ordering borders to be closed. We can include New Zealand's prime minister in that list. The response Ardern led to the pandemic, along with New Zealand's relatively low levels of infections and deaths, added to her international prominence and popularity, to say nothing of her strong standing domestically. But for her coalition partner, the Covid pandemic was politically devastating. Winston Peters had no media airspace as the 2020 general election loomed. He had no platform for the national emergency: that had been taken by Ardern and Director-General of Health Ashley Bloomfield. The virus had co-opted New Zealand First's political messaging which, in campaign mode, often carried a whiff of 'batten down the hatches'. Rejected (or ignored) by the electorate, Peters and his party were exiled from Parliament. Labour experienced the reverse: a clear parliamentary majority unique in the MMP era. And it would thus take control of defence and foreign affairs for term two.

Conclusion

In her initial prime ministerial foreign policy address in 2017, Ardern had drawn connections to her Labour forebears (from Helen Clark and David Lange to Peter Fraser) in highlighting New Zealand's internationalism and multilateralism. Reconfigured for the challenges of the early- to mid-21st century, this meant substituting progress on climate change for the nuclear free movement of the Lange years. But anyone looking back on the remaining part of Ardern's first term would come away wondering whether either issue – climate change or disarmament – sat at the forefront of New Zealand's international thinking. Hopes for a progressive turn in Wellington's approach to the world were bound to be disappointed, not least because foreign policy was a bargain between a Labour prime minister aiming to dominate the centre ground of New Zealand politics and a New Zealand First deputy prime minister and minister of foreign affairs for whom geopolitics was not a dirty word.

One is left wondering what might have happened to New Zealand's outlook on the world if the time machine had been available in late 2017, enabling Ardern to journey forward to late 2020. Such a voyage would have revealed much more than the electoral decimation of the party with more than a little empathy for the power politics model of international relations and the populist nationalism of Donald Trump and Boris Johnson. Ardern's reconnaissance of the international situation at the end of 2020 would also have revealed the Covid pandemic, the serious deterioration in Australia–China relations, and Trump's electoral defeat.

If armed with that foreknowledge when her first government was sworn into office, would Ardern and her Labour colleagues have thought differently about New Zealand's international choices? Would the geopolitical content of New Zealand foreign policy in the 2017–2020 period have been toned down before it began to take off? Would the focus have shifted to the vulnerability of the planet and its peoples? We will never know. But perhaps the second-term agenda of the Ardern government, where New Zealand's external relations are no longer a negotiated exercise in coalition politics, will tell us something about what might have been.

The Campaign, the Results and the Formation of the Government

22

'HERE TODAY, GONE TOMORROW'? NEW ZEALAND ELECTION SIGNS IN 2020

Nigel S. Roberts

Election billboards, hoardings and posters are formally called 'election signs', and prior to the 2020 general election the New Zealand Electoral Commission's website let candidates and parties know that in 'the 9 weeks before election day, you can have election signs that are up to 3 square metres in size.' This was the case throughout New Zealand, but at the same time candidates and parties needed to be aware that 'local councils are responsible for regulating election signs in their region' – for setting the rules 'regulating when, where, and how you can display election signs' (Electoral Commission 2020). Local bodies take their role in this regard seriously. The Porirua City Council, for instance, developed a 15-page document detailing 19 different 'public display sites' for 'electioneering signs and hoardings' (Porirua City Council 2020).

In January 2020, speaking at the first post-Cabinet press conference of the year, the prime minister, Jacinda Ardern (following the examples set by John Key early in 2011 and 2014, and by Bill English in early 2017), announced that the country's ninth MMP general election would be held on Saturday, 19 September. It was no surprise, therefore, that during the weekend of 18–19 July 2020, election signs sprang up throughout New Zealand 'like mushrooms after an autumn shower' (Roberts 2003, p. 280): it was exactly nine weeks prior to the scheduled election.

On 12 August, however, after positive cases of Covid-19 had been detected in an Auckland household, the country's largest city and its immediate surrounds were moved up to Covid-19 alert level 3, while the rest of the country went to alert level 2. A mere five and a half weeks before the general election was scheduled to be held, the ability of about a third of the population of New Zealand to go where it pleased and to attend large gatherings was severely curtailed. Even outside the Auckland region, meetings were restricted to a maximum of a hundred people. Five days later, the prime minister bowed to the inevitable and announced the postponement of the election by four weeks – that is, from 19 September until Saturday, 17 October 2020.

The prime minister's perceived reluctance to alter the previously promulgated date of the election was understandable: it was the first time since the Second World War that a New Zealand election had been postponed for any reason whatsoever. Consequently, when she announced the new date for the election, Ardern also made it clear she would not push the date back again.

In 2020, therefore, election signs were able to be displayed for thirteen weeks – almost a quarter of the year – and not for merely nine weeks. Political parties in New Zealand and candidates standing for election to Parliament thus had an unrivalled opportunity to get their messages across to the electorate at large. What, then, were the messages conveyed by election signs – by billboards, hoardings, placards, and posters – in New Zealand in 2020? How well did the country's political actors make use of what proved to be a uniquely long period to promote their parties, personalities and policies?

20/20 visual acuity

A significant feature of election signs in New Zealand has been that, almost without exception, billboards promoting the major party leaders – that is, the Labour and National party leaders – have concentrated on the party leader alone. Despite the fact that Michael Cullen was Helen Clark's exceptionally able, highly respected, and widely trusted deputy for 12 years, Labour Party election signs in 1996, 1999, 2002, 2005 and 2008 ignored Cullen and concentrated on Clark. Similarly, Bill English – the National Party's equally able deputy leader under John Key – was also overlooked when the party's advertising agents created National's leadership election signs in 2008, 2011 and 2014.

The only exception to this de facto rule about the major parties' promotion of the personalities of their leaders was in 2017, when Andrew Little – the party's leader from November 2014 until August 2017 – appeared on billboards alongside Jacinda Ardern, who had been elected deputy leader of the party six months prior to the 2017 election. However, after Little stepped down as leader on 1 August 2017 and Ardern was catapulted into the leadership of the party less than eight weeks prior to the general election, Labour's election signs reverted to type and focused solely on its leader. They also dropped the words 'A fresh approach', which had accompanied a picture of Little and Ardern, in favour of an equally bland slogan that Ardern had personally put forward when she became the party's leader: 'Let's do this.'

Three years later, Jacinda Ardern was – utterly understandably in light of her widespread popularity – the sole focus of billboards promoting Labour's leadership. A picture of the prime minister with her trademark toothy smile and appropriately wearing a red jacket was accompanied by the exhortation 'Let's keep moving', with a red tick alongside the party's logo and name. These billboards were supplemented by election signs featuring photographs of the prime minister standing slightly but significantly in front of the Labour Party's individual candidates in each of New Zealand's 72 electorates. These hoardings, however, stressed the name of the party's electoral district candidate in large bold type, as well as (but in a considerably smaller standard Roman typeface) the name of the electorate in which the candidate was standing.

As a visual reminder for the country's voters of who was the Labour Party's chief asset in the election, and of who were candidates for the party, Labour's 2020 billboards were appropriately models of 20/20 visual acuity.

Chaos and confusion

In stark contrast, the election signs of the National Party mirrored the chaos and confusion that dogged the party throughout the year of the pandemic. The official opposition's struggle to maintain a semblance of relevance while the government managed the Covid-19 crisis competently and effectively, as well as appalling errors of judgment by Simon Bridges, resulted in his replacement as Leader of the Opposition by Todd Muller on 22 May 2020 (after a vote by National's parliamentary caucus). Auckland Central MP Nikki Kaye shelved her previously announced retirement plans and became Muller's deputy (replacing Paula Bennett, who decided, in the aftermath, that she *did* want to retire from politics).

Five weeks later National unveiled its leadership billboard. For the first time in the MMP era, National had a billboard that featured both its leader and deputy leader. The parallels with what the Labour Party had done in 2017 were immediately obvious: a struggling opposition that lacked confidence in the ability of its leader alone to attract votes was promoting the merits of a popular young female Member of Parliament (Kaye, like Ardern, had not only been born in 1980, but had also first been elected to Parliament in 2008). The billboard trumpeted a three-part slogan: 'Strong Team. More Jobs. Better Economy.' The first two words were laughable in light of the fact that Muller and Kaye's accession to the leadership was a consequence of a bitter internal party coup. Two weeks later, National's election signs were rendered redundant, not to say ridiculous, when Muller abruptly announced his resignation as party leader. Kaye not only followed suit, but also reactivated her retirement plans.

National hastily chose Judith Collins and Gerry Brownlee, respectively, to be the party's third leader and deputy leader in the space of less than eight weeks. Four days later, election signs could legally appear on (authorised) public property. Not surprisingly, the National Party had ditched all its carefully prepared billboards promoting Muller and Kaye, and at the start of what turned out to be a 13-week billboard season, the party was reduced to using signs *sans* pictures – each sign using just two words to ask electors simply to give ticks both to National and to the party's electorate candidate. However, the National Party worked rapidly to repair the situation, and only a week later billboards promoting National's new leadership team appeared on grass verges and street corners. Set against a dark blue background, the party's new leadership election signs featured a photograph of Judith Collins standing in front of Gerry Brownlee. Symbolically, Collins was wearing a light blue jacket as an obvious contrast to Jacinda Ardern's red one. The party opted to retain the slogan used on the Muller and Kaye signs, 'Strong Team. More Jobs. Better Economy.' Given that Collins and Brownlee were National's third pair of leaders in less than two months, the party's continued use of the phrase 'Strong Team' was frankly risible.

Roughly three weeks prior to the election, the National Party fielded a new leadership election sign. This time, Brownlee was left off the billboards. Only Collins appeared on them, and – in an unwittingly appropriate admission – the party stopped promoting its 'Strong Team' theme, instead putting forward a new double-barreled slogan: 'Your Economy. Your Future.' In a style similar to Labour's, National also erected election signs in each electorate, displaying photographs of its leader and of its candidate for the seat. In the middle of the billboards, separating Collins and National's electorate candidate, were the names of the particular candidate and electorate, followed by an exhortation to electors to 'Party Vote National'.

'Party vote . . . today'

Both major parties have, from the earliest days of MMP, been keenly aware of the primacy of the party vote and of the need to harvest party votes. Furthermore, since 2011 increasing proportions of the electorate have cast their ballots prior to election day. In 2011, almost 13 per cent did so; three years later the proportion doing so doubled; and in 2017 early electors accounted for 47 per cent of all the votes cast. In 2020, aided by fears of a Covid-19 outbreak restricting access to polling stations, more than two thirds of those voting in the general election did so prior to Saturday, 17 October. The trend in favour of advance voting in New Zealand was also doubtless assisted by the fact that for a full fortnight before election day, both Labour and National campaign workers plastered an extra, almost identical message across their billboards. A yellow-and-black ribbon tacked across Labour's election signs exhorted electors to 'Party vote Labour today', while an orange-and-white sticker pasted onto National Party election signs urged people to 'Party Vote National Today'. That National was able to use orange as one of the colours for its message raised some eyebrows, because orange is the official colour of the New Zealand Electoral Commission. The National sticker undoubtedly resembled an instruction from the Electoral Commission's 'Orange Guy' mascot, even though parties are specifically told 'You are not allowed to use our trademarked Orange Guy.' It will interesting to see whether parties will again be permitted to sail this close to the wind when campaigning in 2023.

Two ten-seat parties

The Greens – in terms of votes cast, the third largest party in Parliament – had the simplest, and possibly the dullest, election signs. Coloured light green (of course), they contained only five words (other than a mandatory authorisation statement): 'Think ahead. Party Vote Green.' The Green Party also produced a few small placards featuring a photograph of the party's co-leaders, Marama Davidson and James Shaw. The Green Party fought a strenuous and successful two-ticks battle in just one electorate – Auckland Central, where posters urged electors to 'Vote Green Twice' and, to make the message doubly clear, showed tick-marks alongside the phrases 'Party Vote Green' and 'Chlöe Swarbrick for Auckland Central'. The posters were strikingly simple, but at the same time they managed to get the party's message across umlaut and clear.

Although the Green Party and ACT both won ten seats apiece in the 2020 general election (in each case winning one electorate and nine list seats), after special votes were tallied, ACT ended up with 7,726 fewer votes than the Greens and thus became the fourth-largest of the five parties in Parliament. The ACT campaign focused on just one main election sign. It featured a black-and-white photograph of the party's leader (and for six years its sole MP), David Seymour, standing alongside Brooke van Velden, who had played a major role in successfully piloting the End of Life Choice Act 2019 through Parliament and who had been appointed the party's deputy leader. In sharp contrast to the billboards' black-and-white background, the ACT election signs also deployed blue, pink and yellow to highlight the party's pitch: 'Change Your Future / Party Vote ACT'. Of all the parties elected to the House of Representatives, ACT was the only one whose billboards featured a QR ('quick response') code with an invitation to voters to 'scan here for the latest updates'. ACT was also the only parliamentary party to promote its web address on its 2020 election signs.

Back into and back out of Parliament

The Māori Party's principal election sign contained a large colour photograph of the seven candidates it fielded in the Māori electorates. This was something that the Māori Party had done before (in both 2008 and 2014, for example), while the Greens had, likewise, put their seven-member 1999–2002 parliamentary caucus – which they called the 'Green Team' – on the party's 2002 election billboards. Seven people is an almost perfect number for a three square-metre billboard: any more begins to look both cluttered and ridiculous, as evidenced by the Kiwi Party's 2008 billboards which pictured 18 of the 25 candidates on its party list. An even more telling example was the Labour Party's 2014 election sign that pictured all 32 of its MPs who were hoping to be re-elected. The billboard's desperate cri de coeur was reflected in the party's sad electoral performance: it won only 25 per cent of the party votes cast in the 2014 general election – its worst performance in more than 90 years. By contrast, the Māori Party's 2020 election campaign was slick and efficient. Having lost all parliamentary representation in

2017, the party came back from the dead. It not only won an electorate seat – Waiariki, which it had lost in 2017 – but, with a special vote share of the party votes that was almost double its election night share, it also managed, for the first time, to boost the Māori Party's overall representation in Parliament from one (on election night figures) to two.

New Zealand First, on the other hand, did what the Māori Party had done three years earlier: it failed to qualify for any seats in Parliament. Winston Peters, who had been deputy prime minister for the previous three years, went from hero to zero after a lacklustre campaign. The party's predominant election signs reflected the state of its malaise: the billboards contained a colour photograph of Winston Peters alongside a slogan that was so anodyne as to be almost meaningless – 'Back Your Future'. Ironically, though, the nation did back its future by giving the Labour Party the highest share of the votes achieved by any party in a general election since 1951 and, as well, an absolute majority of the seats in Parliament, something that had not happened in any of New Zealand's eight previous proportional representation general elections.

New Zealand First was one of 12 parties that nominated a formal list of candidates and appealed to voters for their party votes during the 2020 general election yet won no seats at all in Parliament. Although the remaining 11 parties garnered a combined total of only 5.2 per cent of all the valid party votes cast in the election, their election signs commanded a considerably larger share of the country's billboard battleground. Two of the minnow parties – Advance New Zealand and the ONE Party – had co-leaders, and both parties displayed colour photographs of both co-leaders on their hoardings. The outlandish conspiracy-theory derived beliefs of Billy Te Kahika, one of Advance New Zealand's co-leaders, attracted a lot of attention during the election campaign, but when the final results of the election were released, the party proved itself unable to attract the support of even 1 per cent of voters.

Devoid of issues

As Claire Robinson (2019, p. 18) has pointed out – and she was referring specifically to New Zealand – if it were not for 'political communication like advertising messages, newspaper headlines and billboard slogans . . . we might not discover the issues over which the election is being fought'. However, New Zealand's 2020 election signs were almost entirely devoid of any mention of the issues confronting the country and being considered during the campaign. This has not always been the case in the MMP era. In 2005, for example, both the Labour Party and the National Party promoted their most prominent policies on their campaign billboards. Labour's main leadership election sign included a picture of a pledge card entitled 'My Commitments to You' signed by the prime minister, Helen Clark; and late in the campaign the party erected massive hoardings specifically promising 'No interest on student loans'. Promises were an even greater feature of National's 2005 election campaign. The party's huge 'Iwi/Kiwi', 'Cabs/Cops', 'Out in no time/Do the whole time' billboards were the most controversial and effective election advertising in New Zealand since National's 1975 'dancing Cossacks' television commercial (see Robinson 2019, pp. 7, 159 and 10 respectively).

Similarly, the minor parties in New Zealand have also, on occasion, used their public election signs to promote a range of policies and promises. In 2002, for example, ACT billboards put forward promises such as a 'Tax cut for every worker' and 'Zero Tolerance for Crime', while the Greens used their election signs in 2002 to argue, 'GE. Keep it in the Lab'.

The one party that used election signs in 2020 to remind electors about its policies was the New Conservative Party. After the Conservative Party won almost 4 per cent of the votes cast in 2014, its founder and first leader stepped down following courtroom battles with a former staffer. The party was almost wiped out in 2017 – when it won less than 0.25 per cent of the votes – but rebranded itself by adding the word 'New' to its name and choosing a new leader. In 2020, the party's billboards contained a range of pithy statements – such as 'Binding Referenda', 'First $20,000 Tax Free', and 'NZ not UN'. One billboard in particular summed up the New Conservative's overall policy stance: alongside a photograph of the party's leader, Leighton Baker, were four words – 'Unkept Promises / No Thanks'. As a campaign strategy, however, the New Conservative's policy-oriented pitch failed to fire, and the party attracted less than 1.5 per cent of the valid votes cast in the general election.

Ephemera: Items of short-lived interest?

The Electoral Commission's *Candidate Handbook for the 2020 General Election* stressed New Zealand's long-standing prohibition of any form of political advertising on election day. Candidates, parties and pressure groups were warned: 'Take down your election and referendum signs and posters before election day. This includes signs and graphics on vehicles, and bumper stickers.' The Commission stressed that on election day 'it's illegal to post or share anything that's likely to influence voters.' (With regard to advance voting, which began on 3 October, it was 'a criminal offence to do anything that can influence voters in an advance voting place [or] within 10 metres of an advance voting place'.)

As a result of these rules governing the conduct of elections in New Zealand, election signs throughout the country disappear almost overnight. If observers miss them during the election campaign, they will not see them on election day or, of course, afterwards. (This is not the case in the United States, for example, where I once photographed a Barack Obama lawn sign that was still on display more than two years after he had been elected to the US Senate!) Consequently, it should not be too great a surprise to learn that archivists and librarians classify election signs as 'ephemera', a dictionary definition of which refers specifically to printed items 'of short-lived interest or usefulness' (Allen 1990, p. 393). The word 'ephemera' is, of course, the plural of 'ephemeron', the origin of which is the Greek word *ephemeros*, meaning 'lasting only one day', or 'short-lived'. Even though the National Library has an Ephemera Collection (National Library of New Zealand 2020), it sadly cannot – and does not – capture, catalogue and classify the vast bulk of New Zealand's 'here today, gone tomorrow' election signs.

As Claire Robinson (2019, p. 11) has noted, previous books in this series of New Zealand general election studies have included

> photographs and ads as illustrations, and some of the more recent individual election analyses have televised ads, billboard images and television excerpts attached to them on DVD. These will be fantastic resources for scholars of the future who want to understand what was happening in our early twenty-first-century elections, provided they can still find the technology to play a DVD.

In order both to illustrate the election signs that have been described and analysed in this chapter and to provide 'scholars of the future' with an additional (and hopefully also 'fantastic') resource to enable them 'to understand what was happening' in New Zealand's MMP elections, a website has been developed especially to exhibit as wide a range as possible of election signs for each of the New Zealand general elections going back as far as the 1996 election, the country's first MMP election.

The URL (the web address) for the website is <www.nigel-roberts.info/New-Zealand-MMP-election-signs.htm>. Hopefully, this resource will mean that for many years to come, election signs in New Zealand will not be 'here today and gone tomorrow', but will instead be here today and accessible tomorrow.

Image 22.1: In 2020, Jacinda Ardern was – utterly understandably in light of her widespread popularity – the sole focus of election signs promoting Labour's leadership.

Image 22.2: As a visual reminder for the country's voters of who was the Labour Party's chief asset in the election, and of who were candidates for the party, Labour's 2020 billboards were appropriately models of 20/20 visual acuity.

Image 22.3: The promotion of the Labour Party's candidates in the Māori electorates used the same template that the party employed to publicise its general electorate candidates.

Image 22.4: For a full fortnight before election day, voters were urged to 'Party vote Labour today'. More than two-thirds of the people who voted in the 2020 New Zealand general election did so prior to (and not on) Saturday, 17 October.

Image 22.5: The National Party unveiled this billboard five weeks after Todd Muller and Nikki Kaye were elected as leader and deputy leader respectively. A mere two weeks later, however, Muller abruptly announced his resignation as party leader, and Kaye followed suit.

Image 22.6: After National hastily chose Judith Collins and Gerry Brownlee as its third leader and deputy leader in less than eight weeks, the party retained the six-word slogan it had used on its Muller and Kaye signs.

Image 22.7: Roughly three weeks prior to the election, the National Party fielded a new leadership election sign that omitted both Brownlee and the party's 'Strong Team' mantra.

Image 22.8: Despite orange being the colour used by the New Zealand Electoral Commission in its advertising, the National Party used orange stickers to urge voters to cast an advance vote.

Image 22.9: The Greens had the simplest, and possibly the dullest, election signs.

Image 22.10: The Green Party fought a strenuous and successful 'two-ticks' battle in Auckland Central, winning an electorate seat for the first time since Jeanette Fitzsimons won Coromandel in 1999 (which she lost three years later).

Image 22.11: The ACT campaign featured just one main election sign with a large black-and-white photograph of Brooke van Velden and David Seymour, the party's deputy leader and leader. Innovatively, the party's billboards also contained a QR code.

Image 22.12: Photographed erecting the Māori Party's principal election sign – which promoted its candidates in all seven Māori electorates – is a group of Māori Party activists (including, on the left both of this photograph and of the billboard, Romaine Ferris, the party's Te Tai Tonga candidate).

Image 22.13: The co-leader of the Māori Party, Debbie Ngarewa-Packer, was ranked first on the party's list and became an MP after the party managed, for the first time, to win a high enough proportion of all the special votes cast in the election to boost its representation in Parliament from one (on election night figures) to two.

Image 22.14: Winston Peters alongside a slogan so anodyne as to be almost meaningless, and which did not help New Zealand First. With only 2.6 per cent of the votes, the party failed to qualify for any seats in Parliament.

Image 22.15: Although the New Conservative Party used election signs to remind electors about its policies, the party attracted less than 1.5 per cent of the votes cast in the 2020 election.

Image 22.16: The outlandish beliefs of Billy Te Kahika, one of Advance New Zealand's co-leaders, attracted a lot of attention during the election campaign, but when the final results were released, the party proved itself unable to attract the support of even 1 per cent of voters.

23

THE 2020 CANNABIS AND EUTHANASIA REFERENDUMS

Luke D. Oldfield and Lara M. Greaves

Introduction

In November 2018, Justice Minister Andrew Little signalled that a referendum 'triple header' might take place on the matters of euthanasia, cannabis and MMP reform (*New Zealand Herald* 2018). The referendum on the End of Life Choice Act (hereafter referred to as 'euthanasia') was to confirm whether someone with a terminal illness or grievous and irremediable medical condition could be assisted in ending their life. Meanwhile, the cannabis reform referendum would question whether a regulated cannabis market should be legalised. Finally, the MMP referendum was to ask about changes to electoral thresholds: such as requiring only 4 per cent of the party vote to gain seats and/or removing the coat-tailing mechanism (allowing a party to gain parliamentary representation if it won at least one electorate seat). In 2019 – contrary to statements made by an MP in his own party – a fourth referendum topic of abortion law reform was also touted by Deputy Prime Minister Winston Peters in response to legislation tabled by Little (Bracewell-Worrall 2019).

Two referendums ended up on the ballot alongside the 2020 general election. In both cases, the referendums were a consequence of politicians opting to defer to the public on contentious issues, as opposed to non-binding citizen-initiated referendums (which arise from widely supported petitions). Referendums in New Zealand can take place either at a general election or via postal ballot, and New Zealand had not seen referendums on more than one topic on the ballot since 1999, when there were two citizen-initiated referendums, one on reducing the size of Parliament to 99 MPs, the other on suggested changes to the criminal justice system (Church 2000). There are problems with holding referendums alongside general elections. The sheer amount of information that voters need to consider in order to process the issues creates extra effort on top of normal candidate and party voting (De Angelis, Colombo and Morisi 2020). In addition, although it was not known at the time, both the 2020 election and the referendums were overshadowed by the Covid-19 pandemic.

Preliminary referendum results were released by the Electoral Commission on 30 October 2020, showing that a decisive number of voters had supported the euthanasia reforms: 1,574,645 (65.2 per cent) voted yes, 815,829 (33.8 per cent) voted no. The final result was little changed: 1,893,290 (65.1 per cent) yes, 979,079 (33.7 per cent) no. In the preliminary results for the cannabis referendum, a narrow majority rejected change: 1,114,485 (46.1 per cent) voted yes, 1,281,818 (53.1 per cent) voted no. Final results, released on 6 November 2020, showed that despite closing the margin further, supporters of the 'yes' vote on cannabis reform had fallen short by a mere 67,662 votes: 48.4 per cent (1,406,973) voted in favour, 50.7 per cent (1,474,635) against.

This chapter outlines some of the protagonists and lobby groups behind each side in both referendums. Public opinion leading into each referendum, and what clues were available within existing research as to their outcomes, will also be examined, followed by analysis of some of the factors influencing the referendum results, and who is likely to be most impacted by the outcomes.

Fierce resistance and some unlikely bedfellows

Both referendum questions were based on legislation that had already been drawn up and approved by Parliament. On euthanasia, voters were asked, 'Do you support the End of Life Choice Act 2019 coming into force?' On cannabis, voters were asked, 'Do you support the proposed Cannabis Legalisation and Control Bill?' The cannabis referendum was originally promised through the 2017 confidence and supply agreement between the Labour and Green parties, although the bill itself was beset with delays and a draft was not released until December 2019. A more complete version was released in April 2020, several months ahead of the election. Left off the ballot were MMP reforms, subsequently featuring in the 2020 cooperation agreement between Labour and the Greens (see this book's Appendix 1). Meanwhile, the Abortion Legislation Act 2020 was enacted in March 2020 through a conscience vote in Parliament without a referendum being held.

There were differing levels of cross-party support for each referendum. Proponents of euthanasia reform included ACT Party leader David Seymour, whose member's bill precipitated the End of Life legislation, later amended to include the referendum. Assisting Seymour was ACT parliamentary staffer Brooke van Velden – elected to Parliament on ACT's party list at the 2020 election – who acted as a lobbyist for the bill, courting support from MPs across the political spectrum. Outside of Parliament, the End of Life Choice Society and Yes to Compassion were prominent lobby groups in favour of euthanasia reform, the former including former Labour party MP (and the party's former president) Maryan Street, who had unsuccessfully tried to introduce a similar bill five years earlier. Conversely, cannabis reform – championed by Green MP Chlöe Swarbrick – had more limited parliamentary backing despite support from former prime minister Helen Clark and the Helen Clark Foundation (a public policy think tank established in 2019). Outside of Parliament, the key pro-change proponents were the New Zealand Drug Foundation and similar groups active in areas of justice, equality and human rights.

Opposition to the euthanasia referendum was considerable. In the lead-up to the 2020 election, interest group involvement from The Care Alliance, Euthanasia-Free New Zealand and Lawyers for Vulnerable New Zealanders aligned with religious groups opposing the bill. A majority of National Party MPs also opposed the legislation, including retiring MP Maggie Barry, a cabinet minister in the previous government. On cannabis reform, a 'Say Nope to Dope' campaign, run by conservative lobby group Family First, sprang up in opposition, quoting a mixture of celebrities and medical professionals in support of their argument. Former prime minister Sir John Key also entered the debate as voting began; he opposed the cannabis bill, claiming that it would make drugs more prevalent and children more inclined to take them.

In contrast to the Cannabis Legalisation and Control Bill, the End of Life Choice Act passed through legislative processes, meaning that it was subject to submissions from the public. More than 39,000 submissions were received, around 90 per cent of which were opposed to euthanasia (Justice Committee 2019). Although the outcome of the referendum demonstrated broad support, this was less clear during the submissions process due to the strong pushback from anti-euthanasia activists.

The mismatch in public submissions to the referendum outcome reflects 'weak majority thought', a phenomenon that can be explained with reference to 20th-century political science theory. Differences in issue intensity (how passionate someone is about a topic) can distort what appears to be the general will of voters (how the majority feel about a topic). Campbell and colleagues (1960) suggest that values are often a predictor of issue intensity. Applying this to euthanasia reform, a minority had a much stronger intensity of opinion – those who were opposed to euthanasia reform were more inclined to be *strongly* against it – when compared to those in favour. Over the last five years this may also have occurred during the select committee phase of legislation relating to water fluoridation (2017) and abortion law reform (2019), both of which seemed to attract weak majority support alongside intense minority opposition.

The politics of change

Polling and research on the topics of euthanasia and cannabis reform over a sustained period gave an indication of what the referendum results were likely to be (for a summary, see Crothers 2020). There had been three previous unsuccessful attempts at legalising euthanasia (two bills in 1995 and 2003 that failed their first reading; and Maryan Street's member's bill, never drawn from the random ballot for such bills). As a result, pollsters had been assessing public opinion on the issue over a period of time. It is relatively difficult to obtain an accurate gauge of public opinion on euthanasia, however, as poll questions can be easily manipulated depending on their wording (Saad 2013). Even naming the issue can be complex and controversial, with terminology varying considerably across interest groups, the media and the specific type of administration of the lethal drugs (Young et al. 2018). Even so, exploring high quality polls with neutral question wording indicates that changing euthanasia law had been a popular policy for some time. A systematic review of research on attitudes over the past 20 years found that, on average, 68 per cent of those polled supported change (Young et al. 2018). Support has been related to a broad range of demographic and attitude variables, including age, ethnicity, socioeconomic status and party affiliation. The most consistent finding across the various studies was that religious people tended to be less supportive of euthanasia. With Pākehā generally supportive of euthanasia change, it was evident from the outset that the euthanasia referendum was likely to produce a majority vote for change.

In contrast to the issue of cannabis reform, the bill to legalise euthanasia was not the consequence of prior agreement among Labour and its support parties. In October 2015 ACT leader David Seymour entered a bill to legalise euthanasia into the member's ballot; it was drawn on 8 June 2017, entirely by chance, and passed its first reading in December 2017. The bill then went through a two-year process, undergoing various significant changes arising out of ACT's desire to obtain support from across the political aisle. The Green Party's support was contingent on the measure being restricted to include only the terminally ill, protecting people with disabilities – as per concerns raised by a submission from the Disability Rights Commissioner (Tesoriero 2018). Throughout the process, MPs opposed to the bill tried (unsuccessfully) to add more than 100 amendments (Cheng 2019).

The End of Life Choice Act 2019 allows for people with a terminal illness, expected to live for six months or less, to end their life. The patient must be the first person to suggest assisted dying and two eligible doctors then need to approve of the person's choice, including confirmation that the person is well informed. The issue was put to a conscience vote in Parliament: MPs were not compelled to vote along party lines. Although the majority of opposition came from National Party MPs, a small contingent of Labour MPs were also opposed. A range of rationales for voting were drawn on by MPs, including the views of their electorates, their personal experiences caring for others, their religious proclivities, and concerns around protecting the vulnerable in terms of age and ethnicity. In November 2019, the bill passed its third and final reading, 69 votes to 51. At the committee of the whole house stage, New Zealand First had made its support conditional on an amendment to take the proposed law to a referendum; the proposal was adopted, 63 to 57. New Zealand thus became the first country in the world to put euthanasia to a national referendum (Graham-McLay 2019).

Polling and research for cannabis reform showed that supporters would have a more difficult time convincing voters. Support for cannabis reform has in the past depended on whether the opinion poll assessed full recreational use (akin to the proposed legislation), decriminalisation (where growing cannabis is not legal but possession is not a criminal offence), or medicinal use only (Crothers 2020). The most popular cannabis policy was allowing it for medicinal use only, with polls regularly finding support in the 80–90 per cent range (Crothers 2020). Decriminalisation was generally less popular, though many polls indicated that it could have reached majority support, depending on the wording of the question. However, polls prior to the announcement of the referendum had generally shown that a majority would not support legalising cannabis for recreational use.

Certain demographic groups have had higher levels of support for cannabis reform. Analysis has shown that younger people are more likely to support the legalisation of recreational cannabis, as are Māori and left-wing voters (Crothers 2020). Supporters of reform have long pointed to surveys, which have shown the majority of New Zealanders have tried cannabis at least once (e.g., over 80 per cent of New Zealanders born in the 1970s) and up to 10 per cent have used it on a regular basis (Poulton et al. 2020). Although not all of those who have tried cannabis would necessarily vote for its legalisation, past use has been associated with support (Boden et al. 2020). Polling during the campaign suggested that the referendum would be close, with varying results depending on polling methods. For instance, the online panel studies commissioned by the Helen Clark Foundation indicated a close contest (Radio New Zealand 2020), whereas some of the phone polls, such as the final pre-election Colmar Brunton poll on the topic, found support for reform 10 points behind (*1 News* 2020).

As noted, the cannabis referendum was part of a confidence and supply agreement between Labour and the Greens after the 2017 election, along with what Little called a 'longstanding commitment' to New Zealand First for a referendum on the topic (Small 2019). The Labour–Green agreement specified the following: 'Increase funding for alcohol and drug addiction services and ensure drug use is treated as a health issue, and have a referendum on legalising the personal use of cannabis at, or by, the 2020 general election.' Indeed, cannabis reform has been part of the Green Party's platform since it entered Parliament in 1999 (Edwards and Lomax 2012). What was not clear from the agreement was what the exact wording of the referendum question would be. In May 2019, the cabinet paper on the 2020 cannabis referendum was proactively released by the government. It argued for firm wording in order to avoid a similar situation to the 2016 UK 'Brexit' referendum, in which a broadly worded referendum won the popular vote, leading to a large amount of effort and controversy as the details were worked out for years after the fact.

Under the Cannabis Legalisation and Control Bill, people aged 20 years or older would be able to access cannabis for recreational use. Eligible people would be able to purchase up to fourteen grams of dried cannabis per day and grow up to two cannabis plants at home for personal use, or up to four per property. Purchasing and possessing cannabis for those under the age of 20 was to remain illegal. There were to be strict potency controls, a licensing regime for commercial growers and an excise tax for the purposes of harm reduction. The bill banned the marketing and advertising of cannabis products and allowed for the promotion of messages and education to prevent cannabis-related harm. The bill did not address medicinal uses, the illegality of driving (or working) under the influence of cannabis, or the production of hemp.

A key difference between the cannabis and euthanasia referendums was the stage in the legislative process they were at before being put to the public. To be passed into law a bill needs to go through three readings – three votes in Parliament – and be subject to scrutiny from a select committee, as well as a 'committee of the whole house' stage, at which there is opportunity for a bill to be debated and voted on, clause by clause, subject to proposed amendments. The euthanasia legislation went through the full legislative process, closely followed by the media throughout the multiple readings and revisions, some emotional and impassioned speeches from MPs, and the votes cast by all MPs, including the prime minister. In contrast, the cannabis measure was simply a draft bill, yet to go through the parliamentary process. As a result, the cannabis bill had less of a public airing than the euthanasia act: as the details of the bill did not get as much scrutiny, there was less opportunity for public input and there was the possibility for details to be changed post-referendum. The lack of long-term media attention or endorsements from politicians through speeches and votes, combined with the potential for the bill to be altered, may have contributed to the public's voting choice and the close final result.

Consequences and criticisms

Voter turnout overall was higher than in 2017, and the highest of any election since 1999. This was widely attributed to the increased availability of advance voting due to the pandemic, but there is some evidence that the two referendums may have also encouraged people to vote. Increases in turnout were not as apparent in voters aged 35 and over (1.13 per cent) as in voters aged 18 to 34 (7.02 per cent of non-Māori, 5.12 per cent of Māori). As cannabis consumption is higher among young adults it is plausible that this may have motivated them to vote in larger numbers (Theodore et al. 2019). The number of special votes cast in 2020 was also an increase on previous years, possibly due to the referendums spurring interest from previous non-voters.

The use of referendums is unlikely to advance the interests of Māori, however. Shortly after the referendum results were released, Associate Professor Khylee Quince said that the results of the cannabis ballot highlighted the difficulties in asking the general population to consider issues which have a disproportionate impact on minorities (Quince 2020). Māori are more likely to be arrested and convicted of a cannabis-related crime than non-Māori (Fergusson, Swain-Campbell and Horwood 2003; Theodore et al. 2020). Cannabis also tends to be identified with Māori, a stereotype reinforced in popular culture despite its widespread consumption across voter demographics (Hokowhitu 2004). The 'Say Nope to Dope' campaign was criticised for reinforcing this stereotype (Taunton 2020). Its campaign against cannabis reform used the picture of a convenience store named 'Kia ora Dopey' with pictures of cannabis leaves superimposed onto the signage (Hawkes 2020). This campaign messaging suggested, incorrectly, that cannabis could be advertised for sale and readily available at corner shops.

It is difficult to ascertain a complete picture of Māori positions on either referendum question because the Electoral Commission did not separate referendum ballots based on Māori or General rolls. Consequently, the only electorate-level data available is that related to special votes, which were overwhelmingly supportive of both cannabis and euthanasia reform. Special votes have favoured the Green Party in every election since 1999 (see this book's chapter 33, by Arseneau and Roberts) and Green voters tend to be younger, with over half their votes previously coming from the 18–45 age bracket (O'Brien 2013). While older Māori cohorts may possibly have been less likely to support euthanasia than the Pākehā majority, such a hypothesis is speculative, with data needed to more completely understand Māori voting on the issue. In future, it would be preferable if the Electoral Commission collected data on referendum votes across electoral rolls so that Māori views can be accurately accounted for. This is particularly important on topics where equity is a concern.

Proponents of cannabis reform lamented the failure of Prime Minister Jacinda Ardern to state her position, which they saw as one of the deciding factors in the narrow referendum loss. Implicit within this argument are two distinct questions. The first is whether Ardern, who stated afterward that she voted 'yes' on both referendums, could have swayed their eventual results. Political science research shows that voters tend to 'follow the leader' on referendum topics. According to data from the New Zealand Attitudes and Values Study, when National MP and prime minister John Key announced a referendum on changing the New Zealand flag in 2015, Labour voters, who had previously been more likely than National voters to want the flag changed, dropped their support for the idea (Satherley et al. 2018). National voters went the opposite way and supported the change, demonstrating that a leader's publicly announced opinions can influence voters.

The second question is whether Ardern had any moral obligation to state her position up front in either of the two referendums. Ardern's socially conservative upbringing may have been a factor in her decision to stay quiet on the subject. The Latter-day Saints Church (for which her father and uncle have been local authorities) is opposed to both euthanasia and the smoking of cannabis. Despite renouncing the religion years earlier, Ardern had tried to strike a balance, stating that she had a real respect for people who have religion as a foundation in their lives and that she also respected people who do not (Smith 2017). A belief that her influence contributed to a positive result might also have put her at odds with conservative Labour MPs in Auckland's south. However, Ardern did vote in favour of euthanasia reform passing through Parliament and had also recently voted in favour of abortion law reform. A more likely explanation is that Ardern was conscious that taking a public stand on the vote would rile socially conservative voters, courted by her centrist politics and decisive leadership in recent crises, including the Covid-19 pandemic. At a time when the prime minister and her party had reached unprecedented levels of support, the raw politics of her decision is apparent: stating how she would vote on either referendum could have amounted to an unnecessary expenditure of political capital.

Aftermath

The prevailing 'no' vote in the cannabis referendum was a message from the electorate that it was not quite ready to embrace comprehensive cannabis law reform. A better question might have been to ask whether the possession of illicit drugs should be treated primarily as a health issue or a criminal issue, which also featured in the 2017 Labour–Green confidence and supply agreement. Such a broad question would have likely removed the stigmatisation of cannabis and the associations that come with it. Furthermore, had such a question on broad drug reform been successful, the government would have had a mandate to decriminalise illicit drugs where appropriate and redirect people with addiction issues away from the courts and into rehabilitation. For opponents of cannabis reform this issue seems won, at least for the time being. While the Green Party is likely to maintain a position of moving the Misuse of Drugs Act away from its punitive underpinnings, the then Minister of Justice Andrew Little ruled out any immediate changes to the law around cannabis possession (Walls 2020).

Unlike the cannabis reforms, where supporters are vowing to fight on, it seems that opponents to euthanasia have accepted the outcome and are now focusing on the implications for their congregations. Senior religious leaders have stated that the practice runs against their core values and will now need to decide whether to perform death and funerary rituals for followers opting to use it (Burrows 2020). While the 'yes' vote has meant that the End of Life Choice Act is now law, it is not yet in practice. In one of Parliament's first post-2020 election sittings, newly elected ACT MP Brooke van Velden sought assurances from Andrew Little that the Ministry of Health, which was now his portfolio, would meet its obligations under the Act: that is, to have the system for assisted dying set up within one year of the referendum for terminally ill people who wished to end their lives. Little responded that he had high expectations the Ministry would meet these commitments.

Conclusion

Referendums, like elections, have winners and losers. In New Zealand, Māori are often those who suffer as a consequence of majority opinion. While it is unclear whether Māori overall opposed or supported euthanasia reform, it is difficult to escape a conclusion that some of the opposition to cannabis law reform was based either on a stereotype that cannabis is primarily abused by Māori or on an indifference to prejudices faced by Māori in the justice system. A silver lining for Chlöe Swarbrick and the Green Party is that voters under 35 turned out in higher numbers than in any election in recent decades, likely connected in part to the two referendum questions, helping Swarbrick win Auckland Central (see this book's chapter 32) and the Greens to increase their parliamentary representation. A referendum 'bump' may also have aided ACT's increase in party vote support (and parliamentary representation).

For all the criticisms of referendums, they do have the effect of identifying majority thought, which can sometimes be unclear during the public submissions process. They can even prompt some who do not feel strongly about a particular topic to at least indicate their preference one way or another. Referendums can also lead to unlikely bedfellows, as MPs choose whether to state their position on a particular issue. While a clear majority in support of the euthanasia act seems to have settled that debate for now, the much smaller majority in opposition to cannabis reform makes it likely that the latter will be revisited at some point in New Zealand's not too distant future.

24

POLITICAL PARTY FUNDING AND THE 2020 ELECTION

Michael Macaulay

Introduction

New Zealand's global reputation as a high trust/high integrity nation is built on many solid foundations. Political party financing is not one of them. In 2013, and again in its 2018 update, Transparency International New Zealand's 'National Integrity Assessment' ranked the country's political parties as among the weakest of institutional democratic pillars in terms of varying categories of integrity (Transparency International New Zealand 2019).

In this century alone, a string of funding scandals has made the headlines (Rashbrooke 2020) and international organisations such as the International Institute for Electoral Assistance (IDEA) continue to point out the many loopholes in New Zealand's systems and processes. Indeed, legislation was amended as recently as 2019 to tighten up some of these funding grey areas.

Whether they were tightened up enough is a different question. In early 2021 the Serious Fraud Office had cases pending against the Labour Party, the National Party and New Zealand First, as well as myriad local government cases, all regarding the legality of political donations. Complicating matters further is that, in the eyes of some commentators, New Zealand already promotes a generous State subsidy for funding, offsetting to some degree the dramatic collapse in political party membership over the last few decades. It is quite the mess, and not what might be expected from a modern democracy, especially not such a supposedly squeaky clean one.

This chapter examines New Zealand's current party funding arrangements, referring to some of the issues that have arisen in the last couple of years. In so doing it tells a story as old as time, showing ways in which our democracy can be – and perhaps is – bought and sold.

Why should we be worried about political party funding?

New Zealand is not alone in its concerns over political parties: the ways in which party funding operates causes consternation all over the world. No matter what the jurisdiction may be, the issues remain more or less the same, revolving around trust, legitimacy and the democratic process.

First, there is the issue of buying one's way directly into politics, and indeed government. In the UK, for example, recent studies confirm long-held public suspicions that party donations lead directly to a seat at the political table. Radford and colleagues (2020) demonstrate the correlation between donations and peerages: major party donors literally buy themselves a seat at the legislative table, effectively becoming legislators through seats in the House of Lords. Perhaps more blatantly still, connections can be seen between campaign funding and appointments in a number of former President Trump's foreign policy choices. For example, it is estimated that around 30 per cent of US ambassadors have been political appointments – personally chosen people without careers in foreign service (Borger 2020). In early 2021, the former President of France, Nicolas Sarkozy, was sentenced to three years' imprisonment on corruption charges relating to party funding, dating back to alleged €50 million undeclared donations by Libyan leader Muammar Gaddafi for Sarkozy's 2007 election campaign (Willsher 2021).

Such activities have long been recognised as influence marketing, which also crosses over into notions of democratic capture and trading in influence. Indeed, Sarkozy was convicted explicitly of influence peddling. Michael Johnston's (2005) work on 'syndromes of corruption' demonstrated that corruption exists all over the world, taking different forms in different political and economic regimes, and with a different legal status in each of them. The syndrome most prevalent in liberal democracies is influence marketing: the legal buying and selling of political power (Johnston 2005), which includes activities such as lobbying, patronage and, of course, political party funding. Not only, in fact, are such activities legal but they are fully commercialised, part of the political furniture.

There is, however, an important distinction to make. As previous studies into political corruption have shown, there is a major difference between *access* and *influence* (Macaulay and Hickey 2011). Some might be surprised by how blatant this can be. In the UK, for example, the Conservative Party advertises a range of different funding mechanisms, culminating in the

'Leaders' Group', an elite membership available to those willing to donate over $50,000 per annum. Here's what that money buys:

> Members are invited to join the Leader and other senior figures from the Conservative Party at dinners, post-PMQ lunches, drinks receptions, election result events and important campaign launches (*The Guardian* 2012).

If an individual would like to meet the British prime minister and have a nice chat over a private lunch, that's how it's done: legally and in full view. In fact, the individual will be mentioned in the register of donors just to ensure that it is all above board.

The Leaders' Group offers a classic example of the problem of access and influence. We can see quite clearly that it provides access to Cabinet ministers, up to and including the prime minister: access is part of the quid pro quo for membership fees. What is not known, however, is where this leads, and whether or not it creates an undue influence in policy decisions.

Distinguishing between these two offers a number of implications. First, whereas the former – access – is relatively easy to demonstrate, the latter is not. Second, it means that the traditional ways of combatting wrongdoing do not necessarily work. Many commentators call for transparency around party donations but, in the cases just noted, the donations are exceedingly transparent. We know who the donors are and what their money is buying. Beyond that there is only speculation as to what the benefits (if any) of that access may be. The limits of transparency have been highlighted in a previous study on UK party funding:

> We used to believe that sunlight was the best disinfectant but now we see it only creates more shadows in which to hide (Macaulay and Hickey 2011).

Too often, issues of political trust appear to focus solely on individual people and specific scandals. What is far more pernicious is trust in the political system itself. The appearance of trading in influence and the concerns around party funding create long-term distrust and unease, not just in political parties but in democratic processes. Populist movements around the world are fuelled partly by distrust in such 'deep state' shenanigans, and there is no large leap from a general feeling of dissatisfaction to anger and conspiracy theories.

To what extent is all this possible in New Zealand? Are fears about people buying access, and perhaps influence, legitimate? Have recent events exacerbated these fears? The answer to all three questions is simple: yes.

2020: Same as it ever was

While 2020 saw yet another outbreak of donation scandals, concerns about party funding date back at least as far as the 1986 Royal Commission on the Electoral System, which found that there was no significant political influence from individuals or groups, nor any corruption in the system. Continuing scandals led to reforms, however, through the 1993 Electoral Act, which required donations of over $10,000 to be declared. A result was that parties simply embraced the loophole of the sub-$10,000 threshold (Rashbrooke 2020). Continued concerns led to the 2007 Electoral Finance Act, quickly repealed in 2009 by the then National government.

Changes and amendments in the law have continued; the legislation was amended as recently as 2019 to try to minimise loopholes for overseas donations. As of January 2020, party secretaries and candidates were not allowed to accept overseas donations above NZ$50. This loophole was closed to minimise potential political influence and 'reduce the risk of foreign money influencing the election process', an interesting development as this was exactly the type of influence that for years we were assured was not possible in New Zealand.

In 2019 the major parties all received substantial amounts of private donations and loans (reported to the Electoral Commission):

- Green Party $339,015.83
- Labour Party $783,919.64
- National Party $1,221,867.08
- NZ First $369,535.17 (plus an additional $44,923.00 in loans).

Nevertheless, the guidelines for political party donations continue to raise potential concerns: there are ample opportunities for donations to remain completely anonymous.

As required by the Electoral Commission (Electoral Commission 2020), every year parties must report:

- every donor who donated over $15,000 during the year
- every contributor who donated over $15,000 during the year

- every anonymous donation over $1,500
- every overseas donation over $1,500
- every contribution from an overseas person over $1,500
- all payments from the Electoral Commission of donations protected from disclosure
- the number of anonymous party donations under $1,500 and the total amount of these donations
- the number of overseas party donations under $1,500 and the total amount of these donations
- the number of all party donations over $1,500 but less than $5,000 and the total amount of these donations
- the number of all party donations over $5,000 but less than $15,000 and the total amount of these donations
- loans over $15,000 entered during the year
- the number and amount of other party loans entered between $1,500 and $15,000.

Donations below $1,500 need not be reported and can remain anonymous. While candidates may only keep up to $50 from overseas, they are allowed to retain up to $1,500 of other anonymous donations. What these regulations offer is a continuation of old loopholes, which recent events demonstrate have been well utilised.

In 2019 Radio New Zealand reported that New Zealand First, since 2017 a coalition partner with Labour, had been receiving loans from an organisation known as the New Zealand First Foundation. According to its official declarations to the Electoral Commission the party had received loans of around $75,000 in 2017 and 2018 respectively, as well as another loan of $45,000 in 2019 from the Foundation. Following investigations by the media it transpired that the Foundation received donations from wealthy supporters, who had offered sums of money that fell just below the threshold that would have forced a legal declaration. Despite the Foundation receiving over $300,000 in donations, the sources of these funds were never revealed (Shand 2019).

The identities of many of the donors have subsequently been discovered. Among them was the person purported to be New Zealand's richest man, Graeme Hart, with records showing two corporate donations to the Foundation of $14,995, $5.01 short of the threshold for declaration (Espiner 2020; Shand and Manch 2020). Concern was noted about donations from the racing industry, not least because Winston

Peters, New Zealand First's leader, was himself the Minister for Racing (among his other roles, including Deputy Prime Minister and Minister of Foreign Affairs).

This information is another manifestation of the problematic dividing line between access and influence. It may well be, for example, that there was no influence sought either directly or indirectly from members of the racing industry while funding the minister responsible for overseeing that same industry. The limits of transparency are also evident: even though it is known that these transactions occurred, it is not known what, if anything, transpired as a result.

When National MP Nick Smith made a speech invoking parliamentary privilege to question the relationship between New Zealand First and the Foundation, he was threatened with a $30 million lawsuit if he raised his questions outside of the parliamentary debating chamber. Even in the legal system, power continues to be brought to bear on proceedings: the parties involved have sought, and won, name suppression through the New Zealand courts on three separate occasions (Espiner 2020).

These scandals are the tip of the iceberg. Major political parties in New Zealand, for example, have also established meet-and-greet opportunities for money, ones that mirror those in the UK and elsewhere. Within the last decade, the National Party's 'Cabinet Club' raised eyebrows for its secrecy and the opportunity it provided for political access. Although shrouded in mystery, it was estimated that under Prime Minister John Key the Cabinet Club averaged NZ$10,000 for membership fees (or donations), which allowed donors to meet for an estimated 53 different lunches and dinners in private gatherings between 2008 and 2014. Even National Party supporters were unhappy with this arrangement: a 2014 poll showed roughly half of National voters considering it 'not a good look' or an outright 'corrupt practice' (Gluck and Macaulay 2017; Trevett 2014).

Labour responded by establishing its own 'President's Club' in 2017, which offered tiered membership (Bronze, Silver, Gold and Platinum) for increasingly large sums of money ($1,000–$5,000+ for the first three tiers; no sum of money was suggested for Platinum membership). No access or influence opportunities were advertised to go along with the donation, although that did not deter media and public scepticism. If nothing else, the President's Club seemed to go against the espoused Labour Party value that:

> All people should have equal access to all social, economic, cultural, political and legal spheres, regardless of wealth or social position, and continuing participation in the democratic process (New Zealand Labour Party 2020).

Equal access does not normally come with a $5,000+ price tag.

It appears, then, that in terms of political party funding New Zealand is as susceptible as other jurisdictions to the many manifestations of trading in influence (Gluck and Macaulay 2017). In the last 20 years alone there has been case after case related to party funding. Winston Peters, for instance, was censured by Parliament in 2008 for not declaring a donation of $100,000. More recently, the scandal around MP Jami-Lee Ross resulted in numerous criminal charges being laid, including some against Ross himself, relating to splitting donations into anonymised chunks, each below the limit needed for declarations.

Learning lessons?

To some commentators, all of the worry over party funding may be a case of misdirection. Perhaps the bigger issue has to do with alternative funding sources. With party memberships having declined, both Labour and National are currently holding only about 10 per cent of the members that they had back in the 1980s. Not only has that source of funding been reduced, it has, more pertinently, eroded party accountability.

Some have argued that in reality New Zealand parties are funded more strongly by the State than by private donors. The Electoral Commission's electoral broadcasting fund was worth $4,145,750 during the 2020 election campaign, available to be used for production costs as well as the purchase of advertising space on television, radio or online during the election period. A much more substantial source of funding comes directly from Parliament itself. Excluding MPs' salaries, political parties were given approximately $50 million in support (Parliamentary Service 2020), leading some commentators to assert that

> In theory, all of these budgets are for Parliamentary purposes, but in reality, they're used for 'the permanent campaign', in which the politicians convert these resources into techniques designed to build their party vote (Edwards 2018).

New Zealand faces a different sort of democratic capture, one already achieved by the principal political parties.

The opacity of funding issues represents a two-fold attack on public trust. On the one hand, these issues contribute to a lack of trust in politicians. Revelations that New Zealand First had been anonymously funded by wealthy businessmen raised doubts about the party's anti-business rhetoric almost comparable to scepticism about Trump 'draining the swamp' while being funded by wealthy corporate donors.

Of far greater import, however, is trust in the political system and the democratic process, and the dangers associated with populist, anti-establishment political movements. Once trust in the system is gone there is far less readiness to adhere to the rule of law, or to believe in the fairness and integrity of election results. A lack of trust leads to a withdrawal from political processes, fuelling further distrust.

Much can be done to prevent this, little of which would be uncontroversial. Consideration can be given to tightening of loopholes: while small-scale anonymous donations may be justified, there can be no excuse for maintaining a system that enables donors to provide thousands of dollars in secret by avoiding the reporting limits. New Zealand is one of the few countries to have specific legislation against trading in influence, although as a fairly nebulous section of the Crimes Act its provisions could be much more tightly drawn (Gluck and Macaulay 2017). The matters before the Serious Fraud Office involving the National Party and the New Zealand First Foundation involved 'obtaining by deception' rather than any specific electoral legislation.

More controversial would be State funding for political parties. It has potential pitfalls, not least of which is an assumed, though rarely tested, lack of popularity with citizens. The last 20 years alone have provided so many problematic examples that it is clear that a proper conversation about the idea needs to be had. The variety of party funding arrangements around the globe is considerable (see, for example, the ACE project's database on party funding: ACE 2020) and the policy is worthy of further exploration. Until then we can be assured of at least two things: that any new loopholes that may be created will be used; and that further funding scandals can be expected to emerge on a fairly regular basis.

25

PERFORMING POLITICS: LEADERS' DEBATES IN THE 2020 ELECTION

Geoffrey Craig

Introduction

The New Zealand election of 2020 was profoundly influenced by the effects of the Covid-19 virus, which significantly impacted on the economy, social life and the national psyche. Evaluations of the past management of the virus and possible future responses to its effects not only dominated election debate but significantly shaped public perceptions of the prime minister, Jacinda Ardern, and a national desire for political continuity. The election was also influenced by the elevation of Judith Collins to the position of leader of the opposition only three months before the election, following Todd Muller's less than two-month tenure in the position, after he had successfully challenged Simon Bridges in May. Collins' ascension to opposition leader generated media excitement and political drama, but the upheavals in the leadership of the National Party over 2020 provided a sharp contrast to the prime minister's competent management of a national crisis over the corresponding period. These respective political fortunes were reflected in public opinion polls prior to the start of the election campaign, with Labour holding a strong lead and the National Party appearing to have little chance of electoral success.

These political circumstances framed the general election campaign and the series of leaders' debates that formed a central part of the election contest. The discussion here will offer an initial overview of the roles and effects of the leaders' debates throughout the election campaign. I will note the prevalence and types of debates throughout the campaign, the legal challenges over participation in the debates, the status of the debates as media events, the role of the debate hosts, and the effectiveness of the debate panel discussions. The analysis will consider the content, performances and reception of each of the major television debates, including a discussion of the smaller party and electorate television debates. The conclusion will be oriented towards the roles of leaders' debates in future elections, and briefly offer some suggestions about the formats of the leaders' debates, including the possibility of reinstating major and minor party shared participation in debates, and the role of debate moderators in eliciting substantive exchanges between debate participants. The chapter, as such, seeks to offer both a review of the leaders' debates in the 2020 election campaign and a critique of the debates with accompanying recommendations for future election campaigns.

The public was once again well served by a large number of televised, streamed and public debates across the country throughout the 2020 election campaign, providing voters with access to party policy positions and opportunities to scrutinise individual candidates. In addition to the major national televised debates, the live-streamed *Press* debate in Christchurch attracted much attention and there were also individual electorate debates, including Māori electorate debates, referendum debates, and specific live-streamed 'themed' debates. Māori electorate debates were hosted on Newshub's *The Hui* programme and on Māori Television. Specific themed debates included the TVNZ Young Voters' debate (*New Zealand Herald* 2020) as well as debates between spokespeople for particular portfolios, most notably between party finance spokespeople (Ensor 2020, Cooke and Manch 2020), but also other policy areas, such as the arts, culture and the creative sector (Brooks 2020). In addition, there were debates about the two referendum topics: the End of Life Choice Act and the cannabis legalisation and control bill (Davison 2020; *1 News* 2020).

It has become almost a regular feature of New Zealand elections that disputes arise over debate participation. The 2020 televised debates were no exception, with issues surrounding the selection of participants from the smaller parties. There were initial expressions of concern about the inclusion of the Advance New Zealand Party in the TVNZ multi-party debate, with TVNZ including the party because its co-leader Jami-Lee Ross was a current MP (Graham-McLay 2020, Te Pou 2020). The Advance New Zealand Party attracted controversy because of its views about Covid-19, 5G and the United Nations, and it barely registered in public opinion polls, despite a presence on social media (Graham-McLay 2020). The Māori Party were also included in the TVNZ minor party debate after challenging an earlier ruling excluding it (Graham-McLay 2020,

Wade 2020). The Advance New Zealand Party also took legal action, against Newshub, after being excluded from the 'Powerbrokers debate' (Owen 2020). The New Conservatives Party took legal action against TVNZ after it was excluded from the network's minor party debate, failing to reach TVNZ's criteria of either polling at 3 per cent or having a seat in Parliament (Wade 2020).

The televised leaders' debates were prominent features of the 2020 election campaign, providing some emphatic performances and giving shape to an overall campaign narrative, but the immediate media and public reception of the debates was often detached from parties' and leaders' prevailing political fortunes. Televised leaders' debates provide a dramatic forum and, as such, the news media require dramatic events and performances to animate an election 'race'. However, the 2020 debates were characterised by a disjuncture between the drama of the events and the campaign's underlying political realities. Public opinion polling prior to the first major party debate showed Labour in a position to govern alone – in accord with the final election result – and the stream of news media reporting occasionally and quietly acknowledged that the 'die might already be cast' (Malpass 2020b). Importantly, the purpose of leaders' debates, and election campaigns in general, is to provide opportunities for political dialogue and public participation and reflection, independent of pre-existing political circumstances and evaluations of whether debates and campaigns facilitate changes in political fortunes or public opinion. The 2020 debates, however, assumed an autonomous status as media events, and their reception was driven by a media framing where the need for a contest and performative distinction overshadowed an evaluation of the merits of the political discourse.

The elevation of the debates as media events was partly realised by the prominent involvement of the debate hosts, who acted more as interviewers of the individual candidates rather than as moderators of exchanges between the party leaders. Both the major networks selected individual hosts for the debates: TVNZ had John Campbell and Jessica Mutch McKay, Newshub had Paddy Gower and Simon Shepherd (hosting the network's multi-party debate). It seems that involvement of a debate panel of journalist questioners, featured in previous campaigns, is no longer the networks' preferred model, with the debates having become vehicles for the promotion of particular political correspondents and broadcasters. TVNZ did include questions from members of the public at the start of debate sections in its opening debate, but there was not the more pervasive inclusion of the public seen in previous campaigns, such as the active involvement of YouTube questioners. The format did not encourage sustained periods of debate between party leaders and often singular questions were posed to individual leaders. The mode of questioning varied considerably across the debate hosts, but in each case the hosts were active agents in the proceedings, often intervening in the party leaders' answers. Of course, hosts will always be prominent figures in debates and they have important functions: voicing concerns of electors, ensuring politicians abide by debate rules, managing conflict between participants, and ensuring that politicians provide reasonable answers to posed questions rather than engaging in obfuscation. The 2020 election debates, however, for all their differences in host style and format, proffered a model of interaction where the moderator was the fulcrum of attention. Jacinda Ardern and Judith Collins spent much of their time attempting to persuade the host of the legitimacy of their position, with the leaders' exchanges limited to short and sharp interruptions to answers. There are virtues to this type of interaction, highlighting processes of accountability, but it also has the effect of channelling and evaluating political discourse through reference to the media framing of issues. What was missing from the televised leaders' debates were substantive, focused exchanges between the political leaders, where policy differences could not only be articulated but also subjected to extended critique by one another. Such interactions would more effectively highlight differences and promote a more challenging political environment, requiring viewers to more actively evaluate competing values, interests and priorities.

The 2020 election debates were also characterised by a decline in the significance of post-debate panel discussions alongside the growing influence of social media on public perceptions. TVNZ commitment to post-debate commentary was weak: the first debate featured only one political scientist in addition to the network's Jessica Mutch McKay and the final TVNZ debate, hosted by Mutch McKay, did not feature a panel at all. Newshub's major party debate featured a panel discussion, hosted by Tova O'Brien, including three journalists and political commentators, where the performances and evaluations of the debate 'victor' were foregrounded in the discussion. (In addition, there were brief, awkward individual appearances by party leaders themselves.) A noteworthy feature was that all of the debate participants were women, countering the traditional masculinist emphasis of political journalism and commentary. The debate panel discussions were nonetheless not set up to allow for a sustained analysis of debate substance, the segments seeming little more than token gestures towards some kind of debate closure. It has been noted previously that post-debate panel discussions have been undermined by practices of two-screen viewing that allow public dissemination of evaluations on social media prior to any post-debate commentary (Craig 2016), shifting the balance of power between commentators and viewers (Anstead and O'Loughlin 2011). Future debates could perhaps acknowledge this contemporary reality, providing more substantive panel discussion and critique of an already unfolding public response. Notwithstanding evidence that a hierarchy of voices persist within social media (Craig 2016, p. 91), social media enables a proliferation of voices (while also amplifying a broadcast media propensity to highlight 'iconic moments' which can, in turn, be deployed for particular political gain). As Venuto (2020) noted:

> Both sides have selected favourable sections from the televised debate to use as evidence of their dominance on social media. . . . These punchy social media messages served on repeat loops will hammer home the exact messaging the politician hopes to get across.

Any evaluation of televised leaders' debates must, as previously suggested (Craig 2016), acknowledge their performative element as well as their televised character, one which prioritises visual presentation, debates' status as a form of entertainment and the length of debate exchanges. While political leaders must be cognisant of the requirements of the genre, imposing upon themselves an appropriate discipline, and viewers must appreciate that the exchanges are not 'debates' in the best sense of the term (involving a consistent and detailed examination of the merits of respective arguments), it nonetheless remains the case that televised leaders' debates are the most high profile and extended opportunities for politicians to speak to the general electorate and for citizens to learn of their respective policy positions, evaluating political leaders through the witnessing of contrasting performances. That said, the 2020 debates highlighted a media propensity to use performance as the evaluative frame in debate discussion, underlining a limited willingness to dissect and judge issues of political content and value. As Van Beynen (2020) wrote:

> The circus-type approach of the debates makes them more of an entertaining spectacle but hinders any enlightening contest of ideas. Information and policy positions elicited by genuine argument and counter-argument are lost in the fray. Zingers and one-liners become more important than real engagement on the issues.

This presentation and framing of the debates, in turn, had the effect of creating something of a disparity between media commentary and public opinion:

> After the first two televised debates, political 'experts' would gather round and talk about how strong Collins had been and how she clearly won. . . . Except a lot of people didn't see that. They saw someone who was practically bullying the Prime Minister. And people really really don't like that (Cormack 2020).

Journalistic focus on performance and debate 'winners' is a long-standing feature of reporting on leaders' debates and election commentary more generally, where the accompanying frequent coverage of opinion polling only exacerbates the 'horse-race' framing of election contests. This type of debate and election reporting, where there is both quantification and personalisation as a basis for political assessment, provides journalism with both a defense of objectivity and a refuge from charges of bias. It also offers a means of avoiding the difficult task of examining the conflicting political and social values underlying political parties' respective policy positions.

TVNZ first leaders' debate

The first major party debate of the 2020 campaign saw strongly contrasting performances from the two participants: National Party leader Judith Collins was trying too hard to make an impact, while Prime Minister Jacinda Ardern was trying too hard *not* to make an impact. Steve Braunias (2020a) wrote after the debate: 'Collins was animated, hooting and scoffing hither and yon, but Ardern was tranquil as a lake, and just as flat.' Collins was generally cast as the 'winner' of the debate, a verdict she was keen to confirm to reporters, although

Luke Malpass (2020a) wrote that while 'Jacinda Ardern lost the first leaders' debate . . . Judith Collins didn't win it', noting how opposition leaders were often judged to have performed well in initial debates in a campaign given they are sharing the same stage as a national leader. The debate did, however, provide the National Party leader with some positive media response and a degree of momentum in the early part of the campaign.

The prime minister's debate performance may have seemed initially confounding, given her noted communication skills and the anticipated scrutiny of the nation. It was the first time she had debated her political rival outside of Parliament. Her performance can be explained partly through reference to the differing requirements of the political and media 'fields' (Bourdieu 1991). As is now customary, TVNZ announced the latest Colmar Brunton public opinion poll results in its news bulletin immediately prior to the debate, showing Labour could govern alone at 48 per cent and National languishing on 31 per cent. As such, Ardern's priority was not so much to perform for the media but more to protect her political interests. While the media field focused on the immediate dynamics of the debate itself, the longer-term requirement, from the prime minister's perspective, was the maintenance of the political status quo and the preservation of Labour's lead. Such a strategy prompted an understated, 'sober' performance which could nonetheless assist Ardern in appearing appropriately prime ministerial in difficult times, in contrast to the provocative Collins, even if such a strategy led to some short-term media criticism. Equally, the debate highlighted that while Ardern is a polished media performer, a more combative debate genre works against her overall approach. Speaking after the debate, Ardern said: 'My view is that politics is not a blood sport. It is a chance for people to see what our ambitions are, where we want to take New Zealand, and I think we had the platform for that tonight.' Responding to criticism, she added: 'I've never done the personal and I won't – that's not how I do politics and that's not how I campaign' (Small 2020). Ardern's political success suggests the wisdom of such a strategy, with the prime minister also signalling some dissatisfaction with the media presentation and adjudication of the debates, an opinion also suggested by other comments after subsequent debates.

While much attention focused on party leaders' performance, the debate did also offer contrasting ideas on issues of national significance.

Topics discussed included: climate change, hospitals, education, tax rates, inequality, housing, farming and the environment, and, not surprisingly, the Covid response. In one point of contrast, Ardern noted her government had raised the minimum wage and would continue to do so, while Collins said the wage level would not be further increased under a National-led government. Collins emphasised the need for reform of the Resource Management Act (RMA) to facilitate more housing development. The National leader stated that farmers felt they were 'bagged all the time' by the government, Labour's leader countering by describing Collins' remarks as representing a 'world that has passed', instead linking future farming development and export growth to greater levels of sustainability. Absent from the debate discussion was any reference to Māori rights and interests, prompting Leonie Hayden (2020) to lament that 'an hour-long discussion about the future of our country took place without any recognition we exist, and it was absolutely heartbreaking.'

The opening TVNZ debate took place without an audience, with Auckland under Covid-19 alert level 2.5, limiting the size of public gatherings. This had the effect of diminishing the drama of the event. Audiences are not merely spectators of debates but contributors to them, an effect strongly evident where Newshub's debate's more active audience involvement animated the event, with an impact on leaders' performances. This contrasting use of audiences for the debates across the two networks replicated a contrast that had been evident in 2017 (Craig 2018). As moderator, John Campbell's familiar, idiosyncratic manner had the effect of rendering the debate less combative, making the subject matter more accessible, and perhaps making the debate participants more comfortable. He still interjected at times with critical questions, such as his querying of whether Judith Collins had really answered the question posed by Auckland City Missioner Chris Farrelly and also whether RMA reform really was the most important response to the housing crisis and income inadequacy. While Campbell's manner fostered a positive and gently critical perspective towards the debate exchanges, visual representations, such as the use of cutaways and split screen shots, were often used to highlight conflict, as when Judith Collins shook her head when Ardern was talking about climate change. Campbell's performance did prompt some criticism about the length of some of his questions and losing his train of thought at one stage (Jennings 2020a). The studio set-up was alienating, with Campbell somewhat marooned, standing before the leaders. As Mark Jennings (2020a) wrote: 'Campbell bobbed and weaved, walked and, at times contorted, his clipboard clutched under an arm or held to his chest. The man needed a podium.'

Newshub leaders' debate

The second debate between the Labour and National leaders took place on Newshub, the debate hosted by national correspondent Patrick Gower. The Newshub debate was framed by the acrimonious first US presidential debate between Joe Biden and Donald Trump a few hours earlier, prompting Sam Sachdeva (2020) to comment that the contrast provided 'a reminder of both the healthier state of our politics and that of our country overall'. The second debate traversed a very broad range of issues, if rather superficially at times, prompted by Gower's demands for short answers. The debate covered some important issues (also discussed in the first debate), such as responses to the Covid-19 crisis, the environment and climate change.

There was a significant point of difference between the two leaders regarding whether companies should repay the Covid-19 wage subsidy if they had remained financially healthy, and there was also contrast over house prices, with Collins saying 'in some cases they will have to go down' while Ardern said 'I want them to stabilise.' The ideological contrast between the two major parties was highlighted in a sequence that covered issues of child abuse, gangs and the methadone crisis, with the National Party leader emphasising law-and-order responses while the Labour leader emphasised the need for public services. Collins agreed with the notion that the right to silence should be abolished in child abuse cases but Ardern declared this had been tried unsuccessfully in Australia. Ardern admitted she had tried cannabis when younger but refused to say how she would vote in the upcoming referendum; Collins said she had not used cannabis and would be voting 'No'. Other topics discussed included the teaching of Te Reo, Pharmac funding, post-election negotiations, gun laws, the controversy over proposed construction at Ihumātao (on ancestral Māori land in south Auckland), and the performance of US president Donald Trump. In a final quickfire round a diverse range of topics were raised, including sugary drinks, gender-neutral bathrooms in schools, subsidising sanitary products, a statue of Kate Sheppard at Parliament, and whether the name of the country should be changed to

'Aotearoa'. In a moment of agreement, both leaders supported an increase to the parliamentary term from three to four years.

The Labour leader was more active and interventionist in the second debate, prompting commentators to observe that 'Jacinda Ardern dropped the bureaucratic speak for a second leaders' debate that was peppered with testy exchanges' (Manch and Cooke 2020). Ryan Bridge (2020) wrote:

> Thankfully for the average punter Ardern dropped the 'double duty' speak, allowing clear messaging on the likes of health, labelling the system 'broken' and asking for another term to fix it. The retort 'Deep breath, Judith' and an acknowledgment Collins was 'very assertive in a debate' were welcome signs there was fight and personality in the Ardern of Round Two.

The National Party leader seemed to have been buoyed by her opening debate performance: 'Collins took things up a notch from an already assertive performance in the first debate, perhaps emboldened by the positive reception that came her way' (Sachdeva 2020). Overall, media commentary opined that there was no clear victor from the second debate, Luke Malpass (2020b) writing: 'It was a strong performance by both leaders and, overall, is best scored a tie.'

Perhaps the most striking difference between the opening two debates was in the performance of the debate moderators. As noted, Campbell was criticised for the length of some of his questions while Gower animatedly fired questions at the debaters, then quickly interrupted answers, often providing commentary about the merits of the answers. Gower generally received positive reviews. Bryce Edwards (2020) wrote that Gower 'was fun, insightful, and a useful inquisitor of the two major party leaders who are vying to be prime minister.' Steve Braunias (2020b) wrote that Gower 'played a stormer. He threw questions at Ardern and Collins willy-nilly, and forced them to answer quickly, driving them sometimes mad, sometimes silly.' It is also possible to conclude, however, that Gower's performance rendered the event less a political debate and more a carnivalesque game show, demanding (for instance) that Ardern and Collins 'quickly give us something visionary' while also (in the quickfire section) interrogating the political leaders on subjects such as how many times per week they ate meat. It is acknowledged that Gower was trying to provoke Ardern and Collins out of their comfort zones and that political discourse has a 'rough and tumble' character, and it is equally recognised that everyday issues are informed by important political dimensions, but the breathless, scattergun manner of the event was frustrating. Ardern and Collins were not given a chance to debate each other about the respective merits of their party policies, although Gower did seek to generate conflict between them, a point observed by Mark Jennings (2020b), who noted that Gower ignored the Labour leader's pleading to be able to answer a question when Collins interrupted her, writing: 'He deliberately ignored . . . [her] because he wanted Ardern to get stuck in and mix it with Collins.' Research by Mark Boyd (2020) shows that the Newshub debate generated the shortest sound bites of all the major debates and that Gower's speaking time was actually greater than Ardern's, the only debate where a moderator's share of speaking time exceeded one of the party leaders. Such debates may align with a social media world where attention levels are increasingly limited, and they may be in accord with public frustrations about politicians' skills of obfuscation, but one of the virtues of televised leaders' debates is that they provide an opportunity for extended discussion of important issues. The extent to which this debate did not fulfil those criteria can perhaps be captured in the prime minister's observation that the event had 'almost a pub quiz feel' and in her comment, in response to Tova O'Brien afterwards, that 'I always prefer a debate where there is a bit more room for people to make their view known.' In this sense, perhaps we should distinguish the lengthier televised leaders' debates from the cut-and-thrust of shorter political interviews, recognising debates' greater opportunities for extended critique and discussion.

Multi-party debates

Under MMP, smaller parties have become electorally more important, highlighted in 2020 by polls suggesting there was a fine line between Labour having to rely on the Greens to form a government and being able to govern alone. Regardless of the eventual outcome, the opportunity for smaller parties to give voice to their policies and to share a national stage is important for the nation's democracy, particularly when it is otherwise difficult for them to gain much news coverage. This partly explains the willingness of some parties to take legal action in bids to appear in the multi-party debates.

The Newshub Powerbrokers debate featured ACT's David Seymour, the Greens' Marama Davidson, the Māori Party's John Tamihere and New Zealand First's Winston Peters. The debate was a lively, good-spirited and casual encounter – with candidates seated on bar stools – and commentators believed that all candidates performed well, although attention focused on the performances of Peters and Tamihere and their interactions with each other. Peters had earlier indicated that he would not take part in the debate, deciding otherwise closer to the event. Much was made of the deputy prime minister's good-humoured and low-key manner in spite of polls suggesting his party would not have a presence in the next Parliament. Jonathan Milne (2020) wrote of the veteran politician: 'Peters didn't win the debate. If this had been a four-person race, he wasn't even a medalist.' Toby Manhire (2020) said of Peters: '. . . he was relaxed, quick, funny, grinning – he appeared not to have a worry in the world . . .' The only non-sitting MP in the debate, Tamihere seemed at ease, entertaining the audience with some good lines, including the observation about David Seymour that 'He's the recipient of the house burning down. It's Judith's job to save the furniture, but what she doesn't understand is David's out the back taking a lot of it out.' More seriously, Tamihere performed strongly on a number of issues, highlighting Māori perspectives, and in particular speaking in defence of those occupying the land at Ihumātao. Thomas Coughlan (2020) wrote: 'Tamihere dominated the debate, taking questions to where he wanted them to go, regardless of the intentions of other people on stage.' The debate covered a number of major policy areas, including Covid, the economy and the housing crisis.

TVNZ's multi-party debate featured the Greens' James Shaw, Winston Peters, David Seymour, John Tamihere and Jami-Lee Ross. Thomas Manch (2020) observed that: 'There was no clear winner, though Seymour was buoyed by his continued success in the polls. Māori Party co-leader John Tamihere . . . took the opportunity to speak forcefully to his constituency.' The debate covered a number of issues, including whether the 5 per cent party-vote threshold for Parliament should be lowered, education and schools, Covid, and which other parties the debate participants could work with in government. David Seymour reiterated his belief that New Zealand needed to be 'Taiwan-smart' in its Covid-19 response, using new technologies to restrict the virus without lockdowns, prompting James Shaw to declare it was 'extraordinary' that a libertarian party would suggest such an imposition on civil liberties. Media commentators criticised Ross' false claims about Covid-19 fatality rates (with comparisons to the flu). While debate chair Jessica Mutch McKay was generally praised for her control over the direction and flow of the debate, the event highlighted the difficulty of providing opportunities for substantive discourse when there are a significant number of debate participants. Russell Palmer noted: 'With more than 16 minutes of ads spread in four blocks across the hour, and five leaders to bounce ideas and insults off one another, last night's debate made for frantic, fractured viewing.' This view was raised by both Seymour and Shaw after the debate, the ACT leader declaring: 'I would've liked there to have been more order and a bit more time to get each person's policy across and less interruption' (Palmer 2020).

The Māori electorate debates screening on Newshub's *The Hui* and Māori Television offered a clear contrast to the major party televised leaders' debates. Debate moderator Mihingarangi Forbes allowed debate participants to answer questions at some length, free from constant interruption. The debates grounded issues in particular electorates, with vox-pops of citizens on the streets outlining their major concerns and debate questions raised by people in the electorate. While particular issues were associated with individual electorates, common concerns were expressed relating to housing, drugs and employment. Māori Television's Whakatau 2020 election coverage also featured Māori electorate debates, hosted by moderator David Jones. These included overviews of individual electorates and results from electorate opinion polls, as well as panel discussions within the body of the debates, accompanied by questions for the debate participants.

Final TVNZ leaders' debate

The final TVNZ leaders' debate, conducted only two days before the election, was significant not so much for the merits of the debate but because it highlighted how having a series of debates across an election campaign helps to construct a campaign narrative reflecting the emerging fortunes of the respective political leaders. The early initiative that the National Party leader gained from strong performances in the opening debates ebbed as the campaign unfolded and election day loomed. Most commentators called the final debate for Ardern or declared it a draw, with much attention focused on Collins' more subdued performance. Simon Wilson (Trevett et al. 2020) observed that 'Collins was less interrupty but seemed to have run out of puff . . .' while Justin Giovannetti (*The Spinoff* 2020) was more forthright: 'Judith Collins is done . . . The tank is empty; she'd so clearly like this all to be done.' In contrast, it was observed that Ardern 'was in the ascendant. She looked like she knew what she was doing. She looked like herself' (Braunias 2020c). Overall, the final debate had less of a combative tone. As Claire Trevett observed, it 'was more of a conversation than the rambunctious debates earlier in the campaign' (Trevett et al. 2020).

Jacinda Ardern's declaration that she would not stay on as opposition leader if Labour did not win the election garnered media attention. The debate was framed with an initial discussion of the latest Colmar Brunton public opinion poll. The two party leaders discussed child poverty, house prices and whether a border exception should be made for agricultural workers from the Pacific. Ardern and Collins also discussed Māori issues with regard to state care for children, inter-generational poverty and the court system. With election day imminent, there was discussion of the influence of minor parties, with Collins pushing the idea that Labour would implement the Greens' proposed wealth tax, a suggestion strongly rejected by Ardern. In their final pitch to the electorate, Ardern said to those still undecided that a vote for Labour was for continuing strong, stable government, Collins that the National Party understands business and has a decisive leader.

The final debate was chaired by Jessica Mutch McKay, the *1 News* Political Editor. The debate took place with an audience, which helped enliven the event, and Mutch McKay was able to use a podium, unlike in the opening TVNZ debate. The studio setting, with both leaders seated behind a curved bench and judicious use of camera angles, provided a more coherent televisual event than the first TVNZ debate. Mutch McKay continued the same process of questioning as in earlier debates, alternating questions to the leaders on broad issues. While enabling a conversation between the two leaders and Mutch McKay and providing opportunities for more extended responses, the debate host was still the fulcrum of attention and evaluating body. Mutch McKay said a call was put out to undecided voters, and many questions received, although their concerns were put to the leaders by the debate host rather than members of the public.

Conclusion

The 2020 televised leaders' debates were a central feature of the election, providing high profile performances and scrutiny of political leaders and their parties' policies. The debates replicated and reproduced the country's political culture, focusing prominently on the two major parties, reflected through the character and performance of their respective leaders. Other parties were acknowledged, yet separated from the major parties, and their debates were not necessarily screened in prime time. Televised leaders' debates, as performance-based media events, always make it a struggle to find an appropriate balance between the merits of particular policies and the communication of those policies by the individual party leaders. It is also a struggle to find appropriate mixes of debates with due regard to participants, formats and the timing of debates over the course of an election campaign. The staging of leaders' debates also poses unique production problems: for instance, particular parties may not agree to sharing a stage with others.

Looking forward to the next election, the debates could be enhanced by greater public participation, through more active audiences (assuming no public health restrictions), the posing of more questions from voters, and more reporting of immediate social media responses to the debates. This would enable the expression of diverse voices and viewpoints and help convey the significance of the public's agency in the election campaign, rather than positing the public only as passive observers of a media spectacle or as disembodied aggregates in opinion poll data. It is also unfortunate that leaders' debates in recent elections have not been able to have representatives from major and smaller parties together on the same stage as in previous elections. Such a format would prompt more nuanced debate, as party leaders negotiate expressions of commonality with potential coalition partners while outlining differences with political adversaries. This format would also more closely reproduce the parliamentary context, conveying some of the complexity of the spectrum of responses to policy issues in contrast to the 'zero-sum' perceptions characterising debates between Labour and National leaders.

While much of the news coverage and commentary about the leaders' debates focused on Judith Collins' more assertive efforts, it is perhaps worth considering the value of Jacinda Ardern's consistent refusal to be more personally combative in the exchanges and her attempts to have the debates oriented more towards substantive discussion. This strategy enabled Ardern to appear prime ministerial in this election campaign, but it also echoed her approach in 2017. The contrast between Ardern's more consultative political style and the combative character of the televised debates was evident throughout Ardern's debate performances as she sometimes vainly, and sometimes successfully, challenged and recast the framing and flow of the discussion. Such attempts highlighted the dominant media structuring of the debates while suggesting an alternative possibility, involving more extended and considered political discourse in the debate exchanges. Televised leaders' debates rightly need to be engaging television, offering lively interactions, but the 2020 televised leaders' debates also highlighted the need to balance such requirements with the offering of space and time for the detailed explanation and examination of policies crucial to viewers' lives.

Ardern's electoral success was, of course, based on a variety of factors, but her debate performances and her stated desire to focus on explaining the merits of her party's policies may have resonated with viewers' wishes. As such, the news media might do well to reconsider their breathless adjudications about the 'winners' of debates, and reflect on whether members of the public might like to hear more from politicians, and less from debate moderators, as they decide who will next govern the country.

26

WHY LABOUR WON – SURVEY FINDINGS AND THE 2020 ELECTION

Stephen Mills, Marcus Downs and Thomas Butt

The lead-up

The polling trend throughout the 2014 to 2017 term pointed to New Zealand First deciding the outcome of the 2017 general election. That proved to be the case. Prior to Covid in the 2017–2020 term, UMR polls pointed to a Labour and Greens government but it was close. In late 2019 New Zealand First, albeit just clinging to 5 per cent, was back in the box seat (Figures 26.1 and 26.2).[1] A generally positive mood and a massive leadership advantage would probably have secured the return of a Labour-led government. But there was little chance and zero expectation of an absolute majority for Labour prior to Covid. The interlocked issues of Jacinda Ardern's leadership and strong support for her government's handling of the pandemic reset the political numbers.

Labour had only just got into play prior to the 2017 election with the change in leadership to Jacinda Ardern. That triggered a shuffling of the Opposition party votes, with Greens and New Zealand First voters going to Labour. That late leadership change did not have much, if any, discernible impact on the National party vote. This time was different. Covid triggered a big shift of National voters across the right–left divide to Labour.

As outlined in Figure 26.3, Colmar Brunton polls showed a stronger pre-Covid position for the centre-right. A Colmar Brunton poll in November 2019 also pointed to a centre-right win. A full set of public poll results in the lead-in to Covid is included in Table 26.1 at the end of this chapter.

The mood

New Zealanders were generally positive about the direction of the country prior to the arrival of Covid. This continued the long-term trend of satisfaction with the government and the prime minister that has lasted since Helen Clark defeated Jenny Shipley in 1999 (Figure 26.4).

The view that the country was heading in the right direction leapt upwards when the pandemic struck and hit record highs for a 30-year-old tracking series. This was an obvious tribute to the government's handling of the pandemic (Figure 26.5).

Leadership

Jacinda Ardern gave Labour a huge advantage on leadership throughout the term (Figure 26.6). This advantage increased when Covid hit.

Jacinda Ardern was as dominant as John Key and Helen Clark in their popularity primes. In April 2020 she hit a peak favourability rating of 83 per cent favourable, 14 per cent unfavourable, narrowly ahead of John Key's best of 81 per cent favourable, 16 per cent unfavourable recorded in October 2009. Helen Clark's peak was 78 per cent favourable, 20 per cent unfavourable in April 2002.

In UMR's post-election survey 59 per cent of Labour voters rated Jacinda Ardern's leadership as 'critically important' in determining their vote. A further 29 per cent rated her leadership as 'one of the main things they considered'. Equivalent 'critically important' ratings for other leaders were 31 per cent for David Seymour from ACT voters and 25 per cent for Judith Collins from National voters.[2]

The prime minister's considerable political strengths, centred on empathy, are captured in an October 2020 word cloud (Figure 26.7). There were few (and only small) negatives for an Opposition to work on.

The three National Party leaders after Bill English struggled to meet the obviously very difficult challenges of being an Opposition during a pandemic. None ever matched the favourability rating English enjoyed when he departed the National Party leadership. Simon Bridges was never popular but, prior to Covid, could perhaps make the case that his all-out attack style was delivering a party vote dividend. Post-Covid his personal ratings were the lowest ever recorded for a National Party leader in UMR tracking. Some belated credit is perhaps due to the much-maligned Labour leaders between Clark and Ardern (Figure 26.8). National arguably compressed the equivalent of nine years of Labour leadership dramas into a year.

Judith Collins was the highest rating of the three National leaders in 2020. Her word cloud highlights a powerful set of positives – tough, strong, determined – but also significant negatives, centred on being too aggressive (Figure 26.9).

The issues

Covid obviously dominated the 2020 election. The three top issues, averaged from monthly polling over 2020 (asking respondents what was the most important issue facing New Zealand today), were the economy, Covid and unemployment (Figure 26.10). None of these featured in 2017. Housing and poverty, the top two issues in 2017, came in fourth and fifth.

Despite some things going wrong, UMR and other public polls consistently showed strong support for the government's management of the pandemic response (Figure 26.11). Critically, the government got in early on the right side (and National on the wrong side) of a public view that saving lives should be the priority, ahead of the economy. The question below (Figure 26.12) does not capture the complexities of the health vs economy trade-off but it was very evident in qualitative research that a segment of voters thought Ardern and the Labour-led government were prioritising health and lives and National were not.

The head-to-head ratings on the 'better government to handle Covid issues' were decisively in Labour's favour (Figure 26.13). This included handling the economic recovery from Covid, where National would perhaps have been expected to prevail. National did spasmodically campaign on the theme that while the Labour-led government had done okay on the immediate health response, National was better suited to the follow-up task of rebuilding the economy. This was the top-rating argument for National voters from a prompted list testing importance of vote-driving factors (see Figure 26.20).

Other issues were overshadowed by Covid but the big movement to Labour drove its head-to-head ratings versus National upwards on all issues tested in UMR's post-election survey (see Figure 26.22). On housing – the top issue in 2017, and one on which Labour had faltered – the party still improved a net 17 points from 2017, leading National in 2020 by 40 per cent to 23 per cent, with 37 per cent seeing no difference or being unsure. Covid also largely removed tax as a campaign issue. Neither a generous temporary tax cut offered by National nor a sustained allegation late in the campaign that Labour would, despite its denials, introduce some form of the wealth tax proposed by the Greens had any serious impact on voting intentions.

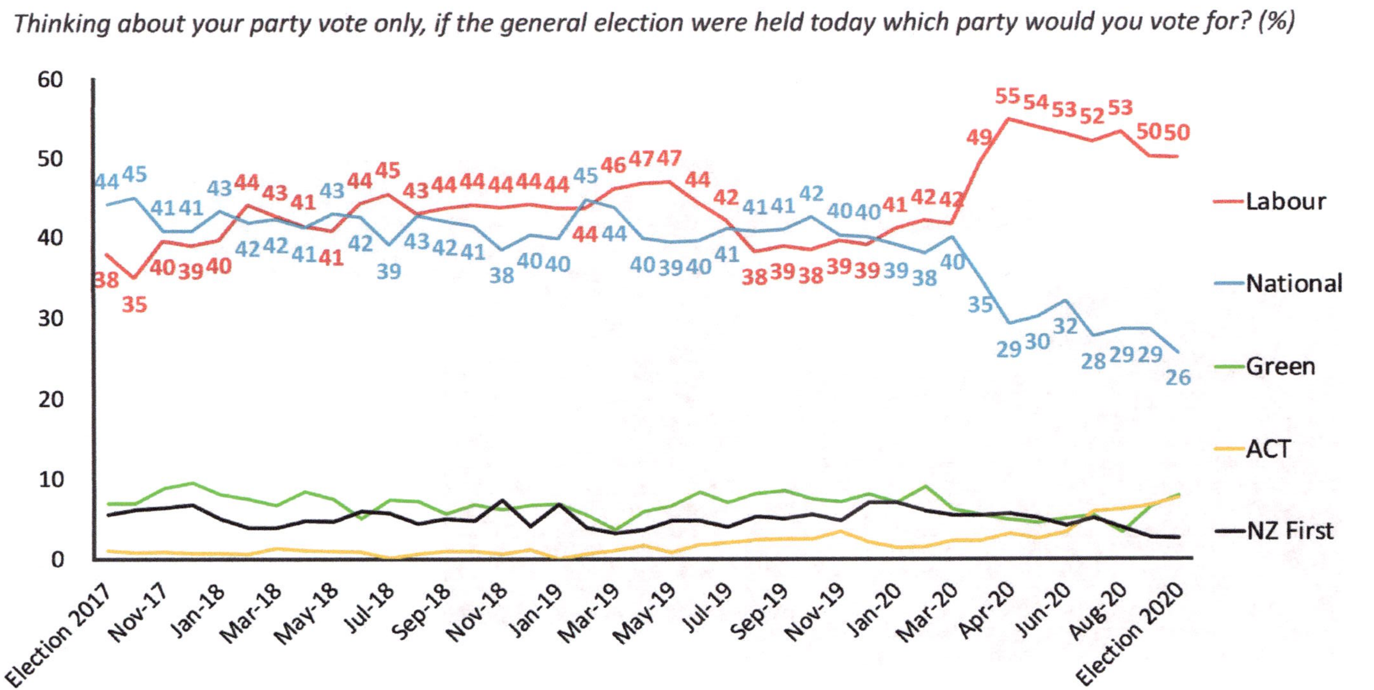

Base: Monthly (n=~1000 per month); Note: results prior to July 2019 are based on telephone omnibus

Figure 26.1: Party vote preferences, 2017–2020

Balance of power: Thinking about your party vote only, if the general election were held today which party would you vote for?

	2017	2018	2019	2020
January		New Zealand First	Left Majority	Left Majority
February		Left Majority	Left Majority	Left Majority
March		Left Majority	Left Majority	Left Majority
April		Left Majority	Left Majority	Left Majority
May		Left Majority	Left Majority	Left Majority
June		Left Majority	Left Majority	Left Majority
July		Left Majority	Left Majority	Left Majority
August		Left Majority	New Zealand First	Left Majority
September		Left Majority	New Zealand First	Left Majority
October	New Zealand First	Left Majority	New Zealand First	
November	New Zealand First	Left Majority	Left Majority	
December	New Zealand First	Left Majority	New Zealand First	

Base: Monthly (n=~1000 per month); Note: results prior to July 2019 are based on telephone omnibus

Figure 26.2: The balance of power (2017–2020)

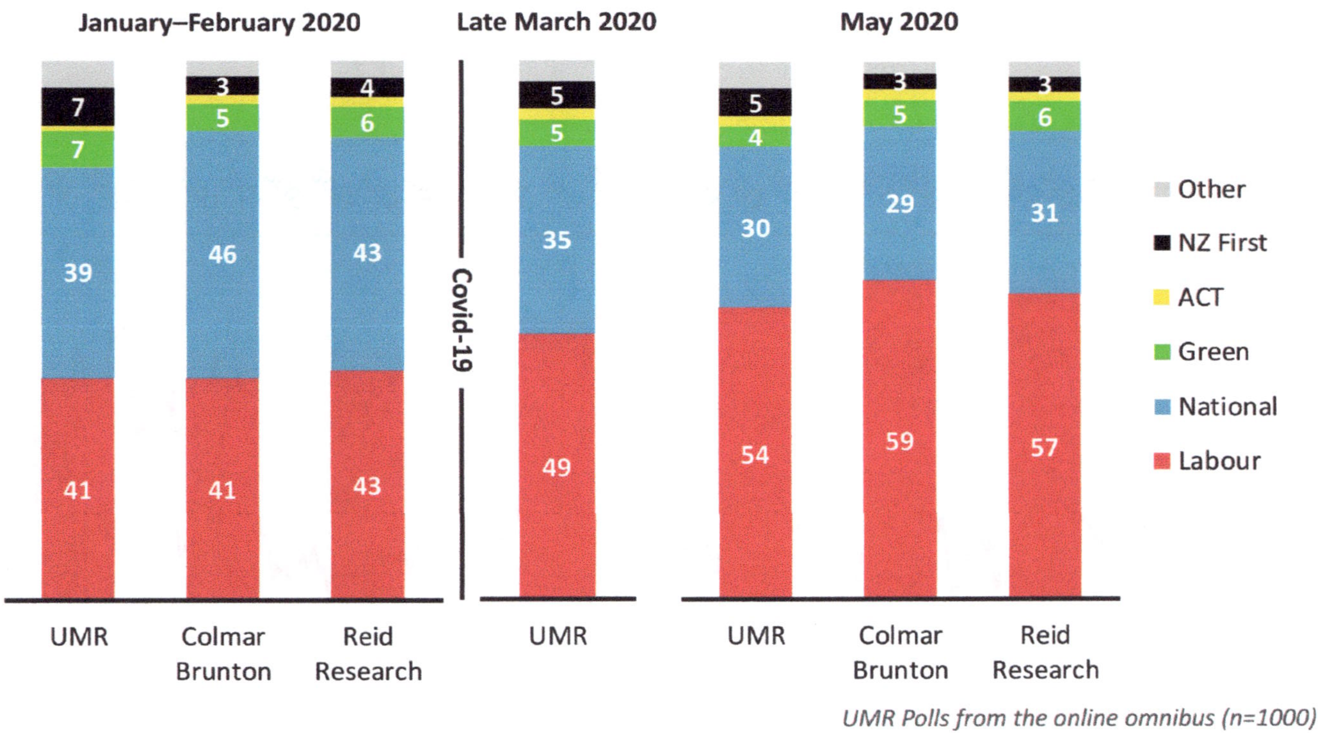

26.3: Polls before and after Covid-19 hit

Direction of New Zealand (1996–2020): Generally speaking, are things in New Zealand heading in the right direction or are they off on the wrong track? (%)

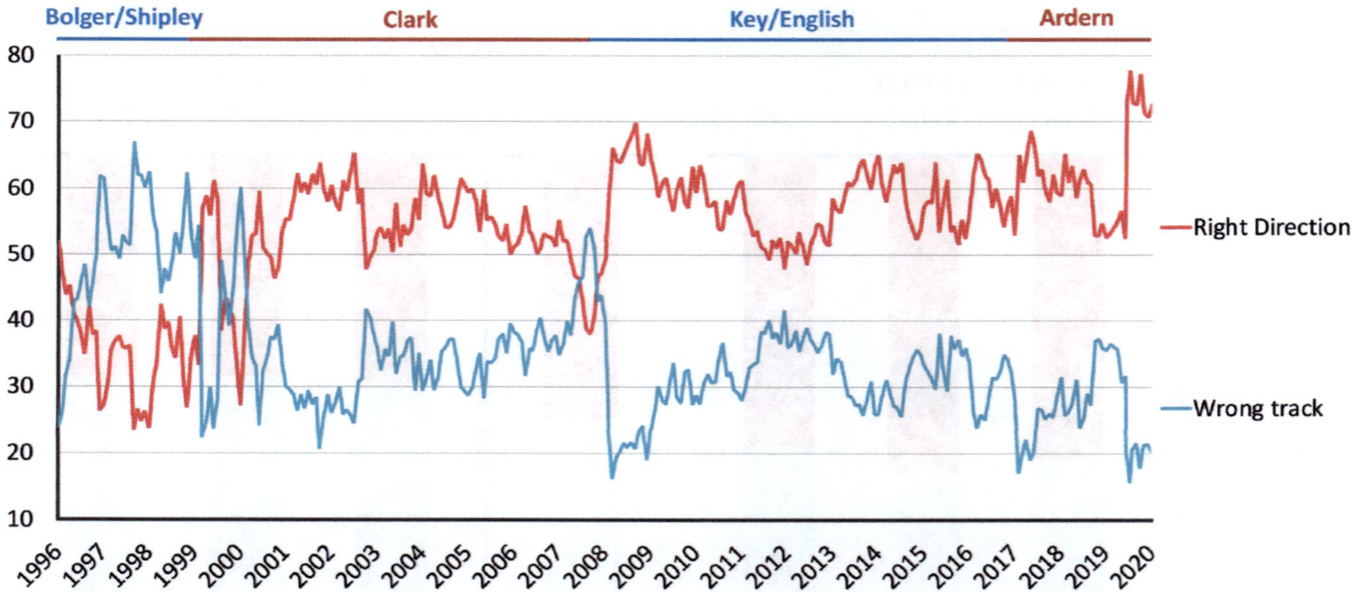

Base: Yearly rolled data. Note: Results prior to July 2019 are based on telephone omnibus

Figure 26.4: The mood – direction of New Zealand (1996–2020)

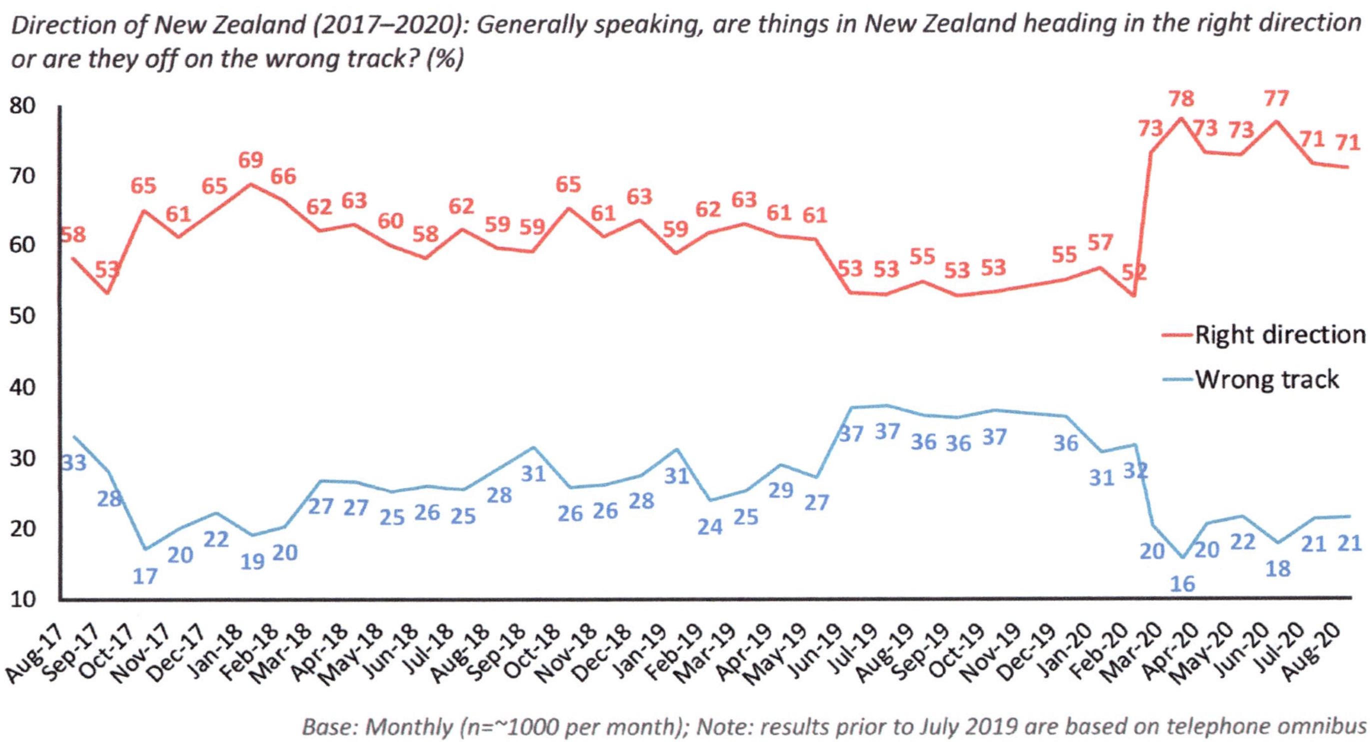

Figure 26.5: The mood – monthly tracking (2017–2020)

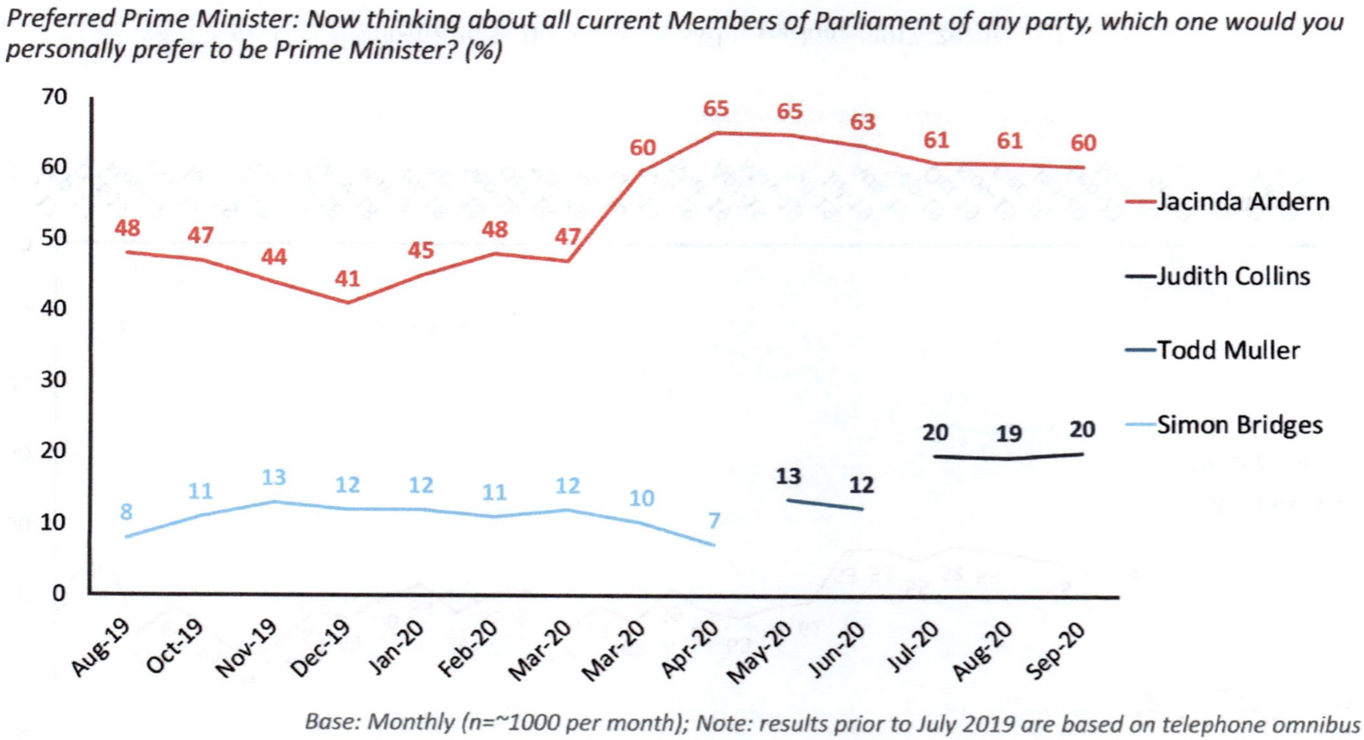

Figure 26.6: Preferred Prime Minister (2019–2020)

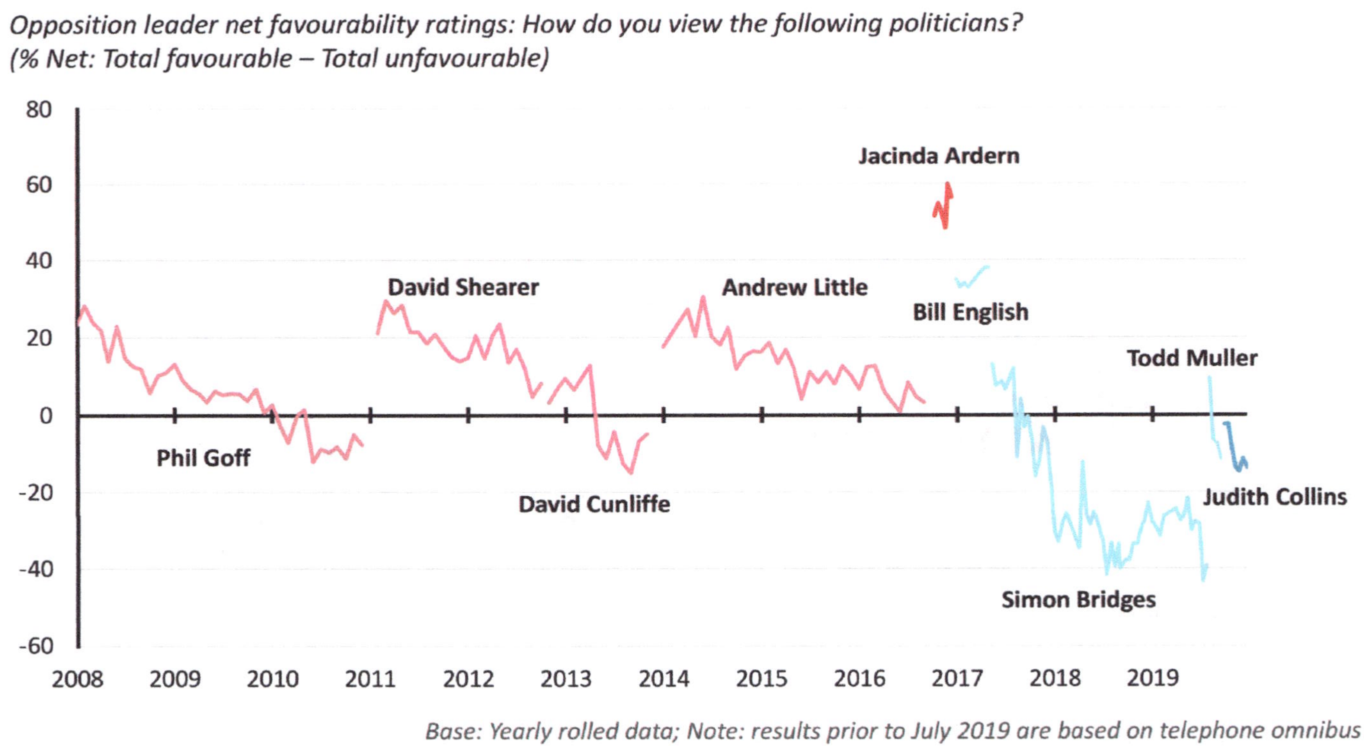

Figure 26.8: Opposition leaders' favourability ratings (2008–2020)

Figure 26.7: 'Word cloud' descriptions of Jacinda Ardern

Judith Collins – word cloud

What one word best describes Judith Collins? (Size of word is relative to the frequency of mentions)

Base: All respondents (n=1,229); Fieldwork: 29 September to 8 October

Figure 26.9: 'Word cloud' descriptions of Judith Collins

What do you think is the most important problem facing the country today?
(Top five issues for each election year)

	2005	2008	2011	2014	2017	2020
1	Healthcare	Economy	Economy	Poverty	Housing	Economy
2	Economy	Crime	Unemployment	Inequality	Poverty	Covid-19
3	Māori issues	Cost of Living	Cost of living	Unemployment	Inequality	Unemployment
4	Education	Healthcare	Poverty	Economy	Immigration	Housing
5	Crime	Politics/ Government	Crime	Housing	Environment	Poverty

Average monthly data from each year. Note: Years prior to 2019 were surveyed over the phone

Figure 26.10: 'The most important problem facing the country today' (2005–2020)

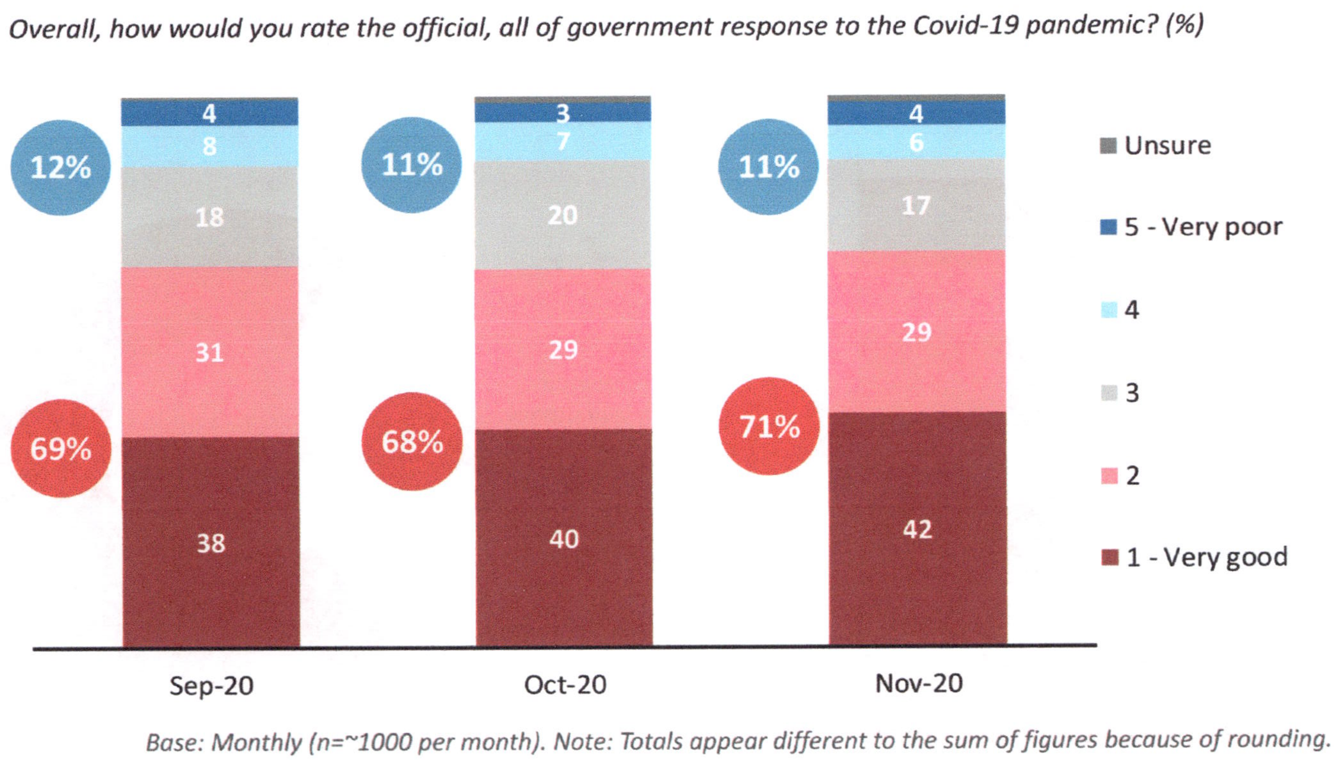

Figure 26.11: The government's handling of the Covid-19 pandemic

Health versus economy: Generally, which do you think is the most important approach in New Zealand's response to Covid-19? (%)

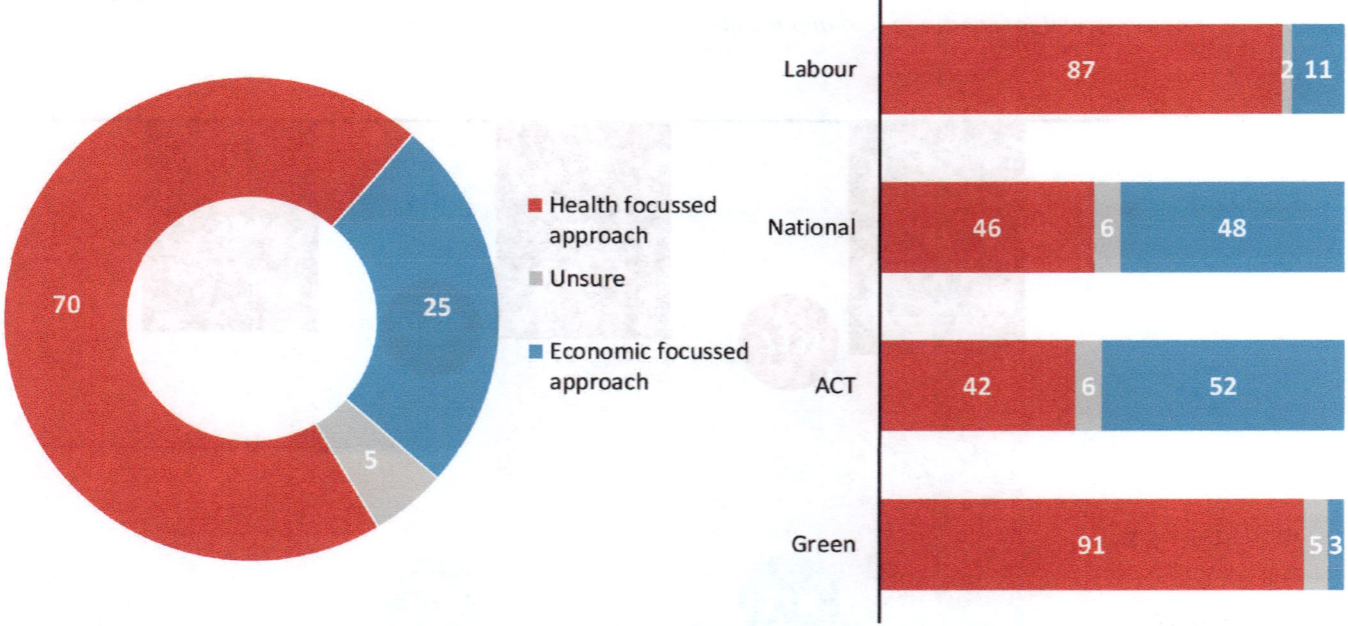

Base: All respondents (n=1,229); Fieldwork: 29 September to 8 October

Figure 26.12: Health versus the economy: the approach to the Covid-19 pandemic

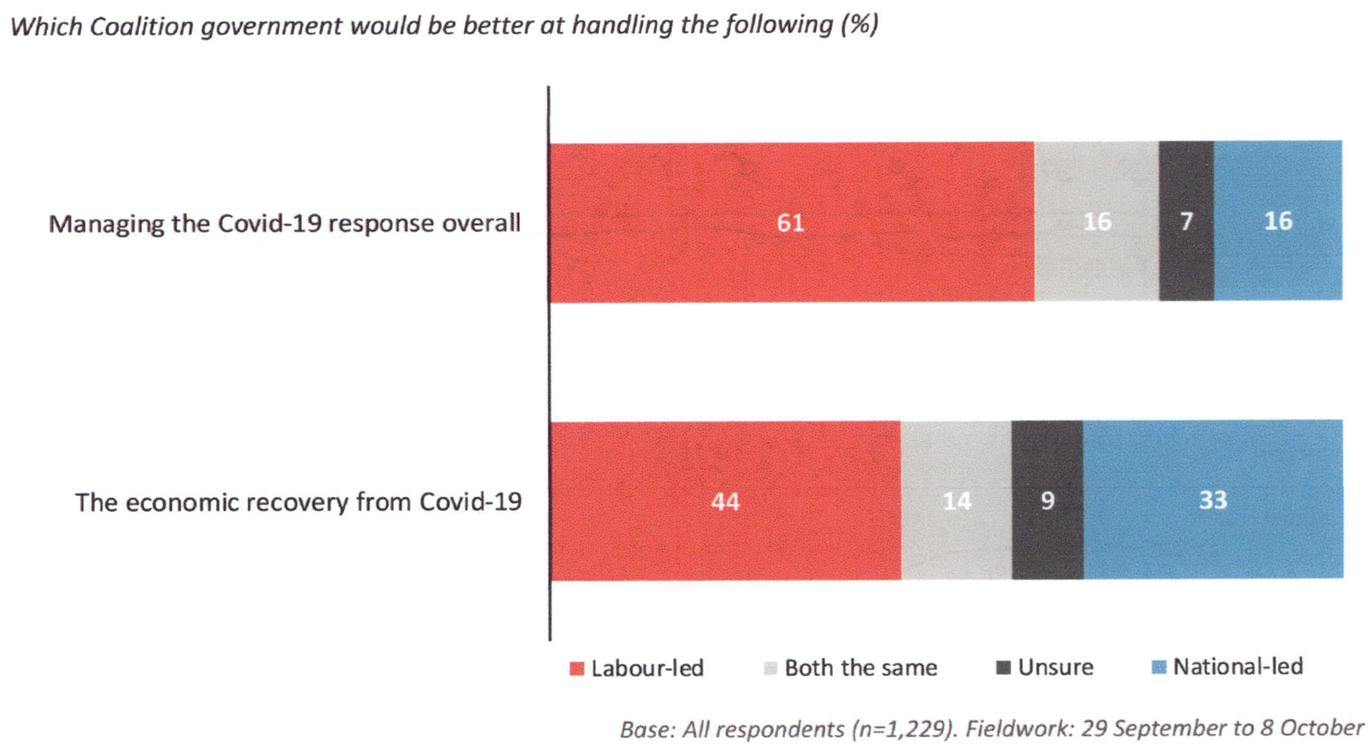

Figure 26.13: Better party for handling the Covid-19 pandemic

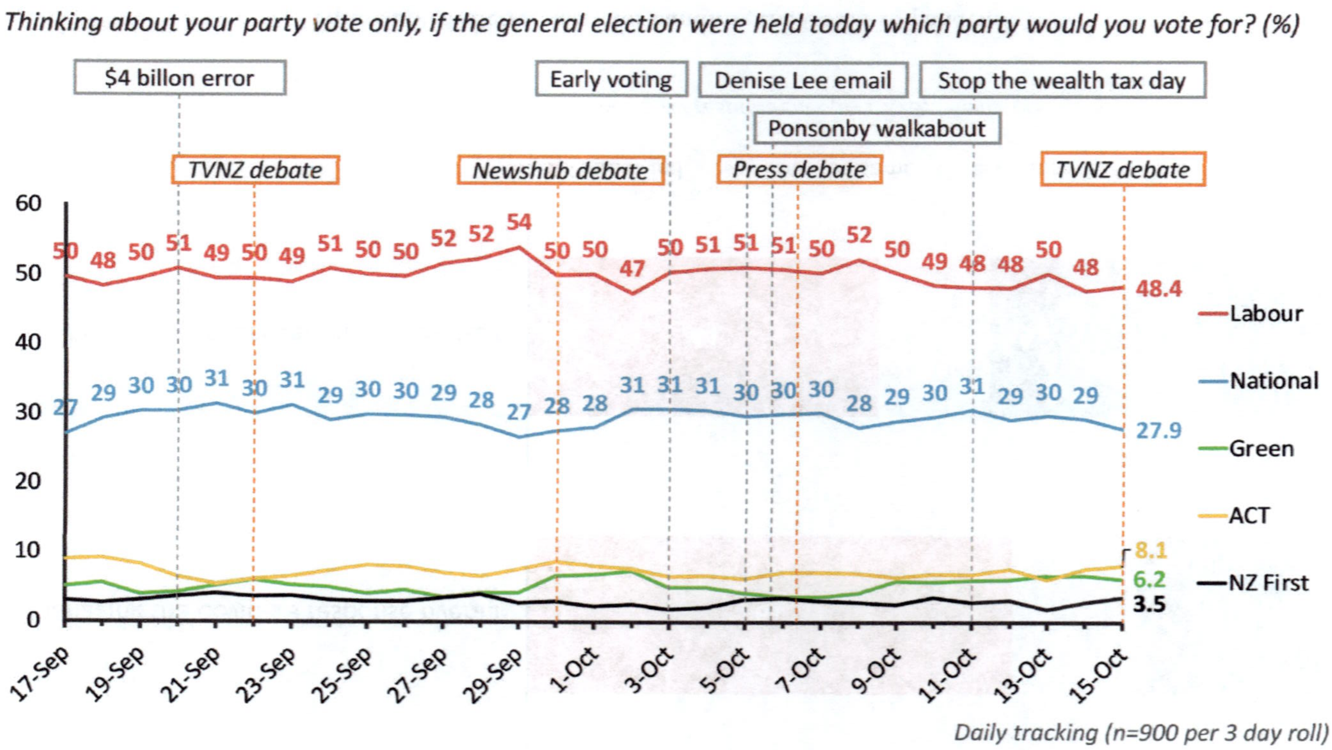

Figure 26.14: Party vote preferences, campaign tracking: 17 September–15 October 2020

National Party slogan: Regardless of your vote, which party do you think [has a . . ./was better at . . .] (%)

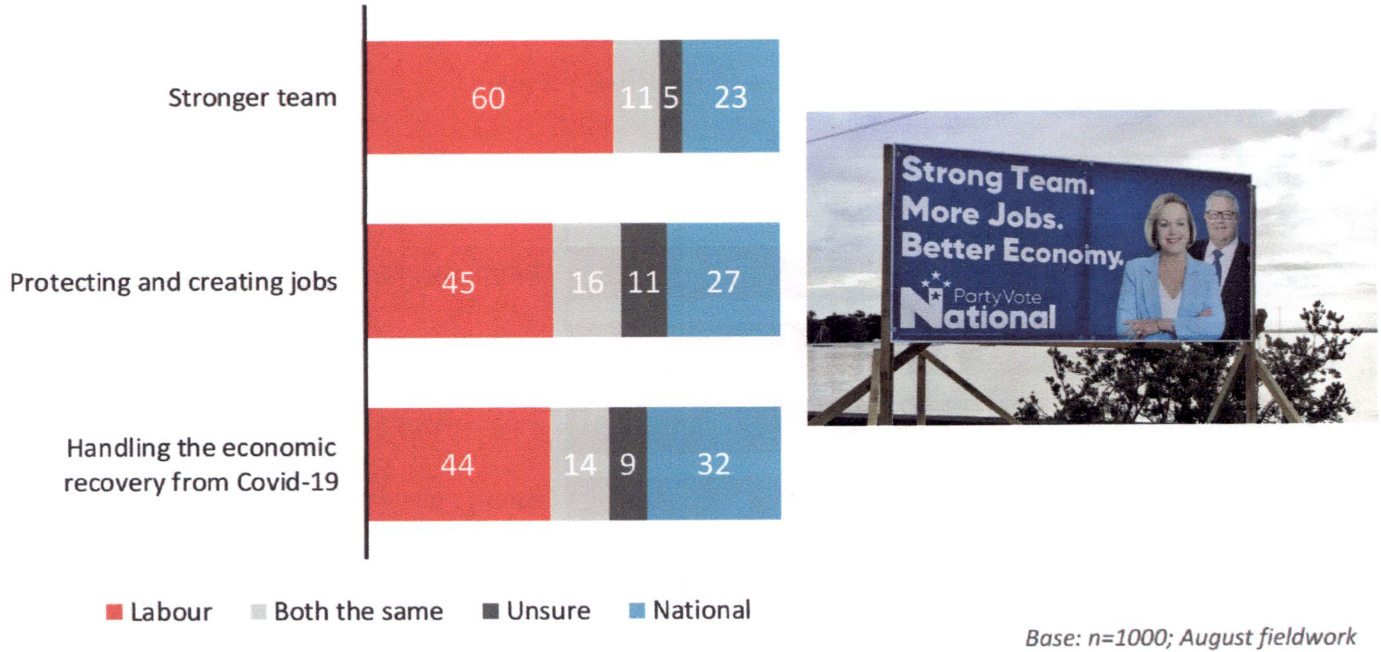

Figure 26.15: Better party, National Party's campaign slogan

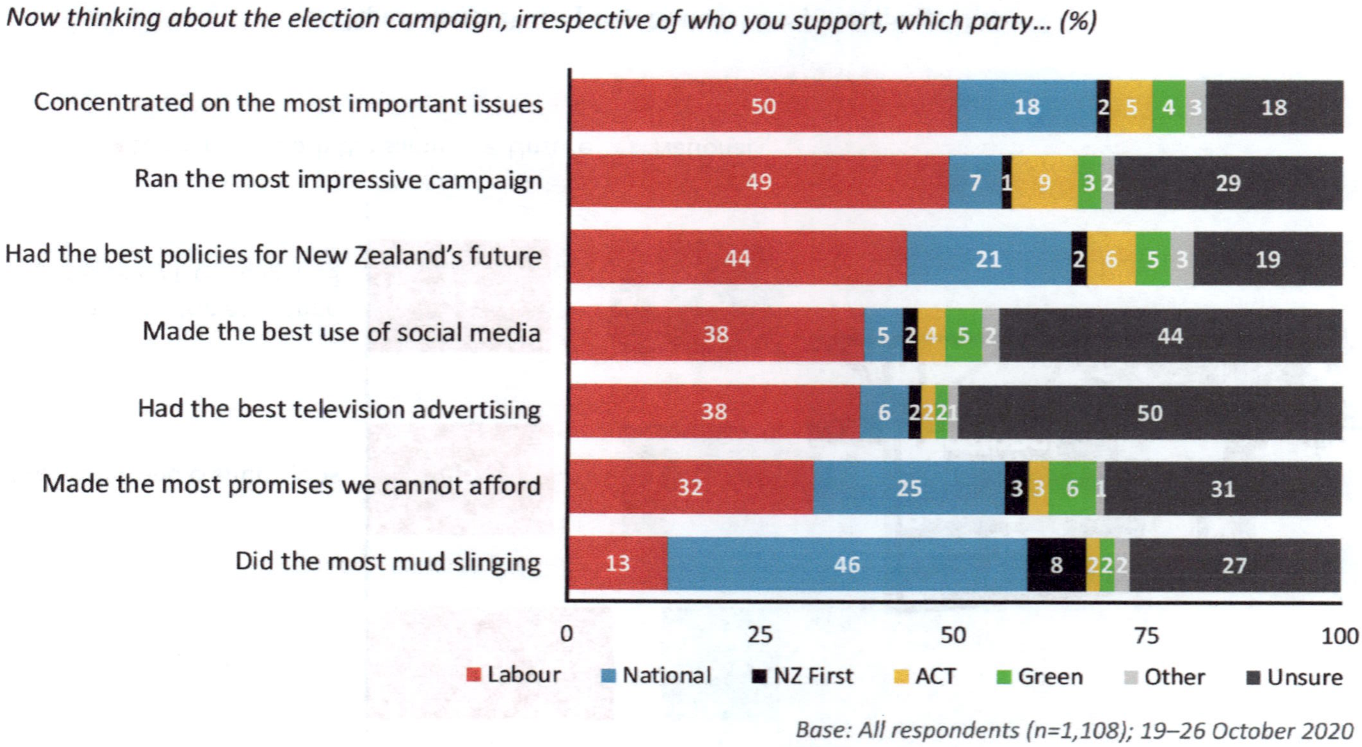

Figure 26.16: Assessments of parties' campaign performance (post-election)

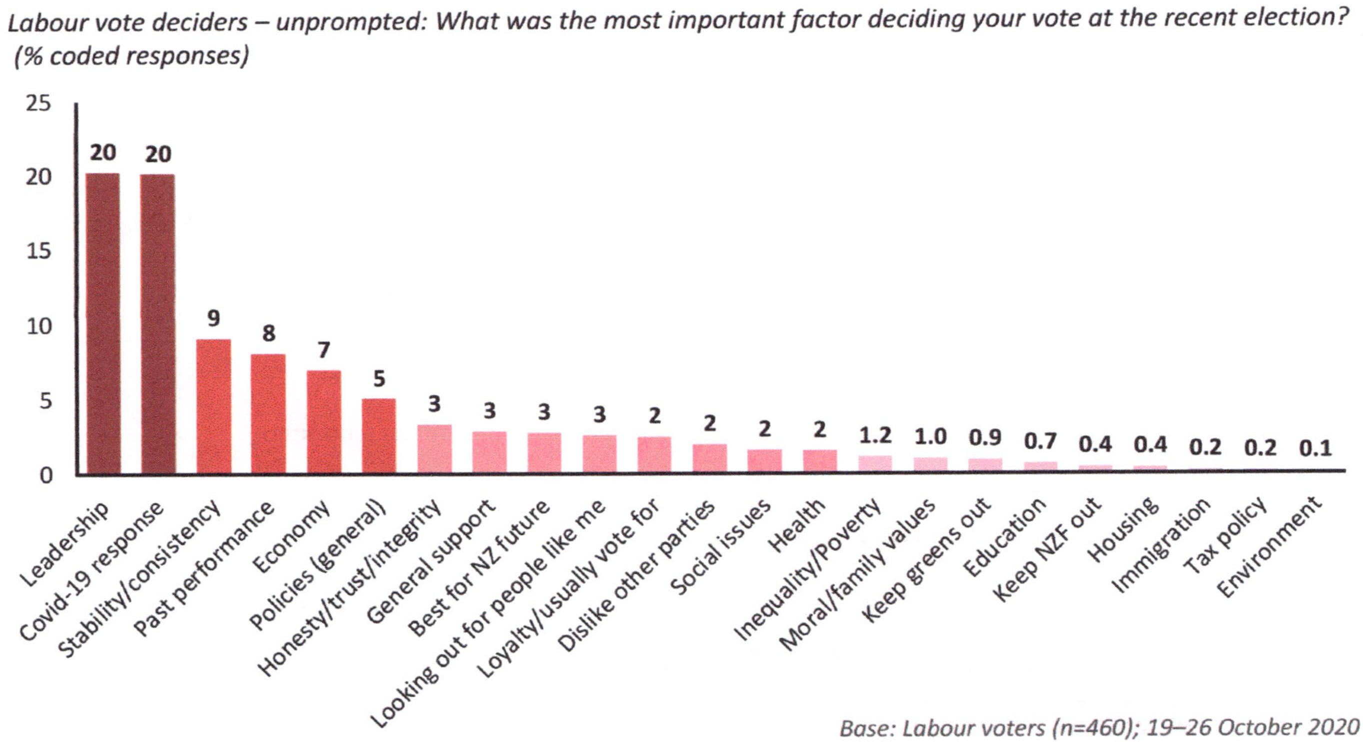

Figure 26.17: Reasons for voting Labour, 2020 election

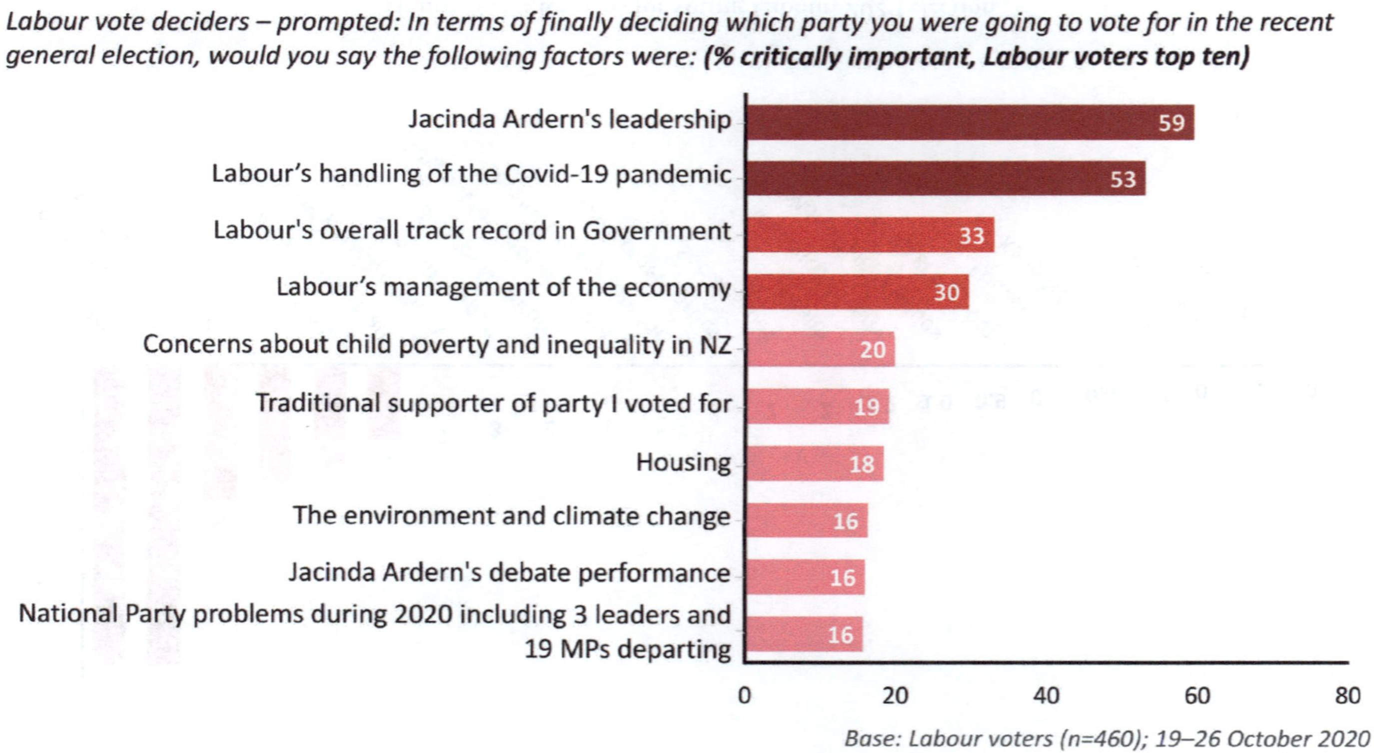

Figure 26.18: 'Critically important' reasons for voting Labour, 2020 election

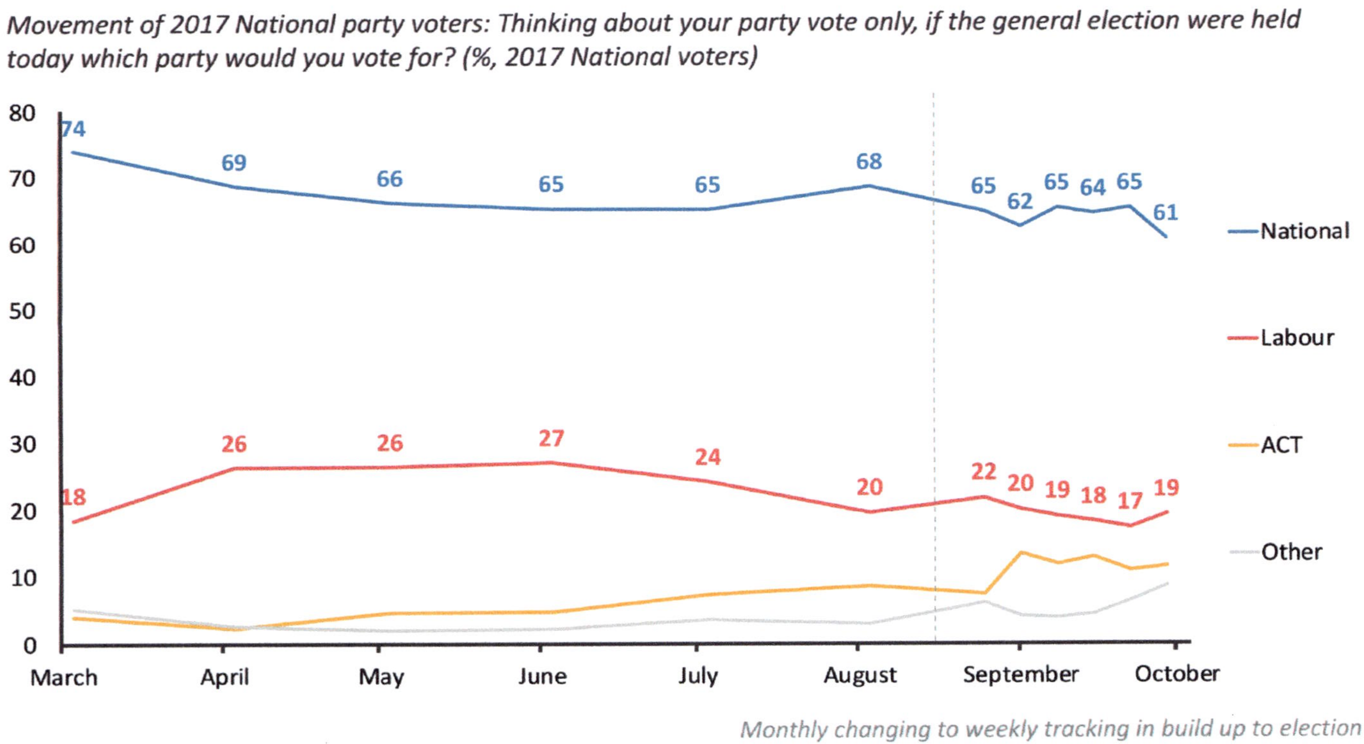

Figure 26.19: Vote intentions (2020) of 2017 National Party voters

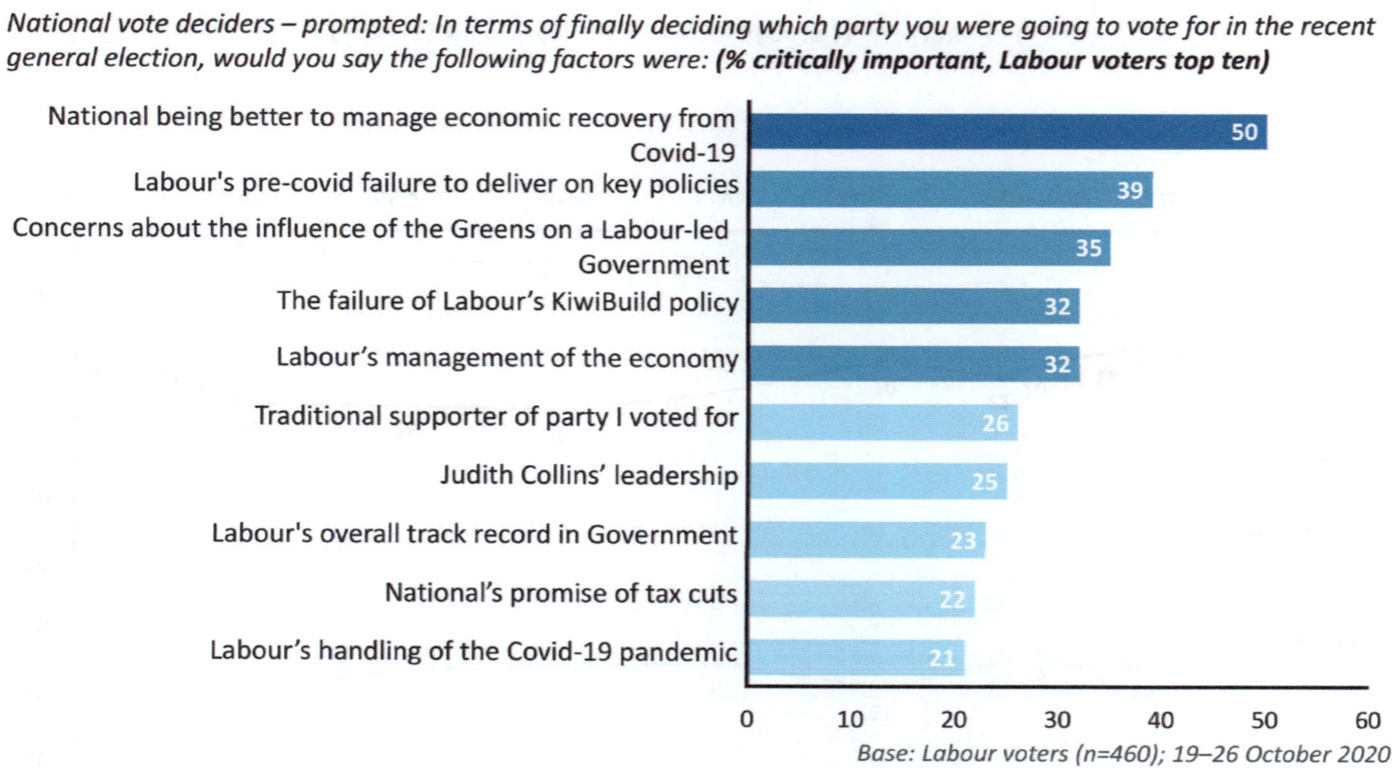

Figure 26.20: 'Critically important' reasons for voting National, 2020 election

Average annual vote 1991–2020: Thinking about this party vote only, if the general election were held today which party would you vote for? (%)

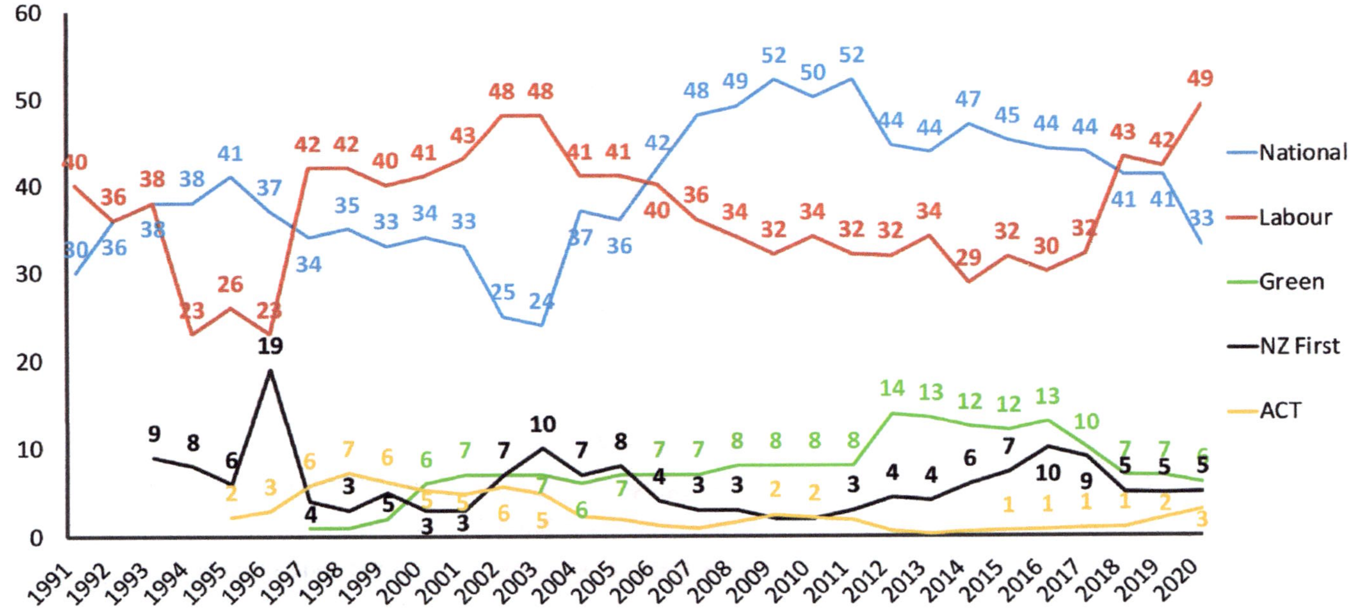

Base: All voters rolled over each year. Note: results prior to July 2019 are based on telephone omnibus

Figure 26.21: Party vote preferences, 1991–2020

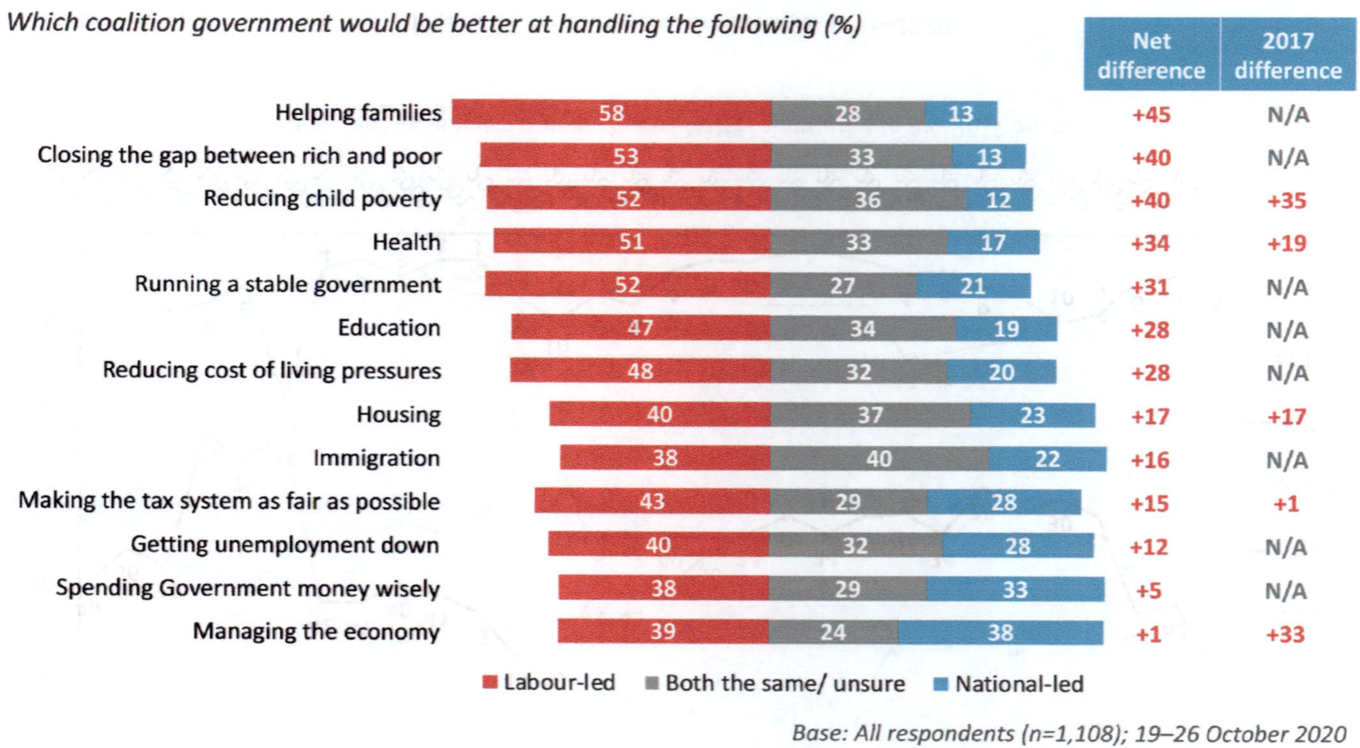

Figure 26.22: Better party by issue (post-election)

The campaign

UMR's campaign tracking showed, despite the dramas, that there was little change over the four-week campaign period (Figure 26.14). Throughout the last month before voting, Labour's vote varied from 47 per cent to 54 per cent and National's from 27 per cent to 31 per cent. Neither policy initiatives, nor bouts of National Party disunity, nor Judith Collins' debate performances moved the needle. Nor was there a late movement of National voters to stop the Greens being part of government. With an assist from a relatively high wasted vote, every daily result produced an absolute majority for Labour.

Highlighting how tough a campaign it was for National, Labour was in front on every one of the three bullet points in National's initial 'Strong Team. More Jobs. Better Economy' slogan (Figure 26.15). Labour also dominated standard campaign responses given in UMR's post-election survey (Figure 26.16). Labour beat National on 'the most impressive campaign' by 49 per cent to 7 per cent, improving on its 2017 campaign advantage of 49 per cent to 24 per cent. In the 2014 campaign National had recorded a 36 per cent to 13 per cent advantage over Labour. National was also seen as doing 'the most mudslinging' by 46 per cent to 13 per cent. The only count going for National was 'made the most promises we cannot afford', where Labour led (on this negative attribute) by 32 per cent to 25 per cent.

Reasons for voting

Respondents in UMR's post-election survey were first asked an open-ended question on their reasons for their party vote choice and then asked to rate the importance of a set of prompted issues in determining their party vote. Labour voters nominated Jacinda Ardern's leadership and the response to Covid-19 as their main reasons for giving Labour their party vote (Figure 26.17). The responses to the prompted questions were almost the same (Figure 26.18). Tables 26.2 and 26.3 (at the end of this chapter) provide full results for these two questions.

UMR polling throughout 2020 showed a proportion of National's 2017 vote going to Labour and ACT. UMR's immediate post-election survey showed 19 per cent of National's 2017 party vote went to Labour and 13 per cent to ACT (Figure 26.19). One view promoted by some in post-election analysis – that there was a large swathe of core National voters voting for Labour only to keep the Greens out of a coalition government – is not borne out by the polling data. As indicated in Figure 26.17, only 0.9 per cent of Labour voters gave 'keeping the Greens out' as the reason for their vote. That translates into about 13,000 voters. Not all were necessarily otherwise National Party voters, but even if they were this represents an exceedingly minor impact on the overall result. Post-election polls by UMR and Colmar Brunton, which showed little or no shift from the election result, also refute the theory of the 'stopping Greens' National voter being important in the final outcome. In any case, once their mission to stop the Greens being part of government was complete this supposed voting bloc would presumably have been free to return to declaring a National vote in polls.

For National voters the main reason given for supporting the party was the economy. When prompted, the top three issues for National voters were 'National being better to manage economic recovery', followed by 'Labour's pre-Covid failure to deliver on key policies' and 'concerns about the influence of the Greens on a Labour-led Government' (Figure 26.20). The latter point did not prevent these 'concerned' voters from voting for National.

The 2023 election

There are many intriguing questions looking forward to the next election, more so than usual given the dramatic result.

A couple to consider.

The usual expectation is that a landslide will be followed by a substantial correction. Many commentators expected Labour's huge leads over National in 2020 polling would be pulled back once the campaign was underway and voters faced 'real choices' in the ballot box. This happened to Labour in 2002 and to a lesser extent to National in 2011 (Figure 26.21). Increasingly, however, in politics everywhere, conventional wisdom does not necessarily apply.

Labour too has an opportunity to build on current perceptions that it is the better economic manager. National's default advantage on this count has massively underpinned its party vote. Labour's usual campaign objective is to neutralise the issue, holding National to no more than a 15–20 point lead. Labour's current lead may not survive outside the Covid context but if Labour can change entrenched perceptions of its economic management credentials, that may reset New Zealand politics. Whether Labour enters a period of Key-like domination of New Zealand politics or whether the 2020 landslide will be seen as a lucky Covid aberration will unfold in the next three years.

A smaller issue will be to see if ACT can hold on to its 7.6 per cent of the vote and re-establish itself as a serious party in New Zealand politics. The committed free-market voter base in New Zealand is around 2 per cent, and possibly even less than that, judging from ACT's performance in the 2011, 2014 and 2017 elections. ACT has previously secured its 5 per cent plus election vote shares by populist forays into law and order, MP perks and race. This time ACT's rise came almost entirely from disaffected National voters.[3] If National is seen as even partly getting more organised and unified, those who voted for them in 2017 are likely to return. For David Seymour, maintaining a strong appeal to the National voters he won this time may prove to be something of a challenge.

Table 26.1: Public polls, mid-late 2019 to early 2020 (pre-Covid-19)

Company (date)	National	Labour	Green	NZ First	ACT	
Colmar Brunton (4–8 Jun 2019)	44	42	6	5	0.7	NZ First decides
Colmar Brunton (20–24 Jun 2019)	45	43	6	3.3	1	Left Majority
Reid Research (2–9 Oct 2019)	44	42	6.3	4.0	1.4	Left Majority
Colmar Brunton (5–9 Oct 2019)	47	40	7	4.2	0.9	Hung parliament
Yougov (7–11 Nov 2019)	38	41	8	8	2	Left Majority
Colmar Brunton (23–27 Nov 2019)	46	39	7	4.7	1.6	Right Majority
Roy Morgan (Jan 2020)	40	40	10.5	2.5	3	Left Majority
Reid Research (23 Jan – 1 Feb 2020)	43	43	5.6	3.6	1.8	Left Majority
Colmar Brunton (8–12 Feb 2020)	46	41	5	3.3	1.7	Right Majority

Table 26.2: 'The most important factor deciding your vote' (post-election)

Unprompted reasons for vote: *What was the most important factor deciding your vote at the recent election? – % Coded*

Column %	Labour (n=460)	National (n=250)	Green (n=71)	ACT (n=75)	NZ First (n=31)
Economy	7	37	3	23	-
Leader/leadership	20	5	1	12	14
Covid-19 response	20	2	2	1	6
Policies (general)	5	10	9	15	5
Past performance	8	5	2	1	3
Stability/consistency	9	2	-	6	-
General support	3	4	4	2	3
Best for NZ future	3	3	4	1	4
Loyalty/usually vote for	2	5	3	-	7
Change	-	8	1	6	4
Moral/family values	1	2	2	4	-
Honesty/trust/integrity	3	0.3	-	-	3
Other strategic vote (e.g. creating strong opposition)	-	0.4	8	7	18
Looking out for people like me	3	2	2	1	-
Dislike others	2	-	4	4	-
Inequality/Poverty	1	-	6	2	-
Social issues	2	1	4	2	-
Tax policy	0.2	3	2	1	3
Environment	0.1	-	14	-	-
Health	2	0.4	1	2	-
Climate change	-	-	13	-	-
Housing	0.4	-	3	3	2
Keep the Greens out	1	-	-	1	-
Education	1	-	-	-	-
Immigration	0.2	-	-	-	6
Keep NZF out	0.4	-	-	-	-
Unsure/no reason	6	10	10	8	22

Table 26.3: 'Critically important' reasons for 'which party you were going to vote for' (post-election)

Prompted reasons for vote: *In terms of finally deciding which party you were going to vote for in the recent general election, would you say the following factors were – % critically important*

Column %	Labour (n=460)	National (n=250)	Green (n=71)	ACT (n=75)	NZ First (n=31)
Jacinda Ardern's leadership	59	17	35	14	31
Labour's handling of the Covid-19 pandemic	53	21	31	11	28
Labour's management of the economy	30	32	14	28	19
Labour's overall track record in Government	33	23	17	22	21
Concerns about the influence of the Greens on a Labour-led Government	9	35	23	39	19
Housing	18	17	14	21	24
National being better to manage economic recovery from Covid-19	5	50	5	29	5
Traditional supporter of party I voted for	19	26	10	13	16
Labour's pre-Covid failure to deliver on key policies	6	39	9	33	13
Concerns about child poverty and inequality in New Zealand	20	12	27	8	14
The failure of Labour's KiwiBuild policy	5	32	8	30	11
The environment and climate change	16	7	53	2	5
Judith Collins' leadership	9	25	14	14	10
Want Greens to push a Labour-led Government to the left including stronger policies on the environment	7	14	60	9	3
Jacinda Ardern's debate performance	16	9	14	4	20
National Party problems during 2020 including 3 leaders and 19 MPs departing	16	6	14	7	7
Want free market economic policies	7	18	2	27	8
National's promise of tax cuts	5	22	4	14	4
Benefits to the regions through the Provincial Growth Fund	8	9	7	4	19
The $4 billion error in National's alternative budget	10	4	9	5	9
Judith Collins' debate performance	5	12	8	7	5
Winston Peters' leadership	6	9	1	5	45
David Seymour's leadership	3	8	2	31	6

27

POPULISM IN THE 2020 CAMPAIGN AND THE DEPARTURE OF NEW ZEALAND FIRST

Margaret Joiner

This chapter looks at New Zealand First's 2020 general election campaign and outcome through the lens of populism. It explores how the once enduring strength of the party's populist ideology was undermined by the rise of competing strong populist ideologies to both the left and right of New Zealand First. This impacted two other factors that have, until this point, accounted for New Zealand First's enduring capacity to assert its relevance as a niche party capable of holding the two main parties to account: the ability to reignite the support of its small electoral constituency and the resilience of the 'Winston Peters' brand (Joiner 2015). The outcome was that New Zealand First suffered its worst election result in the party's history and was not returned to Parliament – for the second time in its lifetime – securing just 2.6 per cent of the party vote.

The outcome in context

Interestingly, New Zealand First's worst election result in history followed its most significant contribution. With over 7 per cent of the party vote at the 2017 election, it had nine seats in Parliament and the balance of power – not the best result the party has had nor the first time it has held the balance of power – but it was what it did with that power that made this contribution significant.

The party decided to change the government and in doing so triggered the incredible rise to celebrity prime minister status of Labour leader Jacinda Ardern. It was an unexpected choice to form a coalition with the less popular major party, Labour having won 46 seats in Parliament compared to National's 56. It took the country in a different direction to what had been widely expected in the lead-up to the election, which was that National would in all probability secure a fourth term.

When Peters announced the decision on 19 October 2017 to form a coalition government with Labour he said it was a choice for change versus a modified status quo. New Zealand First's negotiations with both major parties were influenced by its perception that 'capitalism must regain its responsibility – its human face' (Peters 2017).

At the time, this sentiment aligned to the politics of kindness introduced by Jacinda Ardern, who just two months earlier at Labour's campaign launch had claimed she would 'never stop believing that politics is a place where we can do good', adding that 'we can build a confident and caring nation if we include each and every person, in each and every town and region. That is New Zealand at its best' (Ardern 2017).

With this choice New Zealand First secured four ministers and an under-secretary. Again, this was not the most ministers it had ever secured. Its importance was in the quality of the contribution of these ministers and the stability New Zealand First brought, unlike the 1996 experience where its ministers' inexperience was one of several factors credited with bringing down the government. This time around, New Zealand First ministers secured notable achievements in the portfolios of defence, economic development, seniors, children and foreign affairs. The most publicised of these was in the annual three-billion-dollar Provincial Growth Fund.

The contribution was acknowledged by the Labour Party's Deputy Leader Kelvin Davis, paying tribute to New Zealand First's Tracey Martin for the work she had done as Minister for Children. Similarly, Minister of Foreign Affairs Nanaia Mahuta paid tribute to the work of her predecessor, Winston Peters, at a post-election farewell event she held at Parliament in his honour. This begs the question: how did the party's most significant contribution lead to its worst electoral result?

Party classification, origins and development

New Zealand First's rise and fall between 2017 and 2020 was not unusual for the party, which has experienced significant fluctuations in support across its 27-year life. This has been attributed to the origins of the party. Minor parties can often be classified as 'protest' parties or 'personality' parties. A protest party politicises public reaction to a specific economic, social or religious trend or to an ideological shift in one of the major parties. It aims to create a fairer political system and to highlight the shortcomings of the major parties (Miller 1992). A personality party is driven by a desire to relieve frustrated political ambitions or to preserve and exploit existing autonomy or influence. New Zealand First is a hybrid of both types of party (Joiner 2010).

While small parties often evolve from these classifications, New Zealand First has continued in the personality-protest vein, with its strengths and liabilities. The ebb and flow of its electoral success can be attributed to the tenuous nature of the protest vote; voters seldom fully commit to the alternative small party, retaining their partisan ties to the major party (Chapman 1979). It is also tied to the mercurial nature of the party leader, whose personal popularity has moved up and down over time, inextricably linked to the electoral fortunes of the party. A recent example of this occurred during the 2017 campaign when New Zealand First's polling numbers halved following the news that Peters had been overpaid in his state pension payments over several years (Vowles 2020b).

A party's origins can affect its survivability. New Zealand First was founded in the early 1990s, a period characterised by prolonged economic recession, radical economic and social reforms by both major parties, public distrust of government, National Party disunity, and the rising popularity of the then member for Tauranga, Winston Peters.

From its inception, New Zealand First has been regarded as our purest form of a populist party. Around the world, each populist actor 'emerges because of a particular set of social grievances, which influences its choice of host ideology' to combine with populism, including how it defines 'the people' and 'the elite' (Mudde and Kaltwasser 2017, p. 21). In the case of New Zealand First, the grievances related to the shift to neoliberal economics, and 'the people' were those negatively affected by the government-led reforms; 'the elite' were the political and business leaders driving those changes. Conservative nationalism was the ideology which paired with this New Zealand populism.

These origins gave New Zealand First an enduring capacity to assert its relevance as a niche party capable of holding the two main parties to account. Its leader, with a parliamentary career dating back to 1979, was arguably the country's most resilient politician, and, given that small parties in New Zealand are rarely long-term movements, 24 (non-consecutive) years in Parliament was a remarkable success for New Zealand First.

Speaking on election night 2020, Winston Peters reminded voters of New Zealand First's role and its enduring relevance: 'for 27 years, there's been one party that's been prepared to question the establishment and challenge authority, and tonight more than ever, that force is still needed' (Peters 2020b). But the 2020 campaign saw the most direct competition to date to New Zealand First's role in our party system; while the role is relevant, that competition raised questions on whether New Zealand First still is.

The undermining of the party's populist ideology

Populism has a variety of interpretations. This analysis uses the ideational approach to populism, which defines it as

> a thin-centered ideology that considers society to be ultimately separated into two homogeneous and antagonistic camps, 'the pure people' versus 'the corrupt elite', and which argues that politics should be an expression of the general will of the people (Mudde and Kaltwasser 2017, p. 21).

This definition is useful for the New Zealand context because it accepts that populism rarely exists in isolation, as populist actors combine it with a range of other 'host' ideologies. This has been the practice in New Zealand's party system.

New Zealand First's policy platform has always been defined more by what it opposes than by what it supports. Its recurring populist themes include anti-establishment sentiment and an agenda of anti-corruption, underpinned by an ideology of conservative nationalism. The party continued this policy platform across ten general election campaigns. The populist ideology also allowed the party to take on a centrist position, able to swing left and right. As a former key operative of the party explained, New Zealand First has a 'policy tool box so to speak, with policies to fit the left and the right depending on who it will be working with' (quoted in Joiner 2010).

Opposition to the neo-liberal agenda pursued by both Labour and National has consistently underpinned New Zealand First's policy platform. This was the case in 2020 as well, with Peters' campaign launch speech reminding voters that 'in 1996 New Zealand began modern coalition politics, having rejected the elected dictatorships that produced first Labour and then National governments blindly pursing their neo-liberal revolution without regard to human costs'. New Zealand First's anti-establishment sentiment remained evident as well, with the launch speech claiming that a vote for New Zealand First was a vote to take out some necessary 'insurance against big government and the view that nanny state knows best' (Peters 2020a).

In 2020, however, the strength of this ideology waned, in part because of the rise of competing populist ideologies to both the left and right of the party. On the left Labour strengthened its adoption of a populism of inclusion, building on what it began in 2017. Inclusive forms of populism can be pluralist if a leader's rhetorical approach recognises 'the people' as diverse and encompassing (Vowles and Curtin 2020). The 'host ideology' in this progressive and inclusive style of politics is based on pluralist liberal values. Examples can be found throughout Labour's narrative around the Covid-19 response, including messages to 'Be strong, be kind' and references to New Zealand as 'a team of 5 million'.

Following the populist view of society as separated into two antagonistic camps, if Labour's definition of 'the people' was diverse and encompassing, 'the corrupt elite' were uniform and exclusive. By introducing an opposing populist outlook, Labour relegated New Zealand First's rhetoric and policy platform to the 'corrupt elite' camp, undermining its populist ideology's previously enduring strength. New Zealand First doubled down by reverting to tried and true rhetoric, in opposition to Labour and the Greens' more inclusive position, claiming to have 'opposed woke pixie dust' and to have 'defended socially conservative values, like the right to believe in God' (Peters 2020a).

Compounding this from the right was a different type of populist ideology, with ACT pursuing an anti-establishment rhetoric defined by libertarian values. More broadly, the remarkable revival of the ACT Party, by its sole MP and leader David Seymour, presented the most direct challenge yet to New Zealand First's place in the party system. While New Zealand First and ACT were themselves on opposite ideological poles, their populist strategies were little different, and history has shown that New Zealand's party system cannot easily sustain two such parties. Furthermore, being in opposition – as opposed to New Zealand First's 2017–2020 participation in government – put ACT in a stronger and more convincing position to campaign against 'the establishment'.

Throughout the campaign, and indeed the 2017–2020 period, David Seymour was relentless in his criticisms of the government, including its handling of the Covid-19 response, and its ability to safeguard the economy and small business from the catastrophic impacts of lockdowns and border closures. In the period between 17 August 2020 (when the prime minister announced the new election date of 17 October) and the election, Seymour issued more than 100 press releases criticising the government's actions and highlighting its failings.

Unlike Peters and New Zealand First, who held key roles in government, Seymour represented a genuine opposition, becoming the more logical choice for voters looking for an anti-establishment voice. ACT's competing populist ideology undermined New Zealand First's capacity to assert its relevance as the only small party committed to holding the two main parties to account. The 2020 election result suggests that, at least in 2020, the ACT Party and David Seymour represented a stronger populist force in the view of the electorate.

Inability to reignite the support of its small electoral constituency

The electoral performance of Labour and National – involving significant party vote movement – had a strong impact on New Zealand First, undermining a second factor long associated with its survivability – its ability to reignite the loyal support of its small electoral constituency.

New Zealand First's voter profile has consistently reflected a diverse range of interests and support from across the political spectrum. Its voters shared feelings of protest and of admiration for the party's founder/leader, including his resentment of the social and economic impact of the late 1980s' and early 1990s' neo-liberal reforms. Broadly speaking, New Zealand First's most reliable support base has been made up of elderly, low-income and Māori voters.

The reliability of this support base has been especially evident when voter turnout has been low. New Zealand First's survivability has, to an extent, been linked to the steady decline in New Zealand voter turnout since the early 1950s. In 2011, for instance, when New Zealand First made its first recovery from having lost parliamentary representation, New Zealand experienced a new low in turnout at just over 74 per cent. At that election, 95 per cent of those aged 65 or over voted, compared to just 42 per cent of 18-to-24-year-olds. Conversely, the 2020 election produced the highest voter turnout since 1999, at 82 per cent, including an over 15 per cent increase since 2014 for the 18-to-24-year-old age group (Electoral Commission 2020).

Vote Compass data, comparing voter behaviour from 2017 and 2020, shows that 35 per cent of New Zealand First's 2017 voters – a plurality – switched to Labour in 2020; around 20 per cent of their 2017 vote went to National and ACT; and nearly 15 per cent of New Zealand First's 2017 voters did not vote at all (Vowles 2020a). ACT and Labour did well in provincial and semi-provincial electorates where New Zealand First typically picks up much of its party vote. In 2020 New Zealand First saw a significant decline in its party vote in key electorates on which it has historically relied. In Northland, for instance, it halved its 2017 party vote (5,353 votes, falling to 2,651 votes); in Tauranga, New Zealand First received roughly a third of the votes it had won three years earlier (Electoral Commission 2020).

This analysis of 2020 voter behaviour suggests that Labour's populism of inclusion mobilised the youth vote, and voters more generally, to the detriment of New Zealand First's populist ideology and overall electoral performance. The prime minister's positive rhetoric presumably resonated better with voters than New Zealand First's familiar anti-establishment protest message, weakened by the party campaigning from within government. Other factors also impacted New Zealand First's three broad camps of support – the revival of the Māori party and a strong Labour Māori caucus; the elderly (being the most vulnerable to Covid-19) feeling safer with Labour's careful, cautious approach; and Labour's inclusive outlook reassuring low income earners, making them less inclined to cast a protest vote.

As discussed elsewhere in this book, Covid-19 defined the election and influenced the campaign, with consequences for all parties, including New Zealand First. Social distancing restrictions impacted the practical side of campaigning, making it difficult to connect in person with voters – something Peters had always done well and relied on to bolster his support. Border closures largely removed immigration as a campaign issue, a policy area New Zealand First has historically relied on in attracting a protest vote.

The weakening of the Winston Peters brand

New Zealand First never matured beyond the 'personality type' party, defined by its principal spokesperson and founding leader in the eyes of both the media and the public. This was despite repeated attempts to demonstrate that there was more to the party than its leader and that it was a democratic political party organisation. Before announcing the post-election decision in 2017, for instance, Peters emphasised that the choice was 'made by New Zealand First, and it is its decision, not that of the leader', adding that 'every New Zealand First MP and board member is a witness to that. We consult and that has been the case in our 24 years of existence as a political party' (Peters 2017).

It has been an uphill battle, because Winston Peters personifies New Zealand First. His ability to read and tap into voter sentiment, and to personify the anger and distrust of the electorate, has had a direct impact on the party's electoral outcomes and durability. The 2020 outcome suggests, however, that the personal brand waned along with the populist protest rhetoric. This time around, amidst a highly unusual campaign environment, Peters read it wrong.

Having appointed Ardern to the role of prime minister following the 2017 election, New Zealand First chose to go against, rather than align with, her enormous popularity. Initially, Peters sought to walk the line, claiming at the campaign launch that 'we've been an accelerator for good ideas and a handbrake for bad ones' (Peters 2020a). As the campaign progressed, however, his rhetoric was heavily weighted towards the handbrake. Peters distanced himself and his party from their role in government, rather than focusing on the achievements they had made or contributed to in office.

As in 2017 with Peters' pension payment issue, his popularity was significantly affected, only weeks out from the election, by the Serious Fraud Office (SFO) releasing its decision on the New Zealand First Foundation donations case, which included two charges. Despite not being charged himself, Peters was the subject of considerable negative media attention, contributing to the weakening of his 'brand'. The unfortunate timing of the SFO's decision saw the New Zealand First campaign take a sharp negative turn.

Content analysis by the New Zealand Social Media Study analysed the tone of Facebook posts by parties and their leaders throughout the campaign. The trend for New Zealand First started positive, as one would expect from a government party, but subsequently trended downwards to the point that it ended up with the same ratio as ACT, a strong opposition voice, at about only 30–40 per cent of its Facebook posts being positive (Krewel and Vowles 2020). This compared to 70 per cent for the Green Party, which chose to align closely with Ardern's popularity.

Labour's 2020 landslide has been attributed largely to the unusual campaign environment created by the global pandemic. This view is supported by the fact that before the global pandemic the Ardern administration (and the Labour Party) was down in the polls, with voters frustrated with the party's strong international focus at the expense of delivery at home in key areas such as inequality and housing. Others have regarded Labour's 2020 victory as indicative of a generational shift and a lift in youth political engagement to which both New Zealand First and National failed to respond.

Both factors contributed to a complex, difficult campaign, combining with other influences to bring a decline in the appeal of the Winston Peters 'brand' and New Zealand First's failure to attract enough support to return to Parliament.

Conclusion

The events that gave rise to a historic landslide for Labour worked in the opposite manner for New Zealand First, seeing the small populist party out of Parliament for the second time in its history. This was despite a comparably strong performance in government and a significant contribution to New Zealand's political environment in making possible a Labour-led coalition government following the 2017 election.

What worked for New Zealand First in the past failed to deliver this time around. A successful 'populism of inclusion' on the left relegated New Zealand First to the 'corrupt elite' camp, while ACT's populist campaign from the right attracted a protest vote, further undermining New Zealand First's place as New Zealand's leading populist party. In a complex and unusual campaign environment, New Zealand First failed to reignite the support of its formerly reliable small electoral constituency, and Winston Peters' political strength declined in a campaign defined by the pandemic and New Zealand's response.

Regardless of whether or not New Zealand First returns to Parliament, the 2020 outcome gives cause to consider what our party system and political environment will be like without it. New Zealand First brought stability to MMP politics, as a centrist party able to work with both right and left. Without New Zealand First, small parties such as ACT may come to occupy this position. A perennial topic for the media and commentators – usually voiced around the time of New Zealand First's annual convention – is who will succeed Peters as leader. However, succeeding to the New Zealand First leadership and succeeding to Winston Peters' place in New Zealand politics are by no means the same thing.

As noted, at the 2020 campaign launch Winston Peters declared that a party vote for New Zealand First was a vote to take out some necessary 'insurance against extremism – from either side of politics' (Peters 2020a). New Zealand First has acted as a safety valve for some of the more extreme political sentiments, an 'insurance' against all forms of political extremism, populist or otherwise. This has helped New Zealand's parliamentary parties to remain moderate compared to democracies in Europe and elsewhere that have had anti-establishment parties on the far right and left. New Zealand First's departure from New Zealand's political space may give rise to a broader spectrum of populist responses, something to observe as New Zealand's post-pandemic politics unfold.

28

MĀORI AND THE 2020 ELECTION

Lara M. Greaves and Ella Morgan

In the days after their exit from Parliament following the 2017 election, the then Māori Party co-leader Marama Fox commented that Māori voters had returned to Labour 'like a beaten wife to the abuser' (Horgan 2017). Indeed, while the major story for Māori politics in the 2017 election was the downfall of the Māori Party, in 2020 the main story was its return after Rawiri Waititi unseated Labour's Tāmati Coffey in Waiariki. The return of the Māori Party was even more surprising, given the challenges associated with being a small party outside of Parliament, the media focus on Covid-19, and a substantial victory for Labour overall. This chapter focuses on Māori in the 2020 election. It covers what we see as the major story of the election for Māori: the return of the Māori Party and the contests in the Māori electorates.

While it could seem as though the return of the Māori Party came out of nowhere, the Māori Party underwent a process of renewal after its 2017 defeat. Firstly, both co-leaders resigned. Te Ururoa Flavell went to the tertiary education sector and later became the CEO of Te Wānanga o Aotearoa (the largest Māori tertiary education provider). Marama Fox worked as a consultant; however, her business dealings led to further negative media attention after it was revealed she owed creditors more than $110,000. Secondly, a new executive leadership team was elected: in 2018 Che Wilson and Kaapua Smith were elected as president and deputy president of the party. Both were relatively young (aged 42 and 35 respectively) and represented a generational shift, but the wāhine and tāne co-leader and candidate slots remained open. Later, in April, the party selected its co-leaders: Debbie Ngarewa-Packer and John Tamihere. Ngarewa-Packer, a Taranaki community leader, seabed mining campaigner and former Deputy Mayor of South Taranaki, was set to run in Te Tai Hauāuru. Tamihere, CEO of the Whānau Ora commissioning agency, was announced as the party's candidate for Tāmaki Makaurau. The selection of Tamihere as co-leader was not without its detractors, given his long history in the public eye and tendency to make controversial comments. Notable examples include: referring to his female Labour Party colleagues as 'front bums' and arguing that women received special treatment; victim-blaming comments around the 'Roast Busters' group (Wilson 2019); and, most recently, using a Nazi salute in a 2019 mayoral debate. Tamihere would likely counter criticisms of past controversies with suggestions that he is working class and that, in reality, voters do not care about such talk (Kilgallon 2020).

In 2020, the political context for the Māori Party was likely to be challenging from the outset. As proven by a number of minor parties over the years, including exceptionally well-funded parties (such as the Conservatives, TOP, and Internet-MANA), it is incredibly difficult for a minor party to get into Parliament. Under MMP, a party must gain 5 per cent of the party vote or win an electorate seat to gain representation. In previous years the Māori Party had gained representation through winning a Māori electorate and only ever got to 2.4 per cent of the overall party vote (in 2008). It was clear from these previous party vote results that winning one or more of the Māori electorates should be the strategic focus if the party wished to gain representation again. In addition, the Māori Party faced extra challenges in trying to *return* to Parliament. Such a feat had previously only been achieved with the return of Winston Peters' New Zealand First Party in 2011 after its exit from Parliament in 2008. Being a party with an established name and reputation, especially after pairing with the National Party, meant that the Māori Party had to rebuild its image, identity and relationships with Māori voters.

The 2020 general election presented added challenges for minor parties, as it will no doubt go down in history as the Covid-19 election. Many politicians felt overshadowed by the presence of Jacinda Ardern, who proved popular in the Māori electorates in 2017 (Greaves and Hayward 2020). However, 2019 was also a watershed year for Māori-related policy, with several policy issues capturing broad media attention. Of particular note was the dispute over important heritage land at Ihumātao being used for housing. Members of Save Our Unique Landscape (SOUL; later Protect Ihumātao), a group led by Pania Newton, had been living on the land since 2016 to prevent construction, and led action in the courts,

United Nations, and other protests. In July 2019, land protectors flocked to the site after a trespass notice was issued against SOUL. While the conflict had been de-escalated from its initial level of tension, the issue was not resolved heading into the 2020 election. Additionally, in June 2019, Newsroom published a documentary showing a Māori newborn baby being uplifted by Oranga Tamariki (the Ministry for Children). The investigation and subsequent scandal highlighted structural racism and a lack of Māori input in the child welfare system.

These events were simply part of a broader list of unresolved policy issues including: the underfunding of Whānau Ora (an indigenous community-centred health initiative underpinned by Māori cultural values), the Waitangi Tribunal Hauora report and the push towards an Independent Māori Health Authority, discriminatory referendum laws around the formation of Māori wards in local government, the lack of entrenchment of the Māori electorates, a number of Treaty settlements still to be resolved (including with the largest Iwi, Ngāpuhi), and racism in education. Furthermore, it was clear that due to existing inequities, the emergence of the Covid-19 pandemic would lead to worse outcomes for Māori. This led to multiple Iwi, hapū, and Māori communities instituting road blocks in order to stem the spread of Covid-19, as well as the establishment of Te Rōpū Whakakaupapa Urutā, the National Māori Pandemic Group, to provide advice for Māori communities. However, countering the plethora of issues still to be resolved, in the 2019 budget the Labour Party provided a large amount of targeted funding for Māori, including $480 million in Māori development spending (Horgan 2019). A significant barrier to Māori policy progress was New Zealand First, which had openly talked about being a self-styled 'handbrake' on these issues (Radio New Zealand 2020).

Given the need to rebuild the Māori Party after its 2017 defeat and the challenges associated with Covid-19 and the election, the party's co-leaders indicated that they were happy to take a long-term approach. During the campaign – although he contends he was misquoted – Tamihere even commented that 2020 would not be the year for the Māori Party to return to Parliament, and committed to three elections with the party, telling a journalist '2023's going to be a ripper' (Manch 2020). Multiple commentators also predicted that 2020 would not be the Māori Party's year (e.g., *Waatea News* 2020). Nevertheless, throughout the campaign, the party adopted a core strategy and a clear policy platform.

The Māori Party – strategy, policies and platform

The Māori Party pursued a candidate-vote-only strategy in the Māori electorates. This meant that the candidates explicitly campaigned for only the electorate vote and not the party vote across each of the seven Māori electorates. The appeal behind this strategy was that Māori voters could get a kind of two-for-one deal on Māori representation. The Māori Party pitch was that voting for the Māori Party candidate would mean that Māori would gain a local Māori Party MP, while giving their party vote to the Labour Party would mean that Labour's Māori candidates could enter Parliament on the list. The strategy was best summarised on the party's social media with the slogan: 'Labour want two ticks to keep Māori out, Māori want one tick to get more Māori in' (Māori Party 2020). Indeed, this strategy ultimately (at least partially) paid off, with Rawiri Waititi unseating incumbent Labour MP Tāmati Coffey in Waiariki and the party gaining a second MP (Debbie Ngarewa-Packer) with the special votes, winning 1.2 per cent of the party vote overall.

The Māori Party had a range of clear, specific policies that were announced over an incremental timeline. Increased funding for Māori organisations and initiatives and honouring a Māori worldview were the underlying themes of these policies. Initially, the party announced a 'Whānau First' policy that involved 25 per cent of all government contracts being procured by Māori following the Covid-19 pandemic and nationwide lockdown. Subsequent policies were aimed at upholding Māori freshwater rights and interests, and addressing climate change by establishing a $1 billion fund for Māori community energy projects and ceasing the issuing of oil and gas permits. Economic policies aimed at raising the minimum wage to $25 per hour, as well as large-scale, detailed changes to the benefit system (including changing welfare conditions and creating a targeted, two-tier welfare system). A 'Whānau Build' policy promised changes such as 50 per cent of social housing being made available to Māori first, limiting immigration and foreign purchase of freehold land, and changes to taxation of property. Policies were announced to address issues that had gained lots of media attention in 2020, such as Oranga Tamariki and the racism present in the education system; these policies included establishing an independent Mokopuna Māori entity, making Māori history and te reo Māori core curriculum subjects, and ensuring Māori staff are present in senior positions. Other key policies included adopting recommendations for constitutional transformation put forward by Matike Mai Aotearoa (an independent working group made up of members from the National Iwi Chairs Forum, Māori organisations and Māori academics) and automatically enrolling all Māori on the Māori roll. The Māori Party also proposed changing New Zealand's name to Aotearoa and restoring Māori place names, and increasing funding for kapa haka (Māori performing arts) organisations. While the Māori Party is difficult to place on a traditional Western political science left–right spectrum (Godfery 2015), the positioning of the party across various policy issues in the 2020 campaign seemed to represent a shift to the left. The 2020 Māori Party also ruled out working with National after the election, with Ngarewa-Packer calling the idea 'untenable' (*Te Ao – Māori News* 2020b).

Throughout the 2020 campaign, the Māori Party positioned itself as an 'unapologetic' Māori voice. Māori Party candidates in debates, advertising and on social media highlighted the Māori Party's potential to be an effective opposition in Parliament, one that solely represented Māori. In debates, Māori Party candidates continually emphasised the challenges that Māori faced within the Labour Party; these included the potential for Māori MPs to be overruled by a Labour caucus that was majority Pākehā, and the challenge of representing a Māori voice within a party that was not Māori-centric. The consistent message that Māori Party candidates expressed was that they were Māori in a Māori party rather than Māori in the Labour Party. Labour candidates countered this point by highlighting their actions in government over the last term, and reminded voters of the fact that the Māori Party had been in coalition with the National Party between 2008 and 2017, a move that attracted widespread criticism.

The Māori Party adopted a number of consistent key messages that reinforced its unapologetically Māori stance and the party's key values. The 'Believe in you, believe in me, believe in Māori' slogan, adopted at the start of the campaign, reflected the party's commitment to the 'realisation and fulfilment of all the dreams and aspirations of our people on our terms' (Māori Party 2020). The campaign drew on elements of Māori culture and metaphors in order to communicate key party stances and decisions. Rawiri Waititi, candidate for the Waiariki electorate, often described the party's policies as a 'pou in the ground' (Husband 2020). The use of pouwhenua, traditional Māori carved wooden posts (used to mark territorial boundaries and places of significance), in this context conveys the unapologetic stance at the centre of the party's messaging.

The Māori Party were the second most active party on Facebook throughout the campaign, behind the Labour Party. According to the New Zealand Social Media Study, Tamihere was the most active campaigner on Facebook across all parties, publishing 188 Facebook posts during the campaign period (Victoria University of Wellington 2020). The study's co-leader Dr Mona Krewel noted that the Māori Party's use of social media demonstrated an example of minor parties compensating for a smaller budget with a 'very engaged user of social media': in this case, Tamihere. Krewel characterised many of the Māori Party's posts as 'mobilising', with a large focus on advance voting. The Māori Party used Facebook to provide information about enrolling to vote, overseas voting, voting place locations, election day rules and voting during the advance voting period, along with interactive templates for supporters to post on their own social media pages.

Building on this theme, the Māori Party drew on their kapa haka talents, cultural values, and connections with notable Māori to increase support, all largely showcased through social media. Often Facebook live streams were held, featuring kapa haka performances or karakia (blessings). These online events became more frequent throughout the nationwide Covid-19 lockdown in March–April, continuing through the rest of the campaign. The Māori Party had also built links with a number of influential Māori figures and organisations, many of whom featured on the party's 'Māori conversations' series, where candidates and experts discussed social and political issues and Māori Party policy. The party was once again endorsed by Kiingi Tuheitia and the Kiingitanga, who had previously shown support before the 2017 election. The Mana Movement also endorsed the Māori Party in a statement shared on social media, and early in the campaign SOUL leader Pania Newton appeared in a livestream as part of the 'Māori conversations' series.

The Māori Party also maintained a consistent presence in traditional media. Māori-led election coverage from *The Hui* and Māori Television provided a range of Māori electorate debates (and, crucially, polling). The tone and issues covered in the debates were notably different to those in the general media. The general leaders' debates lacked coverage of Māori issues, to the point that a petition was launched to initiate a Māori-led, Māori-issue leaders' debate; it remains to be seen whether this will be in place for 2023. The tone of the debates within the Māori electorates emphasized whanaungatanga, that is, valuing relationships and a sense of family-like connections between candidates. This carried over to being more inclusive of a range of candidates. Controversially, the debates on both Māori Television and *The Hui* included Billy Te Kahika in Te Tai Tokerau and Hannah Tamaki in Waiariki. Tamaki, leader of Vision New Zealand and the wife of Destiny Church leader Brian Tamaki, had attracted much criticism since the party's formation in 2019 for proposing policies such as a ban on the construction of mosques and drastically reducing immigration (Quinlivan 2019). Advance New Zealand co-leader Billy Te Kahika was widely criticised for spreading misinformation regarding the Covid-19 virus and the 2020 nationwide lockdown. The Māori Party also successfully pushed for inclusion in the TVNZ minor party leaders' debate after arguing the inclusion rules did not adequately take into account the influence of the Māori electorates.

Māori Television commissioned a series of polls across the seven electorates. In Aotearoa, electorate-level polls are rare given their cost and general lack of influence on the composition of Parliament under MMP. However, the Māori electorate polls were important so that voters could assess the Māori Party candidates' chances in any of the electorates and decide whether they could give their party vote to the Māori Party without feeling like it would be 'wasted' if the party didn't reach the 5 per cent party vote threshold. The Māori electorates are challenging to poll for many reasons, including their geographical size, voter confusion over whether they are on the General roll or the Māori roll, the lack of a reliable sampling frame for Māori (i.e., there is no phone list of all Māori to randomly choose from), and so on. However, they provide the best-available systematic attempt at predicting the Māori electorate race outcomes. These polls showed the Māori Party candidate trailing the Labour candidate by 6 per cent in Tāmaki Makaurau, 12 per cent in Waiariki and 18 per cent in Te Tai Hauāuru, indicating that there could be some close races.

Contests in the Māori electorates

Given these polls, the Māori electorates can be split into two categories based on the likelihood of the Māori Party unseating the Labour incumbent. Four electorate contests never looked close. In Te Tai Tokerau (the northernmost Māori electorate), incumbent and number two on the Labour list Kelvin Davis contested the election against the

Māori Party's Mariameno Kapa-Kingi. In Hauraki-Waikato (stretching from the Manukau Harbour and the Coromandel Peninsula to Waihi Beach, the Kaimai Ranges and Matamata in the south) Labour minister Nanaia Mahuta ran against the Māori Party's Donna Pokere-Phillips. Ikaroa-Rāwhiti (encompassing Gisborne, Hawkes Bay, Wairarapa, Hutt Valley and Wainuiomata) was a contest between Labour's Meka Whaitiri, Māori Party candidate Heather Te Au-Skipworth, and Dr Elizabeth Kerekere, who went on to become a list MP for the Green Party. In Te Tai Tonga (the southernmost Māori electorate, comprising the whole of the South Island and part of Wellington), Labour's Rino Tirikatene, of the Tirikatene political dynasty, faced the Māori Party's Tākuta Ferris and Ariana Paretutanganui-Tamati from the Green Party. While the Māori Party candidates across these electorates managed to pick up between 6,255 and 7,597 votes, the eventual margins of victory to the Labour party candidates were all between 6,045 and 9,630 votes.

In contrast, three electorates emerged as potentially winnable for Māori Party candidates: Waiariki, Te Tai Hauāuru and Tāmaki Makaurau. Waiariki (running from Tauranga, Whakatāne and Waihau Bay to Tūrangi in the south, and encompassing Rotorua and Taupō) turned out to be a close-run victory for Māori Party candidate Rawiri Waititi. There were tense times on election night as a narrow gap against Waititi turned into a 415-vote lead by the end of the night. Won by Labour's Tāmati Coffey in 2017, Waiariki was previously held by former Māori Party co-leader Te Ururoa Flavell between 2005 and 2017. Key candidates in 2020 included Coffey, Waititi and Hannah Tamaki, leader of the newly formed Vision New Zealand Party. Waititi, the son-in-law of party leader John Tamihere, ran in the Waiariki seat with the Labour Party in 2014 before announcing support for the Māori Party in 2016. Waititi is also a tohunga of the Ringatū faith (a Māori religious movement, with a large number of members in the Bay of Plenty region). Several notable factors likely contributed to Waititi's victory, including a campaign that drew on Māori culture, his performance across the debates, and Tamaki potentially splitting Coffey's voter base.

Waititi's campaign strategy was unique as it regularly drew on his strong background in kapa haka. Public performances, branded 'kapa haka flash mobs', would take place at public places and gatherings, and were simultaneously livestreamed on Facebook. Other initiatives, such as a Facebook video series entitled 'Waiariki Waiata' and public events such as 'Vote Kapa Vote', similarly utilised kapa haka as a campaign tool and means of bringing together supporters. Waititi continually highlighted the value in kapa haka and eventually announced the party's Toi Māori policy, which promised increased funding for Te Matatini (a national kapa haka and Māori performing arts festival and competition) and a $10 million investment into kapa haka development.

Waititi performed strongly in the candidate debates. During debates, candidates weighed in on a number of local issues unique to the Waiariki electorate, such as the overlapping claims between Tauranga-Moana and Pare Hauraki Iwi groups. The issue stemmed from claims by the Tauranga-Moana Iwi collective that the Crown incorrectly allocated redress to Hauraki Iwi as a result of what Tauranga-Moana have labelled flawed overlapping claims policies and practices. Waititi repeatedly expressed support for Treaty reform and for the Tauranga-Moana Iwi collective and their viewpoint on the issue when questioned in debates, and later reaffirmed his position in videos posted to his Facebook page. Coffey announced that the Labour Māori caucus would attend a hui at Whareroa marae on the overlapping claims issues and argued that there is a need to 'get around the table' and go through a tikanga-based process in order to resolve the issue. However, Coffey was criticised for delaying his response to the issue, and the effectiveness of his actions are yet to be determined. Other issues unique to the electorate included air pollution in Tauranga, Environment Court and High Court challenges to expansion of a water bottling plant in the Otakiri Springs, and the economic effects of Covid-19 on tourism and business in Rotorua.

Another factor contributing to Waititi's victory may have been Hannah Tamaki's decision to run in the electorate. Following the Māori Television debate, arguments emerged regarding Tamaki potentially splitting Coffey's voter base. Paora Stanley, Te Rūnanga o Ngāi Te Rangi Chief Executive, argued that Tamaki had been very active campaigning in poorer urban communities that Coffey had gained votes from in 2017 (*Te Ao – Māori News* 2020a). In the face of an overwhelming victory for the Labour Party and its candidates across even historically National electorates, Waiariki was the one electorate where a Labour incumbent lost, by a margin of just 836 votes; Hannah Tamaki finished third, with 1,171 votes. In summary, there were a number of factors contributing to this result, and there will be varied Māori opinions on why this was the case.

Te Tai Hauāuru (stretching from Ōtorohanga and Tokoroa to the Kāpiti Coast and Porirua at its southern boundary, and including the Taranaki, Manawatu and Whanganui regions) was pegged by the media as the main race to watch. Labour's Adrian Rurawhe only won the electorate by 1,039 votes over the Māori Party candidate in the 2017 election. His only opponent in the 2020 election was Māori Party co-leader Debbie Ngarewa-Packer. Rurawhe has strong links to both the Rātana movement (a Māori religious and political movement) and politics, being the great-grandson of Rātana founder Tahupōtiki Wiremu Rātana, and the grandson of former Western Māori MPs Matiu Rātana and Iriaka Rātana, but he had faced criticism for his lack of a broader public or media profile. It seemed like an electorate that could be won by Ngarewa-Packer.

In debates, Rurawhe continued to highlight the successes of the Labour government over the last term and reminded voters of the actions of the past Māori Party–National coalition. In response, Ngarewa-Packer emphasised the Māori Party stance as standing for Māori, and challenging the government. Other key issues in the electorate that were discussed by candidates included King Country energy hardship and seabed mining. Rurawhe argued that no action had been taken in the last term to address energy hardship due to the difficulties of working with coalition partners, while Ngarewa-Packer argued for a transition to solar panels in the region and additional support in the meantime. Ngarewa-Packer, who has campaigned against seabed mining off the coast of Taranaki, argued for banning it, while Rurawhe highlighted that Labour had ceased the issue of new mining permits. Rurawhe eventually won the electorate, 1,053 votes ahead of Ngarewa-Packer.

Finally, Tāmaki Makaurau (the Auckland region) proved to be an interesting three-way contest between relatively high-profile Māori, Green and Labour party candidates. As previously noted, Māori Party co-leader John Tamihere was a controversial figure who sought to unseat Labour's Peeni Henare. Also contesting the electorate was Green Party co-leader Marama Davidson, who had the highest public profile of the three Green candidates in the Māori electorates. The Māori Television-commissioned poll showed a 6 per cent gap between Henare and Tamihere ten days before election day. It remains to be seen what influence Davidson had on the contest. On the one hand, past work has shown that Māori tend to be either Labour supporters *or* minor party supporters (Sullivan, von

Randow and Matiu 2014), which suggests that Davidson may have taken votes from Tamihere. On the other hand, the Labour and Green parties are both left-wing kaupapa Pākehā parties, so Davidson may have taken votes from Henare. However, quantitative analysis is needed to test this speculation. Ultimately, Henare defeated Tamihere with a margin of 927 votes.

On election night it looked for a while as though Rawiri Waititi would form a 'one man band' of sorts in Parliament, the likes of which we have seen in recent years from United Future's Peter Dunne (2008–2017) and ACT's David Seymour (2014–2020). The day after the election, Tamihere announced that he would stand aside as tāne co-leader in favour of Waititi taking the position. However, there was a tense two-week wait until the final results (including the special votes) were announced. Special votes include those who voted outside of their electorate's geographical region, who enrolled to vote after writ day (a month before the election), or who voted from overseas, plus a range of smaller groups. The special votes must have contained a substantial proportion of Māori Party supporters, as in the final result its party vote increased from 1 per cent to 1.2 per cent, meaning that Ngarewa-Packer joined Waititi in Parliament. The special votes also widened the gap in Waiariki to 836 votes from the 415-vote margin on election night. It may be that those who are enrolled to vote where their hapū/iwi is rather than their current location of residence are more likely to support the Māori Party. In addition, more Māori who do not typically vote may have been motivated to enrol and turn out to vote by the cannabis referendum, an issue that disproportionately affects Māori. Indeed, there was a 7.9 per cent increase in voter turnout for young Māori (aged 18–24) in the 2020 general election (Electoral Commission 2020). Future research should investigate the reasons behind the higher proportion of Māori Party votes in the special votes.

Conclusion

The main story of the 2020 general election for Māori has to be the return of the Māori Party. In the wake of a number of large issues, and contending with huge support for Labour nationwide, the party managed to win the Waiariki electorate and gain a second MP through the party vote. As of the end of 2020, Waititi and Ngarewa-Packer have managed to cause a stir by walking out of Parliament in protest over its speaking rules for smaller parties, Waititi performing a haka for Te Tiriti o Waitangi before taking his Oath of Allegiance, and calling for Te Tiriti to be included in the oath.

More generally, the number of Māori members of Parliament has remained steady, with 23 of Parliament's 120 members being of Māori descent. Since the election, the Labour government has made progress towards addressing Ihumātao, made commitments to introducing legislation regarding the establishment of Māori wards in local government, and appointed Hauraki-Waikato MP Nanaia Mahuta as New Zealand's first female Māori foreign minister, who also wears moko kauae (a traditional Māori chin tattoo for females, representative of whakapapa, hapū and iwi).

Heading into the 2023 election we may see the resurgence of the Māori Party. The presence of two Māori Party MPs creates more of an electoral risk for Labour, given that Parliament brings both the resources and the platform for more effective Māori opposition. There are a number of continuing policy issues that need solving for Māori to ensure equity and aspire to Te Tiriti partnership. Labour did not face strong opposition in the Māori electorates for multiple decades, but now the presence of the Māori Party in Parliament means effective opposition in these electorates across the 2020 term and in the 2023 election. Long term, the Māori Party must balance a number of challenges and opportunities in a trade-off between making change and achieving their policy goals while avoiding being seen as part of the establishment. It is hard out there for a minor party, but is it even harder for a Māori party?

29

ECHOES: THE 2020 ELECTION IN HISTORICAL PERSPECTIVE

Colin James

The 1969 election, the first of 16[1] I covered as a journalist, came at the 'beginning of the end' of 'a time of mildness and hope' and 'a modest affluence for all', as two contemporary writers (M.K. Joseph and Bill Oliver) described the post–World War II period.

A wool price plunge shortly after the 1966 election had forced an exchange rate devaluation which precipitated a long unravelling of the industrial conciliation and arbitration system. An infamous nil wage order by the Arbitration Court in 1968, intended to force a downward adjustment in real household income to make the devaluation stick, was upended by a peace pact by unions, employers and the government. Through 1968 there were rowdy demonstrations by a rising generation against the Vietnam war, nuclear weapons, sport with apartheid South Africa and much else. These eased temporarily in 1969. An opinion poll put Labour marginally ahead a week out from the election. Senior National ministers contemplated defeat.

But Opposition Labour was led by a man too fat to be Prime Minister, according to his secretary, Margaret Hayward.[2] A fight between the Seamen's Union and the decrepit Union Steamship Company flared as election day approached and Labour Minister Tom Shand played it up. Sir Keith Holyoake squeezed into a fourth term which he would not see out as Prime Minister.

This was a 'fishtail' election: National's lead narrowed, then widened at the end. Twelve years later, in 1981, a similar promising poll and promising canvassing signs on the ground for Labour also ended in a 'fishtail', again keeping National in power. Another 1981 light echo with 1969: Labour's leader, Bill Rowling, was outgunned on the hustings by National leader Rob Muldoon, a commanding, though divisive, figure.

Between 1969 and 1981 there were two landslides and a landslip. In 1972 Hayward's 'fat man', Big Norm Kirk, by then trimmed and tailored and backed by a rising cohort of 'modernisers' in key shadow cabinet roles, swept aside Holyoake's successor, Jack Marshall, who had secured a good deal over Britain's entry into the European Economic Community but headed a tiring cabinet. Labour's majority was 55 seats to 32. Kirk's first year in office was stoked by high commodity prices, but these slid in the second year after the collapse of the post-1945 Bretton Woods system, precipitating international currency volatility, and then a dramatic spike in oil prices driven by the Middle East oil-producing nations. New Zealand's already unbalanced economy was skewed further.

Kirk died in 1974, succeeded by Rowling, his Minister of Finance. In 1975, populist Muldoon exactly reversed the 1972 landslide for a 55–32 National majority on promises of economic stability, an unsustainably generous superannuation scheme to wow older voters and resumption of sport, especially rugby, with apartheid South Africa, which appealed to those he called the 'ordinary bloke', whose ally he unequivocally declared himself. Foreshadows of Donald Trump.

In 1978 the landslide reversed again, this time in a landslip. Labour beat National in the popular vote by 0.6 per cent – after opinion polls had given National a 7–9 per cent lead going into the campaign. Boundary and other distortions nevertheless gave National an 11-seat majority over Labour. In 1981 National led 7–10 per cent in pre-campaign polls but Labour again won the popular vote – by 0.2 per cent. And National again beat Labour – but this time by only 47 seats to 43.[3]

By then the 'modest affluence for all' era had fizzled out. High budget and balance of payments deficits, soaring government debt and ever tighter but futile regulation to try to fix the mess marked Muldoon's final years. The noisy protesters of 1968 took control of Labour with some slightly older fellow-travellers. Outside Parliament, divisive street battles in 1981 over a tour by the South African national rugby team, the Springboks, plus rising demands by a new generation of Māori for redress and respect put an end to 'mildness and hope'. Revolution was in the air.

Which is what that rising generation gave us in six years of Labour governments from 1984 and two years of an uncharacteristically radical National government from 1990: a fully independent nation, nuclear-free, on the path towards a bicultural society; a much more open and liberal society; and a deprotected, highly deregulated economy, delivered with massive disruption and seriously high unemployment and inequality.

In 1987 Labour lifted its previous 44 per cent vote to 48 per cent, recruiting large numbers of National-leaning supporters of Labour's pro-market economic reforms. But those reforms were out of character for Labour and cost it growing numbers of its old core wage worker ('ordinary bloke') votes – few Labour MPs were wage workers. After the sharemarket crashed in October 1987 desertions swelled to a flood. MP and former party president Jim Anderton carried off dissident Labourites into a NewLabour party – actually old-Labour wanting a return to pre-reform policies.

In 1990 Labour's vote plunged 13 points to 35 per cent. National stormed to 48 per cent but then in 1993 itself plunged 13 points to 35 per cent. This eerie echo of 1972–75 in reverse came after large numbers rejected National's out-of-character radicalism and members and MPs deserted, notably 1990–91 minister Winston Peters, who formed the populist economic and social nationalist New Zealand First Party, pining for a Muldoon rerun.

There was another eerie echo in the 1993 election – of 1978. A 10-point National opinion poll lead a couple of weeks out from the 1993 election all but evaporated into a tiny 0.4-point lead over Labour in votes – 'bugger the pollsters', National Prime Minister Jim Bolger grumped on election night. With 50 seats out of 95, Bolger had only a one-seat majority over Labour, who had 45 seats, and New Zealand First and the Alliance (Anderton's NewLabour plus the Greens and two other micro-parties), each with two seats. He tempered this by recruiting Labour's Peter Tapsell as Speaker. Helen Clark, newly installed as Labour leader by a coup against Mike Moore, acquiesced because she didn't want another election.

More important, the 1993 election ended another era: that of first-past-the-post single-member constituency voting (FPP). Voters rebuked both old parties for their radical departures from party traditions by backing a referendum replacing FPP with the mixed-member proportional system (MMP) recommended by a royal commission in 1986 and, curiously, put to the vote by Bolger.

Forecasting elections up to 1993 was relatively straightforward: absorb as much information as possible from as many sources as possible, winnow it and work out which of the two old parties would get the most seats. That also required assessing the impact on the two old parties of any significant third parties, such as Social Credit, which won a by-election in 1978, got 16 per cent of the vote and retained that one seat in the general election that year, then won another by-election in 1980 and 21 per cent of the vote in the 1981 general election but ended up with only two seats.

MMP introduced new complications, for voters and for forecasters. Under FPP voters chose a government from the two big parties or voted for something else in protest. Voting for a government was not so straightforward from 1996 because a vote for a small party could end up as a vote for a government which that party chose to join, even if most voters for that small party did not want that big party in power.

I got 1996 wrong. Labour hit its hoped-for target of 28 per cent, thanks in large part to Helen Clark's driving up of the 'worm'[4] in the first leaders' debate. That was not a convincing basis on which to form a coalition government with Jim Anderton's Alliance and National renegade Winston Peters' New Zealand First version of old-National, even though most of those who voted for New Zealand First wanted it to go with Labour. On the other hand, the language Peters had used of National, including that Bolger was not fit to be Prime Minister (he had sacked Peters as a minister in 1991), and the language Bolger and others used of New Zealand First and Peters, strained to breaking point credibility that they could or would work together. But, as Peters' adviser Michael Laws later pointed out in dismay, Peters saw National as 'family'.[5]

In fact it did prove incredible that Peters and National could work together. The family reconciliation was makeshift – and temporary. In November 1997 Jenny Shipley ousted Bolger to make National 'blue' again. In August 1998 she fired Peters, whose party fractured, enough of its MPs backing Shipley to keep her in office.

By 1999 a Labour-led government with the Alliance was an easy bet – they had made up in 1998. It turned out to be a minority government, though one supported by the Greens. Green co-leader Jeanette Fitzsimons won Coromandel when Labour voters got the message that the Greens might be needed for a majority. Had Margaret Wilson, Labour's candidate in Tauranga, told voters to vote for the candidate mostly likely to beat Peters there, his 63-vote plurality over National's Katherine O'Regan would probably have evaporated and New Zealand First would have been removed from Parliament.

The next five elections were easy bets, too. First came nine years of Helen Clark's building a 'third way' to calm middle New Zealand down after the 1980s–90s turmoil. Then nine years of Sirs John Key and Bill English running a moderate-liberal/moderate-conservative party reminiscent of the strong National governments of the 1950s and 1960s, with some rightwards adjustment to Clark's 'third way' policy settings.

The 2002 election was notable for Labour's 11-point slide from its pre-campaign poll ratings to a 41 per cent result – echoes of 1978, 1981 and 1993. But that was overshadowed by National's collapse to 21 per cent in the party vote, though with 31 per cent in the electorate vote it had a base to rebuild from. Anderton's Alliance had disintegrated in 2001 when faced with the need to accept that politics is the 'art of the possible', which limits ideological ventures – a lesson the Greens may be learning now, though that is far from clear yet and may not be known until they are accountable in a two-way coalition with Labour.

For Clark, the Greens were too far off-centre. From 2002 to 2005 she linked up with liberal former Labour and National minister Peter Dunne, who had shacked up with conservative Christians, a marriage of convenience which could not and did not endure. In 2005 Clark turned to New Zealand First, with Winston Peters as Minister of Foreign Affairs.

There was an eruption in Clark's reign: the Māori Party, formed by Labour minister Tariana Turia, who departed Labour when it legislated to overturn a Court of Appeal decision on governance of New Zealand's foreshore and seabed, which some iwi claimed as their right. The Māori seats, long locked into Labour – though they had gone to New Zealand First in 1996 – mostly deserted again in 2005. From 2008 Turia's Māori Party delivered proxy Labour votes to National through nine years of confidence and supply agreements. The gain to Māori was Whānau Ora, Māori-run health and family care.

In 2017, as National was anticipating a fourth term, there came another eruption: Jacinda Ardern. Made Labour leader 53 days before the 2017 election, her younger generation, macro-personality dazzle rescued Labour from 27 per cent in 2011, 25 per cent in 2014 and around 24 per cent and sliding in opinion polls in July 2017. At 37 years of age and with 37 per cent of the vote she formed a three-way coalition and governing arrangement with the ageing Winston Peters and the Greens.

Picking this one correctly required an assumption that National would not or could not replicate 1996 and make whatever policy concessions it would take to stay in power. One clue was that Peters no longer saw himself as 'family' with National. Another was that his party wanted economic policy changes that required movement in Labour's direction. A third was that behind the scenes Jacinda Ardern proved a skilful negotiator, smart and personable. Those clues pointed marginally towards Labour.

Echoes of 1984: the 2017 election marked a substantial generational shift to more than 40 per cent post-baby-boomers in Parliament. Most of the key ministers were of those new X and Y generations. But the Winston Peters 'handbrake', as he called it it, on policy that strayed too far from his take on what middle New Zealand wanted or would tolerate constrained how much 'transformation' (to use Jacinda Ardern's word) could be achieved.

The cost to Peters and New Zealand First in 2020 was a history repeat. In the final year of its previous two stints in government, in 1999 and 2008, New Zealand First polled below 5 per cent leading up to the campaign and finished below 5 per cent in the election. Low polling through 2018 and 2019 and into 2020 pointed to a sub-5 per cent election score. Peters and New Zealand First were duly ejected, with a humiliating 2.6 per cent vote.

The 2020 election will be remembered for Labour's extraordinary vote: for the first time in nearly 70 years, a party topped 50 per cent, even if only by 0.0115194321561 percentage points. That gave it an MMP first: a single-party majority of seats. It will be remembered, too, for National's post-1935 record 18.8 percentage point plunge to 25.6 per cent from 44.4 per cent in 2017. Labour had a 24.4-point lead over National, 4.1 points more than its 20.3 per cent lead in 2002.

Did Labour owe its majority only to Covid-19 and Ardern's intelligent, firm and inclusive management, which pushed her already strong approval ratings stratospheric and triggered turmoil in National? At a guess Covid may have added 5–8 per cent to Labour's score. But pre-Covid, through 2018 and 2019 and into 2020, Labour polled competitively with National and, with the Greens, ahead of National plus ACT. A second term was always more likely than not.

A quick scan of the age of this Parliament's MPs suggests a majority of post-baby-boomers: the new era which the 2017 election foreshadowed. Baby-boomers will hang around, but their influence will wane.

The question now is: will Jacinda Ardern's first unconstrained term in office echo 1984 or 1972? She is in command; just look at her face and her gait now compared with last term. But what commands will she issue?

As in 1969, the 2017 election came after the settled world had begun to fray; in 2020 that fraying had turned to turbulence as the geo-economy and geopolitics rebalanced. That has unsettled the foundations of the 'third way'. Will Ardern in her second term respond to this 'beginning of the end' of the order she grew up in? Will she be vigorously transformative in policy areas such as climate change, ecosystem protection, foreign affairs, tax, health, welfare and housing? That is, will she reposition and reframe Aotearoa New Zealand? That would echo 1984.

Or will Ardern echo Kirk in 1972 and be a pivot, continuing to modestly adjust the 'third way' while pointing in some policy areas (climate change? Māori development?) towards a later government, in 2029 or 2032, made up of Green star Chlöe Swarbrick contemporaries, which might merge necessity with radicalism in a genuinely serious transformation?

30

'WINDOW ON WAIRARAPA': KIERAN McANULTY AND LABOUR'S 2020 CAMPAIGN

Campbell Garrett

Introduction

After one term as a list MP, Kieran McAnulty was elected in 2020 as the electorate representative for the Wairarapa electorate. This chapter examines the conditions and campaign that led to this victory. Of particular focus will be the Covid-19 pandemic, which had a consequential effect on the entire election, including in Wairarapa. This chapter is inspired by, and draws from, Matthew Lamason's (2003) work on the 2002 election campaign in Wairarapa. While demographically and geographically the Wairarapa electorate has not experienced significant change, there has been a drastic political shift in the intervening 18 years and five elections. Lamason introduces Wairarapa as having 'moved from being a National stronghold to a Labour "safe seat" in the space of only one election', and describes a 'calm and comfortable 2002 victory for Labour' (Lamason 2003, p. 175). Labour had not won Wairarapa since. After Georgina Beyer's consecutive victories in the seat in 1999 and 2002, the electorate was carried by National's John Hayes in 2005, 2008 and 2011, and then in 2014 and 2017 by National's Alastair Scott in a series of comfortable victories.

The 2020 election represented the first real chance since Beyer for Labour to win Wairarapa, with incumbent Labour list MP Kieran McAnulty presenting a strong challenge to National's heir apparent Mike Butterick, a first-time candidate. Remarkably, the result on election night was a strong victory for Kieran McAnulty and for the Labour Party – both in Wairarapa and nationally. While the Labour candidate and campaign had been optimistic about the result, such a commanding victory had not been seen as likely. This chapter looks at the electorate – Wairarapa and its political history – and details the campaign and strategy of each of the 2020 Wairarapa candidates, highlighting the most significant factors influencing the 2020 Wairarapa race and its outcome.[1]

The Wairarapa electorate: A National stronghold

The Wairarapa electorate is the fourth largest general electorate in the North Island (Appropriations Review Committee 2018), behind East Coast, Taranaki–King Country and Rangitīkei. It represents a number of largely rural communities with diverse interests and concerns, more so than smaller electorates, such as those in Auckland. The electorate contains areas in five District Councils (South Wairarapa, Carterton, Masterton, Tararua and Central Hawkes Bay) and across three Regional Councils (Greater Wellington, Horizons [Manawatu-Whanganui] and Hawkes Bay). Most of the population is located in Masterton and the rest of the Wairarapa region, whose closest ties are to Wellington. This creates a dichotomy within perceptions of the seat. Wairarapa is generally considered a 'Wellington' electorate although many in the electorate are closer to other centres such as Napier, Hastings or Palmerston North. To give an idea of the scale of the electorate: to drive from one end of it to the other takes close to four hours. At one end is Cape Palliser, the southernmost point of the North Island; at the other is Waipawa, firmly located in Central Hawkes Bay and as close to Rotorua as it is to Wellington. For many in the electorate, then, being considered a 'Wellington' electorate would seem illogical.

The electorate last underwent boundary changes in 2007, when it gained more of the Central Hawkes Bay region, including Waipawa and Waipukurau, which had previously been part of the Hastings-centred Tukituki electorate (Parliamentary Service 2017). As noted, Labour had not won Wairarapa since 2002. The Waipawa and Waipukurau communities, as well as other rural Central Hawkes Bay communities, typically lean towards the National Party. This means that while Labour can point back to Georgina Beyer's success in the seat in 1999 and 2002, geographic changes have moved the seat away from Labour rather than towards it. There were no changes in the 2014 or 2020 redistributions (Representation Commission 2014, 2020). A significant proportion of the electorate's population is located in Central Hawkes Bay, with closer ties to Napier and Hastings; the remainder (in Tararua District) are more closely linked to Palmerston North. Kieran McAnulty, Labour's Wairarapa candidate in 2014, 2017 and 2020, and Alex Walker, Mayor of Central Hawke's Bay District Council, drew attention to this in a request to the Representation Commission (McAnulty and Walker 2020), proposing the electorate be renamed 'Wairarapa and Central Hawkes Bay' in order to recognise the electorate's different communities of interest. While this request was not reflected in the Representation Commission's report, the idea underscored the challenges of representing such a large electorate. Another demonstration of this was in the two other objections to the Wairarapa electorate as part of the 2020 Representation Commission's review. One submission requested that the township of Waipawa remain in the Wairarapa electorate, rather than Tukituki, while a second requested the opposite (Electoral Commission 2020).

McRobie (1989) and Lamason (2003) provide the best histories of the Wairarapa electorate. In New Zealand's early electoral history, Wairarapa was represented by two MPs before being split in 1881 into two electorates: Wairarapa South and Wairarapa North, later replaced by Wairarapa and Masterton. The Wairarapa electorate was largely amalgamated with the Pahiatua electorate in 1996 with the advent of the Mixed-Member Proportional voting system (MMP). This substantially enlarged the electorate, and it grew even further in 2007 with the inclusion of the townships of Waipukurau and Waipawa. The vast size of the electorate, with an exurban connection to Wellington as well as a large provincial centre in Masterton, many rural townships, and connections to both Palmerston North and Napier, makes campaigning difficult. Constituents in different areas have vastly different political needs and priorities, and accessing remote and rural communities can be challenging. This was central to the campaign – each major party candidate made a number of visits to towns and provincial centres across the electorate, even as door-knocking and phone-banking efforts focused on the larger centres such as Masterton and Carterton. Lamason (2003) explains that the size and demographic makeup of Wairarapa makes it a National Party stronghold. Labour have won the electorate only six times since Wairarapa and Masterton were amalgamated to form Wairarapa in 1946. Three of those victories came in the first-past-the-post (FPP) era: 1969 and 1972 through Jack Williams, and 1984 through Reg Boorman. Three victories have come since the advent of MMP: in 1999 and 2002 through Georgina Beyer, and in 2020 with Kieran McAnulty. Conversely, between 1946 and 2020, Wairarapa was won 20 times by National candidates. The neighbouring Pahiatua electorate, abolished and merged into Wairarapa in 1996, was held by National consistently from 1938 to 1993.

This chapter builds on Matthew Lamason's study of the 2002 Wairarapa election campaign. At that election, Georgina Beyer won a comfortable second consecutive victory in the electorate with a majority of 6,372 votes, assisted by the two right-leaning candidates, Ian Buchanan for National and Merepeka Raukawa-Tait for Christian Heritage, splitting the vote. The 2002 and 2020 elections produced National's lowest two party votes since the party's formation in 1936 (it contested its first election in 1938) and were the only two elections at which National's vote dropped below 30 per cent. Another parallel between the two campaigns was the presence of a strong third-party candidate: in 2020, Ron Mark for New Zealand First; in 2002, Merepeka Raukawa-Tait for Christian Heritage. In 2002, Raukawa-Tait claimed that incumbent MP Beyer and National candidate Ian Buchanan would be elected via the Labour and National lists regardless of the result, providing Wairarapa with the possibility of three MPs (though in the end, due to National's poor result, Buchanan was not elected on the list). In 2020, a similar dynamic played out, with both Ron Mark and Mike Butterick campaigning on providing Wairarapa with a second MP as McAnulty was guaranteed a list spot.

The candidates: A crowded field

Eight candidates sought the Wairarapa electorate seat in 2020: Kieran McAnulty (Labour), Mike Butterick (National), Ron Mark (New Zealand First), Celia Wade-Brown (Greens), Warren Butterworth (New Conservatives), Roger Greenslade (ACT), Nigel Gray (Advance New Zealand) and Aileen Haeata (independent).

As noted, 2020 was McAnulty's third consecutive attempt at the seat. In 2017, he significantly reduced incumbent National MP Alastair Scott's majority, entering Parliament as Labour's last list MP on election night. Over the next three years, McAnulty worked and campaigned as the de facto Wairarapa electorate representative in an attempt to win the seat from a largely absent Alastair Scott. This strategy seemed to work with a large cohort of voters – many on the campaign trail suggested that they viewed McAnulty as the electorate MP, some saying they had believed he already was the electorate representative. Broadly, McAnulty's strategy centred on maximising interactions with voters through street corner meetings, candidate and community events, phone calls and door-knocking. The central campaign message was that McAnulty's advocacy as the de facto Wairarapa electorate MP would be better facilitated with the extra resources that come from winning an electorate seat. McAnulty campaigned on the importance of 'having an MP at the heart of Government', ostensibly for the first time since Wyatt Creech in the 1990s. This strategy touted his role as junior Labour Party whip providing access to key government ministers, as well as his high list ranking of 28 (much improved from 38 in 2017) as an indicator of his success in the 52nd Parliament.

Another central theme of McAnulty's Wairarapa campaign was emphasising his local roots. As explained in his campaign video: 'My family have lived and worked here for seven generations. My great-grandmother's great-grandfather founded Featherston' (McAnulty 2020). These local roots, along with his family's farming background, and McAnulty's previous employment as a bookie for the TAB in Masterton, were instrumental in portraying a candidate who was serious about the electorate as well as a regular 'Kiwi bloke'. This was largely in contrast to Alastair Scott – who did not live in the electorate, his main connection to the region being that he owned a vineyard in Martinborough. Emblematic of that image – and helping McAnulty to receive more national coverage – was his signature ute, adorned with Labour colours and advertising for McAnulty. While this image of McAnulty contrasted well with Scott, it was less of a distinction with the new National Party candidate, a sheep and beef farmer who had lived in Wairarapa since 1990. For McAnulty, the 2020 campaign combined ensuring his work was linked in the view of the public to the work of Jacinda Ardern, while also distinguishing himself from the party through his focus on local issues.

The National candidate chosen to replace the retiring Alastair Scott was Mike Butterick, with strong ties to the region. Unlike his predecessor, Butterick lived in the electorate, and would have been a strong advocate for the farming community and for the Wairarapa region had he been elected. Butterick entered public and political life in 2019, when he was involved in the foundation of advocacy group Fifty Shades of Green, which opposed afforestation of farming land. Butterick battled perceptions of his predecessor, Alastair Scott. By 2020, Scott was not a popular figure in Wairarapa, particularly in provincial centres such as Masterton and Carterton. At one debate in Carterton, Butterick was asked his opinion of Scott's time as electorate representative for Wairarapa. The audience laughed at the question, and Butterick's answer was diplomatic: 'I think all the people who have represented Wairarapa over the years have done their utmost . . . I think everyone goes there [to Parliament] with the intention of doing the best they can for the electorate' (*Wairarapa Times-Age* 2020b).

Butterick also had to overcome the challenges of a late selection to the seat. He was not selected until the beginning of June 2020 – less than four months before the election (Burke 2020). The selection process was initially scheduled for 29 March but was delayed by the Covid-19 lockdown that had begun just days before, preventing an in-person selection meeting. The selection outcome was not certain – there were two other candidates for National: Monique Kloeg, a local café owner, and Mark Bridges, school principal and brother of then party leader Simon Bridges (Coltman 2020). While election campaigns in New Zealand are typically short, the time before the campaign begins is key for establishing campaign committee roles, finding volunteers and coordinators, and beginning to increase name recognition. This delay cost Butterick potential campaigning time. In another challenge, the leadership change from Todd Muller to Judith Collins necessitated remaking National Party hoardings, allegedly costing the Wairarapa National Party campaign several thousand dollars. After a rough start to the campaign through no fault of his own, his general campaign strategy was similar to McAnulty's. Butterick was active at street corner meetings, at community events, on social media and at candidate events, with a solid 'ground game' – important for candidates in rural seats.

New Zealand First MP Ron Mark ran for the Wairarapa electorate for a third time. As a two-time Mayor of Carterton, long-time Member of Parliament, and Cabinet Minister in the 52nd Parliament, he represented one of New Zealand First's best opportunities for an electorate win as a ticket back into Parliament. Along with Shane Jones in the Northland electorate, and Tracey Martin in Ōhāriu, Ron Mark was one of just two or three New Zealand First candidates running a genuine electorate campaign. During the 2014 campaign, Mark was able to run as a familiar and trusted face in the region following his Carterton mayoralty, with McAnulty largely unknown. Mark received 23 per cent of the vote to McAnulty's 25 per cent, achieving a credible third place. However, over time, his vote share has declined: to 19 per cent in 2017 and just 7 per cent in 2020. This partly reflects a change in New Zealand First's fortunes nationally. In 2020, New Zealand First failed to return to Parliament. A significant proportion of voters typically vote for a candidate from the same party as their party vote, so the decline in New Zealand First's vote percentage meant Mark was fighting a losing battle in the Wairarapa seat. However, he did manage to win more than double the proportion of votes as a candidate that New Zealand First managed as a party. Meanwhile, polling for McAnulty's Labour campaign in August suggested that fewer New Zealand First voters would give their candidate vote to Mark than in 2017, whereas both McAnulty and Butterick seemed likely to retain higher proportions of Labour and National party supporters, respectively.

Mark positioned himself as a fighter and something of an underdog in the campaign. In a number of interviews and discussions, Mark referred to his upbringing in foster homes and as a ward of the state, before 'making something of himself' in the military. As a committed Minister for both Defence and Veterans, Mark made this another campaign focus, noting his achievements in the humanitarian space with the Defence portfolio, and his advocacy for veterans. However, there is no real New Zealand Defence Force presence in the Wairarapa, so defence and military issues are not front and centre for Wairarapa voters. While not necessarily dissuading voters from supporting Mark, this focus was never likely to win over many of them. One particular challenge for Ron Mark – as well as for Green Party candidate Celia Wade-Brown (and for New Zealand First and the Greens more widely) – is the difficulty of differentiating New Zealand First's achievements from those of the coalition government. Particularly following the Covid-19 pandemic, Labour used its lead role in the coalition and its spotlight during lockdown to take full credit for successful policies, while often shifting the blame for unsuccessful policies to its coalition partners. In debates, this often meant McAnulty, Mark and to a lesser extent Wade-Brown agreed on a number of policies, with Mark pressured to provide a point of difference.

Another former mayor (through of Wellington, not Carterton) Celia Wade-Brown was convinced to run for the Greens in Wairarapa after 2014 and 2017 candidate John Hart declined to do so. A somewhat reluctant candidate, she put her name forward after attending a local meeting ahead of the election, having rejoined the Greens following the end of her mayoralty in 2016. Wade-Brown ran a party-vote-only campaign, at one point explicitly endorsing McAnulty for the electorate vote. This matched with the Greens' campaign across the country, where only two candidates (Chlöe Swarbrick in Auckland Central and Marama Davidson in Tāmaki Makaurau) ran two-tick campaigns. While the Green Party received a slightly higher number of votes than in 2017, Wade-Brown's candidate vote was significantly down on John Hart's 2017 result. This was partly due to her running a more explicit party-vote-only campaign. One notable element of the Green Party (and Wade-Brown) campaign was in hoardings, with none featuring Wade-Brown, while the Greens' Ikaroa-Rāwhiti candidate Elizabeth Kerekere's face featured prominently on hoardings, particularly around Masterton. Although Kerekere was also not running a candidate-vote campaign, she was likely to enter Parliament on the Greens' list, and as such, achieving name recognition was seen as important.

One strategy of Wade-Brown for increasing name recognition – and sharing the Green Party kaupapa – was community meetings (held in cafés rather than on street corners like McAnulty and Butterick). These were important not just for increasing the vote, but also for bringing together the existing Green Party volunteer and member base across the very large electorate. While there was an existing infrastructure, unifying and ensuring that the full membership was engaged was a key element of the campaign. One significant challenge of the Green Party campaign for Wade-Brown was the difficulty of running a party-vote-only campaign, as did ACT, the New Conservative Party and, to a certain extent, Advance New Zealand. Meet-the-candidate and debate-style events are often the primary way to receive campaign attention, particularly in local media, but these events often only invited the so-called 'likely' candidates (Kieran McAnulty, Mike Butterick and Ron Mark). For at least one event – a 'politics in the pub' event in Greytown – Wade-Brown was not initially invited, though she attended anyway. Running a party-vote-only campaign may be less intensive for the candidate and volunteers (and may be better for the relationship between the Greens and the Labour Party); however, it makes receiving campaign coverage harder in media often focused on 'horse race' coverage. In terms of media coverage, Wade-Brown noted that one significant element of her campaign strategy was in gaining (often free) press in local free media – such as the *Carterton Crier*, *Featherston Phoenix*, *Greytown Grapevine* and *Martinborough Star*.

The New Conservative Party's candidate was Warren Butterworth, standing for Wairarapa because his home electorate, Northland, already had a New Conservative Party candidate. Butterworth did have a solid campaign presence, attending several debates, though running a party-vote-only campaign. The Conservative Party did not run a candidate in the 2017 election – they changed their name to the New Conservative Party in November 2017. Butterworth's run for the seat increased the possibility that he could act as a 'spoiler', taking votes away from the National candidate, as Green Party candidates often do to Labour candidates. There was also some (mostly unserious) speculation that some voters may confuse the names of the two 'blue' candidates: Mike Butterick for National and Warren Butterworth for New Conservative. While it is unclear whether this happened in the polling booths, it did happen during the campaign, with voters during question-and-answer sessions in at least one debate confusing the two names, as well as referring to Butterick as Butterfield. Campaigning solely for the party vote, Butterworth was not expecting to be elected to Parliament due to his ranking: 24th out of 24 candidates on the New Conservative party list. As with National's Butterick, Butterworth made anti-afforestation a significant plank of his campaigning. Other elements of Butterworth's campaign matched the party's campaign nationally – anti-abortion, against action on climate change, in favour of lower taxes and very socially conservative policies. While on-the-ground volunteering was not observed, there were a significant number of hoardings, displaying a variety of slogans – 'all life matters', 'keep NZ ours', 'support 1st homebuyers' – seeking to draw upon controversial topics to increase public recognition of New Conservative and to capitalise on the National Party's collapsing support, particularly from conservative and Christian voters.

Roger Greenslade, ACT's candidate, was in his second race for the seat (after 2017). In one of the quirks of the 2020 campaign, Greenslade stood for Wairarapa while living and working in Thailand – standing from overseas as he had done in 2005 and 2017 (*Wairarapa Times-Age* 2020a). Due to this, Greenslade was perhaps the lowest-profile candidate in the race. ACT had fewer hoardings than other parties, none of them including Greenslade. While without a strong campaign presence in Wairarapa, ACT had rapidly risen in nationwide polls. In the lead-up to the election, this created an interesting question – whether Greenslade would draw electorate votes away from Butterick the same way ACT drew party votes away from National. Butterick's hopes for winning the seat depended in part upon ACT receiving fewer candidate votes than party votes. This was partly the case. While Greenslade drew 900 more votes than in 2017, more than 3,500 ACT Party voters out of 4,132 did not give their candidate vote to Greenslade, with two thirds going to Butterick (in 2017, close to half of ACT Party voters also voted for National's Alastair Scott). ACT drew a higher proportion of party votes in Wairarapa than it did nationally, similar to New Zealand First in previous elections. Most of this support likely came from fleeing National voters, which may explain why many ACT voters also provided a candidate vote to the race's main right-of-centre candidate, Butterick.

The Advance New Zealand candidate, Nigel Gray, joined the race late. He quickly gained a solid presence in the campaign, with a scattering of hoardings, some ground game in the electorate, and appearances at the debates. He had a strong social media presence, with a greater following on Facebook than any of the other Wairarapa candidates – including McAnulty and Butterick. This social media presence was largely used to spread conspiracies about Bill Gates, the United Nations, Agenda 2030, Covid-19, and 1080 – all drawn together by Advance New Zealand and the New Zealand Public Party. Many of these conspiracies appeared closely linked with a racist, antisemitic and insane American 'catch-all' conspiracy known as QAnon. While Gray did not explicitly endorse these conspiracies, his candidacy (as well as the Advance New Zealand campaign nationwide) focused on returning 'sovereignty' to New Zealanders in an attempt to excuse bigoted and unsupported policies. Gray briefly received national coverage for suggesting that a large fire at Lake Ōhau Village was deliberately caused by a 'DEW', or 'direct energy weapon' (Wu 2020). In one candidate debate, Gray used his time to criticise the 'takeover' of New Zealand by China and the United Nations, to attack Covid-19 lockdowns, to criticise 1080 and other unnamed drugs, and to lambast the idea of mental health. In another debate, Gray falsely suggested that vaccines cause autism. Particularly in his criticisms of Covid-19 lockdown and doubts of the severity of Covid-19, Gray was a useful foil for McAnulty. In at least one debate, McAnulty took aim at Gray's conspiracism to defend and applaud the Labour Party and Jacinda Ardern's record and leadership on Covid-19. Gray recognised that he was unlikely to win the electorate vote, primarily campaigning for the party vote. In the final results, he achieved just 443 votes, claiming online that the election was 'rigged' because he failed to garner as many votes as even Roger Greenslade, campaigning from Thailand (Gray 2020).

The final candidate was Aileen Haeata. Standing as an independent, she received very little press or attention for her campaign. Haeata had previously run for the Masterton Community Trust during the 2019 local elections, placing last of ten candidates, with 1,709 votes (Masterton District Council 2019). During that election, Haeata expressed support for tikanga and Kaupapa Māori–based solutions to issues facing Masterton, as well as opposition to fluoridation (Tararua District Council 2019; Fluoride Free NZ 2019). She had previously lived in Upper Hutt and Auckland, stating that she could trace her whakapapa back through 45 generations in the Wairarapa region, as part of Rangitāne o Wairarapa (*Wairarapa Times-Age* 2020b). Haeata stated that she was standing to represent the 'downtrodden' and in opposition to the Family Court (Boyack 2020). My own observations were that Haeata attended only one candidate event – the final debate in Carterton. She was not on the official billing, but joined the other candidates anyway before being heckled off after arguing with the debate moderator. Ultimately, Haeata achieved just 109 votes. It proved difficult to establish whether Haeata was actively campaigning. While she may have been knocking on doors or at events in the community, she did not have any hoardings, advertisements or a campaign presence on social media.

Early expectations: Opportunity for Labour?

There were a number of reasons to expect a close election. The political conditions for a Labour victory in the seat were the most favourable since Georgina Beyer's 2002 victory. On a national level, Labour's popularity following the government's handling of the pandemic meant that it was expected to surpass National's vote in a number of usually 'true blue' seats. Additionally, New Zealand First's relative unpopularity in 2020 made a vote for Ron Mark less appealing, with candidate and party votes often going hand in hand. In the electorate, there were additional factors that gave McAnulty hope. The incumbent MP was retiring and his replacement, Mike Butterick, had only been selected in June (New Zealand National Party 2020). This late selection, delayed by the pandemic, reduced the time available to recruit campaign positions, find volunteers and increase name recognition in a large rural electorate where doing so involves significant amounts of time-intensive travel around the region. The campaign was also significantly shortened in its early stages by the pandemic, further limiting opportunities for direct voter contact.

Labour did not have the same issues. McAnulty ran for the Wairarapa seat in 2014 and 2017 and had been an incumbent list MP since 2017, providing a solid base of name recognition and ample opportunity to campaign. Central to the McAnulty campaign was direct voter contact, including street corner meetings that McAnulty had been holding since before his election in 2017. The other party candidates did not represent a significant challenge for either of the two main candidates.

Despite these factors, the fundamentals of the race seemed to remain in Mike Butterick and National's favour. The electorate is more favourable to National than the country as a whole and has trended marginally further towards National over the last three elections (Electoral Commission n.d.). Accounting for trends over the last three elections, National was expected to outperform its nationwide party vote by approximately 5 per cent, with Labour expected to underperform its nationwide party vote by a similar margin. This provided a cushion against National's poor polling nationwide and countered many of the more favourable factors for Labour going into the election. The advantage for National was due to geographic and demographic factors. National generally performs better in rural areas, particularly with farming communities, and with older voters, with the Wairarapa electorate one of the 'oldest' in the country. Despite poor polling, with voters shifting to Labour due to Jacinda Ardern's popularity and the lack of support for National Party leader Judith Collins, there was some anticipation that National's candidate results would be better than those of the party. National electorate candidates were predicted to overperform relative to the party, with voters remaining loyal to their local National MP or candidate while shifting their party-vote support to Labour.

The prospect of having two – or even three – Members of Parliament representing Wairarapa also worked in National candidate Mike Butterick's favour. McAnulty was near-certain to re-enter Parliament on Labour's list. Ron Mark was in a position to return to Parliament if New Zealand First crossed the 5 per cent threshold (or if Shane Jones were to win the Northland electorate). Butterick was unlikely to enter Parliament on the National Party list, being ranked at 58 due to the party's policy of ranking new electorate candidates in National-held seats alphabetically at the bottom of the list. This meant Butterick was able to present an argument to voters that he needed their electorate vote to represent them in Parliament while McAnulty did not. As a result, a main plank of the McAnulty campaign in Wairarapa centred around the necessity of having an MP 'at the heart of Government' – a refrain heard at every campaign event and on every flyer. McAnulty presented the case that in order to expand his advocacy for the region, he required the extra resources provided by the role of electorate MP, particularly in a large seat. Conversely, a main focus of Butterick's campaign was the idea of Wairarapa being represented by multiple Members of Parliament, providing constituents with 'two for the price of one' – an element of the campaign unique to MMP (in FPP, without a party vote or list MPs, the only Members of Parliament were the electorate representatives).

As the campaign wore on, McAnulty and the Labour campaign team remained optimistic. Not only were national polls for Labour holding up at around 50 per cent, but an electorate touch-tone poll taken for the campaign in August – and kept private to a very limited group of the campaign team – put Labour at 44 per cent to National's 30 per cent in the electorate, and McAnulty ahead of Butterick, 45 per cent to 32 per cent. That poll also showed a very positive response to Jacinda Ardern and a very negative response to the leadership of Judith Collins. Given the relatively high number of third-party voters (in the past, mostly for New Zealand First and Ron Mark) in Wairarapa, McAnulty considered that a nationwide party vote for Labour in the mid-forties would be high enough for him to win the seat. There were other positive indicators suggesting a good result for McAnulty and Labour. The volunteer base for Labour was vastly larger than in previous years, as was the number of hoarding sites. Door-knocking in traditional National strongholds of Martinborough and West Masterton returned a surprisingly positive response, and turnout at street corner meetings enabled McAnulty to increase his visibility in the electorate.

Issues in the 2020 election: The Covid campaign

Nationally, the Covid-19 pandemic was undoubtedly the most consequential issue for voters, and for the election more generally, with a significant impact in the Wairarapa. The return of community transmission to New Zealand forced a return to alert levels 2 and 3, and eventually a month-long delay to the election. Among campaign staff, volunteers, MPs, journalists and the voting public, the delay to the election created a kind of 'election fatigue'. More importantly, it also led to a huge shift in national polling, with Labour reaching well above 50 per cent in a series of polls. Overall, perceptions of ineffectual leadership by National Party leaders – Simon Bridges, Todd Muller and Judith Collins – contrasted with Jacinda Ardern's leadership profile, with Labour portrayed as the stable and successful governing option and National in chaos. During the campaign Labour went so far as to paint itself as the heir to the legacy of John Key and Bill English through the leadership of Jacinda Ardern and Grant Robertson.

While the 2020 election could be considered the 'Covid campaign', the pandemic was more a feature of the national campaign than the local campaign in Wairarapa, where local issues of transport and agriculture took priority in many discussions the Labour campaign team had with voters. Much of National's campaign nationally focused on transport and infrastructure announcements, and these became part of the local campaign. Judith Collins visited the electorate to announce new transport projects and fast-tracking of existing projects, briefly putting Labour and the McAnulty campaign on the defensive. Afforestation of farming land in the electorate was also prioritised. National's Mike Butterick's anti-afforestation advocacy had been an early issue in the campaign and dealing with forestry concerns was an early priority for Labour. McAnulty, along with Minister of Forestry Stuart Nash, announced a policy that would require resource consent on certain land proposed for afforestation. This policy, along with claims of hypocrisy from Butterick, who had sold a farm for afforestation several years earlier, reduced the importance of forestry for the remainder of the campaign for most 'urban' voters (*New Zealand Herald* 2020).

Within the transport portfolio, a number of distinct issues were important to the campaign. For McAnulty, the single biggest achievement of the 52nd Parliament was the $196 million funding for upgrades to the Hutt–Wairarapa rail lines, including expected increases to service frequency and resilience. The improvement was a focus for the Labour campaign, with volunteers handing out transport and infrastructure flyers to commuters at train stations in South Wairarapa. Additionally, $10 million in funding for Hood Aerodrome in Masterton as part of the Covid-19 recovery package provided the potential for a return of commercial flights to Masterton. For Butterick's campaign, National's focus on transport and infrastructure included improvements to intersections, roundabouts and bridges in and around Masterton and Martinborough, as well as upgrades to Route 52 between Pōrongahau and Waipukurau. Road safety, as well as overuse of town-centre roads in Masterton and the South Wairarapa towns by trucks, was a central concern to voters at street corner meetings.

Wairarapa: The outcome

More votes were cast in the Wairarapa electorate than in all but 12 electorates, with 45,264 party votes, demonstrating the high levels of engagement and voter contacts achieved by the parties' and the candidates' campaigns. The result (as shown in Table 30.1) was a resounding victory for Kieran McAnulty and for the Labour Party. McAnulty's 22,042 votes – more than any candidate has ever received in Wairarapa – gave him a majority of 6,545 (14.5 per cent) over Butterick. With 48.95 per cent of the vote, McAnulty came closer to a majority of votes than any Wairarapa candidate in the MMP era. While the general expectation among the campaign team was that McAnulty would need a large number of National Party voters to split their vote, this was not reflected in the final result. Labour won the party vote with 47.88 per cent of the vote, 18.8 per cent ahead of National. Kieran McAnulty, Mike Butterick and Ron Mark – the only three candidates seriously competing for the seat – each outperformed their party's vote. Celia Wade-Brown and Roger Greenslade underperformed the Greens' and ACT's party vote, indicating that voters for those two parties were well aware that the contest was between McAnulty and Butterick, and gave their support to one of the two major party candidates.

McAnulty and Labour performed very strongly in advance votes compared to election day votes, a trend absent in 2017. McAnulty won all but one advance voting booth (where McAnulty and Butterick tied, with five votes each). Conversely, Butterick won a majority of election day polling booths. While irrelevant in terms of the overall outcome, Butterick won the election day vote while both McAnulty and Labour achieved tallies greater than 50 per cent in the advance vote count – possibly indicative of McAnulty's 'get out the vote' campaign encouraging early voting, with canvassing during the early voting period (including door-knocking and phone-banking) providing targeted groups of voters with information about their nearest polling booths. It was also consistent with nationwide trends, with left-leaning voters more likely to vote early, and conservative voters more inclined to vote on election day itself.

Table 30.1: The 2020 Wairarapa results

Party	Candidate	Nationwide party vote	Wairarapa party votes		Wairarapa candidate votes	
		%	Votes	%	Votes	%
Labour	Kieran McAnulty	50.01	21,673	47.88	22,042	48.95
National	Mike Butterick	25.58	13,165	29.08	15,497	34.41
NZ First	Ron Mark	2.60	1,545	3.41	3,278	7.28
Green	Celia Wade-Brown	7.86	2,329	5.15	1,359	3.01
ACT	Roger Greenslade	7.59	4,132	9.13	1,076	2.38
New Conservative	Warren Butterworth	1.48	670	1.48	587	1.30
Advance NZ	Nigel Gray	0.99	464	1.03	443	0.98
Independent	Aileen Haeata	-	-	-	109	0.24
Māori Party	-	1.17	125	0.28	-	-
Other parties	-	2.72	1,007	1.95	-	-
Total	-	-	45,264	-	45,027	-
Majority	-	-	8,508	18.80	6,545	14.54

Source: Electoral Commission 2020, 'Official results for the 2020 General Election and referendums', 6 November.

Of course, the Wairarapa results reflected Labour's overall dominance in the 2020 elections. Labour won 17 electorates that had been won by National in 2017, including a number of seats demographically, geographically and politically similar to Wairarapa. A proportion of the Wairarapa victory can be attributed to nationwide developments, reflected in the electorate, with a vastly increased volunteer team, hoarding locations and capacity to campaign in the electorate's far-flung rural areas. Of the 17 seats that went over to Labour, McAnulty holds the second highest majority (6,545) after Whanganui (8,191), an indicator that the victory cannot be wholly attributed to the nationwide climate. Much credit must also go to the candidate, the campaign and to local political factors, including Mike Butterick's late selection and the decline in third-party candidate voting. The magnitude of the 2020 shift in the electorate can be appreciated by noting the swing from a 2,872 vote National majority for Alastair Scott in 2017 to a 6,545 majority for McAnulty in 2020 – a difference of 9,417 votes. This compares to an average electorate swing of around 8,300 towards Labour, the largest swings taking place in Selwyn and Port Waikato (around 15,000 votes).

Conclusion

The 2020 election campaign was peculiar for a number of reasons. It was the first time since 1943 – in the middle of World War II – that a New Zealand election had been delayed. The Covid-19 pandemic utterly dominated all other issues, with polling in Wairarapa placing health as the electorate's most important issue, followed closely by jobs and employment. The pandemic strengthened support for Labour, the governing party, and drastically weakened support for the National Party, which was perceived as an ineffective and unconstructive opposition. This was a Covid campaign and Wairarapa was not immune from the result: a 'red wave' that carried a number of Labour candidates to victory. Such an emphatic victory for Labour and for Kieran McAnulty may well not be repeated, but as with the 2002 campaign, 2020 'allowed for a window on the Wairarapa electorate, offering insights into a number of changes that have taken place in the electorate' (Lamason 2003, p. 190). The Wairarapa electorate proved emblematic of many communities around the country, with voters demonstrating their support for the direction that the Ardern-led coalition government had taken since 2017, and particularly during the Covid-19 pandemic. In addition, strong campaigning from McAnulty as well as other local factors combined to help carry McAnulty and Labour to an impressive Wairarapa victory.

31

A CAMPAIGN FOR THE AGES: CHLÖE SWARBRICK, THE YOUTH VOTE AND THE AUCKLAND CENTRAL ELECTION

Bonnie Hayvice

Prime Minister Jacinda Ardern has frequently referred to the year 2020 as 'unprecedented' (Clench 2020). The results of the country's 53rd general election, which saw Ardern maintain leadership, can also be described in this way. New Zealanders turned stronghold National Party 'blue' electorates 'red', giving Labour 65 seats in Parliament – the first time a party has been able to govern alone since the first MMP (mixed member proportional) election in 1996.

Yet 'unprecedented' success on election night was not reserved for Labour alone. Unexpectedly, Green MP Chlöe Swarbrick secured the Auckland Central electorate seat in a race local media described as 'probably the highest drama contest of the 2020 election' (Braae and Manhire 2020). Swarbrick gained 9,060 votes on election night, 492 votes ahead of Labour candidate Helen White and 1,494 ahead of National candidate Emma Mellow (Radio New Zealand 2020e). In the week following Swarbrick's win, the media concentrated on her ability to harness the youth vote as explanation for her victory over the Labour and National candidates (Cooke 2020c; Davison 2020). This chapter investigates how the youth vote influenced campaigning in the Auckland Central electorate and to what degree Swarbrick's success can be attributed to youth voters in the area.[1]

Focusing on how Swarbrick's support increased reveals how the 'unprecedented' was achieved and why Swarbrick's campaign was underestimated. Considering low youth voting rates internationally, understanding how young politicians such as Swarbrick attract young voters may help relieve engagement concerns (*The Economist* 2017; Levine 2009). However, conditions particular to the 2020 electorate campaign generate reservations with regard to Swarbrick's strategy serving as a blueprint for future candidates.

The Auckland Central electorate

The geography

Auckland Central was established in 1887 after South Island population figures required three seats to be redistributed to the North Island (Parliament 2017). Although in 1890 the electorate was briefly reincorporated into the larger Auckland electorate, in 1905 Auckland was split into three major electorates; Auckland Central has remained an electorate ever since, albeit with slight boundary changes. In 2008, for instance, Point Chevalier moved to the Mount Albert electorate; in 2014, Westmere and Grey Lynn were also transferred to Mount Albert. In 2020, Auckland Central included Grafton, Eden Terrace, Newton, Ponsonby and Auckland's central business district (CBD), as well as Herne Bay, St Mary's Bay, Waiheke Island and Great Barrier Island (Parliament 2017).

The people

More than 60,000 people live in Auckland Central (Parliament 2017). Demographic profiling describes a well-educated, young population, with relatively few children and elderly. Notably, it has the highest proportion of young adults aged 20–29 years (32 per cent) and the lowest proportion of over-65-year-olds (7 per cent). The electorate is well-educated, with 29 per cent of residents (over 15 years of age) having a bachelor's or master's degree, and of mixed ethnicity, with over 60 per cent identifying as 'European', 7 per cent Māori, 4 per cent Pasifika and over 30 per cent Asian. The median annual income as of December 2017 was just over $80,000, the most common occupations being in property, science, finance, accommodation, cafés and restaurants. Considering the electorate's make-up, local candidates tend to campaign for better transport options, a more liveable and vibrant city, and support for small businesses and the homeless (Bhatia 2020; Weekes 2020b).

Political representation

Prior to the 2020 election, National MP Nikki Kaye had held the Auckland Central seat through four election cycles, first winning the seat in 2008. However, Auckland Central is not a strong 'blue' seat, having been held largely by the Labour Party from 1919 to 2008. The only other political party to hold the seat was the left-wing Alliance, whose candidate Sandra Lee won the seat in 1993, losing it three years later. Kaye was considered a hard worker, well respected by local people and businesses (Cheng 2019; Smith 2020a). Swarbrick describes Auckland Central residents as people who respect 'hard work and boots on the ground' (*1 News* 2020c). The electorate's progressive history and Swarbrick's own success in obtaining the seat after Kaye's resignation suggests that Auckland Central voters are not strongly partisan in terms of their parliamentary representation.

The 2020 Auckland Central electorate race

The 2020 Auckland Central election was seen as a high-profile 'three-way race' between the Labour, National and Green candidates (Smith 2020b), partly because incumbent MP Nikki Kaye chose not to seek re-election following a change in National's leadership, leaving the seat open (Satherley 2020). Given the electorate's voting history, with its respect for hard-working, progressive candidates, the idea that a non–National Party candidate could win the seat was not unrealistic. This was particularly true as Labour's Helen White had been only 1,581 votes shy of beating Kaye in 2017, benefitting from Labour's rising national support. The Greens' 2020 decision to run a 'two-tick' campaign in Auckland Central with a high-profile candidate (as opposed to their usual focus on the party vote only) made the electoral outcome much more uncertain (Cooke 2020c).

The candidates – Emma Mellow

Emma Mellow, a 30-year-old communications manager at the ANZ bank, was National's replacement for Nikki Kaye (Kirkness 2020; Orsman 2020b; Weekes 2020c). Mellow's campaign themes followed wider National Party messaging; she told the *New Zealand Herald* on the evening she was selected that the nation's biggest issues centred around jobs (Kirkness 2020). Mellow differentiated herself from Labour and Green candidates by criticising their proposed tax increases, a topic which became a major campaign point later in the year when the Green Party announced its Poverty Action Plan (Green Party 2020), including a proposed 'wealth tax', attacked by National's leader Judith Collins in these terms: 'No Green envy wealth tax with us' (Radio New Zealand 2020d). At the Auckland University Student Association (AUSA) debate on 6 October, Mellow criticised the policy, arguing that Aucklanders did not need added pressure on their household budgets. Mellow's major campaign line was that only National could fix New Zealand's economy, bring jobs and provide infrastructure to Auckland (Hogan 2020b). However, Mellow did identify herself as 'blue-green', recognising that development in Auckland Central needed to be sustainable (Smith 2020b). Like Kaye, Mellow identified more liberally than many other National MPs and candidates, for which Auckland Central voters historically have shown support (Weekes and Thomas 2020). She capitalised on Kaye's support by obtaining her endorsement on social media (Mellow 2020).

Kaye also joined Mellow on the campaign, introducing her to constituents and businesses with whom she had previously developed relationships. While it is always an advantage to have the backing of a well-regarded local MP, this strategy was particularly important for Mellow, whose campaign only began after her relatively late candidate selection on 10 August. Unlike Swarbrick, who was already a high-profile MP and had begun building her campaign much earlier, Mellow had only two months to convince people to give her their vote after the election was postponed by a month due to a Level 3 Covid-19 lockdown in Auckland. In a video Mellow posted to her social media pages, Kaye says that Mellow called over 2,000 households and delivered thousands of campaign letters in her two months' candidacy (Mellow 2020). She also door knocked and visited businesses in an attempt to gain support (Weekes 2020c). Mellow participated in debates with other candidates, ran Facebook Live videos where viewers could ask her questions, and had her own rally with supporters. Overall, Mellow had the difficult task of ensuring previous Kaye supporters transferred their support to her before she could begin making further connections. She ran a strong ground campaign, although its effect was limited due to her late selection and the often negative media associated with wider National Party mishaps (Manch 2020).

The candidates – Helen White

Helen White, an employment lawyer with over 25 years' experience and an advocate for workers' rights, was Labour's Auckland candidate (New Zealand Labour Party 2020a). White also stood in the electorate in 2017 after the previous Labour candidate – Jacinda Ardern – lost to Kaye for the second consecutive time (Orsman 2020a). The combination of Kaye's retirement and National's poor polling (and weak campaign) made White the candidate most likely to win the seat (Weekes 2020b). White's campaign messaging adhered to her party's wider emphasis on safety, stability and 're-building the economy even stronger' (New Zealand Labour Party 2020b). She repeatedly stated that Auckland Central needed Labour representation and a strong Labour voice which could engage with the wider Labour Party (Cooke 2020a). White and Swarbrick agreed on many issues to do with homelessness and increasing public transport options in Auckland Central, but White sought to appeal to voters as the progressive candidate for Auckland Central with the best chance of beating the National candidate (Giovanetti 2020). Concerned about the left vote being split between herself and Swarbrick, much of White's messaging focused on how she was the strategic choice between the two (Cooke 2020c).

White had backing from the prime minister and undertook press opportunities and local walk-abouts with her, on one occasion meeting the cast of *Mary Poppins* shortly after Ardern had been depicted as the title character in British media (Coughlan 2020). White also held a public meeting with former New Zealand prime minister Helen Clark, who endorsed her candidacy (Eventbrite 2020). Ardern's and Clark's support sent the message to voters that if you support Labour you should vote for White. White's ground campaign began in June after New Zealand was lifted out of Level 4 lockdown. She met with local constituents and businesses, campaigning for voters who were likely to place their party vote with Labour, which had grown from 21.7 per cent of Auckland Central voters in 2014 to 37.8 per cent in 2017. Much of White's campaigning was targeted towards Waiheke Island residents (who have historically voted for progressive candidates) and those in Auckland's CBD, where White worked. She held a number of weekend street meetings, although it is reasonable to claim that her full-time job as an employment lawyer limited her personal ground campaign to some extent. Swarbrick – elected to Parliament as a list MP in 2017 – arguably had more time to campaign after the parliamentary dissolution in early September. Kaye's resignation and Swarbrick's strong challenge were unexpected developments, requiring some changes to White's campaign approach and strategy.

Although White benefitted from Labour's growing popularity, as a low-profile candidate running a traditional campaign she did not get much media attention. When the media turned its gaze towards a tightening race, White struggled to provide voters with reasons why they should vote for her instead of the high-profile Greens candidate. When asked directly, White explained her passion for workers' rights and ensuring families had enough money to get by. However, the media often asked White about Swarbrick, her passion for workers' rights overshadowed by strategic messaging that was of limited interest to the electorate.

The candidates – Chlöe Swarbrick

Chlöe Swarbrick had run a high-profile campaign in Auckland's 2016 Mayoral race, finishing third (Donnell 2020). In 2017, she was a candidate in Maungakiekie, gaining nearly 12 per cent of electorate votes despite campaigning only for the Greens' party vote, and entering Parliament on the Green Party list (*Otago Daily Times* 2020). In her three years in Parliament Swarbrick gained a reputation as a hard worker and became a leading voice on mental health and drug law reform issues. Although she was the only elected MP vying for the Auckland Central seat, Swarbrick was positioned in 2020 as a wild-card entry in the electorate race (Weekes 2020a), in part because (despite placing electorate candidates all across New Zealand) the Greens generally only campaign for the party vote. In 2020, both Swarbrick and Green Party Co-Leader Marama Davidson were exceptions to this rule. After demonstrating that their campaigns would help to grow the Greens' party vote, Swarbrick and Davidson were given approval to run 'two-tick' campaigns in Auckland Central and Tāmaki Makarau, respectively (Davidson 2020). Swarbrick also believes she is often underestimated because of her age (Neilson 2020). Despite a political career longer than other candidates, Swarbrick was only 26 years old at the time of the 2020 election.

As the underdog in a three-way race, Swarbrick's presence heightened interest in an already unusual electorate seat contest. She had a large social media following as well as national and international name recognition. White once referred to Swarbrick as a 'celebrity', which was mistakenly interpreted by the media to mean Swarbrick was well known because of her age rather than her substantive track record (*New Zealand Herald* 2020a). Although she subsequently clarified her remarks, claiming she meant for voters to give someone less well known a chance (Hogan 2020a), the media ran with the initial narrative early on in the campaign, bringing people to Swarbrick's defense amid criticism of White (*Newshub* 2020).

Although Swarbrick's messaging aligned with Green Party values, it was more specifically geared towards Auckland Central and why locals should vote for her to represent them. Swarbrick's messaging was consistent throughout the campaign: Auckland Central is her home, she loves it, and she wants to help it reach its full potential (Wilson 2020; Radio New Zealand 2020a). A major campaign strategy involved empowering voters. While this began in response to Auckland Central's low enrolment and voter turnout, it quickly became the go-to response to White asking people to vote strategically for her. Swarbrick reminded voters of the power of their vote, the values of democracy, and claimed (with trademark idealism) that a person should vote for their first choice, not their second or third option. While splitting their vote was a possible outcome, this had little value for Swarbrick, as a split left vote could allow Mellow to win the seat. The alternative, however, saw Swarbrick losing instead to White. Although the two agreed on many issues, Swarbrick did not appreciate White's attempts to get her to withdraw her bid for the seat. Swarbrick wanted to win the 'old fashioned way', supported by her belief that a strong grassroots campaign could win the seat (Davison 2020).

Like Mellow, Swarbrick ran a strong ground campaign, based on months of preparation, with many young volunteers to help her, some unable to vote yet themselves. Like other candidates, Swarbrick called voters, knocked on doors and ran various street meetings for undecided voters. She also held Facebook Live events every day of both lockdowns, at which viewers could ask her questions. There were also activities with volunteers in which Swarbrick participated: planting hundreds of trees on Waiheke Island; collecting roadside rubbish; writing postcards to apartment dwellers, asking for their vote. A stand-up comedy and drag show were among Swarbrick's unique fundraising events, allowing her to establish a candidate office on Karangahape Road (Mandow 2020). Also unique to Swarbrick's campaign was the way she utilised local artists and designers, who helped with everything from social media event banners to the design of her office window. Swarbrick benefitted less from public meetings with Green Party leaders (although both co-leaders did attend her rally) than from the personal following she had gained over her previous three years as a list MP. Swarbrick's idealism helped her appeal to voters as authentic, giving them genuine reasons to vote for her (Cooke 2020c). This also grew Swarbrick's volunteer team, which allowed her to carry out a large grassroots campaign, reaching more voters (Morten 2020).

Through the lens of the youth vote

Swarbrick's win was one of the surprises of election night 2020 (Cormack 2020; *Stuff* 2020). As highlighted, the media and public underestimated Swarbrick because of her age and because she was the Greens' local candidate. In the weeks before election night, two Colmar Brunton polls (Bradbury 2020a, 2020b) positioned Swarbrick behind both White and Mellow, furthering doubts that she could win. The first poll had White at 42 per cent, Mellow 26 per cent and Swarbrick 24 per cent (*1 News* 2020c). Although the gap was closing in the second poll – White at 35 per cent, Mellow 30 per cent and Swarbrick 26 per cent (*New Zealand Herald* 2020b; Radio New Zealand 2020c) – the election night result was unexpected for everyone but Swarbrick, who had consistently claimed that the polls showed a close race and that the winner would be dependent on voter turnout. The unexpected nature of her win had media hypothesising that increased youth voter turnout pushed the result in Swarbrick's favour (Cooke 2020c; Davison 2020). While a third of Auckland Central's population was between 20 and 29 years of age – the largest proportion of this age group for any electorate – this demographic has the country's lowest enrolment and voting rate. Before the 2020 election only 50 per cent of the electorate's residents aged 18–24 years were enrolled; for those aged 25–29 years, the proportion was 48 per cent (Electoral Commission 2020). Swarbrick entered Parliament in 2017, aged 23, and her following included many young New Zealanders who felt represented or inspired by her presence in Parliament (*1 News* 2020d). Low youth voting rates are common worldwide (*1 News* 2020a). It would be a significant achievement if Swarbrick's win were partially due to her having mobilised young voters.

Youth as Swarbrick's target

The 20–29-year-old voter demographic had not yet been captured by either National or Labour candidates, with half of those eligible to vote not even enrolled. Swarbrick sought to mobilise these young voters. By New Zealand law, all eligible voters are required to enrol (New Zealand Government 2020). Criminalising the unenrolled has had limited effect – in any event, none are prosecuted. According to Swarbrick, there is a widespread assumption that young people do not participate in politics because they are apathetic. Instead, Swarbrick understands that young people are used to systems of power which do not work to benefit them. As a result, many young people do not recognise the power of their own vote and are discouraged from participating in politics. A major tactic of Swarbrick's was to empower young people by establishing a strong core message: 'Your vote is powerful'. She reminded young voters and other groups disillusioned with the current political system that not participating only leaves a dysfunctioning political system in place (*1 News* 2020b). She appealed to young voters by reminding them of those who did vote, highlighting individuals (e.g., broadcaster Mike Hosking) and groups (e.g., landlords) largely unpopular with this demographic (*Kava Corner* 2020). The fact that she herself was part of the 20–29-year age group gave her approach added authenticity (Marques 2013): people are more likely to vote for candidates whom they feel represent them (Campbell and Wolbrecht 2006).

Swarbrick and her team created campaign events, like the drag shows and stand-up comedy events mentioned earlier, that were designed explicitly for younger crowds. Such events, very different from more traditional get-out-the-vote strategies, appealed to younger audiences, interested in art or comedy, now finding themselves caught up in politics as well. Art, comedy and politics are of course not mutually exclusive. Swarbrick's campaign included a creative team of young local artists who used a more inventive style of campaign marketing, adding to her appeal, particularly to those disillusioned by traditional politics. Swarbrick actively campaigned for votes through street corner meetings near Auckland university campuses or outside university accommodations. In the final weeks before the election, she spent the majority of her campaign time running street meetings designed to capture the student vote. At the outset, one hall of residence which Swarbrick and volunteers visited had only a 7 per cent enrolment rate.

Youth influence in Mellow's and White's campaigns

The youth vote explanation for Swarbrick's win becomes even more convincing when considering the absence of youth-targeted campaigning by both Mellow and White. While each candidate held street meetings, only Swarbrick's were held in areas with high-density student populations. Mellow tended to hold public meetings in wealthier business communities such as Ponsonby (Wade 2020). White spent the weekend before the election meeting locals in the CBD, Grafton and Eden Terrace. While these are certainly areas with high student populations, there was little effort to encourage students to attend, pointing to a wider issue with White's marketing and messaging. Both White and Mellow did refer to the cross-party parliamentary inquiry into student accommodation in an effort to relate to students' housing and financial struggles. However, Swarbrick had been the MP who pushed for this inquiry earlier in 2020, after Covid-19 exposed the underregulated student accommodation sector (Swarbrick 2020a; Lenihin-Ikin 2020). The Greens also have strong tertiary education policies, including the promise of a universal student allowance (Swarbrick 2020b). While Mellow and White were sympathetic to their concerns, Swarbrick's popularity with students was boosted by her party's highly supportive policy.

Mellow and White did engage with student populations by attending debates run by the University of Auckland's radio station (bFM) and by AUSA. However, their appearances at both arguably only increased support for Swarbrick, who is very comfortable in a debate format, and who empowered voters while offering better solutions to their debt concerns. Mellow and White may well have reduced their time with student populations as a consequence. With Swarbrick in the running, White and Mellow may have chosen to direct resources towards other community groups, reducing campaigning towards students in the belief that Swarbrick was more likely to capture their votes. Without Swarbrick in the race, it is unclear whether Mellow and White would have made the effort to attend student debates (although it is plausible that White or Mellow would have made a greater push to capture student votes if they considered them available). On the other hand, neither National nor Labour candidates thought they needed to mobilise the youth vote in order to win the seat. Both parties traditionally perform well in a country with low youth enrolment and voting participation, making them broadly comfortable with the status quo.

Candidate age and gender

Another influence on the 2020 race – in addition to voters' age – was the age of the candidates. Some scholars might regard Swarbrick's age as a defining feature in her electoral success (Alesina et al. 2015). Swarbrick's age was similarly advantageous in her appeal to environmentally concerned voters, seeking long-term policies that politicians seldom focus on (Marques 2013). Many of today's 'youth issues' can be regarded as intergenerational, such as high unemployment rates, with younger politicians increasingly relating their discourse and policies to economics, employment, work and living standards – all major concerns for those living in the Auckland CBD.

Swarbrick's gender also links to the power of representation and the impact of female politicians as role models. All three major candidates in the 2020 Auckland Central electorate race were women; women candidates in competitive races tend to have a positive impact on women's political engagement, campaign knowledge and media visibility. This was certainly true for Auckland Central, a campaign highlighted as 'one to watch' (Braae and Manhire 2020; Cooke 2020b). This added interest, knowledge and media attention influenced the campaign, ensuring candidates' comments reached larger audiences. Swarbrick also captured the interest and support of other previously underrepresented communities such as the LGBTQIA+ community (*New Zealand Herald* 2020a), who perceived her as their representative.

Grassroots campaigning

A further influence on the 2020 Auckland Central campaign was Swarbrick's campaign dynamics. Swarbrick gathered together a 700-person volunteer base, some as young as 14 years old. Participation can have a significant effect on young people's political awareness (Ødegård, 2017). Swarbrick created a community of supporters, helped by her high profile and track record, and maintained by her ability to come across as 'genuine'. Swarbrick's criticism of the political system (Neilson 2020) – reflecting the opinions of New Zealanders disgruntled with the political system and its effects on issues people care about – showed voters she was 'one of them' (see Bossetta 2018). Her office on Karangahape Road, with its considerable foot traffic, allowed voters to see a candidate in the context of their own home environment, and to view Swarbrick as a good choice for their electorate vote. Swarbrick's campaign was also fun and attractive to voters bored by traditional political posters and campaign videos. In mobilising such a large number of campaign volunteers, she backed up her message to voters that their vote did count – that it did make a difference – by providing people with the resources they needed to actually make a difference, their participation allowing her to do more throughout the campaign period than other candidates, improving her chances of winning the seat.

A major aspect of Swarbrick's grassroots campaign was the personal contact she was able to have with voters, as direct voter contact is central to successful election campaigns targeting potential 'swing voters' (Panagopoulos and Wielhouwer 2008). With strongly partisan voters less likely to switch their vote towards a third-party candidate, Swarbrick spent time and resources talking to undecided voters and people who did not regularly vote. Kevin Arceneaux and Robin Kolodny (2009) adopt 'low information rationality theory' to understand how uninformed voters are persuaded by candidates: interest group endorsements and participation in values-based conversations can assist voters in choosing candidates as if they were fully informed. Both techniques were employed throughout Swarbrick's campaign. Endorsements were actively sought from high-profile Aucklanders, particularly from people across demographics unfamiliar with or less supportive of Swarbrick, as in her endorsement from businesswoman Karen Walker – part of an effort to give people 'permission' to vote for Swarbrick, particularly for those who were supportive yet constrained by their political alignments or other factors. Swarbrick's campaign team was also directed towards values-based discussions when calling, door-knocking and meeting with voters, part of an effort to ensure people voted based on their values and not for strategic reasons, as White was trying to persuade them to do (White 2020). One of the major reasons for people – particularly young people – not engaging with politics is that they do not feel as if they know enough (Arceneaux and Kolodny 2009). Values-based conversations encouraged potential voters to feel that they could have an opinion, and to go out and vote. Increased direct voter contact targeting swing voters and those less well-informed gave Swarbrick an opportunity to increase turnout, contributing to her success.

Successful campaigns contact a variety of constituency groups, a pattern visible in Swarbrick's campaign, which was directed towards students, small businesses and environmentally concerned Aucklanders. Swarbrick used direct voter contact for groups more likely to switch their vote towards her and the Greens. Devoting time and resources to groups of people not known for their dedication to voting (Panagopoulos and Francia 2009) was high-risk but in the end proved cost-effective. Increased voter enrolment and turnout suggests Swarbrick's strategic voter contact paid off, mobilising voters otherwise disconnected from politics.

Covid-19

A third major influence on the 2020 Auckland Central electorate campaigns was the pandemic. It was, in part, responsible for Nikki Kaye's promotion and subsequent resignation, altering the trajectory of the race. Following unpopular comments from Simon Bridges on New Zealand's Covid-19 response and a subsequent drop in his poll ratings, Kaye was promoted, becoming National's deputy leader (Satherley 2020). Swarbrick and White recognised the ambitious task involved in winning a seat belonging to a party's deputy leader and altered their campaign strategies accordingly. Following further internal National Party issues, Kaye stepped down, announcing her retirement. Swarbrick's and White's campaign strategies were again affected. Without an incumbent MP, each had a greater chance of success, particularly given the National Party's failure to select a new candidate until two months out from the election. The pandemic also reduced the National and Green parties' ability to hold the government to account on other political matters, with the country focused on combating the pandemic. This ultimately reduced positive media for both National and the Greens while boosting Labour's popularity, giving White an advantage. Overall, the pandemic and subsequent National Party leadership changes increased Labour's support, changing the landscape of the Auckland Central candidates' campaigns. Without an incumbent MP or *any* National Party candidate for most of the year, White became the one most likely to win the seat (Weekes 2020b), leading to the 'strategic vote' messaging which White ran on for most of the campaign, ultimately contributing to her defeat (Cooke 2020a).

The pandemic also affected the way each candidate campaigned as well as their ability to campaign. The nationwide lockdown beginning in March meant that candidates were unable to meet constituents in person. When there was a renewed community outbreak in August, Auckland went into further lockdown (Tokalau 2020; Whyte 2020), requiring candidates to be more creative in the way they campaigned. Events became socially distanced, with voters contacted via phones and direct mail. During the second lockdown, the ban on campaigning (Radio New Zealand 2020b) meant candidates with lower profiles, like

Mellow and White, struggled to remain visible. While Swarbrick too was unable to actively campaign, her large social media following – tens of thousands of people – allowed her to remain relevant, with Facebook Live videos throughout lockdown providing opportunities for the public to see and engage with her (see Ross and Bürger 2014, on the importance of 'being there' on Facebook; also Heiss and Matthes 2016, on the impact of politicians' participatory Facebook posts on young people's 'political efficacy').

Swarbrick also participated in a discussion on Reddit, and her young supporters made several TikTok videos featuring the candidate. Social media was also used to distribute information regarding campaign events and voting concerns, an effective method given Swarbrick's significant social media following on Instagram. Covid-19 and its impact on in-person campaigning furthered the positive influence this would have for Swarbrick. Changes in campaign tactics can also influence voters' party attachments. Vergeer and colleagues (2013) categorise the changes in political campaigning as pre-modern (direct face-to-face campaigning and newspaper advertising), modern (including televised advertising) and post-modern (ICT campaigning), arguing that as campaigning has diversified across media, voters have become increasingly less attached to particular political parties – a further advantage to Swarbrick, whose party receives significantly fewer votes in Auckland Central than either Labour or National. Using social media to campaign helped her reach large audiences (not all of them Auckland Central residents) and assisted in personalising her campaign.

Summary

While young voter turnout contributed to Swarbrick's success, other major influencing factors on the 2020 Auckland Central result included the candidate's age, her grassroots campaigning and the Covid-19 pandemic. The campaign she created was one she, as a young person herself, would like to be involved in.

Ultimately, Swarbrick's campaign strategy was successful simply because it was better. Although Mellow and White called voters and knocked on doors, Swarbrick and her team called more voters and knocked on more doors. By the end of the campaign Swarbrick's team had reached their target of 10,000 door knocks – one-sixth of total Auckland Central residents and one-sixth of the total number of doors knocked on by Green Party volunteers nationwide (Swarbrick 2020c). Swarbrick's win was less 'astonishing' because her grassroots campaign was Auckland Central's largest, sharing attributes with successful campaigns elsewhere (Panagopoulos and Francia 2009; Panagopoulos and Wielhouser 2008; Beck and Heidemann 2014). The result was an electorate win for a minor party which had not won an electorate seat in over 20 years, all of its parliamentary representatives having come from list seats achieved by MMP's party vote (Orsman 2020c, Orsman 2020d).

Conclusion

In 2017 Chlöe Swarbrick stood in Maungakiekie; receiving 4,060 votes, she placed third, the seat being won by National's Denise Lee. Three years later, Swarbrick received 12,631 votes in Auckland Central, winning the seat: a victory even more assuredly personal – arising out of her campaign, her personality and her impact – when contrasted with Labour's party vote victory, its 16,751 votes more than those cast for National and the Greens combined, by a margin of more than 2,000 votes (Table 31.1).

Table 31.1: The 2020 Auckland Central results

Election Results 2020	**Candidate**	**Party Votes**	**%**	**Candidate Votes**	**%**
Labour	Helen White	16,751	46.21%	11,563	32.48%
National	Emma Mellow	7,680	21.19%	9,775	27.46%
Green	Chlöe Swarbrick	6,937	19.14%	12,631	35.48%
ACT	Felix Poole	2,724	7.52%	588	1.65%
Other Parties	*Other Candidates*	2,151	5.93%	1,046	2.94%
Total valid votes:		**36,243**		**35,603**	
Majority:				**1,068**	

Source: Electoral Commission 2020, 'Official results for the 2020 General Election and referendums', 6 November.

Swarbrick's 12,631 votes – 8,571 more votes than she received three years earlier in Maungakiekie – can also be contrasted with the Greens' 2017 Auckland Central candidate, Denise Roche, who received almost 10,000 votes fewer (2,838 votes) in her third-place finish. At the same time, Swarbrick's win, with 35.5 per cent of the vote, was the lowest proportion of the vote received by any winning electorate candidate in 2020 – a year when many Labour candidates were able to exceed 50 per cent of the vote in winning their seat.

The Auckland Central result for Labour – with a convincing party vote win – was part of its nationwide landslide victory. A consequence was that its unsuccessful Auckland Central candidate, Helen White, ranked 48th on Labour's party list, was also able to join Swarbrick in Parliament, one of 42 first-time MPs. Whether she will be Labour's 2023 Auckland Central candidate in a rematch with Chlöe Swarbrick remains to be seen. If that does occur, it is unlikely that Swarbrick's campaign will be underestimated the second time around. In the meantime, perhaps being underestimated in 2020 – by the public, the media and other parliamentary candidates – was the most significant way age influenced the Auckland Central outcome, allowing Chlöe Swarbrick to be one of the 'stars' on an election night otherwise dominated by news of a Jacinda Ardern-led Labour Party landslide.

32

SPECIAL VOTES AND THE 2020 ELECTION

Therese Arseneau and Nigel S. Roberts

On election night 2017, the National Party appeared to be in pole position to lead a fourth-term government. National, with 58 of 120 seats in the unofficial election-night tally, and ACT – with one seat – were together just two seats shy of a governing majority. Labour's position, on the other hand, seemed less strong: with 45 seats in the preliminary count, it would need the support of both the Greens (then on seven seats) *and* New Zealand First (nine seats), *and* still only have the very slimmest possible majority in Parliament. As Labour leader Jacinda Ardern acknowledged on the night, 'obviously, we hoped for better'.

'Better' came for Labour roughly a fortnight later, after what was then a record haul of special votes was included in the final count: National's election-night total was reduced from 58 to 56 seats, while Labour and Green representation in Parliament rose by one seat apiece, thus widening the overall gap by four seats, which provided the Labour, New Zealand First and Green parties enough of a parliamentary majority (63 government seats versus 57 opposition seats) to govern for a full parliamentary term.

This chapter examines the effects of special votes on the 2020 general election result. It starts with an explanation of what special votes are and a review of their consequences, comparing and contrasting New Zealand elections prior to and since the introduction of the mixed-member proportional representation (MMP) electoral system. The focus then shifts to the most notable aspects of special voting in the 2020 election, including the proportions and partisan impacts of special votes, and whether these were in keeping with the trends of previous MMP elections. Finally, we suggest the likely effects of special voting in future elections, especially in light of new legislation in place that could reduce the number of special votes cast and possibly diminish their importance.

The changed effects of special votes under FPP and MMP

The difference between the election night 'provisional' or 'preliminary' result and the final 'official' result can be significant. The preliminary result is an unofficial count of ordinary votes, that is, of votes cast – either in advance or on election day – by an elector whose name appears on the printed electoral roll in a polling place designated for their electorate. This result is announced on election night; the final result follows about a fortnight later after the official count has been undertaken. This count includes a careful cross-check and recount of all ballot papers tallied on election night; while this recount can result in a small number of changes in the vote total, by far the most significant difference between the preliminary and official results comes from the inclusion of all valid 'special votes' in the final count.

What are these 'special votes'? Electors unable to cast an ordinary vote may instead cast what is formally known as a special declaration vote: if they are voting from overseas, voting outside their electorate, voting remotely away from the supervision of an electoral official, or if they are not on the printed roll for their electorate (because they enrolled after writ day[1] or are on the unpublished roll). Special votes may be cast in advance or on polling day. Most advance votes are ordinary votes and therefore are part of the preliminary result. By contrast, all overseas votes are special votes and are included only as part of the final, official count. Thus, *when* the vote is cast (on election day or in advance) is not significant; however, *where* the vote is cast and when the voter *enrolled* are critical.

In a journal article published less than a year before the 2020 general election, we showed that the introduction of MMP in 1996 resulted in important changes to the impact of special votes, including on the composition of Parliament (Arseneau and Roberts 2019). During 12 successive first-past-the-post (FPP) general elections from 1960 to 1993, special votes resulted in only five seats (affecting a total of just ten candidates) changing from the provisional election night count to the final official result. In contrast, Table 32.1 reveals how different the effect of special votes has been under MMP. In nine MMP elections, special votes have impacted an overall total of 31 seats. This is mainly due to the primacy of party votes under MMP, which are cast and counted in a New Zealand–wide electorate. Therefore, special votes, rather than being divided among many electorates (as they were under FPP), are now consolidated throughout the country as a whole, thus amplifying their effect not only on the composition of Parliament but also, potentially, on the make-up of the government.

Table 32.1: Seats gained and seats lost as a result of special votes cast in New Zealand's nine MMP general elections from 1996 to 2020

	1996	1999	2002	2005	2008	2011	2014	2017	2020	Total seats affected
Labour	0	-3	0	0	0	0	0	+1	+1	5
National	0	-2	0	-1	-1	-1	-1	-2	-2	10
Green	–	+7	+1	0	+1	+1	+1	+1	0	12
NZ First	0	-1	0	0	0	0	0	0	0	1
Alliance	0	-1	0	0	0	0	0	0	0	1
ACT	0	0	0	0	0	0	0	0	0	0
United	0	0	-1	0	0	0	0	0	0	1
Māori	–	–	–	0	0	0	0	0	+1	1
Total seats affected	0	14	2	1	2	2	2	4	4	31

The move to MMP also coincided with a marked change in the partisan hue of special voting. Under FPP, special votes tended to favour the National Party. Figures 32.1 and 32.2 chart the special vote differentials for National and Labour respectively in the 1,070 electorate races in the 12 successive FPP general elections from 1960 to 1993. (Special vote 'differentials' are calculated by comparing a party's or a candidate's share of the special votes cast in the election with their share of the ordinary votes that were counted on election night. If their share of the special votes is higher than their ordinary vote share, then the special vote differential is *positive*; conversely, if their share of the special votes is lower than their share of ordinary votes, then the differential is *negative*.)

Both Figures (32.1 and 32.2) form near-perfect normal distribution curves. The key difference between them is that the National Party's mean differential was positive – the party gained an average of 2.19

per cent more special votes than its share of the votes initially counted on election night, whereas the Labour Party's mean differential was in negative territory. On average, Labour received 1.58 per cent fewer special votes than its share of the initial ordinary vote count.

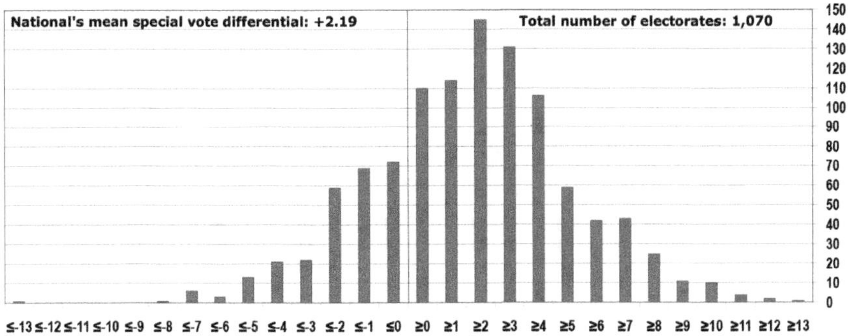

Figure 32.1: National's special vote differentials in FPP general elections from 1960 to 1993

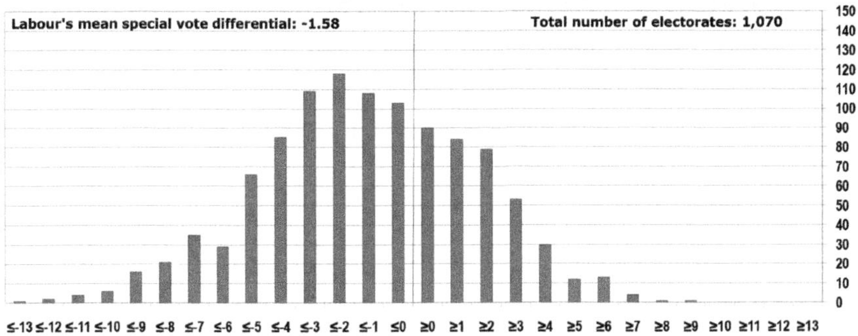

Figure 32.2: Labour's special vote differentials in FPP general elections from 1960 to 1993

Since the implementation of the MMP voting system, however, special votes have favoured the Green and Labour parties. Figure 32.3 shows the special vote differentials for each of the four largest parties (in terms of their overall vote share) during New Zealand's nine MMP general elections. Of the many dramatic facets that the data illustrate, one stands out in particular: the National Party has not benefitted from a positive special vote differential in *any* of the nine MMP elections to date. Not only has the National graph been negative every time, but the party's trend has also been downward. The Greens, on the other hand, have been consistently positive – most strikingly so when the party crossed both MMP's one-seat and five per cent party vote thresholds for parliamentary representation in 1999. As was documented in Table 32.1, the Green Party's special vote differential in 1999 contributed to the fact that 14 seats changed hands after special votes had been tallied in that one election alone.

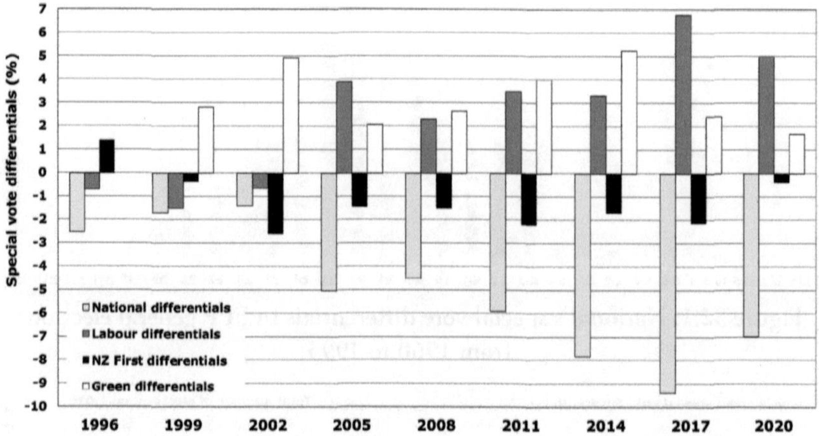

Figure 32.3: Special vote differentials (%) in the nine MMP general elections from 1996 to 2020

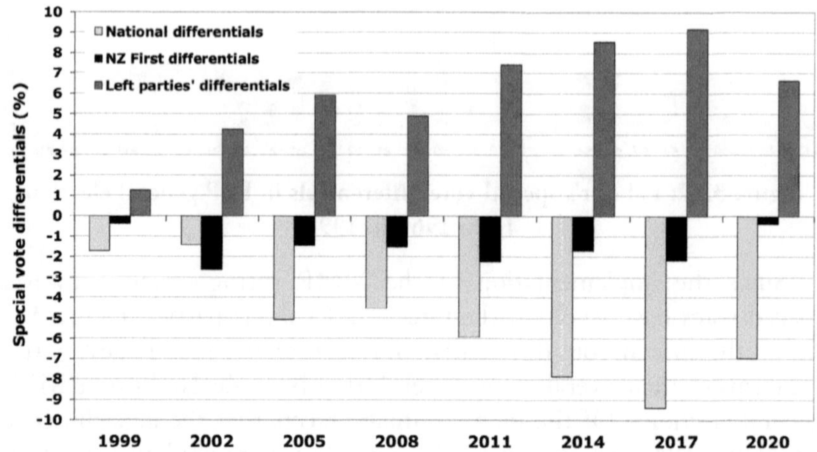

Figure 32.4: Special vote differentials (%) for National, for New Zealand First, and for the Labour and Green parties combined in MMP general elections from 1999 to 2020

Figure 32.4 shows that when votes for the two leading left-of-centre parties in New Zealand politics – the Labour and Green parties – are combined, there was a clear and consistent positive special vote differential for the left in every one of the eight MMP elections contested by both parties. Conversely, the unfailingly negative data for the National Party form a complementary mirror-image on the graph.

Table 32.2 sheds further light on the source of the incremental partisan change in special voting.[2] Focusing first on the Green, Labour and National parties in the general elections from 1999 to 2020, the table breaks down each party's proportional share of votes in five different categories of votes: ordinary votes; overseas votes; party-only special votes; domestic special votes cast prior to election day; and domestic special votes cast on election day. Comparing a party's share of each type of special votes to its share of ordinary votes helps to reveal what underlies the gradual shift in the parties' positive or negative differentials highlighted in Figure 32.3. In Table 32.2, grey boxes signify a category of special votes where a party's percentage is higher than its percentage of ordinary votes; white boxes signify the opposite – a category where the party's share of the provisional count is better than its share of the votes in that category of special votes.

Labour's experience is of gradual but steady and – so far – unrelenting improvement across the special vote categories. In 1999, Labour's ordinary vote share was higher than its share in every category of special votes. In 2002, two special vote categories (party-only vote and specials before election day) outperformed ordinary votes; three special vote categories did so for the next four elections (by adding specials on election day). The final breakthrough came in 2017 and was repeated in 2020 – the overseas votes category favoured Labour as well. This has resulted in a significant overall margin of special votes over ordinary votes for Labour, with the party in positive territory across the board in every category of special votes.

National's special votes journey is perhaps the most striking, especially given its dominance under FPP. From 1999 to 2011, National's special vote share under MMP outperformed its ordinary vote share in only one category – that is, overseas votes. Since 2014, the National Party's share in each of the categories of special votes has been lower than the share of ordinary votes won by the party – and markedly lower in both 2017 and 2020.

Table 32.2: The share (%) of provisional ordinary votes and four types of special votes cast for the Green, Labour, National and Māori parties in New Zealand general elections 1999–2020 (data provided by the Electoral Commission)

		Proportion of Valid Votes (i.e., excludes informals)					
		Ordinary Votes	Overseas Specials	Party-only Specials	Special Votes in Advance	Special Votes on Election Day	Total Votes
1999	Green	4.9	5.7	-	6.1	8.0	5.2
	Labour	38.9	30.7	-	38.4	37.7	38.7
	National	30.7	36.1	-	27.7	28.7	30.5
2002	Green	6.5	14.3	13.6	8.0	11.3	7.0
	Labour	41.32	39.4	44.6	42.3	40.1	41.26
	National	21.1	23.3	14.3	21.0	19.7	20.9
2005	Green	5.1	11.1	5.9	5.6	6.9	5.3
	Labour	40.7	38.3	53.9	41.3	44.7	41.1
	National	39.6	40.9	22.5	38.2	34.8	39.1
	Māori	1.99	0.90	7.67	2.56	3.06	2.12
2008	Green	6.4	13.8	6.9	7.3	8.8	6.7
	Labour	33.7	27.1	46.1	36.1	35.9	34.0
	National	45.4	51.0	28.9	42.2	40.9	44.9
	Māori	2.25	1.35	7.40	3.07	3.28	2.39
2011	Green	10.6	22.7	12.5	12.6	14.4	11.1
	Labour	27.1	21.2	41.0	31.1	29.6	27.5
	National	48.0	48.6	28.6	43.0	43.6	47.3
	Māori	1.36	0.88	4.48	1.58	1.79	1.43
2014	Green	10.0	26.5	12.4	14.1	13.8	10.7
	Labour	24.7	18.0	38.0	29.2	27.3	25.1
	National	48.0	45.4	29.0	39.7	42.1	47.0
	Māori	1.27	0.92	2.96	1.70	1.60	1.32
2017	Green	5.9	15.2	6.2	7.8	6.6	6.3
	Labour	35.8	38.2	52.4	43.6	40.0	36.9
	National	46.0	37.4	26.4	36.5	39.5	44.4
	Māori	1.09	0.90	2.70	1.80	1.50	1.18
2020	Green	7.6	18.9	6.3	8.7	6.7	7.9
	Labour	49.2	53.3	60.1	54.3	52.5	50.0
	National	26.7	15.1	14.3	20.9	21.8	25.6
	Māori	1.09	0.91	3.90	1.80	2.20	1.17

Looking at the Greens, the story is one of relative consistency of positive effects for special votes: a higher proportion in all four categories of special votes in every election from 1999 to 2017. The Greens' 2020 results were a slight exception. Although the party's overall proportion of special votes (7.9 per cent) was higher than its share of the ordinary votes (7.6 per cent), its proportions of party-only special votes (6.3 per cent) and of special votes cast on election day (6.7 per cent) were, for the first time, below the party's share of the election-night count.

The change in the partisan effects of special votes is explained to a large extent by two aspects of MMP. First, under FPP, while Labour's vote was concentrated in relatively few urban and Māori electorates, the National Party had a more optimum geographic spread of votes throughout the general electorates. This resulted in a special vote advantage for National, assisting its electorate candidates, particularly in marginal seats – an advantage which has dissipated under MMP. Second, MMP has also helped to mitigate the negative impact for Labour of special votes cast for smaller parties under FPP, which tended to 'chip away' at Labour's support and were in effect wasted in the 'winner takes all' FPP system (Vowles 2008, p. 172). In contrast, under MMP the votes for smaller parties – provided they go to a party that crosses an MMP threshold and which is aligned to the same bloc – are no longer a liability for Labour, but rather support a potential governing partner. And yet, although the move from FPP to MMP is an important, even fundamental, cause of the changed impacts of special votes since 1996, an in-depth analysis of the 2020 general election finds the advent of MMP – in and of itself – does not provide a full explanation.

What was special about special votes in the 2020 general election?

An extraordinary election

The 2020 general election was remarkable on many counts. Despite a delayed dissolution of Parliament and a postponed election date due to a fresh outbreak of Covid-19, voter turnout was relatively high – more than 82 per cent. The election result itself was striking: Labour achieved a majority of seats – a first for any party under MMP. This historic result was due to an extraordinary confluence of factors, including strong approval of Prime Minister Jacinda Ardern's leadership, especially in dealing with the Covid-19 pandemic, the simultaneous collapse of both National and

New Zealand First, and a record 7.9 per cent vote for parties that did not qualify for seats in Parliament.

The 2020 election represents a high-water mark in terms of both the greatest number (more than half a million) and highest proportion (more than 17 per cent) of special votes. Figure 32.5 not only shows the overall proportions of special votes cast in elections from 1999 to 2020, but also that these proportions rose significantly after 2011. It breaks down the special votes by category – overseas; party-only vote; before election day; on election day – each as a proportion of the total vote. This exercise makes it clear that the source of the growth in special voting has been driven predominantly by special votes cast in New Zealand in advance of election day.

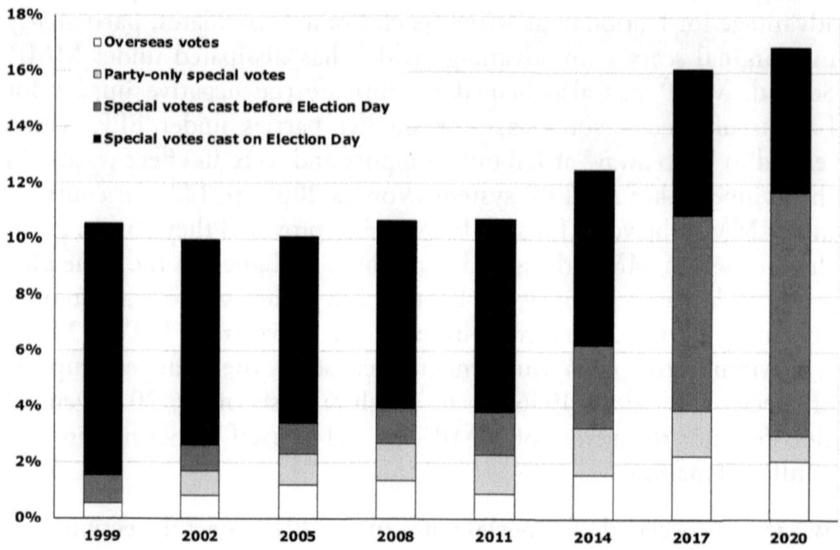

Figure 32.5: The overall proportion of special votes and the type of special votes cast in MMP general elections from 1999 to 2020

The 2020 election's record special-vote count did not lead to the most dramatic change in seat count – the 1999 general election still holds that record; nor did specials alter the type of government formed – special votes confirmed the preliminary result of Labour having a single-party majority in Parliament (indeed, special votes strengthened Labour's majority). However, special votes were critical to another remarkable feature of the 2020 general election result: once special votes were added to its total, Labour became the first party since 1951 to win a majority of the valid votes cast.

Special voting and the Māori Party

Special votes also played an important role in one of the more notable outcomes of the 2020 general election, that is, the return of the Māori Party to Parliament. A small but important feature of Table 32.1 is that from its inception in 2005 through to and including 2017, the Māori Party never once either gained or lost a seat in Parliament after special votes were counted.[3] The 2020 general election proved to be different: for the first time, special votes saw the Māori Party gain a seat. The party's tally increased from one on election night to two. Because the party had crossed MMP's one-electorate-seat threshold (Rawiri Waititi won the Waiariki electorate, which the party had lost three years earlier), it was entitled to its share of all 120 seats in Parliament. On election night data, using the prescribed Sainte-Laguë formula, the Māori Party with 23,938 party votes (1.01 per cent of the provisional votes) qualified for only one seat in the House of Representatives.[4] Once special votes had been counted, however, the Māori Party's 33,630 party votes (1.17 per cent of the total valid votes cast in the election) entitled it to an additional seat in Parliament, and Debbie Ngarewa-Packer, one of the party's two co-leaders, duly took her place in Parliament as a list MP alongside Rawiri Waititi.

What is especially interesting about the fact that the Māori Party gained a seat after special votes had been counted in 2020 is that the party did so because of its positive special vote differential with regard to its *party* votes, despite the fact that the Māori Party 'ran on a campaign of one tick, not two' (Moana Radio 2020). For much of its existence, the Māori Party has promoted the idea that electors in the Māori electorates should cast their electorate votes for the Māori Party's candidates while, at the same time, giving their party votes to the Labour Party. As Lara Greaves has argued, 'the Māori Party's strategy for the election' in 2020 was one in which the party 'specifically asked for seat votes but not party votes' (Cooke and Newton 2020).

Given the Māori Party's emphasis on the harvesting of the electorate – or candidate – votes in the Māori electoral districts, it is not surprising to find (as is shown in Figure 32.6) that the party's mean special vote differential with respect to the electorate vote in the Māori seats during the period from 2005 to 2020 has been positive. Indeed, the party's special vote differential for its electorate votes has – at +2.39 per cent – been even more positive than National's special vote differential was during the FPP era (when it averaged +2.19 per cent during the 1960–1993 period). Although Figure 32.6 is based on only 41 Māori electorate races (there were seven Māori electorates in each of the six general elections from 2005 till 2020, and the Māori Party contested all but one of the seats), it is notable that the results shown in Figure 32.6 also resemble the normal distribution curves portrayed in Figures 32.1 and 32.2. During the MMP era to date, the Māori Party has had a positive special vote differential with respect to its electorate votes on 34 occasions in the Māori electorates, with only seven negative differentials.

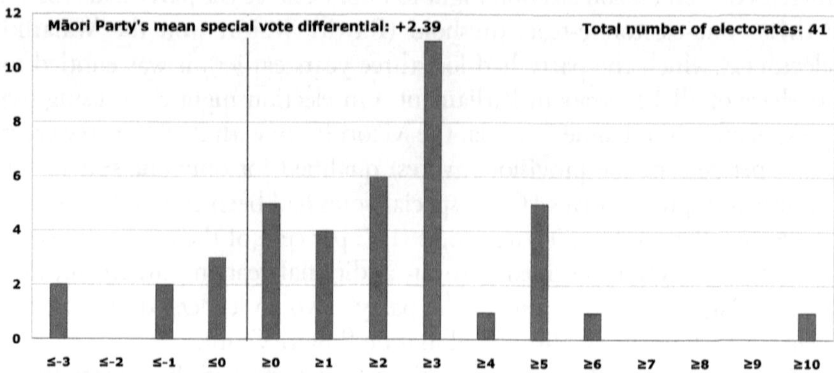

Figure 32.6: The Māori Party's special vote differentials with respect to the electorate vote in the Māori seats from 2005 to 2020

However, under MMP the crucial vote is the party vote, which – by and large – determines the overall distribution of seats in the House of Representatives. Table 32.3 lists the Māori Party's party vote special vote differentials for each of the six general elections from 2005 to 2020. The final line in the table also shows the Māori Party's average special vote differential for the party vote in these six elections.

It is important to note that in every general election that it has contested, the Māori Party's special votes differential was positive. Only one other parliamentary party in New Zealand can make that claim – namely, the Green Party. Despite the fact that the Māori Party has focused primarily on winning the candidate vote in the Māori electorates, in each of the six elections from 2005 to 2020 the party's percentage share of the party vote special votes cast in the election has, without exception, been higher than its share of the ordinary party votes cast in the election. In 2020, the fact that the Māori Party's share of the special votes was 0.9 per cent higher than its share of the ordinary votes cast in the general election made a crucial difference to the party's representation in Parliament.

Table 32.3: The special votes differential for the Māori Party's party votes in the general elections from 2005 to 2020

General election	Special votes differential
2005	+1.26
2008	+1.25
2011	+0.68
2014	+0.46
2017	+0.58
2020	+0.90
Average, 2005–2020	+0.85

The special vote data also reveal that while the Māori Party's gain of a seat due to the specials in 2020 was notable, it was not surprising. Returning to Table 32.2, the consistency of the Māori Party's performance with regard to special votes is striking. Not only has the party's share of the vote increased on the final count in every election since 2005, but it has also done so consistently in three of the four categories of special votes – in advance, on election day and party-only – and underperformed only in the fourth category of special votes, that is, overseas votes.

The party-only category stands out; based on the proportion of valid votes, it is significantly, and consistently, the highest performing category of votes for the Māori Party. Party-only special votes are votes cast by electors who voted for an electorate other than the electorate for which they were qualified to vote: for example, a voter enrolled in Christchurch Central who votes for Christchurch East. Since 2002, the party vote portion of the ballot counts towards the total, but the electorate vote does not.[5] But while this category is high in terms of proportions, Figure 32.5 is a useful reminder that this category of special votes, in terms of the sheer number of votes cast, is relatively small when compared to special votes cast before and on election day. Table 32.4, which examines the Māori Party's special vote categories by number of votes, is therefore illuminating. Although the party's number of special votes (9,334) in 2020 was a record high, the number of party-only special votes (1,003) was lower than in any of the previous five elections, accounting for roughly 10 per cent of the party's special votes. Special votes before and on election day accounted for over 83 per cent and advance special votes were the Māori Party's largest special vote category.

Table 32.4: A breakdown of the number of votes for the Māori Party in the 2005 to 2020 general elections by type of votes (data provided by the Electoral Commission)

Election	Number of Votes						
	Ordinary votes	Overseas special votes	Party-only specials	Special votes before election day	Special votes on election day	Total special votes	Total valid votes
2005	40,777	246	1,941	634	4,665	7,486	48,263
2008	47,201	437	2,268	898	5,176	8,779	55,980
2011	27,094	178	1,395	537	2,778	4,888	31,982
2014	26,680	351	1,203	1,206	2,409	5,169	31,849
2017	23,606	536	1,137	3,268	2,033	6,974	30,580
2020	24,296	568	1,003	4,504	3,259	9,334	33,630
Total	189,654	2,316	8,947	11,047	20,320	42,630	232,284
Total %	*81.65*	*1.00*	*3.85*	*4.76*	*8.75*	*18.35*	*100.00*

The special vote data for the Māori Party suggest that the party might benefit from a change of strategy. Instead of concentrating on the electorate vote and – by comparison at least – letting the party vote look after itself, the party could more actively pursue both the electorate vote and the party vote. When the Māori Party was winning more electorates than the number of seats it would have been entitled to in Parliament on the basis of its party vote – that is, when the Māori Party was winning 'overhang' seats (leading to an increase in the number of MPs from 120), as was the case in 2005, 2008 and 2011 – it possibly made some sense to concentrate on winning electorate votes and to ignore (comparatively at least) the party vote. In 2014, however, not only did the party for the first time not generate an overhang seat in Parliament, but it also for the first time gained a list MP (Marama Fox). Now that the Māori Party has won its second-ever list MP as a result of its positive party-vote special vote performance in 2020, it will be interesting to see whether the party adopts a 'two-tick' approach in 2023.

The advance voting–special voting nexus

The root of the dramatic increase in special voting can be traced back to a seemingly unrelated change to electoral law. In 2010, Parliament changed procedures for advance voting, removing the requirement for electors to make a statutory declaration that they are unable to vote on election day, thus opening the door to 'no excuse' advance voting (see Nicoll 2017; Electoral Commission 2015). As a result, since 2011, increasing proportions of the electorate have cast their ballots prior to election day. In 2011, almost 13 per cent did so; three years later the proportion doing so had doubled; and in 2017 early electors accounted for 47 per cent of all the votes cast. In 2020, aided by fears of a Covid-19 outbreak restricting access to polling stations, more than two thirds of the people who voted in the general election did so prior to Saturday, 17 October.

Intertwined with this were further ongoing reforms that improved voting and enrolment procedures. The Electoral Commission has championed, for example, innovations designed to make advance voting even more accessible, such as situating voting places where people live and work, and remaining open for extended hours, including on weekends. In 2020, partly in response to Covid-19, the Commission greatly improved advance voting accessibility so voters could safely 'vote local' while maintaining appropriate physical distancing (see Electoral Commission 2020). The number of advance voting places increased from 486 in 2014 to 1,522 in 2020 (a 213 per cent increase), the total hours of service increasing from 51,800 hours in 2017 to 85,500 hours in 2020 (a 65 per cent increase).

However, it is the simultaneous improvements in enrolment services in the advance voting period that are key to understanding the corresponding rise in special voting. The Electoral Commission (2018) had long identified the trend of voters enrolling later and closer to election day, and confirmed that the growth in special voting in 2017 – and again in 2020 – was mostly due to an increase in enrolments after writ day. Figure 32.7 uses the Commission's data to illustrate the growth in the electoral roll in the lead-up to the 2020 election and compares it to 2014 and 2017 (using the equivalent days pre- and post-election). All electors who enrol after writ day and then vote in a general election do so by a special vote. Note the significant growth in enrolments from the opening of advance voting and a marked leap in enrolments confirmed after election day with the formal count.

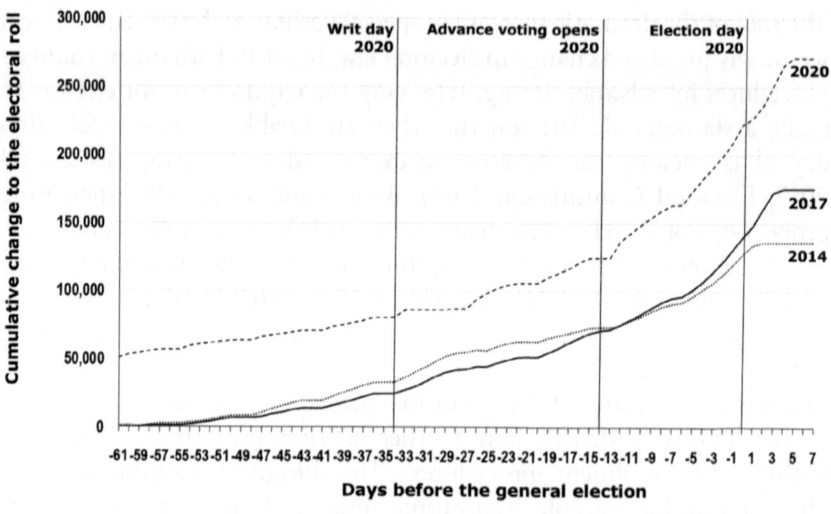

Figure 32.7: The growth in the electoral roll in the lead-up to the 2014, 2017 and 2020 general elections in New Zealand

The growth in post-writ day enrolments – from one election to the next – is striking. Again, underlying this increase was a series of initiatives, such as public education campaigns, including increased use of texting, designed to remind the unenrolled to enrol. Most importantly, in 2017, the advance booths for the first time provided a one-stop enrolling and voting service to allow electors to lodge enrolment forms and vote at advance polling places, and electoral officials to use a digital enrolment-checking function (Electoral Commission 2018, p. 18). A key feature of the 2020 election was the extension of enrolment to include election day: approximately 80,000 voters enrolled and voted on 17 October. According to the Commission, allowing enrolment on election day 'led to a halving of the number of disallowed special votes compared to 2017' (Electoral Commission 2020, p. 18).

It is the greater access to advance voting, when combined with ease of enrolling and voting at the same time at these advance booths, that has been critical to the substantial growth in special votes in 2017 and 2020, and to the growth in the 'domestic specials in advance of election day' category in particular. This not only impacts the rate of special voting but, in turn, likely has a political effect as well. Voters must be enrolled in order to cast a valid vote. The groups most difficult to mobilise to enrol and vote tend to be those more likely to support Labour – those on lower incomes, in rental accommodation, and the young (Vowles 2018, p. 152). They also tend to be more mobile and therefore require ongoing efforts to remain on the electoral rolls. In 2017, in sharp contrast to the 2014 election, enrolments were up in Labour strongholds (defined as the 23 general electorates with Labour Party votes of over 30 per cent in 2014) while enrolments tended to be down in the remaining general electorates (Vowles 2018, pp. 152–153).[6] Although the increased mobilisation and turnout in 2017 was largely driven by the late change of Labour leader (in August 2017, from Andrew Little to Jacinda Ardern), the way in which many of these voters were able to vote was by casting a special vote, assisted by the combination of advance voting and a one-stop enrolment and voting service.

Conclusion

Changing New Zealand's voting system from FPP to MMP was a significant constitutional reform and it had an impact on special voting. However, the lesson from the research for this chapter is that numerous legislative and administrative changes to enrolment and voting practices, albeit less high profile, in conjunction with the move to MMP, are fundamental to understanding the changing proportions and effects of special votes over a period of 60 years.

Looking ahead, what does the future hold for special voting? In its report on the 2017 election, the Electoral Commission (2018) noted that the ability to enrol after writ day and vote outside one's home electorate had increased the accessibility of the New Zealand electoral system (as was reflected in the increase in voter turnout in 2014, 2017 and 2020). The Commission also recognised this greater accessibility comes with a corresponding increase in special votes and, with the potential for significant ongoing growth, has important implications for future elections. Special votes take at least ten times more time and effort to issue and process than ordinary votes, and at their current rate of increase, counting specials might affect the timeliness of the final count – even to the point where 'declaring the final result within the two week period may no longer be possible' (Electoral Commission 2018, p. 31). Furthermore, future election night results might give less and less certainty about the likely final results, which could also impact government formation negotiations. Completing a special vote declaration is more onerous for the voter as well, and – despite recent improvements in this regard – special votes are disallowed at a significantly higher rate than ordinary votes.

Casting an ordinary vote is therefore preferrable both for voters and for electoral officials. Based on the Electoral Commission's (2018) recommendations, Parliament has already passed amendments to the Electoral Act 1993 (Electoral Amendment Act 2020), which will mean that people who enrol after writ day (but before election day) are much more likely to be able to cast an ordinary vote, provided 'the rolls can be marked (manually or electronically) to show the person has applied to vote' (clause 6). As a result, fewer special votes may be cast in future. If so, the 2020 election result may well be remembered for having been (amongst other things) the high-water mark in the proportions of special votes cast in New Zealand general elections, and the impact of special votes on the composition of Parliament.

33

GETTING WHAT YOU'RE GIVEN: GOVERNMENT FORMATION IN 2020

Stephen Church

At first glance, a chapter on government formation in 2020 might seem redundant. After all, the election results delivered Labour a majority of seats, thereby enabling it to govern alone. However, the very fact Labour won a majority, their 'enhanced cooperation agreement' with the Greens, and how this all fits into our previous experience, are worthy of a few brief comments.

Winning a majority under MMP

Winning a majority of seats was undoubtedly an historic result, but should we be that surprised this could happen under MMP? Proportional representation electoral systems have previously delivered single-party majority government elsewhere. Under other MMP systems, the CDU/CSU won a majority in Germany in 1957, and more recently the Scottish Nationalist Party won a majority in 2011 in Scotland. The Single Transferable Vote system has resulted in majority governments for Fianna Fáil in Ireland (1938, 1944, 1957, 1965, 1969 and 1977), and in every election in Malta since the 1950s.

Our electoral system is designed to represent parties in relative proportion to their party vote, although the 5 per cent threshold usually results in successful parties receiving a slightly higher share of seats than their share of the party vote. Accordingly, Labour's majority in 2020 says much more about the distribution of support for parties than the impact of the electoral system.

Over the past decade or so, voting patterns have increased the possibility that a single party would win a majority of seats. In the previous four elections, the leading party fell short of a majority by just a handful of seats: four in 2008, two in 2011, one in 2014, and five in 2017. This reflects a longer trend under MMP of the leading party receiving an increasing share of the vote, since the nadir of 33.87 per cent in the first MMP election in 1996 (see Figure 33.1).

Major party leaders have made unsuccessful pitches for a majority of seats at previous elections, but in 2020 voters appeared to be more receptive to the message that a strong mandate was required to address Covid-19.

Is the party system changing?

The landscape for government formation may also be becoming less complex through other, related changes to the New Zealand party system. The number of parliamentary parties has continued its gradual decline, from a high of eight in 2005 and 2011, to five in 2017 and 2020. One outcome of this is that the current government is the first since 1996 which involves just two parties (although only one was required).

This is also the first government since the 1999–2002 term which does not include participation by a centre party, one which can work with either Labour or National. The removal of New Zealand First from Parliament in 2020, at least for the time being, follows the demise of United Future in 2017. Although the Māori Party has bounced back from being ejected in 2017, based on their own statements prior to the 2020 election (Moir and Patterson 2020) it is difficult to see them working with National in the near future. Once National had also ruled out working with New Zealand First in the lead-up to the election (as it had in 2008 and 2011), there was little space for a viable centre party.[1] If we are seeing the decline of parties who can work both angles, it is likely to make the question of who will form a government more predictable for voters, as the parties fall into clearly identifiable blocs.

No vacancy for electoral accommodations

Since 1996, major parties have used electoral accommodations to signal to voters which minor parties they would prefer to work with in government. By indicating to their supporters in certain seats that they should cast their electorate vote for an aligned minor-party candidate, major parties have attempted to help minor parties circumvent the need to win 5 per cent of the party vote to win representation.

The 2020 election results suggest that the use of electoral accommodations between potential coalition partners may become a thing of the past. Green MP Chlöe Swarbrick won Auckland Central without an assist from Labour (although the Green Party vote was safely over the threshold).[2] ACT won over 5 per cent of the party vote for the first time since 2002, which may lead National to reconsider its longstanding arrangement of not actively contesting the seat of Epsom. Such accommodations may become history anyway if the electorate seat threshold is removed, as part of the government's intention (as stated in the cooperation agreement) to implement the recommendations of the Electoral Commission's 2012 MMP review.

Minor parties in government continued to struggle

The election result for New Zealand First highlighted the challenges for minor parties in government to maintain, let alone increase, electoral support. This has been a common struggle for minor parties participating in any sort of governing arrangement since the advent of MMP, as the election results in Figure 33.2 show.

The notable exception is the Greens, who have increased their share of the vote at three elections, including 2020, after participating in government in some form. This could be a function of the strength of their political brand. It could also be explained by the more distant governing arrangements the Greens have entered into. They have never been in a full coalition, and none of their previous governing arrangements with Labour have been exclusive, as they have shared attention with at least one other minor party. Further, the deals reached by the Greens have always been secondary to those secured by the other parties working with Labour. That is, until now.

Another 'surplus' coalition

Despite its clear majority, Labour decided to work with the Greens. Again, this may not be so surprising when all governments since 2002, with the exception of the government which formed following the 2017 election, have also been examples of 'oversized' or 'surplus' legislative coalitions (i.e. including more parties than strictly necessary). This pattern runs counter to a longstanding theory in political science, which predicts that the government which is most likely to form will be a 'minimum winning coalition', comprising only as many parties as are necessary to win, and no more, so as not to dilute the benefits of office. Overseas experience suggests surplus coalitions arise through political conditions which override the costs of sharing office, such as uniting against the presence of extremist parties, or building supermajorities to achieve constitutional change. Just over one fifth of governments in Western Europe from 1945 to 2015 have been surplus arrangements (Bassi 2017).

In New Zealand, the rationale has been more pragmatic. Surplus coalitions can inoculate against erosion of the government's majority in the short term, such as through defections or by-elections. Since 1987 there has been at least one defection from a parliamentary party per term, except for the 2014–2017 term (although in that term National lost a seat through a by-election). Previous surplus arrangements have also enabled both Labour and National to build alternative legislative coalitions, without having to rely on the same partner for every issue.

In the case of the current government, however, Labour's majority should be sufficient to last the term, and they have not entered into an arrangement with an alternative partner to the Greens. This leaves one further reason – a surplus arrangement can help in building future governing majorities beyond this term. It is probably a recognition by Labour that the 2020 election was contested under unique circumstances, and that the next election may see 'regression to the mean' where it will fall short of a majority on its own.

No room for the Māori Party

If Labour's decision to enter into an arrangement with the Greens was made with an eye to the future, then it is curious that it did not seek a similar arrangement with the Māori Party. The Labour leader stated on election night that she would seek 'as wide a consensus on key issues as possible', and later that 'the principles of MMP should not be ignored' (Coughlan and Cooke 2020). Even if Labour were confident that the close result in Waiariki on election night would be overturned on the final count, it would not have prevented Labour from entering into negotiations with the Māori Party afterwards.

Perhaps Labour's different approach towards the Māori Party, compared to the Greens, reflects a more competitive stance, given the Māori Party's focus on the Māori seats, and potentially a a 'zero-sum' view that all support for the Māori Party must come at the expense of Labour.

Table for one

Apart from the previous government, this administration is a continuation of a pattern since 2008 of having just one party inside Cabinet (in this case, the Greens' two ministers are both outside Cabinet). It is probably too early to say whether this has become a norm, but the experiences of the previous term, and the coalition governments from 1996–2002, underline the challenges of maintaining collective responsibility when two parties are represented in Cabinet.

Length of the negotiations

The government took 20 days to form, from election day to the swearing in of Ministers. Given the clear result, it is a little surprising that this is the fourth longest time to form a government under MMP, after 1996, 2005 and 2017 (the shortest being 11 days in 2008).

The enhanced cooperation agreement

Although the enhanced cooperation agreement with the Greens appears to be a new form of government, it is more accurate to see it as a hybrid of previous arrangements. Like the enhanced confidence-and-supply agreements that have been a feature of the last five governments, this agreement also enables the Greens to hold ministerial posts outside Cabinet and exercise a limited form of collective responsibility for decisions in their portfolios.

But rather than guaranteeing support on confidence-and-supply votes, under this arrangement the Greens have pledged not to vote against the government on matters of confidence and supply. In this respect, it is similar to the earlier cooperation agreements between Labour and the Greens in 2002 and 2005. Seen in this context, the current arrangement is more adaptation than innovation.

A question of confidence

The wording of the confidence provisions in the agreement may be open to interpretation. The agreement states: 'The Green Party agrees to support the Labour Government by *not opposing votes on matters of confidence and supply* for the full term of this Parliament' (emphasis added). I first read that as stating that the Greens would not oppose a confidence vote taking place, rather than not voting against the government in a confidence vote – two very different things. Perhaps that is just pedantry on my part, but it is curious that this agreement did not draw on the clearer wording of previous agreements. For example, the 2005 cooperation agreement stated that 'The Green Party agrees to provide stability to a Labour/Progressive coalition government by co-operating on agreed policy and budget initiatives and not opposing confidence or supply for the term of this Parliament'.

A lack of leverage

The policy content in the enhanced cooperation agreement reflects the Greens' lack of leverage. In announcing the deal, the prime minister said it honoured 'the mandate provided to Labour to form a majority government in our own right' (Coughlan and Cooke 2020). Or, as that noted political theorist – my mother – would say, 'you'll get what you're given'.

Compared to the Greens' enhanced confidence-and-supply agreement last term, which included 35 individual policy commitments, the current agreement identifies three broader 'areas of cooperation' (achieving the purpose and goals of the Zero Carbon Act, protecting our environment and biodiversity, and improving child well-being and marginalised communities), underpinned by twelve actions. Whereas Labour needed the Greens' support last term, this term it is more of a 'nice to have'.

The policy content of the current agreement is also less detailed than the 2002 and 2005 cooperation agreements with Labour. On those occasions the Greens' support was also not essential for the government to maintain confidence, but it did mean that Labour could make progress on initiatives which would not have been supported by United Future or later New Zealand First.

The price of posts

Despite their lack of leverage, it would appear the Greens have done well to negotiate ministerial posts. It suggests that the price of a ministerial post has reduced over time, from full 'boots and all' coalition partnership, to support on confidence and supply, to simply not opposing the government on those essential votes.

However, there are fewer ministerial posts for the Greens this time around, even though there is no third partner to whom other posts must be allocated. Unlike last term, none of the Green ministerial portfolios lead an entire government department or ministry, and Green ministers will not be standing members of Cabinet committees, only attending for items relevant to their portfolios.

Implications for the Budget

The Budget could be an interesting test for the enhanced cooperation agreement. Previously, when minor parties in confidence-and-supply agreements have disagreed with the major party on significant policy matters, they have been called out by opposition parties for continuing to vote for the Budget. Under the current arrangement, there is nothing to prevent the Greens from abstaining on votes, as they did in December 2020 with regard to legislation to introduce a new top marginal tax rate. Potentially, this also extends to the Budget, as the commitment is to not vote against the government on a confidence vote, and the Budget is an implied confidence vote, even if no explicit confidence motion is put by the opposition.

However, abstaining on a Budget vote could create some tension for Green ministers. Although they do not hold any finance or economic portfolios, they will want to be involved in Budget initiatives for their portfolios. For example, the cooperation agreement states that, as the Minister for the Prevention of Family and Sexual Violence, Marama Davidson will be the lead Minister for the whole-of-government response on family and sexual violence, with the mandate to coordinate Budget bids in this area. It would be counterintuitive if the Greens did not vote in favour of the Budget, given that level of involvement in its formulation.[3]

Qualified agreement

This cooperation agreement includes a new twist on the ability for parties to express different views on government decisions. The 'agree to disagree' clause has been a feature of all agreements since 1999, primarily to enable the minor party to express dissent, and has been reserved for the most significant disagreements. Yet the junior partner also has an interest in maintaining a united front when their platforms become government policy. The first two governments under MMP witnessed examples of major party ministers either opposing the policy of the minor party, such as the superannuation referendum agreed as part of the National–New Zealand First coalition, or only providing a lukewarm public endorsement, such as the launch of KiwiBank under the Labour–Alliance coalition agreement (Boston and Church 2003). To address this, the 2002 confidence-and-supply agreement between Labour and United Future included a provision that:

> where there has been full participation in the development of a policy initiative, and that participation has led to an agreed position, it is expected that both parties to this agreement will publicly support the process and outcome.

This provision has been replicated, word for word, in all agreements since then, including the current cooperation agreement, and became the basis for the limited form of collective Cabinet responsibility for the ministerial arrangements which followed. However, the current agreement adds the line: 'This does not prevent the parties from noting where the agreed position deviates from their stated policy.' These differences can even be noted in the relevant Cabinet minute, which brings consideration of party positions even further into Cabinet processes than is already the case (where it is primarily limited to consultation provisions).

It is easy to imagine a scenario where the Greens will draw on this provision to state publicly that the agreed position is heading in the right direction, but does not go as far as they would like, or includes a particular initiative that they do not think will be effective. That may help the Greens to distinguish themselves from Labour, to avoid being subsumed by the major partner as other minor parties have been before them. But the new proviso in the agreement could also underscore the weakness of the Greens' bargaining position, since they cannot use the threat of withdrawing support to secure their ideal policy. In light of the number of portfolios the Greens hold, and the compartmentalisation of their involvement in other decisions, the opportunities to exercise this type of qualified agreement may also be quite limited.

It's all about the numbers

At the risk of stating the obvious, it is the number of seats that is the most important thing about forming a government. By winning a majority of seats on its own, this Labour-led government clearly does not have to think about maintaining numbers, in the sense of holding a coalition of parties together, in the same way that its predecessors did. But it does have to concern itself about maintaining numbers in other respects. It could be the challenge of managing a very large caucus of 65, only slightly smaller than the independently minded caucus of 67 that Jim Bolger led in 1990. Or the longer-term challenge of maintaining an electoral coalition, in the face of high expectations, voter volatility which saw large numbers move to Labour in a matter of months, and the likelihood that, in terms of popularity, this may be as good as it gets. It has been this way since the beginning of responsible government nearly 170 years ago. All prime ministers need to know how to count.

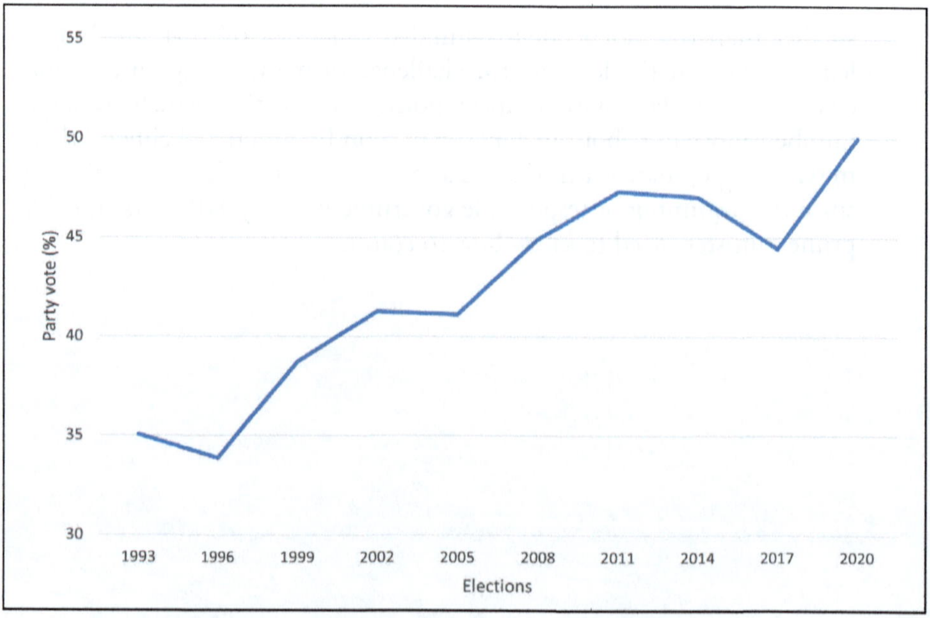

Figure 33.1: Support for the leading party, 1993–2020

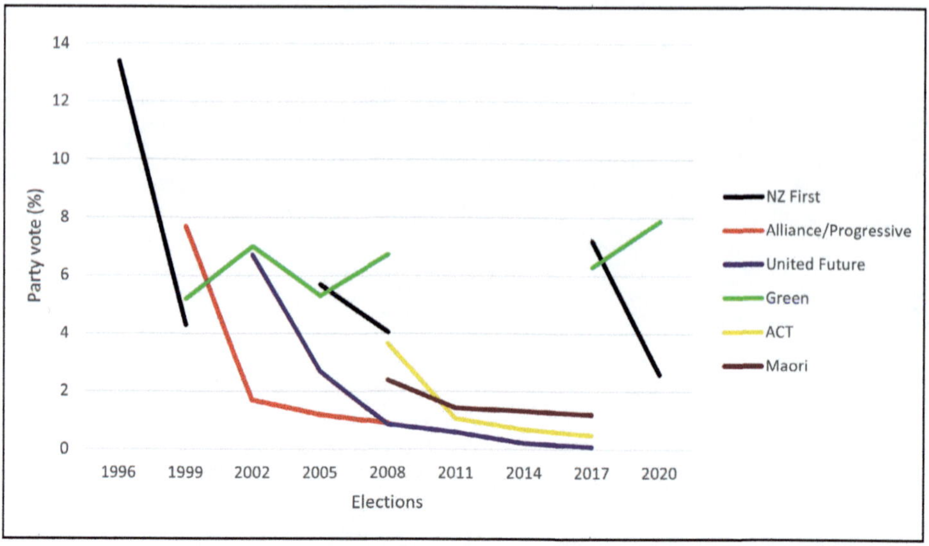

Figure 33.2: Support for minor parties in governing arrangements, 1996–2020

Epilogue

34

JACINDA ARDERN AND POLITICAL LEADERSHIP: THE STORY THUS FAR . . .

Stephen Levine

Political leadership is an important influence on the development and outcome of any political event, and therefore it has been extensively studied. In addition to biographical accounts focusing on individual leaders, analysts have also carried out comparative studies assessing leaders' strengths, weaknesses and overall reputation, and survey-based studies have elicited views – from historians, political scientists, journalists and the public – seeking to identify the 'best' and 'worst' of a country's leaders (as well as those in between), both overall and in terms of the qualities needed for outstanding leadership.

Surveys of 'non-expert' opinion – students and the general public, for instance – generally elicit rankings heavily skewed towards the most recent office-holders, with those more distant in time, whatever their accomplishments, dwelling in the 'largely forgotten' category. Among those assumed to be better informed, the use of explicit criteria in leadership assessment assists in limiting (though by no means eliminating) political biases while recognising that political leadership is a varied and complex exercise, calling on a range of skills, set against an array of hazards and pitfalls.

Notwithstanding diversity in approach, leadership studies often reveal considerable consensus about both the greatest and the least worthy. In the United States, for instance, Abraham Lincoln generally emerges at the top of the presidential heap; the other leaders whose features are carved on Mount Rushmore, in South Dakota, and whose monuments and memorials predominate in the US capital – George Washington, Thomas Jefferson and Theodore Roosevelt – are also regularly cited. Successful leadership in times of war tends to be recognised; failure in such struggles – Lyndon Johnson in Vietnam, for instance – also has consequences.

New Zealand's experience with such rankings (see Sheppard 1998; Johansson and Levine 2013; Smith 2019) also displays considerable continuity of judgment. Among the experts, Premier Richard John Seddon – whose statue stands in front of Parliament House – is invariably highly regarded, as are the first two Labour prime ministers, Michael Joseph Savage and Peter Fraser, the latter a wartime leader. A preference for strong, decisive leaders, generally imbued with progressive instincts, can be discerned, along with a respect for prime ministers who asserted and defended an independent stance with respect to foreign policy, offering moral leadership in the international arena. Norman Kirk's opposition to French nuclear testing in the Pacific and David Lange's adoption of the anti-nuclear cause, leading to New Zealand's formal separation from the ANZUS treaty alliance with the United States and Australia and the adoption of legislation making New Zealand 'nuclear-free', provide prime examples.

Leadership ranking studies typically exclude incumbent leaders, as their record is still unfolding. Indeed, judgment of an individual's leadership qualities and overall record can perhaps never be entirely final, as the passage of years brings new perspectives (and, in many instances, new information), leading to reconsideration and a revised appraisal. Lyndon Johnson's first three years as president – offering enormously effective legislative leadership, with long overdue civil rights legislation and the launch of a 'war on poverty' – would no doubt have placed him among the country's best; the Vietnam War led to the collapse of his presidency and a much lower ranking. Similarly, Woodrow Wilson's domestic programme and his leadership in World War I would have given him a place among the United States' foremost chief executives; a presidency ending in failure (with the Senate's rejection of US membership in the newly established League of Nations) saw him fall short, with the electorate choosing a post-Wilson 'return to normalcy' as its own collective verdict on his tenure.

It can thus be premature to assess a leader's accomplishments and qualities while still in office. Nevertheless, interim judgments can be made, and indeed they are made, if not through historical comparison or by way of systematic criteria, when voters decide whether or not to renew a president's or prime minister's mandate. The 2020 general election, which was accompanied by two referendums, essentially featured a third referendum – on Jacinda Ardern. As in 2017, when her emergence as Labour Party leader only seven and a half weeks before the election transformed the contest, so too in 2020 it was voters' assessments of Jacinda Ardern's character and competence which proved to be the decisive factor in shaping the campaign and the overall result. And as with many other leaders (in New Zealand and internationally), her response in a time of crisis – in a situation comparable to war – became the major factor in shaping voters' perceptions of Ardern's leadership.

Leadership criteria

There are several criteria by which political leadership has been systematically assessed. The first is *effectiveness in maintaining unity and purpose in the leader's political party*. New Zealanders seldom appreciate disunity or chaos in a leader's own party, and with good reason. A leader unable to maintain the confidence of their colleagues can hardly expect to win the untroubled confidence of the electorate. Under MMP, at least until the 2020 election, the need for unity and a collegial shared focus has extended to a leader's supporting cast: coalition parties and support partners.

Leadership strengths are, of course, linked. A further criterion associated with maintaining colleagues' unity involves *parliamentary skills*: the capacity to maintain a parliamentary majority; to dominate opposition parties and leaders; to set the overall agenda; and to maintain a degree of dominance over the news media. In today's environment this also includes *an ability to communicate effectively* with the public, with journalists, and with political party members and supporters, both in person and through all available media.

A leader will inevitably, and rightly, be judged on the strength of *identifiable accomplishments*: managing the economy; obtaining passage of significant, even historic, legislation; contributing to stability where appropriate, to significant positive change where necessary, for New Zealand and, where possible, more globally (as on issues of climate change, human rights, peace and war); and providing the country with international direction and influence in a way that encourages people to be proud to be New Zealanders.

Another important criterion of leadership is *crisis management skills*: the ability to respond effectively to unexpected developments or disasters. While it's not clear that former British prime minister Harold Macmillan actually said that it was 'events' that lent such uncertainty to politics, and such precarity to political leadership, it is evident that the sudden arrival of 'events' – calamities of one kind (political, economic, military) or another (natural, environmental, health-related) – present perhaps the most powerful challenges to a leader's character, competence and courage, separating the transcendent from the time-servers.

Assessments of leadership almost inevitably consider a leader's communication skills as well as what that leader is actually communicating. The first has to do with the ability to get a message across – to express one's views clearly and effectively to colleagues, the media, the public, and important external institutional actors such as the leaders of other countries. The second has to do with the message itself, the particular 'vision' being offered. Whether a leader proves to be memorable may reflect the quality of their rhetoric and the depth of the ideals or issues they have chosen to emphasise and represent: how inspirational their vision is for their own people, in their own time, and perhaps also for future generations.

With these criteria in mind, it is important to recognise that Jacinda Ardern has been prime minister only since October 2017, and leader of the New Zealand Labour Party only since 1 August 2017. This is a very short time in which to assess an individual's competence and contribution. As a result, any assessment can only be regarded as interim and provisional. Much can change, as 'events' develop and as Ardern's own record of leadership and public service continues to be established.

Jacinda Ardern and political leadership

At this stage in Jacinda Ardern's prime ministerial career, her leadership has been displayed most vividly in the 'crisis management' sector. This is in a sense, of course, deeply regrettable; how much better would it have been if New Zealand had not had to experience the March 2019 attacks on the Christchurch mosques, the volcanic eruption on Whakaari / White Island in December 2019, and the 2020 Covid-19 outbreak?

Nevertheless, in each instance, Ardern's strengths as prime minister were much in evidence. She displayed a command of the relevant facts; a determination to uncover causes and deal with consequences; a commitment to the implementation of solutions; and a gift for communicating quickly and clearly with all those affected, and, more broadly, with the New Zealand public, her colleagues and the media. These leadership skills – made explicit by decisions made, actions taken, statements delivered – were complemented by her oft-praised expressions of 'empathy', demonstrating genuine concern in the face of these tragedies.

In responding to each crisis the prime minister has neither been unsure nor unclear, neither overwhelmed nor equivocal. She has not been reluctant or afraid to implement tough policies, whether ordering Covid-19-induced border closures and nationwide lockdowns, or introducing legislation to make the weapons used in the mosque attacks illegal – the latter a display of prime ministerial initiative and power so compelling that the legislation was enacted in less than a month with a parliamentary vote of 119 to 1.

In addition – still on this first crisis of her prime ministership – Ardern acted internationally to address what she considered to be some of the underlying causes of the hate-driven mosque attacks. This led to a shared effort with France's prime minister Emmanuel Macron, with support from the United Nations Secretary-General and many other world leaders and civil society groups, to prevent social media from disseminating hate, bigotry, racism and violence. In doing so the prime minister successfully internationalised New Zealand's response to the mass shooting: an impressive effort for the prime minister of a small, remote country, responding to a massacre less catastrophic, quantitatively, than many other such tragedies elsewhere (particularly in the United States).

In this experience, and again with the Whakaari / White Island eruption and the outbreak of Covid-19, the prime minister displayed focus, clarity, composure, sense of purpose and dignity, qualities that themselves communicated strength and resolve, concern and compassion. Her success was apparent in the respect given to the young prime minister internationally. She did not embarrass the country; quite the contrary. International media and overseas leaders were highly impressed by her demeanour and delivery, in many cases contrasting her approach with far weaker responses elsewhere and declaring New Zealand a world leader in its management of such crises.

Overall, Ardern's leadership style exhibits confidence: an ability to quickly master a situation, to make relevant and sensible decisions, and to communicate those decisions effectively. This confidence is one of the prime minister's most powerful assets. To sum up: when the prime minister has been sorely tested she has been perceived to act forcefully and without hesitation. Her actions, over time, have enhanced confidence in her leadership, both within New Zealand and internationally.

The other leadership criteria, applied to the prime minister, also suggest a positive assessment. The prime minister's first term has had both international successes and domestic legislative accomplishments, including legislation focusing on child poverty and climate change, issues on which she had campaigned in the 2017 election. Ardern also demonstrated an ability to change direction when needed, dismissing Cabinet Ministers seen as 'underperforming', and admitting that policies promoted by her party were no longer to be pursued (for instance, with respect to a capital gains tax and KiwiBuild, the pledge to build 100,000 affordable homes in ten years). A capacity to admit that a particular course of action is not working as planned and needs to be changed – and to do so without losing confidence or support – is a valuable asset, a strength rather than a sign of weakness. A cover-up can be regarded as worse than the original offence, whereas candour and an admitted change of course suggests honesty, strength of character and accountability – a willingness to tell the truth, even when admitting a degree of failure or disappointment.

Ardern remains unrivalled in uniting her historically fractious Labour Party, which has had a tendency to undermine and then replace its leaders. Her party seems well satisfied with her leadership style and the substance of her policies. In her first term she also managed to maintain effective, cordial relations with her coalition partners, New Zealand First and the Green Party – a considerable achievement, given their very different perspectives and priorities. Ardern was yet able to maintain a stable coalition, productive and generally harmonious, and her relationship with the leaders of the two coalition parties appeared to be respectful and congenial despite their policy differences and the fact that each of the three parties were to be competing with one another at the 2020 election.

Ardern has also been successful in maintaining dominance over her parliamentary opposition. She effectively responds to their efforts in Parliament and has consistently maintained a substantial lead over the leader of the National Party – irrespective of who that might be – as 'preferred prime minister' throughout her tenure, leaving the Opposition leader in the difficult position of having to persuade voters that they constitute a credible rival.

Of course, New Zealand's political system is parliamentary, not presidential. The electorate, in 2020, were not able to vote for her directly as prime minister. Even so, there seems little doubt that for many New Zealanders, assessments of her record and of her leadership led them to cast their party vote, at least, as a surrogate for a direct vote for New Zealand's prime minister – a vote cast 'as if' they were voting for the country's leader over the next three years.

Jacinda Ardern's sudden rise to prominence in 2017 – from list MP to Mount Albert MP, to deputy leader then leader of the Labour Party, to Prime Minister – was astonishing. The previous book in this series, *Stardust and Substance*, chronicled the 'Jacindamania' that followed, and the claim by her opponents that she was all 'stardust', no 'substance'. Her ability to connect with the public is exceptional, but the past three years have proven that she has many other leadership skills as well.

Other prime ministers maintained tight control over their parliamentary caucus and were respected for their intelligence and mastery of legislative and policy detail. Ardern's political and managerial skills, and grasp of policy detail, have to date been equally commanding. Other prime ministers, while respected for their strength, were more feared than liked. Ardern, by contrast, seems simply to be admired. Other prime ministers have had to face crises; seldom, for a New Zealand leader, have these come in such quick succession, and probably only the two world wars could rival Covid-19 in its effects on the world's economy and mortality. Other prime ministers were able to establish an international profile, but few have captured as much favourable attention from the international community as she has. In terms of broad public appeal and media support, and with a unified parliamentary team, Ardern has been able to enjoy a position of leadership strength that many of her predecessors would surely have envied.

Conclusion

Over and above his dedication and wartime leadership, Abraham Lincoln is remembered today for his honesty, his humility and his rhetoric, a seriousness of purpose complemented by humour and humanity, whose testament is summed up in words engraved in marble at the back of the Lincoln Memorial: 'In this Temple as in the hearts of the People for whom he saved the Union the memory of Abraham Lincoln is enshrined forever.' These unwished-for circumstances – a civil war – and distinctive personal qualities – honesty, humility and humanity – are not easily captured by a set of categories in a leadership survey. Nor is the extent of public gratitude. Leadership in a crisis situation is not easy – it requires strong measures in the face of uncertain and shifting circumstances, under the close watch of an anxious public. The decisions Ardern made in response to the pandemic – imposing a lockdown; closing borders; requiring people to leave a digital trail of their movements, wear masks and distance themselves from friends and family – could have backfired horribly if she had failed to implement them competently and maintain the trust of her constituents.

In the end, the arc of a prime minister's experience of office will depend on many factors impossible to identify in advance. Jacinda Ardern came to prime ministerial office at a young age – 37 – and now, returned to office three years later, doubtless neither she nor anyone else can know how long she may wish to remain in that position or what future challenges may await. In the long run, anticipating her place in the pantheon of New Zealand's prime ministers, good intentions and a vibrant, inspiring personality, though far from unimportant, will be less decisive than her vision for the country and her ability to make at least the principal elements of that vision a reality. Like all prime ministers, she is certain to face sustained scrutiny from a vigilant media and a determined opposition, but she would appear to have both the time and the talent to become one of New Zealand's most admired political leaders.

This epilogue to an extraordinary election, coming at the end of a uniquely difficult year, is not intended as a comparative exercise. Its purpose is not to assess how Jacinda Ardern, returned to office in spectacular fashion, may be regarded in comparison with New Zealand's former premiers and prime ministers. Others had a 'common touch'; established policies; set precedents; inspired colleagues; overwhelmed adversaries; made effective use of the media; acquired international respect. When Ardern spoke at the December 2017 post-election conference (the precursor to the book *Stardust and Substance*), she was introduced with the sentiment that all New Zealanders, regardless of party, would wish to see the responsibilities of office carried out by the country's new prime minister with dignity, grace, resolve and conviction. The Labour Party's victory at the 2020 elections suggests that much of the electorate, reflecting on the crises faced during Ardern's three-year tenure, felt that she had indeed lived up to these expectations.

During a House of Commons' debate in May 1940, nine months after the start of World War II, Britain's World War I prime minister Lloyd George reflected on what the people expect of their leaders at a time of maximum danger:

> The nation is prepared for every sacrifice so long as it has leadership, so long as the Government show clearly what they are aiming at and so long as the nation is confident that those who are leading it are doing their best.

In confronting Covid-19 – an unprecedented challenge in the lifetime of the New Zealand public – the prime minister, through clarity of purpose, preserved the nation's confidence: no mean feat, and one that proved essential in achieving nationwide unity and compliance.

And what of the future? Jacinda Ardern's outlook – and that of the government she leads – does not appear to be one aiming towards easy victories linked to modest goals. Perhaps, deep down, drawing upon her rhetoric and her government's programmes, her aspirations may not be dissimilar from those articulated by the former UK Chief Rabbi, Professor Jonathan Sacks (honoured in 2005 and appointed to the House of Lords in 2009): 'to accept no illness that can be cured, no poverty that can be alleviated, no injustice that can be rectified'; to work towards a society in which 'all have equal access' not only to the necessities of life (including 'a source of independent livelihood, and a home') but 'to human dignity' (Sacks 2006, p. 108; p. 26).

As for what might be achieved of so principled, ambitious and idealistic an agenda, all that can be said is that we will know later . . .

NOTES

Foreword

1 Doug Kidd (Speaker, 1996–1999) was elected Speaker of the New Zealand House of Representatives following the first MMP election in 1996. He served one term (three years) in that role while MP for the Kaikōura electorate. At the 1999 election he sought re-election as a list-only candidate. Re-elected to Parliament, he lost the position of Speaker when the National Party was unsuccessful at the 1999 election. Labour MP Jonathan Hunt (Speaker, 1999–2005) was a list MP from 1996 to 2005 (having served as MP for New Lynn from 1966 to 1996); Margaret Wilson (Speaker, 2005–2008) served three terms in Parliament as a list MP; Lockwood Smith (Speaker, 2008–2013), having previously been an MP for the Kaipara and Rodney electorates, was elected in 2008 as MP for Rodney, becoming a list MP at the 2011 election; David Carter (Speaker, 2013–2017) was a list MP (having previously been an MP for the Selwyn and Banks Peninsula electorates); and Trevor Mallard (Speaker, 2017–present) became a list MP in 2017 (having previously been an MP for the Hamilton West, Pencarrow and Hutt South electorates) [ed.].

1. Politics in a Pandemic: New Zealand's 2020 election

1 Prime Minister Jacinda Ardern observed 'that whether or not people wear ties in the debating chamber [is] not something I have a particularly strong opinion on. What I do have an opinion on is I don't think it's a particularly good use of Parliament's time to engage in lengthy debate on something that I think most New Zealanders aren't particularly bothered by', adding: 'I don't think most New Zealanders care about ties; they care about housing, they care about jobs, they care about us talking about things that matter' (quoted in Wade 2021).

2 New Zealand's response to Covid-19 will no doubt be the subject of many studies in coming years. Already available is an analysis from a Victoria University of Wellington political scientist, Emeritus Professor Robert Gregory (a contributor to the previous book in this series, *Stardust and Substance*), focusing on 'scientific advice and political realities' (and the implications for policy-making): see Gregory 2021.

4. Growing Green support from a position of government

1 See the Advertising Standards Authority Complaints Board's decision (case number 20/531) at www.asa.co.nz.

6. ACT II

1 The ACT Party, founded in 1994, first stood at a New Zealand general election in 1996, winning eight seats. The party won nine seats in 1999 and again in 2002. Subsequently, for a variety of reasons, the party did less well, winning two seats in 2005, five seats in 2008 and one seat at the 2011, 2014 and 2017 elections. ACT's performance at these elections is chronicled by ACT candidates and leaders in the books comprising this election series, with chapters by David Seymour following the 2014 and 2017 elections [ed.].

7. Jacindamania in Canada: Coverage in the Great White North

1 Part of the reason for delays in Canada around firearms regulations may be attributed to arguments that take into consideration Canadian property owners' need to defend themselves against predatory wildlife, which is less of an issue in New Zealand.

9. 'And the winner is . . . New Zealand': the view from the UK

1 The title for this 2020 chapter, on the view of New Zealand's election as seen from the UK, is taken from Braunias 2020.

2 See, for example, the pen portrait of New Zealand in an article comparing different countries' handling of the pandemic in the *Independent* on 29 September 2020:

> Having emerged miraculously unscathed from the pandemic, New Zealand has developed a reputation for extreme and effective vigilance. Premier Jacinda Ardern has won plaudits for her swift and decisive reaction to the crisis, closing international borders without delay and placing the nation under lockdown in March, operating a strict quarantining system for international arrivals thereafter. While the country plunged into its worst recession in decades, the prioritisation of health and virus elimination appears set to pay dividends in the future.

See also coverage of the fact that New Zealand was ranked first overall and in each category (political stability, economic recovery, virus control and social resilience) in *Bloomberg*'s market crisis management index, published in the second week of October: for instance, Farrer 2020a.

3 For an example of *The Guardian*'s excellent (and often highly entertaining)

weekly review, see 'NZ election weekly briefing: Collins channels Crusher, Ardern smoked out, Peters panned' by Elle Hunt (1 October 2020). Note that much of the coverage there and in other outlets (including the reliably right-wing *Mail*) would have appeared in their online rather than their print editions. Given the reach of the former compared to the latter, however, it would be silly to assume that that meant fewer British readers saw it even if, as in *The Guardian*'s case (and also the *Mail*'s), some of its coverage of the election seemed aimed as much at Australian readers as it was at them. That, incidentally, makes sense since there were around 40,000 registered expat Kiwi voters in Australia compared to only 11,000 or so in the UK (and 4,000 in the US where the online versions of *The Guardian* and the *Mail* do quite good business).

4 For a paradigmatic example, see O'Grady 2020a.

5 The offending (but hardly offensive) tweet ran as follows: 'Are people really discussing Boris Johnson as possible candidate for PM? When I lived in London he was known as the gaffe man! – Jacinda Ardern (@jacindaardern) August 13, 2012.' See Richards 2020 (published in *The National*, very much an SNP supporting newspaper).

6 Langan 2020. For a thoughtful piece on the demise of New Zealand First, see Graham-McLay 2020d. *The Guardian*, not surprisingly perhaps, was the only paper that devoted a relatively substantial piece to the Greens (see Taylor 2020) and the Māori Party (McLachlan 2020b).

10. Jacinda Ardern's election – a European perspective

1 International interest in New Zealand's 2020 election, the country's response to the Covid-19 pandemic and the leadership, personality and outlook of Prime Minister Jacinda Ardern extended widely, beyond Europe – as indicated in some of the other chapters in this section of the book – and within Europe as well. From Poland to Portugal, from Sweden to Spain, from Latvia to Luxembourg, New Zealand's 2020 election and its struggle against Covid-19 – one which it shared with all other nations and peoples – attracted the curiosity of journalists, print and broadcast, and the communities which they served. This chapter provides examples of some of that media curiosity, and the insights achieved by some of the reporters and commentators involved [ed.].

11. A faraway but close relationship – the view from Chile

1 If 'admiration' seems excessive, it might be noted that *The Economist*'s 2020 end-of-year issue included in its 'Leaders' section – the equivalent of its editorial page – a commentary headlined 'Admiration nation', highlighting New Zealand (with praise for Prime Minister Jacinda Ardern and her response to the pandemic) [ed.].

13. The 2020 election: A television journalist's perspective

1 Each of the two National MPs represented South Island electorates. Andrew Falloon, elected to Parliament in 2017 as MP for Rangitata, resigned on 21 July 2020 following reports of 'inappropriate' images being sent to a young woman. Hamish Walker, elected to Parliament in 2017 as MP for Clutha–Southland, announced on 8 July 2020 that he would not be standing for re-election following his unauthorised disclosure of Covid-19 patients' private details. The two MPs' difficulties did little for National's image; while the results in their electorates reflected Labour's nationwide dominance, local disenchantment with what had occurred was no doubt a contributing factor. The Rangitata seat was won by Labour MP Jo Luxton, a list MP who lost to Falloon in 2017; her 2020 result (21,147 votes, against National candidate Megan Hands' 16,739 votes) virtually reversed the 2017 outcome (13,663 votes to Falloon's 19,994 votes). In 2017 Labour lost the party vote in Rangitata by 7,377 votes; in 2020 Labour won the electorate's party vote by 7,374 votes. In 2017 Hamish Walker won Clutha–Southland by more than 14,000 votes, and National won the party vote by more than 12,000 votes. In 2020, in the new seat of Southland, National's Joseph Mooney was elected with a 5,645 vote margin over Labour's Jon Mitchell, but Labour won the party vote, with 15,341 votes to National's 14,244 [ed.].

2 Tova O'Brien's post-election interview with Jami-Lee Ross can be viewed on *Newshub*'s YouTube channel.

16. 'Getting closer to the truth': The 2020 election cartoons as commentary, protest and critique

1 I wish to acknowledge and sincerely thank all the cartoonists whose work has been reproduced in this chapter for their support, interest and generosity in allowing their cartoons to be reprinted here. I also wish to thank *Stuff*, the *Otago Daily Times*, the *New Zealand Herald* and the *Listener* for permission to use the cartoons.

2 During the pandemic Dr Bloomfield was depicted in a Wellington shop window as an apostle, in a display advertising Apostle hot sauce, which compared the sauce's level of spice to the Covid alert level system [ed.].

3 David Clark studied theology at university and is a Presbyterian minister [ed.].

4 See https://twitter.com/domesticanimal/status/1276975875724992512.

5 Email from Malcolm Evans to Mike Grimshaw, 3 February 2021.

17. The 2020 election, the Covid-19 emergency, and the need to improve our response capacity for even more serious threats

1 The author is grateful for the huge collegial support of colleagues in the University of Otago Co-Search team which is focused on researching the public

health aspects of the Covid-19 pandemic and response, notably Dr Amanda Kvalsvig and Professor Nick Wilson.

19. Housing and the Sixth Labour Government

1 The Labour-led government amended the bright-line test in 2018, extending it from two years to five years. In March 2021 the prime minister proposed extending the period to ten years in a further effort to curb speculation and improve housing affordability [ed.].

20. The Christchurch shooting and the 2020 New Zealand election

1 The 'Christchurch Call' was an action plan initiated in May 2019 by New Zealand Prime Minister Jacinda Ardern and French President Emmanuel Macron, bringing together countries and tech companies in an effort to eliminate online terrorist and violent extremist content.

2 The Islamicity Foundation's Islamicity Index, taking the teachings of the Qur'an as its basis, evaluates (and ranks) countries according to the extent to which they do 'the things that Islam says you should do'. According to the Foundation's founder, Hossain Askari, New Zealand's values and practices make the country more Islamic than Muslim-majority countries. Sweden, Iceland, the Netherlands, Switzerland, Denmark and Ireland follow New Zealand in the Foundation's rankings, with the United Arab Emirates (ranked 44th) the highest ranked Muslim-majority country (Carroll 2020).

23. The 2020 cannabis and euthanasia referendums

1 The Greens were part of The Alliance – an alliance of several small parties – competing at the first MMP election (in 1996), with several Green MPs being among the 13 Alliance MPs elected. The Greens subsequently chose to separate from The Alliance, entering Parliament (with seven MPs) at the 1999 election [ed.].

26. Why Labour won – survey findings and the 2020 election

1 Results in this summary are from a mix of UMR nationally representative online polls. These included monthly online surveys undertaken for subscribers to a monthly report, an immediate pre-campaign survey and a post-campaign survey.

2 Winston Peters rated 45 per cent but the sample size of New Zealand First voters was too small to be anything but indicative.

3 A whopping 68 per cent of ACT voters in 2020 had voted for National in 2017; the rest had voted for ACT (13 per cent), Labour (8 per cent) or New Zealand First (4 per cent). Contrary to some commentary there was little shifting from

New Zealand First to ACT. New Zealand First voters from 2017 voted in 2020 as follows: 35 per cent New Zealand First, 29 per cent Labour, 13 per cent National, 10 per cent New Conservative and 4 per cent ACT.

29. Echoes: The 2020 election in historical perspective

1 I missed the 1975 elections. I was in London from 1973 to 1976.
2 '[Norman Kirk] didn't enter my thoughts again except for one occasion when my father predicted he would be Prime Minister before he was finished. I had disagreed. A fat man, I'd said, would never be voted Prime Minister of New Zealand' (Hayward 1981, 'How it began' preface, second unnumbered page).
3 As noted below, Social Credit won one seat in 1978 and two in 1981.
4 The 'worm' was a measure of audience applause displayed on the bottom of the television screen.
5 Michael Laws, *The Demon Profession* (Harper Collins, 1998), p. 373. The full quote is 'Winston regarded his former colleagues with a peculiar sense of familial longing – a connection that refused to be excised or exorcised.'

30. 'Window on Wairarapa': Kieran McAnulty and Labour's 2020 Covid campaign

1 The research for this chapter – particularly the research on the 'ground game' of the campaign – was undertaken while I was an intern for Labour MP Kieran McAnulty, volunteering with the campaign.

31. A campaign for the ages: Chlöe Swarbrick, the youth vote and the Auckland Central election

1 The research for this chapter was undertaken while I was an intern for Green MP Chlöe Swarbrick, taking part in (and observing) the Auckland Central campaign.

32. Special votes and the 2020 election

1 Writ day is the day on which the Governor-General issues a writ – a formal written direction – to the Chief Electoral Officer to hold a general election. In 2020, writ day was Sunday, 13 September. Electors must be enrolled by writ day to be on the printed electoral roll.
2 We would like to express our gratitude to Mr Anthony Pengelly, a staff member at the Electoral Commission, for data he provided to help us with this analysis – particularly with respect to Tables 32.2 and 32.4, and Figures 32.5 and 32.7.
3 It is worth noting that in 2005 – in the first general election the Māori Party contested – the party's share of the special votes cast in the election reduced the number of overhang seats in Parliament by one. Election night figures had the

Māori Party winning four electorates with a party vote that would have won it only two seats in the House of Representatives. The Māori Party's *party vote* 'special votes differential' in 2005 was, as Table 32.3 shows, its best to date, and the party's final valid vote count raised its *party vote* seat entitlement in Parliament to three. However, as the final count also confirmed that the party had won the four electorates it initially held on election night, the party's total number of seats in Parliament was not affected by the specials; however, the total number of seats in Parliament after the 2005 election fell from 122 on the provisional election night count to 121. This explains why Table 32.1 shows National losing a seat as a result of special votes cast in 2005 but does not show any party picking up the lost seat. In every other column of data in Table 32.1, the number of seats lost equals the number of seats gained.

4 All electoral formulas convert votes into seats. The Sainte-Laguë formula does this by taking the actual *number of votes* (i.e., not percentages of the votes) of parties that have qualified for seats in the House of Representatives (either by winning at least 5 per cent of the valid party votes cast throughout the country as a whole or by winning at least one electorate seat in Parliament). The formula divides each qualifying party's number of party votes by successive odd numbers – 1, 3, 5, 7, 9, 11, and so on, and following these divisions then distributes seats in Parliament to the parties with the 120 highest quotients. In the 2020 general election, the highest quotient was 1,443,545 (which was the number of valid party votes won by the Labour Party divided by 1), while – at the other end of the scale – the 119th-highest quotient was 11,210 (which was the Māori Party's 33,630 party votes divided by 3) and the 120th-highest quotient was 11,190.271 (which was the Labour Party's 1,443,545 party votes divided by 129). Because the Labour Party had 65 of the 120 highest quotients, it was entitled to 65 seats in the House of Representatives – and the party was awarded 19 list seats in addition to the 46 electorates it had won. Similarly, because the Māori Party had two of the 120 highest quotients, it was entitled to two seats in the House of Representatives: Debbie Ngarewa-Packer, who was first on the party's list, thus joined her electorate MP colleague Rawiri Waititi in Parliament.

5 Prior to 2002, the entire ballot was disallowed. Note that the *party-only votes* category does not include votes where the voter cast a vote for the correct electorate but did not cast a valid electorate vote (for example by leaving it blank or ticking multiple candidates). These types of votes are fully allowed and are included in the party vote results; however, their electorate vote would be recorded as *informal*.

6 In this instance Vowles considered a Labour 'stronghold' to be an electorate in which the party won more than 30 per cent of the party vote in the 2014 election. By way of context, it should be noted that this reflected Labour's performance in the 2014 election (when it won a mere 25.1 per cent of the vote,

described in chapter 22 of this book as the party's 'worst performance in more than 90 years').

33. Getting what you're given: Government formation in 2020

1 National also stated it was open to working with the Māori Party and that it would continue to encourage National supporters to give their electorate vote to David Seymour in Epsom (Cooke 2020).

2 Although this was the first time under MMP that a general electorate seat has been won by a minor party candidate without the cooperation of a major party, the Māori Party and the Mana Party have won Māori seats without such arrangements. The only other time the Greens have won an electorate seat was when Jeanette Fitzsimons won Coromandel in 1999, with the tacit support of Labour.

3 Conceivably this could lead to a situation where Minister Davidson could be held responsible for these matters even if her party does not ultimately vote in favour of them. For example, the opposition parties could put a case to the Speaker that the cooperation agreement provides the scope for the Minister to be asked parliamentary questions about funding for family and sexual violence prevention.

REFERENCES

1. Politics in a Pandemic: New Zealand's 2020 election

1 News 2020a, 'Nats MP Denise Lee says she "unreservedly supports" Judith Collins after leaked email criticising leader', TVNZ, 6 October.

1 News 2020b, '"You can believe me" – Judith Collins says National won't adopt ACT tax policy if elected', TVNZ, 12 October.

1 News 2020c, 'Trevor Mallard officially re-elected as Speaker: "It is an honour and a privilege"', TVNZ, 25 November.

ACT 2020, 'Change Your Future', flyer.

Adams, Graham 2020, 'A euthanasia referendum in a pandemic', RNZ, 29 June.

Advance New Zealand 2020, 'Court Helps Media Stack Deck Against Democracy', press release, 1 October.

Bonnett, Gill 2020, 'New Zealand First pledges to create rural visa scheme', RNZ, 2 October.

Braae, Alex 2020, 'A revelation in Marton: The Spinoff meets New Zealand's newest Christian party', *The Spinoff*, 18 August.

Brown, Tim 2020, 'Christchurch mosque attacks: Terrorist sentenced to life in jail without parole', RNZ, 7 August.

Cheng, Derek 2020, 'Neck and neck: Nothing between National and Labour–Greens in latest poll', *New Zealand Herald*, 13 February.

Cook, Charlotte 2020, 'The Elevator Pitch: "We believe in people" – Judith Collins', RNZ, 14 September.

Cooke, Henry 2020, 'Election 2020: Labour would make Matariki a public holiday from 2020', *Stuff*, 7 September.

Coughlan, Thomas 2020a, 'National makes enormous recovery in new poll', *Stuff*, 25 June.

Coughlan, Thomas 2020b, 'Election 2020: Jacinda Ardern makes final push in Wellington as election enters home stretch', *Stuff*, 11 October.

Devlin, Collette and Danielle Clent 2020, 'Covid-19: ACT pledges safer, smarter borders, less debt and employment insurance', *Stuff*, 12 July.

Dominion Post 2020a, 'Border bungle blot on record' [editorial], 19 June, p. 12.

Dominion Post 2020b, 'Stunning result in unusual year' [editorial], 19 October, p. 17.

Doyle, Katie 2020, 'Election 2020 with Covid-19 restrictions "the worst campaign environment" – Winston Peters', RNZ, 17 September.

Dreaver, Charlie 2020, 'Greens AGM: Sights set on social equality and animal welfare', RNZ, 25 July.

Electoral Commission 2020, 'Get ready to vote', flyer.

Ensor, Jamie 2020, 'NZ Election 2020: Winston Peters dismisses polls, warns of "Green, Labour nightmare" in animated Duncan Garner interview', *Newshub*, 13 October.

Family First 2020, 'Value Your Vote 2020', flyer.

Forrester, Georgia 2020, 'Election 2020: Jami-Lee Ross will not contest Botany seat in Auckland', *Stuff*, 15 September.

Green Party 2020, 'Think ahead. Party Vote Green', flyer.

Gregory, Robert 2021, 'Covid-19 in New Zealand: Scientific advice and political realities', in Li, Linda Chelan (ed.), *Facts and Analysis: Canvassing Covid-19 Responses*, Hong Kong SAR, City University of Hong Kong Press, pp. 217–232.

Hollingworth, Adam 2020, 'Thirteen firearms owners on ACT Party's election list as it takes aim at New Zealand First', *Newshub*, 28 June.

Jones, Nicholas 2020, 'Election 2020: National leader Judith Collins rules out working with NZ First, says Winston Peters is on way out', *New Zealand Herald*, 18 July.

Manhire, Toby 2020, 'NZ ranked first in world for Covid-19 response communications', *The Spinoff*, 6 May.

McCulloch, Craig 2020a, 'New poll: Labour climbs to 60.9%, National at 25.1%', RNZ, 26 July.

McCulloch, Craig 2020b, 'Judith Collins asked to embrace "Crusher" persona', RNZ, 29 September.

McCullough, Yvette 2020a, 'NZ First the lone voice calling for Christchurch mosque gunman to be sent to Australia', RNZ, 28 August.

McCullough, Yvette 2020b, 'Party vote Green to keep Ardern at helm, Shaw urges', RNZ, 26 September.

Moir, Jo 2020a, 'Power play: Māori Party strategy already undermined by Tamihere', RNZ, 9 March.

Moir, Jo 2020b, 'Jacinda Ardern, Labour soar in new poll', RNZ, 18 May.

Moir, Jo 2020c, 'Judith Collins' bid to underscore "strong team" brand in reshuffle', RNZ, 17 July.

Moir, Jo 2020d, 'NZ First Convention: Peters, caucus joined by 150 members', RNZ, 18 July.

Moir, Jo 2020e, 'Universal Family Benefit part of NZ First plan', RNZ, 19 July.

Moir, Jo 2020f, 'NZ First Leader Winston Peters highlights police, immigration in campaign launch', RNZ, 19 July.

Moir, Jo 2020g, '"Gloves are off" for NZ First and Greens leaders in unofficial election campaign', RNZ, 21 July.

Moir, Jo 2020h, 'National Party admits $4 billion hole in their promised spending', RNZ, 20 September.
Moir, Jo 2020i, 'National "needed to be a unified team with a credible message" – David Carter', RNZ, 23 November.
Moir, Jo and Jane Patterson 2020, 'Māori Party President wary of National partnership: "It kicked us out"', RNZ, 7 February.
National Party 2020, 'Todd Muller resigns as Leader of the Opposition', 14 July.
New Zealand Government 2020, 'What am I voting on?', authorised by the Secretary for Justice.
New Conservative Party 2020, 'Save New Zealand', flyer.
New Zealand Labour Party 2020, 'Let's keep moving', flyer.
One Party 2019, 'One Party – Vote for a Better Future', party website.
Otago Daily Times 2020, 'Peters vs Seymour: "You'd last 10 seconds in the ring with me"', 20 July.
Patterson, Jane 2020a, 'Leader interviews: Judith Collins – "I'm always very confident, particularly when I know I'm right"', RNZ, 10 August.
Patterson, Jane 2020b, 'Leader interviews: Jacinda Ardern says vision not "defined" by Covid-19', RNZ, 10 August.
Patterson, Jane 2020c, 'Leader interviews: Winston Peters – 'One of these days I'll have a lovely retirement – but not yet', RNZ, 10 August.
Patterson, Jane 2020d, 'Green School funding saga continues as Chris Hipkins rejects claims made in James Shaw video', RNZ, 3 September.
Patterson, Jane 2020e, 'National claims $10 billion hole in Labour's economic plan', RNZ, 2 October.
Patterson, Jane 2020f, 'Jacinda Ardern on the year that was', RNZ, 10 December.
Radio New Zealand [RNZ] 2020a, 'Simon Bridges says caucus backs him on ruling out New Zealand First move', 3 February.
RNZ 2020b, 'Donations made to NZ First Foundation referred to police for investigation', 10 February.
RNZ 2020c, 'Jim Bolger backs Todd Muller as potential National leader', *Checkpoint*, 19 May.
RNZ 2020d, 'New poll: National at 29 percent, Labour has best result ever', 21 May.
RNZ 2020e, 'Green Party: Better to spend $1.5b on solar panels than roads', 13 July.
RNZ 2020f, 'PM Jacinda Ardern on Todd Muller resignation: "Politics is a difficult place"', 14 July.
RNZ 2020g, 'Winston Peters ordered to pay nearly $320k in costs for court battle', 20 July.
RNZ 2020h, 'PM Jacinda Ardern on Winston Peters' immigration portfolio coalition requirement', 21 July.
RNZ 2020i, 'Jami-Lee Ross launches Advance New Zealand party', 26 July.

RNZ 2020j, 'Labour launches re-election campaign with $300 million plan to create thousands of new jobs', 8 August.

RNZ 2020k, 'National caucus to vote against cannabis at referendum – Judith Collins', 11 August.

RNZ 2020l, 'Judith Collins calls for James Shaw's resignation over Green School blunder', 2 September.

RNZ 2020m, 'Weather disrupts final act at Parliament', 6 September.

RNZ 2020n, 'Māori Party pledges to change New Zealand's name to Aotearoa, Greens, Labour spell out te reo Māori policy', 14 September.

RNZ 2020o, 'Advance NZ party takes exclusion from debate to court', 29 September.

RNZ 2020p, 'Māori Party promises to establish Māori Parliament', 29 September.

RNZ 2020q, 'Winston Peters holds "important" conference as SFO releases NZ First Foundation investigation statement', 29 September.

RNZ 2020r, 'Cutting benefits off the table in ACT coalition – Judith Collins', 30 September.

RNZ 2020s, 'Court rules against Jami-Lee Ross, Billy Te Kahika over debate exclusion', 1 October.

RNZ 2020t, 'Challenge to minimum voting age fails in High Court', 7 October.

RNZ 2020u, 'Poll shows scarce support for Billy Te Kahika', 8 October.

RNZ 2020v, 'Election 2020: Judith Collins will stay on, no matter what voters decide tomorrow', 16 October.

RNZ 2020w, 'Election 2020: Labour seeking "simplicity" and strong mandate – Jacinda Ardern', 16 October.

RNZ 2020x, 'Dr Shane Reti on "dream" job as National's deputy leader', *Checkpoint*, 10 November.

RNZ 2020y, 'National Party gathers for AGM: "We must give NZers a reason to vote for us"', 21 November.

Robson, Sarah 2020a, 'ACT leader uses campaign launch to slate government's Covid-19 response', RNZ, 12 July.

Robson, Sarah 2020b, 'Judith Collins endorses David Seymour for Epsom – but what about the party's other prospects?', RNZ, 10 August.

Robson, Sarah 2020c, 'Auckland Central: Labour making no deal with the Greens', RNZ, 10 August.

Scoop 2020a, 'Speech: Winston Peters Campaign Launch', 19 July.

Scoop 2020b, '"Safer Kiwi Communities" policy package announced by New Zealand First', 7 October.

Scotcher, Katie 2020a, 'Greens co-leader James Shaw "always disappointed in NZ First" – this time over light rail', RNZ, 12 June.

Scotcher, Katie 2020b, 'Auckland light rail now a campaign matter, Peters says', RNZ, 16 June.

Scotcher, Katie 2020c, 'The outliers: Fears about Te Kahika's controversial Covid-19 views', RNZ, 14 September.

Smith, Anneke 2020, 'New Conservatives fail in bid to feature in TVNZ debate', RNZ, 7 October.

The Economist 2020, 'New Zealand's elections – Labour day', 24 October, p. 20.

Theunissen, Matthew 2020, 'Simon Bridges to face National Party leadership challenge', RNZ, 20 May.

Trevett, Claire 2020, 'New political poll: National drops to 20%, Labour up to 59%', *New Zealand Herald*, 21 May.

Wade, Amelia 2021, 'Tiki vs tie: Parliament neck-tie stoush soon to be tied-up', *New Zealand Herald*, 10 February.

Walls, Jason 2020a, 'Election 2020: Greens co-leader James Shaw says having NZ First in Govt again is a risk not worth taking', *New Zealand Herald*, 26 July.

Walls, Jason 2020b, 'Election 2020: Judith Collins in "bittersweet" campaign launch, attacks Labour as "erratic" and "lazy"', *New Zealand Herald*, 20 September.

Whyte, Anna 2020, 'Judith Collins says it's "onward and upwards" for National after devastating election loss', *1 News*, 20 October.

Wilson, Peter 2020a, 'Spooked MPs opt for unknown Muller to avoid a rout', RNZ, 22 May.

Wilson, Peter 2020b, 'Week in Politics: Shaw still feeling heat as funding issue bubbles on', RNZ, 5 September.

Wilson, Peter 2020c, 'Week in Politics: Labour shows what a majority government can do', RNZ, 4 December.

6. ACT II

Seymour, David 2018, 'The ACT Party: The leader's perspective' in Stephen Levine (ed.), *Stardust and Substance: The New Zealand General Election of 2017*, Victoria University Press, Wellington, pp. 60–66.

7. Jacindamania in Canada: Coverage in the Great White North

Baker, Rochelle 2020, 'Liberal promise on national child care provokes mixed response', *National Observer*, 25 September.

Ball, David 2018, 'Indigenous representation "rising steady" since electoral reform in New Zealand almost 20 years ago, says Maori statistician', *Toronto Star/ Metro Vancouver* edition, 8 November.

Breen, Kerri 2020, '66% of Canadians believe MPs should take a salary cut: poll', *Global News*, 8 May.

Britten, Liam 2018, 'Andrew Weaver wants B.C. to follow New Zealand ban on foreign homebuyers', *CBC News*, 15 August.

CBC 2020a, 'New Zealand's Ardern wins 2nd mandate in election landslide', 17 October (Associated Press).

CBC 2020b, 'New Zealand's Opposition leader steps down 2 months before election', 14 July (Associated Press).

CTV News 2020, 'New Zealand opposition chooses new leader after shock resignation', 14 July (Associated Press).

CTV News staff 2018, 'New Zealand's "First Baby" attends UN General Assembly meeting', *CTV News*, 25 September (with files from Associated Press).

Delvoie, Louis 2020, 'Admirable leaders', *Gananoque Reporter*, 23 October.

Ditchburn, Jennifer 2015, '"Because it's 2015": Trudeau forms Canada's 1st gender-balanced cabinet', *The Canadian Press*, 4 November.

Drolet, Mike 2020, 'New Zealand has chosen its next prime minister – the outcome likely won't surprise, *Global News*, 18 October.

Elghawaby, Amira 2019, 'New Zealand's response to mosque massacre offers lessons for Canada', *Global News*, 26 March.

Fletcher, Tanya 2020, 'Could a 4-day work week boost B.C.'s COVID-plagued economy by spurring more travel?', *CBC News*, 21 May.

Francis, Diane 2018, 'Foreigners are banned from buying property in New Zealand – Canada should do the same', *Financial Post*, 5 January.

Gerster, Jane 2019a, 'Why New Zealand's Jacinda Ardern has the world's attention', *Global News*, 23 March.

Gerster, Jane 2019b, 'Affordable housing: Would copying New Zealand's foreign buyers ban help?', *Global News*, 20 April.

Globe and Mail 2020, 'Ardern leads Labour to landslide N.Z. election victory after successful COVID-19 strategy', 17 October (Reuters).

Google 2020, 'Compare New Zealand election, Jacinda Ardern'; 'Compare Judith Collins, Jacinda Ardern'; 'Compare Todd Muller, Jacinda Ardern'; 'Compare Simon Bridges, Jacinda Ardern'; 'New Zealand election' ('geographic focus: Canada'), *Google Trends Canada*, retrieved 7 December.

Gurney, Matt 2019, 'New Zealand is not showing Canada the way on gun control', *Maclean's*, 1 April.

Harnett, Cindy and Andrew Duffy 2020, 'Greens hang onto three seats, but "time in the sun" over', *Times Colonist*, 24 October.

Hennig, Clare 2018, 'New Zealand minister defends foreign ownership ban as B.C. Greens call for similar policy', *CBC News*, 14 January.

Hutchings, Bob 2019, 'Should Canada ban non-residents from buying homes?', *Toronto Star*, 10 December.

Joseph, Rebecca 2018, 'New Zealand PM makes history with "first baby" at UN General Assembly', *Global News*, 25 September.

Levitz, Stephanie and Joan Bryden 2020, 'Throne speech appears poised to pass vote after COVID-19 benefits boost', *The Canadian Press*, 24 September.

Marshall, James 2020, 'Could Green leader Sonia Furstenau be to B.C. what Jacinda Ardern is to New Zealand?', *Georgia Straight* (Vancouver), 23 October.

Martin, Jesse 2020, 'Canadian Electoral Reform: We know it's needed, but what should it look like?', *Global Conversations* (University of Toronto, Munk School of Global Affairs and Public Policy), 10 March.

Moloney, Anastasia and Nita Bhalla 2020, 'Which countries shatter glass ceilings with gender-balanced cabinets?', *National Post*, 24 November (Reuters).

National Post 2020, '"Crusher" Collins pulls no punches in bid to oust New Zealand's Ardern', 24 July (Reuters).

O'Sullivan, Dominic 2019, 'What Canada can learn from New Zealand on electoral reform', *The Conversation: Canada edition*, 29 October.

Packham, Colin 2020a, 'New Zealand approves euthanasia, set to reject recreational marijuana', *National Post*, 30 October (Reuters).

Packham, Colin 2020b, 'New Zealand approves euthanasia, set to reject recreational marijuana', *The Guardian P.E.I.*, 30 October (Reuters).

Perry, Nick 2020a, 'New Zealand votes to legalize euthanasia but not marijuana, early results show', *Globe and Mail*, 29 October (Associated Press).

Perry, Nick 2020b, 'New Zealand votes against legalizing cannabis, preliminary results show', *Global News*, 29 October (Associated Press).

Perry, Nick 2020c, 'New Zealand votes to legalize euthanasia but not cannabis', *CTV News*, 29 October (Associated Press).

Perry, Nick 2020d, 'New Zealand's Mahuta brings new outlook to foreign affairs', *CP24*, 26 November (Associated Press); and *Toronto City News*, 26 November.

Perry, Nick 2020e, 'AP Interview: Mahuta hits refresh on New Zealand diplomacy', *Yahoo News Canada*, 26 November (Associated Press).

Renzetti, Elizabeth 2019, 'New Zealand's gun ban shows the way. Will Canada be as bold?', *Globe and Mail*, 22 March.

Sanders, Linley 2017, 'Who is Jacinda Ardern? The new "Trudeau-like" leader of New Zealand', *Yahoo Finance (Canada)*, 24 October (Newsweek).

Tencer, Daniel 2018, 'Ban foreign homebuyers from Canada? Be careful what you wish for', *The Huffington Post*, 18 August.

The Chronicle Herald 2020, 'NZ opposition names new leader two months before general election', 15 July (Reuters).

Titleman Colla, Naomi 2020, 'We need female leadership in this time of crisis – handle with care', *Globe and Mail*, 8 June.

Toller, Carol 2019, 'Jacinda Ardern is the leader the world needs right now', *Globe and Mail*, 22 March.

Toronto Sun 2020, 'New Zealand's Jacinda Ardern wins "historic" re-election for crushing COVID-19', 17 October (Reuters).

Villeneuve, Jean-Francois 2020, 'Une ministre des Affaires étrangères maorie pour la Nouvelle-Zélande', *Ici Radio-Canada*, 3 November.

Williams, Melissa 2016, 'There can be no electoral reform without indigenous input', *Globe and Mail*, 8 November.

Withers, Tracy 2017, 'Generational shift: Like Canada, New Zealand chooses a young leader after years of conservative rule', *National Post*, 19 October (Bloomberg News).

8. The 2020 New Zealand election – the view from Australia

Baker, Michael G., Nick Wilson and Andrew Anglemyer 2020, 'Successful elimination of Covid-19 transmission in New Zealand', *The New England Journal of Medicine*, vol. 383, issue 8.

Brockett, Matthew and Ainsley Thomson 2020, 'Ardern's landslide victory shows power of inclusive leadership', *Bloomberg*, 18 October.

Edwards, Bryce 2020, 'Ardern has shone in the coronavirus crisis but a recession could still doom her re-election chances', *The Guardian*, 19 March.

Grattan, Michelle 2020, 'Grattan on Friday: Premiers facing elections play hardball with hard borders', *The Conversation*, 3 September.

Koslowski, Max 2020, '"A lot of work" before there's a trans-Tasman bubble, Ardern says', *Sydney Morning Herald*, 5 May.

New Zealand Herald 2019, 'Jacinda Ardern for Aussie PM? Kiwi leader ranked Australia's most trusted politician', 10 May.

Remeikis, Amy 2020, 'Jacinda Ardern lashes Scott Morrison for "testing" friendship over deportations to New Zealand', *The Guardian*, 28 February.

Sternlicht, Alexandra 2020, 'How New Zealand "eliminated" Coronavirus', *Forbes*, 8 June.

Tavan, Gwenda 2019, 'Issues that swung elections: Tampa and the national security election of 2001', *The Conversation*, 3 May.

Tingle, Laura 2020, 'The High Road: What Australia can learn from New Zealand', *Quarterly Essay*, November.

Walter, James 2020, 'Scott Morrison's biggest failure in the bushfire crisis: An inability to deliver collective action', *The Conversation*, 8 January.

9. 'And the winner is . . . New Zealand': The view from the UK

AP 2020, 'Jacinda Ardern will introduce tax hikes for the richest Kiwis to help pay off coronavirus debt if she wins New Zealand's election', *Mail Online*, 9 September.

Bale, Tim 2018, 'The New Zealand election – the view from the UK' in Stephen Levine (ed.), *Stardust and Substance: The New Zealand General Election of 2017*, Victoria University Press, Wellington, pp. 99–104.

BBC 2020a, 'NZ election: The people left behind in Ardern's "kind" New Zealand', 13 October.

BBC 2020b, 'Former refugee becomes New Zealand's first African MP', 19 October.

BBC 2020c, 'New Zealand appoints first female foreign minister of Maori origin', 5 November.

Braunias, Steve 2020, 'New Zealanders have recognised the good luck that Jacinda Ardern is ours', *Guardian*, 17 October 2020.

Burden, Lizzy 2020, 'New Zealand suffers worst slump since Thirties', *Telegraph*, 18 September.

Carter, Hana 2020, 'Leader in love: Who is Jacinda Ardern's partner Clarke Gayford?', *Sun*, 17 October.

Farrer, Martin 2020a, 'New Zealand's Covid-19 response the best in the world, say global business leaders', *The Guardian*, 8 October.

Farrer, Martin 2020b, 'New Zealand election: the party leaders, in their own words', *The Guardian*, 16 October.

Graham-McLay, Charlotte 2020a, 'Gone to pot: New Zealand cools on legalising cannabis', *The Guardian*, 1 October.

Graham-McLay, Charlotte 2020b, 'Judith Collins: New Zealand's "anti-Ardern" whose hero is Thatcher', *The Guardian*, 14 October.

Graham-McLay, Charlotte 2020c, 'Report card: Jacinda Ardern's government graded on the past three years', *The Guardian*, 12 October.

Graham-McLay, Charlotte 2020d, 'Kingmaker no more: Winston Peters consigned to NZ political history', *The Guardian*, 17 October.

Gregory, Andy 2020, 'One million lives lost: How have key nations fared during the coronavirus pandemic?' *Independent*, 29 September.

Hunt, Elle 2020, 'NZ election weekly briefing: policy on the run, a woke debate, voting begins', *The Guardian*, 8 October.

Langan, Bernard 2020, 'Ardern's landslide brings gay MPs to the fore', *Times*, 19 October.

Marshall, Jonathan 2020, 'More popular abroad than in New Zealand but Jacinda Ardern is set for an emphatic general election victory', *Independent*, 14 October.

McLachlan, Leigh-Marama 2020a, 'Ardern's promise to make Māori new year a public holiday is long overdue', *The Guardian*, 8 September.

McLachlan, Leigh-Marama 2020b, 'The Māori Party defied the odds because Labour has left Indigenous voters wanting', *The Guardian*, 19 October.

Nokise, James 2020, 'The New Zealand election, like watching a political fight through the Calm app', *The Guardian*, 7 October 2020.

O'Grady, Sean 2020a, 'Jacinda Ardern: A beacon of hope in our tumultuous times', *Independent*, 17 October.

O'Grady, Sean 2020b, 'Starmer can learn from Ardern's positive platform', *Independent*, 20 October.

Perry, Nick 2020, 'Ardern promises public holiday to mark Māori new year', *Independent*, 8 September.

Richards, Xander 2020, 'Jacinda Ardern's tweets mocking Boris Johnson resurface after election victory', *The National*, 17 October.

Roach, April 2020, 'Is Jacinda Ardern going to win the New Zealand election?', *Evening Standard*, 14 October.

Roy, Eleanor Ainge 2020a, 'New Zealand election debate: Collins edges it against "passionless" Ardern', *The Guardian*, 22 September.

Roy, Eleanor Ainge 2020b, 'Jacinda Ardern admits cannabis use in heated New Zealand debate', *The Guardian*, 30 September.

Roy, Eleanor Ainge 2020c, 'Danger lurks for Ardern even as her star power dominates New Zealand election', *The Guardian*, 9 October.

Stewart, Ashleigh 2020, 'Jacinda Ardern needs to be more than kind in her next term as New Zealand prime minister', *Independent*, 17 October.

Stickings, Tim 2020, '"We've got someone who was educated in America": New Zealand's Deputy PM brutally ridicules Covid-19 denier then tells him – "Sorry sunshine, wrong place"', *Mail Online*, 14 October.

Taylor, Phil 2020, '"We made history": New Zealand Greens on the rise after voters return to the fold', *The Guardian*, 18 October.

Van Veen, Josh 2020, 'Jacinda Ardern's majority may prove to be her biggest challenge', BBC, 17 October.

10. Jacinda Ardern's election – a European perspective

Abel, Sissi 2020, 'Jacinda Ardern, Neuseelands Mutter Teresa', *Badische Zeitung*, 14 October.

affaritaliani.it 2020, 'Elezioni Nuova Zelanda, Ardern verso il trionfo dopo il successo sul Covid', 14 October.

Barkhausen, Barbara 2020a, 'Der Hass der Neuseeländer auf ihre Premierministerin', *Die Welt*, 12 January.

Barkhausen, Barbara 2020b, 'Lächeln gegen die Krisen', *Neues Deutschland*, 15 October.

Blank, Esther 2020a, 'Bejubelt in der Welt, in Neuseeland kritisiert – die Bilanz von Jacinda Ardern', *Neue Zürcher Zeitung*, 15 October.

Blank, Esther 2020b, 'Wie Jacinda Ardern die politische Kultur Neuseelands verändert', *Neue Zürcher Zeitung*, 21 October.

Borchert, Thomas 2020, 'Friedensnobelpreis 2020 für Greta Thunberg oder Jacinda Ardern: Frauen haben gute Chancen', *Frankfurter Rundschau*, 8 October.

Bröning, Michael 2020, 'Mitte zum Zweck', *Die Zeit*, 16 October.

Campenhout, Charlotte van 2020, 'De vrouw die de Jacinda-mania hoopt Klein te krijgen', *De Standaard*, 14 October.

Delbeke, Korneel 2020, 'Heilige Jacinda halt absolute meerderheid', *De Standaard*, 19 October.

Deutsche Welle 2020, 'Jacinda Ardern steuert auf absolute Mehrheit zu', 17 October.

Fähnders, Till 2020a, 'Ein Erdrutschsieg dank harter Corona Politik', *Frankfurter Allgemeine Zeitung*, 17 October.

Fähnders, Till 2020b, 'Jung, modern und prinzipienfest', *Frankfurter Allgemeine Zeitung*, 18 October.

Friedrich Ebert Stiftung 2021, 'Beteiligung sozialdemokratischer und sozialistischer Parteien an der Regierung in Europa'.

Gorawantschy, Beatrice and Eva Wagner 2020, 'Neuseeland vor den Parlamentswahlen – Wahlkampf in Zeiten der Pandemie', Konrad Adenauer Stiftung, 21 July.

Hansen, Sven 2020, 'Die Anti-Mackerin', *taz*, 18 October.

Hasel, Verena Friederike 2018, 'Staatschefin, Djane, Mutter', *Die Zeit*, 28 July.

Haselsteiner, Felix 2020, 'Klarer Sieg für Premierministerin Jacinda Ardern', *Süddeutsche Zeitung*, 17 October.

Hassenkamp, Milena 2020, 'Ardern gibt nach Trump-Attacken wegen Corona-Fällen Kontra', *Spiegel* online, 18 August.

Hein, Christoph 2020, 'Jetzt muss Ardern die Wirtschaft retten', *Frankfurter Allgemeine Zeitung*, 18 October.

Il Fatto Quotidiano 2020, 'Elezioni Nuova Zelanda, trionfo la premier Jacinda Ardern. I successi dalla pandemia alle stretts sulle armi', 18 October.

Il Post 2020, 'Jacinda Ardern ha vinto le elezioni in Nuova Zelanda', 17 October.

Le Figaro 2020, 'Nouvelle-Zélande: Ardern qualifie de «fausse» la déclaration de Trump sur le virus', 18 August.

Le Monde 2020, 'Nouvelle-Zélande: victoire écrasante de la premiére ministre Jacinda Ardern et des travaillisters lors des législatives', 17 October.

Le Parisien 2020, 'Nouvelle-Zélande: triomphe électoral de Jacinda Ardern', 17 October.

Merkur 2020, 'Jacinda Ardern und ihr "Fünf-Millionen-Team"', 15 October.

Plesse, Gregory 2020, 'Jacinda Ardern, favorite des élections en Nouvelle-Zélande', *Le Figaro*, 16 October.

Radio Erft 2020, 'Jacinda Ardern und ihr 5 Millionen Team', 15 October.

Ratzow, Sandra 2020, 'Die Kümmerin muss liefern', *Die Tagesschau*, 17 October.

Richter, Anke 2020a, 'Sanfte Worte, harte Maßnahmen', *Die Zeit*, 20 April.

Richter, Anke 2020b, 'Neuseelands Überfliegerin', *Der Freitag*, 4 June.

rtlnieuws 2020, 'Premier Nieuw-Zeeland boekt monsterzege na succesvolle aanpak coronavirus', 17 October.

Sanches, Miguel 2020, 'Neuseeland: Historischer Wahlsieg für Jacinda Ardern', *Berliner Morgenpost*, 17 October.

Senzel, Holger 2020, 'Historischer Wahlsieg für Ardern', *tagesschau.de*, 17 October.

Spiegel online 2020, 'Ein TV-Duell mit Anstand', 1 October.

Visser, Jeroen 2020, 'Jacinda Ardern behaalt monsterzege in Nieuw-Zeeland', *de Volkskrant*, 17 October.

von Rohr, Mathiew 2020, 'In Europa geht Corona jetzt erst richtig los', *Der Spiegel*, 19 October.

Wälterlin, Urs 2020a, 'Die Kommunikatorin', *taz*, 30 May.

Wälterlin, Urs, 2020b, 'Jacinda Ardern steuert mit Empathie und harten Maßnahmen auf Wahlsieg zu', *Der Standard*, 16 October.

Wälterlin, Urs 2020c, 'Historischer Erfolg für Ardern', *taz*, 17 October.

Wälterlin, Urs 2020d, 'Ardern will Koalition mit den Grünen', *taz*, 18 October.

Warlimont, Guido 2020, 'Umfragewerte: Regierungen mit strikten Corona-Maßnahmen sind die Krisen-Gewinner', Institut für Weltwirtschaft, 7 September.

Wichert, Silke 2020, 'Die Macht eines ausgewaschenen Sweatshirts', *Süddeutsche Zeitung*, 27 May.

11. A faraway but close relationship – the view from Chile

Apud, Beatriz 2020, Teletrece, Chilean newscast on *Canal 13*, 30 June.
Briones, Ignacio 2020, *ADN Radio*, 23 October.
Caldera, María Betania 2020, 'The two women vying for the government of New Zealand', *El Mercurio*, 16 October.
El Desconcierto 2020, 2 November.
Iglesias, Juan Paulo 2020, 'Christopher Finlayson, former negotiator with the Māori in New Zealand: "In my experience, there is nothing better than forgiveness"', *La Tercera*, 15 August.
Jofré, Valentina 2020, 'Jacinda: Why does everyone love the Prime Minister of New Zealand', *La Tercera*, 20 June.
Plaza Pública 2020, 'Encuesta Plaza Pública: Tercera semana de Septiembre-Estudio N°349', *Cadem*, 21 September.
Villagrán, Juan Manuel 2020, 'Nicolás Ibáñez: Chile has to move towards being a developed country, with a high level of inclusion and social cohesion, like New Zealand', Pulso in *La Tercera*, 17 December.

12. Covering the 2020 election: Platforms and the plague

Bridges, Simon 2020, 'The decision for New Zealand to stay locked down in Level 4 shows the Government hasn't done the groundwork . . .', Facebook, 20 April.
Bretkelly, Sharon 2020, 'The 1pm news scramble', *Newsroom*, 15 September, https://www.newsroom.co.nz/podcast-the-detail/the-1pm-news-scramble.
Burrows, Matt 2020, 'NZ Election 2020: Overweight Kiwi calls out Judith Collins over "bullshit" remarks on obesity in viral post', *Newshub*, 15 October.
Colmar Brunton 2020a, '*1 News* Colmar Brunton Poll 8–12 February 2020', 13 February.
Colmar Brunton 2020b, '*1 News* Colmar Brunton Poll 28 November–2 December 2020', 7 December.
Cooke, Henry 2020a, 'National MPs are twisting Jacinda Ardern's words on social media', *Stuff*, September.
Cooke, Henry 2020b, 'Election 2020: Judith Collins tries to make wealth tax an issue, asking voters to trust her more than Jacinda Ardern', *Stuff*, 11 October.
Cooke, Henry 2020c, 'Election 2020: Judith Collins says she almost rejected National leadership, says fiscal hole and leaks ruined party's chances', *Stuff*, 9 December.
Cooke, Henry and Thomas Coughlan 2020, 'Simon Bridges, the scrapper who couldn't stop scrapping', *Stuff*, 25 May.
Donnell, Hayden 2020, 'Coronavirus: The top 10 Covid-19 briefings of 2020', *Stuff*, 17 November.

Electoral Commission 2020, '2020 General Election official results', 6 November.

Ensor, Jamie 2020, 'NZ Election 2020: Advance voting expected to blast past Electoral Commission target', *Newshub*, 13 October.

Friedman, Uri 2020, 'New Zealand's prime minister may be the most effective leader on the planet', *Atlantic*, 20 April.

Hancock, Farah 2020, 'Election 2020: $200k spent on online ads in one week', *Newsroom*, 1 October.

Harman, Richard 2020, 'National gets desperate', *Politik*, 12 October.

Lowy Institute 2021, 'Covid Performance Index', 9 January.

Malpass, Luke 2020, 'Popularity won't solve Ardern's Winston problem', *Australian Financial Review*, 22 February.

Manch, Thomas 2020, 'Election 2020: A terrible day on the campaign trail for Judith Collins', *Stuff*, 7 October.

McGuire, David et al. 2020, 'Beating the virus: an examination of the crisis communication approach taken by New Zealand Prime Minister Jacinda Ardern during the Covid-19 pandemic', *Human Resource Development International*, vol. 23, no. 4, pp. 361–379.

McKay, Ben 2020, 'Labour on track with final NZ poll', *The West Australian*, 15 October.

Moir, Jo 2020, 'How the Hamish Walker Covid-19 patient detail leak played out', Radio New Zealand, 8 July.

New Zealand Labour (@nzlabour) 2020, 'We've recently seen how vital a strong, well-funded health system is . . .', Twitter, 29 September, 1.30pm.

New Zealand National Party 2020a, 'National rules out working with NZ First', *Scoop*, 2 February.

New Zealand National Party 2020b, 'Groundwork not done to lift lockdown', *Scoop*, 20 April.

New Zealand National Party 2020c, '#LIVE Judith Collins announces economic development policy', Facebook, 6 October.

Newstalk ZB 2020, 'Judith Collins on obesity, Greens' wealth tax and unfair media coverage', 15 October.

Nielsen 2020, 'Nielsen TAM, consolidated data, AP5+, period: 12 March–5 October', 3 November, personal correspondence.

O'Brien, Tova 2020, 'National and Labour neck-and-neck in new Newshub-Reid Research poll', *Newshub*, 9 February.

Oliver, Henry 2020, 'Tova O'Brien is ready for anything', *Metro*, 16 February.

Perlstein, Rick 2020, *Reaganland: America's Right Turn 1976–1980*, Simon and Schuster, New York.

Pullar-Strecker, Tom 2020, 'What 100% renewable energy does to power prices', *Stuff*, September.

Radio New Zealand 2020, 'Wealth tax not a bottom line for Green Party but they will push for it – Shaw', 24 September.

Radio New Zealand 2021, 'Unemployment fell to 4.9% in December quarter', 3 February.

Small, Zane 2020, 'National leader Simon Bridges stands by divisive Facebook post that sparked leadership concerns', *Newshub*, 28 April.

Stuff 2020, 'The Whole Truth', https://interactives.stuff.co.nz/2020/08/election-2020-the-whole-truth/#/.

TVNZ 2020, Tweet about 1 pm coverage, 30 March.

Walls, Jason 2020, 'Covid-19 coronavirus: Inside NZ's favourite reality TV show – the 1 pm press conference', *New Zealand Herald*, 23 April.

Whyte, Anna 2020, '"Why can't we do what Australia's done?" – Bridges says look across Tasman for Covid-19 response', *1 News*, 20 April.

14. A tale of two campaigns – Covid vs chaos: Mainstream media coverage of the lead-up to election 2020

American National Election Study 2016, http://www.electionstudies.org/.

Australian Election Study 2016, http://australianelectionstudy.org/voter_studies.html.

Boyd, Mark 2019, 'Downward spiral? Television news coverage of New Zealand election campaigns 1993–2017', PhD Thesis, University of Auckland.

Boyd, Mark 2020, 'Jacinda Ardern and Judith Collins . . . vs Gower and Campbell', *Sunday Star-Times*, 4 October.

Boyd, Mark and Babak Bahador 2015, 'Media coverage of New Zealand's 2014 election campaign', *Political Science*, vol. 67, no. 2, pp. 143–160.

British Election Study 2017, http://www.britishelectionstudy.com/.

Campbell, Andrew 2020, Prime Minister's Chief Press Secretary (Labour), 'Zoom' interview with Mark Boyd, 22 December.

Carson, Andrea and Brian McNair 2018, 'Still the main source: The established media' in Anika Gauja, Peter Chen, Jennifer Curtin and Juliet Pietsch (eds.), *Double Disillusion: The 2016 Australian Federal Election*, ANU Press, Canberra, pp. 421–452.

Cooke, Henry 2020, 'Election 2020: Judith Collins slams Jacinda Ardern for lack of election policy', *Stuff*, 4 August.

Crotty, William 2018, 'Not an ordinary election', in William Crotty (ed.), *Winning the Presidency 2016*, Routledge, New York, pp. 1–33.

Dillane, Tom 2020, 'TVNZ increase ratings dominance of MediaWorks during lockdown', *New Zealand Herald*, 30 August.

Electoral Commission 2020, '2020 General Election official results', https://elections.nz/media-and-news/2020/2020-general-election-official-results/.

Malpass, Luke 2020, Political Editor, *Stuff*, 'Zoom' interview with Mark Boyd, 21 December.

Miller, Raymond 2014, *Democracy in New Zealand*, Auckland University Press, Auckland.

Mutch McKay, Jessica 2020, Political Editor, *1 News* (TVNZ), 'Zoom' interview with Mark Boyd, 4 December.

New Zealand Election Study 2011–2017, http://www.nzes.org/.

Norris, Pippa et al. 1999, *On Message: Communicating the Campaign*, SAGE, London.

O'Brien, Tova 2021, Political Editor, *Newshub* (TV3), 'Zoom' interview with Mark Boyd, 19 February.

O'Sullivan, Phil 2020, Editor of Newsgathering, *1 News* (TVNZ), 'Zoom' interview with Mark Boyd, 2 December.

Rowe, David 2020, Election Editor, New Zealand Media and Entertainment (NZME), 'Zoom' interview with Mark Boyd, 3 December.

Roy Morgan 2020, 'Readership in New Zealand, 12 months to June 2020', http://www.roymorgan.com/industries/media/readership/readership-new-zealand.

Sharp, Sarah 2004, 'Newspapers', in Janine Hayward and Chris Rudd (eds.), *Political Communications in New Zealand*, Pearson, Auckland, pp. 108–121.

Symons, Todd 2020, Bulletins Editor, *Newshub* (TV3), 'Zoom' interview with Mark Boyd, 3 December.

Trevett, Claire 2020, Senior Writer, *New Zealand Herald* (NZME), 'Zoom' interview with Mark Boyd, 21 December.

Walls, Jason 2020, 'Prime Minister Jacinda Ardern warns voters not to expect big Labour Party policies this election', *New Zealand Herald*, 3 August.

Wilson, Janet 2020, Chief Press Secretary, National, 'Zoom' interview with Mark Boyd, 3 December.

15. Social media, online politics and the 2020 election

Barker, Liz 2004, 'Party websites', in Janine Hayward and Chris Rudd (eds.), *Political Communications in New Zealand*, Pearson, Auckland, pp. 74–91.

Beveridge, Matthew 2015, 'Social media in the 2014 general election', in Jon Johansson and Stephen Levine (eds.), *Moments of Truth: The New Zealand General Election of 2014*, Victoria University Press, Wellington, pp. 287–299.

Chen, Peter John 2009, 'Online media', in Chris Rudd, Janine Hayward and Craig Geoffrey (eds.), *Informing Voters? Politics, Media, and the New Zealand Election 2008*, Pearson, Auckland, pp. 119–141.

de Ronde, Edwin 2010, 'Digital campaigning', in Raymond Miller (ed.), *New Zealand Government & Politics* (5th edn.), Oxford University Press, Victoria, Australia, pp. 312–325.

Election 2020, 'Facebook removes Advance NZ page for repeatedly sharing misinformation', *Stuff*, 15 October.

Fitzjohn, Peter and Rob Salmond 2007, 'The battle of the blog: A phony war?', in Stephen Levine and Nigel S. Roberts (eds.), *The Baubles of Office: The New Zealand General Election of 2005*, Victoria University Press, Wellington, pp. 249–268.

Gender Justice Collective 2020, *Scorecard: Election 2020*, https://www.genderjustice.nz/scorecard_election_2020.

Goode, Luke 2010, 'New media and democracy', in Raymond Miller (ed.), *New Zealand Government & Politics* (5th edn.), Oxford University Press, Victoria, Australia, pp. 431–443.

Hopkins, Kane and Donald Matheson 2005, 'Blogging the New Zealand election: The impact of new media practices on the old game', *Political Science*, vol. 57, no. 2, pp. 93–105.

Kean, Nicola 2010, '2008: The campaign in cyberspace', in Stephen Levine and Nigel S. Roberts (eds.), *Key to Victory: The New Zealand General Election of 2008*, Victoria University Press, Wellington, pp. 192–205.

Kreiss, Daniel, Regina Lawrence and Shannon McGregor 2018, 'In their own words: Political practitioner accounts of candidates, audiences, affordances, genres, and timing in strategic social media use', *Political Communication*, vol. 35, no. 1, pp. 8–31.

Lips, Miriam and Hugo Gong 2009, *The Use of New Media by Political Parties in the 2008 National Election*, Victoria University of Wellington, Wellington.

Murchison, Ashley 2015, 'Changing communications? Political parties and Web 2.0 in the 2011 New Zealand general election', in Guy Lachapelle and Philippe Maarek (eds.), *Political Parties in the Digital Age*, De Gruyter, Berlin, pp. 93–110.

Murchison, Ashley and Anthony Deos 2012, 'What's on their mind? Political parties and Facebook in the 2011 New Zealand general election', in Jon Johansson and Stephen Levine (eds.), *Kicking The Tyres: The New Zealand General Election and Electoral Referendum of 2011*, Victoria University Press, Wellington, pp. 234–246.

Pedersen, Karina 2005, 'New Zealand parties in cyberspace', *Political Science*, vol. 57, no. 2, pp. 107–116.

Pedersen, Karina 2007, 'Electioneering in cyberspace', in Stephen Levine and Nigel S. Roberts (eds.), *The Baubles of Office: The New Zealand General Election of 2005*, Victoria University Press, Wellington, pp. 236–248.

Roper, Juliet 1998, 'New Zealand political parties online: The World Wide Web as a tool for democratization or for political marketing?', in Chris Toulouse and Timothy Luke (eds.), *The Politics of Cyberspace: A New Political Science Reader*, Routledge, London, pp. 69–83.

Ross, Karen and Tobias Burger 2014, 'Face to Face(book): Social media, political campaigning and the unbearable lightness of being there', *Political Science*, vol. 66, no. 1, pp. 46–62.

Ross, Karen, Susan Fountaine and Margie Comrie 2015, 'Facing up to Facebook: politicians, publics and the social media(ted) turn in New Zealand', *Media, Culture & Society*, vol. 37, no. 2, pp. 251–269.

Salmond, Rob 2010, '2008: The YouTube campaign', in Stephen Levine and Nigel S. Roberts (eds.), *Key to Victory: The New Zealand General Election of 2008*, Victoria University Press, Wellington, pp. 206–221.

Shaw, Richard 2009, 'Politics and the internet: The New Zealand research', *Political Science*, vol. 61, no. 2, pp. 5–19.

Victoria University of Wellington 2020a, 'Election 2020: Key social media trends', New Zealand Social Media Study, https://www.wgtn.ac.nz/research/strengths/election.

Victoria University of Wellington 2020b, 'Election 2020: "New Zealanders deserve a positive election," said PM Jacinda Ardern. But are they getting it?', https://www.wgtn.ac.nz/research/strengths/election/Are-New-Zealanders-getting-a-positive-election.

Vowles, Jack 2020, 'Some in the media need to calm down', *Newsroom*, 23 June.

16. 'Getting closer to the truth': The 2020 election cartoons as commentary, protest and critique

Baudrillard, Jean 2003, *The Spirit of Terrorism*, Verso, London/New York.

Chumko, Andre 2020, 'Dr Ashley Bloomfield meets his likeness at Wellington store', *Stuff*, 13 June.

Grant, Ian F. 1987, *The Unauthorized Version: A Cartoon History of New Zealand*, Cassell New Zealand, Auckland.

Grimshaw, Mike 2019, *Bishops, Boozers, Brethren & Burkas: A Cartoon History of Religion in New Zealand*, New Zealand Cartoon Archive, Wellington.

Lamb, Chris 2004, *Drawn to Extremes: The Use and Abuse of Editorial Cartoons*, Columbia University Press, New York.

Molyneux, Vita 2020, 'Advance NZ under fire for altering political cartoonist's work without permission', *Newshub*, 2 October.

O'Brien, Tova 2020, 'Health Minister David Clark brutally throws Dr Ashley Bloomfield under the bus while standing right next to him', *Newshub*, 24 June.

Radio New Zealand 2020, 'New political poll shows National scraping into power and NZ First out of Parliament', 13 February.

TVNZ News 2020, 'Dr Ashley Bloomfield portrayed as "Saint Ashley" in Wellington storefront display', 11 June.

17. The 2020 election, the Covid-19 emergency, and the need to improve our response capacity for even more serious threats

Aylward, Bruce and Wannian Liang 2020, 'Report of the WHO-China joint mission on coronavirus disease 2019 (COVID-19)', *WHO-China Joint Mission on Coronavirus Disease 2019*, World Health Organization, 28 February.

Baker, Michael G., Amanda Kvalsvig and Ayesha J. Verrall 2020, 'New Zealand's COVID-19 elimination strategy', *Med J Aust*, 13 August.

Baker, Michael G., Amanda Kvalsvig, Ayesha J. Verrall, Lucy Telfar Barnard and Nick Wilson 2020, 'New Zealand's elimination strategy for the COVID-19 pandemic and what is required to make it work', *New Zealand Medical Journal*, vol. 133, no. 1512, pp. 10–14.

Baker, Michael G., Amanda Kvalsvig and Nick Wilson 2020a, '6 months after New Zealand's first COVID-19 case, it's time for a more strategic approach', *The Conversation*.

Baker, Michael G., Amanda Kvaslvig and Nick Wilson 2020b, 'A year on from the arrival of COVID-19 in NZ: 5 lessons for 2021 and beyond', *The Conversation*.

Baker, Michael G., Nick Wilson and Andrew Anglemyer 2020, 'Successful elimination of Covid-19 transmission in New Zealand', *New England Journal of Medicine*, vol. 383, e56.

Baker, Michael G., Nick Wilson and Tony Blakely 2020, 'Elimination could be the optimal response strategy for covid-19 and other emerging pandemic diseases', *BMJ*, vol. 371, m4907.

Boyd, Matt, Michael G. Baker and Nick Wilson 2020, 'Border closure for island nations? Analysis of pandemic and bioweapon-related threats suggests some scenarios warrant drastic action', *Australian and New Zealand Journal of Public Health*, vol. 44, no. 2, pp. 89–91.

Carlton, Lauren H. et al. 2021, 'Charting elimination in the pandemic: A SARS-CoV-2 serosurvey of blood donors in New Zealand', *medRxiv*, 1 April.

Cowling, Benjamin J. et al. 2020, 'Impact assessment of non-pharmaceutical interventions against coronavirus disease 2019 and influenza in Hong Kong: an observational study', *The Lancet Public Health*, vol. 5, no. 5, E279–E288.

Every-Palmer, Susanna et al. 2020, 'Psychological distress, anxiety, family violence, suicidality, and wellbeing in New Zealand during the COVID-19 lockdown: A cross-sectional study', *PLoS One*, vol. 15, no. 11, e0241658.

Geoghegan, Jemma L. et al. 2020, 'Genomic epidemiology reveals transmission patterns and dynamics of SARS-CoV-2 in Aotearoa New Zealand', *Nature Communications*, vol. 11, no. 6351, pp. 1–7.

Huang, Sue et al. 2021, 'Impact of the COVID-19 nonpharmaceutical interventions on influenza and other respiratory viral infections in New Zealand', *Nature Communications*, vol. 12, no. 1001, 12 February.

Jefferies, Sarah et al. 2020, 'COVID-19 in New Zealand and the impact of the national response: a descriptive epidemiological study', *Lancet Public Health*, vol. 5, no. 11, e612–e623.

Jenkins, Matthew et al. 2021, 'Silver linings of the COVID-19 lockdown in New Zealand', *PLoS One*, vol. 16, no. 4, e0249678.

Kang, JaHyun et al. 2020, 'South Korea's reponses to stop the COVID-19 pandemic', *American Journal of Infection Control*, vol. 48, no. 9, pp. 1080–1086.

Kvalsvig, Amanda and Michael G. Baker 2021, 'How Aotearoa New Zealand rapidly revised its Covid-19 response strategy: lessons for the next pandemic plan', *Journal of the Royal Society of New Zealand*, vol. 51, pp. S143–S166.

Lu, Ning et al. 2020, 'Weathering COVID-19 storm: successful control measures of five Asian countries', *American Journal of Infection Control*, vol. 48, no. 7, pp. 851–852.

Ministry of Health 2017, 'New Zealand Influenza Pandemic Plan: A framework for action' (2nd edn.), Ministry of Health, Wellington.

New Zealand Government 2021, 'Our health and disability system. Building a stronger health and disability system that delivers for all New Zealanders', Department of Prime Minister and Cabinet, Wellington, April.

Scoop 2021, 'The Independent Panel calls for urgent reform of pandemic preventing and response systems', 13 May [press release, Geneva, Independent Panel for Pandemic Preparedness and Response].

Summers, Jennifer A. et al. 2020, 'Potential lessons from the Taiwan and New Zealand health responses to the COVID-19 pandemic', *Lancet Regional Health – Western Pacific*, vol. 4, no. 100044.

Wang, C. Jason, Chun Y. Ng and Robert H. Brook 2020, 'Response to COVID-19 in Taiwan: Big data analytics, new technology, and proactive testing', *Jama*, vol. 323, no. 14, pp. 1341–1342.

WHO-China Joint Mission 2020, 'Report of the WHO-China Joint Mission on Coronavirus Disease 2019 (COVID-19)', 16–24 February, https://www.who.int/docs/default-source/coronaviruse/who-china-joint-mission-on-covid-19-final-report.pdf.

Wilson, Nick, Lucy Telfar Barnard, Amanda Kvalsvig and Michael G. Baker 2020, 'Potential Health Impacts from the COVID-19 Pandemic for New Zealand if Eradication Fails: Report to the NZ Ministry of Health', Ministry of Health, Wellington, 23 March.

Wilson, Nick, Lucy Telfar Barnard, Jennifer A. Summers, G. Dennis Shanks and Michael G. Baker 2012, 'Differential mortality by ethnicity in three influenza pandemics over a century', *Emerging Infectious Diseases*, vol. 18, no. 1, pp. 71–77.

World Health Organization 2008, 'International health regulations (2005)', World Health Organization.

Wu, Joseph T., Kathy Leung and Gabriel M. Leung 2020, 'Nowcasting and forecasting the potential domestic and international spread of the 2019-nCoV outbreak originating in Wuhan, China: a modelling study', *Lancet*, vol. 395, no. 10225, pp. 689–697.

18. Well-being and the Covid crunch: The economy and the 2020 election

Chapple, Simon 1996, *Full Employment: Whence It Came and Where It Went*, Research Monograph No. 66, New Zealand Institute of Economic Research, Wellington.

Chapple, Simon 2017, 'Corked wine in a cracked bottle', in Jonathan Boston and Derek Gill (eds.), *Social Investment: A New Zealand Policy Experiment*, Bridget Williams Books, Wellington, pp. 355–379.

Chapple, Simon et al. 2020, 'What people said about life under lockdown', *Policy Quarterly*, vol. 16, no. 3, pp. 53–57.

Condon, Christopher, Joao Lima and Paul Jackson 2018, 'Summers warns the biggest economies are not prepared for another recession', *Bloomberg*, 19 June.

Demographia 2020, '16th Annual Demographia International Housing Affordability Survey: 2020', Urban Reform Institute and the Frontier Center for Public Policy.

Fergusson, David et al. 2015, 'Life satisfaction and mental health problems (18 to 35 years)', *Psychological Medicine*, vol. 45, no. 11, pp. 227–36.

Grimes, Arthur 2019, 'New Zealand's well-being approach to budget is not new, but could shift major issues', *The Conversation*, 6 May.

Habibi, Hana, Kate Prickett, Michael Fletcher and Simon Chapple 2021, 'Work circumstances, job loss, and wellbeing during New Zealand's Covid-19 Alert Level 4 lockdown', *New Zealand Economic Papers*, pp. 1–9.

Jacob, Punnoose and Martin Wong 2018, 'Estimating the NAIRU and the Natural Rate of Unemployment for New Zealand', Reserve Bank of New Zealand, Analytical Note Series AN2018/04 March, Wellington.

Karacaoglu, Girol and Joey Au 2018, 'It's *not just* the economy, stupid . . .', in Stephen Levine (ed.), *Stardust and Substance: The New Zealand General Election of 2017*, Victoria University Press, Wellington, pp. 229–250.

Layard, Richard 2011, *Happiness: Lessons from a New Science*, Penguin, London.

Lewis, William Arthur 1954, 'Economic development with unlimited supplies of labour', *Manchester School*, pp. 139–191.

New Zealand Government 2019, 'Wellbeing Budget 2019', The Beehive, Wellington, 7 May.

Reserve Bank of New Zealand 2021, 'Monetary Policy Statement February 2021', Wellington.

Roy, Eleanor Ainge 2019, 'New Zealand's world-first "wellbeing" budget to focus on poverty and mental health', *The Guardian*, 14 May.

Stiglitz, Joseph, Amartya Sen and Jean-Paul Fitoussi 2009, 'Report by the Commission on the Measurement of Economic Performance and Social Progress', Paris, www.stiglitz-sen-fitoussi.fr/en/index.htm.

Winkelmann, Liliana and Rainer Winkelmann 1998, 'Why are the unemployed so unhappy? Evidence from panel data', *Economica*, vol. 65, no. 257, pp. 1–15.

19. Housing and the Sixth Labour Government

1 News 2020, 'Jacinda Ardern says public bears some responsibility for housing crisis after failed taxation attempts', TVNZ, 30 November.

Adams, Amy 2017, 'Helping more rough sleepers into homes', 31 August, The Beehive, Wellington.

Amore, Kate 2016, 'Severe housing deprivation in Aotearoa/New Zealand: 2001–2013', He Kainga Oranga, the Housing and Health Research Programme, University of Otago.

Amore, Kate et al. 2020, 'Severe housing deprivation in Aotearoa New Zealand, 2018', Ministry of Housing and Urban Development, Wellington.

Baker, Michael G. et al. 2013, 'Infectious diseases attributable to household crowding in New Zealand: A systematic review and burden of disease estimate', He Kainga Oranga, the Housing and Health Research Programme, University of Otago.

Carroll, Melanie 2020, 'Just 4092 Kāinga Ora houses meet Healthy Homes standards ahead of mid-2023 goal', *Stuff*, 15 October.

Cook, Charlotte 2020, 'Woman told rats gnawing through pipes in state house "not a health risk"', *Stuff*, 14 July.

Cooke, Henry 2018, 'Housing Ministry opens with budget millions less than Treasury recommends', *Stuff*, 1 October.

Cooke, Henry 2019a, 'Former KiwiBuild boss Stephen Barclay suing Government over departure, says he was on track to meet first year goal', *Stuff*, 28 January.

Cooke, Henry 2019b, 'How KiwiBuild fell down, and whether anything can be saved from the wreckage', *Stuff*, 21 June.

Cooke, Henry 2019c, 'PM takes housing off Phil Twyford in first major reshuffle', *Stuff*, 27 June.

Cooke, Henry 2019d, 'Public housing waitlist at new high with 12,644 households waiting months for housing', *Stuff*, 30 August.

Cooke, Henry 2019e, 'Public housing waitlist nears 14,000 with record-high', *Stuff*, 1 November.

Cooke, Henry 2020a, 'Public housing waitlist hits new record of 14,496', *Stuff*, 13 January.

Cooke, Henry 2020b, 'Waitlist for public housing hits new record as Coronavirus economic crash bites', *Stuff*, 6 July.

Cooke, Henry 2020c, 'Public housing waitlist cracks 20,000 with over 2000 new households in a single month', *Stuff*, 29 October.

Cooke, Henry 2021, 'Public housing waitlist grows by 1000 in two months to new record high as high rents hit the poor', *Stuff*, 20 January.

Dann, Liam 2019, 'More Kiwis support capital gains tax than oppose in new poll', *New Zealand Herald*, 29 March.

Davison, Isaac 2017, 'Vote 2017: Housing immigration and tax dominate Jacinda Ardern and Bill English leaders' debate', *New Zealand Herald*, 31 August.

Fonseka, Dileepa 2020a, 'State paid $3000 a week for "uninhabitable" houses', *Stuff*, 25 August.

Fonseka, Dileepa 2020b, 'Plan to charge for emergency housing back on', *Stuff*, 22 September.

Hickey, Bernard 2020a, 'Kāinga Ora's borrowing limit lifted by $4b', *Newsroom*, 20 January.

Hickey, Bernard 2020b, 'Our housing market is too big to fail', *Newsroom*, 30 August.

Hindley, David 2020, 'NZ vs Ireland building regs', *Build*, 1 December.

Howden-Chapman, Philippa et al. 2007, 'Effect of insulating existing houses on health inequality: Cluster randomised study in the community', *British Medical Journal*, vol. 334, no. 7591, pp. 460–464.

Howden-Chapman, Philippa et al. 2008, 'Effects of improved home heating on asthma in community dwelling children: Randomised controlled trial', *British Medical Journal*, vol. 337, no. 7674, pp. 852–855.

Interest.co.nz 2017, 'New Zealand's "Housing Crisis" dominates domestic issues as New Zealand heads towards September Election 2017', Roy Morgan Research, 28 February.

Johnsen, Sarah and Beth Watts 2014, 'Homelessness and poverty: Reviewing the links', *European Network for Housing Research*, 6 July.

Johnson, Alan et al., 2018, *A Stocktake of New Zealand's Housing*, New Zealand Government, Wellington.

Johnston, Kirsty 2020, 'Revealed: Who's really buying up New Zealand property', *Newstalk ZB*, 6 January.

Kāinga Ora 2020, 'Managed Kāinga Ora properties by number of bedrooms as at 30 September 2020', Kāinga Ora – Homes and Communities, Wellington.

Labour Party, Green Party and Māori Party 2016, 'Ending homelessness in New Zealand: Final report of the Cross-Party Inquiry on Homelessness', New Zealand Parliament, Wellington, 10 October.

Little, Andrew 2016, 'Inquiry presents solutions to homelessness – Govt must act', *Scoop*, 10 October.

Ministry of Housing and Urban Development 2020a, 'Aotearoa/New Zealand Homelessness Action Plan', 18 May, Wellington.

Ministry of Housing and Urban Development 2020b, 'Housing First', 18 May.

Ministry of Housing and Urban Development 2020c, 'June 2020 Public Housing Monthly Update', Wellington.

Ministry of Housing and Urban Development 2020d, 'June 2020 Public Housing Quarterly Report', Wellington.

Ministry of Housing and Urban Development 2020e, 'Government housing dashboard updated – November 2020', Wellington. November.

Nathan, Kim et al. 2019, 'Residential mobility and socioemotional and behavioural difficulties in a preschool population cohort of New Zealand children', *Journal of Epidemiology and Community Health*, vol. 73, no. 10, pp. 947–953.

Nooe, Roger and David Patterson 2010, 'The ecology of homelessness', *Journal of Human Behavior in the Social Environment*, vol. 20, no. 2, pp. 105–152.

Oliver, Jane R. et al. 2017, 'Acute rheumatic fever and exposure to poor housing conditions in New Zealand: A descriptive study', *Journal of Paediatrics and Child Health*, vol. 53, no. 4, pp. 358–364.

Paterson, Ron et al. 2018, *He Ara Oranga: Report of the Government Inquiry into Mental Health and Addiction*, Wellington.

Radio New Zealand 2020, 'House prices inflate at fastest level in 16 years – CoreLogic', 1 December.

Rangiwhetu, Lara, Nevil Pierse and Philippa Howden-Chapman 2017, 'Effects of minor household interventions to block draughts on social housing temperatures: a before and after study', *Kotuitui*, vol. 12, no. 2, pp. 235–245.

Reddy, Patsy 2017, 'Speech from the Throne', The Beehive, Wellington, 8 November [reprinted in *Stardust and Substance: The New Zealand General Election of 2017*, Appendix 3, pp. 510–522].

Reddy, Patsy 2020, 'Speech from the Throne', The Beehive, Wellington, 26 November.

Robson, Sarah 2020, 'Kāinga Ora unaware of how many state houses meet accessibility standards', *New Zealand Herald*, 16 June.

Satherley, Dean and Owen, Lisa 2017, 'Homelessness proves capitalism is a "blatant failure" – Jacinda Ardern', *Newshub*, 21 October.

Schrader, Ben 2018, 'Crisis? What crisis? An overview of the Fifth National Government's housing policies', in Stephen Levine (ed.), *Stardust and Substance: The New Zealand General Election of 2017*, Victoria University Press, Wellington, pp. 281–294.

Shinn, Marybeth 2010, 'Homelessness, poverty and social exclusion in the United States and Europe', *European Journal of Homelessness*, vol. 4, pp. 19–44.

Shorter, Caroline et al. 2018, 'Indoor visible mould and mould odor are associated with new-onset childhood wheeze in a dose-dependent manner', *Indoor Air*, vol. 28, no. 1, pp. 6–15.

Small, Zane 2020, 'Green MP Julie Anne Genter questions Jacinda Ardern ruling out capital gains tax while she's Prime Minister', *Newshub*, 19 November.

Stuff 2019, 'Motels make millions providing emergency housing', 9 November.

Tenancy Services 2019, 'Healthy Homes Standards announced', 24 February, Wellington.

Tenancy Services 2020, 'Residential Tenancies Amendment Act 2020 now in force', 12 August, Wellington.

Tso, Matthew 2020, 'Ministry stops sending emergency housing clients to three "grotty" Lower Hutt motels', *Stuff*, 31 August.

Twyford, Phil 2018, '$100 million to tackle homelessness', 4 May, New Zealand Government, Wellington.

Twyford, Phil 2019, 'Kāinga Ora to build homes and create thriving communities', New Zealand Government, 19 September.

Welfare Expert Advisory Group 2019, 'Wakamana Tāngata – Restoring dignity to social security in New Zealand', Wellington, 26 February.

Wevers, Maarten 2020, 'Register of pecuniary and other specified interests of Members of Parliament: Summary of annual returns at at 31 January 2020', New Zealand House of Representatives, Wellington.

Woods, Megan 2019, 'Kāinga Ora to deliver world-class public housing', New Zealand Government, 19 September.

20. The Christchurch shooting and the 2020 New Zealand election

Al Jazeera 2020, 'Jacinda Ardern wins New Zealand election by landslide', 17 October.

Arab News 2019, 'World reacts to New Zealand terrorist attacks on mosque', 18 March.

Arkilic, Ayca 2020a, 'A year after the Christchurch attacks: What has changed?', Istanbul Bilgi University, Bilgi Prime Youth Blog, 23 October, https://bpy.bilgi.edu.tr/en/blog/year-after-christchurch-mosque-shootings-what-has/.

Arkilic, Ayca 2020b, 'What is Islam's appeal to Māori?', *Newsroom*, 19 August.

Aytekin, Emre and Recep Sakar 2020, 'Yeni Zelanda'da Başbakan Ardern liderliğindeki İşçi Partisi genel seçimden galip çıktı', *Anadolu Ajansı*, 17 October.

BBC 2019, 'Christchurch shootings: Jacinda Ardern calls for global anti-racism fight', 20 March.

Beydoun, Khaled 2019, 'Today I'm a New Zealander', *Al Jazeera*, 23 March.

Bogost, Ian 2019, 'Social media are a mass shooter's best friend', *The Atlantic*, 15 March.

Borissenko, Sasha 2020, '"Jacindamania" set to return Jacinda Ardern as New Zealand PM', *Al Jazeera*, 16 October.

Brown, Tim 2020, 'Christchurch mosque attack victims address gunman: "We did not deserve your actions"', Radio New Zealand, 24 August.

Carroll, Melanie 2020, 'New Zealand ranked the most "Islamic country in the world" in annual index', *Stuff*, 1 November.

Cheng, Derek 2019, 'High-level Turkish delegation visit two days after shooting', *New Zealand Herald*, 17 March.

Christchurch City Council 2021, 'Waipuna/Halswell-Hornby-Riccarton Community Board', https://ccc.govt.nz/the-council/how-the-council-works/elected-members/community-boards/halswell-hornby-riccarton.

CNN Türk 2020, 'Yeni Zelanda'da Başbakan Ardern liderliğindeki İşçi Partisi genel seçimden galip çıktı', 17 October.

Cohen, Richard 2019, 'New Zealand attack shows white supremacy is global terrorist movement', *Southern Poverty Law Center*, 15 March.

Cooke, Henry and Stacey Kirk 2019, 'New Zealand officially on high terror alert, in wake of Christchurch terror attacks', *Stuff*, 15 March.

Devlin, Collette 2020, 'Second tranche of gun laws following March 15 shootings', *Stuff*, 18 June.

Drury, Abdullah 2015, 'Mostly harmless: A short history of the first century of Muslim settlement in New Zealand', *Waikato Islamic Studies Review*, vol. 1, no. 1, pp. 25–49.

Drury, Abdullah 2016, 'Islam's history and integration in the New Zealand society: A convert's view', in Erich Kolig and Malcolm Voyce (eds.), *Muslim Integration: Pluralism and Multiculturalism in New Zealand and Australia*, Maryland, Rowman, pp. 113–129.

Erdoğan, Recep Tayyip 2020, 'Opinion: Recep Tayyip Erdogan: The New Zealand killer and the Islamic State are cut from the same cloth', *Washington Post*, 20 March.

Fifield, Anna 2019, 'New Zealand's prime minister receives worldwide praise for her response to the mosque shootings', *Washington Post*, 19 March.

Fitzgerald, Katie 2019, 'Christchurch terror attack: National haka planned in support of Muslim community', *Newshub*, 20 March.

Foon, Eleisha 2019, 'Muslim local election candidates want "harmony in our society"', Radio New Zealand, 1 September.

Foroutan, Yaqhoob 2017, 'Muslim minority of New Zealand in global context: Demographic perspective', *Journal of Muslim Minority Affairs*, vol. 37, no. 4, pp. 511–519.

Gilbert, Jarrod and Ben Elley 2020, 'Shaved heads and sonnenrads: Comparing white supremacist skinheads and the alt-right in New Zealand', *Kōtuitui: New Zealand Journal of Social Sciences Online*, vol. 15, no. 2, pp. 280–294.

Gillespie, Alexander 2020, 'When life means life: Why the court had to deliver an unprecedented sentence for the Christchurch terrorist', *The Conversation*, 27 August.

Gillespie, Alexander 2021, 'Two years on from the Christchurch terror attack, how much has really changed?', *The Conversation*, 15 March.

Girijashanker, Suraj Kandath 2019, 'Is Jacinda Ardern really the inclusive leader she's been made out to be?', *TRT World*, 10 May.

Greaves, Lara et al. 2020, 'Comparative study of attitudes to religious groups in New Zealand reveals Muslim-specific prejudice', *Kōtuitui: New Zealand Journal of Social Sciences Online*, vol. 15, no. 2, pp. 260–279.

Hart, Lana 2019, 'Kiwi converts to Islam', Radio New Zealand, August 19.

Hürriyet 2020, 'Yeni Zelanda'da Başbakan Ardern liderliğindeki İşçi Partisi genel seçimden galip çıktı', 17 October.

Islamicity Foundation 2020, 'Islamicity Indices', http://islamicity-index.org/wp/.

Keber, Ruth 2013, 'The new Māori Muslims', *North & South*, vol. 324, pp. 44–51.

Keith, Leighton 2019, 'Small town New Zealand not exempt from white supremacists', *Stuff*, 21 March.

Kolig, Erich 2003, 'An accord of cautious distance: Muslims in New Zealand, ethnic relations and image management', *New Zealand Journal of Asian Studies*, vol. 5, no. 1, pp. 24–50.

Kuruvilla, Carol 2019, 'Muslims praise New Zealand Prime Minister for her empathy, actions after attack', *Washington Post*, 18 March.

Manch, Thomas 2020, 'White supremacy rises in New Zealand after March 15 terror attack,' *Stuff*, 17 March.

Mehdi, Syed Zafar 2019, 'Christchurch shooting is "white supremacist terrorism"', *Tehran Times*, March 17.

New Zealand Government 2019a, 'New Zealand bans military style semi-automatics and assault rifles', 21 March.

New Zealand Government 2019b, 'Arms (Prohibited Firearms, Magazines, and Parts) Amendment Bill', New Zealand Parliament.

New Zealand Government 2020, 'A new firearms system focused on safety', 18 June.

New Zealand Parliament 2011, 'Dr Ashraf Choudhary', https://www.parliament.nz/mi/mps-and-electorates/former-members-of-parliament/choudhary-ashraf/.

New Zealand Police 2020, '2019 Firearm law changes (Arms Amendment Bill 2)'.

O'Brien, Abbie 2020, 'The emergence of far-right fringe parties in New Zealand is causing concern for Muslims', *SBS News*, 15 October.

Onnudottir, Helena, Adam Possamai and Bryan S. Turner 2013, *Religious Change and Indigenous Peoples: The Making of Religious Identities*, London, Ashgate.

Öztürk, Bülent 2019, 'Yeni Zelanda Cami Katliamının Batı ve Arap Medyasında Yansıtılma Biçimleri', *Millî Kültür Araştırmaları Dergisi*, vol. 3, no. 1, pp. 32–51.

Paul, Sonali and Robert Birsel 2019, 'New Zealand women don headscarves to support Muslims after shootings', *Reuters*, 22 March.

Pratt, Douglas 2010, 'Antipodean angst: encountering Islam in New Zealand, *Islam and Christian-Muslim Relations*, vol. 21, no. 4, pp. 397–407.

Radio New Zealand 2019a, 'Parliament security increased while security threat level high', 17 March.

Radio New Zealand 2019b, 'Al Noor Mosque imam Gamal Fouda due to join community board', 13 October.

Rahman, Khairiah 2020, 'News media and the Muslim identity after the Christchurch mosque massacres', *Kōtuitui: New Zealand Journal of Social Sciences Online*, vol. 15, no. 2, pp. 360–384.

Rohrlich, Justin 2019, 'People of all faiths are visiting mosques in solidarity after the Christchurch shootings', *Quartz*, 16 March.

Royal Commission of Inquiry 2020, 'Executive Summary', Royal Commission of Inquiry into the Attack on Christchurch Mosques in 15 March 2019.

Sabah 2020, 'Yeni Zelanda'da ilk kez yerli halktan bir kadın Dışişleri Bakanlığına atandı', 2 November.

Sahin, Ayse 2019, 'Why is Turkey at the heart of the Christchurch terrorist's anger?', *TRT World*, 20 March.

Sands, Neil 2019, 'New Zealand opposition dares victorious Ardern to deliver', *The Jakarta Post* and *Agence France-Presse*, 18 October.

Satherley, Dan 2019, 'Jacinda Ardern graces the world's tallest building, the Burj Khalifa', *Newshub*, 23 March.

Scotcher, Katie 2021, New Zealand's terror list needs to be expanded – experts', Radio New Zealand, 22 March.

Shanaah, Sadi et al. 2021, 'Hate begets warmth? The impact of an anti-Muslim terrorist attack on public attitudes toward Muslims?', *Terrorism and Violence*, March.

Shehata, Dina 2020, 'Leading like a woman', *Ahram Online*, 10 March.

Shepard, William 2006, 'New Zealand's Muslims and their organisations', *New Zealand Journal of Asian Studies*, vol. 8, p. 2, pp. 8–44.

Small, Zane and Zac Fleming 2021, 'What to know about second gun buyback and all the other gun law changes', *Newshub*, 22 January.

Spoonley, Paul 2020, 'Far-right extremism still threatens New Zealand, a year on from the Christchurch attacks', *The Conversation*, 11 March.

Star News 2020, 'Election results: Labour landslide, "a very tough night" for National', 17 October.

Statistics New Zealand 2013, '2013 Census', https://www.stats.govt.nz/census/previous-censuses/2013-census/.

Statistics New Zealand 2018, '2018 Census', https://www.stats.govt.nz/2018-census/.

Stuff 2019, 'Armed police guard mosques around New Zealand', 15 March.

Sullivan, Helen 2020, 'Christchurch attack inquiry: the key findings and recommendations', *The Guardian*, 8 December.

Taonui, Rawiri 2019, 'Is Christchurch the capital of white racism in New Zealand?', *Waatea News*, 20 June.

Tehran Times 2019, 'Iran condemns "brutal" terrorist attacks in New Zealand', 15 March.

The Guardian 2019, 'Jacinda Ardern on the Christchurch shooting: "One of New Zealand's darkest days"', 15 March.

The Gulf News 2019, 'Al Nuaimi leads UAE delegation to New Zealand, meets victims' families', 20 March.

The Times of India 2002, 'First-ever Indian MP in New Zealand takes oath', 26 August.

Turkish Ministry of Foreign Affairs 2019, 'Participation of Foreign Minister Mevlüt Çavuşoğlu in the Organization of Islamic Cooperation Emergency Open-Ended Executive Committee Ministerial Meeting, 22 March 2019', https://www.mfa.gov.tr/iit-disisleri-bakanlari-duzeyinde-acil-icra-komitesi-toplantisi.en.mfa.

Ul Khaliq, Riyaz 2020, 'New Zealand all set for general elections', *Anadolu Ajansı*, 16 October.

Utaybi, Abdullah 2019, 'Yeni Zelanda hoşgörüsü', *Asharq al-Awsat*, 24 March.

Walls, Jason 2019, 'Winston Peters achieved the main goal of his visit to Turkey last week – PM Jacinda Ardern', *New Zealand Herald*, 26 March.

Wilson, Chris and Sanjal Shastri 2020, 'Hate crimes against Muslims spiked after the mosque attacks, and Ardern promises to make such abuse illegal', *The Conversation*, 6 October.

Young, Audrey and Claire Trevett 2020, 'Foreign Minister Winston Peters heads to Turkey to "put the record straight" over terrorist attack on mosques', *New Zealand Herald*, 22 March.

21. New Zealand's foreign and defence policy, 2017–2020

Ardern, Jacinda 2018a, 'Speech to New Zealand Institute of International Affairs', 27 February, The Beehive, Wellington.

Ardern, Jacinda 2018b, 'Prime Minister Jacinda Ardern's statement to the United Nations General Assembly', *Stuff*, 28 September.

Ardern, Jacinda, Winston Peters and Ron Mark 2019, 'New Zealand to withdraw from Iraq in June 2020', The Beehive, Wellington, 10 June.

Ayson, Robert 2020, 'New Zealand and the great irresponsibles: coping with Russia, China and the US', *Australian Journal of International Affairs*, vol. 74, no. 4, pp. 455–478.

Block, George 2020, 'Hercules flight over Auckland to announce $1.5 billion deal for defence planes', *Stuff*, 5 January.

Capie, David 2016, 'How new is New Zealand's new language on the South China Sea?', *Incline*, 15 April.

Ensor, Jamie 2019, 'Influx of criminal deportees from Australia a "major irritant" to relationship – Jacinda Ardern', *Newshub*, 1 October 2019.

Greener, Peter 2009, *Timing is Everything: The Politics and Processes of New Zealand Defence Acquisition Decision Making*, ANU E-Press, Canberra.

Mark, Ron Mark 2018, 'New Zealand to buy four P-8A Poseidon Maritime Patrol Aircraft', The Beehive, Wellington, 9 July.

Ministry of Foreign Affairs and Trade 2018, 'Remarks on the Indo-Pacific – Ben King, Deputy Secretary for Americas and Asia', 23 October.

Ministry of Foreign Affairs and Trade 2020, 'Joint Ministerial Statement affirming commitment to ensuring supply chain connectivity amidst the Covid-19 situation', 14 April.

Molyneux, Vita and Alice Wilkins 2019, 'Jacinda Ardern denounces Donald Trump's comments about Democratic congresswomen', *Newshub*, 16 July.

New Zealand Government 2018a, 'Strategic Defence Policy Statement', Ministry of Defence, Wellington, 6 July.

New Zealand Government 2018b, *The Climate Crisis: Defence Readiness and Response*, Ministry of Defence and NZ Defence Force, Wellington, November.

New Zealand Government 2019, *Advancing Pacific Partnerships*, Ministry of Defence, Wellington, p. 5.

New Zealand Government Communications Security Bureau 2018a, 'GCSB Statement', 28 November.

New Zealand Government Communications Security Bureau 2018b, 'Cyber campaign attributed to China', 21 December.

New Zealand Labour Party and New Zealand First Party 2017, 'Coalition Agreement between the New Zealand Labour Party and the New Zealand First Party', Wellington, 2017, p. 6 [reprinted in *Stardust and Substance: The New Zealand General Election of 2017*, Appendix 1, pp. 495–501].

Peters, Winston 2018a, 'Shifting the Dial', Speech to Lowy Institute, 1 March, The Beehive, Wellington.
Peters, Winston 2018b, 'Pacific Partnerships – Georgetown Address, Washington DC', 15 December.
Sachdeva, Sam 2020, 'Slow progress on EU trade talks', *Newsroom*, 22 July.
Smellie, Pattrick 2018, 'PM never saw Peters' pro-US speech before delivery', *Newsroom*, 18 December.
Tobin, Meaghan 2019, 'New Zealand bans Huawei from 5G, China has message for New Zealand', *South China Morning Post*, 17 February.
Walsh, Michael 2021, 'Australia called for a Covid-19 probe: China responded with a trade war', *ABC News*, 3 January.
Yaxley, Louise 2018, 'Jacinda Ardern pressures Australia not to deport Kiwis if they have never set foot in New Zealand', *ABC News*, 2 March.

22. 'Here Today, Gone Tomorrow'? New Zealand election signs in 2020

Allen, R. E. (ed.) 1990, *The Concise Oxford Dictionary of Current English*, 8th edn, Clarendon Press, Oxford.
Electoral Commission 2020, *Candidate Handbook for the 2020 General Election*, Wellington.
National Library of New Zealand 2020, *Ephemera Collection*, Wellington.
Porirua City Council 2020, *Signs Bylaw 2020*, Porirua.
Roberts, Nigel S. 2003, 'All over the place: Billboard battles in 2002', in Jonathan Boston, Stephen Church, Stephen Levine, Elizabeth McLeay and Nigel S. Roberts (eds.), *New Zealand Votes: The General Election of 2002*, Victoria University Press, Wellington, pp. 270–280.
Robinson, Claire 2019, *Promises, Promises: 80 Years of Wooing New Zealand Voters*, Massey University Press, Auckland.

23. The 2020 cannabis and euthanasia referendums

1 News 2020, 'Latest poll shows tightening of results for cannabis, euthanasia referendums', *1 News*, 15 October.
Arseneau, Therese and Nigel Roberts 2019, 'Special voting in New Zealand', *Political Science*, vol. 71, no. 2, pp. 99–122.
Boden, Joseph, Lana Cleland, Bhubaneswar Dhakal and L. John Horwood 2020, 'Attitudes towards cannabis and cannabis law change in a New Zealand birth cohort', *New Zealand Medical Journal*, vol. 133, no. 1515, pp. 79–88.
Bracewell-Worrall, Anna 2019, 'NZ First MP Tracey Martin shares tragic personal connection to backstreet abortion', *Newshub*, 9 August.
Burrows, Matt 2020, 'Euthanasia referendum: Catholic clergy say assisted dying runs against core values, Islamic leader threatens Muslims who choose it with Hell', *Newshub*, 9 November.

Campbell, Angus, Philip E. Converse, Warren E. Miller and Donald E. Stokes 1960, *The American Voter*, University of Chicago Press, Chicago.

Cheng, Derek 2019. 'Scores of proposed amendments could push euthanasia bill well into next year', *New Zealand Herald*, 23 June.

Church, Stephen 2000, 'Crime and punishment: The referenda to reform the criminal justice system and reduce the size of Parliament', in Jonathan Boston, Stephen Church, Stephen Levine, Elizabeth McLeay and Nigel S. Roberts (eds.), *Left Turn: The New Zealand General Election of 1999*, Victoria University Press, Wellington, pp. 184–199.

Crothers, Charles 2020, 'Euthanasia and Cannabis referenda: Research Note on survey research', *The Policy Observatory*, 14 July.

De Angelis, Andrea, Céline Colombo and Davide Morisi 2020, 'Taking cues from the government: Heuristic versus systematic processing in a constitutional referendum', *West European Politics*, vol. 43, no. 4, pp. 845–868.

Edwards, Bryce and Nicola Lomax 2012, '"For a richer New Zealand": Environmentalism and the Green Party in the 2011 New Zealand general election', *Environmental Politics*, vol. 21, no. 6, pp. 994–1000.

Fergusson, David M., Nicola R. Swain-Campbell and L.J. Horwood 2003, 'Arrests and convictions for cannabis related offences in a New Zealand birth cohort', *Drug and Alcohol Dependence*, vol. 70, no. 1, pp. 53–63.

Graham-McLay, Charlotte 2019, 'New Zealand to vote in referendum on euthanasia', *The Guardian*, 13 November.

Hawkes, Arthur 2020, 'Featherston residents say: Nope to dope ad', *Stuff*, 19 September.

Hokowhitu, Brendan 2004, 'Tackling Māori masculinity: A colonial genealogy of savagery and sport', *The Contemporary Pacific*, vol. 16, no. 2, pp. 259–284.

Justice Committee 2019, 'End of Life Choice Bill: As reported from the Justice Committee', New Zealand Parliament, Wellington.

New Zealand Herald 2018, 'Justice Minister Andrew Little flags three referenda could be in the mix at next election', 26 November.

O'Brien, Thomas 2013, 'Leaving the minors: The Green Party of Aotearoa New Zealand and the 2011 General Election', *Representation*, vol. 49, no. 1, pp. 69–81.

Poulton, Richie et al. 2020, 'Patterns of recreational cannabis use in Aotearoa–New Zealand and their consequences: Evidence to inform voters in the 2020 referendum', *Journal of the Royal Society of New Zealand*, vol. 50, no. 2, pp. 348–365.

Quince, Khylee 2020, 'Why referendums are never likely to advance Māori interests', *Stuff*, 14 November.

Radio New Zealand 2020, 'Cannabis referendum: Narrow support for legalisation in latest poll', 6 October.

Saad, Lydia 2013, 'U.S. support for euthanasia hinges on how it's described', *Gallup*, 29 May.

Satherley, Nicole et al. 2018, 'If they say "yes," we say "no": Partisan cues increase polarization over national symbols', *Psychological Science*, vol. 29, no. 12, pp. 1996–2009.

Small, Zane 2019, 'Government reveals details of cannabis referendum', *Newshub*, 7 May.

Smith, Lydia 2017, 'New Zealand prime minister Jacinda Ardern left Mormon church to support LGBT rights', *Independent*, 21 October.

Taunton, Esther 2020, 'Dairy owner shocked to find business used in anti-cannabis campaign', *Stuff*, 21 September.

Tesoriero, Paula 2018, 'Submission of the Disability Rights Commissioner on the End of Life Choice Bill', Human Rights Commission.

Theodore, Reremoana et al. 2020, 'Cannabis, the cannabis referendum and Māori youth: A review from a lifecourse perspective', *Kōtuitui: New Zealand Journal of Social Sciences Online*, 13 May.

Walls, Jason 2020, 'Referendum Results: Prime Minister Ardern explains why she voted for cannabis reform', *New Zealand Herald*, 31 October.

Young, Jessica et al. 2018, 'The euthanasia debate: synthesising the evidence on New Zealander's attitudes', *Kōtuitui: New Zealand Journal of Social Sciences Online*, vol. 14, no. 1, pp. 1–21.

24. Political party funding and the 2020 election

ACE 2020, 'Parties and candidates: Public funding of parties', The Electoral Knowledge Network.

Borger, Julian 2020, 'Trump has given record proportion of ambassador jobs to his own backers', *The Guardian*, 30 May.

Edwards, Bryce 2018, 'State funding of parties is bad for democracy', *Newsroom*, 25 October.

Electoral Commission 2020, 'Rules for party donations and loans', Wellington, https://elections.nz.

Espiner, Guyon 2020, 'The secret case of the NZ First Foundation', Radio New Zealand, 16 October.

Gluck, James and Michael Macaulay 2017, 'Trading in influence: a research agenda for New Zealand?', *Policy Quarterly*, vol. 13, no. 2, pp. 49–55.

Johnston, Michael 2005, *Syndromes of Corruption: Wealth, Power and Democracy*, Cambridge University Press, New York.

Macaulay, Michael and Gary Hickey 2011, 'Corruption in the UK: National Integrity System study', Transparency International UK, London.

New Zealand Labour Party 2020, 'Party information: What are our values and principles?', Wellington.

Parliamentary Service 2020, 'Parliamentary Sector Annual Report 2019/20', Wellington.

Radford, S., A. Mell and S.A. Thevoz 2020, '"Lordy Me!" Can donations buy you a British peerage? A study in the link between party political funding and peerage nominations, 2005–2014', *British Politics*, vol. 15, pp. 135–159.

Rashbrooke, Max 2020, 'A brief history of New Zealand donations scandals', *The Spinoff*, 4 March.

Shand, Matt 2019, 'Who are the donors behind the NZ First Foundation?', *Stuff*, 21 November.

Shand, Matt and Thomas Manch 2020, 'Billionaires among the full list of donors supporting NZ First', *Stuff*, 27 February.

The Guardian 2012, 'Conservative website offers dinner with Cameron to donors', 26 March.

Transparency International New Zealand 2019, *New Zealand National Integrity System Assessment – 2018 update*, Wellington.

Trevett, Claire 2014, 'Cabinet Clubs bad look, even to National voters', *New Zealand Herald*, 18 June.

Willsher, Kim 2021, 'Former French president Nicolas Sarkozy sentenced to jail for corruption', *The Guardian*, 1 March.

25. Performing politics: Leaders' debates in the 2020 election

1 News 2020, 'Should cannabis be legalized?', *1 News*, 20 September.

Anstead, Nick and Ben O'Loughlin 2011, 'The emerging viewertariat and BBC *Question Time*: Television debate and real-time commenting online', *International Journal of Press/Politics*, vol. 16, no. 4, pp. 440–462.

Bourdieu, Pierre 1991, *Language and Symbolic Power*, Polity, Cambridge.

Boyd, Mark 2020, Presentation to the NZPSA Political Communication Network workshop. University of Waikato, Tauranga campus, 26–27 November.

Braunias, Steve 2020a, 'First TV debate between Ardern and Collins avoids being a horror show', *The Guardian*, 22 September.

Braunias, Steve 2020b, 'Score draw for New Zealand leaders in pub quiz-style debate', *The Guardian*, 30 September.

Braunias, Steve 2020c, 'Jacinda Ardern saves best for last in New Zealand election TV debate', *The Guardian*, 15 October.

Bridge, Ryan 2020, 'A sniff of hope for Collins', *Newsroom*, 1 October.

Brooks, Sam 2020, 'Creative differences: Labour, National and the Greens debate 2020 arts policy', *The Spinoff*, 26 September.

Cooke, Henry and Thomas Manch 2020, 'The answers Grant Robertson and Paul Goldsmith didn't have in the Stuff Finance Debate', *Stuff*, 13 October.

Cormack, David 2020, 'Sometimes strength can be a weakness', *New Zealand Herald*, 8 October.

Coughlan, Thomas 2020, 'John Tamihere dominates raucous minor parties debate', *Stuff*, 1 October.

Craig, Geoffrey 2016, *Performing Politics: Media Interviews, Debates and Press Conferences*, Polity, Cambridge.

Craig, Geoffrey 2018, 'Performing politics: Leaders' debates in the 2017 election', in Stephen Levine (ed.), *Stardust and Substance: The New Zealand general election of 2017*, Victoria University Press, Wellington, pp. 351–64.

Davison, Isaac 2020, 'The End of Life Choice Referendum debated on Newstalk ZB', *New Zealand Herald*, 1 October.

Edwards, Bryce 2020, 'Jacinda Ardern vs Judith Collins: A dynamic leaders debate that lacked soul', Radio New Zealand, 1 October.

Ensor, Jamie 2020, 'Paul Goldsmith, Grant Robertson face off over National's fiscal hole in ASB Great Debate', *Newshub*, 23 September.

Graham-McLay, Charlotte 2020, 'New Zealand election TV debate: Fears inclusion of fringe party may "legitimize conspiracy theories"', *The Guardian*, 9 September.

Hayden, Leonie 2020, 'Māori don't exist according to our political leaders so . . . talofa', *The Spinoff*, 23 September.

Jennings, Mark 2020a, 'The leaders' debate: An unmemorable watch', *Newsroom*, 23 September.

Jennings, Mark 2020b, 'Gower gets the debate into top gear', *Newsroom*, 1 October.

Malpass, Luke 2020a, 'Leaders' election debate verdict: Jacinda Ardern lost, but Judith Collins didn't win it', *Stuff*, 22 September.

Malpass, Luke 2020b, 'Election debate verdict: Ardern and Collins draw in round two, but is the die already cast', *Stuff*, 1 October.

Manch, Thomas 2020, 'Pot shots and policy statements in second televised minor party debate', *Stuff*, 9 October.

Manch, Thomas and Henry Cooke 2020, 'Jacinda Ardern, Judith Collins fire up in fierce second leaders debate', *Stuff*, 30 September,

Manhire, Toby 2020, 'Winston Peters looked like a man transformed at the Newshub debate', *The Spinoff*, 2 October.

Milne, Jonathan 2020, 'Powerbrokers debate the beginning of the end', *Newsroom*, 2 October.

New Zealand Herald 2020, 'Fiery exchanges at Young Voters' Debate', 29 September.

Owen, Catrin 2020, 'Advance NZ says it is "unreasonable" to be excluded from Newshub debate', *Stuff*, 30 September.

Palmer, Russell 2020, 'Minor parties' debate becomes a rushed, uninformative melee', Radio New Zealand, 9 October.

Sachdeva, Sam 2020, 'Ardern steps up but Collins holds her own in second debate', *Newsroom*, 1 October.

Small, Zane 2020, 'Judith Collins claims victory in first TV debate as Jacinda Ardern tries to avoid "blood sport"', *Newshub*, 23 September.

Te Pou, Shane 2020, 'Shane Te Pou – why TVNZ should withdraw its debate invitation to the Advance Party', *New Zealand Herald*, 14 September.

The Spinoff 2020, 'Final leaders' debate: The verdicts', 15 October.
Trevett, Claire, Fran O'Sullivan, Audrey Young and Simon Wilson 2020, 'Our experts' verdict: Who will win the election – and with what margin?', *New Zealand Herald*, 16 October.
Van Beynen, Martin 2020, 'Format of leaders' debates needs to change', *Stuff*, 25 September.
Venuto, Damien 2020, 'Jacinda Ardern, Judith Collins or David Seymour: Who's controlling the social media conversation?', *New Zealand Herald*, 1 October.
Wade, Amelia 2020, 'New Conservatives take TVNZ to High Court over debate snub', *New Zealand Herald*, 6 October.

27. Populism in the 2020 campaign and the departure of New Zealand First

Ardern, Jacinda 2017, 'Speech: Let's do this – Labour's election campaign launched', 20 August, New Zealand Labour Party.
Chapman, R. M. 1979, 'The case of the pulled punch: The 1978 election', *Comment*, No. 6, February, pp. 17–20.
Electoral Commission 2020, 'Jump in youth voting', media release, 30 November.
Joiner, Margaret 2015, 'New Zealand First' in Janine Hayward (ed.), *New Zealand Government and Politics*, 6th edn., Oxford University Press, Melbourne, pp. 251–260.
Joiner, Margaret 2010, 'The Life-Cycle of a Small Political Party: The Case of New Zealand First', MA thesis, University of Auckland.
Krewel, Mona and Jack Vowles 2020, 'Election 2020: Key social media trends', The New Zealand Social Media Study, Te Herenga Waka – Victoria University of Wellington.
Miller, Raymond 1992, 'The Minor Parties' in Hyam Gold (ed.), *New Zealand Politics in Perspective*, 3rd edn., Longman Paul, Auckland, pp. 310–325.
Mudde, Cas and Cristóbal Kaltwasser 2017, *Populism: A Very Short Introduction*, Oxford University Press, New York.
Peters, Winston 2017, 'Peters: Post-election announcement speech', New Zealand First Party, 19 October.
Peters, Winston 2020a, 'Speech: Winston Peters campaign launch 2020', New Zealand First Party, 22 July.
Peters, Winston 2020b, 'Election night speech', New Zealand First Party, 17 October.
Vowles, Jack 2020a, 'Where did National's votes go?', *Newsroom*, 10 November.
Vowles, Jack 2020b, 'Populism and the 2017 Election – the background' in *A Populist Exception? The 2017 New Zealand General Election*, ANU Press, Australia.
Vowles, Jack and Jennifer Curtin (eds.) 2020, *A Populist Exception? The 2017 New Zealand General Election*, ANU Press, Australia.

28. Māori and the 2020 election

Electoral Commission 2020, 'Voter turnout statistics for the 2020 General Election', Electoral Commission website, Wellington.

Godfery, Morgan 2015, 'The Māori Party', in Janine Hayward (ed.), *New Zealand Government and Politics* (6th ed.), Oxford University Press, Oxford, pp. 131–139.

Greaves, Lara and Janine Hayward 2020, 'Māori and the 2017 General Election – party, participation and populism', in Jack Vowles and Jennifer Curtin (eds.), *A Populist Exception? The 2017 New Zealand General Election*, Australian National University Press, Canberra, pp. 213–246.

Horgan, Leo 2017, 'Māori have 'gone back like a beaten wife to the abuser' – Marama Fox', *Te Ao – Māori News*, 21 January.

Horgan, Leo 2019, 'A well-meaning Budget 2019 offers almost half a billion for Māori', *Te Ao – Māori News*, 30 May.

Husband, Dale 2020, 'Rawiri Waititi: Unapologetically Māori', *E-Tangata*, 27 September.

Kilgallon, Steve 2020, 'John Tamihere: Why the Māori Party will become important again', *Stuff*, 11 October.

Manch, Thomas 2020, 'Election 2020: John Tamihere on why 2020 isn't the Māori Party's year', *Stuff*, 24 August.

Māori Party 2020, 'Believe in Māori', Facebook, 5 July.

Quinlivan, Mark 2019, 'Hannah Tamaki's Vision NZ says it will ban the construction of mosques, temples and other "foreign buildings"', *Newshub*, 11 November.

Radio New Zealand, 2020, 'Winston Peters says NZ First "staved off any action" on Ihumātao before election', Radio New Zealand, September 25.

Sullivan, Anne, Martin von Randow and Aimee Matiu 2014, 'Māori voters, public policy and privatisation', in Jack Vowles (ed.), *The new electoral politics in New Zealand: The significance of the 2011 election*, Institute for Governance and Policy Studies, Wellington, pp. 141–160.

Te Ao – Māori News 2020a, 'Māori Electoral Debate – Waiariki', Māori Television, 4 October.

Te Ao – Māori News 2020b, 'Māori Party won't work with National', 19 July.

Victoria University of Wellington 2020, '#nzvotes: The dynamics of campaign communication on Facebook', https://www.wgtn.ac.nz/research/strengths/election/facebook-campaign-communication.

Waatea News 2020, 'More penance needed for Māori Party', *Waatea News*, 12 October.

Wilson, Simon 2019, 'John Tamihere on Roast Busters, front bums and running for Auckland mayoralty', *New Zealand Herald*, 26 January.

29. Echoes: The 2020 election in historical perspective

Hayward, Margaret 1981, *Diary of the Kirk Years*, Cape Catley/Reed, Christchurch.

30. 'Window on Wairarapa': Kieran McAnulty and Labour's 2020 Covid campaign

Appropriations Review Committee 2018, *Towards a World-Leading Democracy / Ahu Atu Ai Ki Tētahi Ao-Manapori Arataki: Report of the Seventh Triennial Appropriations Review Committee*, New Zealand Parliament, Wellington.

Boyack, Nicholas 2020, 'Election 2020: Who are the candidates for the Wairarapa electorate?', *Stuff*, 6 October.

Burke, Peter 2020, 'Farmer picked for National in Wairarapa', *Rural News Group*, 2 June.

Coltman, Karen 2020, 'Three choices for National', *Wairarapa Times-Age*, 7 March.

Electoral Commission n.d., 'New Zealand Election Results', Archive | Election Results.

Electoral Commission 2020, 'Boundary Review 2019/20: View Submissions (N43-001, N43-002, N43-003)', Elections NZ.

50 Shades of Green 2019, 'Government urged to pause on zero carbon legislation', *Scoop*, 4 June.

Fluoride Free NZ 2019, 'Elections 2019 – Candidate Responses'.

Gray, N.A. 2020, 'Rigged . . . in more ways than you could count', Facebook, 18 October.

Lamason, Matthew 2003, 'Window on Wairarapa: Georgina Beyer and the 2002 election campaign' in Jonathan Boston, Stephen Church, Stephen Levine, Elizabeth McLeay and Nigel S. Roberts (eds.), *New Zealand Votes: The General Election of 2002*, Victoria University Press, Wellington, pp. 175–191.

Masterton District Council 2019, '2019 Triennial Elections | Declaration of Results', 16 October.

McAnulty, Kieran 2020, 'Back me, so that I can back Wairarapa' [video], Facebook, 27 September.

McAnulty, Kieran and Alex Walker 2020, 'Submission to the electorate boundary review – change of name of Wairarapa electorate', 9 January, Elections NZ.

McRobie, Alan 1989, *New Zealand Electoral Atlas*, GP Books, Wellington.

New Zealand Herald 2020, 'Farmer against forestry conversions is first candidate to seek National selection for Wairarapa', 6 August.

New Zealand National Party 2020, 'Mike Butterick National's new candidate in Wairarapa', Mike Butterick / National Party Candidate for Wairarapa.

Parliamentary Service 2017, 'Wairarapa Electorate Profile', Parliamentary Library, Wellington.

Representation Commission 2014, 'Report of the Representation Commission 2014', Wellington.

Representation Commission 2020, 'Report of the Representation Commission 2020', Wellington.
Tararua District Council 2019, 'Instructions and Candidate Information'.
Wairarapa Times-Age 2020a, 'Roger commits from a distance', 29 July.
Wairarapa Times-Age 2020b, 'Live Stream – Candidates Debate', Facebook, 6 October.
Wairarapa Times-Age 2020c, 'Voting: Who, what, and where', 14 October.
Wu, Crystal 2020, 'Advance NZ denies candidate's claim Lake Ōhau fires were caused by 'direct energy weapon', *Newshub*, 12 October.

31. A campaign for the ages: Chlöe Swarbrick, the youth vote and the Auckland Central election

1 News 2020a, 'Uncertainty for youth vote, as fewer young people enrolled to vote so far this election', TVNZ, 19 July.
1 News 2020b, 'Meet the three women vying to represent Auckland Central after Nikki Kaye's departure', TVNZ, 11 August.
1 News 2020c, 'Auckland Central electorate race narrowing, Q+A Colmar Brunton poll reveals', TVNZ, 4 October.
1 News 2020d, 'Green Party MP Chloe Swarbrick praises "phenomenal" Auckland youth rally turnout', TVNZ, 10 October.
Alesina, Alberto F., Ugo Troiano and Traviss Cassidy 2015, 'Old and young politicians', National Bureau of Economic Research, 2 March.
Arceneaux, Kevin, and Robin Kolodny 2009, 'Educating the least informed: Group endorsements in a grassroots campaign', *American Journal of Political Science*, vol. 53, no. 4, pp. 755–770.
Beck, Paul A. and Erik D. Heidemann 2014, 'Changing strategies in grassroots canvassing: 1956–2012', *Party Politics*, vol. 20, no. 2, pp. 261–274.
Bhatia, Ripu 2020, 'Election 2020: Auckland Central candidates for local MP', *Stuff*, 25 September.
Bossetta, Michael 2018, 'The digital architectures of social media: Comparing political campaigning on Facebook, Twitter, Instagram, and Snapchat in the 2016 U.S. Election', *Journalism & Mass Communication Quarterly*, vol. 95, no. 2, pp. 471–496.
Bradbury, Martyn 2020a, 'Media Watch: Newshub Nation – Auckland Central poll upset – Chloe running 3rd', *The Daily Blog*, 19 September.
Bradbury, Martyn 2020b, 'Q+A Auckland Central Poll – White 35% Mellow 30% Chloe 26%', *The Daily Blog*, 4 October.
Braae, Alex and Toby Manhire 2020, 'The popcorn seats: 21 electorates we'll be glued to on Saturday night', *The Spinoff*, 15 October.
Campbell, David E., and Christina Wolbrecht 2006, 'See Jane run: Women politicians as role models for adolescents', *Journal of Politics*, vol. 68, no. 2, pp. 233–247.

Cheng, Derek 2019, 'Nikki Kaye and Chloe Swarbrick: The race for Auckland Central, Head Girl vs 'High School Dropout', *New Zealand Herald*, 28 November.

Clench, Sam 2020, 'Covid 19 Coronavirus: Sam Clench – Clarity is the quality that makes Jacinda Ardern so effective in a crisis', *New Zealand Herald*, 27 March.

Cooke, Henry 2020a, 'Chlöe Swarbrick could save the Green Party in Auckland, but Labour would have to get out of the way', *Stuff*, 17 July.

Cooke, Henry 2020b, 'Election 2020: The seats to watch in tonight's election', *Stuff*, 17 October.

Cooke, Henry 2020c, 'Election 2020: How Chloe Swarbrick won the campaign of a lifetime and turned a blue seat green', *Stuff*, 19 October.

Cormack, David 2020, 'Election Results 2020: David Cormack – On a night full of drama, the Greens' Chloe Swarbrick steals the show', *New Zealand Herald*, 19 October.

Coughlan, Thomas 2020, 'Election 2020: Jacinda Ardern leans into Mary Poppins on final stretch of campaign', *Stuff*, 15 October.

Davidson, Marama 2020, 'Marama Davidson asks Tāmaki Makaurau for your party vote and your electorate vote', Green Party of Aotearoa New Zealand, 3 May.

Davison, Isaac 2020, 'Chloe Swarbrick says she won Auckland Central "the old-fashioned way"', *New Zealand Herald*, 18 October.

Donnell, Hayden 2020, 'Winners, losers, big losers, and gigantic losers from Election 2020', *The Spinoff*, 19 October.

Electoral Commission 2020, 'Enrolment by General Electorate – Auckland Central Elections', Wellington.

Eventbrite 2020, 'Helen Clark Helen White Event', Auckland, 8 October.

Giovannetti, Justin 2020, 'Election 2020: The battle for Central Auckland is splitting the left', *New Zealand Herald*, 13 October.

Gone By Lunchtime 2020, 'Gone By Lunchtime: The morning after election night, with Chlöe Swarbrick', *The Spinoff*, 18 October.

Green Party of Aotearoa New Zealand 2020, 'Poverty Action Plan'.

Heiss, Raffael and Jörg Matthes 2016, 'Mobilizing for some: The effects of politicians' participatory Facebook posts on young people's political efficacy', *Journal of Media Psychology Theories Methods and Applications*, vol. 28, pp. 123–135.

Hogan, Finn 2020a, 'The Pitch: Helen White', *Newshub*, 5 September.

Hogan, Finn 2020b, 'The Pitch: Emma Mellow makes her case for Auckland Central', *Newshub*, 10 October.

IHeartRadio VOTE 2020 Podcast 2020, 'Listen to Chloe Swarbrick on her phenomenal upset win in Auckland Central', 17 October.

Kava Corner with Chlöe Swarbrick – Episode 4, 2020, https://www.youtube.com/watch?v=wYhamos6jo0.

Kirkness, Luke 2020, 'Election 2020: National names Emma Mellow as Auckland Central replacement for Nikki Kaye', *New Zealand Herald*, 10 August.

Lenihin-Ikin, Isabella 2020, 'Greens planning inquiry into student accommodation', *Newstalk ZB*, 28 May.

Levine, Peter 2009, 'The Civic Opportunity Gap', *Educational Leadership*, vol. 66, no. 8, pp. 20–25.

Manch, Thomas 2020, 'Election 2020: A terrible day on the campaign trail for Judith Collins', *Stuff*, 7 October.

Mandow, Nikki 2020, 'Political campaigning: What A drag', *Newsroom*, 9 October.

Marques, Duarte 2013, 'Young politicians: Different politics?', *European View*, vol. 12, no. 2, pp. 289–297.

Mellow, Emma (@emmamellow) 2020, 'Nikki Kaye is an amazing woman . . .' Twitter, 12 October, 10.14pm.

Morten, Brigette 2020, 'Election 2020: Green MP Chlöe Swarbrick's blueprint for grassroots campaigns in a Covid world', Radio New Zealand, 18 October.

Neilson, Michael 2020, 'Toxic politics: Green MP Chlöe Swarbrick and the "inhuman" nature of Parliament', *New Zealand Herald*, 20 August.

New Zealand Government 2020, 'Enrol to Vote', Wellington, www.govt.nz.

New Zealand Herald 2020a, 'Election 2020: Helen White vs Chloe Swarbrick – war of words erupts over Auckland Central seat', *New Zealand Herald*, 26 July.

New Zealand Herald 2020b, 'Election 2020: Auckland Central poll – tight race between Labour's Helen White and National's Emma Mellow', *New Zealand Herald*, 4 October.

New Zealand Labour Party 2020a, 'Helen White – Candidate for Auckland Central'.

New Zealand Labour Party 2020b, 'Let's Keep Moving – Labour's First TV Ad of the 2020 Campaign'.

Newshub 2020, 'Labour's Auckland Central candidate Helen White mocks Green opponent Chlöe Swarbrick as "celebrity"', 26 July.

Ødegård, Guro 2007, 'Political socialization and influence at the mercy of politicians: A study of a local participation project amongst young people in Norway', *YOUNG*, vol. 15, no. 3, pp. 273–297.

Orsman, Bernard 2020a, 'Helen White: The employment lawyer and pragmatist hoping to win Auckland Central for Labour', *New Zealand Herald*, 13 September.

Orsman, Bernard 2020b, 'Emma Mellow: From humble beginnings to standing for National in Auckland Central', *New Zealand Herald*, 21 September.

Orsman, Bernard 2020c, 'Electorate winners and losers – Chloe Swarbrick's shock win, Gerry Brownlee and Nick Smith tipped out', *New Zealand Herald*, 17 October.

Orsman, Bernard 2020d, 'Chloe Swarbrick pulls off historic win in Auckland Central', *New Zealand Herald*, 18 October.

Otago Daily Times 2020, 'The Greens' Chloe Swarbrick has historic win', 18 October.

Oxenham, Jason 2020, 'Chloe Swarbrick – the MP for K-Rd', *New Zealand Herald*, 11 January.

Panagopoulos, Costas and Peter L. Francia 2009, 'Grassroots Mobilization in the 2008 Presidential Election', *Journal of Political Marketing*, vol. 8, no. 4, pp. 315–333.

Panagopoulos, Costas and Peter W. Wielhouwer 2008, 'Polls and Elections – The Ground War 2000–2004: Strategic Targeting in Grassroots Campaigns', *Presidential Studies Quarterly* vol. 38, no. 2, pp. 347–362.

Parliament 2017, 'Auckland Central: Electoral Profile', Wellington.

Radio New Zealand 2020a, 'Swarbrick says Auckland Central race is "anyone's"', 16 July.

Radio New Zealand 2020b, 'Election campaigning suspended due to new Covid-19 alert', 12 August.

Radio New Zealand 2020c, 'Auckland Central electorate polls show candidates close', 4 October.

Radio New Zealand 2020d, 'Election 2020: Collins doubles down on wealth tax attack', 13 October.

Radio New Zealand 2020e, 'Election 2020: Chlöe Swarbrick wins Auckland Central', 17 October.

Ross, Karen and Tobias Bürger 2014, 'Face to Face(Book): Social Media, Political Campaigning and the Unbearable Lightness of Being There', *Political Science* vol. 66, no. 1, pp. 46–62.

Satherley, Dan 2020, 'How Nikki Kaye went from Deputy Leader to losing "the passion" in just two days', *Newshub*, 16 July.

Smith, Anneke 2020a, 'And then there were three: The race is on for Auckland Central', *Radio New Zealand*, 29 September.

Smith, Anneke 2020b, 'NZ Election 2020: Helen White, Emma Mellow and Chlöe Swarbrick in a three-way race for Auckland Central', *Newshub*, 2 October.

Stuff 2020, 'Election 2020: Greens' Chlöe Swarbrick takes Auckland Central in shock Win', 17 October.

Swarbrick, Chlöe 2020a, 'Greens Work to Secure Inquiry into Wild West Student Accommodation Sector', Green Party of Aotearoa New Zealand, 27 May.

Swarbrick, Chlöe 2020b, 'Tertiary Education Policy', Green Party of Aotearoa New Zealand.

Swarbrick, Chlöe 2020c, 'The Green Party won in Auckland by reaching beyond its own bubble – Chlöe Swarbrick', *The Guardian*, 26 October.

The Economist 2017, 'Not turning out – Millennials across the rich world are failing to vote', 4 February.

Tokalau, Torika 2020, 'Coronavirus: Auckland will be in lockdown during the wettest weeks of August', *Stuff*, 15 August.

Vergeer, Maurice, Liesbeth Hermans and Steven Sams 2013, 'Online Social Networks and Micro-Blogging in Political Campaigning: The Exploration of a New Campaign Tool and a New Campaign Style', *Party Politics*, vol. 19, no. 3, pp. 477–501.

Wade, Amelia 2020, 'Election 2020: Political party leaders, MPs pitch to Auckland business crowd', *New Zealand Herald*, 1 October.

Weekes, John 2020a, 'Election 2020: An uphill battle for Chlöe Swarbrick in Auckland Central', *Stuff*, 9 October.

Weekes, John 2020b, 'Election 2020: Labour's Helen White out in front, but Auckland Central win not guaranteed', *Stuff*, 10 October.

Weekes, John 2020c, 'Election 2020: National's Emma Mellow focused on economy to win Auckland Central', *Stuff*, 19 October.

Weekes, John and Jackson Thomas 2020, 'Election 2020: National picks Emma Mellow for Auckland Central race', *Stuff*, 10 August.

White, Helen 2020, 'Election 2020: Helen White – The voters will decide but I am staying put', *New Zealand Herald*, 8 October.

Whyte, Anna 2020, 'Election date moved to October 17, PM announces – "Gives all parties a fair shot"', *1 News TVNZ*, 17 August.

Wilson, Simon 2020, 'Vote 2020: Simon Wilson's election diary – Why Chloe Swarbrick in Auckland Central?', *New Zealand Herald*, 6 October.

32. Special votes and the 2020 election

Arseneau, Therese and Nigel S. Roberts 2019, 'Special voting in New Zealand, *Political Science*, vol. 71, no. 2, pp. 99–122.

Electoral Commission 2015, *Report of the Electoral Commission on the 2014 General Election*, Wellington.

Electoral Commission 2018, *Report of the Electoral Commission on the 2017 General Election*, Wellington.

Electoral Commission 2020, *Briefing to the Incoming Minister*, Wellington.

Cooke, Henry and Kate Newton 2020, 'Election 2020: How New Zealand split its votes – and caused two upset wins', *Stuff*, 3 December.

Moana Radio 2020, 'Labour wins election by a landslide', Tauranga.

Nicoll, Dave 2017, 'Increase in advance voting could see changes to electoral advertising rules', *Southland Times*, 15 September.

Vowles, Jack 2008, 'Systemic failure, coordination and contingencies: Understanding electoral system change in New Zealand', in Andre Blais (ed.), *To Keep or Change First Past the Post: The Politics of Electoral Reform*, Oxford University Press, Oxford, pp. 163–182.

Vowles, Jack 2018, 'Surprise, Surprise: The New Zealand General Election of 2017', *Kōtuitui: New Zealand Journal of Social Sciences Online*, vol. 13, no. 2.

33. Getting what you're given: Government formation in 2020

Bassi, Anna 2017, 'Policy preferences in coalition formation and the stability of minority and surplus governments', *Journal of Politics*, vol. 79, no. 1, pp. 250–268.

Boston, Jonathan and Stephen Church 2003, 'Government formation after the 2002 general election', in Jonathan Boston, Stephen Church, Stephen Levine, Elizabeth McLeay and Nigel S. Roberts (eds.), *New Zealand Votes: The General Election of 2002*, Victoria University Press, Wellington, pp. 333–360.

Cooke, Henry 2020, 'Simon Bridges rules out working with NZ First after election', *Stuff*, 28 January.

Coughlan, Thomas and Henry Cooke 2020, 'Green Party votes to be part of next government with Labour, *Stuff*, 31 October.

Moir, Jo and Jane Patterson 2020, 'Māori Party President wary of National partnership', Radio New Zealand, 7 February.

34. Jacinda Ardern and political leadership: the story thus far . . .

Johansson, Jon and Stephen Levine 2013, 'Evaluating prime-ministerial performance: The New Zealand experience', in Paul Strangio, Paul 'T Hart and James Walter (eds.), *Understanding Prime-Ministerial Performance*, Oxford University Press, Oxford, pp. 291–317.

Sacks, Jonathan 2006, *Rabbi Jonathan Sacks's Haggadah*, Continuum, New York.

Sheppard, Simon 1998, 'Ranking New Zealand's Prime Ministers', *Political Science*, vol. 50, no. 1, pp. 72–89.

Smith, Katherine 2019, 'The First-Class, the Familiar and the Forgettable: An Analysis of Prime Ministerial Performance in New Zealand', MA thesis, Victoria University of Wellington.

Appendices

APPENDIX 1

COOPERATION AGREEMENT BETWEEN THE NEW ZEALAND LABOUR PARTY AND THE GREEN PARTY OF AOTEAROA NEW ZEALAND

Preamble

1. The Green Party commits to supporting the Labour Government to provide stable government for the term of the 53rd Parliament. The parties commit to working in the best interests of New Zealand and New Zealanders, working to honour Te Tiriti o Waitangi, and building and maintaining public confidence in the integrity of Parliament and our democracy.
2. This agreement builds on the constructive and enduring working relationship between the two parties. It does this by setting out the arrangements between the parliamentary Labour and Green Parties as they relate to the Ministerial portfolios and areas of policy cooperation set out in this agreement.

Nature of agreement

3. The Green Party agrees to support the Labour Government by not opposing votes on matters of confidence and supply for the full term of this Parliament. In addition, the Green Party will support the Labour Government on procedural motions in the House and at Select Committees on the terms set out in this agreement. This will provide New Zealanders with the certainty of a strong, stable Labour Government with support from the Green Party over the next three years.
4. The Green Party will determine its own position in relation to any policy or legislative matter not covered by the Ministerial portfolios and areas of cooperation set out in this agreement. Differences of position within such portfolios and areas of cooperation will be managed in accordance with this agreement.
5. The Labour Government in turn commits to working constructively with the Green Party to advance the policy goals set out in this agreement, alongside Labour's policy programme.

Ministerial positions

6. The Labour Government's priorities for this term centre on a COVID-19 recovery plan. This includes the implementation of Labour's manifesto promises and five point economic plan, with a focus on investing in our people and preparing for the future.
7. The Green Party's aspirations include enabling a Just Transition to a zero-carbon economy; supporting equity, compassion and inclusive communities; ensuring ecosystems, indigenous species and their habitats thrive; and cultivating a flourishing democracy founded on Te Tiriti o Waitangi.
8. This agreement supports the advancement of these priorities by allocating portfolios and establishing areas of cooperation that are consistent with the direction and goals of the Labour Government, as well as contributing to addressing the Green Party's aspirations.
9. The Green Party will hold the following portfolios outside of Cabinet:
   a. Marama Davidson will be appointed to the position of Minister for the Prevention of Family and Sexual Violence and Associate Minister of Housing (Homelessness).
   b. Hon James Shaw will be appointed to the position of Minister of Climate Change and Associate Minister for the Environment (Biodiversity).
10. The Minister for the Prevention of Family and Sexual Violence will be the lead Minister for the whole of government response on family and sexual violence with the mandate to coordinate Budget bids in this area. The Minister will also be a member of the ad hoc Ministerial group on the Child and Youth Wellbeing Strategy.
11. These Ministerial portfolios also reflect areas where Green Party expertise provides a valuable contribution to the Labour Government.
12. Ministers from the Green Party will attend Cabinet Committees for items relevant to their portfolios and receive Cabinet Papers relevant to their portfolios, as provided for in the Cabinet Manual.
13. In addition, the Labour Party will support the nomination of a Green Party Member of Parliament to be the Chair of a Select Committee, as well as a Green Party Member of Parliament in the role of Deputy Chair of an additional Select Committee.

Areas of cooperation

14. The parties will cooperate on agreed areas where the Labour and Green Parties have common goals:
    a. *Achieving the purpose and goals of the Zero Carbon Act* through decarbonising public transport, decarbonising the public sector, increasing the uptake of zero-emission vehicles, introducing clean car standards, and supporting the use of renewable energy for industrial heat.
    b. *Protecting our environment and biodiversity* through working to achieve the outcomes of *Te Mana o te Taiao - Aotearoa New Zealand Biodiversity Strategy 2020*, protecting Kauri, building on pest management programmes, and taking action to minimise waste and problem plastics.
    c. *Improving child wellbeing and marginalised communities* through action on homelessness, warmer homes, and child and youth mental health.
15. These areas of cooperation reflect common goals between the Labour and Green Parties, and represent areas where the policy and experience of the Green Party provides a positive contribution to the Labour Government.
16. The Labour and Green Parties will work together in good faith and cooperate with each other in respect of executive and Parliamentary activities to advance these shared goals, including any public statements. The Prime Minister's letters of expectations to Ministers will reflect the areas of policy cooperation and consultation processes required.
17. Beyond these stated areas of cooperation, it is also the Government's intention to work with political parties from across Parliament (including the opposition) on issues that affect our democracy, including the Electoral Commission's 2012 recommended changes to MMP, electoral finance law, and the length of the Parliamentary term.

Consultation

18. On the areas of cooperation set out in this agreement, or other matters as agreed, the parties commit to undertaking political consultation between the responsible Minister and the appropriate

spokesperson. This process will also apply to Green Party Ministerial portfolio matters.

19. This process, which will be agreed between the parties and set out in a Cabinet Office Circular, will cover:
    a. the initial policy development, including access to relevant papers and drafts of legislation,
    b. the development of Cabinet Papers,
    c. the public communication of the policy to acknowledge the role of the Green Party.
20. The Labour Government will also brief the Green Party on:
    a. the broad outline of the legislative programme,
    b. broad Budget parameters and process.
21. Outside of the areas specified in this agreement, there will be no requirement for consultation, but this could happen on a case by case basis.
22. Where there has been full participation in the development of a policy initiative and that participation has led to an agreed position, it is expected that both parties to this agreement will publicly support the process and outcome. This does not prevent the parties from noting where the agreed position deviates from their stated policy.

Relationship between the parties

23. The Labour and Green Parties will cooperate with each other with mutual respect on the areas set out in this agreement. Cooperation will include joint announcements relating to areas of policy cooperation.
24. The Leader of the Labour Party and the Green Party Co-leaders will meet every six weeks to monitor progress against the areas of cooperation set out in this agreement. The Chiefs of Staff will meet regularly.
25. The parties agree that any concerns will be raised in confidence as early as possible and in good faith, between the Prime Minister's Office and the Office of the Co-leaders of the Green Party. Matters can be escalated to the Chiefs of Staff, and then Party leaders, as required.
26. The parties may establish a process in order to maintain different public positions on the areas of cooperation. The parties agree that matters of differentiation will be dealt with on a 'no surprises' basis.

27. This agreement will evolve as the term of Government progresses, including through opening up potential additional areas of cooperation. Any additional areas of cooperation will be agreed to between the Party leaders and given effect by a letter from the Prime Minister to the relevant Minister.

Cabinet Manual

28. Green Party Ministers agree to be bound by the Cabinet Manual in the exercise of Ministerial Responsibilities, and in particular, agree to be bound by the provisions in the Cabinet Manual on conduct, public duty, and personal interests of Ministers.

Collective responsibility

29. Ministers from the Green Party agree to be bound by collective responsibility in relation to their Ministerial portfolios. When speaking within portfolio responsibilities, they will speak for the Government representing the Government's position in relation to those responsibilities.
30. In accordance with the Cabinet Manual, Ministers from the Green Party must support and implement Cabinet decisions in their portfolio areas. However, Ministers from the Green Party will not be restricted from noting where that policy may deviate from the Green Party policy on an issue. If this is required, it may be noted in the Cabinet minute that on a key issue, the Green Party position differs from the Cabinet decision.
31. When Ministers from the Green Party are speaking about matters outside of their portfolio responsibilities, they may speak as the Co-leader of the Green Party or as a Member of Parliament.
32. Agree to disagree provisions of the Cabinet Manual will be applied as necessary.

Confidentiality

33. Ministers from the Green Party will be bound by the principle of Cabinet confidentiality, as set out in the Cabinet Manual.
34. Where Cabinet papers or other briefings are provided to the Green Party, or where the Green Party is involved in consultation on legislation, policy or budgetary matters, all such material and discussions shall be confidential unless otherwise agreed.

35. In the event that Government or Cabinet papers are provided to the Green Party for the purposes of political consultation they shall be provided to a designated person with the office of the Green Party, who will take responsibility for ensuring they are treated with the appropriate degree of confidentiality.
36. Once confidential information is in the public domain, both parties are able to make comment on the information, subject to any constraints required by collective responsibility or this agreement.

Management of Parliamentary activities

37. Both parties commit to a 'no surprises' approach for House and Select Committee business. Protocols will be established for managing this.
38. The Leader of the House will keep the Green Party informed about the House programme in advance of each sitting session.
39. Consultation on legislation outside of the scope of this agreement will be conducted on a case by case basis. The Green Party will consider its position on each Bill in good faith and advise the relevant Minister and the Prime Minister's Office.
40. The Labour and Green Parties agree to a 'no surprises' approach to new Members' Bills. However, neither party is under any obligation to support the other party's Members' Bills.
41. The Green Party will support the Government on procedural motions in the House and in Select Committees, subject to consultation being undertaken. This excludes urgency, which will be negotiated on a case by case basis. The Labour Party Whip and Green Party Musterer will establish protocols to ensure these processes work effectively to meet the expectations of both parties.
42. The Green Party undertakes to keep full voting numbers present whenever the House is sitting where the Green Party has committed to support the Labour Government and on matters of confidence and supply. The Green Party also undertakes to keep full voting numbers in Select Committee, unless otherwise agreed.

Source: https://www.scoop.co.nz/stories/PA2010/S00117/cooperation-agreement-between-the-nz-labour-party-and-the-green-party-of-aotearoa-nz.htm.

APPENDIX 2

2020 SPEECH FROM THE THRONE

26 November 2020

E aku hoa i te ara o te whai,
Kia kotahi tā tātou takahi i te kō, ko tōku whiwhi kei tō koutou tautoko mai.
Ko tāku ki a koutou, hei whakapiki manawa mōku.
He horomata rangatira te mahi, e rite ai te whiwhinga a te ringatuku, me te ringakape ake, i ōna painga.
Hei ruruhau, hei kaitoko i te ora, hei kaiurungi, hei kaiwhakaawe taumata hou.
He mea pai, i oti tahi
Nāu, nāku, nā tātou.

Honourable Members of the House of Representatives.

It is my privilege to exercise the prerogative of Her Majesty the Queen and open the 53rd Parliament.

In the October election, New Zealanders elected a majority Government for the first time under our Mixed Member Proportional electoral system. The Government not only enjoys the confidence of a clear majority of members in the House of Representatives, it is also privileged to have the confidence of a majority of New Zealanders who voted in the general election. The Labour Government took Office when I swore in the Prime Minister the Right Honourable Jacinda Ardern.

New Zealanders voted for stability and certainty at the election. They have placed huge trust and responsibility in the Labour Government by providing it with a majority mandate to implement the policies it set out during the campaign, while responding to the issues that will inevitably arise, and bringing to bear the same values and strong leadership established in its first term. To add further stability to the New Zealand Government, the Labour Party has agreed to work together with the Green Party of Aotearoa New Zealand through a Cooperation Agreement. This agreement commits the Government to working in the best interests of New Zealand and New Zealanders, working to honour Te Tiriti o Waitangi, and working together on specific policy areas where the Green Party can continue to add expertise and where both parties can achieve mutual gains that advance the goals of the Government.

The Labour Government takes office at a time of unparalleled international crisis. It faces the greatest public health emergency since the global flu pandemic a century ago. The ensuing economic shock represents the largest global downturn since the Great Depression. The health risk posed by the pandemic is greater now than it was when we first closed our borders. The global economic outlook continues to worsen. New Zealand will not be immune to these deteriorating conditions.

In this year of crisis, protecting New Zealand and the lives and livelihoods of New Zealanders has been the urgent and abiding consideration. It remains so. But that does not mark the full extent of what a government can do, and it does not mark the full extent of what this government means to do. Crises do not form an orderly line waiting to be addressed. Three of the country's longest-standing and hardest issues demand continued and determined action: affordable housing and homelessness, child poverty, and the global climate crisis. On each of these areas there is a need to do more and go further. Problems that are decades in the making are not easily or quickly solved. But this Government is committed to relentlessly pursuing progress.

The government means to build on the foundations laid in the first term. New Zealand must continue to tackle these issues, at gathering scale, at gathering speed, and with gathering effect. The Labour Government will have three overarching objectives:

- To keep New Zealanders safe from Covid-19
- To accelerate our economic recovery
- To lay the foundations for a better future

The scale and pace of the recovery offers an opportunity to reshape the way things are done in New Zealand, to innovate and improve our position and our economy. New Zealand's success in fighting the virus means we are better positioned for recovery than many other countries. Already we have seen employment, export and growth numbers that are better than expected. The programme outlined today seeks to make the most of our head start.

Keeping New Zealanders safe from Covid-19

The first objective of the Government will be to keep New Zealanders safe from Covid. In keeping New Zealanders safe, we protect jobs, livelihoods, and strengthen our economy. A strong health response has given the New Zealand economy the best chance at coming back stronger. The Government remains committed to a strategy of elimination, but will always remain open to evolving ways of achieving it.

No system is perfect. That is why we look to continually improve. As we learn more about the virus and other countries' experiences, and as new technologies are developed, there will be opportunities to improve our response. Our response has never been static and we will continue to innovate and learn. The Government will retain and enhance the multiple lines of defence to keep Covid at bay and stamp it out with minimal disruption to the economy and to our everyday lives.

The first layer of defence is our border. With Covid cases increasing around the world, in a growing number of countries, the risk of travelers arriving at the border with Covid increases. The Government will continue to strengthen border protections. Testing, infection control procedures, and professional and quality staffing will remain cornerstones of the response. For those countries where the virus is successfully managed, the Government will look for opportunities for freer travel. Planning for quarantine-free travel zones is currently underway with the Cook Islands, Niue and Australia. We will look to continue to advance these opportunities, but with safety as our priority. We will continue to welcome New Zealanders home. We will also create opportunities for businesses to access the skills they need. The Government will ensure that up to 10 per cent of places in our managed isolation facilities are used by people granted exceptions to enter New Zealand to contribute to accelerating our recovery.

The Government will continue to enhance the next layer of defence, our contact tracing and testing systems, to ensure in the event of cases entering the community it can quickly circle the virus and stamp it out. This will involve investment in ongoing technical enhancements to the Covid Tracer App and looking for ways to increase the use of technology. We have expanded the surveillance testing programme to provide extra protection against pathways for infection. This term we will look for opportunities to take advantage of developments in technology to expand the reach of our early warning system.

Finally, the Government is working to deliver effective and free vaccines to New Zealanders as soon as they are available and safe to administer. Recent news of the progress in vaccine development is welcome and a bright spot on the horizon. This will be a central focus for the Government next year. The Government is working hard to secure supply for New Zealand and to design an immunisation programme to support distribution in New Zealand. New Zealand also has an important role in supporting Pacific countries with access to a Covid-19 vaccine and their rollout of their immunisation programmes. New Zealand's obligations to the Pacific are a core part of the Vaccine Strategy. We are hopeful that 2021 will be the year of the Covid vaccine.

Accelerating the recovery

The Government's Covid recovery plan is already underway. It will now be accelerated as the plans for recovery set out in Labour's election manifesto are implemented.

The New Zealand economy has held up better than expected. Aggressive action to eliminate the virus; strong and early efforts to save jobs and support businesses; and innovative and nimble responses from our businesses have positioned the economy well. But the global picture is bleak. The ongoing impact of Covid on the global economy is the most significant risk to our future growth. The virus' spread abroad will have a downstream impact on our exporters and impact economic activity domestically. New Zealand will be cushioned from that slump by the Government's five-point economic plan to foster jobs and growth:

- $42 billion of infrastructure investment to future proof the economy
- Training and job creation opportunities to support workers and businesses
- Support for small business to grow and thrive
- Programmes to bolster our exports
- Policies that prepare New Zealand for the future by making the most of our competitive advantage in renewable energy and waste reduction.

Investing in infrastructure is at the core of the Government's economic plan. As we begin this term, we already have a record $42.2 billion on the books for infrastructure investment over the next four years in roads and rail, schools and hospitals, houses and energy generation. Waka Kotahi NZ Transport Agency will receive $9.6 billion to invest in new roads and public transport projects that reduce congestion and travel times, support businesses, open up new areas for housing, and increase choice, including safer options for walking and cycling. $3.8 billion is being spent on education facilities, including building new schools and classrooms for 100,000 students and starting the planned upgrade of around 180 schools right across the country over the next 10 years. $3.6 billion has been committed to health, including new hospital facilities in Dunedin, Christchurch, New Plymouth, Auckland and Counties Manukau. Kāinga Ora will invest $9.8 billion across the next four years and the Government is on track to deliver a total of 18,000 public and transitional homes. The Three Waters programme will see a $710 million investment to initiate an overhaul of the nation's drinking, waste and stormwater infrastructure. These investments in housing, transport, schools and hospitals will help future proof our economy as well as create jobs. It also provides a pipeline of work that will provide businesses with confidence and certainty to invest in capacity to undertake these projects.

In addition, over 150 smaller community infrastructure projects will roll out over the coming months and across the term. The Government will invest in community projects like pools and stadiums, local fire stations and surf clubs, and libraries, art galleries, marae and museums – facilities across the country that bring people together to provide support and strengthen communities.

Improving our planning system is also a priority. It will create jobs by making it easier to deliver construction projects while protecting our environment and building the right thing in the right place. The current system is too costly, takes too long, and has not adequately protected the environment. The Government will ensure that New Zealand's resource management system is fit for the future by repealing and replacing the Resource Management Act. The Randerson review provides a sound platform for the Government to advance this work. In the first six months of 2021 the Government intends to release an exposure draft of key elements of the first bill.

Also vital to the recovery is our investment in trades training and apprenticeships. Education is the greatest enabler in our society and one of the biggest levers we can use to improve the productivity of the economy. In the early stages of our Covid response the Government focused heavily on growing training and apprenticeships. It launched a comprehensive support package for apprentices and their employers, assuring job security for existing apprentices and creating openings for new ones. Already thousands of New Zealanders have embraced the opportunity to take up a trade and train for free. These New Zealanders are acquiring new skills and exciting prospects, and at the same time addressing the need to build the workforce that will be required to carry the vast workload of the coming infrastructure projects. The Government will also complete the reform of the vocational education system. As the country rebuilds and more people are looking to retrain, it's now more important than ever that we have a vocational education system that's responsive to the needs of industry and learners.

The Government recognises the need to welcome skilled people from overseas to support New Zealand's economy, and will work alongside industry to help provide for that but it will, as a priority and a starting point, seek to develop New Zealand workforces to meet those skills needed here at home. With many New Zealanders looking for work, we need to do all we can to fill existing job opportunities. While unemployment is lower than expected, the economic fallout has had an impact. The Government will remain focused on creating opportunities for people to get back into work.

History shows that significant economic events have a disproportionate impact on women, Māori and Pacific communities, and our focus will ensure our recovery responds to that. The Government will reinstate the Training Incentive Allowance to assist sole-parents, disabled people and their carers with the costs of getting a degree-level tertiary qualification. It will continue the successful Mana in Mahi and He Poutama Rangatahi programmes which are providing skills and qualifications to unemployed young people. It will also continue to roll out Tupu Aotearoa's expansion across the regions and provide wraparound support for Pacific communities to secure sustainable employment and educational pathways for Pacific peoples of all ages. The government will lift abatement thresholds to ensure that people are not punished by transitioning from a benefit to paid work. It will also support those at risk of long-term unemployment through funding up to an additional 40,000 New Zealanders into work through the Flexi-wage programme.

As well as creating jobs, the Government will remain focused on growing the incomes and wages of New Zealanders, especially those earning the least. It will increase the minimum wage to $20 per hour next year, extend Living Wage guarantees to cleaning, catering and security guards who the public service pays through contractors, implement Fair Pay Agreements to set minimum standards for pay and conditions, and extend sick leave provisions.

The Government will leverage our successful Covid response to position New Zealand globally as a safe and secure place to trade with, to invest in, and eventually, to visit again. The Government will pursue high quality and comprehensive trade agreements that diversify our trade relationships. It will continue to open new opportunities, including through trade deals with the EU and the UK, and the Agreement on Climate Change, Trade, and Sustainability; and by expanding the CPTPP and the Digital Economic Partnership Agreement. The Government will continue to progress our trade relationship with the United States, including into new areas such as digital and green technology.

An important milestone has been accomplished with the conclusion of the China FTA Upgrade, which will provide access into new services markets in China, including e-commerce. The New Zealand Government will continue to support New Zealand exporters doing business with China.

The Pacific regional trade and development agreement PACER Plus will enter into force in December this year. The agreement positions Pacific countries to better engage in international trade. It will make trade easier, will grow jobs, boost sustainable economic growth and contribute to a safer and more prosperous Pacific.

In the Indo-Pacific region, the Government will work to implement the signing of RCEP; and through chairing APEC in 2021, New Zealand will lead on the world stage to drive initiatives for strong regional economic recovery.

The Government will work with industry through Industry Transformation Plans to support the transition and grow high-value export firms. It will continue its investment in innovation, including through the research and development tax credit programme. It will work to implement the primary sector roadmap Fit For a Better World to accelerate the productivity, sustainability and inclusiveness of the primary sector. It will work to support our tourism sector in its transition to a sustainable, low carbon, high skill and high wage industry. It will expand the Innovative Partnerships programme and New Zealand Trade and Enterprise's dedicated international investment attraction team to attract companies to invest and establish in New Zealand.

Small businesses are at the heart of New Zealand's economy and the recovery. The Government will continue to support small businesses with practical support. That will include tackling barriers to innovation and growth as identified by the Small Business Council's Small Business Strategy. The Government has already extended the Small Business Cashflow Scheme for a further three years and extended the interest-free period for another year, and will investigate permanent financing for smaller businesses. The Government will regulate Merchant Service Fees to reduce costs on retailers, and will support small businesses to digitise through digital training or short-courses as part of a new Digital Training programme. The new Minister for the Digital Economy and Communications will work with the technology sector, including through the Digital Technologies Industry Transformation Plan, to help speed growth in jobs and incomes in that important sector.

New Zealand's Covid-19 recovery provides an opportunity to reshape our economy and prepare for the future through investment in energy and waste projects. The Government is committed to the shift away from fossil fuels in order to build a new low-carbon future. It is a shift that will create jobs, improve the environment, and enhance New Zealand's global brand, which our exporters trade on. This term the Government will lay the foundation for the electrification of New Zealand's economy by bringing forward our 100 per cent renewable electricity target to 2030, prohibit the building of new thermal baseload electricity, investigate dry year storage options such as pumped hydro, and invest in emerging technologies like green hydrogen. It will remove barriers to renewable energy generation through a National Policy Statement and also investigate regulatory or market barriers to the uptake of solar micro-generation on residential and commercial buildings. The Government will invest in electrifying and decarbonising industrial and process heat, including by preventing the installation of new low and medium temperature coal-fired boilers, and supporting businesses to replace fossil fuels in industrial heat processes by connecting to the grid. The Government will implement the recommendations of the Prime Minister's Chief Science Advisor by phasing out hard to recycle single-use plastic items and supporting the development of alternatives through a Plastics Innovation Fund. It will also invest in waste infrastructure and projects to enable more efficient recycling, and work with industries to establish regulated product stewardship schemes for priority products.

This economic plan is underpinned by continued responsible management of the Government books. As a consequence of the wider economic outlook and fiscal constraints, it is more important than ever to ensure a balanced approach. This requires investing in our priorities while ensuring that all Government spending decisions are made with particular consideration for the sustainability of the Crown's long-term fiscal position. The Government will continue to ensure vital public services are supported, while keeping a lid on debt. Investments to accelerate the recovery will be prioritised. Ensuring our health and education systems continue to be supported will also be a priority. This will include implementing the Government response to the Health and Disability System review. The efforts of many hardworking and committed health professionals and the health of New Zealanders are hampered by a system that needs fundamental reform. Initial decisions on policy will be taken in 2021.

Laying the foundations for a better future

The Government has marked out the need and importance of taking a broader view of success. Wellbeing will continue to be a priority for Government this term with a focus on reducing child poverty, tackling climate change, and addressing housing. New Zealand's response to Covid would be insufficient if it were to simply return us to the way we were before the virus. Recovering and rebuilding entails determined and connected action by government. That action can, and will, be used to reshape the economy to be more productive, more sustainable, and more equitable. Over the next term it will place a particular focus on sustainability, and pursuing carbon neutrality.

The Government will respond to the first set of Climate Budgets recommended by the Climate Commission, which will set the total emissions permitted for the next fifteen years. The Government will take steps to decarbonise the transport fleet. It will introduce vehicle emissions standards for imported vehicles and incentivise and accelerate the uptake of electric and other low emission vehicles, including by increasing the Low Emissions Vehicles Contestable Fund. In line with the direction set out in the latest Government Policy Statement, it will prioritise investment in public transport, walking and cycling so users have a more accessible, affordable and reliable service, and implement region-specific plans to increase the number of people using public transport and walking and cycling. Supporting the use of public transport is a key element to reducing New Zealand's transport emissions. Given the importance of public transport to New Zealand's future transport system, it will require only zero emissions buses to be purchased by 2025, and aim to decarbonise the public transport bus fleet by 2035.

New Zealand's farmers and growers are creative, innovative and constantly looking to improve their practices. They are taking steps to improve freshwater quality, protect biodiversity and reduce emissions. This will create real value for our exports and is a core part of our New Zealand brand. The Government will bolster these efforts through increased investment in world-leading research that helps us reduce emissions and will support farmers to use integrated farm plans to simplify processes, reduce compliance costs and meet reporting requirements in a coherent way.

The economic impact of Covid will have a disproportionate effect on those least equipped to deal with it. That will require a continued focus and determination in reducing inequality and addressing child poverty. Progress has been made, but there remains much to do. The Government will continue the work from last term that has already seen improvements to the weekly income of around 85,000 sole parents by an average of $100 a week. The Government will continue the overhaul of the welfare system, building on the changes already made, including the indexing of benefits to increases in the average wage. It will extend the Free and Healthy Lunch programme to cover 200,000 students and will add 20 more mobile dental clinics to improve access for children and young people to free oral health care. It will roll out mental health support to all primary and intermediate school age students, and continue to roll out nurses in secondary schools. It will continue to tackle the prevalence of rheumatic fever by expanding the Healthy Homes Initiative to every DHB around the country to ensure more homes are warm, dry and safe.

A focus on housing will be a priority for this Government. Earlier in the year house prices were predicted to fall. Instead they have increased. Globally, low interest rates are having a similar effect. And the situation has rapidly evolved. While it is pleasing to see that efforts to stimulate the economy and support jobs and growth in the wider economy have been effective, the perverse impact on housing affordability will require the Government to continue its focus on this issue. The Government has set out the parameters of what it is prepared to consider during the election campaign. This will not change. But there is room to do more to support both the supply and demand side of housing to see outcomes that are more productive and fair. The Government will review its housing settings with a view to implementing policies that improve access to the housing market for first home buyers.

The Government will continue to focus on homelessness and implementing the Homelessness Action Plan. The Government will review and enhance the Tenancy Tribunal, Tenancy Services' Compliance and Investigations team, regulate property managers, and increase funding to proactively monitor compliance with the Healthy Homes Standards.

In each of these areas – climate, child poverty, and housing – the Government will be guided by its values, and by its commitment to the wellbeing of people, looking beyond GDP to find our measure of success. As part of this focus on wellbeing and creating a fairer New Zealand we will continue to strengthen social inclusion in New Zealand. This is about supporting our diversity and creating a New Zealand where all people feel safe, have equal access to opportunities and do not experience discrimination. This is important as we prepare to receive and respond to the report of the Royal Commission of Inquiry into the Terrorist Attack on Christchurch Mosques on 15 March 2019. Wellbeing might not be as readily reckoned as GDP, but that does not mean it cannot be measured and tracked. Imbalances and deprivation can be recognised and remedied and this Government is determined to do so. Significant levels of government investment in a time of crisis can be a powerful tool for change and it's a tool that is being used. The way we choose to govern is also a tool for change.

Māori–Crown relations

The Government will strengthen the Māori–Crown relationship to ensure that the Crown can grow to be a better Treaty Partner and work in true partnership with Māori. It will continue to work to settle historic Treaty of Waitangi claims. It recognises the importance of te reo Māori as a taonga and the responsibility it has to protect it. Te Ao Māori plays a large part not just in defining who we are as a nation, but in setting us apart from the rest of the world. As such the Government will make Matariki a public holiday, creating a holiday that distinctly recognises and celebrates Te Ao Māori.

The Government will ensure Oranga Tamariki partners with iwi, hapū, and Māori organisations to find appropriate solutions for children in need, and will strengthen Māori housing outcomes through collaborative partnerships, home-ownership models, and papakāinga provision. It will support Whānau Māori enterprise and opportunities through a progressive procurement policy. It will continue to invest in Whānau Ora and support other agencies to implement the Whānau Ora model to get better outcomes for Māori, continue whānau-centred pathways to break the cycle of Māori reoffending, work with other Māori organisations like Te Kōhanga Reo, and look at ways we can expand the Whānau Ora model into communities.

A government for all New Zealanders

New Zealand has entrusted the government with the responsibility of bringing the country through a crisis. Nothing in the programme set out today will come easily. But our opportunities and potential greatly outweigh our problems. In this pandemic we have shown our willingness and capacity to do what must be done. We have more freedoms, are a more open economy and have saved more lives than nearly every other country we normally compare ourselves to. We can rightfully be proud of our success to date as a nation, as a team. But we cannot afford to be complacent, nor stand still. We must keep going.

It is the Government's aim to achieve change alongside consensus. That is why it has committed to being a Government that will govern for all New Zealanders. That does not mean that it can or will represent the views of every New Zealander all of the time. But it does mean it will have a focus on the things that matter most. It means it will be listening to New Zealanders, being pragmatic, doing the things it said it would do and focusing on lasting change. We can recover and we will recover. But that is not enough. We can be better than we were. This government's mission is to make it so.

Nō reira, tēnā koutou, tēnā koutou, tēnā tātou katoa.

Source: New Zealand Government, 'Speech from the Throne', Beehive.govt.nz, 26 November 2020.

APPENDIX 3

MPs IN THE 53RD PARLIAMENT

Labour Party

Kiritapu Allan	(East Coast)
Ginny Andersen	(Hutt South)
Jacinda Ardern	(Mount Albert)
*Camilla Belich	(list)
*Glen Bennett	(New Plymouth)
*Rachel Boyack	(Nelson)
*Rachel Brooking	(list)
*Naisi Chen	(list)
David Clark	(Dunedin)
Tamati Coffey	(list)
Liz Craig	(list)
Kelvin Davis	(Te Tai Tokerau)
Paul Eagle	(Rongotai)
*Barbara Edmonds	(Mana)
Kris Faafoi	(list)
*Shanan Halbert	(Northcote)
Peeni Henare	(Tāmaki Makaurau)
*Emily Henderson	(Whangārei)
Chris Hipkins	(Remutaka)
Willie Jackson	(list)
Anahila Kanongata'a-Suisuiki	(list)
*Ingrid Leary	(Taieri)
*Neru Leavasa	(Takanini)
*Steph Lewis	(Whanganui)
Andrew Little	(list)
*Anna Lorck	(Tukituki)
Marja Lubeck	(list)
Jo Luxton	(Rangitata)

Nanaia Mahuta	(Hauraki-Waikato)
Trevor Mallard	(list)
Kieran McAnulty	(Wairarapa)
*Tracey McLellan	(Banks Peninsula)
Stuart Nash	(Napier)
*Terisa Ngobi	(Ōtaki)
Damien O'Connor	(West Coast-Tasman)
Greg O'Connor	(Ōhāriu)
*Ibrahim Omer	(list)
*Sarah Pallett	(Ilam)
David Parker	(list)
Willow-Jean Prime	(Northland)
Priyanca Radhakrishnan	(Maungakiekie)
*Angela Roberts	(list)
Grant Robertson	(Wellington Central)
Adrian Rurawhe	(Te Tai Hauāuru)
Deborah Russell	(New Lynn)
Jenny Salesa	(Panmure-Ōtāhuhu)
Carmel Sepuloni	(Kelston)
*Gaurav Sharma	(Hamilton West)
Aupito William Sio	(Māngere)
Jamie Strange	(Hamilton East)
Jan Tinetti	(list)
Rino Tirikatene	(Te Tai Tonga)
Phil Twyford	(Te Atatū)
*Tangi Utikere	(Palmerston North)
*Ayesha Verrall	(list)
Louisa Wall	(list)
*Vanushi Walters	(Upper Harbour)
Angie Warren-Clark	(list)
Duncan Webb	(Christchurch Central)
Meka Whaitiri	(Ikaroa-Rāwhiti)
*Helen White	(list)
*Arena Williams	(Manurewa)
Poto Williams	(Christchurch East)
Michael Wood	(Mount Roskill)
Megan Woods	(Wigram)

National Party

Andrew Bayly	(Port Waikato)
David Bennett	(list)
Chris Bishop	(list)
Simon Bridges	(Tauranga)
Simeon Brown	(Pakuranga)
Gerry Brownlee	(list)
Judith Collins	(Papakura)
Jacqui Dean	(Waitaki)
Matt Doocey	(Waimakariri)
Paul Goldsmith	(list)
*Nicola Grigg	(Selwyn)
Barbara Kuriger	(Taranaki-King Country)
Melissa Lee	(list)
*Christopher Luxon	(Botany)
Todd McClay	(Rotorua)
Ian McKelvie	(Rangitīkei)
Mark Mitchell	(Whangaparāoa)
*Joseph Mooney	(Southland)
Todd Muller	(Bay of Plenty)
Simon O'Connor	(Tamaki)
Chris Penk	(Kaipara ki Mahurangi)
Maureen Pugh	(list)
Shane Reti	(list)
*Penny Simmonds	(Invercargill)
Scott Simpson	(Coromandel)
†Nick Smith	(list)
Stuart Smith	(Kaikōura)
Erica Stanford	(East Coast Bays)
Louise Upston	(Taupō)
Tim van de Molen	(Waikato)
*Simon Watts	(North Shore)
Nicola Willis	(list)
Michael Woodhouse	(list)

Green Party

Marama Davidson	(list)
Julie Anne Genter	(list)
Golriz Ghahraman	(list)
*Elizabeth Kerekere	(list)
Jan Logie	(list)
*Ricardo Menéndez March	(list)
Eugenie Sage	(list)
James Shaw	(list)
Chlöe Swarbrick	(Auckland Central)
*Teanau Tuiono	(list)

ACT Party

*Chris Baillie	(list)
*Mark Cameron	(list)
*Karen Chhour	(list)
*Simon Court	(list)
*James McDowall	(list)
*Nicole McKee	(list)
*Toni Severin	(list)
David Seymour	(Epsom)
*Damien Smith	(list)
*Brooke van Velden	(list)

Māori Party

*Debbie Ngarewa-Packer	(list)
*Rawiri Waititi	(Waiariki)

* new Member of Parliament
† Nick Smith resigned from Parliament on 10 June 2021 and was succeeded on 11 June 2021 by Harete Hipango (MP for Whanganui, 2017–2020) from the National Party's list.

Source: https://www.parliament.nz/en/mps-and-electorates/members-of-parliament/

APPENDIX 4

THE GOVERNMENT*

Ministers in the Cabinet

1	Jacinda Ardern	Prime Minister Minister for National Security and Intelligence Minister for Child Poverty Reduction Minister Responsible for Ministerial Services Associate Minister for Arts, Culture and Heritage
2	Grant Robertson	Deputy Prime Minister Minister of Finance Minister for Infrastructure Minister for Racing Minister for Sport and Recreation
3	Kelvin Davis	Minister for Māori Crown Relations: Te Arawhiti Minister for Children Minister of Corrections Associate Minister of Education (Māori Education)
4	Megan Woods	Minister of Housing Minister of Energy and Resources Minister of Research, Science and Innovation Associate Minister of Finance
5	Chris Hipkins	Minister for COVID-19 Response Minister of Education Minister for the Public Service Leader of the House
6	Carmel Sepuloni	Minister for Social Development and Employment Minister for ACC [Accident Compensation Corporation] Minister for Arts, Culture and Heritage Minister for Disability Issues
7	Andrew Little	Minister of Health Minister Responsible for the GCSB [Government Communications Security Bureau] Minister Responsible for the NZSIS [Security Intelligence Service]

		Minister for Treaty of Waitangi Negotiations
		Minister Responsible for Pike River Re-entry
8	David Parker	Attorney-General
		Minister for the Environment
		Minister for Oceans and Fisheries
		Minister of Revenue
		Associate Minister of Finance
9	Nanaia Mahuta	Minister of Foreign Affairs
		Minister of Local Government
		Associate Minister for Māori Development
10	Poto Williams	Minister for Building and Construction
		Minister of Police
		Associate Minister for Children
		Associate Minister of Housing (Public Housing)
11	Damien O'Connor	Minister of Agriculture
		Minister for Biosecurity
		Minister for Land Information
		Minister for Rural Communities
		Minister for Trade and Export Growth
12	Stuart Nash	Minister for Economic and Regional Development
		Minister of Forestry
		Minister for Small Business
		Minister of Tourism
13	Kris Faafoi	Minister of Justice
		Minister for Broadcasting and Media
		Minister of Immigration
14	Peeni Henare	Minister for Defence
		Minister for Whānau Ora
		Associate Minister of Health (Māori Health)
		Associate Minister of Housing (Māori Housing)
		Associate Minister of Tourism
15	Willie Jackson	Minister for Māori Development
		Associate Minister for ACC
		Associate Minister of Justice
16	Jan Tinetti	Minister of Internal Affairs
		Minister for Women
		Associate Minister of Education
17	Michael Wood	Minister of Transport
		Minister for Workplace Relations and Safety

	Deputy Leader of the House
18 Kiritapu Allan	Minister of Conservation
	Minister for Emergency Management
	Associate Minister for Arts, Culture and Heritage
	Associate Minister for the Environment
19 David Clark	Minister of Commerce and Consumer Affairs
	Minister for the Digital Economy and Communications
	Minister for State Owned Enterprises
	Minister of Statistics
	Minister Responsible for the Earthquake Commission
20 Ayesha Verrall	Minister for Food Safety
	Minister for Seniors
	Associate Minister of Health
	Associate Minister of Research, Science and Innovation

Ministers outside Cabinet

Aupito William Sio	Minister for Courts
	Minister for Pacific Peoples
	Associate Minister of Education (Pacific Peoples)
	Associate Minister of Foreign Affairs
	Associate Minister of Health (Pacific Peoples)
	Associate Minister of Justice
Meka Whaitiri	Minister of Customs
	Minister for Veterans
	Associate Minister of Agriculture (Animal Welfare)
	Associate Minister of Statistics
Phil Twyford	Minister for Disarmament and Arms Control
	Minister of State for Trade and Export Growth
	Associate Minister for the Environment
	Associate Minister of Immigration
Priyanca Radhakrishnan	Minister for the Community and Voluntary Sector
	Minister for Diversity, Inclusion and Ethnic Communities
	Minister for Youth
	Associate Minister for Social Development and Employment

Cooperation agreement Ministers

Marama Davidson	Minister for the Prevention of Family and Sexual Violence Associate Minister of Housing (Homelessness)
James Shaw	Minister for Climate Change Associate Minister for the Environment (Biodiversity)

Parliamentary Under-Secretaries

Rino Tirikatene	Parliamentary Under-Secretary to the Minister for Oceans and Fisheries, and to the Minister for Trade and Export Growth (Māori Trade)
Deborah Russell	Parliamentary Under-Secretary to the Minister of Revenue

* As announced on 2 November 2020
Source: Department of the Prime Minister and Cabinet, 'Ministerial List'

CONTRIBUTORS

Jacinda Ardern was elected Leader of the New Zealand Labour Party on 1 August 2017 and was sworn in as Prime Minister on 26 October 2017, and again on 5 November 2020. She was first elected a Member of Parliament at the 2008 election and has been the Member of Parliament for Mount Albert since winning a by-election in that electorate on 25 February 2017. As Prime Minister she contributed a chapter offering her perspective on the 2017 election to *Stardust and Substance: The New Zealand General Election of 2017*.

Ayca Arkilic is a lecturer in political science and international relations at Victoria University of Wellington. Her areas of specialisation include state-diaspora relations, immigration and integration policies, transnationalism, populist nationalism and Islam, with a forthcoming book, *Diaspora Diplomacy: The Politics of Turkish Emigration to Europe*, to be published by Manchester University Press. In 2020 she received a Victoria University of Wellington grant in support of her research focusing on New Zealand's Muslim community.

Therese Arseneau is a senior research fellow in the school of political science and communication at the University of Canterbury. She has contributed to the 2005, 2008, 2011, 2014 and 2017 New Zealand election books in this series, with the 2011, 2014 and 2017 chapters co-authored with Nigel S. Roberts. She was an expert advisor to the New Zealand Electoral Commission both prior to the 2011 electoral referendum and subsequently, in connection with the post-referendum review.

Robert Ayson is Professor of Strategic Studies at Victoria University of Wellington. His research and teaching interests focus on strategic competition and cooperation, with a particular emphasis on security challenges in the Asia-Pacific region. He contributed a chapter on New

Zealand's foreign and defence policies under the governments of prime ministers John Key and Bill English for *Stardust and Substance: The New Zealand General Election of 2017*.

Michael G. Baker is Professor of Public Health at the University of Otago. With research interests which include infectious diseases, environmental health and housing, he was a 2014 recipient of the Prime Minister's Science Prize as a member of He Kāinga Oranga / Housing and Health Research Research Programme. In 2020 he received the Critic and Conscience of Society Award (from Universities New Zealand) and the Public Health Champion Award (from the Public Health Association of New Zealand) for contributions to public health in New Zealand, including his work on the Covid-19 response. In 2020 he was named the *Dominion Post*'s 'Wellingtonian of the Year', the first epidemiologist to be so honoured since the awards were instituted in 1989.

Tim Bale is Professor of Politics at Queen Mary University of London and was a member of the Victoria University of Wellington political science and international relations programme from 1998 to 2003. His study of the impact of television on the 2002 New Zealand general election was published in a previous book in this series, *New Zealand Votes: The General Election of 2002*, and he contributed a chapter on the UK perspective on the 2017 New Zealand election to *Stardust and Substance: The New Zealand General Election of 2017*.

Tina Marie Barton, a New Zealander based in Ottawa, has a Bachelor of Arts degree in political science (Victoria University of Wellington), a Master's degree in economic development and innovation (University of Waterloo) and a background in journalism, communications and policy research. Since 2005 she has worked across the private, public and non-profit sectors in areas related to business, health and community development.

Sarah Hendrica Bickerton is a lecturer in Politics and Policy at the University of Auckland, having previously been a postdoctoral research fellow at its Public Policy Institute. Her doctoral research was on New Zealand women's use of Twitter for political participation construction and she is continuing her research into social uses of technology, technology policy and gender analysis.

Mark Boyd is a lecturer in communication at the University of Auckland. His doctoral dissertation (2019) provided an analysis of television news coverage of New Zealand election campaigns from 1993 to 2017. He was a television and radio journalist for three decades in New Zealand, Australia, the United Kingdom and the United States, and covered elections in all four countries.

Thomas Butt is head of data and analytics for UMR Research. He manages regular political polling and has worked on the last three New Zealand election campaigns as well as several Australian campaigns.

Simon Chapple is Director of the Institute for Governance and Policy Studies at Victoria University of Wellington's School of Government. He has a background as an economist, a policy advisor at both national and international levels, and in public policy research.

Stephen Church, a freelance consultant, has held several advisory positions at Parliament. His 1998 doctoral dissertation at the University of Canterbury won a Wallace Award from the New Zealand Electoral Commission for its contribution to the understanding of party and electoral systems. As a research fellow at Victoria University of Wellington he co-edited (and contributed to) the 1999 and 2002 books in this series of election studies, and his analyses of post-election government formation were published in the three previous election books in this series: *Kicking the Tyres: The New Zealand General Election and Electoral Referendum of 2011*; *Moments of Truth: The New Zealand General Election of 2014*; and *Stardust and Substance: The New Zealand General Election of 2017.*

Judith Collins was elected Leader of the New Zealand National Party on 14 July 2020. She has been a Member of Parliament since 2002 and held several ministerial positions in the governments led by prime ministers John Key and Bill English.

Henry Cooke is chief political reporter for the *Stuff* website and stable of newspapers, based in Parliament's press gallery in Wellington. He has reported on New Zealand politics since 2017 and covered the 2018 midterm elections in the United States.

Geoffrey Craig is a Professor in the School of Communication Studies at Auckland University of Technology (AUT). He has published widely on political communication and on news media coverage, including

Performing Politics: Media Interviews, Debates and Press Conferences (Polity, 2016), focusing on politicians' performances in televised media encounters. His study of leaders' debates during the 2017 election campaign was published in *Stardust and Substance: The New Zealand General Election of 2017*.

Marama Davidson (Te Rarawa, Ngāpuhi, Ngāti Porou) became a Member of Parliament in 2015 and Co-leader of the Green Party of Aotearoa New Zealand in April 2018. She was appointed Minister for the Prevention of Family and Sexual Violence and Associate Minister of Housing (Homelessness) following the 2020 general election.

Marcus Downs is a senior researcher at UMR Research and an advisor at the Research and Evaluation Office, Wellington City Council.

Nicholas Economou is a senior lecturer in political science and international relations at Monash University. He has been a frequent media commentator on politics and has published extensively on Australian politics and political parties. His co-authored chapter offering an Australian view of the 2017 New Zealand election was published in *Stardust and Substance: The New Zealand General Election of 2017*.

Brodie Fraser is a postdoctoral research fellow with He Kāinga Oranga/ Housing and Health Research Programme in the Department of Public Health, University of Otago, Wellington. Following a PhD exploring Takatāpui/LGBTIQ+ homelessness in Aotearoa, Brodie was awarded a University of Otago Division of Health Sciences postdoctoral fellowship to explore Takatāpui/LGBTIQ+ experiences of housing insecurity.

Campbell Garrett, a graduate of Victoria University of Wellington's parliamentary internship programme, was an intern with Labour MP Kieran McAnulty. In 2021 he was appointed to a research position at Parliament in the Labour Leader's Office.

Zareh Ghazarian is a senior lecturer in politics and international relations at Monash University. He has been a frequent media commentator on politics and has published extensively on Australian politics and political parties. His co-authored chapter offering an Australian view of the 2017 New Zealand election was published in *Stardust and Substance: The New Zealand General Election of 2017*.

Lara M. Greaves (Ngāpuhi, Pākehā, Tararā) is a lecturer in New Zealand politics and public policy at the University of Auckland. She is co-editor of *New Zealand Government and Politics*, 7th edition (Oxford University Press, 2021).

Mike Grimshaw, associate professor in sociology at the University of Canterbury, is the author of *Bishops, Boozers, Brethren & Burkas: A Cartoon History of Religion in New Zealand* (New Zealand Cartoon Archive, 2019).

Bonnie Hayvice, a graduate of Victoria University of Wellington's parliamentary internship programme, was an intern with Green MP Chlöe Swarbrick. She is Private Secretary (Executive Support) to Hon. Marama Davidson and Hon. James Shaw.

Chris Hipkins is the Minister of Education, Minister for Covid-19 Response, Minister for the Public Service and Leader of the House. He has served as the Member of Parliament for Remutaka since the 2008 election.

Colin James, among New Zealand's most experienced political journalists, has edited or written numerous studies of New Zealand's politics and elections. He contributed chapters for each of the books in this series, chronicling elections from 1987 through 2020. In 2008 he was awarded an honorary doctorate from Victoria University of Wellington.

Valentina Jofré Méndez, based in Santiago, Chile, is a journalist and has worked as an international reporter for the Chilean newspapers *La Tercera* and *Pulso.*

Margaret Joiner, based in Auckland, is a public policy and government relations specialist with the Trans-Tasman consultancy firm of SenateSHJ, and contributed a chapter on the New Zealand First party to Janine Hayward (ed.), *New Zealand Government and Politics* (Oxford University Press, 6th edition, 2015).

Aljoscha Kertesz is Manager Communications and Public Relations at Caterpillar Energy Solutions in Germany and a freelance journalist writing on German and British politics (with a Master's degree in international relations from Victoria University of Wellington). His chapter on the international media and the election, in *Key to Victory: The New Zealand General Election of 2008*, was the first in this series to look at overseas perceptions of New Zealand elections and politics, a theme developed further with five chapters in the 2017 election book, *Stardust and Substance*, and in this 2020 volume. He has edited several books on German politics, with a volume on former German Chancellor Helmut Kohl forthcoming.

Stephen Levine is a professor of political science at Victoria University of Wellington. He is founder of the university's parliamentary internship programme and has written extensively about New Zealand's politics, elections and international relations. He has been an editor and contributor to books about each of New Zealand's elections under MMP and in 2009 was recognised in the Queen's Birthday Honours List for 'services to education and the Jewish community', appointed an Officer of the New Zealand Order of Merit.

Michael Macaulay is Professor of Public Administration at Victoria University of Wellington's School of Government. His research interests are in ethics, integrity and anti-corruption and he works with government agencies and NGOs in New Zealand and internationally.

Trevor Mallard was first elected a Member of Parliament at the 1984 election, going on to represent the Hutt South electorate from 1996 to 2017. He held several ministerial positions in the Labour-led governments of 1999–2008. Opting in 2017 to stand as a list-only candidate, he returned to Parliament and was elected Speaker of the New Zealand House of Representatives on 7 November 2017, re-elected on 25 November 2020. His reflections on the 2017 election were published as a foreword to *Stardust and Substance: The New Zealand General Election of 2017.*

Stephen Mills is Executive Director of UMR Research, an Australasian issue management market research company founded in 1987. He has worked on over 50 election campaigns in Australia and New Zealand and has written numerous op-ed features on Australasian politics and political polling. Prior to joining UMR he served as a senior political advisor to Prime Minister David Lange and, following his resignation, to then Deputy Prime Minister Helen Clark. He contributed chapters drawing upon UMR survey findings to the two previous books in this election series, *Moments of Truth: The New Zealand General Election of 2014* and *Stardust and Substance: The New Zealand General Election of 2017.*

Ella Morgan (Ngāti Raukawa ki te Tonga) is a graduate student at the University of Auckland. Her graduate research has focused on Mana Wahine and Corrections policy.

Luke D. Oldfield is a doctoral candidate at the University of Auckland and was a Senior Research Assistant on the 2020 New Zealand Election Study.

Tova O'Brien, an experienced interviewer and political journalist, has covered several New Zealand general elections and is Political Editor, *Newshub* (a New Zealand news service available on television, radio and digitally). In 2019 she was named 'Political Journalist of the Year' in the Voyager Media Awards (recognising excellence in New Zealand print and online media).

Nigel S. Roberts is Emeritus Professor of Political Science at Victoria University of Wellington. He has written extensively on New Zealand politics and elections, co-editing, for this series, the books on New Zealand's first five elections under MMP (1996–2008) and contributing chapters (with Therese Arseneau) to the 2011, 2014 and 2017 election books. In 2010 he was appointed an Officer of the New Zealand Order of Merit.

David Seymour was first elected to Parliament at the 2014 election as the Member of Parliament for the Epsom electorate. He is Leader of the ACT Party and served as Parliamentary Under-Secretary to the Minister of Education and to the Minister for Regulatory Reform in the 2014–2017 National-led government. He contributed chapters on ACT's campaigns in *Moments of Truth: The New Zealand General Election of 2014* and *Stardust and Substance: The New Zealand General Election of 2017.*

James Shaw was first elected to Parliament at the 2014 election. He became Co-leader of the Green Party of Aotearoa New Zealand in 2015 and was appointed Minister for Climate Change, Minister of Statistics and Associate Minister of Finance following the 2017 general election, retaining the climate change portfolio and adding Associate Minister for the Environment (Biodiversity) following the 2020 election. His chapter offering a personal perspective on the 2017 campaign was published in *Stardust and Substance: The New Zealand General Election of 2017.*

INDEX